ASP.NET 3.5 Website Pr

CW00569611

ASP.NET 3.5 Website Programming

Problem–Design–Solution

ASP.NET 3.5 Website Programming

Problem–Design–Solution

Chris Love

WILEY

Wiley Publishing, Inc.

ASP.NET 3.5 Website Programming: Problem–Design–Solution

Published by
Wiley Publishing, Inc.
10475 Crosspoint Boulevard
Indianapolis, IN 46256
www.wiley.com

For general information on our other products and services please contact our Customer Care Department within the United States at (877) 762-2974, outside the United States at (317) 572-3993 or fax (317) 572-4002.

Wiley also publishes its books in a variety of electronic formats. Some content that appears in print may not be available in electronic books.

Library of Congress Control Number: 2009928740

About the Author

 **Chris Love** has more than 16 years experience in software design, development, and architecture. He has been the principal developer for more than 300 small- and medium-sized ASP and ASP.NET websites over the past 10 years. These projects have exposed him to a wide range of Microsoft-related technologies to solve real business problems for his clients. He has focused primarily on ASP.NET and VB.NET/C# to produce the majority of his websites. Recently he has been working on applying JQuery to bring more client-side life to his websites, and pursuing a reduction in the size and complexity of his ASP.NET applications by eliminating Web Controls and focusing more on pure HTML markup instead.

Chris's clients rely on his experience and expertise to develop online marketing strategies, including search engine optimization and pay-per-click campaigns. He has begun to leverage this experience along with his ASP.NET know-how to build his own Web properties and practice his technical and marketing theories first-hand.

Chris has been in a leadership role in the local user's group TRINUG for more than 5 years. He frequently presents and organizes Code Camps around the country.

His first book, *ASP.NET 2.0 Your Visual Blueprint for Developing Web Applications* (Wiley), was published in 2007. He has also written two eBooks for WROX on custom HttpHandlers and HttpModules.

Credits

Acquisitions Editor
Paul Reese

Project Editor
Maryann Steinhart

Technical Editor
Cody Reichenau

Production Editor
Daniel Scribner

Copy Editor
Foxxe Editorial Services

Editorial Director
Robyn B. Siesky

Editorial Manager
Mary Beth Wakefield

Production Manager
Tim Tate

**Vice President and
Executive Group Publisher**
Richard Swadley

Vice President and Executive Publisher
Barry Pruett

Associate Publisher
Jim Minatel

Project Coordinator, Cover
Lynsey Stanford

Compositor
Craig Johnson, Happenstance Type-O-Rama

Proofreader
Nate Pritts, Word One

Indexer
Robert Swanson

Cover Image
© Getty Images

Acknowledgments

I am so fortunate to have a great collection of friends and family who have been very supportive over the years. As my .NET experience and knowledge have matured I have been blessed with forming some great relationships in the community. I have to thank everyone who has been supportive in the Triangle .Net User Group over the years. Deciding one night what the group was ultimately changed my career so much for the positive. I encourage each and every reader of this book to seek out any user group in his area.

With that said, there are some specific people to thank. First, Tom, who has been a great friend to me both professionally and personally, and who is always excited when good things happen for me. Beth, you really helped me keep my composure and perspective in the past year with so many things coming at me.

I want to thank all the Microsoft team members with whom I have formed relationships over the last few years. You all have been so helpful to me and anyone else who asked.

Finally, I thank the staff at Wiley for offering me this opportunity. Nothing of this magnitude is without challenges and they have been helpful in solving the many challenges that arose. Producing a book is no small task, but ultimately rewarding. It is always an honor to have the opportunity to share knowledge and experience about something you love with others on the scale possible with a book like this. I know I have learned a lot and I hope to keep learning and sharing.

— *Chris Love*

The publisher gratefully acknowledges **Marco Bellinaso**'s contributions to this book. Marco was the author of *ASP.NET 2.0 Website Programming Problem–Design–Solution* as well as the original TheBeerHouse application. This ASP.NET 3.5 version of the book relies heavily on Marco's book and his application.

Contents

Contents

Contents

Contents

Introduction

Dear reader, thanks for picking up this book, and welcome to the *ASP.NET 3.5 Website Programming: Problem–Design–Solution,* fully updated to ASP.NET version 3.5! The idea for this book was born in 2001, with ASP.NET 1.0, from the desire to have a book that teaches how to create real-world web sites. The first edition was published in 2002, and fortunately it was a success. I believe that this was due to the fact that most ASP.NET books on the market were (and still are) reference-type books, which describe every single control of the framework, and all their methods and properties, but the examples they provide are single-page demos showing how to use a control of a feature. Typically these references don't show how to integrate all ASP.NET features and controls into a single site with rich functionality, which is what readers have to do at work. Designing and implementing a real-world site is very different from creating simple examples, and that's why I think a book like this is helpful for developers facing real problems in their everyday work.

Much of this new edition was rewritten completely from scratch, while trying to preserve as much of the existing application integrity as possible. As a new author for this book I tried to find a balance between the existing Beer House application framework, add some new modules, and integrate some of the great new technologies in ASP.NET 3.5 SP1.

This book is aimed at describing, designing, and implementing a site much like the ones you're probably working on or will be soon, while taking the opportunity to introduce and explain many of the new features that the new great ASP.NET 3.5 Framework offers. I don't hide difficult problems so that the solution can be simpler and shorter to develop; rather, I try to explain most of the problems you'll typically face when writing a modern web site, and provide one or more solutions for them. The result is a web site that features a layout with user-selectable themes, a membership system, a content management system for publishing and syndicating articles, photos, polls, mailing lists, forums, photo gallery, calendar of events, an e-commerce store with support for real-time credit card processing, home page personalization, search engine optimization and localization (refer to Chapter 1 for a more detailed list of features to be implemented). I also decided to write the book in VB.NET, which differs from the previous editions, but source code is available in both C# and VB.NET. I hope you enjoy reading this book, and that it offers guidance that speeds up the development of your next project and makes it more solid, extensible, and well organized.

> You can browse the web site online at www.thebeerhousebook.com.
>
> The author's blog is available at http://professionalaspnet.com. Please keep an eye on it to read about further development and expansion of the sample project.

Who This Book Is For

Let me state up front that this isn't a book for completely novice programmers, or for experienced developers who have never touched ASP.NET and the .NET Framework in general. This book teaches how to write a real-world web site from scratch to deployment, and as such it can't explain every single detail of the technology, but must concentrate on designing and writing actual solutions. To get the most from this book, you should already have had some experience with ASP.NET 2.0, even if not advanced solutions. You're not required to know ASP.NET 3.5, as each chapter will introduce the new controls and features that you'll use in that chapter, providing enough background information to implement the solution. If you then want to learn more about a control, you can check the MSDN official documentation or another reference-type book such as Wrox's *Professional ASP.NET 3.5*. A good reference on search engine optimization principles is Wiley's *Search Engine Optimization: Your Visual Blueprint for Effective Internet Marketing* by Kristopher Jones. I also found Wrox's *Professional LINQ* by Scott Klein very helpful.

What This Book Covers

This book is basically a large case study that starts from the foundation and works its way through to completion with a series of designs and solutions for each incremental step along the way. What sets the Problem–Design–Solution series apart from other Wrox series is the structure of the book and the start-to-finish approach to one completed project. Specifically, this book leads the reader through the development of a complete ASP.NET 3.5 web site that has most of the features users expect to find in a modern content-related and e-commerce site:

- ❑ Account registration, personalization, and themes
- ❑ Site Navigation
- ❑ News and events, organized into categories
- ❑ Opinion polls
- ❑ Newsletter
- ❑ Forums
- ❑ Photo Gallery
- ❑ Calendar of Events
- ❑ E-commerce store with shopping cart and order management
- ❑ Localization

From an administrative point of view, the following features and problems are also covered:

- ❑ Full online back-end administrative section, to manage practically all data from an intuitive user interface
- ❑ Site deployment

The implementation of each of these features provides the opportunity to teach various new features introduced by ASP.NET 3.5, such as the following:

- ❑ ASP.NET AJAX
- ❑ The new `ListView`
- ❑ Entity Framework and LINQ to Entities

Because the book is meant to be a case study of a real-world site, it does not stop at just implementing ASP.NET features; it applies them to typical scenarios. Included are:

❑   Search engine optimization techniques

❑   Error logging and handling

❑   CSS layouts

Not only does this book cover the new features of ASP.NET 3.5, it also demonstrates how to integrate all of them together, for the development of a single full-featured site. All the design options are explained and discussed (including the database design, the data access and business logic components design, and the overall site architecture); at the end of the book you will have learned many of the best practices for web development, based on a solid, scalable, and extensible architecture.

How This Book Is Structured

The book builds a complete project from start to finish. All the chapters (other than the first one) are self-contained modules within the larger project, and are structured in three sections:

❑   **Problem:** This defines the problem or problems to be addressed in the chapter: What do you want to do in this chapter? What features do you want to add to the site and why are they important? What restrictions or other factors need to be taken into account?

❑   **Design:** After the problem is defined adequately, this section describes what features are needed to solve the problem. This will give you a broad idea of how the solution will work or what will be entailed in solving the problem.

❑   **Solution:** After setting up what you are going to accomplish and why (and how that solves the problem defined earlier), we will produce and discuss the code and any other material that will realize the design and solve the problem laid out at the beginning of the chapter. Just as the coverage of the book as a whole is weighted toward solution, so is each chapter. This is where you will get hands-on practice and create the code.

The book is intended to be read from cover to cover, so that you start with nothing and finish with a complete and deployed web site ready to be launched. However, the book follows a modular structure, so every chapter is quite self-contained and implements a module that, if necessary, can be taken out of the proposed sample project and re-used in some other web site.

What You Need to Use This Book

To follow the book by building the project on your own computer, or to run the downloadable and ready-to-use project, you'll need the following:

❑   Windows XP Professional, Windows Vista, Windows 7, Windows Server 2008, Windows Server 2003, or Windows 2000 Professional or Server.

❑   Any edition of Visual Studio 2008, including the freely available Visual Web Developer 2008 Expression Edition. However, Visual Studio 2008 Standard is suggested. You'll be able to follow the book, and run the sample project, even if you don't use a Microsoft editor at all (if, for example, you prefer using Macromedia Dreamweaver MX or some other text editor), because Visual Studio's designers are described and demonstrated in the "Design" section of some chapters, but are not used to write the code in the "Solution" section.

❑ The freely available SQL Server 2008 Express Edition, and possibly SQL Server 2008 Standard Edition.

Conventions

To help you get the most from the text and keep track of what's happening, we've used a number of conventions throughout the book.

> **Boxes like this one hold important, not-to-be forgotten information that is directly relevant to the surrounding text.**

Notes, tips, hints, tricks, and asides to the current discussion are offset and placed in italics like this.

As for styles in the text:

❑ New terms and important words are *highlighted* when introduced.

❑ Keyboard combination strokes look like this: Ctrl+A.

❑ File names, URLs, and code within the text look like so: `persistence.properties`.

❑ Code is presented in two different ways:

```
We use a monofont type with no highlighting for most code examples.
We use gray highlighting to emphasize code that is of particular importance in
the present context, or to indicate where new code is added.
```

Source Code

As you work through the examples in this book, you may choose either to type in all the code manually or to use the source code files that accompany the book. All of the source code used in this book is available for download at `http://thebeerhouse.codeplex.com/`. Once at the site, you can either download the current source code by selecting the files under 2.0 Production – WebForms. This site is shared with the MVC edition as well, so be aware of that. You can also download the source code by selecting the Source Code tab and following the instructions on the page.

If for any reason the source is not available at CodePlex, we will keep a copy available for download at `www.wrox.com`. Once at the site, simply locate the book's title (either by using the Search box or by using one of the title lists) and click the Download Code link on the book's detail page to obtain all the source code for the book.

Because many books have similar titles, you may find it easiest to search by ISBN; this book's ISBN is 978-0-470-18758-6.

Once you download the code, just decompress it with your favorite compression tool. Alternately, you can go to the main Wrox code download page at http://www.wrox.com/dynamic/books/download .aspx to see the code available for this book and all other Wrox books.

Errata

We make every effort to ensure that there are no errors in the text or in the code. However, no one is perfect, and mistakes do occur. If you find an error in one of our books, like a spelling mistake or faulty piece of code, we would be very grateful for your feedback. By sending in errata you may save another reader hours of frustration and at the same time you will be helping us provide even higher quality information.

To find the errata page for this book, go to www.wrox.com and locate the title using the Search box or one of the title lists. Then, on the book details page, click the Book Errata link. On this page you can view all errata that has been submitted for this book and posted by Wrox editors. A complete book list including links to each book's errata is also available at www.wrox.com/misc-pages/ booklist.shtml.

If you don't spot "your" error on the Book Errata page, go to www.wrox.com/contact/techsupport .shtml and complete the form there to send us the error you have found. We'll check the information and, if appropriate, post a message to the book's errata page and fix the problem in subsequent editions of the book.

p2p.wrox.com

For author and peer discussion, join the P2P forums at p2p.wrox.com. The forums are a Web-based system for you to post messages relating to Wrox books and related technologies and interact with other readers and technology users. The forums offer a subscription feature to e-mail you topics of interest of your choosing when new posts are made to the forums. Wrox authors, editors, other industry experts, and your fellow readers are present on these forums.

At http://p2p.wrox.com you will find a number of different forums that will help you not only as you read this book, but also as you develop your own applications. To join the forums, just follow these steps:

1. Go to p2p.wrox.com and click the Register link.
2. Read the terms of use and click Agree.
3. Complete the required information to join as well as any optional information you wish to provide and click Submit.
4. You will receive an e-mail with information describing how to verify your account and complete the joining process.

You can read messages in the forums without joining P2P but in order to post your own messages, you must join.

Once you join, you can post new messages and respond to messages other users post. You can read messages at any time on the Web. If you would like to have new messages from a particular forum e-mailed to you, click the Subscribe to this Forum icon by the forum name in the forum listing.

For more information about how to use the Wrox P2P, be sure to read the P2P FAQs for answers to questions about how the forum software works as well as many common questions specific to P2P and Wrox books. To read the FAQs, click the FAQ link on any P2P page.

1

Introducing the Project: TheBeerHouse

This chapter introduces the project that we're going to develop in this book. I'll explain the concept behind the sample website that is the subject of this book, but as you read along you should keep in mind that this is a general-purpose, data-driven, content-based style of website that can easily be modified to meet the needs of a myriad of real-world website requirements. Although we'll use many of the older features of ASP.NET, the clear focus of this book is on showing you how to leverage the powerful new features of ASP.NET 3.5 SP1 such as ASP.NET AJAX, and the ADO.NET Entity Framework. I'll also integrate some basic search engine optimization techniques and third-party services for social networking and SPAM filtering to make a much richer site.

This book follows a "Problem–Design–Solution" approach in each chapter: the Problem section explains the business requirements for the module designed in that chapter; the Design section is used to develop the roadmap for meeting those requirements, and the Solution section is where we write the code to implement our design. This is unlike traditional computer books because the focus is not on teaching basic concepts but rather on showing you how to apply your knowledge to solve real-world business problems.

If you are new to ASP.NET, this is perhaps not the best book to start with, but if you're generally familiar with the basic concepts of web development and ASP.NET (any version of ASP.NET), you're ready to put that knowledge to use, and perhaps you want to learn about the new features in ASP.NET 3.5 SP1. Then, fasten your seat belt!

TheBeerHouse was originally created by Marco to serve as an online presence for a local pub in his hometown of Bologna, Italy. It was meant to serve as a way to reach out to the pub's mostly young clientele. This is still the primary goal of the site, but as technology matures, so does the average user's expectations of a site. The success of the site has driven website traffic and demand for TheBeerHouse merchandise much higher. This demand means a new site is needed to help extend the brand and the sharing of information with patrons. It also provides an opportunity to upgrade the underlying plumbing with some new technologies for both the user interface and the business layers.

Problem

Although the owner has always used traditional, printed marketing ads for her pub, and has a popular website, she wants to expand into social networking because many of her patrons are already active on Facebook, Twitter, and other popular social networking sites. Retaining features with which users are familiar is important because users are used to reading about new specials and events, and receiving newsletters with promotions and coupons. Now you want to extend their capability to browse photos of past events and to see a true calendar of upcoming events. Since the typical patron of TheBeerHouse is a young student who is active online, these upgrades should go a long way in extending TheBeerHouse brand, and, hopefully, profits!

The owner also realizes that, just as online marketing and frontend experiences have evolved, so has the technology that drives the Internet. Building a flexible and scalable business tier is also important to the owner. Object Relational Mapping (ORM) frameworks have come of age since the last version of the site. She is also interested in building some client software for back-office management with Windows Presentation Foundation (WPF) and maybe even a mobile client in the next phase, so creating a common business library is very important.

Design

At the beginning of a project, you think about your client's needs and how you might meet those needs, and possibly even expand on them to give your client more functionality than the minimum needed, while still staying within your time limits and budgetary guidelines. In this scenario your client is a pub owner who wants to have a website to promote her pub, providing online information about upcoming events, reports about past events, and more. The current site can be expanded in many ways, to create a new site that has a lot more interesting things, good for its users (who are also potential customers for the physical pub) and for the store owner. We can begin by writing down a list of features that a modern content-based site should have, and a few reasons why they are useful:

❑   The site will need to provide a rich interactive user experience (now known as UX). The experience users have on the website directly affects the impression they have of the pub. This means that users must find information and desired activities easy to browse and interact with.

Attention should also be given to cross-browser compatibility, that is, ensuring that the site looks good and behaves well on different platforms and browsers. While Internet Explorer is still the dominant browser, FireFox, Opera, and Safari are growing in popularity. You can't know in advance which browser your customers will use, as you might in the case of an intranet site for a corporation, for example.

❑   A successful content-based site owes its popularity to its users. Loyal users who regularly visit the site, help write content, and participate in polls and special events are those who guarantee that the site will keep growing. To build a vibrant community of active members, users must have some sort of *identity*, something that describes and distinguishes them from other members. Because of this, the site needs a registration feature, as part of a larger authentication/ authorization infrastructure. This will also be used to grant and restrict access to some areas of the site.

❑ Extending the concept of identity and interaction is leveraging popular social networking sites like Facebook, MySpace, Twitter, and YouTube. These sites will give TheBeerHouse another avenue of extending its brand, interacting with patrons, and allowing them to interact with TheBeerHouse site. Most social networking sites, such as Twitter, have available APIs that can be used by the site to publish content. Twitter allows you to post and monitor your Twitter feed through any client you want. All of these external sites have been designed to add value to the overall experience for a patron of TheBeerHouse.

❑ The site needs a constant supply of fresh content to stay alive and vibrant. If the content becomes stale, visitors will lose interest in the site and won't visit it anymore. A pub's site can't be very good unless it has regular updates about upcoming events, parties, and concerts. What's the point in visiting the site if it doesn't display photos that were shot at the last party? To facilitate a constant stream of new content, the site needs some mechanism that enables the editor to easily update it with dynamic content. The content should also be thoughtfully organized so that visitors can find, and even subscribe to, the type(s) of information in which they are most interested. Furthermore, the editor who will be in charge of the content updates will probably not be a technical person, so you must build some simple administration pages that make updates easy, even for nontechnical people.

❑ The Beer House owes much of its success to its nightly entertainment, themed parties and other events. The new site includes a Calendar of Events for visitors to keep track of what is happening at the Beer House.

❑ Once the site has new content ready to be read, the site's manager must have some way to inform its users about this. Not all users visit the site every day, so the site manager must be proactive and notify the customers about recent updates. If customers have registered on the site, providing their e-mail address, they might also have requested to receive a newsletter notifying them about recent changes and additions to the site. Of course, there are also other ways to syndicate news, such as exposing RSS (Really Simple Syndication) feeds to which a user can register and then control from their favorite RSS reader, and get automatic notifications about news without having to visit the site daily to get the information.

❑ A site like this can also be a good opportunity to get feedback from customers about a variety of issues: What do they like most in a pub? What brand of beer do they prefer? Do they want to listen to live music while drinking with friends, or perhaps they don't like all that noise? Establishing some kind of user-to-site communication is important, and if you get a good number of responses, it can even lead to strategic decisions and changes that may improve the business.

❑ If the presence of some sort of user-to-site communication is important, user-to-user communication may be even more so, because that's the central point of creating a community of loyal users, who come to the site frequently to chat, discuss the news posted on the site, ask for suggestions from the others about upcoming events, and more. This translates into more traffic on the site and a feeling of membership that will pay off in both the short and long run.

❑ Once the store has a user base, the store's owner may decide to expand it so that it supports an online store. In fact, the pub already offers a catalog of products for beer enthusiasts, such as glasses, T-shirts, key chains, and more. If the site has a lot of traffic, it may be a good way to promote these products so that people can place orders without even visiting the pub in person. And once users see a product and like it, they can rate that product to tell other people how much they like it. The online store must be easy to manage by nontechnical people, because it might possibly be the pub's owner who adds and edits products, and manages the orders. Thus, there must be a module with a simple and intuitive UI that automates as many operations as possible, and guides the user through the tasks.

❑ Demonstrating how lively and fun TheBeerHouse is very important in fostering dedicated patrons. Photos and videos are a great way to share this atmosphere. Adding a photo gallery to the site and taking advantage of YouTube.com and other video-sharing sites are great ways to share what life is like in TheBeerHouse.

❑ With the site offering news and articles, lists of products, user-to-user discussions, and other dynamic content, it's easy to imagine that the home page could easily become crowded, and possibly more difficult to read and understand because of too much information. It would be good if the user herself could build her own home page, according to what she is interested in. Maybe she wants to read about upcoming events but doesn't care about shopping online for gadgets? Great, you want to give her the capability to do that, by adding and deleting content to and from the home page, or maybe just moving around the existing content so that it's placed and organized in a way that she finds more comfortable and useful for her. This type of customization is done on some large sites such as Windows Live and My MSN, for example, and is a great example of personalization, which helps encourage users to decide to register on the site.

❑ As mentioned previously, the pub is typically visited by a lot of customers coming from many different countries, and the pub's owner expects the same to happen on the website. Because of this, the site must be partially or fully translated into multiple languages, making it easy for most users to understand it. Not only must text be translated, but information such as dates and numbers should also be displayed according to the user's preferred locale settings, so that nobody will misunderstand an announcement about an upcoming party or event.

❑ Optimizing the site for search engine exposure is also a high priority. Adding social networking features to the online strategy should help gain valuable inbound links to assist with search engine ranking. But you still need to make sure that common search engine optimization techniques are applied to the site to help with overall ranking and placement of the site for targeted keyword phrases.

To recap everything in a few words, the TheBeerHouse site will have everything a modern content-based site will have, including dynamic articles and news, polls for user-to-site communication, forums for user-to-user communication, newsletters and RSS feeds to notify members about new content on the site, an e-commerce store for selling products online, home page personalization, and content localization. It will also have a photo gallery, calendar of events, social networking, and OpenId integration. Although the sample project is built around a fictitious pub, you'll recognize in this list of requirements the common features of the majority of content- and commerce-based sites you find online now, and sites that you're likely to develop in the near future, or maybe even sites you're developing right now.

Solution

The Solution section of each chapter will contain the instructions and actual code for implementing all the features and requirements outlined and designed in the previous sections. However, this first chapter gives you a more detailed description of exactly what the following chapters will cover, so that you can get a good idea of what the final result will be like.

In Chapter 2, you'll build the site's design, the graphics, and the layout that are shared among all pages of the site, through the use of master pages and nested master pages. You will also use themes and Cascading Style Sheets (CSS) to create a couple of different visual appearances for the same master page, and create a mechanism to enable users to select their own favorite theme from a drop-down list, so that they can change the colors and overall appearance of the site according to their taste and possible visual impediments. Finally, a flexible and easy-to-maintain navigation system will be built by means of a custom `SiteMapProvider` and the `Menu` and `SiteMapPath` controls.

In Chapter 3, you'll lay down the foundations for building a flexible, and easily configurable and instrumented site. First, a data access layer (DAL) will be built from the ADO.NET Entity Framework and a SQL Server database. Then a business logic layer will be built on the top of the DAL to expose the data in an object-oriented way, with the required validation logic, transaction management, event logging, and caching. Finally, you'll look at the UI and presentation layer, which take advantage of the new `ListView` control and ASP.NET AJAX to quickly generate complex, interactive, and feature-rich, data-driven pages.

In Chapter 4, you'll integrate the membership infrastructure introduced in ASP.NET 2.0 into the site, to create user registration forms and supporting logic to authenticate/authorize users. You'll also see how to use the `Profile` module, which allows you to declaratively define user-level properties that are automatically persisted to a durable medium, quite different from the well-known traditional `Session` state variables, which last only as long as the user browses the site on one occasion. You will also see how to take advantage of ASP.NET AJAX's built-in membership, role, and profile interfaces. You will build a complete management console to enable administrators to see the list of members, disable members that behave badly on the site, and view and edit each user's profile.

In Chapter 5, you'll build a sort of content management system, a module that enables administrators to completely manage the site's articles from an intuitive UI, accessible also by nontechnical users. The module will integrate with the built-in membership system to secure the module and track the authors of the articles, and will have a syndication service that publishes an RSS feed of recent content for a specific category, or for every category, and will support ratings and comments, among many other features. It will also automatically post matching content on Twitter, alerting followers about new content and make use of user and search-engine-friendly URLs, that take advantage of the article title in the URL and a custom URL Rewriting HttpModule. The result will be quite powerful, enabling the editor to prepare richly formatted content in advance, and schedule it for automatic publication and retirement, so that the site's content updates are as simple as possible, and require the least effort and time. At the end of the chapter, you will have experienced a many of the things you can do with the new `ListView` control, the ADO.NET Entity Framework, interacting with external APIs and custom HttpHandlers.

In Chapter 6, you'll implement a solution for creating and managing multiple dynamic polls on the website. It will feature an administration console for managing the polls through a web browser and a user control that enables you to plug different polls into any page you want with just a couple of lines of code, as well as a history page for viewing archived polls.

In Chapter 7, the site will be enriched with a complete module for sending out newsletters to members who registered for them in their profile page. The module will enable you to send out the e-mail newsletters from a background thread, instead of the main thread that processes the page request, so that the page won't risk timeouts, and more important, so that the editor will not be left with a blank page for minutes at a time. AJAX will be used to implement real-time feedback about the newsletter being sent in the background. Finally, end users will be able to look at past newsletters listed on an archive page. To implement all this, you'll use advanced features such as multithreaded programming, the new script callback feature, and new classes for sending e-mails.

In Chapter 8, you'll create a forums system from scratch, which supports multiple sub-forums with optional moderation; lists threads and replies through custom pagination and with different sorting options; has wide support for standard RSS feeds, configurable user rating, signatures, and quoting; and offers other features typical of most recent forum software. Complete administration features (for deleting, editing, approving, moving, and closing threads and posts) will also be provided.

In Chapter 9, you'll add a working e-commerce store with most of the essential features, including a complete catalog and order management system; a persistent shopping cart; integrated online payment via credit cards; product ratings; product stock availability; rich formatting of a product's descriptions, including text and images; configurable shipping methods and order statuses; and much more. All this will be implemented in relatively few pages, since it will leverage the good foundations built in previous chapters, such as the built-in membership and profile systems, and other features and controls, such as the `ListView`, `Wizard`, and `MultiView` controls.

In Chapter 10, you'll add a photo gallery that features the capability for administrators to add and manage photo albums, photos, and descriptive data about the photos. It also implements an AJAX lightbox to add some special effects when viewing an image.

In Chapter 11, you'll add an event calendar to which TheBeerHouse staff will add events at each of their locations. Patrons can subscribe to these events via RSS or add them to their calendar applications via an `iCal` object. This will be done by using the `Calendar` control and a custom `httpHandler`. New events will also be published directly to TheBeerHouse Twitter feed.

In Chapter 12, you'll make the site's home page fully localizable to an additional language and will support the user's preferred locale settings when displaying dates and numbers. All this can be done easily with ASP.NET, thanks to its automatic resource generation, implicit and explicit localization expressions, strongly typed and dynamically compiled global resources, and good Visual Studio Designer support.

Finally, in Chapter 13, you'll look the different ways to deploy an ASP.NET site, either on a local IIS server or to a remote production site, or to an inexpensive shared hosting server. The ASP.NET compilation model enables you do use a simple `XCOPY` deployment that includes everything, but lacks protection of source code, and takes a little time to compile on first requests. If that's a problem for you, you will see how you can use the new command-line tools and Visual Studio's wizards to precompile the site and generate one or more compiled assemblies to deploy. You'll also learn how to deploy the local SQL Server Express database to a remote full-featured SQL Server instance, and how you can create installer packages for distributing the application to automate as many installation tasks as possible.

Summary

You now have an overview of an aggressive plan to develop a highly functional content-based website that shows you how to use ASP.NET 3.5, ASP.NET AJAX, the ADO.NET Entity Framework, and various external APIs to their full capacity. This chapter gave you a broad idea about what we're going to discuss, design, and implement throughout the rest of the book.

In each chapter, you'll learn something new about ASP.NET and web programming, and at the end of the book you will have created a real-world site with most of the features required by modern content-centric sites and e-commerce stores. Furthermore, the site you develop in this book may provide a good deal more functionality than any site you've designed in the past, and the relatively small development effort will enable you to do more than you thought possible in a small amount of time. One of Microsoft's key goals with the .NET platform is to help you "fall into the pit of success." ASP.NET is designed to make developers' jobs easier: to reduce the amount of effort required to implement common functionality, thereby giving them more time to focus on business needs, and enabling them to offer more advanced functionality to empower users and site administrators, while keeping the site maintainable and scalable. This book will help you judge whether Microsoft has met this goal. Let the adventure begin!

2

Developing the Site Design

The first step in developing a new site is to develop the visual site design, consisting of the site's overall layout, use of graphics, and user interaction elements. Today the visual architecture defines more than just the "look and feel" from the user's perspective; it also means the ease of use and encouraging user interaction. You start by establishing the user experience you want people to have, and then you design the plumbing behind the scenes that will provide that user experience. Some basic considerations that affect the user's experience are the menu and navigation, use of images, organization of elements on the page, and use of AJAX.

The menu must be intuitive and should be augmented by navigation hints such as a site map or *breadcrumbs* that can remind users where they are, relative to the site as a whole. Breadcrumbs in this context refer to a set of small links on the page that form a trail that enables users to back up to a previous page by clicking on the link segment for a page higher in the page hierarchy.

Consider the specific ASP.NET features before writing any code, so you can take advantage of the work that's already been done by Microsoft. By laying a good foundation for the technical architecture, you can improve code reusability and enhance maintainability. This chapter looks at the overall visual layout of the site and explains how you can take advantage of powerful features such as master pages and themes. Master pages are used to group functionality into templates that provide the common elements shared by many pages, and themes enable users to customize certain aspects of the site to give them a unique look and feel that appeals to them (also called *skinning*).

Problem

Over the last few years the .NET development community has begun to work hard toward creating great user interfaces for its applications. We really started seeing a good effort made in this direction with the introduction of ASP.NET AJAX and now with Windows Presentation

Foundation (WPF) and Silverlight. The marketplace has really driven this paradigm change through competition and users' demanding it. It is more than just having pretty graphics and whiz-bang features; it has to do with just plain usability. Users do not want to have to think; an application should just work.

Many developers start out writing source code without paying attention to the primary goal of the site: to provide a simple but highly functional graphical application for users to interact with. This is not acceptable in today's competitive world. Developing the user interface seems like a very basic task, but if it is not done properly, you may have to revisit it several times during development. Every time you go back and change fundamental features it will require a certain amount of rework, not to mention a whole new round of unit, integration, and user acceptance testing. Even worse, if you take the user interface too lightly, you will likely end up regretting it because users may choose not to visit your site. There are various elements to consider when creating the site design. First, you must convince yourself of one simple fact: appearance *is* important! You should repeat this out loud a couple of times.

If your site doesn't look appealing or if interacting with the site is not natural, people may regret being there. It's easy for a developer to get caught up with the difficult tasks of organizing source code into classes and coding the business logic — the cosmetics of the site just don't seem so important, right? Wrong! The user interface is the first thing presented to the end user and, more importantly, your customer if you are a typical developer. If it is ugly, unclear, and basically unusable, chances are good the user will be left with a bad impression of the site and the company behind it. Sadly, this will happen regardless of how fast and scalable the site is.

In addition, you need to consider that not all users have the same opinion about a site template. Some users may find it difficult to read text in a site with a specific color scheme and prefer a different color scheme that might be unclear to many others. It's very difficult to make everybody happy with a single template and color scheme. That's why some sites have multiple color schemes and possible layouts available from which users can choose, enabling them to customize their own user experience according to their personal taste — and possibly physical impediments such as color blindness. Studies have shown that a surprising number of people suffer from partial color blindness that makes it hard for them to distinguish certain colors, so they must be able to select colors they can distinguish but that still appear somewhat pleasant.

> The term UX (an acronym for "user experience") has become very common in the last 2–3 years when referencing software. When AJAX started coming of age a few years ago, the interaction that website visitors had with the site or application started increasing. The release of WPF and Silverlight (and I'll have to throw Adobe Flex in here, too) has driven users' expectations even higher. This does not mean that a site needs to be completely done in Silverlight to be acceptable these days, but gone are the days of blinking and clashing text, as well as the visible postback model. Users expect to feel comfortable while using an application, knowing that everything is going as they expect. This means that they should not have to struggle to understand how an application works, and so forth. A good example in the new version of the Beer House is the use of pure AJAX to allow users to comment on articles. The topic of UX is really outside the scope of this book; however, I hope this upgrade adds several good UX improvements not in the previous edition.

After you choose the layout and colors to use, you need to ensure that the site will look the same on different browsers. A few years ago, Internet Explorer (IE) was the absolute dominant browser among Windows users, and if you were developing a technical site targeted at Windows developers, you could assume that the majority of your user base would use IE to browse the site, and thus develop and test it only against IE. However, Firefox, Opera, Safari, and now Google Chrome are gaining noticeable market share among Internet users, not to mention browsing from other operating systems, such as Linux and Mac OS. To make things a little more complicated Microsoft is getting close to releasing Internet Explorer 8, which promises to be ACID 2 compliant, a standard test to measure a site's compliance with CSS standards.

You are not targeting just a small niche of users (i.e., not just Windows developers but all people that go to your client's pub), and because there are other popular browsers besides Internet Explorer, it is absolutely necessary to ensure that your site works well for the most popular browsers. If you ignore this and just target IE, Firefox users may come to the site and find a layout much different from what they expect, with the wrong alignments, sizes, and colors, with panels and text over other elements — in other words, a complete mess. As you can guess, a user who is presented such an ugly page will typically leave it, which means losing a potential client or customer for the online store. At the very least, this person's visit would have generated page views and, thus, banner impressions.

Because you don't want to lose visitors, we'll make sure the new Beer House site renders and works properly in as many browsers as we can. Typically, if you can make the site work consistently in Internet Explorer, Firefox, and Chrome, it will work in the other browsers as well. The real key is testing against the popular browser engines, Internet Explorer, Gecko (Firefox), and WebKit (Chrome).

Designing the user interface layer doesn't mean just writing the HTML for a page; it also involves the navigation system and the capability of the webmaster or site administrator (if not the end user) to easily change the appearance of the site without requiring them to edit the actual content pages (which are numerous). Once you're done with the site's home page, developing all the other pages will take much less time because the home page establishes layout and navigation elements that will apply throughout the site. And if you need to modify something in the site's layout (for example, adding a new poll box to be displayed on the right-hand side of any page), you will be able to do this easily if you've developed a common user interface shared among many pages. This is why it's definitely worth spending some additional time thinking about a well-designed UI foundation layer instead of firing up Visual Studio .NET and starting to code right away. This is really a strategic decision that can save you hours or even days of work later. Remember that fundamental changes applied later in the development phase will require more time and effort to implement. Figure 2-1 shows the new Beer House in the Mozilla and WebKit engines.

> **The previous version of the Beer House made the use of Web Parts, which is a concept brought over from SharePoint to allow users to move content around the page. I chose to remove that chapter from the book because the use of Web Parts is very minimal, and it drastically adds to the weight of the pages. This technology was not revised in ASP.NET 3.5 either. If you need to see how to implement Web Parts in your site, then I recommend the 2.0 version of this book.**

Figure 2-1

Design

In this section, I'll take the problems described in the first section and discuss how to solve them by devising a technical system design. In practice, you will design and implement the following:

❑ A good-looking graphical template (layout) that appears the same with all major browsers, and a mechanism to dynamically apply different color schemes and other appearance attributes to it.

❑ A way to easily share the created template with all pages of the site, without physically copying and pasting the entire code in each page.

❑ A navigation system that enables users to easily find resources on the site and clearly tells users where they currently are in the site map, enabling them to navigate backward.

❑ A way to apply not only a common design to all pages of the site, but also a common behavior, such as counting page views or applying the user's favorite style to the page.

I'll describe how you can utilize some of the features in ASP.NET when implementing your reusability, menu, navigation, and customization requirements. I'll also review how to utilize CSS layouts to build an easy-to-manage template that is also search engine optimization (SEO) friendly. Later, in the "Solution," section, you'll put these powerful new features into action!

Designing the Site Layout

When you develop a site design, you typically create a mock-up with a graphics application such as Adobe Photoshop, Jasc Paint Shop Pro, Paint.NET, or just a piece of paper to show you what the final site may should look like before you do any specific layout or coding in HTML. Once you have a mock-up, you can show it to the various model users, testers, and managers, who can then decide whether to apply it to the front of the application. You might create a simple picture like the one shown in Figure 2-2, in which you show how the content will be laid out in the various areas of the page.

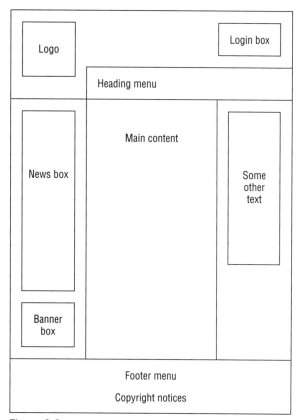

Figure 2-2

This is a typical three-column layout, with a header and footer. When the layout is approved, you must recreate it with real graphics and HTML. It makes sense to do this in the graphics program because, on average, it takes much less time for a web designer to produce these mock-ups as images than as real HTML pages. Once the client approves the final mock-up, the web designer can cut the mock-up image into small pieces and use them in an HTML page.

Creating a mock-up is not always easy for those of us who aren't very artistic by nature. For a medium or large company, this is not a problem because there is usually a professional designer to create the graphical design, and then the developers (people like you and me) build the application around it, or the designer creates a nice design to fit the application you create. Sometimes it can be helpful to enlist

the assistance of a third-party company if you're faced with creating the graphical design by yourself —
you can, in effect, subcontract that one aspect of the site to someone more artistically talented, and they
can make you a site template. This can also mean licensing a prebuilt template from a company like
TemplateMonster (www.templatemonster.com). For the purposes of creating the website discussed
in this book, I used an image of three beer steins I found doing a search for "beer" through Creative
Commons (creativecommons.org), a large collection of free resources such as images and videos. Next, I
wanted to decide on a consistent color scheme and used http://kuler.adobe.com, a site that demonstrates color schemes, to help me find just the right scheme, "Dark Beer." I then created some supporting
graphics, consisting of some gradients and a logo in Paint.NET. Paint.NET is a graphic design program
that is similar to Adobe Photoshop, but written entirely in .NET and available for free. Combining all
this made a site design that I could use as a starting point.

I kept things pretty simple, so I did not have to do too much work to get the layout of the site together. I
really needed to get started with defining the stylesheets in the Dark Beer theme to apply the graphics
and the color scheme to the site.

Technologies Used to Implement the Design

ASP.NET 3.5 SP1 is the overriding technology that makes the site work. This runs on the web server
and takes advantage of the functionality provided by the .NET Framework. However, ASP.NET does
not run on the user's computer; instead, it dynamically generates the elements that a browser uses to
render a page. The elements that are sent down to the browser consist of HTML, images, and Cascading
Style Sheets (CSS), which provide colors, sizes, and alignments for various items in the HTML. ASP.NET
also generates some JavaScript procedural code that is also sent down to the browser to handle data
validation and to tell the browser how to interact with the web server.

HTML is created in several ways. You can use the visual form designer in Visual Studio to drop controls onto the form, and this automatically creates the markup for the controls that ultimately emit
HTML. You can hand-edit or author your own HTML code in the .aspx files to give it features that
aren't easily specified in the form designer. Last, HTML can be dynamically generated by your code or
by classes in the .NET Framework, HttpHandlers are the best example of this.

Using CSS to Define Styles in Stylesheet Files

It is not possible to give an exhaustive explanation of CSS in this book, but I'll cover some of the general
concepts. You should consult other sources for complete details about CSS. The purpose of CSS is to
specify how visual HTML tags are to be rendered by specifying various stylistic elements such as font
size, color, alignment, and so on. These styles, called Selectors, can be included as attributes of HTML
tags, or they can be stored separately and referred to by Class, by ID or by defining a rule for a specific
HTML element.

Sometimes HTML files have the styles hard-coded into the HTML tags as attributes, as in the following
example:

```
<div style="align: justify; color: red; background-color:
yellow; font-size: 12px;">some text</div>
```

This is bad because it is difficult to modify these stylistic elements without going into all the HTML
files and hunting for the CSS attributes. It also adds volume to each page being downloaded, thus
hurting the overall perceived performance of the pages. Instead, always put the style definitions in a

separate stylesheet file with an extension of `.css`; or if you insist on including styles inside an HTML file, at least define them in a `<style>` section at the top of the HTML file.

> There are many blogs and websites that focus entirely on Web Design and CSS. A quick search will give you a pretty good list to start with. Some books you might want to reference include:
>
> *Mastering Integrated HTML and CSS* by Virginia Debolt (`www.wiley.com/WileyCDA/WileyTitle/productCd-047009754X.html`), HTML, XHTML
>
> *CSS Bible* by Steven Schafer, (`www.wiley.com/WileyCDA/WileyTitle/productCd-0470128615.html`)
>
> *Beginning CSS* by Richard York, (`www.wiley.com/WileyCDA/WileyTitle/productCd-0470096977.html`)
>
> *CSS Instant Results* by Richard York (`www.wiley.com/WileyCDA/WileyTitle/productCd-047175126X.html`)

Maintaining style definitions in a separate stylesheet file makes the site more maintainable, increases performance and minimizes the administrative effort required to maintain styles and to enforce a common look and feel among many pages. You often hear the term "separation of concerns" in terms of application architecture; it applies to web development of user interfaces with CSS. The idea is to separate as much of the design concerns from the application code as possible. Keeping styles in a file means that there is only one place where you need to manage elements when you need to adjust a style. Using inline style definitions is no different from repeating a routine multiple times in code. In programming terms, it means that you can refactor a style definition to a central location instead of repeating it in each page of markup. This is a common theme you will see in modern ASP.NET with the use of master pages, themes, and user controls.

Let's assume that the client wants to change some styles of a site that's already in production. If you've hard-coded styles into the HTML elements of the page, then you'd have to look in many files to locate the styles to change, and you might not find them all, or you might change something else by mistake — this could break something! However, if you've used style classes stored separately in CSS files, then it's easier to locate the classes that need to be changed, and your HTML code will be untouched and safe.

Furthermore, CSS files can make a site more efficient. The browser will download the CSS file once and then cache it on the client. The browser will use the cached instance of the .css file and not download all the styles again, so each subsequent request will be much smaller, and therefore faster to download. In some cases, this can dramatically speed up the loading of web pages in a user's browser.

On top of downloading fewer resources, this can also help with rendering tables, which browsers do more slowly than a series of DIV and SPAN elements. That's because browsers wait until the entire contents of a table have been downloaded before rendering it to the user. Tables are good for tabular data, and that is what they should be used for. While using stylesheet layouts is tougher to become familiar with, it can be a much more flexible way to create a site layout.

While many sites use multiple stylesheet files, I personally like to have just one. The reason is that each file will need to be downloaded and thus add to the time required to download the content. While the hit may seem to be negligible, it all adds up. On the flip side, organizing related styles into specific files can be very helpful in managing styles. It can also add to confusion and duplication of styles, meaning that efforts get overwritten during rendering. The ultimate choice will come down to the needs of the application and your personal management style.

When you group CSS styles, you can create `Selectors`, which syntactically resemble classes or functions. You can assign them a class name, preceded by a period (.), to allow them to be referenced in the `class=` attribute of HTML tags. You can also associate an HTML element with an element name simply by creating a style rule with the same name as the element. For example, H1 maps to the `<h1>` element. You can also refer to specific elements by their client-side ID; just precede the name of the style rule with a # followed by the ID of the element. Finally, you can combine class, element, and ID selectors to create complex style rules.

> For a more detailed explanation of CSS `Selectors` I recommend visiting the W3C recommendations, `www.w3.org/TR/CSS2/selector.html`.

If you use a stylesheet `Selector`, an ID, or element selectors, and you want to change the font size of all corresponding HTML elements , you only need to find that style rule and change that single occurrence in order to change many visual HTML elements of that given type. If the stylesheet is defined in a separate file, you will benefit even more from this approach, because you will change a single file and *n* pages will change their appearance accordingly.

Here is an example of how you can redefine the style of a `DIV` object by storing it in a separate file named `styles.css`. First, define a new class called mystyle in a file called `mystyles.css` as follows:

```
.mystyle
{
    align: justify;
    color: red;
    background-color: yellow;
    font-size: 12px;
}
```

Then, in the .aspx or .htm page, you will link the CSS file to the HTML as follows:

```
<head>
    <link href="/styles.css" text="text/css" rel="stylesheet" />
    <!-- other metatags... -->
</head>
```

Finally, you write the HTML DIV tag and specify which CSS class you want it to use:

```
<div class="mystyle">some text</div>
```

Note that when the style was declared, I used the dot (.) prefix for the class name. You have to do this for all of your custom style `Selectors`.

If you want to define a style to be applied to all HTML elements of a certain kind (for example, to all <p> paragraphs, or even the page's <body> tag) that don't have another explicit class associated with them, you can write the following specification in the stylesheet file:

```
body
{
    margin: 0px;
    font-family: Verdana;
    font-size: 12px;
}


p
{
    align: justify;
    text-size: 10px;
}
```

This sets the default style of all body tags and all <p> (paragraph) tags in one place. However, you could specify a different style for some paragraphs by stating an explicit class name in those tags.

Yet another way to associate a Selector to a HTML object is by ID, which you will see used as we start defining the layout for the new Beer House site. You define the Selector name with a # prefix, as follows:

```
#header
{
    padding: 0px;
    margin: 0px;
    width: 100%;
    height: 184px;
    background-image: url(images/HeaderSlice.gif);
}
```

Then you could use the id attribute of the HTML tag to link the CSS to the HTML. For example, this is how you could define an HTML division tag and specify that you want it to use the #header style:

```
<div id="header">some text</div>
```

You typically use this approach for single objects, such as the header, the footer, the container for the left, right, center column, and so on. If you need to apply a style to multiple elements in a page, use a class Selector.

Finally, you can mix the various approaches. Suppose that you want to give a certain style to all links in a container with the sectiontitle style, and some other styles to links into a container with the sectionbody style. You could do it this way:

In the .css file

```
.sectiontitle a
{
    color: yellow;
}
```

```
.sectionbody a
{
    color: red;
}
```

In the .aspx/.htm file

```
<div class="sectiontitle">
<p>some text</p>
<a href="http://www.wrox.com">Wrox</a>
<p>some text</p>
</div>

<div class="sectionbody">
<p>some other text</p>
<a href="http://www.wiley.com">Wiley</a>
<p>some other text</p>
</div>
```

Avoid Using HTML Tables to Control Layout

Often developers will use HTML tables to control the positioning of other items on a web page. This was considered the standard practice before CSS matured, but many developers still use this methodology today. I admit it took me a long time to make the switch. Although this is a very common practice, the W3C officially discourages it (www.w3c.org/tr/wai-webcontent), saying "Tables should be used to mark up truly tabular information ("data tables"). Content developers should avoid using them to lay out pages ("layout tables"). Tables for any use also present special problems to users of screen readers." In other words, HTML tables should be used for displaying tabular data on the page, not to build the entire layout of the page. For that, you should use container elements (such as DIVs) and their style attribute, possibly through the use of a separate `<style>` section or a separate file. This is ideal for a number of reasons:

❑   If you use container elements and a separate stylesheet file to define appearance and position, you won't need to repeat this definition again and again, for each and every page of your site. This leads to a site that is both faster to develop and easier to maintain once you have a standard set of templates to build pages.

❑   The site will load much faster for end users. Remember that the stylesheet file will be downloaded by the client only once, and then loaded from the cache for subsequent requests of pages until it changes on the server. If you define the layout inside the HTML file using tables, the client instead will download the table's layout for every page, and thus it will download more bytes, with the result that downloading the whole page will require a longer time. Typically, a CSS-driven layout can trim the downloaded bytes by up to 50%, and the advantage of this approach becomes immediately evident. Furthermore, this savings has a greater impact on a heavily loaded web server — sending fewer bytes to each user can be multiplied by the number of simultaneous users to determine the total savings on the web server side of the communications.

❑   Screen readers, software that can read the text and other content of the page for blind and visually impaired users, have a much more difficult job when tables are used for layout on the page. Using a table-free layout can increase the accessibility of the site. This is a very important requirement for certain categories of sites, such as those for public administration and government agencies. Few companies are willing to write off entire groups of users over simple matters like this.

❑   CSS styles and DIVs provide greater flexibility than tables. You can, for example, have different stylesheet files that define different appearances and positions for the various objects on the page. By switching the linked stylesheet, you can completely change the appearance of the page, without changing anything in the content pages themselves. With dynamic ASP.NET pages, you can even change the stylesheet at runtime and, thus, easily implement a mechanism that enables end users to choose the styles they prefer. And it's not just a matter of colors and fonts — you can also specify positions for objects in CSS files and therefore have one file that places the menu box on the upper-left corner of the page and another one that puts it on the bottom-right corner. Because we want to allow users to pick their favorite styles from a list of available themes, this is a particularly important point.

❑   CSS enables you to target different classes of devices in some cases without requiring new HTML markup, such as mobile devices like PDAs or smartphones. Because of their constrained screen size, it is necessary to adapt the output for them, so that the content fits the small screen well and is easily readable. You can do this with a specific stylesheet that changes the size and position of some containers (placing them one under the other, rather than in vertical columns), or hide them completely. For example, you might hide the container for the banners, polls, and the header with a big logo. Try to do this if you use tables — it will be much more difficult. You'll have to think about a custom skinning mechanism, and you'll need to write separate pages that define the different layouts available. This is much more work than just writing a new CSS file.

Note that the preceding discussion refers to avoiding the use of tables for the site's overall layout. However, using tables is acceptable to create input forms with a tabular structure because otherwise too much CSS code would be required to be easily writeable and maintainable. It's also not very likely that you'll need to dynamically change the layout of the input form, so you don't need all the flexibility of CSS for that, and using HTML tables is more immediate.

Sharing the Common Design among Multiple Pages

Once you finish creating your beautiful site design, you need to find a way to quickly apply it to *n* pages, where *n* could be dozens or even hundreds of pages. Master pages are used to control the overall layout of the site. They have replaced the common ASP.NET 1.1 practice of using a series of user controls on every page. With Visual Studio 2008, it becomes very natural to develop with nested master pages.

Enter the Master Page Model

ASP.NET 2.0 introduced a master page feature that enables you to define common areas that every page will share, such as headers, footers, menus, and so on. A master page enables you to put the common layout code in a single file and have it visually inherited in all the content pages. A master page contains the overall layout for your site. Content pages can inherit the appearance of a master page, and place their own content where the master page has defined a `ContentPlaceHolder` control.

What actually happens at runtime is that the content of the master page and the content page are merged together as one cohesive unit. Behind the scenes, the master page actually injects itself in the child control hierarchy of the `Page` class itself (see `www.odetocode.com/Articles/450.aspx`). If you think about it, this makes perfect sense because the `MasterPage` class inherits the `UserControl` class, it is just a special user control in reality.

Once the master page has injected itself into the content page's control tree, it then looks for corresponding Content controls for each of the ContentPlaceHolders declared in the master page's markup. In this action, the overall layout is produced and the page proceeds to build itself as expected. Figure 2-3 illustrates the hierarchy being implemented with master pages.

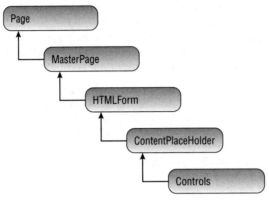

Figure 2-3

All of this magic actually happens after the PreInit event, but before the Init event of the content page. This means that the content page's master page must be set in the PreInit event and not after it. Generally, this will be done in the @Page Directive or the web.config file. But there are occasions where you want to define the actual master page at runtime, such as when you open your site up to layout customizations by the end user. You just have to remember to do this in the PreInit event handler or an InvalidOperationException will be thrown when your page is executed.

An example is worth a thousand words, so let's see how this concept turns into practice. A master page has a .master extension. Because it is an extended version of a UserControl, it can be programmed in the same fashion. The following is code for a master page that contains some text, a header div tag, and a footer div tag. It also defines a ContentPlaceHolder control between the header and the footer:

```
<%@ Master Language="VB" AutoEventWireup="true"
CodeFile="MasterPage.master.vb" Inherits="MasterPage" %>

<html>
<head id="Head1" runat="server">
   <title>The Beer House</title>
</head>

<body>
<form id="Main" runat="server">
   <div id="header">The Beer House</div>
   <asp:ContentPlaceHolder ID="MainContent" runat="server" />
   <div id="footer">Copyright 2008 WROX</div>
</form>
</body>
</html>
```

As you see, it is extremely similar to a standard page or user control, except that it has a `@Master` directive at the top of the page instead of a `@Page` or `@Control` directive, and it declares one or more `ContentPlaceHolder` controls where the .aspx pages will add their own content. The master page and the content page will merge at runtime — therefore, because the master page defines the `<html>`, `<head>`, `<body>`, and `<form>` tags, you can easily guess that the content pages must not define them again. Content pages define the content for the master's `ContentPlaceHolder` controls and nothing else. The following extract shows an example of a content page:

```
<%@ Page Language="VB" MasterPageFile="~/MasterPage.master" AutoEventWireup="false"
CodeFile="MyPage.aspx.vb" Inherits="MyPage" Title="The Beer House - My Page" %>

<asp:Content ID="MainContent" ContentPlaceHolderID="MainContent" Runat="Server">
    My page content goes here...
</asp:Content>
```

The first key point is that the `@Page` directive sets the `MasterPageFile` attribute to the virtual path of the master page to use. The content is placed into `Content` controls whose `ContentPlaceHolderID` must match the ID of one of the `ContentPlaceHolder` controls of the master page. In a content page, you can't place anything but `Content` controls, and other ASP.NET controls that actually define the visual features must be grouped under the outermost `Content` controls. Another point to note is that the `@Page` directive has a new attribute, `Title`, that allows you to override the value specified in the master page's `<title>` metatag. If you fail to specify a `Title` attribute for a given content page, then the title specified on the master page will be used instead.

Figure 2-4 illustrates the master page feature.

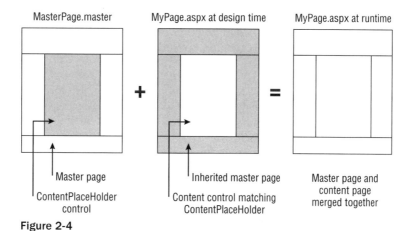

Figure 2-4

When you edit a content page in Visual Studio in Design or Split View, it properly renders both the master page and the content page in the form designer, but the master page content appears to be "grayed out." This is done on purpose as a reminder to you that you can't modify the content provided by the master page when you're editing a content page. Figure 2-5 shows the home page in design mode. Notice how its master page is listed in the top-right corner (`CRMaster.master`), and the elements contained in the master pages are rendered in the editor but are disabled.

Figure 2-5

I'd like to point out that your master page also has a code-behind file that could be used to write properties and functions that could be accessed in the .aspx or code-behind files of content pages. This is because the master page is actually a user control, so working in a master page is almost identical to working with a user control.

When you define the ContentPlaceHolder in a master page, you can also specify the default content for it, which will be used in the event that a particular content page doesn't have a Content control for that ContentPlaceHolder. Here is a snippet that shows how to provide some default content:

```
<asp:ContentPlaceHolder ID="MainContent" runat="server">
    The default content goes here…
</asp:ContentPlaceHolder>
```

Default content is helpful to handle situations in which you want to add a new section to a number of content pages, but you can't change them all at once. You can set up a new ContentPlaceHolder in the master page, give it some default content, and then take your time in adding the new information to the content pages — the content pages that haven't been modified yet will simply show the default content provided by the master.

Setting the MasterPageFile attribute at the page level may be useful if you want to use different master pages for different sets of content pages. If, however, all pages of the site use the same master page, it's easier to set it once for all pages from the web.config file, by means of the <pages> element, as shown here:

```
<pages masterPageFile="~/Template.master" />
```

If you still specify the `MasterPageFile` attribute at the page level, however, that attribute will override the value in `web.config` for that single page.

Nested Master Pages

You can take this a step forward and have a master page be the content for another master page. In other words, you can have nested master pages, whereby a master page inherits the visual appearance of another master page, and the .aspx content pages inherit from this second master page. The second-level master page can look something like the following:

```
<%@ Master Language="VB" MasterPageFile="~/MasterPage.master"
AutoEventWireup="false" CodeFile="MasterPage2.master.vb"
Inherits="MasterPage2" %>

<asp:Content ID="Content1" ContentPlaceHolderID="MainContent" Runat="Server">
   Some other content...
   <hr style="width: 100%;" />
   <asp:ContentPlaceHolder ID="MainContent" runat="server" />
</asp:Content>
```

Because you can use the same ID for a `ContentPlaceHolder` control in the base master page and for another `ContentPlaceHolder` in the inherited master page, you wouldn't need to change anything in the content page but its `MasterPageFile` attribute, so that it uses the second-level master page.

This possibility has great promise because you can have an outer master page that defines the very common layout (often the company-wide layout), and then other master pages that specify the layout for specific areas of the site, such as the online store section, the administration section, and so on. Visual Studio 2005 did not have design-time support for nested master pages, making it very difficult to manage development with nested master pages. Visual Studio 2008 has resolved that issue and made working with master pages much easier all around. In this version of the Beer House I will leverage several uses of nested master pages to allow a more flexible design of the site. There will be child master pages to define two- and three-column layouts.

Other improvements around master pages in Visual Studio 2008 make it easier to see how styles are applied to the layout, even through all the layers of master pages. While I tend to spend most of my time working with the layout in the Source View, it is nice to be able to switch to Design View to get a decent idea of how things are actually shaping up without launching the site. Figure 2-6 illustrates the principle of nested master pages.

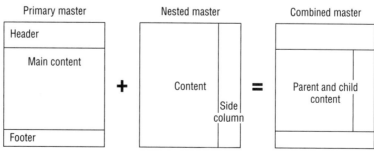

Figure 2-6

Accessing the Master Page from the Content Page

You also have the capability to access the master page from a content page, through the page's `Master` property. The returned object is of type `MasterPage`, which inherits directly from `UserControl` (remember that I said master pages are similar to user controls) and adds a couple of properties. It exposes a Controls collection, which allows you to access the master page's controls from the content page. This may be necessary if, for example, in a specific page you want to programmatically access a control on the master page, such as a `TextBox`, `Button`, or the like. Accessing the Controls collection directly would work, but would require you to do a manual cast from the generic `Control` object returned to the right control type, such as a `TextBox` or `Button`. A much better, and objected-oriented, approach is to add custom properties to the master page's code-behind class. In fact you can create public properties and functions in a `MasterPage`'s code-behind that can be accessed from the content page. The following example wraps a property to enable or disable personalization. This is what you could write in the `MasterPage`'s code-behind:

```
Private _enablePersonalization As Boolean = False
Public Property EnablePersonalization() As Boolean
    Get
        Return _enablePersonalization
    End Get
    Set(ByVal value As Boolean)
        _enablePersonalization = value
    End Set
End Property
```

Now in the content page you can add the following line after the `@Page` directive:

```
<%@ MasterType VirtualPath="~/MasterPage.master" %>
```

With this line you specify the path of the master page used by the ASP.NET runtime to dynamically create a strongly typed `MasterPage` class that exposes the custom properties added to its code-behind class. I know that it seems a duplicate for the `MasterPageFile` attribute of the `@Page` directive, but that's how you make the master page properties visible in the content page. You can specify the master type not just by virtual path (as in the preceding example) but also by name of the master page's class, by means of the `TypeName` attribute. Once you've added this directive, in the content page's code-behind file (or in a `<script runat="server">` section of the .aspx file itself), you can easily access the master page's `EnablePersonalization` property in a strongly typed fashion, as shown here:

```
Protected Sub Page_Load(ByVal sender As Object, ByVal e As System.EventArgs)
Handles Me.Load
    If Not IsPostBack Then
        Me.Master.EnablePersonalization = True
    End If
End Sub
```

When I say "strongly typed" I am implying that you'll have Visual Studio IntelliSense on this property, and that's true: Type **Me.Master.** and when you press that second period, you'll see your new property in the IntelliSense list!

This methodology of accessing master objects from content pages is particularly useful when you want to put common methods in the master page, to be used by all the pages that use it. If we didn't have access to a strongly typed `MasterPage` object built at runtime by ASP.NET, you'd need to use reflection to access those methods, which is slower and certainly much less immediate to use (in this case, it would have been easier to put the shared methods in a separate class that every page can access).

You can cast the `Master` property to the master page type at runtime as well. This comes in handy when you set the master page at runtime. You just have to know what the actual type the master page is for your content page. By doing this, you can access any public members of the actual master page's class, including assigning event handlers.

Another thing to remember when using nested master pages is keeping track of which master page is actually being referenced. If you are using nested master pages then the `Master` property of the class returns a reference to that master page, not its master page. To access the parent master page, you need to access the content page's master page's master page. Wow! Say that a few times real fast!

```
Protected Sub Page_Load(ByVal sender As Object, ByVal e As System.EventArgs) _
Handles Me.Load
    If Not IsPostBack Then
        Me.Master.Master.EnablePersonalization = True
    End If
End Sub
```

Switching Master Pages at Runtime

The last thing I want to describe in this introduction to master pages is the capability to dynamically change the master page used by a content page at runtime. That's right; you can have multiple master pages and pick which one to use after the site is already running. You do this by setting the page's `MasterPageFile` property from within the page's `PreInit` event handler, as follows:

```
Protected Sub Page_PreInit(ByVal sender As Object, ByVal e As EventArgs)
    Me.MasterPageFile = "~/OtherMasterPage.master"
End Sub
```

The `PreInit` event was new in ASP.NET 2.0, and you can only set the `MasterPageFile` property in this event handler because the merging of the two pages must happen very early in the page's life cycle (the `Load` or `Init` event would be too late).

When changing the master page dynamically, you must make sure that all master pages have the same ID for the `ContentPlaceHolder` controls, so that the content page's `Content` controls will always match them, regardless of which master page is being used. This exciting possibility enables you to build multiple master pages that specify completely different layouts, allowing users to pick their favorite one. The downside of this approach is that if you write custom code in the master page's code-behind file, you will need to replicate it in the code-beside class of any page; otherwise, the content page will not always find it. In addition, you won't be able to use the strongly typed `Master` property, because you can't dynamically change the master page's type at runtime; you can only set it with the `@MasterType` directive.

This problem can be mitigated by creating a common base `MasterPage` class each of the `MasterPage` variations inherit from. Any common member of the master pages would be contained in the parent class. For example you would want to have the `EnablePersonalization` property defined in the common base class and, thus, available to any of the master page variations.

While changing a `MasterPage` at runtime is pretty cool, a more common practice used on the web is changing stylesheets to produce a different layout. Because we've decided to use a table-free layout, we can completely change the appearance of the page (fonts, colors, images, and positions) by applying different styles to it. ASP.NET provides a mechanism called themes to help us accomplish just that.

Creating a Set of User-selectable Themes

Themes were a new feature in ASP.NET 2.0 that enabled users to have more control over the look and feel of a web page. A theme can be used to define color schemes, font names, sizes and styles, and even images (square corners versus round corners, or images with different colors or shades). The concept of "skin" support was also new in ASP.NET 2.0. It is really an organized extension of CSS but applied at a control level. Individual users can select a theme from various options available to them, and the specific theme they choose determines a "skin" that specifies which visual stylistic settings will be used for their user session. Skins are server-side relatives of CSS stylesheets. A skin file is similar to a CSS file, but, in contrast to CSS, a skin can override various visual properties that were explicitly set on server controls within a page (a global CSS specification can never override a style set on a particular control). You can store special versions of images with themes, which may be useful if you want several sets of images that use a different color scheme based on the current skin. However, themes do not displace the need to use CSS; you can use both CSS files and skin files to achieve a great deal of flexibility and control.

> *A special note about Web Controls and CSS: out of the box most do not render the content using container controls and instead use tables. A good example is the* Menu *control, which the default version does not even function correctly in IE 7 and above. This can be very inefficient and make your pages heavy. There is a set of "CSS Friendly Control Adapters" that you can download to change the way the some of the default Web Controls are rendered in the browser (*http://cssfriendly.codeplex.com/*). While we will not cover the use of the control adapters in this book, it is worth your time to check out.*

A theme is a group of related files stored in a subfolder under the site's /App_Themes folder, which can contain the following items:

❑ Stylesheet .css files that define the appearance of HTML objects.

❑ Skin files that define the appearance of server-side ASP.NET controls. You can think of them as server-side stylesheet files.

❑ Other resources, such as images.

One cool thing about the way ASP.NET implements themes is that when you apply a theme to the page (you'll learn how to do this shortly), ASP.NET automatically creates a <link> metatag in each page for every .css file located in the theme's folder at runtime. You should be aware the links generated by Themes are in alphabetical order. This is very important because CSS rules are applied in a specific order and you may have rules overridden if they are applied in an unexpected order. This is good because you can rename an existing CSS file or add a new one, and all your pages will still automatically link to all of them. This is especially important because, as you will see, you can dynamically change the theme at runtime (as you can do with the master page), and ASP.NET will link the files in the new theme's folder, thus changing the site's appearance to suit the preferences of individual users. Without this mechanism, you would need to manually create all the <link> metatags at runtime according to the theme selected by the user, which would be a pain.

As mentioned, themes can contain skin files. These are files with a .skin extension that contain one or more declarations of ASP.NET controls, such as the following one:

```
<asp:TextBox runat="server" BorderStyle="Dashed" BorderWidth="1px" />
```

Everything is the same as a normal declaration you would put into an .aspx page, except that in the skin file you don't specify the controls' ID. Once you apply the theme to your page(s), their controls will take on the appearance of the definitions written in the skin file(s). For a TextBox control, it may not seem such a great thing, because you could do the same by writing a style class for the <input> HTML element in a .css stylesheet file. However, as soon as you realize that you can do the same for more complex controls such as the Calendar or the GridView control, you will see that it makes much more sense. Those controls don't have a one-to-one relationship with an HTML element, and thus you could not easily define their style with a single class in the classic stylesheet file. Note that not every control, nor every attribute of the skinable controls, can be styled via skins.

You can have a single .skin file in which you place the definition for controls of any type, or you can create a separate .skin file for every control type, such as TextBox.skin, DataGrid.skin, Calendar.skin, and so on. At runtime, these files will be merged together in memory, so it's just a matter of organizing things the way you prefer.

To apply a theme to a single page, you use the Theme attribute in the @Page directive:

```
<%@ Page Language="VB" Theme="DarkBeer" MasterPageFile="~/TBHMain.master" … %>
```

To apply it to all pages, you can set the theme attribute of the <pages> element in web.config, as follows:

```
<pages theme="DarkBeer" masterPageFile="~/TBHMain.master" />
```

As for master pages, you can also change the theme programmatically, from inside the PreInit event of the Page class. For example, this is how you apply the theme whose name is stored in a Session variable:

```
Protected Sub Page_PreInit(ByVal sender As Object, ByVal e As EventArgs)
    If Me.Session("CurrentTheme") IsNot Nothing Then
        Me.Theme = Me.Session("CurrentTheme")
    End If
End Sub
```

In Chapter 5, we will improve this mechanism by replacing the Session variables with Profile properties.

> **When you use the** Theme **attribute of the** @Page **directive (or the** theme **attribute in** web.config**), the appearance attributes you specify in the skin files override the same attributes that you may have specified in the** .aspx **files. If you want themes to work like** .css **stylesheets — whereby you define the styles in the** .skin **files, but you can override them in the** .aspx **pages for specific controls — you can do that by linking to a theme with the** StylesheetTheme **attribute of the** @Page **directive, or the** styleSheetTheme **attribute of the** <pages> **element in** web.config**. Try not to confuse the** Theme **attribute with the** StylesheetTheme **attribute.**

So far, I've described unnamed skins — namely, skins that define the appearance of all the controls of a specific type. However, in some cases you will need to have a control with an appearance that differs from what you've defined in the skin file. You can do this in three different ways:

1. As described previously, you can apply a theme with the `StylesheetTheme` property (instead of the `Theme` property), so that the visual properties you write in the .aspx files override what you write in the skin file. However, the default behavior of the theming mechanism ensures that all controls of some type have the same appearance, which was intended for situations in which you have many page developers and you can't ensure that everyone uses attributes in the .aspx pages only when strictly required.

2. Disable theming for that control only, and apply the appearance attributes normally, as in the following code:

```
<asp:TextBox runat="server" ID="btnSubmit" EnableTheming="False"
    BorderStyle="Dotted" BorderWidth="2px" />
```

3. Use a named skin for a control, which is a skin definition with the addition of the `SkinID` attribute, as shown here:

```
<asp:Label runat="server" SkinID="FeedbackOK" ForeColor="green" />
<asp:Label runat="server" SkinID="FeedbackKO" ForeColor="red" />
```

When you declare the control, you'll need to use a matching value for its `SkinID` property, such as the following:

```
<asp:Label runat="server" ID="lblFeedbackOK"
    Text="Your message has been successfully sent."
    SkinID="FeedbackOK" Visible="false" />

<asp:Label runat="server" ID="lblFeedbackKO"
    Text="Sorry, there was a problem sending your message."
    SkinID="FeedbackKO" Visible="false" />
```

In my opinion, this is the best way to go, because it enables you to define multiple appearances for the same control type, all in a single file, and then apply them in any page. Additionally, if you keep all style definitions in the skin files instead of in the pages themselves, you'll be able to completely change the look and feel of the site by switching the current theme (which is the intended purpose behind themes). Otherwise, with hard-coded styles, this is only partially possible.

In the "Solution" section of this chapter, you'll use themes to create a few different visual representations for the same master page.

Creating a Navigation System

The `Menu` control and the use of a static `SiteMap` file to define navigation are useful for relatively static sites, but a truly dynamic and growing site like the Beer House needs a way to grow and adjust as new content is added to the site. While the main navigation of the site will stay fairly static, the use of the `BreadCrumb` navigation control will benefit from a full and accurate site map.

ASP.NET sites are dynamic and grow and expand all the time. Many are a content management system if you actually look at them objectively. An online store, for example, routinely changes its catalog and, thus, the overall site map.

Because the vast majority of ASP.NET sites are driven by a backend database, typically SQL Server, we will create a custom `SiteMapProvider` driven by a table in the database. The nice thing about driving from a site map table is we can add and remove nodes to and from the overall map as needed. This means that each time there is a new article, event, photo, or poll added to the site it can be added to the site map table. It also means that, when an article expires or content is removed from the site, it can be removed from the site in real time.

Maintaining the site map in the database will also make it easier for search engine spiders to crawl our site. We will create a custom `HttpHandler` to render a SiteMaps.org-compliant site map.

In addition to showing the menu, you want to provide users with a visual clue as to where they are and some way to allow them to navigate backward from their current location to the home page. This is usually done through the use of *breadcrumbs,* a navigation bar that shows links to all pages or sections, starting from the home page, that the user visited to arrive on the current page, such as the following:

```
Home > Store > Shopping cart
```

With this navigation system, the user can go back two pages without pressing the browser's Back button and without starting over from the home page and trying to remember the path previously followed. With ASP.NET, you can add a breadcrumb bar with a single line of code by declaring an instance of the `SiteMapPath` control on the page:

```
<asp:SiteMapPath ID="SiteMapPath1" runat="server" />
```

As usual, this control has a number of properties that enable you to fully customize its look and feel, as you'll see in practice in the "Solution" section.

Creating XHTML-Compliant and -Accessible Sites

All ASP.NET built-in standard controls render well-formatted XHTML 1.0 Transitional code by default. XHTML code is basically HTML written as XML, which means it must comply with much stricter syntax rules. For example, all attribute values must be enclosed within double quotation marks, all tags must have a closing tag or must be explicitly self-closing (e.g., no more `<br>` and `<img src="...">`, but `<br />` and `<img src="..." />`), and nested tags must be closed in the right order (e.g., no more `<b><p>hello</b> Chris</p>` but `<p><b>Hello</b> Chris</p>`). In addition, many HTML tags meant to format the text, such as `<font>`, `<center>`, `<s>`, and the like are now deprecated and should be replaced by CSS styles (such as `font-family: Verdana; text-align: center`). The same is true for some attributes of other tags, such as `width` and `align`.

The reasoning behind this new standard is to attain a greater separation of presentation and content (something I've explained earlier) and to create cleaner code — code that can be read by programs that work with XML data. The fact that ASP.NET automatically renders XHTML code, as long as you use its controls, is a great time saver for the developer and makes the process of getting used to XHTML smoother. The official W3C documentation about XHTML 1.0 can be found at `www.w3.org/TR/xhtml1/`.

> **W3C's online HTML validator (`http://validator.w3.org`) allows you to supply your HTML, which it analyzes and then provides you with a list of improper markup. You can supply your HTML by pasting the code in the browser and submitting it, uploading a file, or pointing the validator to a public URL.**

At the top of every top-level master page (one without a parent) or Web Form not using a master page, you will find the following markup:

```
<!DOCTYPE html PUBLIC "-//W3C//DTD XHTML 1.0 Transitional//EN"
"http://www.w3.org/TR/xhtml1/DTD/xhtml1-transitional.dtd">
```

This is a directive telling the browser which version of HTML or XHTML the page is using. If this directive is omitted, the browser will render the page in Quirks mode. This is a mode in which the browser assumes the page is invalid, and therefore the page may not render correctly in the browser. The !DOCTYPE directive is required for XHTML compliance.

As for accessibility, the W3C defines a set of rules meant to ease the use of the site by users with disabilities. The official page of the Web Content Accessibility Guidelines 1.0 (commonly referred as WCAG) can be found at www.w3.org/TR/WCAG10. Section 508 guidelines were born from WCAG, and must be followed by U.S. federal agencies' sites, as well as by the sites of most companies that want to do business with the U.S. government. You can read more at www.section508.gov. For example, you must use the alt attribute in <img> tags to provide an alternate text for visually impaired users, so that screen readers can describe the image, and you must use the <label> tag to associate a label to an input field.

Other guidelines are more difficult to implement and are not specifically related to ASP.NET, so you can check out the official documentation for more information. ASP.NET makes it easier to follow some of the simpler rules, such as those mentioned previously. For example, the Image control has a GenerateEmptyAlternateText property that, when set to true, generates alt="" (setting AlternateText="" would generate nothing instead), and the Label control has the AssociatedControlID property that is set to the name of an input control and at runtime generates the <label> control for it (this should be used together with the AccessKey property, to create shortcuts to the input field).

If you want to read more about XHTML, accessibility, and the ASP.NET features that pertain to this subject, you can refer to the following online articles: Alex Homer's "Accessibility Improvements in ASP.NET 2.0 — Part 1" (www.15seconds.com/issue/040727.htm) and "Accessibility Improvements in ASP.NET 2.0 - Part 2" (www.15seconds.com/issue/040804.htm), or Stephen Walther's "Building ASP.NET 2.0 Web Sites Using Web Standards" (http://msdn.microsoft.com/en-us/library/aa479043.aspx).

Sharing a Common Behavior among All Pages

Master pages and themes do a great job of sharing the same design and look and feel among all pages of the site. However, you may also want the pages to share some common behavior, that is, code to run at a certain point of their life cycle. For example, if you want to log access to all pages so that you can build and show statistics for your site, you have to execute some code when the page loads. Another case where you need to run some code for every page is when you need to set the page's Theme property in the PreInit event handler. It's true that you can isolate the common code in an external function and just add a line of code to execute it from within each page, but this approach has two drawbacks:

❑　You must never forget to insert that line to call the external function when you design a new page. If multiple developers are creating .aspx pages — which is often the case — you will need to make sure that nobody forgets it.

❑ You may want to run some initialization from inside the PreInit event and some other code from the Load event. In this case, you have to write two separate xxxInitialize methods, and add more lines to each page to call the proper method from inside the proper event handler. Therefore, don't rely on the fact that adding a single line to each page is easy, because later you may need to add more and more. When you have hundreds of pages, I'm sure you'll agree that going back and modifying all the pages to add these lines is not a workable solution.

These two disadvantages are enough to make me discard that option. Another option is to write the common code in the master page's code-behind. This may be a very good choice in many situations. Not in our case, however, because we must handle the PreInit event, and the MasterPage class (and its base classes) does not have such an event. You can handle the Init or Load events, for example, but not PreInit, so we must think of something else.

In the previous editions of this book, there was a BasePage class from which all the content pages would inherit, instead of inheriting directly from the standard System.Web.UI.Page class. I believe this is still the best option, because you can handle any page event from inside this class by overriding the On*XXX* methods, where *XXX* is the event name.

The snippet that follows is a basic skeleton for such a custom base class that inherits from Page and overrides the OnPreInit and OnLoad methods:

```
Public Class BasePage
Inherits System.Web.UI.Page

Protected Overrides Sub OnPreInit(ByVal e As System.EventArgs)

        ' add custom code here...

MyBase.OnPreInit(e)
End Sub

Protected Overrides Sub OnLoad(e as EventArgs)

        ' add custom code here

    Mybase.OnLoad(e)
End Sub
End Class
```

The classes in the pages' code-behind files will then inherit from your custom BasePage, rather than the standard Page, as shown here:

```
Public Partial Class Contact
    Inherits BasePage

    ' normal page code here...

End Sub
```

You still need to change some code in the code-behind class of every page but, once that's done, you can later go back to BasePage, add code to the existing methods or overload new methods, and you will not need to modify any additional lines in the code-behind classes. If you take this approach initially, you'll modify the code-behind classes one by one as you create them, so this will be easy and it gives you a future-proof design.

Solution

Now that we have laid out the visual requirements of the site, it's time to start working on the layout. You can go about this many different ways. If you are working with a designer, they will most likely work on a complete layout in Photoshop and provide a PSD file. Designers can often create some pretty amazing layouts. What I have experienced over the years, though, is that some of those designs are not flexible enough for dynamic sites that ASP.NET data-driven applications require because the content is variable. For this reason, you should strive to be a part of the design process to advise the designers about what ramifications their choices may have on the actual implementation.

I have learned to keep my site designs simple, flexible, and manageable, over the years. So, the layout that I created for this version of the Beer House consists of a stock photo under Creative Commons license and some supporting graphics I created using Paint.NET. The layout is applied by CSS stylesheets, as part of a theme. This choice means that I can quickly change the color scheme and supporting graphics simply by changing the stylesheet or theme applied to the site or even the page.

First, create a new website project in Visual Studio .NET 2008 (File ➪ New Web Site or Shift+Alt+N). You can create a project by specifying a folder on the file system (instead of specifying a web location) if you select File System in the Location drop-down list, as shown in Figure 2-4. You can also specify a location via Http or Ftp as well. Also notice that, in Visual Studio 2008, you can also specify the framework version the site will be developed against. You can select 3.5 (which you will want to keep to build the application in this book), 3.0, or 2.0. The reason you can do this with Visual Studio 2008 is the .NET Common Language Runtime (CLR) for each of these platforms is built around version 2.0, so in essence the 3.x versions of the .NET Framework are merely additions to the 2.0 release.

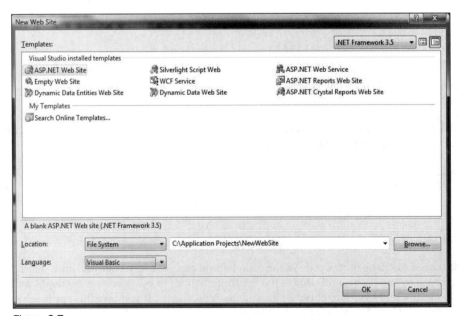

Figure 2-7

This enables you to create an ASP.NET project without creating a related virtual application or virtual directory in the IIS metabase (the metabase is where IIS stores its configuration data), and the project is loaded from a real hard disk folder, and executed by an integrated lightweight web server (called ASP. NET Development Server) that handles requests on a TCP/IP port other than the one used by IIS (IIS uses port 80). The actual port number used is determined randomly every time you press F5 to run the website in debug mode or Ctrl+F5 to run without debug mode. For example, it handles requests such as `http://localhost:1168/ProjName/Default.aspx`. This makes it much easier to move and back up projects, because you can just copy the project's folder and you're done — there's no need to set up anything from the IIS Management console. In fact, Visual Studio 2008 does not even require IIS unless you choose to deploy to an IIS web server, or you specify a web URL instead of a local path when you create the website project.

If you've developed with any previous version of ASP.NET or Visual Studio prior to 2005, I'm sure you will welcome this option. I say this is an option because you can still create the project by using a URL as project path — creating and running the site under IIS — by selecting HTTP in the Location drop-down list. I suggest you create and develop the site by using the File System location, with the integrated web server, and then switch to the full-featured IIS web server for the test phase. VS2008 includes a deployment wizard that makes it easier to deploy a complete solution to a local or remote IIS web server. For now, however, just create a new ASP.NET website in a folder you want, and call it TheBeerHouse35.

> **The integrated web server was developed to make development and quick testing easier. However, you should never use it for final quality assurance or integration testing. Use IIS for that. IIS has more features, such as caching, HTTP compression, and many security options that can make your site run very differently from what you see in the new integrated ASP.NET Development Server.**
>
> **One of the reasons for this is that all requests for any resource are passed through the development web server and processed by the ASP.NET engine. This means that any images, stylesheets, and so forth will be processed by the entire ASP.NET pipeline. Therefore, you may notice some minor differences between the experience with the development web server from a production deployment using IIS 6 or 7. All testing prior to approving a production push should be done in as close to real environment as possible to ensure that the application functions as desired the final environment.**

After creating the new website, right-click on `Default.aspx` and delete it. We'll make our own default page soon.

Creating the Site Design

Creating the master page with the shared site design is not that difficult once you have a mocked-up image (or a set of images if you made them separately). Basically, you cut the logo and the other graphics and put them in the HTML page. The other parts of the layout, such as the menu bar, the columns, and the footer, can easily be reproduced with HTML elements such as DIVs. Figure 2-8 shows the site layout. It is composed of an image found under a Creative Commons license and a few custom-created graphics. I used Paint.NET to create the simple Beer House logo and a gradient background for the menu. The remaining elements are a collection of DIV elements and cascading stylesheets.

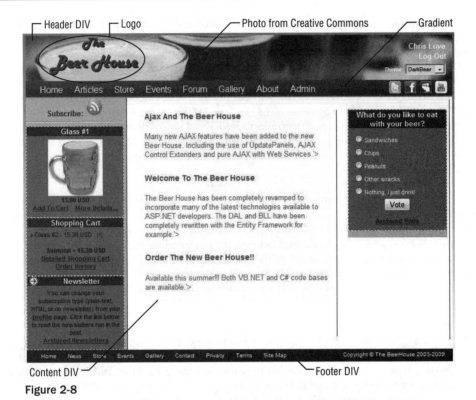

Figure 2-8

In this book I am assuming a certain amount of familiarity with ASP.NET and Visual Studio .NET. More specifically, I assume that you have a working knowledge of the basic operation of any previous version of Visual Studio .NET. Therefore, the steps I explain here focus on the changes in version 2.0–3.5 but do not cover every small detail. If you are not comfortable following the steps presented here, consult a beginner's book on ASP.NET before tackling this project.

Creating the Master Page

After creating the website, create a new master page file (select Website ➪ Add New Item ➪ Master Page, and name it TBHMain.master), and then use the visual designer to add the ASP.NET server-side controls and static HTML elements to its surface. However, when working on laying out a page, I've found that the visual designer cannot provide the flexibility and control I desire. I find it easier to work directly in the Source View and write the code by hand. As I said earlier, creating the master page is not much different from creating a normal page; the most notable differences are just the @Master directive at the top of the file and the presence of ContentPlaceHolder controls where the .aspx pages will plug in their own content. What follows is the code that defines the basic layout for the new Beer House site in the file TBHMain.master:

```
<%@ Master Language="VB" CodeFile="TBHMain.master.vb" Inherits="TBHMain" %>

<%@ Register Src="controls/FooterCopyright.ascx" TagName="FooterCopyright"
TagPrefix="uc1" %>
<%@ Register Src="controls/ThemeSelector.ascx" TagName="ThemeSelector"
TagPrefix="uc2" %>
<!DOCTYPE html PUBLIC "-//W3C//DTD XHTML 1.0 Transitional//EN"
"http://www.w3.org/TR/xhtml1/DTD/xhtml1-transitional.dtd">
<html xmlns="http://www.w3.org/1999/xhtml">
<head id="Head1" runat="server">
    <title>The Beer House</title>
    <asp:ContentPlaceHolder ID="head" runat="server">
    </asp:ContentPlaceHolder>
</head>
<body runat="server" id="pageBody">
    <form id="form1" runat="server">
    <div id="dHeader">
    ...
    </div>
    <div id='dContainer'>
        <asp:ContentPlaceHolder ID="MainContent" runat="server">
        </asp:ContentPlaceHolder>
    </div>
    <div id="dMainfooter">
        ...
    </div>
    </form>
</body>
</html>
```

> Similar to the way that the table content does not render until the entire table has
> been downloaded, all rendering is stopped as soon as JavaScript is encountered.
> By specification, all browsers stop everything until the entire script is loaded and
> evaluated; this mean loaded either from the server or inline scripts. This is why
> pushing any JavaScript routines to dedicated files instead of inline scripts is vital
> to a web application's performing fast.

A page is composed of a series of nested DIV elements, such as the header, content, and footer areas. Inside each of these DIV elements will be more DIV or SPAN tags that further define the actual layout of the page. Something of interest in the new layout is that it leverages nested master pages. This gives us the flexibility of defining multiple implementations of a classic two- or three-column layout. For example, the home page is a three-column layout where the main content section is the wider than the two side columns. There are two nested master pages used in the site, one with a narrow column to the left of the primary content, the other with a narrow column to the right of the main content.

The primary master page is a collection of DIVs that are used throughout the site, such as the header, the main content area, and the footer. At the top of the layout architecture is a main DIV with the ID of dHeader. This DIV contains the markup that defines the common header used in the layout, the header, and horizontal navigation. Inside the dHeader element there are two child DIV tags, dMainHeader and dMainNav.

```
<div id="dHeader">
    <div id="dMainHeader">
```

```
        </div>
        <div id="dMainNav">
        </div>
    </div>
```

The dHeader, dContent, and dMainFooter elements share common positioning style rules, so they have a common style definition. This definition is used to position the elements in the horizontal center with a width of 780 pixels and no border. Further, the use of a background image is defined to start at the top-left corner with no scrolling.

> Why 780 pixels? Until recently a large majority of computer users had a screen resolution of 800 × 600 pixels, so a browser set to full screen would only have 800 pixels available to it horizontally. Add a vertical scroll bar 20 pixels wide and you have 780 pixels. Even with the advent of higher screen resolutions and much larger monitors, sticking to this rule is generally a good idea. Average users are still in the 1024 × 768 or just slightly higher resolutions. Advanced users will go much higher, but with the added real estate, most users do not go full screen with their browsers. The style definitions can be altered to allow the page to fill 100% of the horizontal space, but in the case of this layout, the header background image will not extend to fill anything past 780 pixels. Background images do not scale using CSS, but rather repeat. This means that setting the width of the Beer House to 100% width would cause the header image to repeat. The ultimate decision is usually a matter of personal preference rather than a functional decision.

Here are the style properties shared by all of the main layout elements:

```
div#dHeader, div#footer, div#dContainer
{
    background-position: 0 0;
    background: none repeat scroll 0 0;

    border: none;
    width: 780px;
    margin: auto;
}
```

Creating the Header Element

The dMainHeader DIV is composed of several child DIV elements for the logo, login elements, and theme selection.

```
<div id="dMainHeader">
        <div id="dLogo">
            <img src="~/images/tbh_logo.gif" runat="server"
alt="The Beer House" enableviewstate="false" />
        </div>
        <div id="dLoginLinks">
            <div id="dLoginMenu">
                <a id="btnDisplayLogin"
href="javascript:DisplayLoginHandler();"
class="LoginLink">Login</a></div>
```

```
            <div id="dLogoutMenu">
                <div id="dUserName">
                </div>
                <a id="btnDisplayLogout" href="javascript:logoutHandler();"
class="LoginLink">Log Out</a>
            </div>
        </div>
        <div id="dThemeselector">
            <uc2:ThemeSelector ID="ThemeSelector1" runat="server" />
        </div>
</div>
```

Each of these elements has further style rules used to define their positioning and visual representations. The dMainHeader uses a background-image (the beer steins from Creative Commons), a height of 80 pixels, and width of 780 pixels. clear is set to both, clearing the element's floating inheritance from its parent element. both designates both left and right clearing.

```
/* Header Elements */

#dMainHeader
{
    background-image: url('images/bh_header.png');
    clear: both;
    color: #800000;
    float: left;
    height: 80px;
    padding: 0;
    width: 780px;
}

H1.dMainHeader
{
    font-size: 24px;
    font-weight: bold;
    color: #996633;
}

#dLogo
{
    width: 480px;
    float: left;
    margin-right: 40px;
    margin-left: 40px;
}

#dLoginLinks
{
    width: 200px;
    float: right;
    margin-top: 10px 5px 0 0;
    padding-right: 10px;
    padding-top: 10px;
}
```

```
/* Login */

#dLoginMenu
{
    text-align: right;
    display: none;
}

#dLogoutMenu
{
    text-align :right;
    display: none;
}

a.LoginLink:link
{
    padding: 2px 1px 2px 1px;
    color: #FFFFFF;
    font-size: Small;
    text-decoration: none;
    font-weight: bolder;
}

a.LoginLink:visited
{
    padding: 2px 1px 2px 1px;
    color: #FFFFFF;
    font-size: Small;
    text-decoration: none;
    font-weight: bolder;
}

a.LoginLink:active
{
    padding: 2px 1px 2px 1px;
    color: #FFFFFF;
    font-size: Small;
    text-decoration: none;
    font-weight: bolder;
}

a.LoginLink:hover
{
    padding: 2px 1px 2px 1px;
    color: #FFFFFF;
    font-size: Small;
    text-decoration: none;
    font-weight: bolder;
}

/* Themes */
#dThemeselector
{
    text-align: right;
```

```
      height: 80px;
      padding: 2px;
      font-size: 10px;
      margin-top: 50px;
      margin-right: 10px;
      color: #FFFFFF;
}

#dThemeselector select
{
    color: black;
    background-color: #e1e1e1;
    font-size: 10px;
}
```

Creating a Menu with CSS

The next section in the header is the site's primary horizontal navigation, composed of a specially styled unordered list (<UL>). There are actually two child DIVs in the dMainNav DIV: dMenu and dSocial. The first DIV is the traditional menu; the second is a series of image links pointing to Beer House pages on various social networking sites. Following is a list of the dMainNav's style properties; they define the background gradient image, dimensions, and position of the element.

```
#dMainNav
{
    background: url(images/menu_bg.gif) repeat-x;
    float: left;
    padding: 2px 0 0px 0;
    top: 85px;
    height: 28px;
    bottom: 100px;
    left: 1px;
    width: 780px;
    font-family: Arial, Helvetica, sans-serif;
}
```

The horizontal menu is defined by a series of style selectors applied to the UL and its child elements. The most important rule to notice is the one applied to the list items (<LI>). It defines how each of the list items is rendered in the list, which is inline. This tells the browser not to render the list as a stacked list of elements, but rather as if it is normal text or horizontal. Once this is defined, the remaining rules define the actual appearance, such as spacing, size, and colors for the elements in the list. Collectively, these rules define a list of horizontal links that compose a nice horizontal menu. The resulting HTML output is much thinner than the output of the Menu control, which outputs a large set of nested tables to accomplish the same effect. Similar rules are applied to the dSocial element to display the social site icon links. Following is the HTML markup:

```
<div id="dMenu">
<ul>
            <li><a href="<% =ResolveUrl("default.aspx") %>">
<span>Home</span></a></li>
                <li><a href="<% =ResolveUrl("showcategories.aspx") %>">
<span>Articles</span></a></li>
                <li><a href="<% =ResolveUrl("ShowDepartments.aspx") %>">
```

```
<span>Store</span></a></li>
                <li><a href="<% =ResolveUrl("BrowseEvents.aspx") %>">
<span>Events</span></a></li>
                <li><a href="<% =ResolveUrl("ShowForums.aspx") %>">
<span>Forum</span></a></li>
                <li><a href="<% =ResolveUrl("BrowseAlbums.aspx") %>">
<span>Gallery</span></a></li>
                <li><a href="<% =ResolveUrl("About.aspx") %>">
<span>About</span></a></li>
                <li id="liAdmin"><a href="<% =ResolveUrl("Admin") %>">
<span>Admin</span></a></li>
            </ul>
</div>
```

Here are the styles applied to the menu:

```
#dMenu
{
    width: 550px;
    float: left;
}

#dMenu ul
{
    clear: left;
    float: left;
    width: 100%;
    list-style: none;
    margin: 1px 0 0 0;
    padding: 0;
}

#dMenu ul li
{
    display: inline;
    list-style: none;
    margin: 0;
    padding: 0;
}

#dMenu ul li a
{
    display: block;
    float: left;
    margin: 0 0 0 1px;
    padding: 3px 10px;
    text-align: center;
    color: #FFFFFF;
    text-decoration: none;
    position: relative;
    left: 15px;
    font-size: medium;
}
```

```
#dMenu ul li a:hover
{
    background: transparent;
    color: #CECECE;
}

#dMenu ul li a.active, #dMenu ul li a.active:hover
{
    font-weight: bolder;
}

#dMenu ul li a span
{
    display: block;
}
```

Creating the Footer Section

The footer section is a collection of two DIVs — one for navigation and one for a copyright notice. The menu is, again, a UL and applies similar style rules as the primary navigation. The other DIV contains the site's copyright notice — more on that later.

```
<div id="dMainfooter">
<div id="footermenu">
            <ul>
                <li><a href="<% =ResolveUrl("default.aspx") %>">
<span>Home</span></a></li>
                <li><a href="<% =ResolveUrl("showcategories.aspx") %>">
<span>News</span></a></li>
                <li><a href="<% =ResolveUrl("ShowDepartments.aspx") %>">
<span>Store</span></a></li>
                <li><a href="<% =ResolveUrl("BrowseEvents.aspx") %>">
<span>Events</span></a></li>
                <li><a href="<% =ResolveUrl("BrowseAlbums.aspx") %>">
<span>Gallery</span></a></li>
                <li><a href="<% =ResolveUrl("Contact.aspx") %>">
<span>Contact</span></a></li>
                <li><a href="<% =ResolveUrl("Privacy.aspx") %>">
<span>Privacy</span></a></li>
                <li><a href="<% =ResolveUrl("Terms.aspx") %>">
<span>Terms</span></a></li>
                <li><a href="<% =ResolveUrl("SiteMap.aspx") %>">
<span>Site Map
</span></a></li>
            </ul>
        </div>
        <div id="footerCopyright">
            <uc1:FooterCopyright ID="FooterCopyright1" runat="server"
CompanyName="The BeerHouse"
            StartYear="2003" EnableViewState="false" />
        </div>

</div>
```

There are some more elements that complete the main master page for the login dialog, and those will be explained in Chapter 4. The remaining element is nested between the header and footer elements and contains a `ContentPlaceHolder` control named `MainContent`.

Creating the Main Content Sections in Nested Master Pages

There are two more master pages used in the site, plus another for the site's administration. The remaining two master pages; `LCMaster.master` (2-Column layout with thin right column and left primary content) and `CRMaster.master` (another 2-Column layout with a thin left column and right primary content). Both of these master pages are nested master pages from the primary master page. Inside each of these master pages is a `Content` control that corresponds to the `MainContent` `ContentPlaceHolder` of the `TBHMain.master` page. Each of these child master pages contains two DIV elements, one for the primary content of the page and one for a side column with ancillary content. The side column contains a link to the site's overall RSS feed and then a `ContentPlaceHolder` control that lets the actual page set the remaining content.

```
<div id='left-column'>
        <div id="dRSS">
            <a href="thebeerhouse.rss">Subscribe:
                <img id="Img1" runat="server" src="~/images/beercap.gif" border="0"
 alt="Follow The BeerHouse via RSS." /></a>
            <hr />
        </div>
        <asp:ContentPlaceHolder ID="RightColumn" runat="server">
        </asp:ContentPlaceHolder>
</div>
<div id='right-main-content'>
        <asp:SiteMapPath runat="server" ID="TBHSiteMapPath"
CssClass="tbhSiteMapPath" ParentLevelsDisplayed="2">
        </asp:SiteMapPath>
        <asp:ContentPlaceHolder ID="CenterColumn" runat="server">
        </asp:ContentPlaceHolder>
</div>
```

The primary content DIV contains a `SiteMapPath` control and a `ContentPlaceHolder`. I'll discuss the `SiteMapPath` in more detail in the next chapter. I want to point out here the use of a DIV element with a specific name. In the preceding example, the content DIV is named `right-main-content`. The other child master page uses `left-main-content`. This allows different style rules to be defined for each element to position them either on the left or right side of the page.

When pages are rendered by ASP.NET, the markup will contain the DIV elements in the desired nesting hierarchy. The reason the columns are contained within a wrapping DIV element is to keep the footer element below the dynamic content rendered by the site. The two columns apply style rules that define their float or horizontal position and their width:

```
#left-main-content, #right-main-content
{
    background-color:#FFF;
    margin:5px;
    min-height:400px;
    width:570px;
}

#left-main-content
```

```
{
    border-right:thin solid #000080;
    float:left;
}

#right-main-content
{
    border-right:thin solid #000080;
    float:right;
}

#right-column, #left-column
{
    background-color: #E6BB70;
    margin: 4px;
    min-height: 190px;
    width: 180px;
}

#right-column
{
    float: right;
    left: 380px;
}

#left-column
{
    clear:left;
    float: left;
    margin-right: 5px;
}
```

A quick tutorial on the CSS Box Model is in order. Every element in HTML is defined as a box or a rect-angle. The position of the box is determined by the Top, Left, Right, and Bottom values, which are either an integer value or a percentage. There are different unit types, but I use pixels (px) throughout this book to keep it simple. Generally I use absolute positioning, but this may vary from relative to static as needed. When absolute positioning is used the values for the position are calculated from the containing element, which would be the body, a DIV, and so on. As you will see by examining the lay-out of the new Beer House, this helps control where content is rendered (see Figure 2-9).

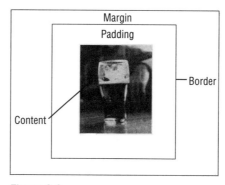

Figure 2-9

In the actual Box Model, there are three important value groups to understand: margin, border, and padding. The margin is the effective space around the box from another element. Think of it as cellspacing in a table. The border defines a line that designates one or more of the sides of the box and can have its style, width, and color defined. Padding refers to the space between the border and the actual content of the element. Effective use of these values enables you to produce some pretty stunning layout effects.

Figure 2-10 shows these concepts being applied to the About page.

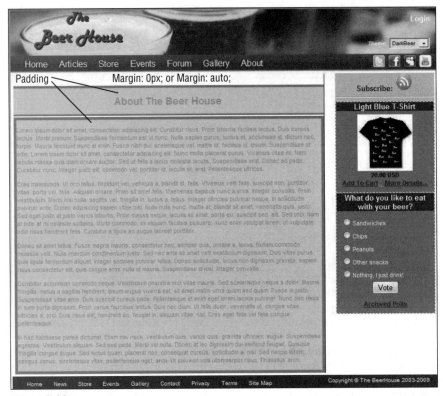

Figure 2-10

Creating a Three-Column Layout

A three-column layout that keeps the footer below all the page's content is often referred to as the Holy Grail of CSS layouts.

The only page in the new Beer House that uses a three-column layout is the home page. I chose to use the two-column layouts on the remaining pages because I wanted more room for the actual content. The home page, however, needs to expose as much content as possible to the visitor, so using three columns on the page — a column on each side of 180 pixels in width and a center column — made the most sense. The difference between a three-column layout and a two-column layout is that one of the thin columns is contained within the larger content DIV element. This keeps the footer element from overlapping any of the content elements.

```
<div id="MainColHome">
        <div id="center-main-content">
            /* Main Content */
        </div>
        <div id="right-column">
                /* Side Content */
        </div>
</div>
```

Following are the style rules applied to the layout elements:

```
#center-main-content
{
    background-color:#FFFFFF;
    border-right:thin solid #000080;
    float:left;
    margin:5px;
    min-height:400px;
    width:360px;
}

#left-main-content, #right-main-content
{
    background-color:#FFF;
    margin:5px;
    min-height:400px;
    width:570px;
}

#left-main-content
{
    border-right:thin solid #000080;
    float:left;
}

#right-main-content
{
    float:right;
}
```

Binding a BreadCrumb to the SiteMap

Helping users know where they are in the site is not just a feature but a requirement to help users feel comfortable using your site. BreadCrumb navigation is a common way to let users see where they are in the site from a hierarchical perspective, meaning that it not only provides a visual representation but also lets users quickly navigate back up the site tree.

The SiteMapPath control was introduced with a series of navigation controls in ASP.NET 2.0. It is used to create a BreadCrumb navigation strip for a website and relies on the presence of a site map as part of the website; to be more specific, it automatically works with the site's SiteMapProvider. Again, I will cover creating a data-driven custom SiteMapProvider after we establish how to use the Entity Framework.

The `SiteMapPath` creates a link from each of the nodes in the hierarchy to the current page. There is a node for each parent URL above the current page, so it shows users where they are in relation to the rest of the site.

Creating the First Theme

It's time to create the first theme for the master page: `DarkBeer`. There are two ways to do this that are functionally equivalent. You could add a new folder to the project named `App_Themes` and then a new subfolder under it called `DarkBeer`. Alternately, you could let Visual Studio assist you: select Website ➪ Add Folder ➪ Theme Folder, and name it `DarkBeer` (the `App_Themes` folder is created for you in this case). The `App_Themes` folder is special because it uses a reserved name, and appears in gray in Solution Explorer. Select the `App_Themes\DarkBeer` folder, add a stylesheet file to this folder (select Website ➪ Add New Item ➪ Stylesheet, and name it `Default.css`). The name you give to the CSS file is not important because all CSS files found in the current theme's folder will automatically be linked by the .aspx page at runtime.

I could go on and on about how and why the styles are defined the way they are, but that would make an entire book to itself. My advice is to carefully study the CSS used to create this layout and adjust it to your liking. A great resource to get up to speed on CSS layouts is www.csszengarden.com. There you will find a large set of examples using the same HTML page but with various stylesheets or themes applied to the site.

All images pointed to in this stylesheet file are located in an Images folder under `App_Themes/DarkBeer`. That keeps together all related objects that make up the theme. The ASP.NET engine sort of fakes things and automatically maps them correctly for you when the page renders.

Creating a Sample Default.aspx Page

Now that you have a complete master page and a theme, you can test it by creating a sample content page. To begin, add a new web page named `Default.aspx` to the project (select the project in Solution Explorer and choose Website ➪ Add New Item ➪ Web Form), select the checkbox called Select Master Page in the Add New Item dialog box, and you'll be presented with a second dialog window from which you can choose the master page to use — namely, `Template.master`. When you select this option, the page will just contain `Content` controls that match the master page's `ContentPlaceHolder` controls, and not the `<html>`, `<body>`, `<head>`, and `<form>` tags that would be present otherwise. You can put some content in the central `ContentPlaceHolder`, as shown here:

```
<%@ Page Language="vb" AutoEventWireup="false" CodeBehind="Default.aspx.vb"
 Inherits="TBH_Web35._Default"
    MasterPageFile="~/CRMaster.Master" %>
<%@ Import Namespace="System.IO" %>
<%@ Register Src="controls/RSSReader.ascx" TagName="RSSReader" TagPrefix="uc3" %>
<asp:Content ID="CenterColumnContent" ContentPlaceHolderID="CenterColumn"
runat="Server">
    <div id="MainColHome">
        <div id="center-main-content">
            <asp:ListView ID="lvArticles" runat="server">
                <LayoutTemplate>
                    <div id="itemPlaceholder" runat="server" />
```

```
                </LayoutTemplate>
                <EmptyDataTemplate>
                    <p>
                        Sorry there are no articles available at this time.</p>
                </EmptyDataTemplate>
                <ItemTemplate>
                    <div class="Homearticlebox">
                        <div class="articletitle">
                            <a class="articletitle" href='<%# ResolveUrl("~/" &
SEOFriendlyURL( _
                        Settings.Articles.URLIndicator & "\" & Eval("Title"),
".aspx")) %>'>
                                <%# HttpUtility.HTMLEncode(Eval("Title")) %></a>
                        </div>
                        <div class="articleabstract">
                            <p>
                                <%# Eval("Abstract") %>'></p>
                        </div>
                    </div>
                </ItemTemplate>
                <AlternatingItemTemplate>
                    <div class="Homearticlebox">
                        <div class="articletitle">
                            <a class="articletitle" href='<%#
ResolveUrl(SEOFriendlyURL("~/" & _
                        Path.Combine(Settings.Articles.URLIndicator, Eval("Title")),
 ".aspx")) %>'>
                                <%# HttpUtility.HTMLEncode(Eval("Title")) %>
</a></div>
                        <div class="articleabstract">
                            <p>
                                <%# Eval("Abstract") %>'></p>
                        </div>
                    </div>
                </AlternatingItemTemplate>
            </asp:ListView>
        </div>
        <div id="right-column">
            <uc1:PollBox ID="PollBox1" runat="server" />
            <uc3:RSSReader ID="RSSReader1" runat="server" />
        </div>
    </div>
</asp:Content>
<asp:Content ID="leftColumnContent" ContentPlaceHolderID="RightColumn"
runat="Server">
    <uc1:Featuredproduct ID="Featuredproduct1" runat="server" />
    <uc1:ShoppingCartBox ID="ShoppingCartBox1" runat="server" />
    <uc1:NewsletterBox ID="NewsletterBox1" runat="server" />
</asp:Content>
```

You could have also added the Theme attribute to the @Page directive, setting it equal to "DarkBeer".
However, instead of doing that here, you can do it in the web.config file, once, and have it apply
to all pages. Select the project ⇨ Website ⇨ Add New Item ⇨ Web Configuration File. Remove the

MasterPageFile attribute from the code of the Default.aspx page, because you'll also put that in web.config, as follows:

```
<?xml version="1.0"?>
<configuration xmlns="http://schemas.microsoft.com/.NetConfiguration/v2.0">
   <system.web>
       <pages theme="DarkBeer" masterPageFile="~/CRMaster.master" />
       <!-- other settings here... -->
   </system.net>
</configuration>
```

Why select a master page from the New Item dialog box when creating Default.aspx, *just to remove the master page attribute immediately afterward? Because that way, VS2008 will create the proper* Content *controls and not the HTML code of a normal page.*

Creating the Second Theme

To test the user-selectable theming feature described earlier in the chapter, we must have more than one theme. Thus, under the App_Themes folder, create another folder, named LightBeer (select the project, right-click Add Folder ⇨ Theme Folder, and name it DomesticBeer), and then copy and paste the whole Default.css file from the DarkBeer folder, modifying it to make it look different.

In the provided example, I've changed most of the containers so that no background image is used, and the header and footer are filled with simple solid colors, like the left and right columns. Not only is the size for some elements different but the position is as well. The positions of the left and right columns in particular (which use absolute positioning) are completely switched, so that the container named leftcol is docked on the right border, and the rightcol container is docked on the left. This is done by changing just a couple of style classes, as shown here:

```
body
{
    font-family: Arial, Helvetica, sans-serif;
    font-size: 12px;
    background-color: #FFCC00;
}

div#dHeader, div#footer, div#dContainer
{
    background-position: 0 0;
    background: none repeat scroll 0 0;

    border: none;
    width: 780px;
    margin: auto;
}

/* Header Elements */

#dMainHeader
{
    clear: both;
    color: #800000;
```

```
    float: left;
    height: 80px;
    padding: 0;
    width: 780px;
    background-color: #CC6600;
}

H1.dMainHeader
{
    font-size: 24px;
    font-weight: bold;
    color: #996633;
}

#dLogo
{
    width: 480px;
    float: left;
    margin-right: 40px;
    margin-left: 40px;
}
```

This is the power of DIVs and stylesheets: change a few styles, and the colors change and there are no background images. This was a pretty simple example, but you can push this much further and create completely different layouts, with some parts hidden and others made bigger, and so on.

Creating the ThemeSelector User Control

You now have a master page, with a couple of themes for it, so now you can develop a user control that will display the list of available themes and allow the user to pick one. Once you have this control, you will plug it into the master page, in the "themeselector" DIV container. Before creating the user control, create a new folder named "Controls", inside of which you'll put all your user controls so that they are separate from the pages for better organization (select the project, right-click Add Folder ➪ Regular folder, and name it Controls). To create a new user control, right-click on the Controls folder, select Add New Item ➪ Web User Control, and name it ThemeSelector.ascx. The content of this .ascx file is very simple and includes just a string and a DropDownList:

```
<%@ Control Language="VB" AutoEventWireup="false" CodeFile="ThemeSelector.ascx.vb"
  Inherits="MB.TheBeerHouse.UI.Controls.ThemeSelector" %>
<asp:DropDownList runat="server" ID="ddlThemes" AutoPostBack="True"
  meta:resourcekey="ddlThemesResource1" />
```

Note that the drop-down list has the AutoPostBack property set to true, so that the page is automatically submitted to the server as soon as the user changes the selected value. The real work of filling the drop-down list with the names of the available themes, and loading the selected theme, will be done in this control's code-behind file, and in a base page class that you'll see shortly. In the code-behind file, you need to fill the drop-down list with an array of strings returned by a helper method and then select the item that has the same value as the current page's Theme:

```vb
Public Partial Class ThemeSelector
    Inherits System.Web.UI.UserControl
    Protected Sub Page_Load(ByVal sender As Object, ByVal e As EventArgs)
        ddlThemes.DataSource = Helpers.GetThemes()
        ddlThemes.DataBind()

        ddlThemes.SelectedValue = Me.Page.Theme
    End Sub
End Class
```

The `GetThemes` method is defined in a `Helpers.vb` file that is located in the root folder of the TBHBLL class library; you will have to compile the library after any changes before those changes can be used by the site. You'll read more about the compilation model later in the book, and especially in Chapter 13 about deployment.

> Going forward with the new Beer House application, you will need a class library as part of the overall solution. This can easily be added by selecting File ⇨ Add ⇨ New Project from the Visual Studio menu. That invokes the Add New Project dialog, in which you select Class Library.
>
> You work is still not done, and we will cover more of the details in remaining chapters. But you need to add a reference to the class library in your website. You can do this by right-clicking on the root node of the website and selecting Add Reference from the context menu. Select the Projects tab in the dialog, double-click the name of your new class library, and you have a reference. You will have to compile the class library before any changes you make can be used by the website.
>
> Several supporting classes are discussed in the rest of the chapter. While you can just as easily place them in the App_Code folder, for the purposes of this book, I will be including these classes in a supporting class library. There will be more details on this process in the next chapter.

The `GetThemes` method uses the `GetDirectories` method of the `System.IO.Directory` class to retrieve an array with the paths of all folders contained in the `~/App_Themes` folder (this method expects a physical path, not a URL — you can, however, use a URL to point to the physical path by using the `Server.MapPath` method). The returned array of strings contains the entire path, not just the folder name, so you must loop through this array and overwrite each item with that item's folder name part (returned by the `System.IO.Path.GetFileName` static method). Once the array is filled for the first time, it is stored in the ASP.NET cache, so that subsequent requests will retrieve it from there, more quickly. The following code shows the entire content of the `Helpers` class (`Helpers.vb`):

```vb
Imports System.IO
Imports Microsoft.VisualBasic
Imports System.Collections.Specialized
Imports System.Web
Imports System.Web.Caching
Imports System.Web.UI
Imports System.Web.UI.WebControls

Namespace UI
    Public NotInheritable Class Helpers
```

```
'
' Returns an array with the names of all local Themes
'
Public Shared Function GetThemes() As String()
If Not IsNothing(HttpContext.Current.Cache("SiteThemes")) Then
Return DirectCast(HttpContext.Current.Cache("SiteThemes"), String())
Else
Dim themesDirPath As String = HttpContext.Current.Server.MapPath("~/App_Themes")
                ' get the array of themes folders under /App_Themes
            Dim themes As String() = Directory.GetDirectories(themesDirPath)
                For i As Integer = 0 To themes.Length - 1
                    themes(i) = Path.GetFileName(themes(i))
            Next
                Dim dep As New CacheDependency(themesDirPath)
                HttpContext.Current.Cache.Insert("SiteThemes", themes, dep)

Return themes
End If

End Function
    End Class
End Namespace
```

Now that you have the control, go back to the master page, and add the following line at the top of the file in the Source view to reference the external user control:

```
<%@ Register Src="Controls/ThemeSelector.ascx" TagName="ThemeSelector"
TagPrefix="uc2" %>
```

Then, declare an instance of the control where you want it to appear — namely, within the "themeselector" container:

```
<div id="themeselector">
   <uc2:ThemeSelector id="ThemeSelector1" runat="server" />
</div>
```

The code that handles the switch to a new theme can't be placed in the DropDownList's SelectedIndexChanged event, because that happens too late in the page's life cycle. As I said in the "Design" section, the new theme must be applied in the page's PreInit event. Also, instead of recoding it for every page, we'll just write that code once in a custom base page. Our objective is to read the value of the DropDownList's selected index from within our custom base class, and then we want to apply the theme specified by the DropDownList.

You can't access the controls and their values from the PreInit event handler because it's still too early in the page's life cycle. Therefore, you need to read the value of this control in a server event that occurs later: the Load event is a good place to read it. However, when you're in the Load event handler, you won't know the specific ID of the DropDownList control, so you'll need a way to identify this control, and then you can read its value by accessing the row data that was posted back to the server, via the Request.Form collection.

And there is a remaining problem: you must know the ID of the control to retrieve its value from the collection, but the ID may vary according to the container in which you place it, and it's not a good idea to hard-code it because you might decide to change its location in the future. Instead, when the control is first created, you can save its client-side ID in a static field of a class, so that it will be maintained for the entire life of the application, between different requests (postbacks), until the application shuts down (more precisely, until the application domain of the application's assemblies is unloaded). Therefore, add a `Globals.vb` file to the supporting class library, and write the following code inside it:

```
Imports System.Web.Configuration
Imports Microsoft.VisualBasic

Public NotInheritable Class Globals

    Public Shared ThemesSelectorID As String = String.Empty

End Class
```

Then, go back to the `ThemeSelector`'s code-behind file and add the code to save its ID in that static field:

```
Imports TheBeerHouse
Imports TheBeerHouse.UI

Namespace UI.Controls
    Partial Class ThemeSelector
        Inherits System.Web.UI.UserControl

        Protected Sub Page_Load(ByVal sender As Object, ByVal e As
System.EventArgs) Handles Me.Load
            If Globals.ThemesSelectorID.Length = 0 Then
                Globals.ThemesSelectorID = ddlThemes.UniqueID
            End If

            ddlThemes.DataSource = Helpers.GetThemes()
            ddlThemes.DataBind()

            ddlThemes.SelectedValue = Me.Page.Theme
        End Sub
    End Class
End Namespace
```

You're ready to create the custom base class for your pages, and this will just be another regular class you place in `UI` folder in the class library and that inherits from `System.Web.UI.Page`. You override its `OnPreInit` method to do the following:

1. Check whether the current request is a postback. If it is, check whether it was caused by the `ThemeSelector` drop-down list. In ASP.NET, all pages with a server-side form have a hidden field named `"__EVENTTARGET"`, which will be set with the ID of the HTML control that causes the postback (if it is not a Submit button). To verify this condition, you can just check whether the `"__EVENTTARGET"` element of the `Form` collection contains the ID from the drop-down list, based on the ID read from the `Globals` class.

2. If the conditions of point 1 are all verified, you retrieve the name of the selected theme from the `Form` collection's element with an `Id` equal to the ID saved in `Globals`, and use it for setting the page's `Theme` property. Then, you also store that value in a `Session` variable. This is done

so that subsequent requests made by the same user will correctly load the newly selected theme and will not reset it to the default theme.

3. If the current request is not a postback, check whether the `Session` variable used in point 2 is empty (null) or not. If it is not, retrieve that value and use it for the page's `Theme` property.

The following snippet translates this description into real code:

```
Namespace TheBeerHouse.UI
    Public Class BasePage
        Inherits System.Web.UI.Page
        Protected Overloads Overrides Sub OnPreInit(ByVal e As EventArgs)
            Dim id As String = Globals.ThemesSelectorID
            If id.Length > 0 Then
                If Me.Request.Form("__EVENTTARGET") = id AndAlso Not
    String.IsNullOrEmpty(Me.Request.Form(id)) Then
                    Me.Theme = Me.Request.Form(id)
                    Me.Session("CurrentTheme") = Me.Theme
                Else
                    If Me.Session("CurrentTheme") IsNot Nothing Then
                        Me.Theme = Me.Session("CurrentTheme").ToString()
                    End If
                End If
            End If

            MyBase.OnPreInit(e)
        End Sub
    End Class
End Namespace
```

The downside of the approach used here is that the selected theme is stored in a session variable, which is cleared when the session ends — namely, when the user closes the browser or when the user does not make a page request for 20 minutes (the duration can be customized). A much better solution would be to use Profile properties, which are persistent between sessions and also have other advantages. You'll examine this feature of ASP.NET — and modify this code to use it — in Chapter 5.

The last thing you have to do is change the default code-behind class for the `Default.aspx` page so that it uses your own `BasePage` class instead of the default `Page` class. Your custom base class, in turn, will call the original `Page` class. You only need to change one word, as shown here (change `Page` to `BasePage`):

```
Public Partial Class _Default
    Inherits TheBeerHouse.UI.BasePage
    Protected Sub Page_Load(ByVal sender As Object, ByVal e As EventArgs)
    End Sub
End Class
```

You're done! Run the project; by default, you'll see the home page shown earlier in Figure 2-7 (except for the login box, which doesn't contain anything so far — it will be filled in Chapter 5) with the `DarkBeer` theme applied to it. If you pick the `LightBeer` item from the `ThemeSelector` drop-down list, the home page should change to something very similar to what is shown in Figure 2-11.

Figure 2-11

The same page with the `LightBeer` theme applied is shown in Figure 2-12.

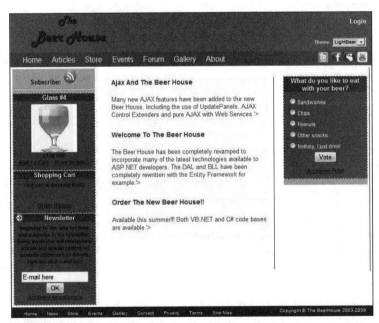

Figure 2-12

Creating Consistent Sidebar Content

The user control elements in the sidebar boxes have a consistent layout and style applied to them. Each content box is composed of a wrapper DIV element and two child DIVs. The first child DIV is the content's title bar. The second child element is the actual content. Notice how style classes are applied to the elements; remember, these elements are repeated several times on each page. Therefore, you need to apply the style settings using the `class` attribute:

```
<div class="SideBarbox">
    <div class="SideBarTitle">
        <asp:Image ID="imgArrow" runat="server" ImageUrl="~/images/arrowr.gif"
  GenerateEmptyAlternateText="True" meta:resourcekey="imgArrowResource1" />
        Newsletter
    </div>
    <div class="SideBarContent">
/* Content Goes Here */
    </div>
</div>
```

Here are the corresponding styles:

```
/* Side Bar Box */

.SideBarbox
{
    padding: 0px 1px 3px 1px;
    font-size: 11px;
    text-align: center;
    border: 1px dashed #FFFFFF;
    background-color: #CC6600;

}

.SideBarbox a
{
    color: #521300;
    font-weight: bold;
}

.SideBarTitle
{
    font-family: Arial, Helvetica, sans-serif;
    font-size: small;
    font-weight: bold;
    color: #FFFFFF;
    background-color: #800000;
}

.SideBarTitle img
{
    float: left;
    margin-left: 3px;
    margin-right: 3px;
```

```
}

.SideBarContent
{
    padding: 6px;
}
```

Figure 2-13 shows an example of these styles in action.

Figure 2-13

Another Small Touch of Style

A single page (`Default.aspx`) is not enough to test everything we've discussed and implemented in this chapter. For example, we haven't really seen the `SiteMapPath` control in practice, because it doesn't show any link until we move away from the home page, of course. You can easily implement the `Contact.aspx` and `About.aspx` pages if you want to test it. I'll take the `Contact.aspx` page as an example for this chapter. The final page is represented in Figure 2-14.

Figure 2-14

Summary

In this chapter, you've built the foundations for the site's user interface layer. You've designed and implemented nested master pages with common HTML and graphics, making it easy to change the layout and the graphics of the site by modifying a single file. You have seen how to create a variety of two- and three-column page layouts using CSS. You've also used themes to create a couple of different visual appearances for the same master page. You've created a mechanism to enable users to dynamically pick their own favorite theme from a drop-down list, so that they can change the appearance of your site to meet their needs and desires. You have also created a lean set of menus using Unordered List and stylesheets. You have also added a `SiteMapPath` control to display breadcrumb navigation based on the `SiteMapProvider` we will build in a later chapter. Finally, you've used a custom `BasePage` class to provide not just a common look and feel among the pages but also some common behavior. All in all, you've already developed some significant new features, but with comparatively few lines of code. In the next chapter, we'll continue to talk about foundations, but for the business layer and data layers.

3

Planning an Architecture

This chapter lays the groundwork for the rest of the book by creating a number of basic services that will be shared among all future modules: configuration classes to process custom sections and elements in `web.config`, base business classes and the Entity Framework model, caching strategies, and more. I'll show you the `ListView` control introduced in ASP.NET 3.5, and we'll build an *n*-tier architecture to manage interacting with the database.

Problem

Our website is made up of a number of separate modules for managing dynamic content such as articles, forums, photo galleries, events, and polls, and sending out newsletters. However, all the modules have a number of common "design" tasks that you must deal with:

- ❑ Create a sound Entity Framework model that will manage the data access.

- ❑ Create a base for a business logic layer to manage interaction with the Entity Framework and to validate data.

- ❑ Expand and customize the business object architecture generated by the Entity Framework Wizard to expose the data retrieved by the data access layer in an object-oriented format. This will leverage the use of partial classes introduced in .NET 2.0.

- ❑ Separate the business logic code from the presentation code (user interface) so that the site is much more maintainable and scalable. This is called a *multi-tier design*.

- ❑ Support the caching of business objects to save the data you've already fetched from the data store so that you don't have to make unnecessary fetches to retrieve the same data again. This results in less CPU, and database resource usage and less network traffic, resulting in better general performance.

- ❑ Create a class library to house various components and classes that compose the core infrastructure of the application.

❏ Handle and log exceptions to help diagnose problems in the event of a system failure and to provide an audit trail.

❏ Standardize a common user interface methodology to display list of records, details, and administrative editing.

❏ Create a custom configuration section to hold site specific data.

❏ Create a common location in which to store information about each page or resource in the site so that it can be distributed as needed.

❏ Create a data-driven custom `SiteMapProvider` that will allow automatic updating of content as it is added to and removed from the site.

❏ Create a custom SiteMap.org `HttpHandler` to produce the appropriate feed, based on the current site structure.

❏ Create an infrastructure to ensure optimized search engine techniques.

❏ Create an RSS infrastructure to syndicate items from the site, such as articles, photos, and the like.

The task in this chapter is to devise a common set of classes and guidelines to address these problems so that the common classes can be utilized by the various modules to be covered in later chapters. Once you finish this chapter, you'll have a foundation upon which to build, and you can even distribute the development of future modules to various other developers, who can leverage the same common code to build each module.

Design

The "Problem" section identified many core tasks that must be addressed before we can proceed to building the site. Having a solid foundation is the most important aspect of building any application, in software development this starts with the operating system and bubbles its way up. We have established the use of the Windows platform and .NET as the application framework, so some core architecture decisions need to be made to implement the solution to the problems.

The .NET Framework now has so many ways to solve just about every problem you can have in an application that sometimes the hardest thing is to decide which solution to leverage. By defining a solid foundation, the Beer House will have a highly performant, flexible, and extendible architecture.

Creating a Common Class Library

Class libraries are way to contain custom objects and resources in a common location that can be used by multiple applications. A class library is simply a .NET assembly or `.dll` file that can be added to the Global Assembly Cache (GAC) and referenced directly by any application on the machine, or added to the application's folder to be loaded at runtime. Housing common objects in one location makes the code more portable and manageable for large applications and systems. For example, the Beer House uses the web as a common user interface but is considering expanding the application's frontend to WPF and Silverlight in the near future. Separating common business logic and resources means that the user interface layer or application can be thinner and code will not need to be modified on the backend to implement the new media.

In the previous edition of this book, the majority of this code was added to the App_Code folder. In this edition most, of this code is added to a class library referenced by the web application. I am going to use just one class library, but as the application code grows, it will be beneficial to break this code into even more focused class libraries, such as Data, UI, SEO, and so on.

Adding a Class Library to a Visual Studio Solution

Visual Studio 2008 provides a couple of ways to add a new class library to a project; you can select File Add New Project, or you can right-click on the root node of the solution in the Solution Explorer window and select Add New Project from the context menu. Either way, the Add New Project dialog opens (see Figure 3-1). Select Visual Basic in the Project Types list, and choose Class Library from the Visual Studio installed templates.

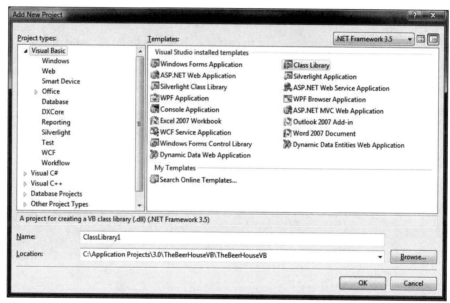

Figure 3-1

The new Class Library project is added to the solution with an initial class `Class1`. Delete that class file; you'll add files for the real classes as you work through this book.

For the website to leverage the class library, it must reference the library. Right-Click on the website's root and select Add Reference from the context menu. The Add Reference dialog (see Figure 3-2) displays. Change to the Projects tab and select the new class library.

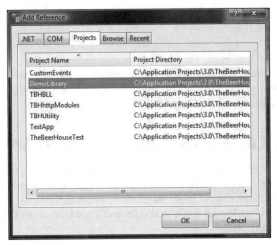

Figure 3-2

This adds a reference to the class library in the website. The class library should define a root namespace that can be assumed by all the classes contained in the library. That's not a requirement, but it makes things easier to manage. This is done by opening the properties page for the project by right-clicking the root of the class library project and selecting Properties at the bottom of the context menu. The page shown in Figure 3-3 is displayed, and the Root Namespace can be defined.

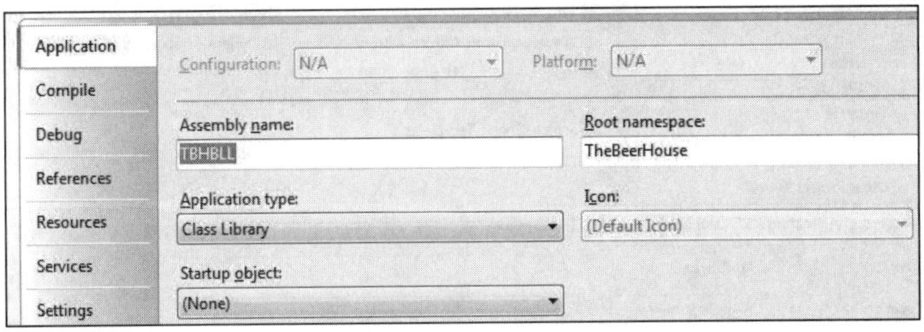

Figure 3-3

The namespace can be automatically imported by the website project by opening the site's property page the same way and selecting the References tab. At the bottom of the References tab is the Imported Namespaces section (see Figure 3-4). This section lists all the available namespaces with a checkbox. Namespaces that are imported on a global level are checked, if TheBeerHouse namespace is not selected, then it can be selected, making it available to all the pages and classes within the site.

You can designate any available namespace to be imported. Because the TheBeerHouse.Bll namespace is part of the referenced TBHBLL class library, it can be imported at an application level. Because that namespace is used quite a bit in the site, this very nice convenience saves you the trouble of importing it over and over.

Figure 3-4

Designing a Layered Infrastructure

If you have not heard of *n*-tier architecture, you will become familiar with it as you read through this book. As software development has evolved over the years, we have learned to separate logic or work into separate layers, typically a data store, and data access, business logic, and presentation layers. While there are times when these layers can be subdivided further, this is typically what you will see in most applications. Here are descriptions of each layer:

❑ **Data store:** Where the data resides. This can be a relational database, an XML file, a text file, or a proprietary storage system, such as SQL Server, Oracle or MySQL.

❑ **Data access layer:** The code that takes care of retrieving and manipulating the raw data saved in the data store.

❑ **Business logic layer:** The code that takes the data retrieved by the data access tier and exposes it to the client in a more abstracted and intuitive way, hiding low-level details such as the data store's schema, and adding all the validation and authorization logic that ensures that the input is safe and consistent.

❑ **Presentation layer (user interface):** The code that defines what a user should see on the screen, including formatted data and system navigation menus. This layer will be designed to operate inside a web browser in the case of ASP.NET, but there are so many more user interfaces in use today. WPF and Silverlight are some of the emerging new technologies to build desktop and web interfaces. Mobile applications are also increasing in demand as well. So never think your application will just be a web application.

Depending on the size of the project, you might have additional tiers, or some tiers may be merged together. For example, in the case of very small projects, the data access and business tiers may be merged together so that a single component takes care of retrieving the data and exposing it in the UI in a more accessible way. The SQLDataSource, AccessDataSource, and XmlDataSource controls introduced with ASP.NET 2.0, as well as the LinqDataSource and EntityDataSource controls introduced in ASP.NET 3.5, combine the UI, business, and data access layers into one layer in what is known as Line-of-Sight architecture, meaning that there is direct communication between the database and the user interface.

When discussing multi-tier architecture and design, the terms *tier* and *layer* are frequently used interchangeably, but there's actually a subtle difference between them: tiers indicate a physical separation of components, which may mean different assemblies (DLL, EXE, or other file types if the project is not all based on .NET) on the same computer or on multiple computers, whereas layers refer to a logical separation of components, such as having distinct classes and namespaces for the DAL, BLL, and UI code. Therefore, tiers are about physical separation and units of deployment, but layers are about logical separation and units of design.

In the last edition of this book the classes for the business, data tier, and utility classes were merged into the website in an effort to reduce the overhead of maintaining the code base. The argument was made that separating these classes is fine for large, enterprise-level sites but is not that good for small and medium applications. This is correct; now that the App_Code folder in ASP.NET 2.0 is available, it does help at least with organizing code for a website.

The Beer House business is increasing, and the demand for the site is growing. The owners are also starting to look into creating customized mobile, WPF desktop applications (for point of sale), SharePoint integration, and even Silverlight in a future version. This is a common scenario in today's world, and you need a strong, robust backend infrastructure with the capability to quickly add multiple frontend interfaces.

So, in this version of the Beer House, all the supporting classes that can be reused in multiple applications are placed in a class library. Eventually, you will want to separate the various classes into more targeted class libraries. But for this project, having one class library will keep it cleaner.

This book uses the Entity Framework as a data access layer. One of the main features of the Entity Framework is that it's inherently designed to be leveraged against any backend data store. Data providers, such as Oracle, DB2, or MySQL, can easily build custom providers that work with Entity Framework to access their database. So, in essence, the Entity Framework is the data provider layer for this version of theBeerHouse application.

The Entity Framework provides a rich foundation on which to build a data model for the application, while abstracting the actual data store from the rest of the application. The Entity Framework Wizard generates the data model and supporting classes to interact with the model and the Entity Framework. These classes can be extended and added upon to make a rich business logic layer.

> **In the previous editions of this book the root namespace was MB, which stands for Marco Bellinaso. Because the application is built around the Beer House, I removed that level of the namespace, making `TheBeerHouse` the top-level namespace.**

Choosing a Data Store

Having an infrastructure that is flexible when it comes to choosing a data store is important for some. If you are producing an application as a vendor who has clients that use different data stores for example. Most businesses chose a database vendor and stick with them rather that change every few years. Generally, in creating an application that will only be used internally, architecting for a data store change is not as important, because a change that drastic typically means drastic changes to the application itself.

But it is nice knowing that the core application architecture can easily support these types of changes, not only in the choice of the backend data store but also in all components of the application. Since the Entity Framework is designed to be flexible toward the backend database this gives you an instant advantage because we do not need to concern ourselves with that code. If the Beer House decides to change from SQL Server to another data store technology or vendor, as long as there is an ADO.NET data provider for that platform, the application can quickly be modified.

The Beer House has not changed its choice of database, SQL Server. So you will continue to build the application on top of SQL Server, but because the application is using Entity Framework, it will be built around the entities in the data model, rather than the data schema of the database.

Designing the Data Access Layer

The data access layer (DAL) is the code that executes queries to the database to retrieve data, and to update, insert, and delete data. It is the code that's closest to the database, and it must know all the database details — the schema of the tables, the name of the fields, stored procedures, views, and so on. Keep database-specific code separated from your site's pages for a number of reasons:

❑ The developer who builds the user interfaces (i.e., the pages and user controls) may not be the same developer who writes the data access code. In fact, for midsized to large sites, they are usually different people. The UI developer may ignore most things about the database but still provide the user interface for it, because all the details are wrapped into separate objects that provide a high-level abstraction of the table, the stored procedure and field names, and the SQL to work with them.

❑ Typically, some queries that retrieve data will be used from different pages. If you put them directly into the pages themselves, and later you have to change a query to add some fields or change the sorting, you'd have to review all your code and find every place where it's used. If, instead, the data access code is contained in some common DAL classes, then you'd just need to modify those, and the pages calling them will remain untouched.

❑ Having hard-coded queries inside web pages would make it extremely difficult to migrate to a new relational database management system (RDBMS) or to support more than one RDBMS. Plus, they are often an easy target of SQL Injection attacks because the developers who hard-coded queries often neglect to parameterize the queries.

Introduction to the Entity Framework

In 2006, Microsoft announced a new data framework, ADO.NET vNext. This has since become the ADO.NET Entity Framework (EF) and was released with .NET 3.5/Visual Studio 2008 SP1 in August of 2008. The Entity Framework is an entry from Microsoft into the object relational mapping (ORM) space. ORMs are data frameworks aimed at bridging the gap between data stores (databases) and applications. Entity Framework is an example of an ORM; Linq to SQL, nHibernate, Wilson ORM, and many others are also available for the .NET platform. All have attractive features and provide a way to abstract the database from the application to make it easier for developers to program an application based on business needs and not the database schema.

The Entity Framework's Entity Data Model (EDM) is composed of several elements and is ultimately based on Dr. Peter Chen's Entity Relationship (ER). ER is the conceptual representation of business elements and the relationships they have with each other. The EDM is what really differentiates the Entity Framework from other ORM products. The EDM builds a layer of abstraction above the ER model, but preserves the concepts of entities and their relationships.

What the Entity Framework does provide is a consistent way to program against a model that is abstracted away from the way the data is actually stored. As applications have evolved, the data is no longer necessarily stored in a manner that is easy to conceptualize in an application. Data is often optimized for speed, indexing, and other considerations for the actual data store technology, which can create a problem — often referred to as an impedance mismatch — when you're trying to efficiently create applications around the data model. This is where EF becomes a valuable tool to the developer because it abstracts the complex data storage schemas from the developer. The developer can then simply concern herself with the business entity model when architecting solutions.

The actual data model for the Beer House is pretty straightforward, so we will not be dealing with this issue as you might have to in more complex applications. All the entity mappings in the Beer House are one-to-one, instead of being an entity composed of related data in many tables.

The EDM (see Figure 3-5) consists of two concepts: entities and relationships. An entity is a thing, such as an article or an article category. A relationship is an association, such as the category an article belongs or a list of comments for the article. Article Categories, Comments, and Articles are all entities or things; the association they have to each other is the relationship. Typically, you can think of these as tables and foreign key relationships, and often this is how the model will be generated.

Figure 3-5

A group of entities is called an `EntitySet`, which is a collection of entities such as Articles, Categories, and Comments. The `EntitySet` class implements `IList`, `ICollection`, `IList(of TEntity)`, `ICollection(of TEntity)`, `IEnumerable(of TEntity)`, `IEnumerable`, and `IListSource`. By implementing these interfaces, it provides a rich set of members to manage a collection of entities in a fashion familiar to those used to working with generics. Similarly, `AssociationSets` are a collection of associations. An `EntityContainer` wraps a group of entities and associations.

Entity SQL

The EF introduces a new query language, Entity SQL (ESQL), which supports inheritance and polymorphism. These two concepts are not supported in existing SQL languages. Entity SQL does not query against the data store but against the modeled objects composed from the data store. Therefore, it needs to work against objects but still retain a familiar SQL-like syntax to make programming easier.

This also means that ESQL is not bound to a specific backend data store. For example, SQL Server SQL is slightly different than Oracle's SQL and IBM's SQL, and so forth. This abstraction frees developers from having to be tightly concerned with the vendor-specific version of SQL. The following ESQL code example shows how to retrieve a list of articles and their comments when at least one comment exists for the article.

```
Select a, a.Comment
From ArticlesModel.Articles as a
Where a.Comment.Count > 0
```

The Entity Framework comes with built-in support for SQL Server but has already been extended too many other vender platforms. Vendors need to simply create or modify existing ADO.NET data providers.

You may be asking yourself how does the Entity Framework actually communicate with the data store, or where is the actual SQL? Entity framework does the lifting for you because it creates an optimized, parameterized SQL query to communicate with the database. You can still use existing stored procedures and create your own, but you do lose some LINQ to Entities flexibility in querying over the results. Basically, calling a stored procedure returns a result set or just performs an action, and there is no `IQueryable` result to query against.

ESQL Parameterized Concepts

Using Parameterized SQL and ESQL is important to guarding against SQL Injection attacks. No platform is immune to potential SQL Injection attacks, but they are easily prevented. Most SQL Injection attacks are successful because of lazy coding habits. Using stored procedures has long been a common way to protect against these attacks because the parameters passed to the procedure are done using a `SQLParameter` object.

SQL Injection attacks are a common way that hackers attack a website by injecting SQL code into a poorly written website. This is usually done by passing a SQL string as a parameter to a Web Form. The reason it works is that many web developers hard-code SQL statements into their application and do a string concatenation to insert parameter values. Hackers simply inject their desired SQL as a form parameter, terminating the original SQL statement and causing theirs to be executed. There are many examples on the web that go into great detail on specific attacks, and if you have not investigated this issue, I encourage you to do so. Use parameterized SQL statements to guard against these attacks.

Continued

EF provides the same parameterization methodologies, but you still have the capability to pass values unchecked to an ESQL query. This should never be done. The `ObjectParameter` class acts just like the `SQLParameter` class used to directly pass parameters to ad hoc queries and stored procedures, as shown in the following code snippet.

```
Using lArticlectx As New ArticlesEntities()

Dim queryString As String = _
            "SELECT VALUE Article FROM Articles " & _
            "AS Article WHERE Article.Approved = @as"

Dim ArticleQuery As New ObjectQuery(Of Article)(queryString, _
                            lArticlectx)

' Add parameters to the collection.
ArticleQuery.Parameters.Add(New ObjectParameter("as", True))

Dim lArticles As ObjectResult(Of Article) =
ArticleQuery.Execute(MergeOption.NoTracking)

        Dim lArticle As Article
        For Each lArticle In lArticles
            Console.WriteLine("Title: {0}", lArticle.Title)
Next
```

A platform specific Entity Framework provider typically extends an existing vendor-specific ADO. NET data provider by creating platform optimized syntax to interact with the database. This is a very nice feature because now you as the developer do not have to worry about this and have the freedom to build your application in the language you prefer, such as C# or VB.NET.

The EF introduces the `EntityClient` that runs on top of the ADO.NET providers. It leverages the existing `Connection`, `Command`, and `DataReader` objects with which all .NET developers should be familiar by now. There are special classes for each of these familiar objects, `EntityConnection`, `EntityCommand`, and `EntityReader`. You will not need to be concerned with using these objects in the scope of this book, but it is nice to know that you can leverage them if you want.

Object Services

Object Services is a layer of abstractions that sits on top of the `EntityClient`. It acts a bridge between the application and the datastore. The `EntityClient` is responsible for the ORM aspects, and Entity Framework and object querying. You can think of Object Services as the workhorse of EF. The Object Services layer takes LINQ or ESQL queries, passes them to the `EntityClient` and returns an `IQueryable(of T)`. The `EntityClient` is the data provider, customized for the data store.

What is more important to understand about the Object Services is the `ObjectContext`, which provides the interface for the developer to interact with the entities and, ultimately, the database. The `ObjectContext` also tracks changes to entities through the `ObjectStateManager`. That's because each entity is attached to the context. While an entity can be detached or retrieved unattached, this is not done by default. Attached entities can have their changes tracked (optimistic concurrency) by the `ObjectStateManager`. This is an important feature to understand, and you'll see how to take advantage of it when we revisit how to implement EF in the solution section.

LINQ to Entities

Since Language Integrated Query (LINQ) was introduced with the release of .NET 3.5, there have been many implementations of LINQ, such as LINQ to Objects, LINQ to XML, LINQ to SQL, LINQ to DataSets, and so on. Entity framework has its own implementation of LINQ as well, LINQ to Entities. LINQ to Entities is a very thin layer built on top of Object Services that takes advantage of the `ObjectQuery` class to perform queries.

LINQ to SQL was the first LINQ extension released that allowed developers to interact with SQL Server. The big difference is LINQ to Entities does not talk directly to the database but instead queries the Entity Framework that does the talking. This means that LINQ to Entities can talk to any data store as long as there is an EF provider for the platform. LINQ queries are converted to expression trees and executed against the Object Services layer and return an `IQueryable(of T)` result (see Figure 3-6).

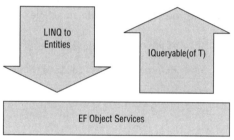

Figure 3-6

The EF `ObjectServices` layer exposes a conceptual view of the data, which is ideal for LINQ queries to manipulate. This gives the developer a Transact SQL–like programming experience in the application and development environment. LINQ also adds lambda expressions, making for an even richer development experience. Because the queries are written in the application, the developer has development aides, such as IntelliSense, compile-time syntax checking, and so forth, to make building queries against the Entity Model much easier. LINQ to Entities gives the developer the ability to create strongly typed queries that will have any errors in syntax caught by the compiler.

To perform LINQ to Entities, the application must reference `System.Core.dll` and `System.Data.Entity.dll`. It must also import the `System.Linq` and `System.Data.Objects` namespaces. Of course, the application must either contain or reference an Entity Data Model as well.

Many of the LINQ to SQL concepts are supported by LINQ to Entities, but there are a few instances where things are done slightly differently or are not supported at all.

The LINQ standard query operators are supported, so query results can be shaped, filtered, sorted, and grouped. Common operators like `Select`, `Where`, `Join`, and `OrderBy`, and the `aggregate` and `set` operators are all supported. For more details read more about standard query operators on MSDN at `http://msdn.microsoft.com/en-us/library/bb738551.aspx`.

A LINQ to Entities query is executed by creating an expression tree that is executed by EF against the data source. All EF queries are executed using deferred execution, meaning that they must be either explicitly executed or are not executed until they are used. The concept of implicit and deferred execution is important to understand when discussing ORM frameworks. You will also hear the term *lazy loading* in reference to deferred loading. This means that data is not actually loaded or queried from the database until it is explicitly requested.

In the following example, a Linq to SQL statement is used to load an article's comments into a `ListView` control, using deferred execution.

```
Using linqToSqlContext as new L2SDataContext()

lvComments.DataSource = linqToSqlContext.Articles.First().Comments
lvComments.DataBind()

End Using
```

Using the same pattern with an EF model will result in 0 comments being returned because EF does not support lazy loading. Instead, you must explicitly load the comments as illustrated in the following snippet because you have to tell EF you want to include an article's comments:

```
Using EFContext as new EFDataContext()

lvComments.DataSource = EFContext.Articles.Include("Comments").First().Comments
lvComments.DataBind()

End Using
```

Or

```
Using EFContext as new EFDataContext()

Dim lArticle as List(of Articles) = EFContext.Articles
lArticle.Comments.Load()
lvComments.DataSource = lArticle.Comments
lvComments.DataBind()

End Using
```

The reason for this is to make developers aware that they are accessing the database. The first example eagerly loads the list of comments when the article is retrieved. The second example explicitly loads the list of comments only when they are needed. Eagerly loading typically results in fewer hits on the database, which makes DBAs happy but can put more pressure on system memory because more data is loaded that may not be used; it also causes the extra data to travel across the wire. Explicit loading ultimately results in more hits on the database but uses less memory as well as resulting in a lighter load being sent across the wire. Ultimately, the choice is up to you, based on your system design and overall demands.

Because queries are deferred, multiple queries can be executed at once. The query variable actually stores the commands, as they are added and not executed until the command is iterated over. For example, you could designate a query to retrieve a list of articles, another to retrieve a list of categories and yet another query to get a list of approved comments against the same `DataContext`. These queries will not be executed until at least one is explicitly executed; that causes all three to be exectuted against the data store simultaneously. If you look at the connection string generated by the Entity Data Model Wizard, you will see that it sets `MultipleActiveResultSets= true`. `MultipleActiveResultSets` (MARS) allows applications to execute more than one SQL statement on a connection in the same request. EF leverages MARS by executing any statements that need to be executed in a single transaction, thus increasing application performance.

Immediate execution is done whenever a scalar query is executed, `Avg`, `Max`, `Sum`, `Min`, and so forth. These queries require all the query results to be returned so that the scalar value can be calculated. Immediate execution can also be forced by calling one of the enumeration methods: `ToArray`, `ToDictionary` and `ToList`. These methods return the results to a corresponding collection object.

Extending Entity Framework in an N-Tier Environment

The Visual Studio Entity Framework experience provides a helpful visual Designer to create and manage the Entity Model. The wizard creates a strongly typed `ObjectContext` and one or more custom entity classes derived from `EntityObject`. These objects can be easily extended using the partial class model, introduced in .NET 2.0.

While it may not be obvious at first glance, the Entity Framework is easily integrated into a standard *n*-tier model. The Entity Framework itself sits on top of the actual data access layer, ADO.NET 3.5. Above the Entity Framework sits a custom business layer. But the bridge between the Entity Framework and the business logic layer is a thin layer of customized objects that further customize the Entity Framework services.

The *n*-tier architecture used in the Beer House consists of a custom `ObjectContext` class generated by the Entity Model Wizard, a series of entity repositories, and custom entity classes generated by the wizard and extended. The `Repository` model is similar to the `Active Record` model, except the entity just holds data that composes an object, for example a `SiteMapInfo` in the `SiteMap`. Instead of the entity also containing members responsible for retrieving records from the database, the `Repository` class contains members responsible for interacting with the database, such as doing standard CRUD operations. The Entity Data Model Wizard creates a series of classes that represent each of the entities and a derived `ObjectContext` with some basic members for interacting with EF. The classes the wizard generates are all marked partial, as are some of the class members. For example, each property in an entity has an `OnChanging` and `OnChanged` partial method. These partial methods can be extended or defined in your own partial class. The following code example demonstrates the generated `SiteMapInfo`'s `SiteMapId` property code.

```
<Global.System.Data.Objects.DataClasses.EdmScalarPropertyAttribute(
EntityKeyProperty:=true, IsNullable:=false),
        Global.System.Runtime.Serialization.DataMemberAttribute()> _
        Public Property SiteMapId() As Integer
            Get
                Return Me._SiteMapId
            End Get
            Set
                Me.OnSiteMapIdChanging(value)
                Me.ReportPropertyChanging("SiteMapId")
                Me._SiteMapId =
Global.System.Data.Objects.DataClasses.StructuralObject.SetValidValue(value)
```

```
                        Me.ReportPropertyChanged("SiteMapId")
                        Me.OnSiteMapIdChanged
                End Set
        End Property
        Private _SiteMapId As Integer
        Partial Private Sub OnSiteMapIdChanging(ByVal value As Integer)
        End Sub
        Partial Private Sub OnSiteMapIdChanged()
        End Sub
```

The two partial members are stubbed out in the generated class and marked as partial. These methods can be defined in your extension class, most likely to add some sort of validation to the process of changing the value. For example if the SiteMapId is out of an expected range of numbers, maybe a description is too long or a phone number is unacceptable. In the following example the SiteMapId has to be greater than 0; if it is a negative value, an ArgumentException is thrown. This exception can then be caught and handled appropriately, rather than letting the invalid data get caught by the database or, worse yet, committed to the database.

```
        Public Class SiteMapInfo

            Private Sub OnSiteMapIdChanging(ByVal value As Integer)
                If value < 0 Then
                    Throw New ArgumentException("The SiteMapId cannot be less than 0.")
                End If
            End Sub

        End Class
```

The code generated by the wizard creates two types of classes, a custom ObjectContext class with some helper methods to facilitate interacting with the Entity Model and a EntityObject for each entity. Figure 3-7 shows these relationships.

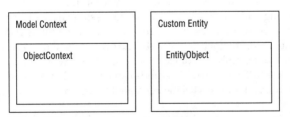

Figure 3-7

The custom ObjectContext class not only wraps up all the members of the ObjectContext but also provides read-only properties that represent an ObjectQuery of each of the entities in the model. This makes querying each of the entity types fairly trivial as well as making LINQ queries much simpler. The following example shows the property that represents a collection of SiteMapInfos in the database:

```
Public ReadOnly Property SiteMaps() As Global.System.Data.Objects.ObjectQuery(
Of SiteMapInfo)
Get
```

```
            If (Me._SiteMaps Is Nothing) Then
                Me._SiteMaps = MyBase.CreateQuery(Of SiteMapInfo)("[SiteMaps]")
            End If
            Return Me._SiteMaps
    End Get
    End Property
    Private _SiteMaps As Global.System.Data.Objects.ObjectQuery(Of SiteMapInfo)
```

 In this code, `SiteMaps` is of type `ObjectQuery(Of SiteMapInfo)`. The `CreateQuery` call processes the ESQL statement `"[SiteMaps]"` to return a collection of `SiteMapInfo` objects. The `Get` accessor also checks to see if the collection has already been built before it makes the query to the database, adding a little performance gain.

If you are familiar with basic LINQ syntax, the next example should be easy. The property exposes the data as an `ObjectQuery(T)`, which can be further manipulated or used as is. `ObjectQuery(T)` is a query that uses the `ObjectContext` connection and metadata information to perform a query against an entity model. Before an `ObjectQuery(T)` actually executes the query against the entity model it can be further transformed, such as adding a `Sort By` or `Where` clause to the query. In the example, `Categories` is exposed as an `ObjectQuery(T)`, and you can see how to retrieve a list of active `SiteMapInfos` using basic LINQ syntax.

```
    Public Function GetSiteMapNodes() As List(Of SiteMapInfo)

    Dim lSiteMapNodes As List(Of SiteMapInfo)

    SiteMapctx.SiteMaps.MergeOption = MergeOption.NoTracking
    lSiteMapNodes = (From lSiteMapNode In SiteMapctx.SiteMaps _
                Where lSiteMapNode.Active = True _
    Order By lSiteMapNode.SortOrder).ToList()

    Return lSiteMapNodes

    End Function
```

In the example, I set the `MergeOption` to `NoTracking`, which means that the entities returned will not be attached to the context. This is important when returning collections of entities that will not need to have their state tracked by the context. This is common when caching content, and I will show this in practice later as I explore how a repository will be architected and results cached.

As I continue explaining how the Entity Framework can be leveraged in theBeerHouse application, I will continue to expand the model into a true *n*-tier architecture by extending the generated entity objects and creating corresponding object repositories to manage the queries to and from the database.

Generating an Entity Framework Data Model

While there are command-line tools to generate a model for the Entity Framework, Visual Studio 2008 SP1 has a built-in wizard that takes care of making all the necessary code for a valid model. Once you have a model built with the wizard, you have a graphical surface to manage the model from, making it easy to apply updates and customize the model.

To add an Entity Model to a website, WPF application, or class library, first you add a new ADO.NET Entity Data Model to the project. This is added just like any new item, by right-clicking the root node or folder in the project and selecting Add New Item from the context menu (or by using the keyboard shortcut Ctrl+Shift+A) to open Visual Studio's Add New Item dialog (see Figure 3-8). For theBeerHouse application I am going to add the model to the class library I am creating to hold the business side of the application.

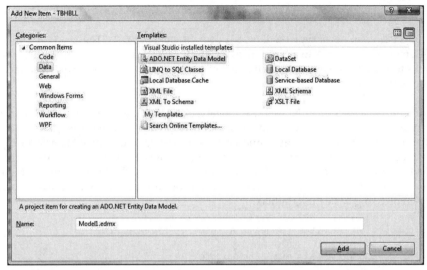

Figure 3-8

You will find the ADO.NET Entity Data Model item in the Common items, but you can probably find it more quickly by selecting the Data node in the Categories tree on the left side of the dialog.

Once you select the model type, give it a valid name. In this case, I am adding the SiteMap table that will be the foundation of all the navigation in the site and naming it SiteMapModel.

Click the Add button on the New Item dialog to start the Entity Data Model Wizard. In the first window (see Figure 3-9), select the option Generate From Database.

The next screen in the wizard builds the connection string needed by the Entity Framework to connect to the data source. If you already have a valid Entity Framework connection string available, you will see it in a drop-down at the top of the window. If you do not have a connection string or you need to create a new one, click the New Connection button to open the Connection Properties dialog (see Figure 3-10).

This should be a familiar dialog if you have ever set up a connection string from a Microsoft development tool like SQL Management Studio or Visual Studio. To use this dialog, enter the server name or address. If you are connecting to a database on your development machine, you can use (local) or just a "." as shown in Figure 3-10. Note that you can connect to a database file if you are using SQL Express. The connection string will be slightly different, but because the wizard creates it for you, there is nothing you need to do different in the rest of the wizard. Just use the connection dialog to make the connection to your SQL Express database the way you normally would.

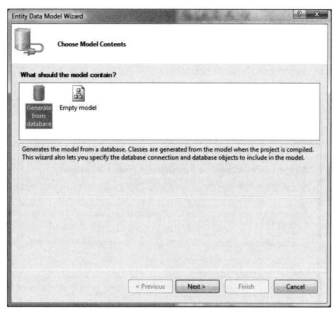

Figure 3-9

Figure 3-10

Once you have created the connection string to the data source, you will notice the name has been predefined and consists of the server name, a period, the name of the database, another period, and dbo.

The Entity Connection String (outlined in Figure 3-11) shows you the real connection string used by the Entity Framework to connect to the data source.

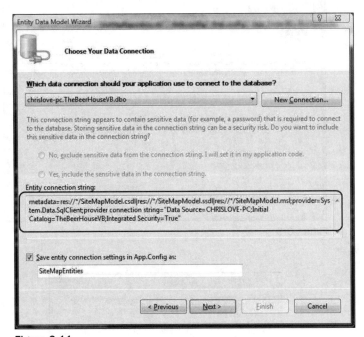

Figure 3-11

Notice that there is more information in this connection string than in a traditional .NET connection string. The Wizard will ultimately place a copy of the model's connection string in either web.config (if being added directly to a web site project) or app.config (if being added to a Class Library or non-web application project) as shown in the following snippet:

```
<connectionStrings>
<add name="TheBeerHouseEntities"
connectionString="metadata=res://*;provider=System.Data.SqlClient;
provider connection string=&quot;Data Source=.;
Initial Catalog=TheBeerHouseVB;
Integrated Security=True;
MultipleActiveResultSets=True&quot;"
providerName="System.Data.EntityClient"/>
</connectionStrings>
```

An Entity Framework connection string is actually composed of a series of semicolon-delimited values; metadata, provider, and provider connection string. The metadata pair specifies a pipe-delimited list of directories, files, and resources that contain metadata and mapping information for the Entity Framework.

The wizard typically creates a generic value for this "res://*". This value tells the Entity Framework to load any possible values from the application, including all referenced assemblies and anything else that might be in the bin folder.

For a more detailed explanation of the Entity Framework Connection String please refer to the following MSDN article: `http://msdn.microsoft.com/en-us/library/cc716756.aspx`.

Typically, the metadata will point to a file resource containing the EDM and metadata mapping; these values can be stored as a resource in an assembly. In this case, the values need to be supplied in the following format: `res://<assemblyFullName>/<resourceName>`. `assemblyFullName` would be the same complete format you would use to register an assembly in the references section of the `web.config` file; assembly file name, version, culture, and `PublicKeyToken`. The `resourceName` value points to the specific resource embedded in the assembly.

But the metadata value can be used to specify the location of particular resources that define the Entity Model. For example, the CSDL (Conceptual Schema Definition Language), SSDL (Store Schema Definition Language), and MSL (Mapping Specific Language) files. When the wizard generates the model for you, the content of these files is stored in the Designer file, `.edmx`. Unless you plan on generating the CSDL, SSDL, and MSL at the command line, you will never have to deal with these model definition files. In fact, it is in your best interest to not modify the content of these sections; remember that they are generated sections in the Designer file when using the wizard, because they are not well documented and very interrelated. The wizard generates a Designer file that contains each of these sections for the model. You can read more detail on these sections on MSDN (`http://msdn.microsoft.com/en-us/library/bb399604.aspx`); because intimate knowledge of these sections is not needed to work with Entity Framework I will not pursue them any further. Any changes you want to make to these sections can be done through the Designer in Visual Studio and will be done correctly.

The provider pair specifies the type of provider for the Entity Framework to use. Remember Entity Framework is not database-specific, and various providers are available to work with it. When working with SQL Server, this value is `System.Data.SQLClient`, which is the familiar namespace we have been using since the beginning of .NET to connection to SQL Server.

The Provider Connection String pair is where the value of the more traditional connection string is located. So, if you have an existing connection string to connect to the database, you can still use that; you would need to place it in this section of the Entity Framework–specific connection string.

At the bottom of the wizard, check the box to Save entity connection settings in App.Config as. That stores the connection string in the config file of the application, which will save you work later because the wizard will create the correct connection string instead of you having to do it.

> **Creating an Entity Model in a class library causes the wizard to add an** `App.Config` **file to the class library. Because this is a DLL and not an application, it is not used directly, it but should be referenced to copy the connection string for your application, whether it is a website (`web.config`) or desktop application (`app.config`). Of course, if you generate the Entity Model within a website (in the** `App_Code` **folder), the connection string is added to the** `web.config` **file.**

Clicking the Next button takes you to the Choose Your Database Objects page (see Figure 3-12), which displays a list of tables, views, and stored procedures you can use to build the model. For this example, you are going to build a model around the site map, so expand the Tables node and scroll down the list of tables till the `SiteMap` table is displayed. Check the node so that it will be used to build the model. If there were more tables to add to the model, you would check them as well. You will do this in later chapters.

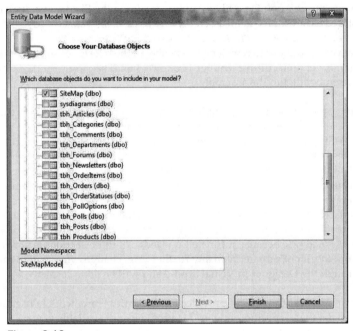

Figure 3-12

At the bottom of the page, specify the name of the Entity Model, in this case enter `SiteMapModel`. This will be used to identify the Entity Model and context for the site map. Click Finish to create the model. When the model has been created, the Designer will be displayed, showing a list of entities in the model. This looks a lot like the class diagram that was introduced with Visual Studio 2005, as shown in Figure 3-13.

Before you save the model, rename the entity something other than `SiteMap` to avoid confusion with the `SiteMap` already built into the .NET framework. I chose `SiteMapInfo`. It is also smart to change the Entity Set Name. The wizard will call it `SiteMapSet`, which just does not sound natural; I changed it to `SiteMapInfos`.

You can change both of these values by selecting the SiteMap entity in the Model Designer and pressing F4. This opens the entity's properties, which allows you to modify these properties as shown in Figure 3-14.

Figure 3-13

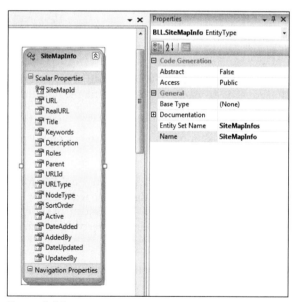

Figure 3-14

Additionally, you can change the property names in the entity by bringing up their property window or clicking on the name itself in the Designer. You can change even more of a property's values in the Properties window (see Figure 3-15), accessed by selecting the property in the Designer and pressing F4.

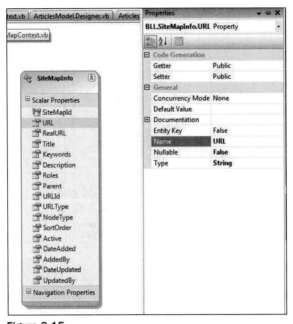

Figure 3-15

Each property has a getter and a setter, and the access modifier can be changed from the default `Public` to `Internal`, `Private`, or `Protected`. It is interesting to note the getter and setter of a property can have differing access modifiers.

To make the Entity Framework check for optimistic concurrency on the property, change the Concurrency Mode to `Fixed`.

You can also set a default value for the property, which you should do for the Active field in the tables. This field is used to indicate if a record has been deleted, so it should be set to true. As I review more entities in the site, you will see that there are a few other fields that should have default values. These default values are assigned to the properties backing property. For example Active's backing property, `_Active : Private _Active As Boolean = true`.

Active is a new field added to each of the tables in the database from previous versions of the BeerHouse. I was taught early in my career when dealing with records in a database to rarely actually delete a record from the database. In many cases, there are legal reasons for this, but practically it can make running your application much easier. A common scenario is that a user accidentally deletes a record from the database; if you physically deleted the record from the database, you would have to either go through a full database restore to return the record or reenter the record. The first resolution is a major task that may or may not be allowed by the system DBAs. The latter method often means you have corrupted data, since the original data is gone along with any relationships and activity trail. If you add the extra Active field to a table, you can simply flip the bit to true or false. If a record needs to be restored, this can be done with a simple operation, instead of a major one.

The `Documentation` property gives you a place to store a long description and a summary for the entity. `Entity Key` is true if the field is part of the primary key of the associated table(s). Typically, you will want to let the wizard determine this for you.

The `Name` property is the `Name` used to access the value of the field. For example, you may have a field name that is not the friendliest of names or more commonly the name of a relationship. Later I will explain the architecture of the Articles module, which has a relation between the Articles table and the Categories table. There is only one category per article, so renaming the property to `Category` makes more sense.

`Nullable` indicates if the field accepts null values or not. This actually sets the `EdmScalarPropertyAttribute`'s `IsNullable` property. This basically indicates that the database field can accept null as a valid value.

Finally, the `Type` property indicates what type of object is represented by the property. For example, value types like `String` and `Integer` or any custom object you may want to use.

> The actual classes created by the Entity Framework Model Wizard are located in a code-behind file associated with the model's `.edmx` file. If you expand the node for the Designer, you will see this file. It contains the custom `ObjectContext` and entity classes for the model. Try to avoid customizing the code in this file because any future changes to the model will result in them being overwritten by the code generator. I will make a few slight modifications to the file to make sure that the classes are part of the correct namespace, but that is it. All other modifications will be done in partial classes.

Customizing Relationships

I want to step ahead a little and talk about customizing relationships in the Designer. Because the `SiteMap` consists of just one table, I am going to use the model for the `Articles` module. I will go over this model in detail in Chapter 5, but for now I want to focus on the relationships.

When an entity has a relationship to another entity a `Navigational Property` is generated. This will be initially defined as the name of the foreign entity. So, in the case of an Article, it has a many-to-one relationship to `Categories` and a one-to-many relationship to `Comments`. Just like the names of the entities, the name of the `Navigational Property` can be changed. Just click on the name in the entity and change it to the desired name. The `Navigational Property` can also be opened and the name changed there as well.

Notice the other `Navigation` properties are disabled (see Figure 3-16). That's because they are tied to the underlying data store and should not be changed in the Designer.

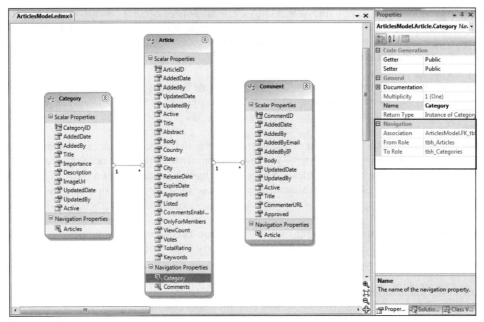

Figure 3-16

Examining the Generated Entity Model

After customizing any values in the entity Designer, save the model. Behind the Designer is a code-behind file (in this case, `SiteMapModel.Designer.vb`) that contains a custom `ObjectContext` class and a custom `EntityObject` class to represent any entities.

Back in the Data Connection step of the wizard, it asks the developer to designate the Model Namespace value, for the `SiteMap` model, I designated `SiteMapEntities` as the name. This value is used as the name of the custom `ObjectContext` class the wizard generates.

```
Partial Public Class SiteMapEntities
    Inherits Global.System.Data.Objects.ObjectContext
```

Each model has one class that derives from `System.Data.Objects.ObjectContext`, `SiteMapEntities` in this case. The `System.Data.Objects.ObjectContext` class actually does the heavy lifting to interact with the Entity Framework. The `ObjectContext` class has numerous methods and properties and the `SavingChanges` event. I'll explain many of these as I review how the repositories work.

The following table describes the class's methods.

Method	Description
AcceptAllChanges	Accepts all changes made to objects in the object context.
AddObject	Adds an object to the object context.
ApplyPropertyChanges	Applies property changes from a detached object to an object already attached to the object context.

Method	Description
Attach	Attaches an object or object graph to the object context when the object has an entity key.
AttachTo	Attaches an object or object graph to the object context in a specific entity set.
CreateEntityKey	Creates the entity key for a specific object, or returns the entity key if it already exists.
CreateQuery(T)	Creates an ObjectQuery(T) in the current object context by using the specified query string.
DeleteObject	Marks an object for deletion.
Detach	Removes the object from the object context.
Dispose	Releases the resources used by the object context.
Equals	Determines whether the specified Object is equal to the current Object. (Inherited from Object.)
ExecuteFunction(TElement)	Executes the given stored procedure or function against the data source to return an ObjectResult(T).
GetObjectByKey	Returns an object that has the specified entity key.
Refresh	Overloaded. Updates specific objects in the object context with data from the data source.
SaveChanges	Overloaded. Persists all updates to the data source.
TryGetObjectByKey	Returns an object that has the specified entity key.

Here's a look at the properties of the ObjectContext class:

Property	Description
CommandTimeout	Gets or sets the timeout value, in seconds, for all object context operations.
Connection	Gets the connection used by the object context.
DefaultContainerName	Gets or sets the default container name.
MetadataWorkspace	Gets the metadata workspace used by the object context.
ObjectStateManager	Gets the object state manager used by the object context to track object changes.

The SavingChanges event occurs when changes are saved to the data source.

ObjectContext Constructors

The custom `ObjectContext` has three public constructors: one parameterless, one that accepts a `connectionString`, and one that accepts a connection string and an existing `EntityConnection`.

```
Public Sub New()
        MyBase.New("name=SiteMapEntities", "SiteMapEntities")
        Me.OnContextCreated
End Sub

Public Sub New(ByVal connectionString As String)
        MyBase.New(connectionString, "SiteMapEntities")
        Me.OnContextCreated
End Sub

Public Sub New(ByVal connection As
Global.System.Data.EntityClient.EntityConnection)
        MyBase.New(connection, "SiteMapEntities")
        Me.OnContextCreated
End Sub
```

Typically, the first constructor will be used, taking advantage of the settings in the `web.config` connections element. But depending on the way your application is configured you may want to use the second constructor.

As I evolve the business architecture, I will start explaining the use of a class repository. The repository classes create a context used to interact with the entity model. Therefore the repostories will ultimately be responsible for passing along the connection string value to the context, as shown in the following example:

```
Private _SiteMapctx As SiteMapEntities
Public Property SiteMapctx() As SiteMapEntities
Get
              If IsNothing(_SiteMapctx) Then
                  _SiteMapctx = New SiteMapEntities(GetActualConnectionString())
              End If

              Return _SiteMapctx
End Get
Set(ByVal Value As SiteMapEntities)
              _SiteMapctx = Value
End Set
End Property


Public Sub New(ByVal sConnectionString As String)
        ConnectionString = sConnectionString
        CacheKey = "SiteMap"
End Sub

Public Sub New()
        ConnectionString = Globals.Settings.DefaultConnectionStringName
        CacheKey = "SiteMap"
End Sub
```

Mom's Website

Dark Green	# 1a882f	26, 136, 47
Light Green	# 5da969	93, 169, 105
White	# ffffff	255, 255, 255

http://barnicat.netreadystaging.com/

Username: paulbarni

password: paulbarni

The Default ObjectQuery

The next major member is the `SiteMaps` property, an `ObjectQuery(of SiteMapInfo)`. Remember that I named the site map entity `SiteMapInfo` to avoid confusion with other classes already in use in the .NET Framework. An `ObjectQuery` is special generic class that represents a collection of entities returned from a query (select statement) through the Entity Framework.

```
Public ReadOnly Property SiteMapInfos()
As Global.System.Data.Objects.ObjectQuery(Of SiteMapInfo)
        Get
            If (Me._SiteMapInfos Is Nothing) Then
                Me._SiteMapInfos = _
                    MyBase.CreateQuery(Of SiteMapInfo)("[SiteMapInfos]")
            End If
            Return Me._SiteMapInfos
        End Get
End Property
Private _SiteMapInfos As Global.System.Data.Objects.ObjectQuery(Of SiteMapInfo)
```

The property checks to see if it has already created a list of `SiteMapInfo` objects; if not, it calls `CreateQuery` to get an `ObjectQuery` of `SiteMapInfo` objects. The `CreateQuery` method accepts a query string and an optional `ObjectParameter` collection. It returns an `ObjectQuery` that allows you to construct queries against the `SiteMapInfo` entity. Think of an `ObjectQuery` as a generic `List(of T)`, but it has special features that allow it to be queried by LINQ. Notice that the private `_SiteMapInfos` variable is an `ObjectQuery` of `SiteMapInfo` objects.

The `SiteMapInfos` property is defined so LINQ to Entities can be executed to return data. The LINQ engine uses the `ObjectQuery` to work its magic.

Updating an Entity

There is only one method to the custom context, `AddToSiteMaps`, which accepts a `SiteMapInfo` object. This method is basically a helper method that allows new or disconnected entity objects to be added and updated within the context.

```
Public Sub AddToSiteMaps(ByVal siteMapInfo As SiteMapInfo)
    MyBase.AddObject("SiteMaps", siteMapInfo)
End Sub
```

When entities are retrieved from the database via the Entity Framework, they are returned attached to the context by default so that the framework can manage changes to each entity and subsequent concurrency issues.

Entities can exist without being attached to a context; they are just normal objects after all. TheBeerHouse application uses detached entities in many instances, typically when a list of entities is cached. In order to save any entity through the Entity Framework, it must be attached to the context and the `AddToSiteMaps` helper method manages this operation by calling the `ObjectContext`'s `AddObject` method. It passes the name of the data set and the entity it belongs to.

Adding the entity to the context adds the object to the `ObjectStateManager`, which is used by the `ObjectContext` to manage how to treat an entity when the `SaveChanges` method is called. When

SaveChanges is called the Entity Framework context will perform any necessary insert, update, or delete operations needed by iterating over an internal collection of entities. Each will have an assigned EntityState value to indicate the type of operation to be performed: Added, Modified, Deleted, Detached or Unchanged.

Working with the Partial Custom ObjectContext Class

All the classes generated by the Entity Framework Wizard are partial and use partial members where appropriate. If you are not familiar with partial classes they allow you to literally split a class across multiple files. Partial classes were introduced with the .NET 2.0 Framework and primarily used to split the generated user interface support code from the code used to program the page in an ASP.NET site or forms in a Windows application. This provides a nice clean surface to write the business code of the page.

The feature has been leveraged by the Entity Framework generated classes as well. Think of the classes generated by the Entity Framework classes as the user interface support code generated by Visual Studio for a Web Form that has been separated out.

Taking advantage of the partial class methodology the custom ObjectContext class, SiteMapEntities, can be extended by adding a new partial class to the project, also named SiteMapEntities.

```
Public Class SiteMapEntities

        Private Sub SiteMapEntities_SavingChanges(ByVal sender As Object,
    ByVal e As System.EventArgs) Handles Me.SavingChanges
            Dim typeEntries = (From entry _
            In Me.ObjectStateManager.GetObjectStateEntries(EntityState.Added Or
    EntityState.Modified) _
            Where TypeOf entry.Entity Is IBaseEntity).ToList()

            For Each ose As System.Data.Objects.ObjectStateEntry In typeEntries

                Dim lBaseEntity As IBaseEntity = DirectCast(
    ose.Entity, IBaseEntity)

                If lBaseEntity.IsValid = False Then
                    Throw New BeerHouseDataException(
    String.Format("{0} is Not Valid", lBaseEntity.SetName), "", "")
                End If

            Next

        End Sub
    End Class
```

For the purposes of theBeerHouse architecture, I am going to add one event handler, SavingChanges. This event provides a way to intercept any changes being made to the context, that is, the objects being modified, added or deleted from the database. While I have not covered it yet, I am leveraging an interface called IBaseEntity that has an IsValid property that must be implemented by each of the entity objects, more about that shortly.

The `SavingChanges` event handler iterates through any new or modified entities and makes sure the `IsValid` property returns true. If the entity does not meet its defined requirements to be a valid object a custom exception is thrown, keeping the update from executing.

A list of `SiteMapInfo` objects that have either an `Added` or `Modified` state is retrieved by calling the `GetObjectStateEntries`, passing in an ORed list of `EntityStates`. The list is then iterated over, casting each entity to an `IBaseEntity` object so the `IsValid` property can be checked.

Notice the use of LINQ to create the list of entries? This is a relatively basic LINQ query that returns a List of `ObjectStateEntry` objects. I will certainly go over more LINQ statements as this book progresses.

Designing the Business Logic Layer

The DAL discussed in the previous section is made from the Entity Framework and some supporting classes that retrieve data from the database by running SQL queries and returning as a collection of custom entities that wrap the fields of the retrieved data. The data returned by the DAL is still raw data, even though it's wrapped in objects. These entity objects do not add any functionality per se; they are just strongly typed containers with a series of properties that map to the underlying data, typically a series of immutable properties and validation logic to represent data. Immutable properties wrap calculated values that cannot be explicitly set. Each entity can have its own logic that defines if it is in a valid or acceptable state. The BLL consumes data from the Entity Framework and exposes it to the UI layer adding validation logic, and adds instance and static methods to delete, edit, insert, and retrieve data in class repositories.

For a domain object, or entity, named `Employee` that represents an employee, there may be a property named `Boss` that returns a reference to another entity, `Employee` that represents the first object's boss. In middle-sized to large projects, there are usually dozens, hundreds, or maybe even thousands of such entities, with relationships between them. This object-oriented and strongly typed representation of any data provides an extremely strong abstraction from the database, which merely stores the data, and it provides a simple and powerful set of classes for the UI developer to work with, without needing to know any details about how and where the raw data will be stored, how many tables are in the database, or which relationships exist between them. This is one of the primary goals of the Entity Framework and why it is an ideal choice to use as the data access layer and the support classes it generates.

In the previous edition of the book, the Active Record pattern was used. This pattern adds a series of methods to interact with the DAL to manage data. This means an entity not only holds the data for one record, but it also holds the members to interact with the DAL. This is many developers' their pattern of choice, but if you believe in separation of concerns this will not work. The Repository Pattern separates the entity object from the worker methods. The worker methods are separated into a helper class known as a repository. Some take it so far as to create a corresponding interface for the members of the repository so that inversion of control and mocking can be done more easily. I also think this architecture is good because it identifies what the object is responsible for. It is commonly known as separation of concerns, but I like to think of it as delegating responsibility to objects that specialize in specific tasks, as managers should do with their people.

This makes the UI developer's job easier, and makes it possible for us to change low-level database structures without breaking any of the UI code (which is one of the primary reasons for using a multi-tier design). This can require more development time initially, and more talented and experienced developers to create this design (which is why you're reading this book) than would be required if you just used a `DataSet` to pass data around, but in the long run it pays off in the form of easier maintainability and increased reliability. The Entity Framework Wizard helps by generating a good base to start building a solid business layer.

Once you have a well-designed, completed BLL using entities and repositories, developing the user interface will be very easy, and can be done by less experienced developers in less time, so some of the upfront time you spend early in the project can be recovered later when you develop the UI.

Figure 3-17 illustrates the relationship between the Entity Framework and the entity repository.

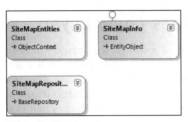

Figure 3-17

Building a Repository

The Active Record pattern contains a series of methods that interact with the database. These methods (I call them worker methods) make the record's object active, so to speak. An active record places all the worker methods in the entity object, which means that it is all one self-contained class, but that can lead to architecture issues as the application grows. This is a very popular pattern to use and keeps things pretty simple to manage. There are fewer objects to instantiate and manage; the problem that arises is separating concerns. Because all the business methods are built into the class, you cannot separate these from the values in the record itself.

Introducing the Repository Pattern

Over the past few years I found myself creating classes to hold and self-validate records held in my databases. Because I wanted all my sites to follow a standard *n*-tier architecture, I designed a partner class that would hold all the members to perform any business logic and talk to the data access layer. This is known as the *Repository Pattern*.

The Repository Pattern separates the worker methods into a separate repository class and leaves the data specific members in the entity. By isolating the members responsible for managing data access, the repository can not only be separated into a separate tier but can also easily be transformed into a portable interface.

> *IoC containers such as Castle Windsor are used by many to allow them to program against a business domain without needing a real backend data store. The basic principle is to program against interfaces rather than actual objects. This way, you can easily swap providers to a different data store without having to reprogram the application. I decided not to go this far because the Entity Framework handles managing communication to any database you might use.*

Reviewing a Repository

A repository is a class that contains members that interact with the data layer and validates data. Just like many other cases in programming there are always common methods and routines that are repeated throughout an application and across applications. These pieces of code should be refactored into either a common base class to derive from or a utility class that can be called from all sorts of objects in an application.

```
Imports System.Web
Imports System.Web.Caching
Imports System.Security.Principal

Namespace BLL

Public MustInherit Class BaseRepository
Implements IDisposable
```

In the previous edition of the book, a `BizObject` class was created to contain many of these methods. This version takes that class and changes it to a base repository class and adds some new functionality. The class, `BaseRepository`, is a `MustInherit` (VB.NET) or `abstract` (C#), which means it cannot be used directly but must be inherited by a subclass that can be instantiated.

The next thing to note is it implements the `IDisposable` interface, which means that it implements a `Dispose` method. Interestingly enough this interface method is not really implemented in the `BaseRepository` itself, but marked as `MustOverride` (abstract in C#) in the derived class.

```
        Private disposedValue As Boolean = False          ' To detect redundant calls

        ' IDisposable
        Protected MustOverride Sub Dispose(ByVal disposing As Boolean)

#Region " IDisposable Support "
        ' This code added by Visual Basic to correctly implement the
disposable pattern.
        Public MustOverride Sub Dispose() Implements IDisposable.Dispose
```

This pattern is automatically created by Visual Studio when the `IDisposable` interface is implemented in a class. The `Dispose` method is used to clean up any resources created by the class that need to be released. In the case of a repository class, it needs to at least ensure that the `ObjectContext` object is disposed of.

```
        Private disposedValue As Boolean = False          ' To detect redundant calls

        ' IDisposable
        Protected Overrides Sub Dispose(ByVal disposing As Boolean)
            If Not Me.disposedValue Then
                If disposing Then

                    If IsNothing(_SiteMapctx) = False Then
                        _SiteMapctx.Dispose()
```

```
                        End If

                   End If

             End If
             Me.disposedValue = True
        End Sub

        ' This code added by Visual Basic to correctly implement the
    disposable pattern.
             Public Overrides Sub Dispose()

                   Dispose(True)

                   GC.SuppressFinalize(Me)
             End Sub
```

The first things defined in the BaseRepository class are a couple of constants that can be used by the child repositories, DefPageSize and MAXROWS. The DefPageSize constant is used when performing paging operations and is used as a default value for how many records the result or page will contain. The MAXROWS constant is set to the MaxValue an integer can be. This can be used as a limiting value to the number of records a query can contain.

```
Public Const DefPageSize As Integer = 50
Protected Const MAXROWS As Integer = Integer.MaxValue
```

The next section is a set of properties that help manage caching data in memory. The first two relate to caching, EnableCaching and CacheDuration. These values can be set at runtime but have default values, so they do not have to be set each time. If EnableCaching is set to false, then any data will not be cached from that instance of the repository. It also means that, if there is a cached version of the result set, it will not be used and a query will be made to the database. The CacheDuration value specifies how many seconds a result set will be stored in memory.

```
#Region " Properties "

        'Needs to be definable in the config file and stored in the app cache
        Private _enableCaching As Boolean = True
        Private _cacheDuration As Integer = 0

        Protected Property EnableCaching() As Boolean
            Get
                Return _enableCaching
            End Get
            Set(ByVal value As Boolean)
                _enableCaching = value
            End Set
        End Property

        Protected Property CacheDuration() As Integer
            Get
                Return _cacheDuration
            End Get
            Set(ByVal value As Integer)
```

```
            _cacheDuration = value
        End Set
End Property

Private _cacheKey As String = "CacheKey"
Public Property CacheKey() As String
    Get
        Return _cacheKey
    End Get
    Set(ByVal Value As String)
        _cacheKey = Value
    End Set
End Property
```

```
#End Region
```

The `CacheKey` property is used by inheriting repositories as a prefix to the objects and collections they cache. The reason that a common `CacheKey` property is a member of the `BaseRepository` class is to help with managing the purging of cache objects. As repositories retrieve entities they can place them in memory as a named cache object. This will typically be a list of entities but can be individual entities as the situation warrants. Each cached object will have a name associated with it to access it. As entities are added to and updated in the data store, the cache may need to be purged, or possibly all the cached objects of a specific type may need to be purged. By prefixing all the cache objects with a common key for the repository, there should be a uniform way to access these objects.

If you examine the `CacheData` method in the code sample that follows, you can see that it takes a `key` and `data` to cache. The `key` is a string passed to it to identify the `data` being cached. The method checks to make sure that the data being passed in is not null and inserts it into the repository's `Cache` object. For this example, the `Cache` object is simply the current context's cache object.

```
#Region " Cache "

    Protected Shared ReadOnly Property Cache() As Cache
        Get
            Return HttpContext.Current.Cache
        End Get
    End Property

    Protected Shared Sub CacheData(ByVal key As String, ByVal data As Object)
        If Not IsNothing(data) Then
            Cache.Insert(key, data, Nothing, _
                DateTime.Now.AddSeconds(120), TimeSpan.Zero)
        End If
    End Sub

    Protected Sub PurgeCacheItems(ByVal prefix As String)
        prefix = prefix.ToLower
        Dim itemsToRemove As New List(Of String)

        Dim enumerator As IDictionaryEnumerator = Cache.GetEnumerator()
        While enumerator.MoveNext
            If enumerator.Key.ToString.ToLower.StartsWith(prefix) Then
                itemsToRemove.Add(enumerator.Key.ToString)
```

```
                End If
        End While

        For Each itemToRemove As String In itemsToRemove
                Cache.Remove(itemToRemove)
        Next
    End Sub

#End Region
```

The `PurgeCacheItems` method accepts a `prefix`, which should correspond to the repository's `CacheKey` property. As I start examining the repositories, you will start to see that a repository may cache data in various forms based on a variety of data filters.

The next section of code focuses on the Entity Framework connection string. There is a `ConnectionString` property and a `GetActualConnectionString` function that returns the actual connection string from the site's configuration file. The `ConnectionString` property actually refers to the name of the connection string in the connection string section of the configuration file. This methodology forces the storage of the connection string in the configuration file and keeps it from being hard-coded as a piece of the application.

```
Private _connectionString As String = "Set the ConnectionString"
Public Property ConnectionString() As String
Get
                Return _connectionString
End Get
Set(ByVal Value As String)
                _connectionString = Value
End Set
End Property

Protected Function GetActualConnectionString() As String
Return ConfigurationManager.ConnectionStrings(ConnectionString).ConnectionString

End Function
```

The `GetActualConnectionString` function calls the `ConfigurationManger`'s `ConnectionStrings` collection and retrieves the connection string for the model.

The following code comes from the `SiteMapRepository`'s constructor methods. The first one accepts the name of a connection string and uses it, making it flexible enough to use a different connection string if needed. The second method uses the `ConnectionString` property from the `TheBeerHouseSection` class. A class that manages access to the site's custom configuration section. Both constructors set the `CacheKey` to "SiteMap".

```
Public Sub New(ByVal sConnectionString As String)
ConnectionString = sConnectionString
CacheKey = "SiteMap"
End Sub

Public Sub New()

    ConnectionString = Globals.Settings.DefaultConnectionStringName
```

```
CacheKey = "SiteMap"

End Sub
```

The next section of code I want to discuss is what I call user information properties. At one time, they were contained in the BaseObject class, but because they can be used in many places outside of the repository or entity classes, I moved them to the Helpers class. The first property, CurrentUser, returns a reference to the current IPrincipal object. This simply wraps a call to the HttpContext.Current .User call. The CurrentUserName property returns the username if the user has been authenticated; if not, then it returns an empty string. Notice how it uses the CurrentUser property to reduce the amount of code it uses.

Both of these properties are used throughout the application concerning user authentication. You will see shortly that the CurrentUser property will play a role in extending the authentication properties of entities.

```
Protected Shared ReadOnly Property CurrentUser() As IPrincipal
Get
                Return HttpContext.Current.User
        End Get
End Property

Protected Shared ReadOnly Property CurrentUserName() As String
Get
                Dim userName As String = String.Empty
                If CurrentUser.Identity.IsAuthenticated Then
                    userName = CurrentUser.Identity.Name
                End If
                Return userName
        End Get
End Property

Protected Shared ReadOnly Property CurrentUserIP() As String
Get
                Return HttpContext.Current.Request.UserHostAddress
        End Get
End Property
```

The final property is CurrentUserIP, which returns a string of the client IP address. This is obtained from the Request's UserHostAddress property. This property is important because it can be used to analyze where the user is logged for analysis and authentication purposes, and so forth. As I introduce new concepts in later chapters, we will integrate Akismet spam comment filtering and wants the client IP address to determine if the comment is potentially spam or not. The CurrentUserIP property makes it very convenient to obtain this value.

The EncodeText function takes a string and encodes it so that it can be safely displayed in HTML. First, it runs the string through the HtmlEncode method, then it replaces double spaces with the HTML-encoded   and line returns with a <br> tag.

```
Protected Shared Function EncodeText(ByVal content As String) As String
                content = HttpUtility.HtmlEncode(content)
```

```
            content = content.Replace("  ", "   ").Replace("\n", "<br>")
            Return content
    End Function
```

The next method is `ConvertNullToEmptyString`, which is a safety method to make sure that the application does not attempt to use a null string. If a null string is used in an application, an exception will typically be thrown, converting it to an empty string is a safe way to keep this from happening. A null string happens when a string is created but not initialized.

```
    Protected Shared Function ConvertNullToEmptyString(ByVal input As String) As String
            If String.IsNullOrEmpty(input) Then
                Return String.Empty
            Else
                Return input
            End If
    End Function
```

More members can be added in a similar manner that can be used by child classes.

Examining a Repository

It all starts with a `BaseRepository` class that contains some common properties and methods that will be used by all the repositories in the BLL. It is marked as `MustInherit`, (*abstract* in C#), meaning that it cannot be instantiated on its own and must be inherited by another class and it can be instantiated. The `BaseRepository` class only provides common helper properties and methods that help you work with data.

The next class in the hierarchy is the `BaseArticleRepository` class, which contains one key member, `Articlesctx`. The `Articlesctx` property wraps around an `ArticlesEntities` object `ArticlesEntities` is a customized `ObjectContext` object created by the Entity Framework Wizard. The `Articlesctx` property wraps around a private variable. The property checks to see if an `ArticlesEntities` context has already been created, and if not, creates one and returns it. The structure and relationship of these classes is illustrated in Figure 3-18.

```
    Private _Articlesctx As ArticlesEntities
    Public Property Articlesctx() As ArticlesEntities
    Get
    If IsNothing(_Articlesctx) Then
                _Articlesctx = New ArticlesEntities(GetActualConnectionString())
            End If
            Return _Articlesctx
        End Get
        Set(ByVal Value As ArticlesEntities)
            _Articlesctx = Value
        End Set
    End Property
```

The reason why there is a `BaseArticleRepository` class is that the news module consists of three entity types: `Article`, `Category`, `Comment`. I have created a targeted repository for each entity. In this example, I am showing the `ArticleRepository` class. The `ArticleRepository` class contains a series of methods to interact with the Entity Framework and database to retrieve, insert, update, and delete articles. I will detail the members in Chapter 5. The `BaseArticleRepository` holds common members used by each of the child repositories. In this case, it is a set of constructors and the `ArticleContext` object. Each of these members is used by the child repositories.

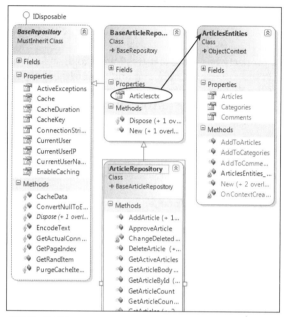

Figure 3-18

Examining an Entity Class

The Entity Framework Model Wizard generates a series of partial classes that can be extended to integrate custom logic and properties. Each entity in the Entity Model is derived from the `System.Data` `.Objects.DataClasses.EntityObject` class. This ensures each entity contains some base members that allow it to interact with the EF Object Services.

The `Article` class consists of a partial class distributed across two files. The Entity Framework Wizard generates the core class that consists of properties, methods, and events related to the data that represents a news article. All custom entities inherit from `EntityObject` and extend its functionality. The entity's class is adorned with attributes that describe it to the Entity Framework.

```
<Global.System.Data.Objects.DataClasses.EdmEntityTypeAttribute(
NamespaceName:="ArticlesModel", Name:="Article"), _
    Global.System.Runtime.Serialization.DataContractAttribute(
IsReference:=True), _
    Global.System.Serializable()> _
    Partial Public Class Article
        Inherits Global.System.Data.Objects.DataClasses.EntityObject
```

Each entity contains at least a series of properties that represent data. They are prefixed with a series of attributes that describe the property to the Entity Framework. Examining the code sample that follows for the `ArticleID` property, you can see it is an `EntityKeyProperty` and is not nullable. I assume that you are familiar with how tables are defined in SQL Server, so looking at these attributes, you can quickly ascertain this property probably represents at least one of the primary key fields in a table. In this case, it is the primary key in the database, and it is the primary key of the entity as well. Remember, an entity does not have to actually have a one-to-one mapping with database tables.

The setter portion of the property has some features I want to discuss. First, there are a couple of extra methods defined below it: `OnArticleIDChanging` and `OnArticleIDChanged`. These are both marked as partial methods, meaning that you can create another partial class to extend these methods and give them body. Typically, if you had some sort of custom validation logic that needed to be executed, extending these methods would be a good idea.

```
<Global.System.Data.Objects.DataClasses.EdmScalarPropertyAttribute(
EntityKeyProperty:=True, IsNullable:=False), _
Global.System.Runtime.Serialization.DataMemberAttribute()> _

Public Property ArticleID() As Integer
Get
                Return Me._ArticleID
End Get
Set(ByVal value As Integer)
                Me.OnArticleIDChanging(value)
                Me.ReportPropertyChanging("ArticleID")
                Me._ArticleID =
Global.System.Data.Objects.DataClasses.
StructuralObject.SetValidValue(value)
                Me.ReportPropertyChanged("ArticleID")
                Me.OnArticleIDChanged()
End Set
End Property
Private _ArticleID As Integer
Partial Private Sub OnArticleIDChanging(ByVal value As Integer)
End Sub
Partial Private Sub OnArticleIDChanged()
End Sub
```

This example creates the body of the `OnArticleIdChanging` method in a custom extension to the `Article` class to validate the value is 0 or greater. If it is not, a new `ArgumentException` is thrown explaining the issue.

```
Private Sub OnArticleIDChanging(ByVal value As Integer)
If value < 0 Then
Throw New ArgumentException("The ArticleId cannot be less than 0.")
    End If
End Sub
```

The next items to note are the calls to the `ReportPropertyChanging` and `ReportPropertyChanged` methods in the `Set` accessor of the `ArticleID` property. The `ReportPropertyChanging` method is part of the `EntityObject` class and is called to notify the `IEntityChangeTracker` that the value is about to change, so it can cache the initial value. Similarly, the `ReportPropertyChanged` method is called to commit the cached value and call the `EntityMemberChanged` method. This collectively works with the state manager to manage the current state of the entity. So, when the `SaveChanges` method is called on the entity context, it will know which entities to commit to the database.

The next thing to examine in the generated code is how references are handled. In the case of an article, it needs to belong to a category, which is a many to one foreign key relationship. This is indicated by the `EdmRelationshipNavigationPropertyAttribute` attribute. This attribute does the linking between the entity and the related entity. In this case, it defines the foreign key relationship to the category. The `Category` property manages the value of the category entity to which the article belongs.

```
<Global.System.Data.Objects.DataClasses.EdmRelationshipNavigationPropertyAttribute(
"ArticlesModel", "FK_tbh_Articles_tbh_Categories", "tbh_Categories"), _
Global.System.Xml.Serialization.XmlIgnoreAttribute(), _
Global.System.Xml.Serialization.SoapIgnoreAttribute(), _
Global.System.Runtime.Serialization.DataMemberAttribute()> _
Public Property Category() As Category
Get
                Return CType(Me,
Global.System.Data.Objects.DataClasses.IEntityWithRelationships)
.RelationshipManager.GetRelatedReference(Of Category)(
"ArticlesModel.FK_tbh_Articles_tbh_Categories", "tbh_Categories").Value

End Get
        Set(ByVal value As Category)
                CType(Me,
Global.System.Data.Objects.DataClasses.IEntityWithRelationships)
.RelationshipManager.GetRelatedReference(Of Category)(
"ArticlesModel.FK_tbh_Articles_tbh_Categories", "tbh_Categories").Value = value
        End Set
End Property

<Global.System.ComponentModel.BrowsableAttribute(False), _
Global.System.Runtime.Serialization.DataMemberAttribute()> _
Public Property CategoryReference() As
Global.System.Data.Objects.DataClasses.EntityReference(Of Category)
Get
                Return CType(Me,
Global.System.Data.Objects.DataClasses.IEntityWithRelationships)
.RelationshipManager.GetRelatedReference(Of Category)(
"ArticlesModel.FK_tbh_Articles_tbh_Categories", "tbh_Categories")
End Get
Set(ByVal value As Global.System.Data.Objects.DataClasses.EntityReference(
Of Category))
                If (Not (value) Is Nothing) Then
                    CType(Me,
Global.System.Data.Objects.DataClasses.IEntityWithRelationships)
.RelationshipManager.InitializeRelatedReference(Of Category)(
"ArticlesModel.FK_tbh_Articles_tbh_Categories", "tbh_Categories", value)
                End If
End Set
End Property
```

The `CategoryReference` property is of type `EntityReference(Of Category`. An `EntityReference` represents the navigational relationship between an article and a category in this case. If the relationship were one-to-many, it would have an associated `EntityCollection` property, which is the case for article comments. But since the article can only belong to one category, the `Category` property is simply a single category entity.

```
<Global.System.Data.Objects.DataClasses.EdmRelationshipNavigationPropertyAttribute(
"ArticlesModel", "FK_tbh_Comments_tbh_Articles", "tbh_Comments"), _
Global.System.Xml.Serialization.XmlIgnoreAttribute(), _
Global.System.Xml.Serialization.SoapIgnoreAttribute(), _
Global.System.Runtime.Serialization.DataMemberAttribute()> _
Public Property Comments() As
Global.System.Data.Objects.DataClasses.EntityCollection(Of Comment)
Get
                Return CType(Me,
Global.System.Data.Objects.DataClasses.IEntityWithRelationships)
.RelationshipManager.GetRelatedCollection(Of Comment)(
"ArticlesModel.FK_tbh_Comments_tbh_Articles", "tbh_Comments")
End Get
Set(ByVal value As Global.System.Data.Objects.DataClasses.EntityCollection(
Of Comment))
                If (Not (value) Is Nothing) Then
                    CType(Me,
Global.System.Data.Objects.DataClasses.IEntityWithRelationships)
.RelationshipManager.InitializeRelatedCollection(Of Comment)(
"ArticlesModel.FK_tbh_Comments_tbh_Articles", "tbh_Comments", value)
                End If
End Set
End Property
```

Notice the difference between the `Comments` property and the `Category` property is comments are a one-to-many relationship and, thus, require a collection of comments. In short, an `EntityCollection` represents the many end of the relationship.

The IBaseEntity Interface

In the last edition of this book, a common base class, `BizObject`, that contained several helper methods and properties. Since entities are derived from the `EntityObject`, this cannot be done in this architecture. Since most of helper members actually help in the interaction with the database, it does not make sense to hold those methods in the entity object structure anyway. Instead, I created the `IBaseEntity` interface that all entities should implement. This interface is pretty simple, it contains an `IsValid` and a `SetName` Property.

```
Public Interface IBaseEntity
    ReadOnly Property IsValid() As Boolean
    Property SetName() As String

    ReadOnly Property CanEdit() As Boolean
    ReadOnly Property CanRead() As Boolean
    ReadOnly Property CanDelete() As Boolean
    ReadOnly Property CanAdd() As Boolean

End Interface
```

Earlier, I talked about using the `IsValid` property in the entity object; it is used to determine if the object satisfies a set of rules that determine if the object is complete. Each entity is responsible for checking the data to ensure that it is valid in its own unique fashion. For example, a `SiteMapInfo` entity should have at least a URL, a `RealURL`, and a `Title` to be considered valid. These are the minimum requirements needed to be able to actually function in the scope of the navigation infrastructure. If these values have not been set, then this entity is not valid and should not be committed. If these conditions are met, the property returns true; if not, it returns false, indicating that it is either not ready or cannot be used.

```
Public ReadOnly Property IsValid() As Boolean Implements IBaseEntity.IsValid
Get
If String.IsNullOrEmpty(URL) = False And _
                String.IsNullOrEmpty(RealURL) = False And _
                String.IsNullOrEmpty(Title) = False Then
            Return True
        End If
        Return False
End Get
End Property
```

The `SetName` property is used when the name of the entity's set is needed. We will investigate these instances as we examine how modules are designed.

Extending an Entity

While the Entity Data Model Wizard generates a class that inherits from `EntityObject`, which contains series of properties to represent each field in the entity, it has built-in limitations. The entity classes can be extended by using partial classes and partial methods. Each generated property follows a pattern with the usage of EDM attributes, a common setter pattern, a private variable to hold the value, and pair of partial methods to indicate the value is changing and has changed.

```
<Global.System.Data.Objects.DataClasses.EdmScalarPropertyAttribute(
EntityKeyProperty:=True, IsNullable:=False), _
Global.System.Runtime.Serialization.DataMemberAttribute()> _
Public Property SiteMapId() As Integer
Get
            Return Me._SiteMapId
End Get
Set(ByVal value As Integer)
            Me.OnSiteMapIdChanging(Value)
            Me.ReportPropertyChanging("SiteMapId")
            Me._SiteMapId =
Global.System.Data.Objects.DataClasses.StructuralObject.SetValidValue(Value)
            Me.ReportPropertyChanged("SiteMapId")
            Me.OnSiteMapIdChanged()
End Set
End Property
Private _SiteMapId As Integer
Partial Private Sub OnSiteMapIdChanging(ByVal value As Integer)
End Sub
Partial Private Sub OnSiteMapIdChanged()
End Sub
```

Within the property setter, the OnSiteMapIDChanging method is called, allowing an opportunity to perform custom validation on the value being passed to the property. While the value can be validated, the only way to stop the process is to throw an exception.

```
Private Sub OnSiteMapIdChanging(ByVal value As Integer)
If value < 0 Then
                Throw New ArgumentException("The SiteMapId cannot be less than 0.")
End If
End Sub
```

After the changing event is executed, the ReportPropertyChanging method is called, letting the Entity Object Services indicate a value is changing. The object services then knows to track the property for changes in the ObjectStateManager. The tracking is completed by calling the ReportPropertyChanged method.

Finally, similarly to the OnSiteMapIDChanging method, the OnSiteMapID_Changed method is called at the end of the setting. Again, custom validation can be performed in this partial method.

Extending the generated entity class is done by creating custom members in a customized partial class. A common method of extending the entity is to create immutable properties that manipulate values. In this example, an article's Average rating is calculated by ensuring that there is at least one vote and averaging the TotalRating by the number of Votes.

```
Public ReadOnly Property AverageRating() As Double
        Get
            If Me.Votes >= 1 Then
                Return CDbl(Me.TotalRating) / CDbl(Me.Votes)
            Else
                Return 0.0
            End If
        End Get
End Property
```

There is no limitation on how much an entity can be directly extended by adding members by extending the partial class generated by the Entity Data Model Wizard.

Caching Data for Better Performance

In every site- or web-based application, there is some data that doesn't change very often, which is requested very frequently by a lot of end users. Examples are a list of article categories, an e-store's product categories and product items, a list of countries and states, and so on. The most common solution to increase the performance of your site is to implement a caching system for that type of data, so that once the data is retrieved from the data store, it will be kept in memory for some interval, and subsequent requests for the same data will retrieve it from the memory cache, avoiding a round trip to the database server and running another query. This will save processing time and network traffic and, thus, produce faster output to the user. In ASP.NET 1.x, the System.Web.Caching.Cache class was commonly used to cache data. The cache works as an extended dictionary collection, whereby each

entry has a key and a related value. You can store an item in cache by writing `Cache.Insert("key",
data)`, and you retrieve it by writing `data = Cache["key"]`. The `Insert` method of the `Cache` class
has a number of other overloads through which you can specify either the cached data's expiration time
or how long the data will be kept in the cache, and whether it is a sliding interval (a sliding interval is
reset every time the cached data is accessed), plus a dependency on a file or other cached item. When
the dependent file is changed, the expiration time is reached, or the interval passes, the data will be
purged from the cache, and at the next request, you will need to query the data directly from the database, storing it in the cache again.

Choosing a Caching Strategy That Fits Your Needs

The `Cache` class, which was greatly improved with the release of ASP.NET 2.0, has not changed in ASP.
NET 3.5. Support for `CacheDependency` is still available and its child `SQLCacheDependency` is supported in tandem with Entity Framework. In fact, it has nothing to do with Entity Framework because
entities and objects are cached after they are returned from Entity Framework; the `SQLDependency`
simply hooks the cache object into database changes based on the dependency.

It is important to disconnect entities from the context before caching them because tying them to a particular context adds overhead and causes issues when trying to work with the entities against another
context. The proper way to retrieve entities that will be cached is by setting the entity set's `MergeOption`
to `NoTracking`. This retrieves the entities without their being attached to the context being used, reducing
the overhead needed to retrieve them and have them in a state that is not attached to the context. The following method shows retrieving a list of `SiteMapInfo` with `MergeTracking` turned off to allow caching
the results.

```
Public Function GetSiteMapNodes() As List(Of SiteMapInfo)

Dim lSiteMapNodes As List(Of SiteMapInfo)

If EnableCaching AndAlso Not IsNothing(Cache(key)) Then
            lSiteMapNodes = CType(Cache(key), List(Of SiteMapInfo))
End If

SiteMapctx.SiteMaps.MergeOption = MergeOption.NoTracking
            lSiteMapNodes = (From lSiteMapNode In SiteMapctx.SiteMaps _
                Order By lSiteMapNode.SortOrder).ToList()

    If EnableCaching Then
            CacheData(key, lSiteMapNodes)
    End If

Return lSiteMapNodes

End Function
```

Looking at the `GetSiteMapNodes` function you can see that it also checks the `EnableCaching` property to verify that caching is enabled, and if so, it checks to see if the results already exist. If they do, it
returns the results; if not, then it retrieves the values form the database. Again, if caching is enabled, it
will cache the results before returning the them.

It is interesting the Entity Framework team is working on a transparent caching mechanism that will be data-store-agnostic. For now there is a way it can be done and detailed in a blog entry by the Entity Framework Design team; http://blogs.msdn.com/efdesign/archive/2008/07/09/ transparent-caching-support-in-the-entity-framework.aspx. *The idea being that EF will cache the results and manage purging stale data from the cache. This would all happen above the DAL but below the object services layer. This way, it is done before any query is passed to the data store but still below where any queries would have access to query the cached data instead. The ultimate idea is to make caching a first-class or natural part of EF.*

Transaction Management with ADO.NET Entity Framework

Transactions are automatically managed within the same object context by the Entity Framework Object Services. This includes multiple operations that are dependent on successful completion of queries or transactions that depend on distributed systems, such as e-mail or Microsoft Message Queue (MSMQ). Entity Framework operations can also be executed within a `System.Transactions Transaction` to ensure that the requirements are met.

The use of transactions and Object Services requires the following considerations: only operations against the data source are transacted, `SaveChanges` will use any existing transaction to perform the operation, and if none exists, it will create one. Changes to objects in the object context are not accepted until the entire transaction is complete. If you retry an operation within a transaction the `SaveChanges` method should be called with `acceptChangesDuringSave` set to false, then `AcceptAllChanges` should be called after the transaction operations have completed. Avoid calling `SaveChanges` after calling `AcceptAllChanges`; this will cause the context to reapply all the changes to the data source.

Storing Connection Strings and Other Settings

The `web.config` file is composed of multiple sections of related elements that are used by the application to determine how the site should work. There are numerous sections provided by ASP.NET out of the box, but this can be extended to add custom sections. The Beer House site contains numerous configuration sections for each of the modules that help define module defaults, paths, and so forth.

The BLL will need the caching settings, and the user interface will need other settings, such as the recipient's e-mail address for e-mail sent from the site's Contact Us form, the prefix for their subject lines (so that it's easy to spot them among all the other e-mails, and one to set up a rule to move them to a dedicated folder in your favorite e-mail client program). All these settings are saved in the `web.config` file, so it's easy for an administrator to change them using only a text editor. Anytime the `web.config` file is changed, ASP.NET will automatically reload it, and its modified settings will be used for new users, and will not require you to restart the IIS application (which would have terminated any users already online) because changes to the `web.config` file will automatically recycle the application.

Connection string settings have their own dedicated section in `web.config`: `<connectionStrings>`. Here's an example that shows how to store a connection string and give it a shorter and friendlier name that will be used to retrieve it later from code, or from other configuration elements of `web.config`:

```
<connectionStrings>
<remove name="LocalSqlServer"/>
<add name="TheBeerHouseEntities"
connectionString="metadata=res://*;provider=System.Data.SqlClient;
```

```
provider connection string=&quot;Data Source=.;
Initial Catalog=TheBeerHouseVB;Integrated Security=True;MultipleActiveResultSets=
True&quot;"
 providerName="System.Data.EntityClient"/>
<add name="LocalSqlServer" connectionString="Data Source=.;
Integrated Security=True;Initial Catalog=TheBeerHouseVB;"
 providerName="System.Data.SqlClient"/>
</connectionStrings>
```

These connection strings settings are referenced by many other configuration elements — for example, the element that configures the ELMAH system (Error Logging Modules and Handlers, which is used to log details about exceptions and gracefully handle them), or the SQL-dependency caching settings. By default, all these elements have a connectionStringName attribute set to LocalSqlServer (remember the EF has a different connection string, so having a traditional connection string is very important), which refers to a connection string pointing to a local SQL Server database called ASPNETDB.MDF — for convenience, we'll use that same file name for our database. If you choose to rename the file, you can create a new connection string element under <connectionStrings>, and change all elements' connectionStringName attribute to your new connection string name. A more drastic option would be to remove the LocalSqlServer entry from machine.config, and then register it again with the new connection string.

By doing this, all modules pointing to the LocalSqlServer setting will take the new connection string, and you won't have to change their individual connectionStringName attribute. However, I generally don't recommend changing machine.config because it creates deployment issues, and any syntax error in that file can render the whole web server (not just that site) inoperable. And, of course, a web hosting provider is not going to let you make this change. I mention it only for completeness and because it might be the right solution on a tightly controlled corporate intranet web server, for example.

To retrieve the connection strings from code, there's a new class called System.Web.Configuration. WebConfigurationManager, which has a ConnectionStrings dictionary property to retrieve the connection string by name, as follows (note the square brackets used to index into the dictionary):

```
Dim connString as = WebConfigurationManager.ConnectionStrings(
    "LocalSqlServer").ConnectionString
```

This class also has an AppSettings dictionary property that lets you read the values stored in the <appSettings> section. However, a better option would be to create a class that reads from a custom section in web.config, so each subapplication would have its settings isolated from one another. You just write a class that inherits from the System.Configuration.ConfigurationSection class and decorate its public properties with the ConfigurationProperty attribute to indicate that they need to be filled with settings read from the web.config file, and the actual reading will be done for you when your getter reads that setting from your base class! For elements nested under a parent custom section, you need to create a new class that inherits from ConfigurationElement (instead of ConfigurationProperty) and, again, define your properties with the ConfigurationProperty attribute. Here's an abbreviated example:

```
Public Class TheBeerHouseSection
    Inherits ConfigurationSection

    <ConfigurationProperty("defaultConnectionStringName",
DefaultValue:="LocalSqlServer")> _
```

```vbnet
        Public Property DefaultConnectionStringName() As String
            Get
                Return CStr(Me("defaultConnectionStringName"))
            End Get
            Set(ByVal value As String)
                Me("DefaultConnectionStringName") = value
            End Set
        End Property

        <ConfigurationProperty("articles", IsRequired:=True)> _
        Public ReadOnly Property Articles() As ArticlesElement
            Get
                Return CType(Me("articles"), ArticlesElement)
            End Get
        End Property

    End Class


    Public Class ArticlesElement
        Inherits ConfigurationElement

        <ConfigurationProperty("ratingLockInterval", DefaultValue:="15")> _
        Public Property RatingLockInterval() As Integer
            Get
                Return CInt(Me("ratingLockInterval"))
            End Get
            Set(ByVal value As Integer)
                Me("ratingLockInterval") = value
            End Set
        End Property

    End Class
```

This `TheBeerHouseSection` class will be mapped to a custom configuration section. It has a property named `DefaultConnectionStringName` that maps a `"defaultconnectionstringname"` attribute, which has a default value of `"LocalSQLServer"`. It also has the `Articles` property of type `ArticlesElement`, which maps to a subelement named `articles` with the `RatingLockInterval` Integer attribute. Note that the `ConfigurationProperty` attribute of the `ArticlesElement` property has the `IsRequired` option set to true, meaning that the element is required to be present in the `web` `.config` file. The other properties do not have this constraint because they have a default value.

Once the class is ready you must register it in the `web.config` file and define the mapping to a section named `"site"`, as follows:

```xml
<configuration xmlns="http://schemas.microsoft.com/.NetConfiguration/v2.0">
    <configSections>
        <section name="theBeerHouse" type="TheBeerHouse.TheBeerHouseSection,
TBHBLL, Version=3.5.0.1, Culture=neutral, PublicKeyToken=null"/>
    </configSections>

<theBeerHouse defaultConnectionStringName="TheBeerHouseEntities"
siteDomainName="[Add Your Base URL Here]">
```

```
<articles RatingLockInterval="10" />
</theBeerHouse>

    <!-- other configuration sections... -->
</configuration>
```

To read the settings from code, you use the `WebConfigurationManager`'s `GetSection` to get a reference to the `"theBeerHouse"` section, and cast it to the `TheBeerHouseSection` type. Then, you can use its properties and subproperties:

```
Public Shared ReadOnly Settings As TheBeerHouseSection = _
    CType(WebConfigurationManager.GetSection("theBeerHouse"), TheBeerHouseSection)
```

This book's sample site requires a number of settings for each module, so there will be a single custom configuration section with one subelement for each module. Each module will have its own connection string and caching settings. However, it's useful to provide some default values for these settings at the section level, so that if you want to use the same connection string for all modules, you don't have to specify it separately for each module, just once for the entire site. In the "Solution" section of this chapter, you'll see the custom section class, while the module-specific elements will be added in their specific chapters later in the book. Also in this chapter, we'll develop a class to map a subelement named `contactForm` with settings for sending the e-mails from the Contact Us page (the subject line's prefix, and the To and CC fields).

User Interface

With the data and business layers covered, it is time to start defining how the data will be presented to and collected from the user. ASP.NET provides a great set of resources to produce a very rich interface for customers and staff to be productive and interactive with theBeerHouse site. Layout issues were discussed in the preceding chapter, so here we'll discuss design issues pertaining to a common pattern for displaying and administering data.

A Base Page Class

When adding a new Web Form (Page) to an ASP.NET website, Visual Studio automatically adds the corresponding code-behind file with a class for the page that inherits from `System.Web.UI.Page`. When building an application like theBeerHouse, there is always common code that each page uses. Adding redundant code is a sign of poor programming because it adds unnecessary maintenance to the application.

In the previous edition of the book, a `BasePage` class was leveraged to contain those common members. This class inherits from `System.Web.UI.Page` and, thus, inherits all the features of the `Page` class needed by the `BasePage` class. As you examine the code of theBeerHouse site, there will be other page classes that inherit from the `BasePage` class. For example, there is an `ArticlePage` class that contains common members related to article management.

```
Public Class BasePage
    Inherits System.Web.UI.Page
```

I am going to review a few of the new members I have added to the `BasePage` class since the last edition. The first members manage moving Hidden Fields (think `ViewState`) to the bottom of the page.

A hidden field is used by pages to hold values that need to be passed back to the server but not displayed to the user. The reason they exist is because the web is stateless, meaning that each request or action against the site is a completely independent action. Cookies and hidden fields are used to link requests from the server's perspective.

ViewState is unique to ASP.NET and is used to hold a variety of values, typically for web controls, but it is not limited to that duty. One of the problems with the ViewState is that it can get very bloated very quickly. It is also rendered at the top of the content. There are two problems with this; it hurts search engine optimization and it hurts perceived client-side performance.

I have seen a few studies that show search engines tend to only index the topmost parts of the content of a page. This means that if the content you want to get indexed has been pushed down the page by a large ViewState, it might not be indexed because the ViewState counts towards those precious bytes.

Large ViewState aside, page content is rendered as it is received by the browser, and hidden fields at the top of the page only hinder this by being at the front of the content stream. There are many factors that play into how fast content is rendered, but that is way outside the scope of this book. However, moving these hidden fields to the bottom of the page is important to help rendering and on-page SEO. There are drawbacks to this technique because there are many instances where ASP.NET AJAX is involved because it relies on the ViewState being present to properly function. So, if you have the ViewState moved to the bottom of the page and have issues with AJAX functioning properly, then return the ViewState to the top of the page.

Since hidden fields are injected into the content rendered by the page typically at the top of the content by ASP.NET the request has to be intercepted right after it has been rendered by the page and any controls but before it is sent down the wire. The Page class has a Render method that can be overwritten, which provides the opportunity needed to massage the content.

The BasePage class has a MoveHiddenFields Boolean property that tells the custom Render method if it should move the hidden fields to the bottom of the page. One problem I have seen with moving the hidden fields is that some controls do not execute correctly because they are looking for those fields during the page load event processing. For example, the FCKEditor does not function if the hidden fields are moved.

```vb
Private _moveHiddenFields As Boolean = True
Public Property MoveHiddenFields() As Boolean
        Get
                Return _moveHiddenFields
        End Get
        Set(ByVal Value As Boolean)
                _moveHiddenFields = Value
        End Set
End Property

Private Function MoveHiddenFieldsToBottom(ByVal html As String) As String
        Dim sPattern As String = "<input type=""hidden"".*/*>|
<input type=""hidden"".*></input>"
        Dim mc As MatchCollection = Regex.Matches(html, sPattern, _
                RegexOptions.IgnoreCase & RegexOptions.IgnorePatternWhitespace)
```

```
Dim sb As New StringBuilder

For Each m As Match In mc

    sb.AppendLine(m.Value)
    html = html.Replace(m.Value, String.Empty)

Next

    Return html.Replace("</form>", sb.ToString & "</form>")
End Function
```

If `MoveHiddenFields` is true the custom `Render` method calls the `MoveHiddenFieldsToBottom` method, passing the string that contains the HTML to be rendered in the browser. This method uses a regular expression to match all the hidden fields and loop through them, removing them and appending them to a `StringBuilder`. Once the loop is done, all the hidden fields have been stripped from the HTML, but the last line of the method inserts them back in at the very bottom of the `<form>` tag. It is important to insert the hidden fields before the form tag close because they need to be included in the post back to the server managed by the form.

```
Protected Overrides Sub Render(ByVal writer As System.Web.UI.HtmlTextWriter)

        Dim stringWriter As New System.IO.StringWriter
        Dim htmlWriter As New HtmlTextWriter(stringWriter)
        MyBase.Render(htmlWriter)
        Dim html As String = stringWriter.ToString()

        If MoveHiddenFields Then

            html = MoveHiddenFieldsToBottom(html)

        End If

        writer.Write(html)

End Sub
```

Finally, the `Render` method writes the optimized HTML to the `HTMLTextWriter`, which ultimately sends the content down the wire to the client. The overall process incurs negligible overhead to optimize the page content.

The next element I want to discuss is the `PrimaryKeyId` property. This a common pattern used to check for the existence of a primary key being passed in the URL or stored in the page's `ViewState`. It first checks to see if the value has been stored in the `ViewState`, and if not, it then checks to see if it was passed in the URL's `QueryString`. If either of those criteria is not met, then it returns 0. This value will be used in pages to retrieve content, such as an article, from the database.

```
Public Property PrimaryKeyId(ByVal vPrimaryKey As String) As Integer
        Get
                If Not IsNothing(ViewState(vPrimaryKey)) AndAlso
    IsNumeric(ViewState(vPrimaryKey)) Then
                    Return CInt(ViewState(vPrimaryKey))
```

```
                    ElseIf Not IsNothing(Request.QueryString(vPrimaryKey))
        AndAlso IsNumeric(Request.QueryString(vPrimaryKey)) Then
                        ViewState(vPrimaryKey) = CInt(Request.QueryString(vPrimaryKey))
                        Return CInt(Request.QueryString(vPrimaryKey))
                    End If
                    Return 0
            End Get
            Set(ByVal Value As Integer)
                    ViewState(vPrimaryKey) = Value
            End Set
    End Property
```

In this example, the `ArticleId` property of the `ArticlePage` class calls the `PrimaryKeyId` property to retrieve the value.

```
Public Property ArticleId() As Integer
Get
                    Return PrimaryKeyId("ArticleId")
End Get
Set(ByVal Value As Integer)
                    PrimaryKeyId("ArticleId") = Value
End Set
End Property
```

There are other members of the `BasePage` class that will be used as the balance of the book is presented. There are also helper classes or what I think of as utility classes that are also used to contain common methods. The reason they are important is these methods are not page-specific (meaning tied to a specific page) and might need to be used in other classes. For example, the site takes advantage of user controls and Web Parts as part of its UI architecture. They will need to access some of these methods, too.

Introducing the ListView Control

The `ListView` control is new in ASP.NET 3.5 and combines the functionality of the `Repeater`, `GridView`, and `Datalist` controls but adds the capability to page and sort the data naturally. While it is not as lightweight as the `Repeater` or `DataList` control, it is pretty close and adds the paging and sorting capabilities built into the `GridView` control. Editing capabilities are also available with the `ListView` control, but I will not leverage this feature. All these features make it a very rich tool to display tables of data on the web.

Most examples and demos of the `ListView` control show how to bind the control to one of the `DataSource` controls. While the previous edition of this book leveraged the `ObjectDataSource` control and there is an `EntityDataSource` control, I will not use them to bind data. This technique is often not done in high-demand production sites and reduces an *n*-tier architecture to a flat model by making databinding line of sight to the database. Since it is very easy to bind collections to a `ListView` from a business layer, I have opted to use this technique.

Once data is bound to a `ListView`, it is displayed in an ordered fashion by using templates. If you have ever used a `Repeater`, a `DataList`, or templates to build the layout of a `GridView`, this will seem like second nature. There are a few new twists to the template model used in the `Repeater` and `DataList` controls, but they are minor. The `ListView` offers a rich set of possible templates to control how data is displayed to the end user.

Template Name	Description
LayoutTemplate	Identifies the root template that defines the main layout of the control. It contains a placeholder object, such as a table row (tr), div, or span element. This element will be replaced with the content that is defined in the ItemTemplate template or in the GroupTemplate template. It might also contain a DataPager object.
ItemTemplate	Identifies the data-bound content to display for single items.
ItemSeparatorTemplate	Identifies the content to render between single items.
GroupTemplate	Identifies the content for the group layout. It contains a placeholder object, such as a table cell (td), div, or span that will be replaced with the content defined in the other templates, such as the ItemTemplate and EmptyItemTemplate templates.
GroupSeparatorTemplate	Identifies the content to render between groups of items.
EmptyItemTemplate	Identifies the content to render for an empty item when a GroupTemplate template is used. For example, if the GroupItemCount property is set to 5, and the total number of items returned from the data source is 8, the last row of data displayed by the ListView control will contain three items as specified by the ItemTemplate template, and two items as specified by the EmptyItemTemplate template.
EmptyDataTemplate	Identifies the content to render if the data source returns no data.
SelectedItemTemplate	Identifies the content to render for the selected data item to differentiate the selected item from the other displayed items.
AlternatingItemTemplate	Identifies the content to render for alternating items to make it easier to distinguish between consecutive items.
EditItemTemplate	Identifies the content to render when an item is being edited. The EditItemTemplate template is rendered in place of the ItemTemplate template for the data item being edited.
InsertItemTemplate	Identifies the content to render when an item is being inserted. The InsertItemTemplate template is rendered in place of an ItemTemplate template at either the start of the items displayed by the ListView control or the end. You can specify where the InsertItemTemplate template is rendered by using the InsertItemPosition property of the ListView control.

The ListView displays data using a set of templates, allowing declarative and code-behind databinding. It actually uses a nested layout structure where everything starts with the LayoutTemplate and proliferates from there. The only real requirement for the LayoutTemplate is that it contains at least one control marked as a placeholder.

For the administration pages of theBeerHouse application, I use a table to create the layout of the
`ListView` control. The first row of the table contains the header row of the data. In the example, there
are Title, Edit, and Delete column. These columns are mapped to the `Title` property of the bound entities, followed by a column that contains image buttons that will either link to a page to edit the record
or delete the record from the database.

```
<asp:ListView ID="lvSiteMap" runat="server">
<LayoutTemplate>
                <table cellspacing="0" cellpadding="0" class="AdminList">
    <THead>
                    <tr class="AdminListHeader">
                        <td>Title</td>

    <td>Edit</td>

    <td>Delete</td>
</tr>
        </THead>
        <TBody>
<tr id="itemPlaceholder" runat="server"></tr>
        </TBody>
    </table>

</LayoutTemplate>
</asp:ListView>
```

The next row is changed to a server control by adding the `runat="server"` attribute. It has the ID of
`itemPlaceholder`, which is important because this tells the `ListView` to use this control to add items
to the list. In this case, the item templates should be a table row <tr> with the appropriate table cells <td>.

```
<EmptyDataTemplate>
<tr>
<td colspan="3"><p>Sorry there are no Categories available at this time.</p></td>
</tr>
</EmptyDataTemplate>
<ItemTemplate>
<tr>
<td class="ListTitle"><a href='<%# String.Format(
"AddEditSiteMap.aspx?categoryid={0}", Eval("siteMapid")) %>'>
<%# Eval("Title") %></a>
</td>
<td><a href="<%# String.Format(
"AddEditSiteMap.aspx?categoryid={0}", Eval("siteMapId")) %>">
<img src="../images/edit.gif" alt="" width="16" height="16"
class="AdminImg" /></a>
</td>
<td><asp:ImageButton runat="server" ID="ibtnDelete" ImageAlign="Middle"
 ImageUrl="~/Images/Delete.gif" AlternateText="Delete Node" /></td>
</tr>
</ItemTemplate>
```

The actual templates are declaratively defined as the table row to fill the placeholder control designated in
the `LayoutTemplate`. The first template is the `EmptyDataTemplate`. It defines what is displayed if there
are no records returned from the data source. Figure 3-19 shows an example of how this page looks.

Figure 3-19

The next template is the `ItemTemplate`, it defines how data is displayed in each row. An `AlternatingItemTemplate` that defines the layout for every other row is also available, giving you a chance to change the visual appearance on every other row.

The template use declarative databinding, which is code embedded between `<%# %>`. The data is actually bound to the `ListView` in the code-behind. The binding methods take advantage of the Using syntax that uses an object that implements the `IDisposable` interface to clean up its resources in a transparent fashion. In the example, a `CategoryRepository` is created and the `GetCategories` method is called to bind the records to the `ListView`.

```
Private Sub BindCategories()

    Using Categoryrpt As New CategoryRepository

        lvCategories.DataSource = Categoryrpt.GetCategories()
        lvCategories.DataBind()

    End Using

End Sub
```

I think it is important to note a difference between the previous edition of the book, where data was retrieved in small chunks or pages of data and this version. The former version involved getting a matching row count for the full set of records matching the query results and doing math behind the scenes. This was done to reduce the amount of data carried across the wire from the database, but this approach causes more hits on the database.

I like to cache data in memory to reduce the number of times I need to hit the database. The ListView has the logic baked into it to correctly calculate the number of pages, how to display the navigation in the DataPager, and so forth. So, I think trying to duplicate this effort is not a productive use of time.

Paging and Sorting the ListView

Manipulating the records displayed in the ListView is important to make it effective; this is typically done by paging and sorting the data. The ListView provides built-in mechanisms to help make developing these routines easy.

ASP.NET 3.5 added the DataPager control, which is a complementary control designed to page through the ListView control contents. It is added to the LayoutTemplate in the position in which you want it to appear. I tend to add it at the bottom, but you are not limited to that. It can actually be added outside the ListView control all together, the DataPager control has a PageControlId property that needs to be set to the id of the ListView.

```
<div class="pager">
<asp:DataPager ID="pagerBottom" runat="server" PageSize="15">
            <Fields>
                    <asp:NextPreviousPagerField ButtonCssClass="command"
 FirstPageText="«" PreviousPageText="<" RenderDisabledButtonsAsLabels="true"
ShowFirstPageButton="true" ShowPreviousPageButton="true"
ShowLastPageButton="false" ShowNextPageButton="false" />
<asp:NumericPagerField ButtonCount="7" NumericButtonCssClass="command"
CurrentPageLabelCssClass="current"
NextPreviousButtonCssClass="command" />
<asp:NextPreviousPagerField ButtonCssClass="command" LastPageText="»"
NextPageText=">" RenderDisabledButtonsAsLabels="true"
ShowFirstPageButton="false" ShowPreviousPageButton="false"
ShowLastPageButton="true" ShowNextPageButton="true" />
</Fields>
</asp:DataPager>
</div>
```

The DataPager control causes the ListView control to post back to the server and cause the PagePropertiesChanged event to be executed. In PagePropertiesChanged, the data needs to be rebound to the control; the ListView takes care of rendering the proper page.

```
Private Sub lvSiteMap_PagePropertiesChanged(ByVal sender As Object,
ByVal e As System.EventArgs) Handles lvSiteMap.PagePropertiesChanged
BindSiteMapNodes()
End Sub
```

The ListView content can be sorted as well. The only requirement is to add a postback control (Button, LinkButton, or ImageButton,) with the CommandName of "Sort" and a CommandArgument with the name of the sort criteria. The ListView automatically handles changing the sort order from ascending to descending. The same PagePropertiesChanged event used to manage paging. The ListView has the SortExpression and SortDirection properties that can be used to build the query to retrieve the data. I hope you see why I chose not to retrieve just the page of records that will displayed and instead chose to cache the full recordset to be manipulated by the ListView.

Using the Update Panel with the ListView Control

ASP.NET 3.5 has added the ASP.NET AJAX framework to the user interface tools that can be quickly integrated in a site to build rich user interfaces. The framework is a set of JavaScript methods built to mirror the .NET Framework in organization, classes, and methods that help build client-side functionality. It has a set of web controls: `ScriptManager`, `ScriptManagerProxy`, `UpdatePanel`, `Timer`, and `UpdateProgress`.

Each page that needs to use the ASP.NET AJAX framework must have a `ScriptManager` control. When a master page is used the content page must have a `ScriptManagerProxy` control, so the content page can leverage the `ScriptManager` on the master page.

The `UpdatePanel` control is the poor man's JavaScript helper, it allows blocks of content to be contained in the `UpdatePanel` control and all requests are automatically converted to AJAX instead of a traditional postback. This means that you do not have to lift a finger to change an existing page that performs postbacks to the server to change those postbacks to an asynchronous operation. This means the user will not have to see the page flicker associated with the postback.

The `ListView` control works naturally inside an `UpdatePanel` control, making the paging and sorting methods work asynchronously. Once the page is working an `UpdatePanel` just needs to be added with the `ListView` embedded in the panel's `ContentTemplate`.

```
    [f0000.xxx]    [f0000.xxx]    [f0000.xxx]    [f0000.xxx]    [f0000.xxx]
    [f0000.xxx]    [f0000.xxx]    [f0000.xxx]<asp:UpdatePanel runat=
"server" ID="uppnlComments">
<ContentTemplate>
<asp:ListView ID="lvComments" runat="server">
<LayoutTemplate>
```

Nothing more is required; the `UpdatePanel` will make the postback to the server; that, in turn, causes the normal page request to be performed on the server. The updated content is then parsed by the `UpdatePanel`, and it manages updating the `ListView` content based on the server's response. It is that simple! I will go over some more involved AJAX scenarios in later chapters.

A Standard Administration Form

In the previous edition of theBeerHouse application, `FormViews` were used to bind data to edit and insert records into the database. In this edition, I am going to slim things down a bit in the user interface and take more control in the code-behind. The edit form is laid out in a table, with the appropriate controls used to represent the data. These can be a `TextBox`, `CheckBox`, `DropDownList`, and so forth. When possible, controls and extenders from the ASP.NET AJAX control toolkit are used. At the bottom of the form is a series of buttons to perform inserting, updating, deleting, or canceling.

One of the reasons I do not like to use the `FormView` and `DetailView` controls is that they tend to limit the capability to customize the display, or add complexity to the form that ultimately defeats the purpose the `View` controls are meant to serve.

The ASP.NET AJAX Control Toolkit is a set of controls and control extenders that Microsoft produces the toolkit and maintains it on CodePlex at `www.codeplex.com/AjaxControlToolkit`. It is a community project though which anyone, including you, can suggest changes and report bugs. The source code of the entire toolkit is available for downloading, so you can make changes and examine how the controls are built. Figure 3-20 shows how the AddEdit form for the Category entity looks.

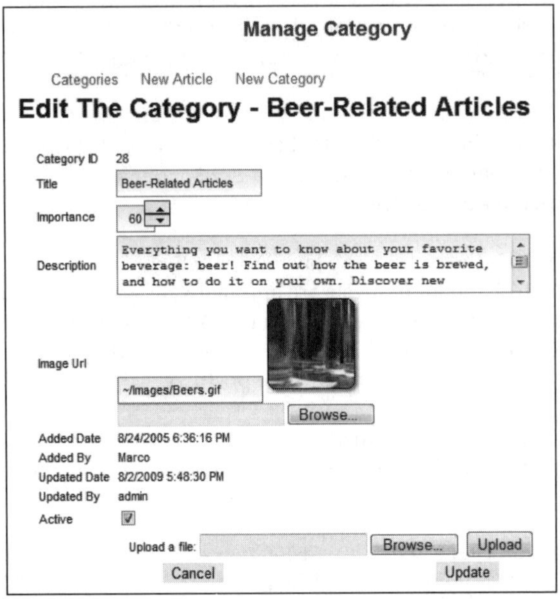

Figure 3-20

The administrative form's code-behind is responsible for retrieving the entity, displaying the data, updating the data, and storing it. All this responsibility is handled by five methods: the `Page Load` event handler, `ClearItems`, the `Bind Entity` method, and the `Cancel` and `Submit` event handlers. The page also inherits from the `AdminPage` class or possibly a descendant of the `AdminPage` class.

The `AdminPage` contains a `PreInit` event handler that sets the `MoveHiddenFields` to false. This is done because the `FCKEditor` is used on many of the administration pages and does not work when the hidden fields are moved.

```
Private Sub Page_PreInit(ByVal sender As Object,
ByVal e As System.EventArgs) Handles Me.PreInit

MoveHiddenFields = False

End Sub
```

The remaining properties of the `AdminPage` are to help manage primary keys that I detailed earlier.

In the `Page Load` event handler checks to see if a primary key was passed to the form, and if so, then binds the entity to the controls; if not, it clears the form.

```
    Protected Sub Page_Load(ByVal sender As Object,
ByVal e As System.EventArgs) Handles Me.Load
```

```
        If Not IsPostBack Then

            If CategoryId > 0 Then
                BindCategory()
            Else
                ClearItems()
            End If

        End If

    End Sub
```

The `ClearItems` method is called when the form is being loaded to add a new entity to the database. Notice the last item in the method sets the status literal control text to instruct the user what to do. The status control is used to provide feedback to the user as to the status of the form.

```
    Private Sub ClearItems()

        ltlCategoryID.Text = String.Empty
        ltlAddedDate.Text = String.Empty
        txtTitle.Text = String.Empty
        txtImportance.Text = String.Empty
        txtDescription.Text = String.Empty
        txtImageUrl.Text = String.Empty
        ltlUpdatedDate.Text = String.Empty
        iLogo.Visible = False

        ltlStatus.Text = "Create a New Category."

    End Sub
```

The bind method, `BindCategory` in the example, retrieves the entity that corresponds to the primary key value passed to the page. It then binds the data to the appropriate controls as needed.

```
    Private Sub BindCategory()

        Using Categoryrpt As New CategoryRepository

            Dim lCategories As Category = Categoryrpt.GetCategoryById(CategoryId)

            If Not IsNothing(lCategories) Then

                ltlCategoryID.Text = lCategories.CategoryID
                ltlAddedDate.Text = lCategories.AddedDate
                ltlAddedBy.Text = lCategories.AddedBy
                txtTitle.Text = lCategories.Title
                txtImportance.Text = lCategories.Importance
                txtDescription.Text = lCategories.Description

                If String.IsNullOrEmpty(lCategories.ImageUrl) = False Then
                    txtImageUrl.Text = System.IO.Path.GetFileName(
lCategories.ImageUrl)
                    iLogo.ImageUrl = lCategories.ImageUrl
```

```
        Else
            iLogo.Visible = False
        End If

        cbActive.Checked = lCategories.Active
        ltlUpdatedDate.Text = lCategories.UpdatedDate
        ltlUpdatedBy.Text = lCategories.UpdatedBy

        ltlStatus.Text = String.Format("Edit The Category - {0}.",
lCategories.Title)
        Else
            CategoryId = 0
            ltlStatus.Text = "Create a New Category."
        End If

    End Using

End Sub
```

The Submit button's click event manages changing, updating or creating a new entity. First, it gets a copy of the existing version of the entity if a primary key value has been supplied.

Then each field gets updated if the value has been changed. This is done because the Entity Framework will create a SQL Update command that updates only the changed fields, making it perform slightly better.

```
Private Sub UpdateCategory()
    Using Categoryrpt As New CategoryRepository

        Dim lCategory As Category

        If CategoryId > 0 Then
            lCategory = Categoryrpt.GetCategoryById(CategoryId)
        Else
            lCategory = New Category()
        End If

        lCategory.Title = txtTitle.Text
        lCategory.Importance = CInt(txtImportance.Text)
        lCategory.Description = txtDescription.Text

        lCategory.ImageUrl = GetItemImage(fuImageURL, txtImageUrl)
        lCategory.Active = cbActive.Checked

        lCategory.UpdatedBy = UserName
        lCategory.UpdatedDate = Now

        If lCategory.CategoryID = 0 Then
            lCategory.Active = True
            lCategory.AddedBy = UserName
            lCategory.AddedDate = Now
        End If

        If Not IsNothing(Categoryrpt.AddCategory(lCategory)) Then
```

```
                    IndicateUpdated(Categoryrpt, "Category", ltlStatus, cmdDelete)

                    cmdUpdate.Text = "Update"
                    IndicateUpdated(Categoryrpt, "Category", ltlStatus, cmdDelete)
                    Dim sURL As String = SEOFriendlyURL( _
                        Settings.Articles.CategoryUrlIndicator & "/" &
lCategory.Title, ".aspx")
                        Dim sRealURL As String =
String.Format("BrowseArticles.aspx?Categoryid={0}", lCategory.CategoryID)

                    CommitSiteMap(lCategory.Title, sURL, sRealURL, _
                        lCategory.Description.Substring(0,
If(lCategory.Description.Length >= 200, 199, lCategory.Description.Length - 1)), _
                        If(String.IsNullOrEmpty(lCategory.Title) = False,
lCategory.Title, String.Empty), "Category")

                Else
                    IndicateNotUpdated(Categoryrpt, "Category", ltlStatus)
                End If

            End Using

    End Sub
```

After the fields have been updated, the `UpdatedBy` and `UpdatedDate` values are set to the current username and the current time. It then checks to see if it is a new entity or an update to an entity by checking the `CategoryId` value. If it is greater than 0, then the entity's repository `Update` method is called. If not then the entity is added to the database by calling the `AddCategory` method.

Based on the result of the `Add` or `Update` method, the status message is updated to reflect the outcome.

When the Cancel button is clicked, it causes the response to be sent to the entity's list administration page.

```
Private Sub btnCancel_Click(ByVal sender As Object,
ByVal e As System.EventArgs) Handles cmdCancel.Click
        Response.Redirect("ManageCategories.aspx")
End Sub
```

Clicking the Delete button calls the `Delete` method of the entity's repository class. According to the outcome of the `Delete` method, the page's status is updated to let the user know what happened.

```
Protected Sub cmdDelete_Click(ByVal sender As Object,
ByVal e As System.EventArgs) Handles cmdDelete.Click

        Using Categoryrpt As New CategoryRepository
            If Categoryrpt.DeleteCategory(CategoryId) Then
                Response.Redirect("ManageCategories.aspx")
            Else
                ltlStatus.Text = "Sorry the Category was not Deleted."
            End If
        End Using

    End Sub
```

Error Logging

Tracking exceptions with any application is very important to understand what has happened when something goes wrong. No matter how many unit, integration, and manual tests are created and rerun, every application will eventually hit a moment where something goes wrong and an exception is thrown. Fortunately, there are numerous ways to log exceptions in .NET applications.

In the last edition of this book, Marco showed how to use health monitoring and instrumentation to log and monitor an application. This is a great way to plug into the application and track down issues. Another popular choice is the Logging Application Block available in the Microsoft Enterprise Library, `http://microsoft.com/patterns`. But I wanted to add to the choices for monitoring your applications with the Error Logging Modules and Handlers (ELMAH) components, `www.raboof.com/Projects/ELMAH`.

ELMAH is a free utility built by Atif Aziz and added to by several members of the ASP.NET community. It is a class library with a collection of `httpModules` and `httpHandlers` to log and report application exceptions. The real power ELMAH offers ASP.NET developers is ease of configuration and multiple means to alert site administrators to issues. You can read more details about implementing ELMAH in an article by Scott Mitchell and Atif Aziz, `http://msdn.microsoft.com/en-us/library/aa479332.aspx`.

With ELMAH, exceptions can be logged to a SQL database, XML file, e-mail, or a variety of other data stores. This provides a very flexible reporting platform. The e-mail option is particularly helpful because this can be set up to alert several administrators at once. The database and XML options keep a permanent record of exceptions that later can be reviewed, transformed, or brought into a reporting platform, such as SQL Server Reporting Services.

Errors are logged by a custom `httpModule` that hooks into the ASP.NET pipeline's `OnError` event. The same error information is logged that is displayed in the error page, also known as the Yellow Screen of Death by many. Once the exception is logged, processing continues without interfering with the normal user experience.

For production sites, it is a good idea to designate an error page to be displayed instead of the default exception reporting page. This creates a better user experience when things are not going so well. It also suppresses sensitive error information from being rendered to the user. This is not only abrasive to a typical user, but it also exposes information that can be very valuable to a hacker for launching a successful attack against the application.

Once exceptions are logged, they can be retrieved through a set of custom `httpHandlers` that provide a secure and organized reporting infrastructure. The main reporting interface is a nonexistent page with the `.axd` extension, shown in Figure 3-21. This extension is commonly used in ASP.NET as a resource extension for content streamed by custom `httpHandlers`. The handler produces a page that lists all the errors in the log, allowing you to page through exceptions if there are many that have been logged. Each exception in the list has a link that will display a detailed report of the exception.

The detailed exception shows the exception details and the page's trace log. This is the same trace information that would be displayed at the bottom of the page if tracing were enabled. All this information is helpful to trace the source of the exception and examine the state of the request.

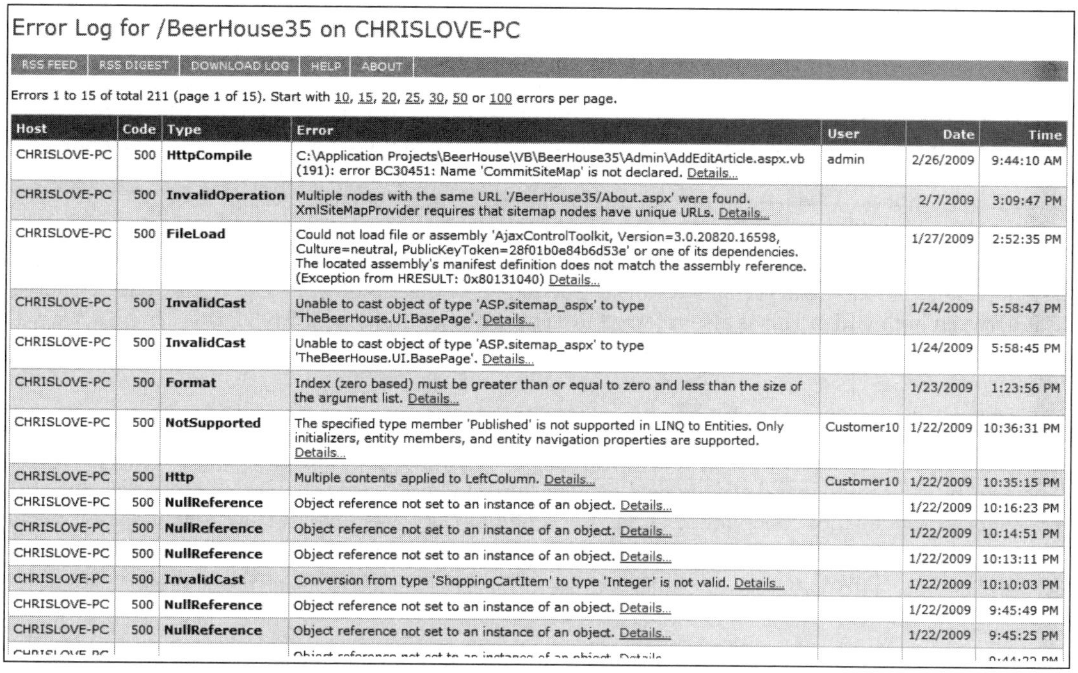

Figure 3-21

The report information can be protected by configuring ELMAH to require authentication. ELMAH automatically leverages the ASP.NET authentication configured for the site, protecting this sensitive information from prying eyes.

Another feature I like about ELMAH as an error-logging and reporting tool is that it also provides and RSS feed that can be used to monitor a site for exceptions.

Search Engine Optimization Techniques

Search engine visibility or placement is one of the most important aspects of any public website. Obtaining high rankings is one of the most important aspects of online marketing and can be the difference between success and failure for many online businesses. Obtaining those top positions can be extremely difficult, but it is not impossible.

While this book is not going to cover details of search engine fundamentals, there are standard things that can be done from a technical perspective that can be done to make an ASP.NET website more search-engine-friendly. The pages of an ASP.NET site should contain site-, page-, and content-level optimizations, much of which can be controlled or aided by good application architecture.

Site-Level Optimizations

Search engines are known for penalizing sites for duplicate content, which can commonly happen when multiple URLs can retrieve the same content. While search engines have gotten a lot better, accounting for common duplications, such as www and non-www access, it helps to have only one true URL for content.

The www/non-www Canonical Issue

The first way this needs to be addressed is eliminating the ability for visitors to use the www alias of the website. Second-level domains, and third-level domains controlled by site owners, should be the way a site is accessed. The www prefix to a domain is really an artifact from the early days of the web and stands for World Wide Web. It was prepended to the domain to indicate the protocol being used as a domain alias or CNAME. When the Internet gained mainstream traction, this did not change. A good website should respond to both the www alias and the actual domain.

The problem with this is that search engines will index both URLs, potentially earning a duplicate content penalty; if not, it will certainly dilute the actual score the search engine gives the page by spreading it between both URLs. This is also referred to as canonicalization. In ASP.NET, this can be dealt with in either the `global.asax` file or a custom `httpModule`.

Use 301 Redirects Properly

Inevitably, you will one day restructure your site by changing the landscape of the URLs used on the site, or retiring content and adding new content. It could be a simple change like changing the URL `~/ShowProduct.aspx?ProductId=3` to `~/Gadgets-for-beer-fanatics/Beer-Cap.aspx`. But whatever the need, using 301 redirects not only tells visitors where the content is located but also tells search engines how to reindex existing resources on your site in a way that will not cause you to lose your rankings.

A 301 redirect refers to the HTTP status code sent from the server to the client. In this case, a status code of 301 tells the client that the resource requested has been permanently moved to a new location, which is added to the response location header.

This technique is also good for ensuring against duplicate content issues discussed in the previous section. In the previous product example, the old URL still works and, ultimately, is what the ASP.NET engine actually processed, but this URL should not be used as the way to access the content. While not using the old URL on the site is one way to eliminate the URL from being indexed, there is no 100% way to eliminate this link from being indexed. What must be done is a 301 redirect for the URL to the new URL at the site application level.

Search-Engine-Friendly URLs and Site Structure

Organizing the structure of a website is another important aspect of search engine optimization because it not only tells the search engines about the content but also guides potential visitors looking at results to click on a page. URLs should be organized by category, department, or other logical groups. In the case of theBeerHouse application, there are various application modules that produce content of different types. News, for example, can be identified by the `'News'` container, which is analogous to a folder or directory. From there, each article is contained within a selected category and, finally, the title of the article. A sample article URL might be represented by `'~/News/Beer-related-articles/Top 10-of-brewing-methods.aspx'`. This relays the content of the article is about brewing methods and is a topic about beer. It also indicates it is a news article, also important in identifying the content. So, a person searching for online articles about brewing beer could feel pretty confident that this might be the article for them, and they will be more likely to visit the site.

Notice that "-" is used to separate words in the example of the URL. This is done intentionally to deline-ate words in a URL because it is thought that search engines tend to understand this better. It is also easier for visitors to quickly look at a URL and isolate the words into a readable format. If you simply URLEncode *an article's title, it replaces spaces with "+", which is not as easy for a human to distin-guish between words. There are some cases, such as "Beer-related" that contain dash that will have to be dealt with in the core architecture, but this can be handled in ASP.NET.*

Page-Level Optimizations

It has long been known that having the proper content on a page helps you get better search engine vis-ibility. In the early days of the Internet, sites could rely on the content of their header tags to get them reasonable visibility in most cases. That is not as true today but is still a very relevant task that should be done for each page in a site. This includes having valid, targeted content in the page's Title, and META tags.

The Title Tag

The Title tag is one of the most important pieces of the page because it is one of the primary factors search engines use to determine the content of the page. It is also used as the page's clickable text in the search engine results and is displayed at the top of the browser every time it is displayed. The text of the Title tag should be compelling, relevant, and less than 65 characters long. Search engines typically do not display more than 65 characters in their results.

Figure 3-22 shows the results for my blog on live.com. I have highlighted the Title tag used to link to my blog from the result list.

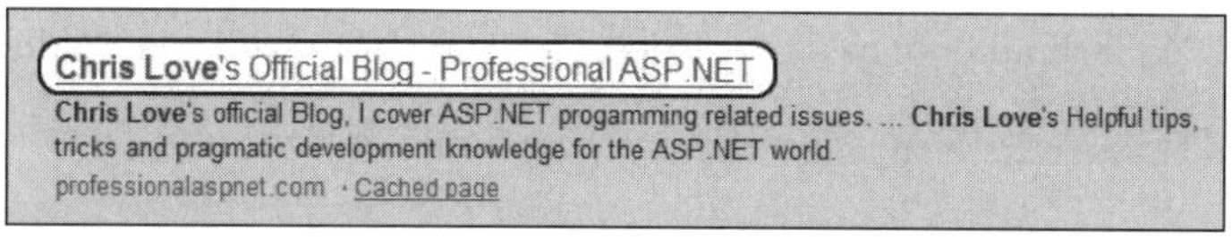

Figure 3-22

Viewing the source of my blog's home page, you will see the same text contained in the Title tag.

```
<head>
<title>Chris Love's Official Blog - Professional ASP.NET</title>
</head>
```

All Title tags in the site should be unique and should never start with "Welcome to. . . ." If you do a quick search for "Welcome to" you will see how many sites are indexed for that term. The title should include content that describes the page's content and is targeted to specific keyword phrases if at all possible. Generic terms like "Welcome to" just reduce the relevance of the page. Avoiding this common mistake could be the difference between a first page listing and a fifth page listing.

The Description META Tag

The Description META tag no longer carries the significance it once had with place in search engine results, but it is very important for each page to have a unique description. The content of the Description META tag is often used by search engines as the description in the search results. Having a relevant description will help a site get more visitors from search engines. If this tag is not added to a page, the search engine is forced to assume the description from other sections of the page, thus taking it out of your control.

Searching for "Chris Love" on Live.com returns the following result. I have highlighted the content located in the title tag of my blog, Figure 3-23. Notice how it appended more content from the page to help add more content to the result? I will talk more about this shortly.

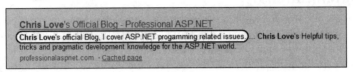

Chris Love's Official Blog - Professional ASP.NET
Chris Love's official Blog, I cover ASP.NET progamming related issues. ... Chris Love's Helpful tips, tricks and pragmatic development knowledge for the ASP.NET world.
professionalaspnet.com · Cached page

Figure 3-23

Viewing the source of my blog's home page, you can see the Description META tag and see where Live.com gathered the initial content for the description in the search result.

```
<meta name="description" content="Chris Love's official Blog,
I cover ASP.NET programming related issues." />
```

The Keyword META Tag

Like the Description META tag, the Keyword META tag is not leveraged by search engines to determine placement and indexing, but it should still be used to add a list of relevant phrases for each page. The reason this is no longer used by search engines is that it was spammed by many in the mid-1990s to gain higher rankings. Yet it should not be disregarded, as it can always add some value to the page.

```
<meta name="keywords" content="ASP.NET, VB.NET, C#, Silverlight,
SQL Server, SharePoint" />
```

Add a Robots META Tag

One of the most direct ways to talk to a search engine spider is through the robots.txt file, but each page can also contain a Robots META tag to further dictate how a search engine can index a page. The Robots META tag can contain a collection of the following directives: index, noindex, follow, nofollow. The index directives tell the search engine if it should index the content or not. The following directive tells tell it not to follow the links on the page.

```
<META NAME="robots" CONTENT="index, nofollow"/>
```

You can only use one directive per action, either follow or nofollow, for example. You can also use all and none to tell the spider to index and follow or noindex and nofollow, respectively.

Use Header Tags and Modifiers

Using Header Tags, such as <H1>, and modifier tags tell search engines to use the enclosed text with higher relevance when ranking the page.

Header tags, such as <H1>, <H2>, and the like, are used to indicate important phrases; typically, they help segment or outline a document's content, too. They add value to the visitor because they can serve as a section title; for example, Use Header Tags and Modifiers would be an `<H4>`, if this entire chapter were a page. `<H1>` carries the highest significance, and the significance progressively decreases at each level.

```
<H1>Planning an Architecture</H1>
<H2>Search Engine Optimization Techniques</H2>
<H3>Page Level Optimizations</H3>
<H4>Use Header Tags</H4>
```

Search engines are looking text that is emphasized, and header tags do just that. Often you will want to wrap keyword phrases in header tags to help set them apart. This also forces you to write more targeted content.

You do not have to rely upon header tags to provide emphasis; text modifiers also add value to phrases. A modifier is simply a tag that should make a phrase stand out from the surrounding text, `<Strong>`, `<B>`, `<I>` and `<EM>` are all modifiers. So, as you compose the text of a page and design the layout, consider how these tags will be used to draw attention to the text they contain. The use of header and modifier tags helps to identify the content on the page a search engine should emphasize when ranking it.

Use Valid HTML

Valid HTML is important to help search engines spider and parse the content of a web page. Invalid HTML can hinder a spider from properly reading the content. If a spider tries to parse an improperly formatted HTML element, this could cause the spider to stop processing the page or cause it to improperly read the page. It can also cause the page to not render properly in some browsers, resulting in users becoming frustrated with the site.

The World Wide Web Consortium (W3C) creates the standards for HTML and Cascading Style Sheets. They also provide a handy online tool to validate the markup of a page, http://validator.w3.org. By using this tool, you can quickly identify potential problems that might keep spiders or visitors from reading a page.

Company Information and Privacy Pages

While it is not proven the common thinking among the search engine optimization community is that including a Company Information or About Us and a Privacy Policy pages adds to a site's credibility. Search engines are known to look for common features of a site to distinguish a valid site from a spam site. Simply adding these two pages to the site can add value for overall search engine placement, not to mention customer satisfaction.

> *The Direct Marketing Association has an online tool to help create a privacy policy for your website. You can access its online generation tool at* www.dmaresponsibility.org/PPG.

Navigation

Creating a sound navigation system for a data-driven website is a fundamental component of a successful website. This includes one that allows the URLs to be naturally understood by both users and search engines alike. The ASP.NET `SiteMapProvider` can also be dynamically driven from the database. There should also be an available `SiteMap.org` file for spiders to know the most current version of the site's structure.

URL Rewriting

Building web applications has long meant leveraging the QueryString to pass parameters to the application. For example, to retrieve an article in theBeerHouse application an ArticleId parameter would be added to the URL, ShowArticle.aspx?articleid=28. While this is not terribly bad, it can quickly become a long series of parameters. There is a great deal of competition in the market to garner search engine visibility for targeted keywords. It is equally important to reduce potential attack surfaces for potential hackers to hit. URL Rewriting can help in both of these cases.

Creating friendly URLs is pretty easy in ASP.NET, but it does require the use of a custom httpModule. An httpModule is registered with the ASP.NET application and allows developers to create an event handler or a series of event handlers to hook into the ASP.NET life cycle.

In short, httpModules are classes that implement the IhttpModule interface, which requires methods to handle the Init and Dispose methods. Each module must also be registered in the site's web.config file, in the httpModules section. Once the module is registered the ASP.NET engine will call the Init method when the application first starts. The Dispose method is called when the application is closed.

```
<httpModules>
<add name="URLRewrite" type="URLRewrite"/>
<add name="ScriptModule" type="System.Web.Handlers.ScriptModule,
System.Web.Extensions, Version=3.5.0.0, Culture=neutral,
PublicKeyToken=31BF3856AD364E35"/>
</httpModules>
```

In the Init method, you are not limited to what you can do, but generally event handlers are wired to specific life cycle events. For the case of URL rewriting, it is advisable to intercept the request in the AuthorizeRequest event.

```
Public Sub Init(ByVal context As System.Web.HttpApplication)
Implements System.Web.IHttpModule.Init
AddHandler context.AuthorizeRequest, AddressOf AuthorizeRequest
End Sub
```

This provides the capability to intercept the request, check to see if the requested URL should be rewritten, rewrite the requested URL using the RewritePath method if necessary, and proceed with the request. For theBeerHouse application, URL rewriting leverages the list of entities in the site's site map, stored in the database. Each module that creates a potential URL in the site must be responsible for storing its URLs in the SiteMap database table.

Custom SiteMap

Maintaining an up-to-date map of theBeerHouse application is important for two reasons: breadcrumbs and search engines. Breadcrumbs are a way to provide the user a sense of where they are and how to easily navigate back up the tree. Letting search engines know what the site currently consists of is important so that your content gets indexed. It is also helpful to leverage a custom site map so that URL rewriting can be done easily.

To maintain a central site map for the site, it should be stored in a table in the site's database, Figure 3-24. The table needs to store the URL, the actual URL on the site, a title, description, keywords, a reference to a parent URL, what type of node it is, and a value to indicate its order with sibling nodes.

Of course, the table should have a `SiteMapId` primary key and fields that indicate if the node is active, and when it was added or updated and by whom.

SiteMap
- SiteMapId
- URL
- RealURL
- Title
- Keywords
- Description
- Roles
- Parent
- URLId
- URLType
- NodeType
- SortOrder
- Active
- DateAdded
- AddedBy
- DateUpdated
- UpdatedBy

Figure 3-24

There are two URL-related fields: the URL and the `RealURL`. The URL field holds the path from the site's domain that will be publically available. In other words, this will be the URL used by visitors to access the page but not necessarily the URL to the item in the site. For example, articles will be accessed by requesting a `URLEncoded` version of the article's title suffixed with the `.aspx` extension. This URL is mapped to the traditional `ShowArticle.aspx?ArticleId=X url` that was used in the previous edition of theBeerHouse application.

Custom SiteMapProvider

In the previous edition of this book, a `SiteMap.xml` file was used to manage the nodes in the `SiteMapProvider`. This is fine when a site is small and does not change very often. But theBeerHouse site is a dynamic application that can change quite often. A physical file needs to be maintained on each change in the site. Since changes to the site are made in the database this can be leveraged for a custom `SiteMapProvider` based on the database.

Jeff Prosise wrote a few articles for *MSDN* magazine in 2006 (http://msdn.microsoft.com/en-us/magazine/cc163657.aspx) that walked through creating a SQL `SiteMapProvider`, which serves as a good starting point to be creating a custom provider for theBeerHouse application. A good custom `SiteMapProvider` will quickly build a site map for the site, based on the page hierarchy stored in the database, and honor any security requirements.

The custom provider inherits from `StaticSiteMapProvider`, an abstraction of the `SiteMapProvider` class. A custom `SiteMap` provider must be registered in the `web.config`'s `system.web` section.

```
<siteMap defaultProvider="TBHSiteMapProvider" enabled="true">
<providers>
<add name="TBHSiteMapProvider" type="TheBeerHouse.TBHSiteMapProvider"
  securityTrimmingEnabled="true"/>
```

```
    </providers>
  </siteMap>
```

There can be more than one provider registered in the site. The `SiteMapPath` control and the `SiteMapDataSource` control can both designate which provider to use if more than one is registered.

SiteMaps.org File

A few years ago Google created a standard way for site owners to let the search engine's spiders know what content comprises the site. Later, other search engines, such as Yahoo.com and Live.com, adopted the standard, which is known as a `SiteMap.org` site map file. It is an XML document containing information about the URL. The details of the site map format are available at `SiteMap.org`.

```
<?xml version="1.0" encoding="UTF-8"?>
<urlset xmlns="http://www.sitemaps.org/schemas/sitemap/0.9">
   <url>
      <loc>http://www.example.com/</loc>
      <lastmod>2005-01-01</lastmod>
      <changefreq>monthly</changefreq>
      <priority>0.8</priority>
   </url>
</urlset>
```

The search engine spiders use this file to know what to index. It also tells them when the content was last updated, how often it changes, and a priority. Knowing if a URL has changed since a spider last visited it allows the search engine to avoid spidering the resource if it has not changed. This is a big bandwidth and resource saver for sites because the spider should not request resources that have not changed since it last visited.

Custom SiteMap File httpHandler

When the search engine spider comes to your site, it will begin its quest by asking for the latest `sitemap.xml` file. You can, and typically will, register another site map file name with each search engine, if you want; in that case, it will ask for that file. No matter, the spider tries to consume the up-to-date site map file. Since the website is a living application that changes its composure at any time, maintaining a static file is not feasible. Because the site map information is stored in the database, it can be retrieved as needed to compose the site map file.

A custom `httpHandler` is an ideal way to compose the required XML from the information stored in the database. A custom `httpHandler` is one of the core elements used to compose content in ASP.NET. In fact the `Page` class is actually an `httpHandler`. A custom `httpHandler` is a class that implements the `IHttpHandler` interface and can either register as the handler for specific requests, or a generic handler, the `.ashx` file, that is requested directly from the client.

```
Imports System.Linq
Imports System.Xml.Linq
Imports System.Web
Imports TheBeerHouse.BLL
Imports <xmlns:xsi="http://www.w3.org/2001/XMLSchema-instance">

Public Class SiteMapsHandler
    Implements IHttpHandler
```

The `IHttpHandler` interface requires two methods are implemented by the class: `IsReusable` and `ProcessRequest`. The `IsReusable` property indicates to the ASP.NET engine if the `httpHandler` can be used simultaneously by more than one request. In other words, is there anything in the handler that has to be mutually exclusive with other requests. For requests that produce static output, this can be true; with dynamic requests, this can vary depending on what the handler is performing.

The `ProcessRequest` method is invoked by the ASP.NET engine to begin actual processing and composition of the content sent to the client. A reference to the current context is passed to `ProcessRequest`; this gives the handler access to the `Request` and `Response` objects.

```
Public Sub ProcessRequest(ByVal context As System.Web.HttpContext)
Implements System.Web.IHttpHandler.ProcessRequest

        BaseContext = context
        CreateSiteMap()

        Response.Flush()
        Response.End()

End Sub
```

The site map handler composes the site map content in a method called `CreateSiteMap`. Since the site map format is XML, the `Response.ContentType` or MIME type is set to "application/xml". Before composing the XML content, a request is made to the database to retrieve the site map nodes by creating a `SiteMapRepository` and retrieving a `List(of SiteMapInfo)` entities.

In VB.NET the map is composed using XML Literals; in C#, it requires a little more complex coding using the LINQ `XDocument` classes.

Using XML Literals is a very intuitive way to compose and parse XML content in .NET that were introduced with VB 9 (.NET 3.5). With XML Literals XML can be processed in a declarative manner in a VB class member. Instead of having to deal with unnatural classes, XML is managed in its natural format, making it much easier to see XML structure in the code.

> **Site map files can contain no more than 50,000 URLs and can be no more than 10MB in size, which can be an issue for large sites. HTTP compression (GZIP or Deflate) can be used to reduce the size of the files as they are transported to the spider. The SiteMap.org protocol allows for multiple site map files to be specified by providing a site map index file that lists all the site map files. There can be no more than 1000 index files, and the index file itself cannot exceed 10MB in size.**

```
<?xml version="1.0" encoding="UTF-8"?>
<sitemapindex xmlns="http://www.sitemaps.org/schemas/
sitemap/0.9">
    <sitemap>
        <loc>http://www.example.com/sitemap1.xml.gz</loc>
        <lastmod>2004-10-01T18:23:17+00:00</lastmod>
    </sitemap>
    <sitemap>
        <loc>http://www.example.com/sitemap2.xml.gz</loc>
        <lastmod>2005-01-01</lastmod>
    </sitemap>
</sitemapindex>
```

To create a site map using XML Literals, it is ideal to paste the required components of a valid site map into the code itself, then manipulate the code snippet to produce the desired dynamic output. The XML content is set to an XDocument object, xSiteMap. The site map XML is composed by integrating a LINQ query using declarative syntax much as you would do in ASP.NET to integrate server-side coding using the <% %> syntax. The LINQ query is a select statement executed on the list of SiteMapInfo entities, returning a list of <url> elements that compose the resulting site map file.

VB.NET

```
Private Sub CreateSiteMap()

    Response.ContentType = "application/xml"

    Dim lsiteMapNodes As List(Of SiteMapInfo)

    Using siteMaprpt As New SiteMapRepository
        lsiteMapNodes = siteMaprpt.GetSiteMapNodes
    End Using

    Dim xSiteMap As XDocument = <?xml version="1.0" encoding="UTF-8"?>
    <urlset xmlns="http://www.sitemaps.org/schemas/sitemap/0.9">
            <%= From lSiteMapNode In lsiteMapNodes.AsEnumerable _
        Select <url>
            <loc><%= lSiteMapNode.URL %></loc>
            <lastmod><%= lSiteMapNode.DateUpdated %></lastmod>
            <changefreq>weekly</changefreq>
            <priority>0.8</priority>
            </url> %>
    </urlset>

    Response.Write(xSiteMap.ToString)

End Sub
```

Finally, the xSiteMap content is written to the Response content by calling the ToString method.

Composing the content in C# is not quite as simple because it requires more formal use of the LINQ to XML classes. I call the special classes in the LINQ namespace related to XML "X classes" because they are all prefixed with X followed by the object type: XDocument, XElement, and XAttribute, for example.

C#

```
private void CreateRSSFeed()
{
    TheBeerHouseSection Settings = Helpers.Settings;
    this.Response.ContentType = "application/xml";
    using (ArticleRepository lArticlectx = new ArticleRepository())
    {
        List<Article> lArticles = lArticlectx.GetActiveArticles();
```

```
                var xRss = new XDocument(new XDeclaration("1.0", "utf-8", "yes"),
        new XElement("rss",
                        new XAttribute("version", "2.0"),
                          new XElement("channel",
                          new XElement("title",
"The Beer House Articles"),
                          new XElement("link", "http://www.TheBeerHouseBook.com/"),
                          new XElement("description",
                              "RSS Feed containing The Beer House News Articles."),

                from item in lArticles
                    select
                        new XElement("item",
                            new XElement("title", item.Title),
                            new XElement("description", item.Abstract),
                            new XElement("link",
Helpers.SEOFriendlyURL(Settings.Articles.URLIndicator +
"/" + item.Title, ".aspx")),
                            new XElement("pubDate",
item.ReleaseDate.ToString())
                        )
                    )
                )
            );
            this.Response.Write(xRss.ToString());
        }
        this.Response.Flush();
        this.Response.End();
    }
```

Once the content of the document is composed, the request is wrapped up by flushing the content to the browser and ending the response.

Before this handler can respond to the request for sitemap.xml, it has to be registered in the httpHandlers section of the web.config file. All the request for the sitemap.xml file are GET requests, so the verb should reflect that and the path is set to "sitemap.xml", limiting the scope of this handler to only that resource name.

```
<add verb="GET" path="sitemap.xml" validate="false"
type="TheBeerHouse.SiteMapsHandler, TBHBLL, Version=3.5.0.1,
Culture=neutral, PublicKeyToken=null"/>
```

Once the handler is registered the only thing left is to verify that the sitemap.xml file is properly composed and served. Retrieving the file in a browser should produce the desired content as shown in Figure 3-25.

Because the site map handler composes the XML from the database, each time a spider requests the document you can be assured that the content is up to date, ensuring that your site is properly indexed by each search engine.

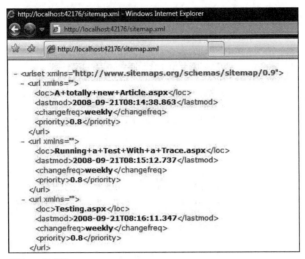

Figure 3-25

Solution

The "Solution" section of this chapter is thinner than those found in most of the other chapters. In fact, in this chapter you've been presented with some new controls and features that won't be part of a common custom framework but will be used in most of the upcoming chapters as parts of other classes to be developed. The discussion about the DAL and BLL design will be extremely useful for the next chapters, because they follow the design outlined here. Understand that ASP.NET 3.5 already has a number of built-in common services to handle many of your general framework-level needs, which allows you to focus more of your time and efforts on your specific business problems. The rest of the chapter shows the code for the small base classes for the DAL and the BLL, the custom configuration section, and the code for raising and handling web events.

TheBeerHouse Configuration Section

Following is the code for the classes that map the `<theBeerHouse>` custom configuration section, and the inner `<contactForm>` element, whose meaning and properties were already described earlier:

```
Public Class TheBeerHouseSection
    Inherits ConfigurationSection

    <ConfigurationProperty("defaultConnectionStringName",
DefaultValue:="LocalSqlServer")> _
    Public Property DefaultConnectionStringName() As String
        Get
            Return CStr(Me("defaultConnectionStringName"))
        End Get
        Set(ByVal value As String)
            Me("DefaultConnectionStringName") = value
        End Set
```

```
      End Property

      <ConfigurationProperty("devSiteName", DefaultValue:="BeerHouse35")> _
      Public Property devSiteName() As String
          Get
              Return CStr(Me("devSiteName"))
          End Get
          Set(ByVal value As String)
              Me("devSiteName") = value
          End Set
      End Property

      <ConfigurationProperty("siteDomainName", DefaultValue:="localhost")> _
      Public Property SiteDomainName() As String
          Get
              Return CStr(Me("siteDomainName"))
          End Get
          Set(ByVal value As String)
              Me("siteDomainName") = value
          End Set
      End Property

      <ConfigurationProperty("defaultCacheDuration", DefaultValue:="600")> _
      Public Property DefaultCacheDuration() As Integer
          Get
              Return CInt(Me("defaultCacheDuration"))
          End Get
          Set(ByVal value As Integer)
              Me("defaultCacheDuration") = value
          End Set
      End Property

      <ConfigurationProperty("contactForm", IsRequired:=True)> _
      Public ReadOnly Property ContactForm() As ContactFormElement
          Get
              Return CType(Me("contactForm"), ContactFormElement)
          End Get
      End Property
```

The `TheBeerHouseSection` class must be mapped to the `<theBeerHouse>` section through a new element under the `web.config` file's `<configSections>` section. Each module has its own custom configuration section that resides within `theBeerHouse` element. Once you've defined the mapping, you can write the custom settings as follows:

```
<theBeerHouse defaultConnectionStringName="TheBeerHouseEntities"
siteDomainName="[Add Your Base URL Here]">
<contactForm mailTo="thebeerhouse@wrox.com"/>
<articles pageSize="10" twitterUrserName="[Username]"
twitterPassword="[Password]" enableTwitter="true"
 akismetKey="12abcdf23456" enableAkismet="True"/>
<polls archiveIsPublic="true" votingLockByIP="false"/>
<newsletters fromEmail="thebeerhouse@wrox.com"
fromDisplayName="TheBeerHouse" archiveIsPublic="true"
hideFromArchiveInterval="10"/>
```

```
<forums threadsPageSize="8" hotThreadPosts="10"
bronzePosterPosts="10" silverPosterPosts="20"
goldPosterPosts="50"/>
<store sandboxMode="true" businessEmail="thebeerhouse@wrox.com"/>
</theBeerHouse>
```

To make the settings easily readable from any part of the site, you will add a public field of type
`TheBeerHouseSection` in the `Globals` class and set it as follows:

```
Public NotInheritable Class Globals
    Public Shared ReadOnly Settings As TheBeerHouseSection = _
        CType(WebConfigurationManager.GetSection("theBeerHouse"),
TheBeerHouseSection)

End Class
```

The `WebConfigurationManager` class is used to access configuration content, including custom sections
such as `TheBeerHouseSection`. As you can notice in the preceding code, `TheBeerHouseSection` is
retrieved and the values are cast into a `TheBeerHouseSection` object.

To see how these settings are actually used, let's create the `Contact.aspx` page, which enables users to
send mail to the site administrator by filling in a form online. Figure 3-26 shows the page at runtime.

Figure 3-26

The following code is the markup for the page, with the layout structure removed to make it easier to follow:

```
Your name: <asp:TextBox runat="server" ID="txtName" Width="100%" />
<asp:RequiredFieldValidator runat="server" Display="dynamic" ID="valRequireName"
    SetFocusOnError="true" ControlToValidate="txtName"
    ErrorMessage="Your name is required">*</asp:RequiredFieldValidator>

Your e-mail: <asp:TextBox runat="server" ID="txtEmail" Width="100%" />
<asp:RequiredFieldValidator runat="server" Display="dynamic" ID="valRequireEmail"
    SetFocusOnError="true" ControlToValidate="txtEmail"
    ErrorMessage="Your e-mail address is required">*</asp:RequiredFieldValidator>
<asp:RegularExpressionValidator runat="server" Display="dynamic"
    ID="valEmailPattern"  SetFocusOnError="true" ControlToValidate="txtEmail"
    ValidationExpression="\w+([-+.']\w+)*@\w+([-.]\w+)*\.\w+([-.]\w+)*"
    ErrorMessage="The e-mail address you specified is not well-formed">*
</asp:RegularExpressionValidator>

Subject: <asp:TextBox runat="server" ID="txtSubject" Width="100%" />
<asp:RequiredFieldValidator runat="server" Display="dynamic" ID="valRequireSubject"
    SetFocusOnError="true" ControlToValidate="txtSubject"
    ErrorMessage="The subject is required">*</asp:RequiredFieldValidator>

Body: <asp:TextBox runat="server" ID="txtBody" Width="100%"
    TextMode="MultiLine" Rows="8" />
<asp:RequiredFieldValidator runat="server" Display="dynamic" ID="valRequireBody"
    SetFocusOnError="true" ControlToValidate="txtBody"
    ErrorMessage="The body is required">*</asp:RequiredFieldValidator>

<asp:Label runat="server" ID="lblFeedbackOK" Visible="false"
    Text="Your message has been successfully sent." SkinID="FeedbackOK" />
<asp:Label runat="server" ID="lblFeedbackKO" Visible="false"
    Text="Sorry, there was a problem sending your message." SkinID="FeedbackKO" />

<asp:Button runat="server" ID="txtSubmit" Text="Send" OnClick="txtSubmit_Click" />
<asp:ValidationSummary runat="server" ID="valSummary"
    ShowSummary="false" ShowMessageBox="true" />
```

When the Send button is clicked, a new `System.Net.Mail.MailMessage` is created, with its To, CC, and Subject properties set from the values read from the site's configuration; the From and Body are set with the user input values, and then the mail is sent:

```
Protected Sub txtSubmit_Click(ByVal sender As Object,
ByVal e As System.EventArgs) Handles txtSubmit.Click
        Try
            ' send the mail
            Dim msg As New MailMessage
            msg.IsBodyHtml = False
            msg.From = New MailAddress(txtEmail.Text, txtName.Text)
            msg.To.Add(New MailAddress(Globals.Settings.ContactForm.MailTo))
            If Not String.IsNullOrEmpty(
Globals.Settings.ContactForm.MailCC) Then
                msg.CC.Add(New MailAddress(
```

```
Globals.Settings.ContactForm.MailCC))
                End If
            msg.Subject = String.Format( _
                Globals.Settings.ContactForm.MailSubject, txtSubject.Text)
            msg.Body = txtBody.Text
            Dim client As New SmtpClient()
            client.Send(msg)
            ' show a confirmation message, and reset the fields
            lblFeedbackOK.Visible = True
            lblFeedbackKO.Visible = False
            txtName.Text = String.Empty
            txtEmail.Text = String.Empty
            txtSubject.Text = String.Empty
            txtBody.Text = String.Empty
            Exit Try

        Catch ex As Exception
            lblFeedbackOK.Visible = False
            lblFeedbackKO.Visible = True
        End Try
    End Sub
```

The SMTP settings used to send the message must be defined in the web.config file, in the
<mailSettings> section, as shown here:

```
<configuration xmlns="http://schemas.microsoft.com/.NetConfiguration/v2.0">
    <system.web> <!-- some settings here...--> </system.web>
    <system.net>
        <mailSettings>
            <smtp deliveryMethod=" Network " from="thebeerhouse@wrox.com">
                <network defaultCredentials="true" host="(localhost)" port="25" />
            </smtp>
        </mailSettings>
    </system.net> </configuration>
```

Implementing Good Search Engine Optimization Techniques

Applying good search engine optimization techniques is not always the easiest thing to do from a
programming perspective, but creating a good SEO-friendly architecture can make this very easy to
accomplish.

The URLRewrite httpModule

In the "Design" section of this chapter, I talked about various search engine optimization techniques
that should be employed to help the site earn better search engine placement. Two of those techniques
involved search-engine-friendly URLs and 301 redirecting requests going to one version of the domain
instead of both the www alias and the actual domain name. Both of these tasks can be handled in a
custom httpModule called URLRewrite.

If you are not familiar with httpModules, they are part of the foundation of the ASP.NET model and
provide a means to hook into the ASP.NET pipeline to intercept requests and modify them according to

your business rules. In this case, the module will intercept the request, analyze the requested URL, and reroute it as necessary.

A custom `httpModule` implements the `IHttpModule` interface, which consist of two methods: `Init` and `Dispose`. The `Dispose` method is the same as I discussed earlier; it is called when the module is being destroyed and allows you to release any resources that may be opened by the module. In the case of the `URLRewrite` module, there are no ongoing resources in use, so this method will be empty.

```
Imports Microsoft.VisualBasic
Imports System.IO
Imports TheBeerHouse.BLL
Imports System.Web
Imports System.Text.RegularExpressions

Public Class URLRewrite
    Implements IHttpModule
```

There is one variable declared in the module, wwwRegex, a regular expression used to match the requested URL to see if "www." has been used. If you are not familiar with regular expressions or feel a little intimidated with the syntax, I encourage you to investigate them further. They are a great way to parse text efficiently. Another nice thing is they are essentially language agnostic, meaning that they are used with just about every platform and programming language. There are a few subtle differences across languages, but they seem to be minor.

This regular expression looks for a URL string that contains "http://www." or "https://www.", which is important because this is a way to catch SSL and non-SSL requests. The expression looks almost exactly like the pattern I am trying to catch. The first deviation is the ? after `https`. This tells the regular expression parser to look for 0 or 1 of the previous characters. The next deviation is \., which is simply an escape character "\" to tell the parse to look for a period.

```
Private Shared wwwRegex As New Regex("https?://www\.",
RegexOptions.IgnoreCase Or RegexOptions.Compiled)
```

The next parameter combination is the regular expression options for the `Regex` object. In this case, `Regex` is instructed to ignore the case of the characters it is matching and to compile the expression. Compiling the expression means that it will be part of the assembly and perform slightly faster. The `RegexOptions Enum` can be ORed together, as shown in the example. There are many other options available for regular expressions that can be used to control how an expression performs its matching.

The `Init` method is called by the ASP.NET engine the first time a request is made to the website. This method is called only once, and it is typically used to register event handlers. In the `URLRewrite` module, I am registering a single event handler to intercept the `BeginRequest` event. There are over 20 events in the ASP.NET page life cycle. I talk about these and many more concepts related to `httpModules` in a WROX BLOX, *Leveraging httpModules for Better ASP.NET Applications*, which is available from the WROX website.

```
Public Sub Dispose() Implements System.Web.IHttpModule.Dispose

End Sub

Public Sub Init(ByVal context As System.Web.HttpApplication)
```

```
Implements System.Web.IHttpModule.Init
        AddHandler context.BeginRequest, AddressOf BeginRequest
    End Sub
```

All the events in the ASP.NET page life cycle have the standard Microsoft event signature: an Object named sender and an EventArgs object named e. The sender object is the application, an HttpApplication object. The BeginRequest method uses this parameter by casting the sender to an HttpApplication object named app. I then create local variables for the Request and Response objects as well to save some coding.

Following the declaration of those variables the method declares a series of variables; sRequestedURL, bWWW, and redirectURL. The sRequestedURL variable holds the URL requested by the user, converted to lower case. This is important because all string comparisons are case sensitive. The bWWW Boolean variable is a flag that indicates if there was a match to the regular expression to catch requests made using the www. prefix. The redirectURL variable is initially set to an empty string and will ultimately be set to the real URL if the method needs to perform a 301 redirect.

```
Private Sub BeginRequest(ByVal sender As Object, ByVal e As EventArgs)
        Dim app As HttpApplication = CType(sender, HttpApplication)
        Dim Request As HttpRequest = app.Request
        Dim Response As HttpResponse = app.Response

        Dim sRequestedURL As String = Request.Url.ToString.ToLower

        Dim bWWW As Boolean = wwwRegex.IsMatch(sRequestedURL)
        Dim redirectURL As String = String.Empty
        If bWWW Then
            redirectURL = wwwRegex.Replace(sRequestedURL,
String.Format("{0}://", Request.Url.Scheme))
        End If

        Rewrite(app)

    End Sub
```

If there was a match to the regular expression, then the RegEx object is used to perform a quick replace to remove the www. from the URL and set the updated version to redirectURL. The next section of code checks to see if the redirectURL contains any text, and if so, then proceeds to do a 301 redirect. Before the redirect, it does another check to see if the URL ends with "default.aspx," which is important because you need to minimize the use of default.aspx as the home page. Again, this is to avoid duplicate content penalties.

Here is an interesting situation that ASP.NET poses: this will only check for the use of "default .aspx" if the user requested "http://www.thebeerhouse.com/default.aspx" and not "http:// thebeerhouse.com/default.aspx". The reason goes to the root of ASP.NET and IIS. The ASP.NET engine is an ISAPI filter that is registered with IIS to process request for specified file name extensions, such as .aspx. You can map any extension you like to be processed by the ASP. NET engine; just realize there will be a slight bit of added overhead for this choice. In fact, you could do a wildcard mapping, which means you tell IIS to use the ASP.NET engine to process all requests to the site. If you wanted to use URLs that did not have a file extension you would have to do this for example. That is also the way you can get around the "default.aspx" issue.

> **If you make a request to the core domain without specifying a file, IIS will, by default, change the URL and append the default file to the end of the URL and process it accordingly. In this case,** `default.aspx` **has been configured to be the default page for the site and, because it has the** `.aspx` **extension, it will be processed by the ASP.NET engine. If the request did not append the default file name to the requested URL, it would not be processed by ASP.NET, which is not what we want.**

So, why did I check for this in the `BeginRequest` method? In this case, the 301 redirect is being sent back to the client without `default.aspx` appended, which means the search engine will only see the actual domain as the URL. The file name is appended only on the server. If this were checked, say in the regular expression, it would cause an infinite loop because the module would be continually sending 301 redirect notices to the browser or spider because each request would keep having `default` `.aspx` appended to the end of the URL. Figure 3-27 shows an example of the expected result.

Figure 3-27

This still leaves us with a potential hole in the module to allow duplicate content to be indexed by the search engine. Unfortunately, without mapping every request through the ASP.NET engine, it leaves to the URL the responsibility to not use any links to the home page of the site with `default.aspx` file appended. This takes discipline, and there is no good answer as to how to avoid this without investing in a third-party ISAPI filter.

The last piece of the duplicate content checking code actually performs the 301 redirect. The `RedirectLocation` of the `Response` object is set to the `redirectURL` variable. The `StatusCode` property of the `Response` is set to 301. The `StatusCode` refers to the HTTP Status code returned to the client (a browser or search engine spider) that lets the client know how the request was processed. For example, a normal request returns a status of 200; one where the user is not authenticated to access the resource returns a 403 status code. This tells the client what to do next. In the case of a 301 status code, the client knows it should look for the `Location` header to see where the URL has been permanently moved to. Search engines see this and know not to index the first URL and instead index the new URL.

Finally, if the requested URL does not need to be redirected from the www version, it still needs to be checked against the site map. The `Rewrite` method accepts the `requestedPath` and a reference to the `HttpApplication` object.

```
    Private Sub Rewrite(ByVal app As HttpApplication)

        Using lSiteMapRst As New SiteMapRepository()
            Dim lSiteMap As SiteMapInfo =
lSiteMapRst.GetSiteMapInfoByURL(
Path.GetFileName(app.Context.Request.RawUrl))

            If Not IsNothing(lSiteMap) Then
                HttpContext.Current.RewritePath(lSiteMap.RealURL)
            End If
        End Using

    End Sub
```

The logic in the `Rewrite` method is wrapped in a using statement, where a new `SiteMapRepository` object is created. In the using statement the `GetSiteMapInfoByURL` method is called, passing the file name of the requested resource. The reason the file name is used instead of the domain portion of the URL is that should be the same value for every request.

The `GetSiteMapInfoByURL` method makes a simple LINQ query over the `SiteMap` and returns either the first match to the requested URL or nothing. The return statement wraps the LINQ query in `()` and called the `FirstOrDefault` method, which returns the first object matching returned from the data source or null if there are no matches in the database. If just `First` was used and there were no matches, it would throw an exception; `FirstOrDefault` manages that scenario.

```
Public Function GetSiteMapInfoByURL(ByVal URL As String) As SiteMapInfo

    Return (From lai In SiteMapctx.SiteMaps _
        Where lai.URL = URL).FirstOrDefault

End Function
```

The next line of code checks to see if a match was found; if there was, then the requested path is rewritten by calling the `RewritePath` method. This method does not do a 301 redirect; it actually transforms the requested URL to the desired URL and lets the ASP.NET engine continue processing the request. In essence, it tricks the engine into thinking the client requested a URL they didn't. The only trick you need to have is a way to transform the requested URL to the URL you want ASP.NET to process. There are several ways to manage this; I have found that, for larger sites, it is easier to do this with a database table maintaining various types of information that makes up a page and using that as the ultimate transform. Regular expressions are also very popular.

> Microsoft has also recently released the ASP.NET MVC framework, which is featured in the MVC version of the Beer House (*ASP.NET MVC Problem–Design–Solution*). It uses a routing subsystem that has been made available to all forms of ASP.NET to leverage. You can find more information about using the Route subsystem at `http://msdn.microsoft.com/en-us/library/system.web.routing.aspx`.

Page-Level Optimizations

Implementing good search engine practices not only helps the site garner better search engine placement but also makes the overall user experience on the site better. In the base page class, there are several properties to manage the page description, keywords, and other META tag members.

In ASP.NET, there are two basic types of controls: web and HTML. While the web controls garner the vast majority of attention, the HTML controls are very useful. For search engine optimization purposes, the `HtmlMeta` control renders a META tag used for description, keywords, and other tags. The `BasePage` class contains a method that creates an `HtmlMeta` control and adds it to the page's header, composing it with the appropriate tag name and value. It takes care to work with both a master page and a page without a master template.

```
Public Sub CreateMetaControl(ByVal sTagName As String, ByVal TagValue As String)

        Dim meta As New HtmlMeta()
        meta.Name = sTagName
```

```
        meta.Content = TagValue

    If Not IsNothing(Master) AndAlso Not IsNothing(Master.Page) Then
        Master.Page.Header.Controls.Add(meta)
    Else
        Page.Header.Controls.Add(meta)
    End If

End Sub
```

Similarly, retrieving the value of a META tag is just as important. This is done by interrogating the page for the metatag control. This is done by using the FindControl method and returning the content of the control.

```
Public Function GetMetaValue(ByVal sTagName As String) As String

    Dim meta As HtmlMeta

    If Not IsNothing(Master) Then
        meta = Master.Page.Header.FindControl(sTagName)
    Else
        meta = Page.Header.FindControl(sTagName)
    End If

    If Not IsNothing(meta) Then
        Return meta.Content
    End If

    Return String.Empty

End Function
```

The BasePage class contains targeted properties to get and set the values of these metatags. The setter creates the META tag by calling the CreateMetaControl method. It gets the value by calling the GetMetaValue method.

```
Protected Property PageKeyWords() As String
    Get
        Return GetMetaValue("KEYWORDS")
    End Get
    Set(ByVal value As String)
        CreateMetaControl("KEYWORDS", value)
    End Set
End Property
```

Configuring ELMAH

The nice thing about configuring ELMAH is that it takes very little effort. First, you download the library, http://code.google.com/p/elmah. You can download a setup project or the source code and compile your own copy.

Once the ELMAH library has been compiled or installed on the development machine, a reference to ELMAH needs to be added to theBeerHouse site, Figure 3-28. Right-click on the root node of the site, and select Add Reference. Then find the ELMAH library either in the machine's GAC or browse for the DLL.

Figure 3-28

The next step is to add a couple of entries in the site's web.config file. First, add a sectionGroup element to the configSection of the web.config file. You can grab this and copy it from the supplied sample site that comes with the ELMAH library.

```
<sectionGroup name="elmah">
<!-- NOTE! If you are using ASP.NET 1.x then remove the
                requirePermission="false" attribute from the section
                elements below as those are only needed for
                partially trusted applications in ASP.NET 2.0 -->
<section name="security" requirePermission="false"
type="Elmah.SecuritySectionHandler, Elmah"/>
<section name="errorLog" requirePermission="false"
type="Elmah.ErrorLogSectionHandler, Elmah"/>
<section name="errorMail" requirePermission="false"
type="Elmah.ErrorMailSectionHandler, Elmah"/>
<section name="errorFilter" requirePermission="false"
  type="Elmah.ErrorFilterSectionHandler, Elmah"/>
</sectionGroup>
```

Once the ELMAH sectionGroup has been added to the configuration, the actual ELMAH section can be added to the file. The ELMAH section contains several child elements that allow configuration of the various pieces of the tool. The first section is security, which has only one attribute, allowRemoteAccess. This can be set to 0 to allow anyone to access the ELMAH reports. If ELMAH is to be protected, the value can be any of the following: true, yes, on, and 1.

```
<elmah>
<security allowRemoteAccess="0"/>
```

```
<errorLog type="Elmah.SqlErrorLog, Elmah" connectionStringName="LocalSqlServer"/>
<errorFilter>
<test>
<equal binding="HttpStatusCode" value="404" valueType="Int32"/>
</test>
</errorFilter>
</elmah>
```

The `errorLog` element, which defines which type of data store the errors are logged. For theBeerHouse site the errors are logged to SQL Server and the same database with the rest of the site's data. Notice that the `connectionStringName` is not set to the same connection string as the Entity Framework's connection string. That's because the Entity Framework has all the metadata built into the string. There are many other potential data stores that can be used with ELMAH, such as an XML or SQLLite file.

The next section is the `errorFilter` element. It holds a series of rules that can be used to limit the errors that are logged. The preceding example is designed to eliminate 404 or page not found errors. This keeps certain errors from being overreported and clogging up the logs.

If you want errors sent to an e-mail address, then the `errorMail` section needs to be properly configured.

```
<errorMail
    from="error@thebeerhouse.com"
    to="info@thebeerhouse.com"
    subject="Exception in the Beer House Site"
    async="true"
    smtpPort="25"
    smtpServer="mail.thebeerhouse.com"/>
```

For ELMAH to actually log errors, the modules must be registered. This is actually a set of modules; notice that the e-mail module is optional. `HttpModules` are registered in the `httpModules` element of the `system.web` section.

```
<add name="ErrorLog" type="Elmah.ErrorLogModule, Elmah"/>
<!--
            Uncomment the entries below if error mail reporting
            and filtering is desired.
    -->
<add name="ErrorMail" type="Elmah.ErrorMailModule, Elmah"/>
<add name="ErrorFilter" type="Elmah.ErrorFilterModule, Elmah"/>
```

The final configuration steps register the ELMAH custom handler to report the errors. Like `http-Modules`, `httpHandlers` are registered in the `httpHandlers` section of the system.web configuration section.

```
<add verb="POST,GET,HEAD" path="elmah.axd"
type="Elmah.ErrorLogPageFactory, Elmah"/>
```

Summary

This chapter provided several guidelines for building a flexible, easily configurable and instrumented site. First, we discussed implementing the Entity Framework for data access. Next, we covered a business logic layer built on the top of the DAL, which exposes the data in an object-oriented way, with the required validation logic, event logging, and caching. Finally, we examined the user interface presentation layer, which takes advantage of the new `ListView`, and `UpdatePanel` controls to quickly generate complex and feature-rich data-enabled UI controls. In the "Solution" section, we created custom configuration sections and implemented the ELMAH framework.

You now have a good foundation to start building the site upon! In the next chapter, you'll discover the ASP.NET's Membership system to manage user's account subscriptions and profiles and will build a complete administration area for managing users, profiles, preferences, roles, and security settings.

4

Membership and User Profiling

The sample website developed in this book contains dynamic content such as news, events, newsletters, polls, forum posts, and more. It can be considered a content-based site, where significant parts of the site can be easily changed or updated by privileged users (this functionality is sometimes called a *content management system*), although it differs from many content-based sites because we've also added an important e-commerce section that enables our investors to earn a healthy return on their investment.

Here's a secret (although not a well-kept one) for any content-based site that you want to be successful: build a vigorous and thriving community of users! If you have a lot of loyal users, you can be sure that the site will increase its user base and, thus, its size, its popularity, and your revenues. You want to encourage users to register for a free account on the site, so you can enable them to customize their view, participate in message forums, and even order merchandise from e-commerce pages. Once they obtain a free account, they will be a member of the site. Membership is a form of empowerment — they will feel special because they are a member, and you want to reward their loyalty by enabling them to customize certain visual aspects, and to remember their settings on their return visits.

To track members, it is necessary to have some sort of identity to describe and distinguish them from other members and, more importantly, from anonymous users who have not logged in. This chapter will explain how to develop user registration functionality and user profiles. The user account will also be used to grant or deny access to special restricted pages of the site. The profile will be used by modules developed later in this book to customize content and give users a public "virtual face," visible to other members and users.

Problem

In reality, a membership system is a requirement for most websites — not just for community and content-based sites. Sites typically have a number of administration pages to which visitors should not have access. The administration section can be a complete application in itself or just a couple of simple pages to allow people to change some settings. However, you always need to identify each user who tries to access those restricted pages and check whether they are authorized to do so.

The process of identifying a user is called *authentication,* and the process of determining what access a user has is called *authorization*. Unfortunately, it's easy to confuse these terms, so it helps to think of the root words: authenticate (who are you?) and authorize (now that I know you, what are you allowed to do?). The authentication and authorization processes are part of the site's membership system, which includes the creation of new user accounts, the management of the user's credentials (including protection mechanisms such as encryption and password recovery in case passwords are lost or forgotten), and roles associated with an account.

For the sample site, the membership system must be complete because it will be used by administrators and editors to access protected areas, and by users who want to have their own identity within the community, post messages to the forums, and be recognized by other members. It must enable users to create their account interactively without administrator intervention and to update their profile information on demand.

Administrators must also be able to see a list of registered users and to control them. For example, if there is a user who regularly posts spam or offending messages to the forum, a good administrator (or forum moderator) will want to temporarily or permanently disable this user's account. Conversely, if a user always behaves well and respects the site's policies, an administrator may decide to promote him or her to the status of moderator, or even editor. In other words, modifying user account settings and their roles should be an easy thing to do, because the administrator may need to do it frequently. Thus, we require an easy-to-use administration section to manage user accounts.

To make it easier to manage security permissions, we'll create roles that are basically a group of users who have special permission in addition to the normal user permissions. For example, the Administrators role will be used to designate certain individuals who will have the capability to manage user accounts and site content.

Although a membership system is necessary for common security-related tasks, other things are needed in order to build an effective community of happy users. The users expect to have some benefits from their registration. For example, they could receive newsletters with useful information (with links back to the website), and they could customize the home page so that it highlights the type of content they are most interested in. Furthermore, their preferred site template could be saved and restored between sessions. All this information makes up what's called a *user profile*. Implementing a system for profiling the user is a good thing not just for the end user but also for the site administrators. Among the information stored in the profile is the user's age, gender, and full address. A savvy administrator could later make use of such data in a variety of ways:

❑　**To customize the user appearance for registered and profiled users:** For example, the news and events modules developed in the next chapter will use the details stored in the user's profile to highlight with different colors the news and events that happen in the user's country, state, or city, to identify the items closest to home. This rather simple feature can improve the user experience, and gives users an incentive to provide such personal details in their profile.

❑ **To implement targeted marketing:** For example, you could send a newsletter about a concert or some other event to all users that reside in a particular country, state, or city. You can do the same with banners or text notices on the site. Multiple criteria could be used for targeting the sponsored news, other than that from the user's location: it could be chosen according to age, gender, or a combination of multiple conditions. The more details you have about your users, the more chances you have to sell advertisement spaces on your site(s) to external companies, or to effectively use the ad possibilities yourself.

❑ **To offer a choice of identity authorization:** Username and passwords have been the traditional means to be authenticated on websites for years and are still the standard means to identify yourself. There are a few problems with the traditional username and password combinations because they require users to keep track of numerous combinations across all the sites the users visit and such combinations have been coming under more and more scrutiny these days. To resolve these issues, new identity management mechanisms have been introduced: OpenID and CardSpace. Offering a choice of authentication mechanism makes the site more usable by more visitors.

❑ **To implement authentication via ASP.NET AJAX:** AJAX was created to make a better user experience for visitors. ASP.NET AJAX leverages Forms authentication, the membership provider, and profile services via web services.

The site administrator will need an intuitive console from which she can see and edit the profile of any user — to remove an offending signature or avatar image (an avatar image is a small picture of a user, or a "cool" signature picture a user wants to display next to his or her name) used in the forums.

Design

To recap, the "virtual client" has commissioned a membership system that handles the following operations and features:

❑ Users must be able to create new accounts independently, by filling out an online registration form.

❑ Users must be able to later change their own credentials or recover them if they forget them.

❑ The administrator must be able to grant or deny access to specific sections or individual pages by certain users. The permissions should be editable even after deploying the site, without requiring the intervention of a developer to change complex code or settings.

❑ The administrator must be able to temporarily or permanently suspend a user account, for example, when a user does not respect the site's policy of conduct.

❑ The administrator should be able to see summary and statistical data such as the number of total registered users and how many of them are online at a particular time. The administrator may also want to know when specific users registered, and the last time they logged in.

❑ A profiling system should enable each registered user to save data such as site preferences and personal details in a data store (such as a database), so that the information will be remembered on future visits. The administrator must be able to view and edit the profile of each user.

ASP.NET 2.0 introduced some great features that help to develop the membership subsystem.

Password Storage Mechanisms

There are basically three methods for storing passwords, with each one offering different trade-offs between security and the convenience of developers, administrators, and users.

1. The most convenient method of password storage for developers and administrators is to store the password as plain text in a database field. This is also convenient for users because you can easily e-mail a user's password to them in case they forget it. However, this is the least secure option because all of the passwords are stored as plain text — if your database were compromised by a hacker, he'd have easy access to everyone's password. You need to be extremely careful about locking down your database and ensuring that you secure your database backup files.

2. To enhance the security of password storage, you can encrypt the passwords before storing them in a database. There are many ways to encrypt passwords, but the most common method is *symmetric encryption*, which uses a guarded system password to encrypt all user passwords. This is two-way encryption: you can encrypt a password and also decrypt it later. This offers medium convenience for developers but still offers a lot of convenience for users because you can still e-mail them a forgotten password.

3. The highest level of security requires a form of encryption that prevents administrators and developers from gaining access to any user's password. This uses a one-way type of encryption known as hashing. You can always encrypt a password by hashing the password with a proven algorithm, but you can never decrypt it. Therefore, you store the hashed version of the password, and later, when you want to verify a user's password when he logs in again, you can perform the same hashing algorithm on whatever he types in as his password. You can then compare this hash against the hash you stored in the database — if the two match, then you know the user entered his password correctly. This offers a low amount of convenience to developers, administrators, and users because it's not possible to e-mail forgotten passwords. Instead, if a user forgets his password, your only choice is to change the user's password to a known value and then save the hash for his new password.

Hashing (method 3) was used in the first edition of this book, but it caused a lot of confusion for administrators and frustration for users because people generally prefer having the option of "recovering" a lost password without requiring a new one. We will use symmetric encryption (method 2) in this edition, but please keep in mind that password hashes should always be used to protect websites containing financial data or other very sensitive data (such as medical records, test scores, etc.). Most users would *not* like to see their super-secret banking password mailed to them in an e-mail message, and most don't even want bank employees to have access to passwords. A bank employee who is trusted today might become a disgruntled former employee tomorrow, and it's nice to know that he won't be taking your password with him!

Authentication Modes: Windows Security or Custom Login Form?

The first thing you have to decide when you set up a security mechanism for a website is whether you want to use Windows or Forms authentication. Windows authentication is the easiest to set up and use, while Forms authentication requires you to create a custom database and a login form. Windows security is usually the best choice when you are developing an intranet site for which all users who have access to the site are also users of a company's internal network (where they have domain user accounts). With Windows security, users enjoy the capability to use restricted web pages without having to formally log in to the website; the page is executed under the context of the user requesting it, and security restrictions are automatically enforced on all resources that the code tries to access and use (typically files and database objects). Another advantage is that Windows will securely store and encrypt user credentials so that you don't have to.

However, the requirement to have a local network account is a huge disadvantage that makes it a bad choice for Internet sites. If you use Windows security for users located outside of a company's network, the company would be required to create a network user account for each website user, which makes it slow for users to gain access and expensive for companies to administer. While you could conceivably write some code to automate the creation of Windows network accounts, and could write a login page that uses Windows impersonation behind the scenes, it just doesn't make sense to employ Windows security with those nasty workarounds in our context (a public website with possibly thousands of users). Instead, it makes more sense to use Forms authentication, and store user account credentials and related profile data in a custom database.

The Let's Do Everything on Our Own Approach

Designing a module for handling user membership and profiling is not easy. It may not seem particularly difficult at first: you can easily devise some database tables for storing the required data (roles, account credentials, and details; the associations between roles and accounts; and account profiles) and an API that allows the developer to request, create, and modify this data. However, things are rarely as easy as they appear at first!

You must not downplay the significance of these modules because they are crucial to the operation of the website, and properly designing these modules is important because all other site modules rely on them. If you design and implement the news module poorly, you can go back and fix it without affecting all the other site's modules (forum, e-commerce, newsletter, polls, etc.). However, if you decide to change the design of the membership module after you have developed other modules that use it, chances are good that you will need to modify something in those modules as well. The membership module must be complete but also simple to use, and developers should be able to use its classes and methods when they design administration pages. They should also be able to create and edit user accounts by writing just a few lines of code or, better yet, no code at all. ASP.NET 1.1 provided a partial security framework that allowed you to specify roles that could or could not access specific pages or folders by specifying role restrictions in `web.config`. It also took care of creating an encrypted authentication cookie for the user, once the user logged in. The developer, though, was completely responsible for all the work of writing the login and registration pages, authenticating the user against a database of credentials, assigning the proper roles, and administering accounts. In the first edition of this book, we did everything ourselves with custom code. The solution worked fine but still suffered from a couple of problems:

❏　The developer had to perform all security checks programmatically, typically in the `Page_Load` event, before doing anything else. If you later wanted to add roles or users to the ACL (access control list) of a page or site area, you had to edit the code, recompile it, and redeploy the assembly.

❏　The membership system also included user profiling. The database table had columns for the user's first and last name, address, birth date, and other related data. However, the table schema was fixed, so if you wanted to add more information to the profile later, you had to change the database, the related stored procedures, and many API methods, in addition to the user interface to insert the data.

Things could have been made more flexible, but it would have been more difficult to develop. You have to weigh the advantages of design extensibility against the time and effort required to implement it. Fortunately, ASP.NET has full-featured membership and profiling systems out of the box! Yes, that's right, you don't have to write a single line of code to register users, protect administrative pages, and associate a profile with the users, unless you want to customize the way they work (for example, to change the format in which the data is stored, or the storage medium itself).

This section introduces the built-in security and profiling framework of ASP.NET; after that, you will learn how to profitably use it in your own project instead of "rolling your own" solution.

The Membership and MembershipUser Classes

ASP.NET 2.0 included many features to help developers solve common problems quickly; one of these features is the Membership and Role providers. The principal class of the ASP.NET's security framework is `System.Web.Security.Membership`, which exposes a number of static methods to create, delete, update, and retrieve registered users. The following table describes the most important class methods.

Method	Description
CreateUser	Creates a new user account.
DeleteUser	Deletes the specified user.
FindUsersByEmail	Returns an array of users with the specified e-mail address. If SQL Server is used to store accounts, the input e-mail can contain any wildcard characters supported by SQL Server in LIKE clauses, such as % for any string of zero or more characters, or _ for a single character.
FindUsersByName	Returns an array of users with the specified name. Wildcard characters are supported.
GeneratePassword	Generates a new password with the specified length, and the specified number of non-alphanumeric characters.
GetAllUsers	Returns an array with all the registered users.
GetNumberOfUsersOnline	Returns an integer value indicating how many registered users are currently online.
GetUser	Retrieves a specific user by name.
GetUserNameByEmail	Returns the username of a user with the given e-mail address.
UpdateUser	Updates a user.
ValidateUser	Returns a Boolean value indicating whether the input credentials correspond to a registered user.

Some of these methods (`CreateUser`, `GetAllUsers`, `GetUser`, `FindUsersByName`, `FindUsersByEmail`, and `UpdateUser`) accept or return instances of the `System.Web.Security.MembershipUser` class, which represents a single user, and provides quite a lot of details about it. The following tables describe the instance properties and methods exposed by this class.

Property	Description
Comment	A comment (typically entered by the administrator) associated with a given user.
CreationDate	The date when the user registered.
Email	The user's e-mail address.
IsApproved	Indicates whether the account is enabled and whether the user can log in.
IsLockedOut	Indicates whether the user account was disabled after a number of invalid logins. This property is read-only, and the administrator can only indirectly set it back to false, by calling the `UnlockUser` method described below.
IsOnline	Indicates whether the user is currently online.
LastActivityDate	The date when the user logged in or was last authenticated. If the last login was persistent, this will not necessarily be the date of the login, but it may be the date when the user accessed the site and was automatically authenticated through the cookie.
LastLockoutDate	The date when the user was automatically locked out by the membership system, after a (configurable) number of invalid logins.
LastLoginDate	The date of the last login.
LastPasswordChangedDate	When the user last changed his or her password.
PasswordQuestion	The question asked of users who forget their password — used to prove it's really the user.
UserName	The user's username.

Method	Description
ChangePassword	Changes the user's password. The current password must be provided.
ChangePasswordQuestionAndAnswer	Changes the question and answer asked of a user who forgets his or her password. Requires the current password as input (so someone can't change this for somebody else).

Continued

Method	Description
GetPassword	Returns the current password. Depending on how the membership system is set up, it may require the answer to the user's password question as input and will not work if only a password hash is stored in the database.
ResetPassword	Creates a new password for the user. This is the only function to change the password if the membership system was set up to hash the password.
UnlockUser	Unlocks the user if she was previously locked out by the system because of too many invalid attempts to log in.

When you change a user property, the new value is not immediately persisted to the data store; you have to call the UpdateUser method of the Membership class for that. This is done so that with a single call you can save multiple updated properties and, thus, improve performance.

By using these two classes together, you can completely manage the accounts' data in a very intuitive and straightforward way. It's outside the scope of this book to provide a more exhaustive coverage of every method and overload, but I can show you a few examples about their usage in practice — please consult MSDN for all the details on these classes. Following is some code for registering a new account and handling the exception that may be raised if an account with the specified username or e-mail address already exists:

```
Dim msg As String = "User created successfully!"
Try
    Dim newUser As MembershipUser = Membership.CreateUser("Marco",
"secret", "mbellinaso@wrox.com")
Catch exc As MembershipCreateUserException
    msg = "Unable to create the user. "
    Select Case exc.StatusCode
        Case MembershipCreateStatus.DuplicateEmail
            msg += "An account with the specified e-mail already exists."
            Exit Select
        Case MembershipCreateStatus.DuplicateUserName
            msg += "An account with the specified username already exists."
            Exit Select
        Case MembershipCreateStatus.InvalidEmail
            msg += "The specified e-mail is not valid."
            Exit Select
        Case MembershipCreateStatus.InvalidPassword
            msg += "The specified password is not valid."
            Exit Select
        Case Else
            msg += exc.Message
            Exit Select
    End Select
End Try
lblResult.Text = msg
```

If you want to change some of the user's information, you first retrieve a `MembershipUser` instance that represents that user, change some properties as desired, and then update the user, as shown here:

```
Dim user As MembershipUser = Membership.GetUser("Marco")
If DateTime.Now.Subtract(user.LastActivityDate).TotalHours < 2 Then
    user.Comment = "very knowledgeable user; strong forum participation!"
End If
Membership.UpdateUser(user)
```

Validating user credentials from a custom login form requires only a single line of code (and not even that, as you'll see shortly):

```
dim isValid as Boolean = Membership.ValidateUser("Marco", "secret")
```

In the "Solution" section of this chapter, you will use these classes to implement the following features in the site's Administration area:

- ❑ Retrieve the total number of users and determine how many of them are currently online.

- ❑ Find users by partial username or e-mail address.

- ❑ Display some information about the users returned by the search, listed in a grid, such as the date of the user's last activity and whether they are active or not. In another page we will display all the details of a specific user and will allow the administrator to change some details.

The Provider Model Design Pattern

I use the term data store to refer to any physical means of persisting (saving) data — this usually means saving data in a database or in Active Directory, but .NET abstracts the actual data storage mechanism from the classes that manipulate the data. The provider class is the one that stores the data on behalf of other classes that manipulate data. This provider model design pattern, introduced in Chapter 3, is pervasive in .NET since the 2.0 release — you can frequently "plug in" a different backend provider to change the mechanism used to save and retrieve data. The `Membership` class uses a secondary class (called a *membership provider*) that actually knows the details of a particular data store and implements all the supporting logic to read and write data to/from it. You can almost think of the `Membership` class as a business layer class (in that it only manipulates data), and the `provider` class as the data access class, which provides the details of persistence (even though a pure architect might argue the semantics). Two built-in providers are available for the Membership system, and you can choose one by writing some settings in the `web.config` file. The built-in providers are the ones for SQL Server (`SqlMembershipProvider`) and for Active Directory (`ActiveDirectoryMembershipProvider`), but you can also write your own or find one from a third party (for use with Oracle, MySQL, DB2, and so on, or perhaps XML files). Figure 4-1 illustrates the provider model design pattern.

I find that the use of the provider model provides tremendous flexibility, because you can change the provider used by the `Membership` API under the hood without affecting the rest of the code, because you just access the `Membership` "business" class from the pages and the other business classes, and not the providers directly. Actually, you may even ignore which provider is used, and where and how the data is stored (this is the idea behind abstraction of the data store). Abstraction is obviously provided to users in the sense that they don't need to know exactly how their data will be stored, but now we also have abstraction for developers because they, too, don't always need to know how the data is stored!

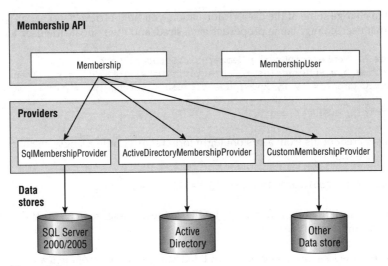

Figure 4-1

To create a new provider, you can either start from scratch by building a completely new provider that inherits directly from System.Web.Security.MembershipProvider (which in turn inherits from System.Configuration.Provider.ProviderBase) or you can just customize the way some methods of an existing provider work. For example, let's assume that you want to modify the SqlMembershipProvider so that it validates a user's password to make sure that it's not equal to his username. You simply need to define your own class, which inherits from SqlMembershipProvider, and you can just override the CreateUser method like this:

```
Class SqlMembershipProviderEx
    Inherits SqlMembershipProvider
    Public Overloads Overrides Function CreateUser(ByVal username As String,
ByVal password As String, ByVal email As String,
ByVal passwordQuestion As String, ByVal passwordAnswer As String,
ByVal isApproved As Boolean, _
    ByVal providerUserKey As Object, ByRef status As MembershipCreateStatus)
As MembershipUser
        If username.ToLower() = password.ToLower() Then
            status = MembershipCreateStatus.InvalidPassword
            Return Nothing
        Else
            Return MyBase.CreateUser(username, password, email,
passwordQuestion, passwordAnswer, isApproved, _
            providerUserKey, status)
        End If
    End Function
End Class
```

The provider model design pattern is also very useful in the migration of legacy systems that already use their own custom tables and stored procedures. Your legacy database may already contain thousands of records of user information, and you want to avoid losing them, but now you want to modify your site to take advantage of the new Membership class. Instead of creating a custom application to migrate data to a new data store (or using SQL Server DTS or SQL Server Integration Services to copy the data from your tables to the new tables used by the standard `SqlMembershipProvider`), you can just create your own custom provider that directly utilizes your existing tables and stored procedures. If you're already using a business class to access your account's data from the ASP.NET pages, then creating a compliant provider class may be just a matter of changing the name and signature of some methods. Alternatively, you can follow this approach: keep your current business class intact but make it private, and then move it inside a new provider class that delegates the implementation of all its methods and properties to that newly private legacy business class. The advantage of doing this instead of just using your current business class "as is" is that you can change to a different data store later by just plugging it into the membership infrastructure — you wouldn't have to change anything in the ASP.NET pages that call the built-in `Membership` class.

Once you have the provider you want (either one of the default providers, a custom one you developed on your own, or a third-party offering), you have to tell ASP.NET which one you want to use when you call the `Membership` class' methods.

The `web.config` file is used to specify and configure the provider for the Membership system. Many of the default configuration settings are hard-coded in the ASP.NET runtime instead of being saved in the `Machine.Config` file. This is done to improve performance by reading and parsing a smaller XML file when the application starts, but you can still modify these settings for each application by assigning your own values in `web.config` to override the defaults. You can read the default settings by looking at the `Machine.config.default` file found in the following folder (the "*xxxxx*" part should be replaced with the build number of your installation):

```
C:\<Windows Folder>\Microsoft.NET\Framework\v2.0.xxxxx\CONFIG
```

What follows is the definition of the <membership> section of the file, where the `SqlMembershipProvider` is specified and configured:

```
<system.web>
   <membership>
      <providers>
         <add name="AspNetSqlMembershipProvider"
            type="System.Web.Security.SqlMembershipProvider, System.Web,
               Version=2.0.0.0, Culture=neutral, PublicKeyToken=b03f5f7f11d50a3a"
            connectionStringName="LocalSqlServer"
            enablePasswordRetrieval="false"
            enablePasswordReset="true"
            requiresQuestionAndAnswer="true"
            applicationName="/"
            requiresUniqueEmail="false"
            passwordFormat="Hashed"
            maxInvalidPasswordAttempts="5"
            passwordAttemptWindow="10"
            passwordStrengthRegularExpression=""
         />
      </providers>
   </membership>

   <!-- other settings... -->
</system.web>
```

You can register more providers inside the `<providers>` section and choose which one you want to use by specifying its name in the `defaultProvider` attribute of the `<membership>` element (not shown above). Another attribute of `<membership>` is `userIsOnlineTimeWindow`, which specifies how many minutes after the last activity a user is still considered online. That is, if a user logs in, brings up one page, but then closes her browser immediately, she will be counted as being online for this number of minutes. We need this kind of parameter because we have no definite way to know when a user has left the site or closed down his or her browser. You can test this by checking the value returned by `Membership.GetNumberOfUsersOnline` as users come to your site and then leave.

For this site, we will use SQL Server 2008 Developer Edition, a simple version of SQL Server Enterprise Edition designed for developers to install on their local development workstation. It is not a full enterprise-powered version, but it is great for a developer to test against.

More Details about SqlMembershipProvider

In the last code snippet, you saw the default settings used to register the `SqlMembershipProvider`. The following table lists the attributes you can specify when you register the provider, in the `<provider>` element.

Attribute	Description
applicationName	The name of the web application; used if you want to store data on user account's for multiple websites in a single database.
connectionStringName	The name of the connection string, registered in the `<connectionStrings>` section of `web.config`, that points to the SQL Server database used to store the data.
	Important: This is not the actual connection string! This is only a name that refers to `web.config`, where the actual connection string is stored.
description	A description for the provider.
enablePasswordReset	Indicates whether you want to enable the methods and controls for resetting a password to a new, auto-generated one.
enablePasswordRetrieval	Indicates whether you want to enable the methods and controls that allow a user to retrieve her forgotten password.
maxInvalidPasswordAttempts	The maximum number of invalid login attempts. If the user fails to log in after this number of times within the number of minutes specified by the `passwordAttemptWindow` attribute, the user account is "locked out" until the administrator explicitly calls the `UnlockUser` method of a `MembershipUser` instance representing the specific user.

Attribute	Description
minRequiredNonalphanumericCharacters	The minimum number of non-alphanumeric characters a password must have to be valid.
minRequiredPasswordLength	The minimum number of characters for a valid password.
name	The name used to register the provider. This is used to choose the provider by setting the defaultProvider attribute of the \<membership\> element.
passwordAttemptWindow	The number of minutes used to time invalid login attempts. See the description for maxInvalidPasswordAttempts.
passwordFormat	Specifies how the password is stored in the data store. Possible values are Clear, Encrypted, and Hashed.
passwordStrengthRegularExpression	The regular expression that a password must match to be considered valid.
requiresQuestionAndAnswer	Indicates whether the user must respond to a personal secret question before retrieving or resetting her password. Questions and answers are chosen by users at registration time.
requiresUniqueEmail	Indicates whether the same e-mail address can be used to create multiple user accounts.

By default, minRequiredPasswordLength *is set to 7 and* minRequiredNonalphanumericCharacters *is set to 1, meaning that you must register with a password that is at least seven characters long and contains at least one non-alphanumeric character. Whether you leave these at their default settings or change them to suit your needs, remember to list these values on your registration page to let users know your password requirements.*

These attributes let you fine-tune the membership system. For example, the capability to specify a regular expression that the password must match gives you great flexibility to meet stringent requirements. But one of the most important properties is certainly passwordFormat, used to specify whether you want passwords to be encrypted, or whether you just want a hash of them saved. Passwords are hashed or encrypted using the key information supplied in the \<machineKey\> element of the configuration file (you should remember to synchronize this machine key between servers if you will deploy to a server farm). The default algorithm used to calculate the password's hash is SHA1, but you can change it through the validation attribute of the machineKey element. Storing passwords in clear text offers the best performance when saving and retrieving the passwords, but it's the least secure solution. Encrypting a password adds some processing overhead, but it can greatly improve security. Hashing passwords provides the best security because the hashing algorithm is one-way, which means that the passwords cannot be retrieved in any way, even by an administrator. If a user forgets her password, she can only reset it to a new auto-generated one (typically sent by e-mail to the user). The best option always depends on the needs of each particular website: if I were saving passwords for an e-commerce site on which I might also save user credit card information, I would surely hash the password and use a Secure Sockets Layer (SSL) connection in order to have the strongest security. For our content-based website, however, I find that encrypting passwords is a good compromise. It's true that we're also building a small e-commerce store, but we're not going to store very critical information (credit cards numbers or other sensitive data) on our site.

> Never store passwords in clear text. The small processing overhead necessary to encrypt and decrypt passwords is definitely worth the increased security and, thus, the confidence that the users and investors have in the site.

Exploring the Default SQL Server Data Store

Even though the ASP.NET membership system is prebuilt and ready to go, this is not a good reason to ignore its design and data structures. You should be familiar with this system to help you diagnose any problems that might arise during development or deployment. Figure 4-2 shows the tables used by the `SqlMembershipProvider` class to store credentials and other user data. Of course, the data store's design of other providers may be completely different (especially if they are not based on relational databases).

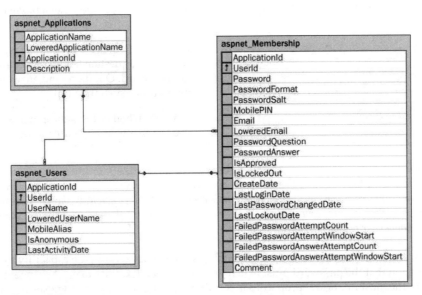

Figure 4-2

The interesting thing you can see from Figure 4-2 is the presence of the `aspnet_Applications` table, which contains a reference to multiple applications (websites). Both the `aspnet_Users` table and the `aspnet_Membership` table contain a reference to a record in `aspnet_Applications` through the `ApplicationId` foreign key. This design enables you to use the same database to store user accounts for multiple sites, which can be very helpful if you have several sites using the same database server (commonly done with corporate websites or with commercial low-cost shared hosting). In a situation where you have a critical application that requires the maximum security, you'll want to store the membership data in a dedicated database that only the site administrator can access. If you are using a SQL Server 2008 Express Edition database, it this requires you to use your own private database, deployed as a simple file under the `App_Data` special folder. In addition to these tables, there are also a couple of views related to membership (`vw_aspnet_MembershipUsers` and `vw_aspnet_Users`) and a number of stored procedures (`aspnet_membership_xxx`) for the CRUD (`Create`, `Read`, `Update`, and `Delete`) operations used for authorization. You can explore all these objects by using the Visual Studio's Server Explorer window or SQL Server Management Studio, as shown in Figure 4-3.

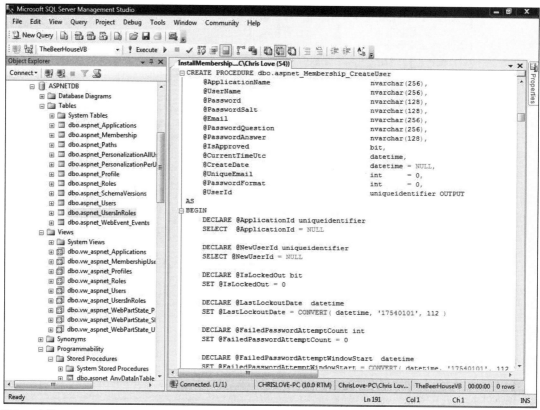

Figure 4-3

If you configure the provider so that it uses the default SQL Server Express database named `ASPNETDB` located under the `App_Data` folder, the ASP.NET runtime will automatically create all these database objects when the application is run for the first time! Because we are using this database for our site, we don't need to do anything else to set up the data store. However, if you're using a full edition of SQL Server 2008, you'll need to set up the tables manually by running the `aspnet_sql.exe` tool from the Visual Studio 2008 command prompt. You can find the `aspnet_sql.exe` in the `C:\<Windows Folder>\Microsoft.NET\Framework\v2.0.xxxxx\` folder if you want to just open it by hand. This little program lets you to choose an existing database on a specified server, and it creates all the required objects to support membership, along with caching, profiles, personalization, and more. Figure 4-4 shows a couple of screens generated by this tool.

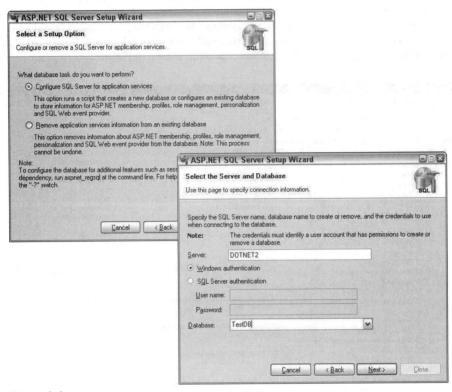

Figure 4-4

The Graphical Login Controls

As you saw earlier, creating, validating, and managing users programmatically requires only a few lines of code. But what about writing no code at all? That's actually possible now, thanks to the new Login family of controls introduced with ASP.NET 2.0. These controls provide a premade user interface for the most common operations dealing with membership and security, such as creating a new account, logging in and out, retrieving or resetting a forgotten password, and showing different output according to the authenticated status of the current user. Figure 4-5 shows the Visual Studio IDE with the Login controls section of the Toolbox. It also shows a CreateUserWizard control dropped on a form, and its Smart Tasks pop-up window.

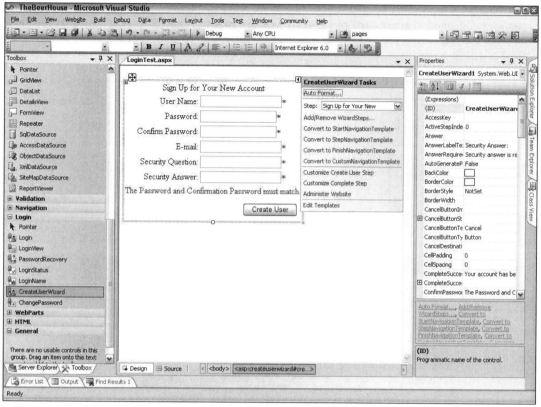

Figure 4-5

The CreateUserWizard Control

A wizard is an ASP.NET feature used to create a visual interface for a process that involves multiple steps. Each step has a separate visual panel or frame containing its own group of controls. After the user fills in values for controls of each step, he can press a link to advance to the next step in the wizard.

The CreateUserWizard control creates a user interface for a user to register, by providing the username, password, and e-mail address. The secret question and answer are also requested, but only if the current membership provider has the requiresQuestionAndAnswer attribute set to true; otherwise, these two last textboxes are hidden. When the Submit button is clicked, the control calls Membership .CreateUser under the hood on your behalf. By default, the code produced by the designer (and visible in the Source View) is:

```
<asp:CreateUserWizard ID="CreateUserWizard1" runat="server">
  <WizardSteps>
    <asp:CreateUserWizardStep runat="server">
    </asp:CreateUserWizardStep>
    <asp:CompleteWizardStep runat="server">
    </asp:CompleteWizardStep>
  </WizardSteps>
</asp:CreateUserWizard>
```

It contains no appearance attributes, and the control will look plain and simple, with the default font, background, and foreground colors. However, you can specify values for all the attributes used to control the appearance. An easy way to do that is by clicking Auto Format from the Smart Tasks window and selecting one of the premade styles. Figure 4-6 shows the control in the Elegant style.

Figure 4-6

The corresponding source code was automatically updated as follows:

```
<asp:CreateUserWizard ID="CreateUserWizard1" runat="server"
    BackColor="#F7F7DE" BorderColor="#CCCC99" BorderStyle="Solid"
    BorderWidth="1px" Font-Names="Verdana" Font-Size="10pt">
    <WizardSteps>
        <asp:CreateUserWizardStep runat="server">
        </asp:CreateUserWizardStep>
        <asp:CompleteWizardStep runat="server">
        </asp:CompleteWizardStep>
    </WizardSteps>
    <SideBarStyle BackColor="#7C6F57" BorderWidth="0px"
        Font-Size="0.9em" VerticalAlign="Top" />
    <SideBarButtonStyle BorderWidth="0px" Font-Names="Verdana"
        ForeColor="#FFFFFF" />
    <NavigationButtonStyle BackColor="#FFFBFF" BorderColor="#CCCCCC"
        BorderStyle="Solid" BorderWidth="1px" Font-Names="Verdana"
        ForeColor="#284775" />
    <HeaderStyle BackColor="#F7F7DE" BorderStyle="Solid" Font-Bold="True"
        Font-Size="0.9em" ForeColor="#FFFFFF" HorizontalAlign="Left" />
    <CreateUserButtonStyle BackColor="#FFFBFF" BorderColor="#CCCCCC"
        BorderStyle="Solid" BorderWidth="1px" Font-Names="Verdana"
        ForeColor="#284775" />
    <ContinueButtonStyle BackColor="#FFFBFF" BorderColor="#CCCCCC"
        BorderStyle="Solid" BorderWidth="1px" Font-Names="Verdana"
        ForeColor="#284775" />
    <StepStyle BorderWidth="0px" />
    <TitleTextStyle BackColor="#6B696B" Font-Bold="True" ForeColor="#FFFFFF" />
</asp:CreateUserWizard>
```

Back in Chapter 2, we discussed the disadvantages of having the appearance properties set in the .aspx source files, in comparison to having them defined in a separate skin file as part of an ASP.NET theme. Therefore, I strongly suggest that you *not* leave the auto-generated appearance attributes in the page's source code, but instead cut and paste them into a skin file. You can paste everything except for the ID property and the <WizardSteps> section, as they are not part of the control's appearance.

The `<WizardSteps>` section lists all the steps of the wizard. By default it includes the step with the registration form, and a second one with the confirmation message. You can add other steps between these two, and in our implementation we'll add a step immediately after the registration form, where the user can associate a profile to the new account. The wizard will automatically provide the buttons for moving to the next or previous step, or to finish the wizard, and raise a number of events to notify your program of what is happening, such as `ActiveStepChanged`, `CancelButtonClick`, `ContinueButtonClick`, `FinishButtonClick`, `NextButtonClick`, and `PreviousButtonClick`.

If the available style properties are not enough for you, and you want to change the structure of the control, that is, how the controls are laid down on the form, you can do that by defining your own template for the `CreateUserWizardStep` (or for the `CompleteWizardStep`). As long as you create the textboxes with the IDs the control expects to find, the control will continue to work without requiring you to write code to perform the registration manually. The best and easiest way to find which ID to use for each control is to have Visual Studio .NET convert the step's default view to a template (click the Customize Create User Step link in the control's Smart Tasks window), and then modify the generated code as needed. The code that follows is the result of Visual Studio's conversion and the deletion of the HTML layout tables:

```
<WizardSteps>
    <asp:CreateUserWizardStep runat="server">
        <ContentTemplate>
        <b>Sign Up for Your New Account</b><p></p>
        User Name: <asp:TextBox ID="UserName" runat="server" />
        <asp:RequiredFieldValidator ID="UserNameRequired" runat="server"
            ControlToValidate="UserName" ErrorMessage="User Name is required."
            ValidationGroup="CreateUserWizard1">*</asp:RequiredFieldValidator>
        <br />
        Password: <asp:TextBox ID="Password" runat="server" TextMode="Password" />
        <asp:RequiredFieldValidator ID="PasswordRequired" runat="server"
            ControlToValidate="Password" ErrorMessage="Password is required."
            ValidationGroup="CreateUserWizard1">*</asp:RequiredFieldValidator>
        <br />
        Confirm Password: <asp:TextBox ID="ConfirmPassword" runat="server"
            TextMode="Password" />
        <asp:RequiredFieldValidator ID="ConfirmPasswordRequired" runat="server"
            ControlToValidate="ConfirmPassword"
            ErrorMessage="Confirm Password is required."
            ValidationGroup="CreateUserWizard1">*</asp:RequiredFieldValidator>
        <asp:CompareValidator ID="PasswordCompare" runat="server"
            ControlToCompare="Password" ControlToValidate="ConfirmPassword"
            ErrorMessage="The Password and Confirmation Password must match."
            ValidationGroup="CreateUserWizard1"></asp:CompareValidator>
        <br />
        E-mail: <asp:TextBox ID="Email" runat="server" />
        <asp:RequiredFieldValidator ID="EmailRequired" runat="server"
            ControlToValidate="Email" ErrorMessage="E-mail is required."
            ValidationGroup="CreateUserWizard1">*</asp:RequiredFieldValidator>
        <br />
        Security Question: <asp:TextBox ID="Question" runat="server" />
        <asp:RequiredFieldValidator ID="QuestionRequired" runat="server"
            ControlToValidate="Question" ErrorMessage="Security question is required."
            ValidationGroup="CreateUserWizard1">*</asp:RequiredFieldValidator>
        <br />
```

```
        Security Answer: <asp:TextBox ID="Answer" runat="server" />
        <asp:RequiredFieldValidator ID="AnswerRequired" runat="server"
            ControlToValidate="Answer" ErrorMessage="Security answer is required."
            ValidationGroup="CreateUserWizard1">*</asp:RequiredFieldValidator>
        <br />
        <asp:Literal ID="ErrorMessage" runat="server" EnableViewState="False" />
        </ContentTemplate>
    </asp:CreateUserWizardStep>
    <asp:CompleteWizardStep runat="server">
    </asp:CompleteWizardStep>
</WizardSteps>
```

> **All of the various validation controls are declared with a** `ValidationGroup` **property set to the control's name, that is,** `CreateUserWizard1`**. The** `CreateUserWizard` **creates a Submit button with the same property, set to the same value. When that button is clicked, only those validators that have the** `ValidationGroup` **property set to the same value will be considered. This is a powerful feature of ASP.NET that you can use anywhere to create different logical forms for which the validation is run separately, according to which button is clicked.**

For the custom-made Create User step of the wizard, the Question and Password fields are not automatically hidden if the current membership provider has the `requiresQuestionAndAnswer` *attribute set to false, as would happen otherwise.*

You can also set up the control so that it automatically sends a confirmation e-mail to users when they complete the registration process successfully. The setup is defined by the `CreateUserWizard`'s `<MailDefinition>` subsection, and consists of the sender's e-mail address, the mail subject, and a reference to the text file that contains the e-mail's body. The following code shows an example:

```
<asp:CreateUserWizard runat="server" ID="CreateUserWizard1">
    <WizardSteps>
        ...
    </WizardSteps>
    <MailDefinition
        BodyFileName="~/RegistrationMail.txt"
        From="yourname@yourserver.co"
        Subject="Mail subject here">
    </MailDefinition>
</asp:CreateUserWizard>
```

The `RegistrationMail.txt` file can contain the `<% UserName %>` and `<% Password %>` special placeholders, which at runtime will be replaced with the values taken from the new registration's data. To send the mail, you must have configured the SMTP server settings in the `web.config file`, through the `<mailSettings>` element and its subelements, as shown in the following code:

```
<configuration xmlns="http://schemas.microsoft.com/.NetConfiguration/v2.0">
    <system.web> <!-- some settings here...--> </system.web>
    <system.net>
        <mailSettings>
            <smtp deliveryMethod=" Network " from="thebeerhouse@wrox.com">
```

```
                  <network defaultCredentials="true" host="(localhost)" port="25" />
            </smtp>
        </mailSettings>
    </system.net> </configuration>
```

The Login Control

The `Login` control does exactly what its name suggests: it allows the user to log in. It provides the user interface for typing the username and password, and choosing whether the login will be persistent (saved across different sessions) or not. For the default simple appearance, you just need to declare the control as follows:

```
<asp:Login ID="Login1" runat="server" />
```

However, if you apply the Elegant prebuilt style to it, it will look as shown in Figure 4-7.

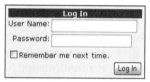

Figure 4-7

Under the covers, this control calls the `Membership.ValidateUser` method to check whether the provided credentials are found in the data store, and if so, it calls `FormsAuthentication` `.RedirectFormLoginPage` to create the encrypted authentication ticket, saves it into a client cookie, and redirects the user to the page that he or she originally tried to access before being redirected to the login page. The control exposes a lot of properties: many are for changing its appearance (colors, fonts, etc.), and others enable you to specify whether you want to show a link to the registration page (`CreateUserText` and `CreateUserUrl` properties), a link to the page to recover a forgotten password (`PasswordRecoveryText` and `PasswordRecoveryUrl` properties), and whether the control should be hidden when the user is already logged in (the `VisibleWhenLoggedIn` property). Of course, you can completely customize the way the `CreateUserWizard` control looks, by defining a template. Here's an example:

```
<asp:Login ID="Login1" runat="server">
    <LayoutTemplate>
        Username: <asp:TextBox ID="UserName" runat="server" />
        <asp:RequiredFieldValidator ID="UserNameRequired" runat="server"
            ControlToValidate="UserName" ErrorMessage="User Name is required."
            ValidationGroup="Login1">*</asp:RequiredFieldValidator>
        Password: <asp:TextBox ID="Password" runat="server" TextMode="Password" />
        <asp:RequiredFieldValidator ID="PasswordRequired" runat="server"
            ControlToValidate="Password" ErrorMessage="Password is required."
            ValidationGroup="Login1">*</asp:RequiredFieldValidator>
        <asp:CheckBox ID="RememberMe" runat="server" Text="Remember me next time." />
        <asp:Literal ID="FailureText" runat="server" EnableViewState="False" />
        <asp:Button ID="LoginButton" runat="server" CommandName="Login"
        Text="Log In" ValidationGroup="Login1" />
    </LayoutTemplate>
</asp:Login>
```

Remember that the only important thing is that you give textboxes, buttons, labels, and other controls the specific IDs that the parent control expects to find. If you start defining the template from the default template created by VS2008, this will be very easy.

The ChangePassword Control

The ChangePassword control allows users to change their current password through the user interface shown in Figure 4-8.

Figure 4-8

This control is completely customizable in appearance, by means of either properties or a new template. As with the CreateUserWizard control, its declaration can contain a <MailDefinition> section, where you can configure the control to send a confirmation e-mail to the user with her new credentials.

The PasswordRecovery Control

The Password Recovery control enables users to recover or reset their password, in case they forgot it. The first step, shown in Figure 4-9, is to provide the username.

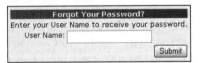

Figure 4-9

For the next step, the user will be asked the question he or she chose at registration time. If the answer is correct, the control sends the user an e-mail message. As expected, there must be the usual MailDefinition, along with the current password, or a newly generated one if the membership provider's enablePasswordRetrieval attribute is set to false or if the provider's passwordFormat is hashed.

The LoginStatus, LoginName, and LoginView Controls

These last three controls are the simplest ones, and are often used together. The LoginName control shows the name of the current user. It has a FormatString property that can be used to show the username as part of a longer string, such as "Welcome {0}!", where the username will replace the {0} placeholder. If the current user is not authenticated, the control shows nothing, regardless of the FormatString value.

The LoginStatus control shows a link to log out or log in, according to whether the current user is or is not authenticated. The text of the liks can be changed by means of the LoginText and LogoutText properties, or you can use graphical images instead of plain text, by means of the LoginImageUrl and LogoutImageUrl properties. When the Login link is clicked, it redirects the user to the login page specified in the web.config file's <forms> element, or to the Login.aspx page if the setting is not present. When the Logout link is clicked, the control calls FormsAuthentication.SignOut to remove the client's authentication ticket, and then can either refresh the current page or redirect to a different one according to the values of the LogoutAction and LogoutPageUrl properties.

The LoginView allows you to show different output according to whether the current user is authenticated. Its declaration contains two subsections, <AnonymousTemplate> and <LoggedInTemplate>, where you place the HTML or ASP.NET controls that you want to display when the user is anonymous (not logged in) or logged in, respectively. The code that follows shows how to display the login control if the user is not authenticated yet, or a welcome message and a link to log out otherwise:

```
<asp:LoginView ID="LoginView1" runat="server">
  <AnonymousTemplate>
    <asp:Login runat="server" ID="Login1" />
  </AnonymousTemplate>
  <LoggedInTemplate>
    <asp:LoginName ID="LoginName1" runat="server" FormatString="Welcome {0}" />
    <br />
    <asp:LoginStatus ID="LoginStatus1" runat="server" />
  </LoggedInTemplate>
</asp:LoginView>
```

Integrating ASP.NET AJAX Authentication

Since ASP.NET 2.0 was released Microsoft has released an AJAX framework to build rich user interfaces. It was originally an add-on to the .NET Framework, but became part of the framework with the 3.5 release. The ASP.NET AJAX framework is a natural extension of programming with .NET, except that it is a JavaScript framework that executes in the browser. The main benefit of the ASP.NET AJAX framework is the capability to program in JavaScript the way you can against the .NET Framework. This should drastically reduce the learning curve needed for ASP.NET programmers to leverage this AJAX framework. While there are great AJAX frameworks available, such as JQuery, ASP.NET AJAX is specifically designed to integrate tightly with the server-side aspects of ASP.NET, such as the Membership and Profile providers.

The ASP.NET AJAX framework is composed of a series of pseudo-namespaces and -classes. I use the prefix "pseudo" because there are no true object-oriented concepts in JavaScript. But the ASP.NET AJAX framework provides a series of common classes that can be used to build the rich user experiences demanded by users today. For more information on the AJAX namespaces and classes visit http://msdn.microsoft.com/en-us/library/bb397536.aspx.

The Sys.Services namespace contains a set of classes that interact with the Membership, Role, and Profile providers on the server through web services. The Authentication class is the proxy class used to interact with the Membership provider. This class has two members, Login and Logout. The

`Login` method performs forms authentication and sets the authentication cookie upon successful authentication. The following table describes the arguments to `Login`:

Argument	Description
Username	The account's username.
Password	The account's password.
isPersistent	A Boolean flag indicating to forms authentication whether to save the users' authentication token so they are not required to authenticate themselves next time.
redirectURL	URL to take the user to after a successful authentication.
customInfo	Reserved.
loginCompletedCallback	The function name the script calls when the login is completed.
failedCallback	Name of the function the script calls when an authentication fails.
userContext	Custom data that is passed to the callback function.

Similarly, the `Logout` function clears the form's authentication cookie, and the user must log back in to the site to access secured content areas. The `Logout` function takes a series of arguments, too:

Argument	Description
redirectUrl	The URL the user is redirected to after logging out.
logoutCompletedCallback	The callback function the script calls when the logout is complete.
failedCallback	The callback function the script calls if the logout fails.
userContext	Custom data that is passed to the callback function.

Before forms authentication can be executed using ASP.NET AJAX, it must be enabled to do so in the `web.config` file. If you are creating a new website with Visual Studio 2008, there will be a line in the `web.config` file that needs to be uncommented to enable grant access from the application's services. The section is actually part of the `system.web.extensions` section, which holds the key to implementing the ASP.NET AJAX interfaces to profiles and roles:

```
<system.web.extensions>
<scripting>

<webServices>

    <authenticationService enabled="true" requireSSL="false" />

    <profileService enabled="true" readAccessProperties="FirstName, LastName" />
```

```
        <roleService enabled="true" />

    </webServices>

    <scriptResourceHandler enableCompression="true" enableCaching="true" />
    </scripting>
    </system.web.xtensions>
```

Once these sections have been officially added to the site, client-side script can be written to access these providers.

Setting Up and Using Roles

An authentication/authorization system is not complete without support for roles. Roles are used to group users for the purpose of assigning a set of permissions, or authorizations. You could decide to control authorizations separately for each user, but that would be an administrative nightmare! Instead, it's helpful to assign a user to a predetermined role and give him the permissions that accompany the role. For example, you can define an Administrator's role to control access to the restricted pages used to add, edit, and delete the site's content, and only users who belong to the Administrators role will be able to post new articles and news. It is also possible to assign more than one role to a given user. In ASP.NET 1.x, there wasn't any built-in support for roles in Forms authentication — roles were only supported with Windows security. You could have added role support manually (as shown in the first edition of this book), but that required you to create your own database tables and write code to retrieve the roles when the user logged in. You could have written the code so that the roles were retrieved at runtime — and then encrypted together by the authentication ticket on a client's cookie — so that they were not retrieved separately from the database with each request. Besides taking a considerable amount of development time that you could have spent adding value to your site, it was also a crucial task: any design or implementation bugs could impact performance, or even worse, introduce serious security holes. The good news is that as of 2.0 ASP.NET has built-in support for roles, and it does it the right way with regard to performance, security, and flexibility. In fact, as is true in many other pieces of ASP.NET (membership, sessions, profiles, personalization), it is built on the provider model design pattern: a provider for SQL Server is provided, but if you don't like some aspect of how it works, or you want to use a different data store, you can write your own custom provider or acquire one from a third party.

The role management is disabled by default to improve performance for sites that don't need roles — role support requires the execution of database queries, and consequent network traffic between the database server and the web server. You can enable it by means of the `<roleManager>` element in the `web.config` file, as shown here:

```
    <roleManager enabled="true" cacheRolesInCookie="true" cookieName="TBHROLES" />
```

This element allows you to enable roles and configure some options. For example, the preceding code enables role caching in the client's cookie (instead of retrieving them from the database on each web request), which is a suggested best practice. Unless specified otherwise, the default provider will be used, with a connection string to the default local SQL Server Express database (the ASPNETDB file under the App_Data folder). If you want to use a different database, just register a new provider within the `<roleManager>` element, and choose it by setting the roleManager's defaultProvider attribute.

`System.Web.Security.Roles` is the class that allows you to access and manage role information programmatically. It exposes several static methods, the most important of which are listed in the following table.

Method	Description
AddUserToRole, AddUserToRoles, AddUsersToRole, AddUsersToRoles	Adds one or more users to one or more roles.
CreateRole	Creates a new role with the specified name.
DeleteRole	Deletes an existing role.
FindUsersInRole	Finds all users who belong to the specified role and who have a username that matches the input string. If the default provider for SQL server is used, the username can contain any wildcard characters supported by SQL Server in LIKE clauses, such as % for any string of zero or more characters, or _ for a single character.
GetAllRoles	Returns an array with all the roles.
GetRolesForUser	Returns an array with all the roles to which the specified user belongs.
GetUsersInRole	Returns the array of usernames (not `MembershipUser` instances) of users who belong to the specified role.
IsUserInRole	Indicates whether the specified user is a member of the specified role.
RemoveUserFromRole, RemoveUserFromRoles, RemoveUsersFromRole, RemoveUsersFromRoles	Removes one or more users from one or more roles.
RoleExists	Indicates whether a role with the specified name already exists.

Using these methods is straightforward, and you will see some practical examples in the "Solution" section of this chapter, where we implement the administration console to add and remove users to and from roles.

The roles system integrates perfectly with the standard `IPrincipal` security interface, which is implemented by the object returned by the page's `User` property. Therefore, you can use the `User` object's `IsInRole` method to check whether the current user belongs to the specified role.

The SQL Server provider retrieves and stores the data from and to the tables `aspnet_Roles` and `aspnet_UsersInRoles`. The latter links a user from the `aspnet_Users` table (or another user table, if you're using a custom membership provider for a custom database) to a role in the `aspnet_Roles` table. Figure 4-10 shows the database diagram, again, updated with the addition of these two tables.

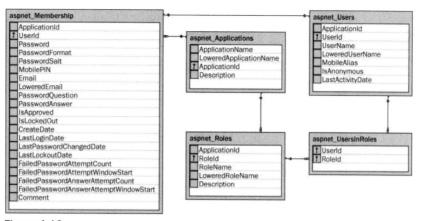

Figure 4-10

Using Roles to Protect Pages and Functions against Unauthorized Access

Basically, you have two ways to control and protect access to sensitive pages: you can do it either imperatively (programmatically) or declaratively (using a `config` file). If you want to do it by code, in the page's `Load` event you would write something like the following snippet:

```
If Not Roles.IsUserInRole("Administrators") Then
    Throw New System.Security.SecurityException("Sorry, this is a restricted
function you are not authorized to perform")
End If
```

When you don't pass the username to the `Roles.IsUserInRole` method, it takes the name of the current user, and then "forwards" the call to the `IsInRole` method of the current user's `IPrincipal` interface. Therefore, you can call it directly and save some overhead by using the following code:

```
If Not Me.User.IsInRole("Administrators") Then
    Throw New System.Security.SecurityException("Sorry, this is a restricted
function you are not authorized to perform")
End If
```

When `Roles.IsUserInRole` *is called with the overload that takes in the username (which is not necessarily equal to the current user's username), the check is done by the selected role's provider. In the case of the built-in* `SqlRoleProvider`, *a call is made to the* `aspnet_UsersInRoles_IsUserInRole` *stored procedure.*

The biggest disadvantage of imperative (programmatic) security is that to secure an entire folder, you have to copy and paste this code in multiple pages (or use a common base class for them). Even worse, when you want to change the ACL (access control list) for a page or folder (because, for example, you want to allow access to a newly created role), you will need to change the code in all those files! Declarative security makes this job much easier: you define an `<authorization>` section in a `web.config` (either for the overall site or for a subfolder), which specifies the users and roles who are allowed to access a certain folder or page. The following snippet of `web.config` gives access to members of the Administrators role, while everyone else (*) is denied access to the current folder's pages:

```
<configuration xmlns="http://schemas.microsoft.com/.NetConfiguration/v2.0">
    <system.web>
        <authorization>
            <allow roles="Administrators" />
            <deny users="*" />
        </authorization>
        <!-- other settings... -->
    </system.web>
</configuration>
```

Authorization conditions are evaluated from top to bottom, and the first one that matches the user or role stops the validation process. This means that if you switched the two preceding conditions, the `<deny>` condition would match for any user, and the second condition would never be considered; as a result, nobody could access the pages. This next example allows everybody except anonymous users (those who have not logged in and who are identified by the `?` character):

```
<authorization>
    <deny users="?" />
    <allow users="*" />
</authorization>
```

If you want to have different ACLs for different folders, you can have a different `<authorization>` section in each folder's `web.config` file. As an alternative, you can place all ACLs in the root `web.config`, within different `<location>` sections, as in this code:

```
<configuration xmlns="http://schemas.microsoft.com/.NetConfiguration/v2.0">
    <system.web>
        <!-- settings for the current folder -->
        <authorization>
            <allow users="*" />
        </authorization>
    </system.web>

    <location path="Admin">
        <!-- settings for the Admin sub-folder -->
        <system.web>
            <authorization>
                <allow roles="Administrators" />
                <deny users="*" />
            </authorization>
        </system.web>
    </location>

    <location path="Members">
        <!-- settings for the Members sub-folder -->
        <system.web>
            <authorization>
                <deny users="?" />
                <allow users="*" />
            </authorization>
```

```
            </system.web>
        </location>
    </configuration>
```

The path attribute of the `<location>` section can be the name of a subfolder (as shown above) or the virtual path of a single page. Using the `<location>` section is the only way to declaratively assign a different ACL to specific individual pages, since you can't have page-level `web.config` files. Although it's possible to restrict individual pages, it's more common to restrict entire subfolders.

Programmatic security checks are still useful and necessary in some cases, though, such as when you want to allow everybody to load a page but control the visibility of some visual controls (e.g., buttons to delete a record, or a link to the administration section) of that page to specific users. In these cases, you can use the code presented earlier to show, or hide, some server-side controls or containers (such as `Panel`) according to the result of a call to `User.IsInRole`. Alternatively, you can use a `LoginView` control that, in addition to its sections for anonymous and logged-in users, can also define template sections visible only to users who belong to specific roles. The next snippet produces different output according to whether the current user is anonymous, is logged in as a regular member or is logged in and belongs to the Administrators role:

```
<asp:LoginView ID="LoginView1" runat="server">
    <AnonymousTemplate>anonymous user</AnonymousTemplate>
    <LoggedInTemplate>member</LoggedInTemplate>
    <RoleGroups>
        <asp:RoleGroup Roles="Administrators">
            <ContentTemplate>administrator</ContentTemplate>
        </asp:RoleGroup>
    </RoleGroups>
</asp:LoginView>
```

Note that in cases where the currently logged-in user is also in the Administrators role, the `LoginView` control only outputs the content of the `<Administrators>` section, not that of the more general `<LoggedInTemplate>` section.

Finally, roles are also integrated with the site map, which lets you specify which roles will be able to see a particular link in the `Menu` or `TreeView` control that consumes the site map. This is a very powerful feature that makes it easy to show a user only the menu options he is actually allowed to access! For example, if you want the Admin link to be visible only to Administrators, here's how you define the map's node:

```
<siteMapNode title="Admin" url="~/Admin/Default.aspx" roles="Administrators">
```

However, to enable this to work you must also register a new provider for the SiteMap system (in the `<siteMap>` section of the `web.config` file), and set its `securityTrimmingEnabled` attribute to `true`. Registering the provider for the site map is very similar to registering a provider for the membership or roles system; in the "Solution" section you will see code examples to illustrate this.

Integrating ASP.NET AJAX Roles Service

Like the Authentication service, ASP.NET AJAX provides an interface to leverage Roles through web services on the client. The service has to be turned on by enabling in the `web.config` (shown in the previous section on authentication). The `Sys.Services.RoleService` class has three methods that need to be discussed: `Load`, `IsUserInRole`, and `Roles`.

The `Load` method loads the roles for the currently authenticated user. The Roles themselves are stored in client-side memory if the call to the load function is successful.

Argument	Description
loadCompletedCallback	The function that is called when the load operation has completed. The default is null.
failedCallback	The function that is called if loading has failed. The default is null.
userContext	User context information that is passed to the callback functions.

The `IsUserInRole` function checks to see if the current user belongs to a specified role and takes one parameter, role, which is the name of the role to check. The function returns `true` if the current user belongs to the role; otherwise, it returns `false`.

The `Roles` function returns an array listing all the roles that the current user belongs to. The `Load` method must be called before accessing the `Roles` function; otherwise, no roles will be returned.

Setting Up and Using User Profiles

In the ASP.NET 1.x days, if you wanted to associate a profile with a registered user, you typically added a custom table to your database, or stored them together with the user credentials, in the same table. You also had to write quite a lot of code for the business and data access layers, to store, retrieve, and update that data from your web pages. ASP.NET provides a built-in mechanism to manage user profiles, in an easy, yet very complete and flexible, way. This feature can save you hours or even days of work! The Profile module takes care of everything — you just need to configure what the profile will contain, that is, define the property name, type, and default value. This configuration is done in the root `web.config` file, within the `<profile>` section. The following snippet shows how to declare two properties: `FavoriteTheme` of type `String`, and `BirthDate` of type `DateTime`:

```
<configuration xmlns="http://schemas.microsoft.com/.NetConfiguration/v2.0">
   <system.web>
      <profile>
         <properties>
            <add name="FavoriteTheme" type="String" />
            <add name="BirthDate" type="DateTime" />
         </properties>
      </profile>
      <!-- other settings... -->
   </system.web>
</configuration>
```

Amazingly, that is all you need to do to set up a profile structure! When the application is run, the ASP. NET runtime dynamically adds a `Profile` property to the `Page` class, which means that you will not find such a property in the Object Browser at design time. The object returned is of type `ProfileCommon` (inherited from `System.Web.Profile.ProfileBase`); you will not find this class in the Object Browser either, or on the documentation, because this class is generated and compiled on-the-fly, according to the properties defined in the `web.config` file. The result is that you can just access the page's `Profile` property and read/write its subproperties. The following code demonstrates how to read the values of the current user's profile to show them on the page when it loads, and then updates them when a Submit button is clicked:

```
Protected Sub Page_Load(ByVal sender As Object, ByVal e As EventArgs)
    If Not Me.IsPostBack Then
        ddlThemes.SelectedValue = Me.Profile.FavoriteTheme
        txtBirthDate.Text = Me.Profile.BirthDate.ToShortDateString()
    End If
End Sub

Protected Sub btnSubmit_Click(ByVal sender As Object, ByVal e As EventArgs)
    Me.Profile.FavoriteTheme = ddlThemes.SelectedValue
    Me.Profile.BirthDate = DateTime.Parse(txtBirthDate.Text)
End Sub
```

Even though you can't see these properties in the Object Browser, Visual Studio is smart enough to compile this class in the background when the `web.config` file is modified, so you get full IntelliSense in the IDE, just as if the `Profile` properties were built-in properties of the `Page` class, like all the others. Figure 4-11 shows the IDE with IntelliSense in action.

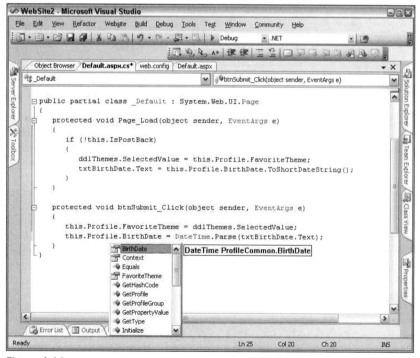

Figure 4-11

> **Having a class dynamically generated by Visual Studio with all the custom profile properties (and the IntelliSense for them) doesn't just speed up development but also helps developers reduce inadvertent coding errors. In fact, this class provides strongly typed access to the user's profile, so if you try to assign a string or an integer to a property that expects a date, you'll get a compile-time error, and you can correct the problem immediately!**

When you define a profile property, you can also assign a default value to it, by means of the `defaultValue` attribute:

```
<add name="FavoriteTheme" type="String" defaultValue="Colorful" />
```

The default value for strings is an empty string, not null, as you may have thought. This makes it easier to read string properties, because you don't have to check whether they are null before using the value somewhere. The other data types have the same default values that a variable of the same type would have (e.g., zero for integers).

When you declare profile properties, you can also group them into subsections, as shown here:

```
<profile>
    <properties>
        <add name="FavoriteTheme" type="String" />
        <add name="BirthDate" type="DateTime" />
        <group name="Address">
            <add name="Street" type="String" />
            <add name="City" type="String" />
        </group>
    </properties>
</profile>
```

The `Street` property will be accessible as `Profile.Address.Street`. Note, however, that you can't define nested groups under each other but can only have a single level of groups. If this limitation is not acceptable to you, you can define your own custom class with subcollections and properties, and reference it in the `type` attribute of a new property. In fact, you are not limited to base types for profile properties; you can also reference more complex classes (such as `ArrayList` or `Color`), and your own enumerations, structures, and classes, as long as they are serializable into a binary or XML format (the format is dictated by the property's `serializeAs` attribute).

The Profile system is built upon the provider model design pattern. ASP.NET comes with a single built-in profile provider that uses a SQL Server database as a backing store. However, as usual, you can build your own providers or find them from third parties.

Accessing Profiles from Business Classes

Sometimes you may need to access the user's profile from a business class, such as we are doing in this book. The `Profile` property is dynamically added only to the ASPX pages' code-behind classes, so you can't use it in those situations. However, you can still access it through the `Profile` property exposed by the current `HttpContext`. The `HttpContext` class is the container for the current web request — it's used to pass around objects that are part of the request: forms, properties, `ViewState`, and so on.

Anytime you process a page, you will have this `HttpContext` information, so you can always pull a `Profile` class instance out of the `HttpContext` class. The returned type is `ProfileBase`, though, not the `ProfileCommon` object generated on-the-fly that enabled you to use IntelliSense and access properties in a strongly typed manner. Therefore, the resulting `Profile` class instance read from the `HttpContext.Current.Profile` will not be strongly typed. No problem — just create a `ProfileBase` object and use its methods to retrieve values. I have added a series of methods to the `Helpers` class to help with this in the Beer House. The first step is a series of overloaded `GetUserProfile` methods that return a `ProfileBase` object. The `Create` method has two overloads, one that accepts just the username and one that accepts the username and if they are authenticated. I created three versions of the `GetUserProfile` method, one to handle each of the `Create` overloads and one to automatically retrieve the profile for the current user, passing in his or her authentication status.

```
Public Shared Function GetUserProfile() As ProfileBase
        Return ProfileBase.Create(CurrentUserName,
CurrentUser.Identity.IsAuthenticated)
End Function

Public Shared Function GetUserProfile(ByVal vUserName As String) As ProfileBase
        Return ProfileBase.Create(vUserName, CurrentUser.Identity.IsAuthenticated)
End Function

Public Shared Function GetUserProfile(ByVal vUserName As String,
ByVal isAuthenticated As Boolean) As ProfileBase
        Return ProfileBase.Create(vUserName, isAuthenticated)
End Function
```

The next method to investigate is the `ProfileBase.GetProfileGroup` method. It accepts the name of the profile group you want to access and returns it as a `ProfileGroupBase` object. In the following example, I return the `ProfileGroup` as an object instead of a `ProfileGroupBase`. This seems to make it easier to cast the group as a custom object, such as the shopping cart, if needed.

```
Private Shared Function GetProfileSubGroup(ByVal profile As ProfileBase,
ByVal vSubGroup As String) As Object
        Return profile.GetProfileGroup(vSubGroup)
End Function
```

The `ProfileBase`'s `GetPropertyValue` and `SetPropertyValue` can be used to access and update profile values. If a value is a member of a `SubGroup`, you simply need to access the `SubGroup` and call these methods from it. The wrapper methods that follow demonstrate using the `PropertyValue` functions.

```
Public Shared Function GetProfileSubGroupStringProperty(
ByVal profile As ProfileBase, ByVal vSubGroup As String,
ByVal vProperty As String) As String
      If Not IsNothing(profile) AndAlso Not
IsNothing(profile.GetProfileGroup(vSubGroup)) Then
          Return profile.GetProfileGroup(vSubGroup).GetPropertyValue(vProperty)
      Else
          Return String.Empty
      End If
End Function

Public Shared Function GetProfileSubGroupIntegerProperty(ByVal profile As
```

```
ProfileBase, ByVal vSubGroup As String, ByVal vProperty As String) As Integer
     If Not IsNothing(profile) Then
         Return GetProfileSubGroup(profile, vSubGroup).GetPropertyValue(vProperty)
     Else
         Return 0
     End If
End Function

Public Shared Function GetProfileSubGroupObjectProperty(ByVal profile As
ProfileBase, ByVal vSubGroup As String, ByVal vProperty As String) As Object
     If Not IsNothing(profile) Then
         Return GetProfileSubGroup(profile, vSubGroup).GetPropertyValue(vProperty)
     Else
         Return Nothing
     End If
End Function

Public Shared Function GetProfileTheme(ByVal profile As ProfileBase) As String
     Return GetProfileSubGroupStringProperty(profile, "Preferences",
"Theme").ToString
End Function

Public Shared Sub SetProfileTheme(ByVal profile As ProfileBase,
ByVal sTheme As String)
     GetProfileSubGroup(profile, "Preferences").setpropertyvalue("Theme", sTheme)
End Sub

Public Shared Function GetSubscriptionType(ByVal profile As ProfileBase) As
  SubscriptionType
     Return CType(GetProfileSubGroupStringProperty(profile, "Preferences",
"Newsletter"), SubscriptionType)
End Function
```

As we proceed through the application, you will see places where these helper methods are used, such as in the Newsletter module:

```
' retreive all subscribers to the plain-text and HTML newsletter
Dim subscribers As New List(Of SubscriberInfo)

For Each user As MembershipUser In Membership.GetAllUsers
Dim userProfile As ProfileBase = Helpers.GetUserProfile(user.UserName, False)
     If Not Helpers.GetSubscriptionType(userProfile) <> SubscriptionType.None Then
         Dim subscriber As New SubscriberInfo(user.UserName, user.Email, _
             Helpers.GetProfileFirstName(userProfile), _
             Helpers.GetProfileLastName(userProfile),
Helpers.GetSubscriptionType(userProfile))
             subscribers.Add(subscriber)
             Newsletter.Lock.AcquireWriterLock(Timeout.Infinite)
             Newsletter.TotalMails += 1
             Newsletter.Lock.ReleaseWriterLock()

     End If
Next
```

An option that I did not employ in the Beer House is to create a custom profile class that inherits from `ProfileBase` and automatically instantiates itself with properties that map to the profile properties defined in the `web.config`. Lee Dumond does a great job explaining this on his blog, `http://leedumond.com/blog/getting-strongly-typed-profile-properties-from-a-class-library/`. Either way works just fine and the choice is yours.

Accessing the Profile for Users Other Than the Current User

So far, all the examples have shown how to read and write the profile for the current user. However, you can also access other users' profiles — very useful if you want to implement an administration page to read and modify the profiles of your registered members. Your administrator must be able to read and edit the profile properties for any user. The `ProfileCommon` class exposes a `GetProfile` method that returns the profile for any specified user, and once you obtain this profile instance you can read and edit the profile properties just as you can do for the current user's profile. The only difference is that after changing some values of the retrieved profile, you must explicitly call its `Save` method, which is not required when you modify the profile for the current user. (In the case of the current user, `Save` is called automatically by the runtime when the page unloads.) Here's an example of getting a profile for a specified user and then modifying a property value in that profile:

```
Dim profile As ProfileCommon = Profile.GetProfile("Marco")
profile.BirthDate = New DateTime(1980, 9, 28)
profile.Save()
```

Adding Support for Anonymous Users

The preceding code works only for registered users who are logged in. Sometimes, however, you want to be able to store profile values for users who are not logged in. You can explicitly enable anonymous identification support by adding the following line to `web.config`:

```
<anonymousIdentification enabled="true"/>
```

After that, you must indicate what properties are available to anonymous users. By default, a property is only accessible for logged-in users, but you can change this by setting the property's `allowAnonymous` attribute to `true`, as follows:

```
<add name="FavoriteTheme" type="String"
    allowAnonymous="true" defaultValue="Colorful" />
```

This is useful to allow an anonymous user to select a theme for his current session. This would not be saved after his session terminates because we don't have an actual user's identity to allow us to persist the settings. Another important concern regarding profiles for anonymous users is the migration from anonymous to authenticated status. Consider the following situation: a registered user comes to the site and browses it without logging in. He or she then changes some profile properties available to anonymous users, such as the name of the favorite theme. At some point, he or she wants to access a restricted page and needs to log in. Now, because the favorite theme was selected while the user was anonymous, it was stored into a profile linked to an anonymous user ID. After the user logs in, he or she then becomes an authenticated user with a different user ID. Therefore, that user's previous profile settings are loaded, and the user will get a site with the theme selected during a previous session, or the default one. What you wanted to do, however, was to migrate the anonymous user's profile to the authenticated user's profile at the time he or she logged in. This can be done by means of the `Profile_MigrateAnonymous` global event, which you can handle in the `Global.asax` file. Once this event is raised, the

`HttpContext.Profile` property will already have returned the authenticated user's profile, so it's too late for us to save the anonymous profile values. You can, however, get a reference to the anonymous profile previously used by the user and then copy values from it to the new profile. In the "Solution" section, you will see how to implement this event to avoid losing the user's preferences.

Integrating the ASP.NET AJAX Profile Service

Along with the `Authentication` and `Roles`, the `Sys.Services.ProfileService` class provides client-side access to the `Profile` service. There are two main functions to become familiar with: `Load` and `Save`. The `Load` function loads the user's profile into client memory. The method accepts an array of profile properties to load, along with the typical callback function names. If null is passed into the `Load` function, the full set of profile properties is loaded.

```
Sys.Services.ProfileService.load(null,

LoadCompletedCallback, ProfileFailedCallback, null);
```

The `profileServer` also has to be enabled in the `web.config` file, as shown earlier. When you enable the `ProfileService` class, you have to explicitly define what fields can be read and which fields can be written to. You cannot create new profile fields through the `ProfileService`. You also cannot change the Read/Write status of a property through the service.

`Readonly` properties are defined as a comma-separated list in the `readAccessProperties` value. A similar list can be set to the `witeAccessProperties`. The list does not have to match, and it can overlap.

```
<profileService enabled="true" readAccessProperties="FirstName, LastName" />
```

OpenId Identity Services

One of the usability problems all users face with the web is managing a never-ending list of passwords. The technical term that embodies the challenges and solutions to this real-world issue is "identity." The marketplace has been creating some solutions to this problem; Microsoft, for example, introduced CardSpace with the release of .NET 3.5. The developer community has also created a technology called OpenId. The reality is the two technologies are very complementary because CardSpace targets the more secure websites requiring SSL, such as sites used in online banking. OpenId is more general purpose and ideal for a site that is not mission critical, although it could be sufficient to address sites that are. Because the Beer House is a simple site that does not have a SSL certificate, which is currently required by CardSpace, we will integrate OpenId authentication as an option for our users.

OpenId was originally created by Brad Fitzpatrick as the identity system for LiveJournal. It has matured into a system that is ultimately managed by the OpenId Foundation, http://OpenId.net. The main paradigm change that OpenId brings to the table is the concept that instead of a username/password combination, an identity relies on a URL. For example, http://TheBeerHouse.MyOpenId.net. Instead of providing a username and password to the site, known as the Relaying party, the user supplies an OpenId URL. The Relaying party, your website, then redirects the user to the OpenId provider at the URL. The URL can point to any number of providers; there is no one single OpenId provider. Here, the user is authenticated, typically through a username and password, but that is not an absolute requirement, and upon successful authentication, the user is redirected back to the Relaying party.

Typically, a user remains authenticated with their OpenId provider, usually through a persistent cookie, but this is also not a requirement. Once authenticated on the site, the user decides what information he or she wants to share with the Relaying party. The user can decide at this point if he or she is comfortable sharing the required and optional data with the Relaying party. I try to keep these requests as minimal as possible to create a valid user account in the ASP.NET membership provider. If this is the user's first experience authenticating with my site, he or she will need to have an account to authenticate against. So the create user process is drastically changed from the `CreateUserWizard` process also described in this chapter.

When a user creates an OpenId account he or she will supply the provider with much of this information. As part of the OpenId protocol the Relaying party tells the identity provider what fields it requires to perform a successful authentication; it can also request optional information. Before the user tells the identity provider to trust the Relaying party, the user is asked if he or she is comfortable sharing personal information with the Relaying party. Figure 4-12 illustrates the steps required to perform OpenId authentication.

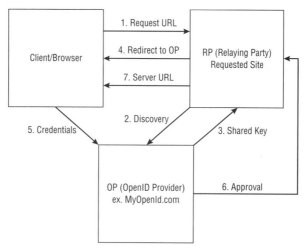

Figure 4-12

Ultimately, the user is more in control of his or her personal identification and has one central location in which to store this data. This should help the user when trying to authenticate with numerous sites, and save time in the registration process because the same information can be seamlessly passed back to the relaying party without having to be reentered by the user.

Designing Our Solution

So far, we have described the general features of the membership and profile services, and we can now build upon this knowledge and design exactly how we can implement these features in our particular website. Here's the summary of our design objectives regarding membership and profile features, and a description of the corresponding web pages:

❑   A login box will be visible in the top-right corner of each page whenever the user is anonymous. After the user logs in, the login box will be hidden. Instead, we'll show a greeting message and links for Logout and Edit Profile.

❏ A faux login dialog box will be displayed using ASP.NET AJAX and CSS that allows users to authenticate themselves using either ASP.NET AJAX or OpenId. The dialog box is embedded in the main master page for the site and will be hidden by default. It will perform authentication by calling the membership services built into ASP.NET AJAX. If a user wants to authenticate him- or herself using OpenId, an additional interface will provide for it.

❏ A `Register.aspx` page will allow new users to register (create their own account), and we'll populate it with some profile settings upon registration. The profile will have the following first-level properties: `FirstName` (`String`), `LastName` (`String`), `Gender` (`String`), `BirthDate` (`DateTime`), `Occupation` (`String`), and `Website` (`String`). A profile group named `Address` will have the following subproperties: `Street`, `PostCode`, `City`, `State`, and `Country`, all of type `String`. Another group, named `Contacts`, will have the following string subproperties: `Phone` and `Fax`. A final group, named `Preferences`, will have the `Theme`, `Culture`, and `Newsletter` properties. The `Theme` property is the only one that will be made available to anonymous users.

❏ Our `PasswordRecovery.aspx` page will allow users to recover forgotten passwords; it can e-mail the password to the user's e-mail address that is on file. This is possible because we'll configure the membership module to encrypt the password, instead of storing it as a hash (a hashed password is a one-way encryption that is not reversible). We had to decide whether we wanted the best possible security (hashing) or a more user-friendly encryption method that enables us to recover the user's password. In our scenario, we've determined that the user-friendly option is the best choice.

❏ Our `EditProfile.aspx` page will only be accessible to registered members, and it will allow them to change their account's password and the profile information they set up at registration time.

❏ We'll create some administration pages to allow the administrator to read and edit all the information about registered users (members). A `ManageUsers.aspx` page will help the administrator look up records for members by either their username or e-mail address (searches by partial text will also be supported). Among the data returned will be their username, e-mail address, when they registered or last accessed the site, and whether they are active or not. A second page, `EditUser.aspx`, will show additional details about a single user, and will allow the administrator to enable or disable the account, assign new roles to the user, remove roles from the user, and edit the user's personal profile.

Solution

We'll get right into the implementation because we've already covered the basic material and our objectives in the "Design" section of this chapter. Now we'll put all the pieces together to create the pages and the supporting code to make them work. These are the steps used to tackle our solution:

1. Define all the settings required for membership, roles, and profiles in `web.config`.

2. Create the login box on the master page, and the "access denied" page. To test the login process before creating the registration page, we can easily create a user account from the ASP.NET Web Administration Tool.

3. Create the registration and profiling page.

4. Create the password recovery page.

5. Create the page to change the current password and all the profile information.

6. Design profiles to save the user's favorite theme, and handle the migration from an anonymous user to an authenticated user so we won't lose his theme preference.

7. Create the administration pages to display all users, as well as edit and delete them.

The Configuration File

Following is a partial snippet of the `web.config` file (located in the site's root folder) used to configure the authentication type, membership, role manager, profile, and site map provider (in this order):

```
<configuration xmlns="http://schemas.microsoft.com/.NetConfiguration/v2.0">
    <!-- other settings... -->
    <system.web>
        <authentication mode="Forms">
            <forms cookieless="AutoDetect"
                loginUrl="~/AccessDenied.aspx" name="TBHFORMAUTH" />
        </authentication>

        <membership defaultProvider="TBH_MembershipProvider"
            userIsOnlineTimeWindow="15">
            <providers>
                <add name="TBH_MembershipProvider"
                    connectionStringName="LocalSqlServer"
                    applicationName="/"
                    enablePasswordRetrieval="true"
                    enablePasswordReset="true"
                    requiresQuestionAndAnswer="true"
                    requiresUniqueEmail="true"
                    passwordFormat="Encrypted"
                    maxInvalidPasswordAttempts="5"
                    passwordAttemptWindow="10"
                    minRequiredPasswordLength="5"
                    minRequiredNonalphanumericCharacters="0"
                    type="System.Web.Security.SqlMembershipProvider, System.Web,
Version=2.0.0.0, Culture=neutral, PublicKeyToken=b03f5f7f11d50a3a"
                    />
            </providers>
        </membership>

        <roleManager enabled="true" cacheRolesInCookie="true"
            cookieName="TBHROLES" defaultProvider="TBH_RoleProvider">
            <providers>
                <add name="TBH_RoleProvider"
                    connectionStringName="LocalSqlServer"
                    applicationName="/"
                    type="System.Web.Security.SqlRoleProvider, System.Web,
Version=2.0.0.0, Culture=neutral, PublicKeyToken=b03f5f7f11d50a3a"
                    />
```

```
            </providers>
        </roleManager>

        <anonymousIdentification cookieless="AutoDetect"  enabled="true"/>

        <profile defaultProvider="TBH_ProfileProvider">
            <providers>
                <add name="TBH_ProfileProvider"
                    connectionStringName="LocalSqlServer"
                    applicationName="/"
                    type="System.Web.Profile.SqlProfileProvider, System.Web,
Version=2.0.0.0, Culture=neutral, PublicKeyToken=b03f5f7f11d50a3a"
                    />
            </providers>
            <properties>
                <add name="FirstName" type="String" />
                <add name="LastName" type="String" />
                <add name="Gender" type="String" />
                <add name="BirthDate" type="DateTime" />
                <add name="Occupation" type="String" />
                <add name="Website" type="String" />
                <group name="Address">
                    <add name="Street" type="String" />
                    <add name="PostalCode" type="String" />
                    <add name="City" type="String" />
                    <add name="State" type="String" />
                    <add name="Country" type="String" />
                </group>
                <group name="Contacts">
                    <add name="Phone" type="String" />
                    <add name="Fax" type="String" />
                </group>
                <group name="Preferences">
                    <add name="Theme" type="String" allowAnonymous="true" />
                    <add name="Culture" type="String" defaultValue="en-US" />
                    <add name="Newsletter"
type="MB.TheBeerHouse.BLL.Newsletters.SubscriptionType" />
                </group>
            </properties>
        </profile>

        <machineKey validationKey="287C5D125D6B7E7223E1F719E3D58D17BB967703017E1BBE28
618FAC6C4501E910C7E59800B5D4C2EDD5B0ED98874A3E952D60BAF260D9D374A74C76CB741803"
            decryptionKey="5C1D8BD9DF3E1B4E1D01132F234266616E0D5EF772FE80AB"
            validation="SHA1"/>

        <siteMap defaultProvider="TBH_SiteMapProvider" enabled="true">
            <providers>
                <add name="TBH_SiteMapProvider"
                    type="System.Web.XmlSiteMapProvider"
                    securityTrimmingEnabled="true"
                    siteMapFile="web.sitemap"
                />
            </providers>
```

```
            </siteMap>
        </system.web>

        <location path="EditProfile.aspx">
            <system.web>
                <authorization>
                    <deny users="?" />
                    <allow users="*" />
                </authorization>
            </system.web>
        </location>

        <system.net>
            <mailSettings>
                <smtp deliveryMethod="Network">
                    <network defaultCredentials="true" host="vsnetbeta2" port="25"
                        from="mbellinaso@wrox.com"></network>
                </smtp>
            </mailSettings>
        </system.net>
    </configuration>
```

As you can see, a provider is defined and configured for all modules that support this pattern. I specified the provider settings even though they are often the same as the default providers found in machine.config.default, because I can't be sure whether the defaults will always be the same in future ASP.NET releases, and I like to have this information handy in case I might want to make further changes someday. To create these settings, I copied them from machine.config.default, and then I made a few tweaks as needed.

I defined a Newsletter profile property as type TheBeerHouse.BLL.Newsletters.SubscriptionType, which is an enumeration defined in the SubscriptionType.vb file located under /Newsletter in the class library:

```
Namespace BLL.Newsletters

    Public Enum SubscriptionType As Integer
        None = 0
        PlainText = 1
        Html = 2
    End Enum

End Namespace
```

To configure the cryptographic keys, we need to set the validationKey and decryptionKey attributes of the machineKey element. Because we are configuring the membership module to encrypt passwords, we can't leave them set at AutoGenerate, which is the default. You can find some handy utilities on the Internet that will help you set these values. You can check the following Microsoft Knowledge Base article for more information: http://support.microsoft.com/kb/313091. This article shows how to implement a class that makes use of the cryptographic classes and services to create values for these keys. Alternatively, if you want an easier way to create these keys, check out this online tool: www.aspnetresources.com/tools/keycreator.aspx.

I want to reiterate a point I made earlier in this chapter: if you'll be deploying your application to a web farm (more than one web server configured to distribute the load between the servers), then you need to specify the same machine keys for each server. In addition to password encryption, these keys are also used for session state. By synchronizing these keys with all your servers, you ensure that the same encryption will be used on each server. This is essential if there's a chance that a different server might be used to process the next posting of a page.

Creating the Login Box

The user interface for user authentication is fairly common across all websites; a username, password textbox combination, an optional Remember Me checkbox, a link to register on the site, and a link to retrieve a lost password. Something like this is ideal to collect together in a user or Web Control, which is exactly with the ASP.NET team did in ASP.NET 2.0. The Login control combined all these common user interface elements into a fully customizable control that seamlessly works with the membership provider.

Now it's time to fill that <div> with the code for the login box. ASP.NET typically uses customizable templates to control the visual rendering of many controls. In this section, we will customize the default user interface of the login controls by providing our own template. Using custom templates offers the following advantages:

1. You have full control over the appearance of the produced output, and you can change many aspects of the behavior. For example, our custom template can be used with validator controls, and you can set their SetFocusOnError property to true (this defaults to false in the default template). This property specifies whether the validator will give the focus to the control it validates if the client-side validation fails. This is desirable in our case because we want the focus to go to the first invalid control after the user clicks the Submit button if some controls have invalid input values.

2. If you don't redefine the TextBox controls, the SetInputControlsHighlight method we developed in Chapter 2 will not find them, and thus the textboxes will not get the special highlight behavior that gives users a visual cue as to which TextBox currently has the focus.

Here's the complete code that uses a LoginView to display a login box. This login box contains links to register a new account or to recover a forgotten password when the user is anonymous, or it will contain a welcome message, a logout link, and a link to the EditProfile page if the user is currently logged in:

```
<div id="loginbox">
<asp:LoginView ID="LoginView1" runat="server">
   <AnonymousTemplate>
      <asp:Login ID="Login" runat="server" Width="100%"
         FailureAction="RedirectToLoginPage">
         <LayoutTemplate>
            <table border="0" cellpadding="0" cellspacing="0" width="100%">
               <tr>
                  <td width="60px">Username:</td>
                  <td><asp:TextBox id="UserName" runat="server" Width="95%" /></td>
                  <td width="5px" align="right">
                     <asp:RequiredFieldValidator ID="valRequireUserName"
                        runat="server" SetFocusOnError="true" Text="*"
```

```
                        ControlToValidate="UserName" ValidationGroup="Login" />
                    </td>
                </tr>
                <tr>
                    <td>Password:</td>
                    <td><asp:TextBox ID="Password" runat="server"
                        TextMode="Password"  Width="95%" /></td>
                    <td width="5px" align="right">
                        <asp:RequiredFieldValidator ID="valRequirePassword"
                            runat="server" SetFocusOnError="true" Text="*"
                            ControlToValidate="Password" ValidationGroup="Login" />
                    </td>
                </tr>
            </table>
            <table border="0" cellpadding="0" cellspacing="0" width="100%">
                <tr>
                    <td><asp:CheckBox ID="RememberMe" runat="server"
                        Text="Remember me"></asp:Checkbox></td>
                    <td align="right">
                        <asp:ImageButton ID="Submit" runat="server"
                            CommandName="Login" ImageUrl="~/images/go.gif"
                            ValidationGroup="Login" />
                    </td>
                    <td width="5px" align="right"> </td>
                </tr>
            </table>
            <div style="border-top: solid 1px black; margin-top: 2px">
                <asp:HyperLink ID="lnkRegister" runat="server"
                    NavigateUrl="~/Register.aspx">Create new account
                </asp:HyperLink><br />
                <asp:HyperLink ID="lnkPasswordRecovery" runat="server"
                    NavigateUrl="~/PasswordRecovery.aspx">I forgot my password
                </asp:HyperLink>
            </div>
        </LayoutTemplate>
    </asp:Login>
</AnonymousTemplate>
<LoggedInTemplate>
    <div id="welcomebox">
        <asp:LoginName ID="LoginName1" runat="server"
            FormatString="Hello  {0}!" /><br />
        <small>
        <font face="Webdings">4</font>
        <asp:HyperLink ID="lnkProfile" runat="server" Text="Edit Profile"
            NavigateUrl="~/EditProfile.aspx" />
        <font face="Webdings">3</font><br />
        <font face="Webdings">4</font>
        <asp:LoginStatus ID="LoginStatus1" Runat="server" />
        <font face="Webdings">3</font>
        </small>
    </div>
</LoggedInTemplate>
</asp:LoginView>
</div>
```

Absolutely no code is needed in the master page's code-behind files. In fact, because we used the right IDs for the textboxes and other controls in the template sections of the Login control, it will continue working autonomously as if it were using the default UI. To test the control, first create a new user through the ASP.NET Website Configuration Tool described earlier, and then try to log in. In Figure 4-13, you can see what the home page looks like from an anonymous user's and an authenticated user's point of view.

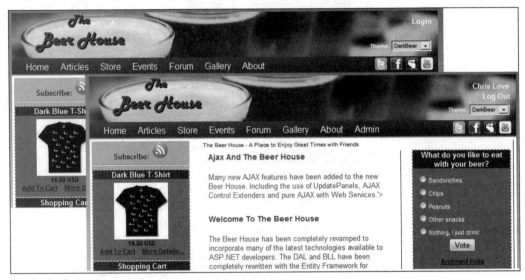

Figure 4-13

Observe the login box in the first window (only displayed for anonymous users), and the new greeting message and links in the second window that are displayed after the user logs in. Also, note that an Admin link is visible on the second browser's menu bar. That Admin link only appears for users who have been assigned the Administrators role. The web.sitemap file is used to generate the menu, and the item representing the Admin link was modified by adding the roles attribute, which was set to Administrators:

```
<siteMap xmlns="http://schemas.microsoft.com/AspNet/SiteMap-File-1.0" >
    <siteMapNode title="Home" url="~/Default.aspx">
        <!-- other items -->
        <siteMapNode title="Admin" url="~/Admin/Default.aspx"
            roles="Administrators" />
    </siteMapNode>
</siteMap>
```

Of course, you can test the site-map-controlled menu by assigning the Administrators role to your sample user. You can even do this role assignment from the online configuration application!

The AccessDenied.aspx Page

If you look a few pages back, you'll see that the loginUrl attribute of the web.config's <forms> is set to AccessDenied.aspx. As its name clearly suggests, this is the URL of the page we want to redirect control to when the user tries to access a protected page to which he doesn't have permission. In many cases, you would place the login box in this page, hence the attribute name (loginUrl). In our case, however, we have a site that lets anonymous users access many different pages, and we only require the user to log in to gain access to a small number of pages, so we want to make sure the login box is visible from any page when the user is anonymous. The login box invites users to log in if they already have an account, or to register if they don't have one. This AccessDenied page is also loaded when users try to log in but give invalid credentials, or when they are already logged in but they don't have a role required by the page they requested. Therefore, the page has three possible messages, and the following code uses three labels for them:

```
<div id="ContentTitleDiv">
    <asp:Literal runat="server" ID="ltlTitle"></asp:Literal></div>
<div id="ContentBodyDiv">
    <asp:Image ID="imgLock" runat="server" ImageUrl="~/images/lock.gif"
ImageAlign="left"
        AlternateText="Access denied" />

    <asp:Label runat="server" ID="lblLoginRequired" Font-Bold="true">
You must be a registered user to access this page. If you already have an account,
please login with
your credentials in the box on the upper-right corner. Otherwise <a
href="Register.aspx">click here</a> to register now for free.
    </asp:Label>
    <asp:Label runat="server" ID="lblInsufficientPermissions" Font-Bold="true">
Sorry, the account you are logged with does not have the permissions required to
access this page.
    </asp:Label>
    <asp:Label runat="server" ID="lblInvalidCredentials" Font-Bold="true">
The submitted credentials are not valid. Please check they are correct and try
again.
If you forgot your password, <a href="PasswordRecovery.aspx">click here</a> to
recover it.
    </asp:Label>
</div>
```

Since OpenId has been added to the authentication options, the Login control has been changed to have a LayoutTemplate defined. This affords us the flexibility of using the built-in authentication logic that comes with the Login control but lets us extend the available layout to include some extra controls to work with OpenId. When you create a custom layout for the Login control or any of the stock membership controls, special care must be taken to create controls with the same ID values the stock control uses. Otherwise the control will look for them and throw exceptions.

```
<asp:Login runat="server" ID="adLogin" CreateUserUrl="~/Register.aspx"
Width="300">
    <LayoutTemplate>
        <table border="0" cellpadding="0" cellspacing="0" width="100%">
            <tr>
                <td width="60px">
                    <asp:Label runat="server" ID="lblUserName"
AssociatedControlID="UserName" Text="Username:"
                        meta:resourcekey="lblUserNameResource1" />
                </td>
                <td>
                    <asp:TextBox ID="UserName" runat="server" Width="95%"
```

```
                Columns="30" meta:resourcekey="UserNameResource2" />
                                </td>
                                <td width="5px" align="right">
                                        <asp:RequiredFieldValidator ID="valRequireUserName"
runat="server" SetFocusOnError="True"
                                                ControlToValidate="UserName" Text="*"
ValidationGroup="Login" meta:resourcekey="valRequireUserNameResource1" />
                                </td>
                        </tr>
                        <tr>
                                <td>
                                        <asp:Label runat="server" ID="lblPassword"
AssociatedControlID="Password" Text="Password:"
                                                meta:resourcekey="lblPasswordResource1" />
                                </td>
                                <td>
                                        <asp:TextBox ID="Password" runat="server"
TextMode="Password" Width="95%" meta:resourcekey="PasswordResource2" />
                                </td>
                                <td width="5px" align="right">
                                        <asp:RequiredFieldValidator ID="valRequirePassword"
runat="server" SetFocusOnError="True"
                                                ControlToValidate="Password" Text="*"
ValidationGroup="Login" meta:resourcekey="valRequirePasswordResource1" />
                                </td>
                        </tr>
                </table>
                <table border="0" cellpadding="0" cellspacing="0" width="100%">
                        <tr>
                                <td>
                                        <asp:CheckBox ID="RememberMe" runat="server"
Text="Remember me" meta:resourcekey="RememberMeResource1">
                                        </asp:CheckBox>
                                </td>
                                <td align="right">
                                        <asp:ImageButton ID="Submit" runat="server"
 AlternateText="Login" CommandName="Login"
                                                ImageUrl="~/images/go.gif" ValidationGroup="Login"
 meta:resourcekey="SubmitResource1" />
                                </td>
                                <td width="5px" align="right">
                                         
                                </td>
                        </tr>
                </table>
                <table border="0" cellpadding="0" cellspacing="0" width="100%">
                        <tr>
                                <td>
                                        <asp:TextBox runat="server" ID="txtOpenId" Width="200"
class="openid_identifier" />
                                </td>
                                <td>
```

```
                                    <asp:ImageButton runat="server" ID="btnLogon"
AlternateText="Login Using OpenId"
                                        ImageUrl="~/images/open-id-login.gif"
onclick="btnLogon_Click" /><br />
                            </td>
                            <td width="5px" align="right">
                                 
                            </td>
                        </tr>
                    </table>
                    <div style="border-top: solid 1px black; margin-top: 2px;
padding-top: 2px">
                        <asp:HyperLink ID="lnkRegister" runat="server" NavigateUrl=
"~/Register.aspx" meta:resourcekey="lnkRegisterResource1">Create new
account</asp:HyperLink><br />
                        <asp:HyperLink ID="lnkPasswordRecovery" runat="server"
 NavigateUrl="~/PasswordRecovery.aspx"
                        meta:resourcekey="lnkPasswordRecoveryResource1">
I forgot my password</asp:HyperLink>
                    </div>
                </LayoutTemplate>
        </asp:Login>
```

The `Page_Load` event handler in the code-behind file contains the logic for showing the proper label and hiding the other two. You need to do some tests to determine which of the three cases applies:

❑   If the querystring contains a `loginfailure` parameter set to `1`, it means that the user tried to log in but the submitted credentials were not recognized.

❑   If the user is not authenticated and there is no `loginfailure` parameter on the querystring, it means that the user tried to access a page that is not available to anonymous users.

❑   If the current user is already authenticated and the page is loaded anyway, it means the user does not have sufficient permission (read "does not belong to a required role") to access the requested page.

Here is how to translate this description to code:

```
Partial Public Class AccessDenied
    Inherits BasePage

    Protected Sub Page_Load(ByVal sender As Object, ByVal e As System.EventArgs)
Handles Me.Load
        lblInsufficientPermissions.Visible = Me.User.Identity.IsAuthenticated
        lblLoginRequired.Visible = Not (Me.User.Identity.IsAuthenticated) AndAlso _
            String.IsNullOrEmpty(Me.Request.QueryString("loginfailure"))
        lblInvalidCredentials.Visible = Not (Me.Request.QueryString("loginfailure")
 = Nothing) AndAlso _
            Me.Request.QueryString("loginfailure") = "1"

        If OpenID.IsOpenIdRequest Then
            Dim data As OpenIdData = OpenID.Authenticate()
```

```
            If data.IsSuccess Then

                    Dim mu As MembershipUser = Membership.GetUser(data.Identity)

                    If IsNothing(mu) Then
                            mu =
Membership.GetUser(Membership.GetUserNameByEmail(data.Parameters("email")))
                    End If

                    If IsNothing(mu) Then
                            Response.Redirect(String.Format(
"Register.aspx?fullname={0}&email={1}&dob={2}&gender={3}
&postcode&{4}&country{5}", _
                            data.Parameters("fullname"), data.Parameters("email"),
data.Parameters("dob"), _
                            data.Parameters("gender"), data.Parameters("postcode"),
  data.Parameters("country")))
                    End If

                    FormsAuthentication.RedirectFromLoginPage(mu.UserName,
adLogin.RememberMeSet)

            End If

        End If

    End Sub
```

Implementing OpenId Authentication

Now that OpenId has been explained, it is time to actually implement it in the Beer House. There are several ASP.NET solutions available (http://code.google.com/p/dotnetopenid), including full-blown libraries with Web Controls and the like. However, for now I want to keep the implementation simple, and Mads Kristensen provides a bare bones implementation (http://blog.madskristensen .dk/post/OpenId-implementation-in-Csharp-and-ASPNET.aspx) that is easy to integrate. This is a single-class solution that handles the base needs of interacting with an identity provider. It takes care of all the fundamental requirements of requesting an OpenId authentication through the designated OpenId URL (identity provider) and managing the subsequent response.

If the user decides to authenticate using OpenId, the btnLogon click event is fired to initiate the OpenId process. A simple call to the shared Login method, with some key parameters, and the process is managed for us.

```
        Protected Sub btnLogon_Click(ByVal sender As Object, ByVal e As
    System.Web.UI.ImageClickEventArgs)
            Dim success As Boolean =
    OpenID.Login(DirectCast(adLogin.FindControl("txtOpenId"), TextBox).Text, _
                            "email,fullname",
    "country,language,nickname,dob,gender,postcode")

            If Not success Then
                Response.Write("The OpenID is not valid")
```

```
                End If
        End Sub
```

The `Login` method takes the user's `OpenId` URL (identity), a comma-separated list of required parameters (`email` and `fullname`) and a comma-separated list of optional parameters. The method then builds a `StringDictionary` of values to pass the `OpenId` URL and redirects the user to their URL.

```
    Public Shared Function Login(ByVal identity As String, ByVal requiredParameters As
    String, ByVal optionalParameters As String) As Boolean
            Try
                Dim dic As StringDictionary = GetIdentityServer(identity)
                Dim server As String = dic("openid.server")
                Dim delgate As String = If(dic("openid.delegate"), identity)

                If Not String.IsNullOrEmpty(server) Then
                    Dim redirectUrl As String = CreateRedirectUrl(requiredParameters,
    optionalParameters, delgate, identity)

                    ' Add the provided data to session so it can be tracked after
    authentication
                    Dim data As New OpenIdData(identity)
                    HttpContext.Current.Session("openid") = data

                    HttpContext.Current.Response.Redirect(server + redirectUrl, True)
                End If
            Catch generatedExceptionName As Exception
            End Try

            Return False
    End Function
```

Once users complete the verification and confirmation process at their `OpenId` provider they are redirected back to the Access Denied page. In a similar fashion, as we check to see if the page is in a `PostBack` or not, the `Page Load` event handler checks to see if the page is being loaded in response to an `OpenId` request, if so and the authentication was successful, the user is reconciled with an account and authenticated.

```
    Public Shared ReadOnly Property IsOpenIdRequest() As Boolean
            Get
                ' All OpenID request must use the GET method
                If Not HttpContext.Current.Request.HttpMethod.Equals("GET",
    StringComparison.OrdinalIgnoreCase) Then
                    Return False
                End If

                Return HttpContext.Current.Request.QueryString("openid.mode") _
    IsNot Nothing
            End Get
    End Property
```

The `OpenId.Authenticate` method returns an `OpenIdData` object, which contains all the requested data, including if the authentication was successful (`isSuccess`), the user's `OpenId` identity and any returned parameters.

```
Public Shared Function Authenticate() As OpenIdData
      Dim data As OpenIdData = DirectCast(HttpContext.Current.Session("openid"),
OpenIdData)

      ' Make sure the client has been through the Login method
      If data Is Nothing Then
         Return New OpenIdData(String.Empty)
      End If

      Dim query As NameValueCollection = HttpContext.Current.Request.QueryString

      ' Make sure the incoming request's identity matches the one stored in session
      If query("openid.claimed_id") <> data.Identity Then
         Return data
      End If

      data.IsSuccess = query("openid.mode") = "id_res"

      For Each name As String In query.Keys
         If name.StartsWith("openid.sreg.") Then
             data.Parameters.Add(name.Replace("openid.sreg.", String.Empty),
query(name))
         End If
      Next

      HttpContext.Current.Session.Remove("openid")
      Return data
End Function
```

The following routine first checks to see if there is an account that corresponds to the OpenId Identity value, if not it tries to retrieve the membership by the e-mail supplied by the identity provider. If the account still cannot be reconciled the user is then passed to the Register page with the supplied credentials in tow. I chose to place this code in the main MasterPage's Page Load event handler.

```
If OpenID.IsOpenIdRequest Then
Dim data As OpenIdData = OpenID.Authenticate()
If data.IsSuccess Then

            Dim mu As MembershipUser = Membership.GetUser(data.Identity)

            If IsNothing(mu) Then
                mu = Membership.GetUser(Membership.GetUserNameByEmail(
data.Parameters("email")))
            End If

            If IsNothing(mu) Then
                Response.Redirect(String.Format("Register.aspx?fullname=
{0}&email={1}&dob={2}&gender={3}&postcode&{4}&country{5}", _
                data.Parameters("fullname"), data.Parameters("email"),
data.Parameters("dob"), _
                data.Parameters("gender"), data.Parameters("postcode"),
data.Parameters("country")))
            Else
                FormsAuthentication.RedirectFromLoginPage(mu.UserName,
```

```
adLogin.RememberMeSet)
            End If
    End If

    End If
```

Figure 4-14 shows the Access Denied page.

Figure 4-14

The UserProfile Control

The user interface and the logic required to show and update a user's profile are contained in a user control named `UserProfile.ascx` and placed under the `Controls` folder. Profile properties can be edited in the registration page, the page that users access to change their profile, and the site's administration area, so it makes sense to put this code in a user control that can easily be reused in multiple places. The user interface part consists of simple HTML code to lay out a number of server-side controls (textboxes and drop-down lists) that will show users their profile properties and let them edit those properties:

```
<%@ Control Language="VB" AutoEventWireup="true" CodeFile="UserProfile.ascx.vb"
 Inherits="UserProfile" %>
<div class="sectionsubtitle">Site preferences</div>
<p></p>
<table cellpadding="2">
  <tr>
    <td width="130" class="fieldname">Newsletter:</td>
```

```
            <td width="300">
               <asp:DropDownList runat="server" ID="ddlSubscriptions">
                  <asp:ListItem Text="No subscription" Value="None" Selected="true" />
                  <asp:ListItem Text="Subscribe to plain-text version"
                     Value="PlainText" />
                  <asp:ListItem Text="Subscribe to HTML version" Value="Html" />
               </asp:DropDownList>
            </td>
      </tr>
      <tr>
         <td class="fieldname">Language:</td>
         <td>
            <asp:DropDownList runat="server" ID="ddlLanguages">
               <asp:ListItem Text="English" Value="en-US" Selected="true" />
               <asp:ListItem Text="Italian" Value="it-IT" />
            </asp:DropDownList>
         </td>
      </tr>
</table>
<BR/>
<table cellpadding="2" width="95%">
    <tr>
         <td><img alt="Avatar" src="<%= GetAvatarURL() %>" /></td>
         <td><a href="http://www.gravatar.com">More About Gravatar</a></td>
    </tr>
    <tr>
       <td style="width: 110px;" class="fieldname"><asp:Label runat="server" ID=
"lblAvatarUrl" AssociatedControlID="txtAvatarUrl" Text="Avatar Url:" /></td>
       <td><asp:TextBox runat="server" ID="txtAvatarUrl" Width="99%" /></td>
    </tr>
    <tr>
       <td class="fieldname"><asp:Label runat="server" ID="lblSignature"
AssociatedControlID="txtSignature" Text="Signature:" /></td>
       <td><asp:TextBox runat="server" ID="txtSignature" Width="99%"
MaxLength="500" TextMode="multiLine" Rows="4" /></td>
    </tr>
</table>
<p></p>
<div class="sectionsubtitle">Personal details</div>
<p></p>
<table cellpadding="2">
    <tr>
       <td width="130" class="fieldname">First name:</td>
       <td width="300">
          <asp:TextBox ID="txtFirstName" runat="server" Width="99%"></asp:TextBox>
       </td>
    </tr>
    <tr>
       <td class="fieldname">Last name:</td>
       <td>
          <asp:TextBox ID="txtLastName" runat="server" Width="99%" />
       </td>
    </tr>
    <tr>
```

```
            <td class="fieldname">Gender:</td>
            <td>
               <asp:DropDownList runat="server" ID="ddlGenders">
                  <asp:ListItem Text="Please select one..." Value="" Selected="True" />
                  <asp:ListItem Text="Male" Value="M" />
                  <asp:ListItem Text="Female" Value="F" />
               </asp:DropDownList>
            </td>
         </tr>
         <tr>
            <td class="fieldname">Birth date:</td>
            <td>
               <asp:TextBox ID="txtBirthDate" runat="server" Width="99%"></asp:TextBox>
               <asp:CompareValidator runat="server" ID="valBirthDateFormat"
                  ControlToValidate="txtBirthDate"
                  SetFocusOnError="true" Display="Dynamic" Operator="DataTypeCheck"
                  Type="Date" ErrorMessage="The format of the birth date is not valid."
                  ValidationGroup="EditProfile">
                  <br />The format of the birth date is not valid.
               </asp:CompareValidator>
            </td>
         </tr>
         <tr>
            <td class="fieldname">Occupation:</td>
            <td>
               <asp:DropDownList ID="ddlOccupations" runat="server" Width="99%">
                  <asp:ListItem Text="Please select one..." Value="" Selected="True" />
                  <asp:ListItem Text="Academic" />
                  <asp:ListItem Text="Accountant" />
                  <asp:ListItem Text="Actor" />
                  <asp:ListItem Text="Architect" />
                  <asp:ListItem Text="Artist" />
                  <asp:ListItem Text="Business Manager" />
                  <%-- other options... --%>
                  <asp:ListItem Text="Other" />
               </asp:DropDownList>
            </td>
         </tr>
         <tr>
            <td class="fieldname">Website:</td>
            <td>
               <asp:TextBox ID="txtWebsite" runat="server" Width="99%" />
            </td>
         </tr>
      </table>
<p></p>
<div class="sectionsubtitle">Address</div>
<p></p>
<table cellpadding="2">
      <tr>
         <td width="130" class="fieldname">Street:</td>
         <td width="300">
            <asp:TextBox runat="server" ID="txtStreet" Width="99%" />
         </td>
```

```
        </tr>
        <tr>
           <td class="fieldname">City:</td>
           <td><asp:TextBox runat="server" ID="txtCity" Width="99%" /></td>
        </tr>
        <tr>
           <td class="fieldname">Zip / Postal code:</td>
           <td><asp:TextBox runat="server" ID="txtPostalCode" Width="99%" /></td>
        </tr>
        <tr>
           <td class="fieldname">State / Region:</td>
           <td><asp:TextBox runat="server" ID="txtState" Width="99%" /></td>
        </tr>
        <tr>
           <td class="fieldname">Country:</td>
           <td>
              <asp:DropDownList ID="ddlCountries" runat="server"
                 AppendDataBoundItems="True" idth="99%">
                 <asp:ListItem Text="Please select one..." Value="" Selected="True" />
              </asp:DropDownList>
           </td>
        </tr>
   </table>
   <p></p>
   <div class="sectionsubtitle">Other contacts</div>
   <p></p>
   <table cellpadding="2">
        <tr>
           <td width="130" class="fieldname">Phone:</td>
           <td width="300"><asp:TextBox runat="server" ID="txtPhone" Width="99%" /></td>
        </tr>
        <tr>
           <td class="fieldname">Fax:</td>
           <td><asp:TextBox runat="server" ID="txtFax" Width="99%" /></td>
        </tr>
   </table>
```

There is a custom `StateDropDownList` control that was added to the class library project (in the controls folder). It derives from the `DropDownList` control and overrides the `Init` method to bind the states. The `DataTextField` and `DataValueField` names are set and the `CreateDataSource` method is called. This populates the list. There are two additional properties, `IncludeCanada` and `IncludeUS`. These are simple Boolean flags that tell the `CreateDataSource` method if it should bind the provinces and states for each of the two countries. I hope you can see that this control could be expanded to include all the states, provinces, or any other geographical region for any of the numerous countries on the globe. But for simplicity's sake I limited it to these two countries.

```
<ToolboxData("<{0}:StateDropDownList runat=server></{0}:StateDropDownList>")> _
Public Class StateDropDownList
        Inherits DropDownList

        Protected Sub CreateDataSource()

                Me.Items.Clear()

                If IncludeUS And IncludeCanada Then
```

```vbnet
            Me.Items.Add(New ListItem("Choose a State/Province", "0"))
        ElseIf IncludeUS And IncludeCanada = False Then
            Me.Items.Add(New ListItem("Choose a State", "0"))
        ElseIf IncludeUS = False And IncludeCanada Then
            Me.Items.Add(New ListItem("Choose a Province", "0"))
        End If

        If IncludeUS Then
            Me.Items.Add(New ListItem("Alabama", "AL"))
            Me.Items.Add(New ListItem("Alaska", "AK"))
            Me.Items.Add(New ListItem("Arizona", "AZ"))

'All 50 US States, but could add all terrirtories too!
            Me.Items.Add(New ListItem("Wisconsin", "WI"))
            Me.Items.Add(New ListItem("Wyoming", "WY"))
        End If

        If IncludeCanada Then
            Me.Items.Add(New ListItem("British Columbia", "BC"))
            Me.Items.Add(New ListItem("Manitoba", "MB"))
            Me.Items.Add(New ListItem("New Brunswick", "NB"))
            Me.Items.Add(New ListItem("Newfoundland and Labrador", "NL"))
            Me.Items.Add(New ListItem("Northwest Territories", "NT"))
            Me.Items.Add(New ListItem("Nova Scotia", "NS"))
            Me.Items.Add(New ListItem("Nunavut", "NU"))
            Me.Items.Add(New ListItem("Ontario", "ON"))
            Me.Items.Add(New ListItem("Prince Edward Island", "PE"))
            Me.Items.Add(New ListItem("Quebec", "QC"))
            Me.Items.Add(New ListItem("Saskatchewan", "SK"))
            Me.Items.Add(New ListItem("Yukon Territories", "YT"))
        End If

    End Sub

    <Category("Control Flags"), DefaultValue("True")> _
    Public Property IncludeCanada() As Boolean
        Get
            If Not IsNothing(ViewState("Canada")) Then
                Return CBool(ViewState("Canada"))
            End If
            Return True
        End Get
        Set(ByVal Value As Boolean)
            ViewState("Canada") = Value
        End Set
    End Property

    <Category("Control Flags"), DefaultValue("True")> _
    Public Property IncludeUS() As Boolean
        Get
            If Not IsNothing(ViewState("US")) Then
                Return CBool(ViewState("US"))
            End If
            Return True
        End Get
```

```
                        Set(ByVal Value As Boolean)
                            ViewState("US") = Value
                        End Set
                End Property

                Protected Overloads Overrides Sub OnInit(ByVal e As EventArgs)

                        Me.DataTextField = "Text"
                        Me.DataValueField = "Value"
                        CreateDataSource()
                        MyBase.OnInit(e)
                End Sub

        End Class
```

There is also a `DropDownList` control that enables users to select their country. This is another custom Web Control that derives from the `DropDownList` control. The control's `Init` method is overridden to set the control's data source, a list of countries, and their corresponding codes:

```
<ToolboxData("<{0}:CountryDropDownList runat=server></{0}:CountryDropDownList>")> _
Public Class CountryDropDownList
        Inherits DropDownList

        Protected Sub CreateDataSource()

                Me.Items.Clear()

                Me.Items.Add(New ListItem("Choose a Country", "0"))
                Me.Items.Add(New ListItem("United States", "US"))
                Me.Items.Add(New ListItem("Canada", "CA"))
                Me.Items.Add(New ListItem("Afghanistan", "AF"))
                Me.Items.Add(New ListItem("Albania", "AL"))
                Me.Items.Add(New ListItem("Algeria", "DZ"))

'Long list of Countries here!
                Me.Items.Add(New ListItem("Zambia", "ZM"))
                Me.Items.Add(New ListItem("Zimbabwe", "ZW"))

        End Sub

        Protected Overloads Overrides Sub OnInit(ByVal e As EventArgs)

                Me.DataTextField = "Text"
                Me.DataValueField = "Value"
                CreateDataSource()
                MyBase.OnInit(e)

        End Sub

End Class
```

Persisting Properties through the New Control State

Because this control will be used in the administration area to read and edit the profile for any user, it needs a public property that stores the name of the user for whom you are querying. In ASP.NET 1.*x*, the typical way to make a property value persistent across postbacks is to save it in the control's ViewState collection, so that it is serialized into a blob of base-64 encoded text, together with all the other property values, and saved in the __VIEWSTATE HTML hidden field. This is better than session state because it doesn't use server resources to save temporary values because the values are saved as part of the overall page. The user won't see the hidden values, but they are there in the user's browser and he'll post them back to the server along with the other form data each time he does a postback. The problem with view state is that it can be disabled, by setting the page's or control's EnableViewState property to False. Disabling this feature is a common way to minimize the volume of data passed back and forth across the network. Unfortunately, controls that use view state to store values will not work correctly if view state is disabled on any particular host page. To resolve this issue, ASP.NET 2.0 introduced a new type of state called *control state,* which is a similar to view state, except that it's only related to a particular control, and it can't be disabled. Values that a control wants to save across postbacks can be saved in the control state, while values that are not strictly necessary can go into the view state. In reality, both categories of values will be serialized and saved into the same single __VIEWSTATE field, but the internal structure makes a difference between them. With the view state, you would just read and write the property value from and to the control's ViewState object from inside the property's accessor functions. To use control state, you need to do the following:

1. Define the property so that it uses a private field to store the value.

2. Call the parent page's RegisterRequiresControlState method, from the control's Init event handler. This notifies the page that the control needs to store some control state information.

3. Override the control's SaveControlState method to create and return an array of objects you want to save in the control state. The array values consist of the property values you need to be persisted, plus the base class' control state (this always goes into the array's first slot).

4. Override the LoadControlState method to unpack the input array of objects and initialize your properties' private fields with the values read from the array.

Following is the complete code needed to define and persist a control's UserName property:

```
Partial Class UserProfile
    Inherits System.Web.UI.UserControl

#Region " Properties "

    Public ReadOnly Property FirstName() As String
        Get
            Return FullName.Split(" ")(0)
        End Get
    End Property

    Public ReadOnly Property LastName() As String
        Get
            Return FullName.Split(" ")(FullName.Split(" ").Length - 1)
```

```vb
            End Get
    End Property

    Public ReadOnly Property FullName() As String
        Get
            Return Request("fullname")
        End Get
    End Property

    Public ReadOnly Property EMail() As String
        Get
            Return Me.Request.QueryString("Email")
        End Get
    End Property

    Public ReadOnly Property DOB() As String
        Get
            Return Request("dob")
        End Get
    End Property

    Public ReadOnly Property Gender() As String
        Get
            Return Request("gender")
        End Get
    End Property

    Public ReadOnly Property PostCode() As String
        Get
            Return Request("postcode")
        End Get
    End Property

    Public ReadOnly Property Country() As String
        Get
            Return Request("country")
        End Get
    End Property

#End Region

    Private _userName As String = String.Empty
    Public Property Username() As String
        Get
            If String.IsNullOrEmpty(_userName) Then
                Return Helpers.CurrentUser.Identity.Name
            End If
            Return _userName
        End Get
        Set(ByVal value As String)
            _userName = value
        End Set
    End Property

    Protected Sub Page_Init(ByVal sender As Object, ByVal e As System.EventArgs)
```

```
Handles Me.Init
        Me.Page.RegisterRequiresControlState(Me)
    End Sub

    Protected Overrides Sub LoadControlState(ByVal savedState As Object)
        Dim ctlState As Object() = CType(savedState, Object())
        MyBase.LoadControlState(savedState)
        _userName = CStr(ctlState(1))
    End Sub

    Protected Overrides Function SaveControlState() As Object
        Dim ctlState() As Object
        ReDim ctlState(1) ' Initializes the array with 2 objects
        ctlState(0) = MyBase.SaveControlState()
        ctlState(1) = _userName
        Return ctlState
    End Function
End Class
```

This is somewhat more complicated than the older method of using the host page's view state, but you gain the advantage of independence from that page's configuration. You have to weigh the added complexity against the needs of your application. If you'll have a large application with many pages, it is probably wise to use control state because you can't be sure if one of the host pages might have view state disabled (in a large system it's almost guaranteed that some pages will have it disabled). Also, if your controls might be used by other applications within your company, or even other companies, you should definitely use control state to give you the added peace of mind to know that your controls will always work.

Loading and Editing a Profile

Now you can write some code for handling user profiles within a control. In the control's code-behind, you should handle the Load event to load the specified user's profile, so you can populate the various input controls with profile values. If no username is specified, the current user's profile will be loaded:

```
Protected Sub Page_Load(ByVal sender As Object, ByVal e As System.EventArgs)
Handles Me.Load
        If Not Me.IsPostBack Then

            ' if the UserName property contains an empty string, retrieve the profile
            ' for the current user, otherwise for the specified user
            Dim profile As ProfileBase = GetProfile()
            ddlSubscriptions.SelectedValue = profile.GetProfileGroup("Preferences")
.GetPropertyValue("Newsletter").ToString
            ddlLanguages.SelectedValue = profile.GetProfileGroup("Preferences")
.GetPropertyValue("Culture")
            txtFirstName.Text = profile.GetPropertyValue("FirstName")
            txtLastName.Text = profile.GetPropertyValue("LastName")

            If String.IsNullOrEmpty(Gender) Then
                ddlGenders.SelectedValue = Gender
            Else
                ddlGenders.SelectedValue = profile.GetPropertyValue("Gender")
```

```
            End If

            If Not profile.GetPropertyValue("BirthDate") = DateTime.MinValue Then
                txtBirthDate.Text = profile.GetPropertyValue("BirthDate")
.ToShortDateString
            End If
            ddlOccupations.SelectedValue = profile.GetPropertyValue("Occupation")
            txtWebsite.Text = profile.GetPropertyValue("Website")
            txtStreet.Text = profile.GetProfileGroup("Address")
.GetPropertyValue("Street")
            txtCity.Text = profile.GetProfileGroup("Address").GetPropertyValue("City")
            txtPostalCode.Text =
profile.GetProfileGroup("Address").GetPropertyValue("PostalCode")
            ddlState.SelectedValue =
profile.GetProfileGroup("Address").GetPropertyValue("State")

            If String.IsNullOrEmpty(Country) Then
                ddlCountry.SelectedValue = Country
            Else
                ddlCountry.SelectedValue =
profile.GetProfileGroup("Address").GetPropertyValue("Country")
            End If

            txtPhone.Text = profile.GetProfileGroup("Contacts")
.GetPropertyValue("Phone")
            txtFax.Text = profile.GetProfileGroup("Contacts").GetPropertyValue("Fax")
            txtAvatarUrl.Text = GetAvatarURL()
            txtSignature.Text = profile.GetProfileGroup("Forum")
.GetPropertyValue("Signature")
        End If
End Sub
```

This control doesn't have a Submit button to initiate saving profile values, so create a public method named SaveProfile that the host page will call when needed:

```
    Public Sub SaveProfile()
        ' if the UserName property contains an emtpy string, save the
current user's profile,
        ' othwerwise save the profile for the specified user
        Dim profile As ProfileBase = GetProfile()

        profile.GetProfileGroup("Preferences").SetPropertyValue("Newsletter",
CType([Enum].Parse( _
            GetType(SubscriptionType), ddlSubscriptions.SelectedValue),
SubscriptionType))
        profile.GetProfileGroup("Preferences").SetPropertyValue("Culture",
ddlLanguages.SelectedValue)
        profile.SetPropertyValue("FirstName", txtFirstName.Text)
        profile.SetPropertyValue("LastName", txtLastName.Text)
        profile.SetPropertyValue("Gender", ddlGenders.SelectedValue)
        If txtBirthDate.Text.Trim().Length > 0 Then
            profile.SetPropertyValue("BirthDate", DateTime.Parse(txtBirthDate.Text))
```

```
        End If
        profile.SetPropertyValue("Occupation", ddlOccupations.SelectedValue)
        profile.SetPropertyValue("Website", txtWebsite.Text)
        profile.GetProfileGroup("Address").SetPropertyValue("Street", txtStreet.Text)
        profile.GetProfileGroup("Address").SetPropertyValue("City", txtCity.Text)
        profile.GetProfileGroup("Address").SetPropertyValue("PostalCode",
txtPostalCode.Text)
        profile.GetProfileGroup("Address").SetPropertyValue("State",
ddlState.SelectedValue)
        profile.GetProfileGroup("Address").SetPropertyValue("Country",
ddlCountry.SelectedValue)
        profile.GetProfileGroup("Contacts").SetPropertyValue("Phone", txtPhone.Text)
        profile.GetProfileGroup("Contacts").SetPropertyValue("Fax", txtFax.Text)
        profile.GetProfileGroup("Forum").SetPropertyValue("AvatarUrl",
txtAvatarUrl.Text)
        profile.GetProfileGroup("Forum").SetPropertyValue("Signature",
txtSignature.Text)
        profile.Save()

    End Sub
```

The Register Page

Users can create an account for themselves through the `Register.aspx` page that is linked just below the login box. This page uses the `CreateUserWizard` control described earlier. The first step is to create the account; the user interface for this is implemented by our custom template. The second step allows the user to fill in some profile settings, and uses the `UserProfile` control we just developed. The registration code that follows is pretty long, but it should be easy to follow without further comments:

```
    <asp:CreateUserWizard runat="server" ID="CreateUserWizard1" AutoGeneratePassword
="False"
        ContinueDestinationPageUrl="~/Default.aspx"
          FinishDestinationPageUrl="~/Default.aspx">
        <WizardSteps>
            <asp:CreateUserWizardStep ID="CreateUserWizardStep1" runat="server">
                <ContentTemplate>
                    <div class="sectiontitle">
                        Create your new account</div>
                    <p>
                    </p>
                    <table cellpadding="2">
                        <tr>
                            <td style="width: 110px;" class="fieldname">
                                <asp:Label runat="server" ID="lblUserName"
AssociatedControlID="UserName" Text="Username:" /></td>
                            <td style="width: 300px;">
                                <asp:TextBox runat="server" ID="UserName" Width="100%" />
</td>
                            <td>
                                <asp:RequiredFieldValidator ID="valRequireUserName"
runat="server" ControlToValidate="UserName"
```

```
                                    SetFocusOnError="true" Display="Dynamic" ErrorMessage
="Username is required."
                                    ToolTip="Username is required." ValidationGroup=
"CreateUserWizard1">*</asp:RequiredFieldValidator>
                        </td>
                    </tr>
                    <tr>
                        <td class="fieldname">
                            <asp:Label runat="server" ID="lblPassword"
AssociatedControlID="Password" Text="Password:" /></td>
                        <td>
                            <asp:TextBox runat="server" ID="Password" TextMode=
"Password" Width="100%" /></td>
                        <td>
                            <asp:RequiredFieldValidator ID="valRequirePassword" runat=
"server" ControlToValidate="Password"
                                    SetFocusOnError="true" Display="Dynamic" ErrorMessage=
"Password is required."
                                    ToolTip="Password is required." ValidationGroup=
"CreateUserWizard1">*</asp:RequiredFieldValidator>
                            <asp:RegularExpressionValidator ID="valPasswordLength"
runat="server" ControlToValidate="Password"
                                    SetFocusOnError="true" Display="Dynamic"
ValidationExpression="\w{5,}" ErrorMessage="Password must be at least 5
characters long."
                                    ToolTip="Password must be at least 5 characters long."
ValidationGroup="CreateUserWizard1">*</asp:RegularExpressionValidator>
                        </td>
                    </tr>
                    <tr>
                        <td class="fieldname">
                            <asp:Label runat="server" ID="lblConfirmPassword"
AssociatedControlID="ConfirmPassword"
                                    Text="Confirm password:" /></td>
                        <td>
                            <asp:TextBox runat="server" ID="ConfirmPassword" TextMode=
"Password" Width="100%" /></td>
                        <td>
                            <asp:RequiredFieldValidator ID="valRequireConfirmPassword"
runat="server" ControlToValidate="ConfirmPassword"
                                    SetFocusOnError="true" Display="Dynamic" ErrorMessage=
"Confirm Password is required."
                                    ToolTip="Confirm Password is required." ValidationGroup
="CreateUserWizard1">*</asp:RequiredFieldValidator>
                            <asp:CompareValidator ID="valComparePasswords" runat=
"server" ControlToCompare="Password"
                                    SetFocusOnError="true" ControlToValidate=
"ConfirmPassword" Display="Dynamic"
                                    ErrorMessage="The Password and Confirmation Password
must match." ValidationGroup="CreateUserWizard1">*</asp:CompareValidator>
                        </td>
                    </tr>
```

```
                <tr>
                    <td class="fieldname">
                        <asp:Label runat="server" ID="lblEmail"
AssociatedControlID="Email" Text="E-mail:" /></td>
                    <td>
                        <asp:TextBox runat="server" ID="Email" Width="100%" Text=
'<%# Email %>' ></asp:TextBox></td>
                    <td>
                        <asp:RequiredFieldValidator ID="valRequireEmail" runat=
"server" ControlToValidate="Email"
                            SetFocusOnError="true" Display="Dynamic" ErrorMessage=
"E-mail is required." ToolTip="E-mail is required."
                            ValidationGroup="CreateUserWizard1">*
</asp:RequiredFieldValidator>
                        <asp:RegularExpressionValidator runat="server" ID=
"valEmailPattern" Display="Dynamic"
                            SetFocusOnError="true" ValidationGroup=
"CreateUserWizard1" ControlToValidate="Email"
                            ValidationExpression="\w+([-+.']\w+)*@\w+([-.]\w+)*\.
\w+([-.]\w+)*" ErrorMessage="The e-mail address you specified is not
well-formed.">*
</asp:RegularExpressionValidator>
                    </td>
                </tr>
                <tr>
                    <td class="fieldname">
                        <asp:Label runat="server" ID="lblQuestion"
AssociatedControlID="Question" Text="Security question:" /></td>
                    <td>
                        <asp:TextBox runat="server" ID="Question" Width=
"100%" /></td>
                    <td>
                        <asp:RequiredFieldValidator ID="valRequireQuestion" runat=
"server" ControlToValidate="Question"
                            SetFocusOnError="true" Display="Dynamic" ErrorMessage=
"Security question is required."
                            ToolTip="Security question is required."
ValidationGroup="CreateUserWizard1">*</asp:RequiredFieldValidator>
                    </td>
                </tr>
                <tr>
                    <td class="fieldname">
                        <asp:Label runat="server" ID="lblAnswer"
AssociatedControlID="Answer" Text="Security answer:" /></td>
                    <td>
                        <asp:TextBox runat="server" ID="Answer" Width=
"100%" /></td>
                    <td>
                        <asp:RequiredFieldValidator ID="valRequireAnswer" runat=
"server" ControlToValidate="Answer"
                            SetFocusOnError="true" Display="Dynamic" ErrorMessage=
"Security answer is required."
```

```
                                        ToolTip="Security answer is required." ValidationGroup=
        "CreateUserWizard1">*</asp:RequiredFieldValidator>
                            </td>
                        </tr>
                        <tr>
                            <td colspan="3" style="text-align: right;">
                                <asp:Label ID="ErrorMessage" SkinID="FeedbackKO" runat=
        "server" EnableViewState="False"></asp:Label>
                            </td>
                        </tr>
                    </table>
                    <asp:ValidationSummary ValidationGroup="CreateUserWizard1" ID=
        "ValidationSummary1"
                        runat="server" ShowMessageBox="True" ShowSummary="False" />
                </ContentTemplate>
            </asp:CreateUserWizardStep>
            <asp:WizardStep ID="WizardStep1" runat="server" Title="Set preferences">
                <div class="sectiontitle">
                    Set-up your profile</div>
                <p>
                </p>
                    All settings in this section are optional. The address information is
        required only if you want to order products from our e-store. However, we ask
        you to fill in these details in all cases, because they help us know our target
        audience, and improve the site and its contents accordingly. Thank you for your
        cooperation!
                <p>
                     </p>
                <uc1:UserProfile ID="UserProfile1" runat="server" />
            </asp:WizardStep>
            <asp:CompleteWizardStep ID="CompleteWizardStep1" runat="server">
            </asp:CompleteWizardStep>
        </WizardSteps>
        <MailDefinition BodyFileName="~/RegistrationMail.txt" From=
    "webmaster@effectivedotnet.com"
            Subject="The Beer House: Your registration ">
        </MailDefinition>
    </asp:CreateUserWizard>
```

The `CreateUserWizard`'s `<MailDefinition>` section contains all the settings needed for sending the confirmation mail. The most interesting property is `BodyFileName`, which references a disk file containing the mail's body text. In this file, you will typically write a welcome message, and maybe the credentials used to register, so that users will be reminded of the username and password that they selected for your site Following is the content of `RegistrationMail.txt` that specifies the body text:

```
Thank you for registering to The Beer House website! Following are the
credentials you selected for logging in:
UserName: <% UserName %>
Password: <% Password %>

See you online!
- The Beer House Team
```

This example is e-mailing the username and password because this is a low-risk site, and we chose user-friendliness over the tightest possible security. Besides, I wanted to demonstrate how to use placeholders in the body text file (<% UserName %> and <% Password %>). For serious e-commerce sites or in situations where your company (or your client) doesn't approve of e-mailing usernames and passwords, do not follow this example!

The page's code-behind file is impressively short: you only need to handle the wizard's FinishButtonClick event and have it call the UserProfile's SaveProfile method. The code that implements the registration it not placed here because it's handled by the user control:

```
Protected Sub CreateUserWizard1_FinishButtonClick(ByVal sender As Object,
ByVal e As System.Web.UI.WebControls.WizardNavigationEventArgs)
Handles CreateUserWizard1.FinishButtonClick
       UserProfile1.SaveProfile()
End Sub
```

Figure 4-15 shows the registration page on the first step of the wizard.

Figure 4-15

Figure 4-16 shows the second step, enabling users to set up their profile.

Figure 4-16

The PasswordRecovery Page

Under the login box is a link to PasswordRecover.aspx, which allows a user to recover a forgotten password, by sending an e-mail with the credentials. The page uses a PasswordRecovery control with a custom template for the two steps (entering the username and answering the secret question). The code follows:

```
<%@ Page Language="VB" MasterPageFile="~/Template.master" AutoEventWireup="true"
   CodeFile="PasswordRecovery.aspx.vb" Inherits="PasswordRecovery"
   Title="The Beer House - Password Recovery" %>
<asp:Content ID="MainContent" ContentPlaceHolderID="MainContent" Runat="Server">
<div class="sectiontitle">Recover your password</div>
<p></p>If you forgot your password, you can use this page to have it sent to you
by e-mail. <p></p>
<asp:PasswordRecovery ID="PasswordRecovery1" runat="server">
    <UserNameTemplate>
        <div class="sectionsubtitle">Step 1: enter your username</div>
        <p></p>
        <table cellpadding="2">
          <tr>
            <td width="80" class="fieldname">Username:</td>
            <td width="300">
                <asp:TextBox ID="UserName" runat="server" Width="100%" />
```

```
            </td>
            <td>
                <asp:RequiredFieldValidator ID="valRequireUserName" runat="server"
                    ControlToValidate="UserName" SetFocusOnError="true"
                    Display="Dynamic" ErrorMessage="Username is required."
                    ValidationGroup="PasswordRecovery1">*
                </asp:RequiredFieldValidator>
            </td>
        </tr>
        <td colspan="3" align="right">
            <asp:Label ID="FailureText" runat="server" SkinID="FeedbackKO"
                EnableViewState="False" />
            <asp:Button ID="SubmitButton" runat="server" CommandName="Submit"
                Text="Submit" ValidationGroup="PasswordRecovery1" />
        </td>
    </table>
</UserNameTemplate>
<QuestionTemplate>
    <div class="sectionsubtitle">Step 2: answer the following question</div>
    <p></p>
    <table cellpadding="2">
        <tr>
            <td width="80" class="fieldname">Username:</td>
            <td width="300">
                <asp:Literal ID="UserName" runat="server" />
            </td>
            <td></td>
        </tr>
        <tr>
            <td class="fieldname">Question:</td>
            <td><asp:Literal ID="Question" runat="server"></asp:Literal></td>
            <td></td>
        </tr>
        <tr>
            <td class="fieldname">Answer:</td>
            <td><asp:TextBox ID="Answer" runat="server" Width="100%" />
            </td>
            <td>
                <asp:RequiredFieldValidator ID="valRequireAnswer" runat="server"
                    ControlToValidate="Answer" SetFocusOnError="true"
                    Display="Dynamic" ErrorMessage="Answer is required."
                    ValidationGroup="PasswordRecovery1">*
                </asp:RequiredFieldValidator>
            </td>
        </tr>
        <tr>
            <td colspan="3" align="right">
                <asp:Label ID="FailureText" runat="server"
                    SkinID="FeedbackKO" EnableViewState="False" />
                <asp:Button ID="SubmitButton" runat="server" CommandName="Submit"
                    Text="Submit" ValidationGroup="PasswordRecovery1" />
            </td>
```

```
            </tr>
          </table>
        </QuestionTemplate>
        <SuccessTemplate>
          <asp:Label runat="server" ID="lblSuccess" SkinID="FeedbackOK"
            Text="Your password has been sent to you." />
        </SuccessTemplate>
        <MailDefinition
          BodyFileName="~/PasswordRecoveryMail.txt"
          From="webmaster@effectivedotnet.com"
          Subject="The Beer House: your password">
        </MailDefinition>
      </asp:PasswordRecovery>
    </asp:Content>
```

The body of the mail sent with the credentials is almost the same as the previous one, so we won't show it again here. Figure 4-17 shows a couple of screenshots for the two-step password recovery process.

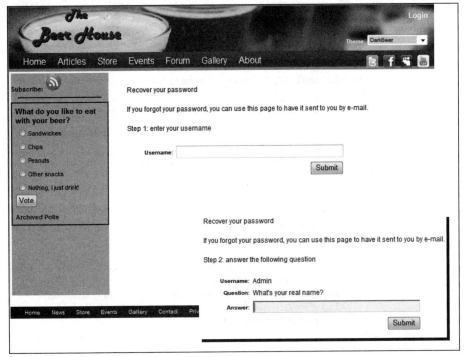

Figure 4-17

The EditProfile Page

Once users log in, they can go to the EditProfile.aspx page, linked in the top-right corner of any page, and change their password or other profile settings. The password-changing functionality is implemented by way of a custom ChangePassword control, and the profile settings functionality is handled by the

UserProfile control we already developed. Following is the code for the EditProfile.aspx file (with some layout code removed for clarity and brevity):

```
<div class="sectiontitle">
   Change your password</div>
<p>
</p>
<asp:ChangePassword ID="ChangePassword1" runat="server">
    <ChangePasswordTemplate>
        <table cellpadding="2">
            <tr>
                <td style="width: 110px;" class="fieldname">
                    <asp:Label runat="server" ID="lblCurrentPassword"
AssociatedControlID="CurrentPassword"
                        Text="Current password:" />
                </td>
                <td style="width: 300px;">
                    <asp:TextBox ID="CurrentPassword" TextMode="Password"
 runat="server" Width="100%"></asp:TextBox>
                </td>
                <td>
                    <asp:RequiredFieldValidator ID="valRequireCurrentPassword"
 runat="server" ControlToValidate="CurrentPassword"
                        SetFocusOnError="true" Display="Dynamic"
ErrorMessage="Password is required."
                        ToolTip="Password is required."
ValidationGroup="ChangePassword1">*</asp:RequiredFieldValidator>
                </td>
            </tr>
            <tr>
                <td class="fieldname">
                    <asp:Label runat="server" ID="lblNewPassword"
 AssociatedControlID="NewPassword" Text="New password:" />
                </td>
                <td>
                    <asp:TextBox ID="NewPassword" TextMode="Password"
runat="server" Width="100%"></asp:TextBox>
                </td>
                <td>
                    <asp:RequiredFieldValidator ID="valRequireNewPassword"
 runat="server" ControlToValidate="NewPassword"
                        SetFocusOnError="true" Display="Dynamic"
ErrorMessage="New Password is required."
                        ToolTip="New Password is required."
ValidationGroup="ChangePassword1">*</asp:RequiredFieldValidator>
                    <asp:RegularExpressionValidator ID="valPasswordLength"
runat="server" ControlToValidate="NewPassword"
                        SetFocusOnError="true" Display="Dynamic"
ValidationExpression="\w{5,}" ErrorMessage="New Password must be at
least 5 characters long."
                        ToolTip="New Password must be at least 5 characters long."
ValidationGroup="ChangePassword1">*</asp:RegularExpressionValidator>
                </td>
            </tr>
```

```
            <tr>
                <td class="fieldname">
                    <asp:Label runat="server" ID="lblConfirmPassword"
AssociatedControlID="ConfirmNewPassword"
                        Text="Confirm password:" />
                </td>
                <td>
                    <asp:TextBox ID="ConfirmNewPassword" TextMode="Password" runat=
"server" Width="100%"></asp:TextBox>
                </td>
                <td>
                    <asp:RequiredFieldValidator ID="valRequireConfirmNewPassword"
runat="server" ControlToValidate="ConfirmNewPassword"
                        SetFocusOnError="true" Display="Dynamic" ErrorMessage=
"Confirm Password is required."
                        ToolTip="Confirm Password is required." ValidationGroup=
"ChangePassword1">*</asp:RequiredFieldValidator>
                    <asp:CompareValidator ID="valComparePasswords" runat="server"
ControlToCompare="NewPassword"
                        ControlToValidate="ConfirmNewPassword" SetFocusOnError=
"true" Display="Dynamic"
                        ErrorMessage="The Confirm Password must match the New
Password entry." ValidationGroup="ChangePassword1">*</asp:CompareValidator>
                </td>
            </tr>
            <td colspan="3" style="text-align: right;">
                <asp:Label ID="FailureText" runat="server" SkinID=
"FeedbackKO" EnableViewState="False" />
                <asp:Button ID="ChangePasswordPushButton" runat="server"
CommandName="ChangePassword"
                    Text="Change Password" ValidationGroup="ChangePassword1" />
            </td>
        </table>
        <asp:ValidationSummary runat="server" ID="valChangePasswordSummary"
ValidationGroup="ChangePassword1"
            ShowMessageBox="true" ShowSummary="false" />
    </ChangePasswordTemplate>
    <SuccessTemplate>
        <asp:Label runat="server" ID="lblSuccess" SkinID="FeedbackOK" Text=
"Your password has been changed successfully." />
    </SuccessTemplate>
    <MailDefinition BodyFileName="~/ChangePasswordMail.txt" From=
"webmaster@effectivedotnet.com"
        Subject="The Beer House: password changed">
    </MailDefinition>
</asp:ChangePassword>
<p>
</p>
<hr style="width: 100%; height: 1px;" noshade="noshade" />
<div class="sectiontitle">
    Change your profile</div>
<p>
</p>
```

All settings in this section are required only if you want to order products
from our e-store. However, we ask you to fill in these details in all cases,

because they help us know our target audience, and improve the site and its
contents accordingly. Thank you for your cooperation!

```
    <p>
    </p>
    <uc1:UserProfile ID="UserProfile1" runat="server" />
    <table cellpadding="2" style="width: 525px;">
        <tr>
            <td style="text-align: right;">
                <asp:Label runat="server" ID="lblFeedbackOK" SkinID="FeedbackOK" Text
="Profile updated successfully"
                    Visible="false" />
                <asp:Button runat="server" ID="btnUpdate" ValidationGroup=
"EditProfile" Text="Update Profile"
                    OnClick="btnUpdate_Click" />
            </td>
        </tr>
    </table>
```

In the code-behind, you don't have to do anything except handle the Update Profile Submit button's
Click event, where you call the UserProfile control's SaveProfile method, and then show a confirmation message:

```
Protected Sub btnUpdate_Click(ByVal sender As Object, ByVal e As System.EventArgs)
Handles btnUpdate.Click
    UserProfile1.SaveProfile()
    lblFeedbackOK.Visible = True
End Sub
```

Figure 4-18 shows part of this page at runtime.

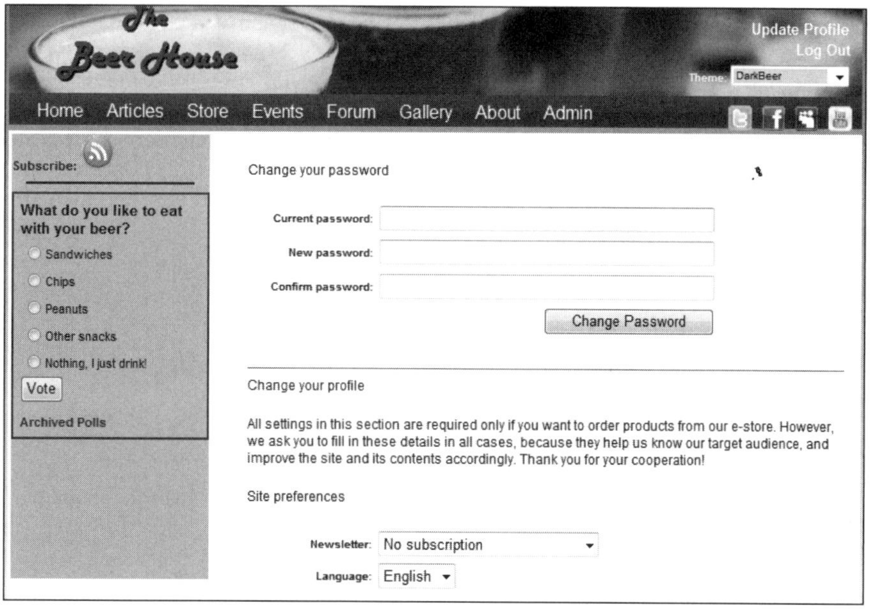

Figure 4-18

The last thing to do on this page is to ensure that anonymous users — who, of course, don't have a password or profile to change — cannot access this page. To do this, you can create a `<location>` section for this page in the root `web.config` and then write an `<authorization>` subsection that denies access to the anonymous user (identified by `"?"`) and grant access to everyone else. This is the code you should add to the `web.config` file:

```
<configuration xmlns="http://schemas.microsoft.com/.NetConfiguration/v2.0">
    <system.web> <!-- some settings here...--> </system.web>
    <location path="EditProfile.aspx">
        <system.web>
            <authorization>
                <deny users="?" />
                <allow users="*" />
            </authorization>
        </system.web>
    </location>
</configuration>
```

Creating an AJAX Login Dialog

The access denied page is great for protecting resources from users that do not have permission to view them, but in today's competitive market, richer user experiences are driving competition. With the use of some CSS, AJAX, and the ASP.NET AJAX AuthenticateService, we can add a rich login experience that offers both username/password and `OpenId` authentication. This solution consists of two DIV tags that are hidden by default and located at the bottom of the page's markup. When the user clicks the Login link located in the page's header, the faux login dialog is rendered on top of the page. The `PopUpBackGround` DIV has an opaque gray background that simulates the feel of the site being disabled and even a sense of security. This looks somewhat similar to the experience a user has when they use CardSpace. Since the DIV is set to expand to the full size of the browser window, the user cannot click or interact with anything on the page, also fostering this sense of security.

Layered on top of the `PopUpBackGround` DIV is the `LoginDlg` DIV. This DIV contains the controls needed to collect the user's credentials or `OpenId` URL. It is composed of some HTML markup and HTML input elements. Raw HTML elements are used because Web Controls are much more complicated to work with when AJAX is involved because of the names generated by the ASP.NET framework on the server. While working with Web Controls is possible, it is very complicated compared to using pure HTML elements.

```
<div id="PopUpBackGround">
</div>
<div id="LoginDlg">
    <div id="dLoginError" />
    <div id="AnonymousView">
        <img src="~/images/lock.gif" runat="server" hspace="5" vspace="12" align
="left" alt="Login to the Beer House." />
        Username:
        <input id="txtUsername" type="text" onkeypress="ValidateLoginValues();"
/><br />
        Password:
        <input id="pwdPassword" type="password" onkeypress=
"ValidateLoginValues();" /><br />
```

```
            <input id="chkRememberMe" type="checkbox" />Remember Me<br />
            <input id="btnCancel" type="button" value="Cancel" /><input id=
"btnLogIn" type="button"
                value="Login" /><br />
            <a href="~/Register.aspx" runat="server" class=
"LoginDialog">Register</a> 
            <a href="~/PasswordRecovery.aspx" runat="server" class="LoginDialog">
Retrieve Password</a><br />
            <div id="dOpenId">
                Login with your OpenId.<br />
                <asp:TextBox runat="server" type="text" ID="txtOpenId" class=
"openid_identifier_dlg" />
                <asp:Button runat="server" ID="btnLoginOpenId" Text="Go" />
            </div>
        </div>
        <div id="LoggedInView" style="display: none;">
            Logged in.<br />
            <input id="btnLogOut" type="button" value="Log Out" />
        </div>
    </div>

<div id="dLoginLinks">
<div id="dLoginMenu">

<a id="btnDisplayLogin" href="javascript:DisplayLoginHandler();" class=
"LoginLink">Login</a></div>
<div id="dLogoutMenu">
        <div id="dUserName"></div>

<a id="btnDisplayLogout" href="javascript:logoutHandler();" class=
"LoginLink">Log Out</a>
</div>
</div>
```

The corresponding style properties:

```
/* Modal Dialog */
#PopUpBackGround
{
    z-index: 1400;
    position: fixed;
    top: 0;
    left: 0;
    height: 100%;
    width: 100%;
    background-color: #333333;
    filter: alpha(opacity=70);
    opacity: 0.7;
    display:none;
}

#LoginDlg
{
    background-color : White;
```

```
        left: 275px;
        top: 150px;
        width:325px;
        height : 190px;
        z-index : 1500;
        position :fixed;
        border: thin ridge #CC6600;
        padding: 2px 2px 2px 2px;
        display :none;
    }
```

The username and password input fields both call the `ValidateLoginValues` function as keys are pressed. This does a couple of things; it checks to see if the user pressed the Enter key and verifies that there is text in each field before the authentication occurs. Users typically try pressing the Enter key to submit the page instead of clicking buttons, so handling this action is important.

```
function ValidateLoginValues() {

    if (event.which || event.keyCode) {
        if ((event.which == 13) || (event.keyCode == 13)) {

            Username = $get('txtUsername');
            Password = $get('pwdPassword');

            if (Username.value.length > 0 && Password.value.length > 0) {

                ProcessEnter('btnLogIn');

            } else {

                alert('You must enter both a Username and a Password to authenticate.');

            }
        }
    }
}
```

The `ProcessEnter` function simulates the Submit button being pressed, thus initiating the authentication process.

```
function ProcessEnter(btnSubmit) {

    if (event.which || event.keyCode) {
        if ((event.which == 13) || (event.keyCode == 13)) {
            $get(btnSubmit).click();
            return false;
        }
    } else {
        return true;
    };

}
```

The reason that you do not have to explicitly hook up a method to the Submit button's click event is it was registered in the site's JavaScript file when it was loaded. The ASP.NET AJAX framework has the concept of wiring event handlers in a very similar fashion as we do in server-side code. The $addHandler method takes the element ID, the client-side event name and the function to associate to manage this for us. Here are some examples from the Beer House's TBH.js file:

```
// Hook up the click events of the log in and log out buttons.
if ($get('btnLogIn') != null) {
    $addHandler($get('btnLogIn'), 'click', loginHandler);
}
if (null != $get('btnLogOut')) {
    $addHandler($get('btnLogOut'), 'click', logoutHandler);
}
if (null != $get('btnCancel')) {
    $addHandler($get('btnCancel'), 'click', CancelLoginHandler);
}
```

Here are the corresponding client-side functions:

```
var ssa = Sys.Services.AuthenticationService;

function CancelLoginHandler() {
    $get('LoginDlg').style.display = 'none';
    $get('PopUpBackGround').style.display = 'none';
}

function loginHandler() {
    var username = $get('txtUsername').value;
    var password = $get('pwdPassword').value;
    var isPersistent = $get('chkRememberMe').checked;
    var customInfo = null;
    var redirectUrl = null;
    // Log them in.
    ssa.login(username,
                        password,
                        isPersistent,
                        customInfo,
                        redirectUrl,
                        onLoginComplete,
                        onError);

}

function logoutHandler() {
    // Log them out.
    var redirectUrl = null;
    var userContext = null;
    ssa.logout(redirectUrl,
                        onLogoutComplete,
                        onError,
                        userContext);
}
```

The `loginHandler` function gets the username and password supplied by the user and calls the Authentication Services Login method. It passes the name of the function to call upon a completed login (`onLoginComplete`) and when an error occurs (`onError`).

The `onLoginComplete` function checks the result, meaning whether authentication was successful, and changes the on-screen display of different sections of the page for an authenticated user. If the authentication failed, a simple alert dialog is displayed to inform the user that the credentials failed authentication.

```
function onLoginComplete(result, context, methodName) {

    if (result) {
        // Logged in.  Hide the anonymous view.
        $get('LoggedInView').style.display = 'block';
        $get('AnonymousView').style.display = 'none';
        $get('LoginDlg').style.display = 'none';
        $get('PopUpBackGround').style.display = 'none';

        $get('dLoginMenu').style.display = 'none';
        $get('dLogoutMenu').style.display = 'block';

        LoadProfile();
        loadRoles();

    } else {
        alert('Sorry those Credentials did not work.');
        $get('txtUsername').value = '';
        $get('pwdPassword').value = '';

    }
}
```

Similarly, when a user logs out of the site, the visible display of the page is changed.

```
function onLogoutComplete(result, context, methodName) {
    $get('dLoginMenu').style.display = '';
    $get('dLogoutMenu').style.display = 'none';
    $get("adminView").style.display = 'none';
}
```

A simple error alert dialog is displayed if an exception was thrown. This method passes the exception message to the alert dialog. That's not necessarily the best idea for security or user-friendliness, but it serves the purpose for now.

```
function onError(error, context, methodName) {
    alert(error.get_message());
}
```

If you review the `onLoginComplete` function, you will see that it calls the `LoadProfile` function. This function loads the profile service and provides access to the user's associated profile settings. Once the profile is loaded, the site displays a simple welcome message containing the user's first name.

```
var profileService = Sys.Services.ProfileService;
var propertyNames = new Array();

// Loads the profile of the current
```

```
// authenticated user.
function LoadProfile() {

    Sys.Services.ProfileService.load(null,
    OnLoadCompleted, OnProfileFailed, null);

}

// Reads the profile information and displays it.
function OnLoadCompleted(numProperties, userContext, methodName) {

    firstName = Sys.Services.ProfileService.properties.FirstName;

    if (firstName.length > 0){
        alert("Welcome " + firstName);
    }

}
```

The ShowProfileInfo function checks to see if a full name can be displayed; if so, it sets the
innerHTML of the dUserName DIV, located in the site's header, to a link for the user to edit his profile
with his name hyperlinked. If the full name cannot be composed, then the user simply sees an Update
Profile link in the same location.

```
function ShowProfileInfo() {

    if (null != $get('dUserName')) {

        if (undefined != Sys.Services.ProfileService.properties.FirstName &&
            undefined != Sys.Services.ProfileService.properties.LastName) {

            $get('dUserName').innerHTML =
                '<a href="editprofile.aspx">' +

            Sys.Services.ProfileService.properties.FirstName + ' ' +
            Sys.Services.ProfileService.properties.LastName + '</a><BR/>' +
            '<a href="ProfileEdit.aspx">Edit Profile</a>';

        } else {
            $get('dUserName').innerHTML =
                '<a href="editprofile.aspx">Update Profile</a><BR/>'
        }
    }

}
```

Another function called by onLoginComplete is the loadRoles. It calls RoleService to load the role
information for the site. Like the authentication and profile services, it also has on complete, failed, and
error method callbacks that need to be set.

```
function loadRoles() {
    Sys.Services.RoleService.load(onLoadRolesCompleted, onLoadRolesFailed, null);
}

function onLoadRolesCompleted(result, userContext, methodName) {
    if (Sys.Services.RoleService.isUserInRole("Administrators")) {
```

```
            $get("adminView").style.display = '';
            $get("adminView").innerHTML = "Hello Admin";
        }
    }

    function onLoadRolesFailed(error, userContext, methodName) {
        alert(error.get_message());
    }
```

If the user wants to authenticate him- or herself via OpenId, this is handled by calling the GoOpenId function. This will open the user's OpenId URL so he can be authenticated.

```
    function GoOpenId() {
        OpenIdURL = $get(txtOpenId);
        window.open(OpenIdURL.value, 'MyOpenId', null, null);
    }
```

Persisting the Favorite Theme between Sessions

In Chapter 2, we created a base page class from which all other pages inherit. One of the tasks of this class is to set the page's Theme property according to what is stored in a Session variable, which tells us what theme the user selected from the Themes drop-down list near the top-right corner. The problem with Session variables is that they only exist as long as the user's session is active, so we'll have to store this value in a persistent location. Thankfully, it turns out that we have a great place to store this — in the user profile. The following code highlights the changes done to the base page to allow us to save the Profile.Preferences.Theme property in the user's profile, and because we're putting it in the base page class, we will not have to do this in all the other pages:

```
Private Sub Page_PreInit(ByVal sender As Object, ByVal e As System.EventArgs)
Handles Me.PreInit

Dim id As String = Helpers.ThemesSelectorID


If String.IsNullOrEmpty(id) = False Then

            ' if this is a postback caused by the theme selector's dropdownlist,
            ' retrieve the selected theme and use it for the current page request

If Me.Request.Form("__EVENTTARGET") = id AndAlso _
                Not String.IsNullOrEmpty(Me.Request.Form(id)) Then
            Me.Theme = Me.Request.Form(id)
            Helpers.SetProfileTheme(profile, Me.Theme)
        Else
            ' if not a postback, or a postback caused by controls other then
            ' the theme selector,
            ' set the page's theme with the value found in the user's profile,
            ' if present
            If Not String.IsNullOrEmpty(Helpers.GetProfileTheme(profile)) Then
                Me.Theme = Helpers.GetProfileTheme(profile)
            End If
```

```
                End If
    End If

    End Sub
```

As mentioned before, we must also handle the `Profile_MigrateAnonymous` global event, so that when an anonymous user selects a theme and then logs in, his or her favorite theme will be migrated from the anonymous profile to the authenticated one. After this, the old profile can be deleted from the data store, and the anonymous ID can be deleted as well. Following is the complete code:

```
Sub Profile_MigrateAnonymous(ByVal sender As Object, ByVal e As
ProfileMigrateEventArgs)
      ' get a reference to the previously anonymous user's profile
      Dim anonProfile As ProfileBase = ProfileBase.Create(e.AnonymousID)
      ' if set, copy its Theme to the current user's profile
      If Not String.IsNullOrEmpty(anonProfile.GetProfileGroup("Preferences")
.GetPropertyValue("Theme")) Then
          Profile.Preferences.Theme = anonProfile.GetProfileGroup("Preferences")
.GetPropertyValue("Theme")
      End If
      ' delete the anonymous profile
      ProfileManager.DeleteProfile(e.AnonymousID)
      AnonymousIdentificationModule.ClearAnonymousIdentifier()
End Sub
```

The Administration Section

Now that the end-user part of the work is done, we only have the administration section to complete. The `~/Admin/Default.aspx` page linked to the Admin menu item is the administrator's home page, which contains links to all the administrative functions. First, we will develop the page used to manage users and their profiles. To protect all the pages placed under the Admin folder against unauthorized access, you should add a `web.config` file under this `~/Admin` folder, and write an `<authorization>` section that grants access to the Administrators role and denies access to everyone else. In the Design section is a sample snippet to demonstrate this.

The Admin Master Page

In Chapter 2, we discussed the use of master pages and CSS to create a consistent user interface for the public facing website. The same techniques are just as important for the site's administration. The administrative section has its own dedicated master page, which primarily differs from the public site's layout by having an accordion panel to use for navigation in the admin area.

The `Accordion` control is actually a part of the ASP.NET AJAX control toolkit, a set of free controls produced by Microsoft that extend the ASP.NET AJAX framework (`www.codeplex.com/AjaxControlToolkit`). The version I am using with this site is 3.0.20820; you should check the project's page to use the most current bits as they change from time to time.

The `Accordion` control allows multiple panes to be defined, but only one is visible at a time. Each of the panels is collapsible, meaning that they are neatly hidden from the user when they are not needed.

The user can select the pane he or she wants to see by clicking on the visible header. In the Beer House administrative section, the header defines a module's administrative pages and tasks.

```
<ajaxToolkit:Accordion ID="aAdminMenu" runat="server" FadeTransitions="false"
 FramesPerSecond="100"
 TransitionDuration="250" CssClass="accordion" HeaderCssClass="header"
ContentCssClass="content" RequireOpenedPane="True" AutoSize="None">
<Panes>

<ajaxToolkit:AccordionPane ID="apArticles" runat="server">

<!-- Content (ListView) -->

</ajaxToolkit:AccordionPane>

<!-- Other Panes -->
</Panes>
</ajaxToolkit:Accordion>
```

Inside each pane is a dedicated ListView containing links to the administrative duties of the module. Typically, this includes links to manage any items as well as adding new items. The lists are actually manually built by calling a series of methods in a AdminMenuItems class, but you could drive them from a table or configuration setting. Considering the size and scope of the Beer House site, it is simpler to create a class to manually build the navigation. Each of the methods in the AdminMenuItems class is a shared method that builds an ArrayList of AdminMenuItems. An AdminMenuItem contains a MenuName, ImageURL and URL property. The MenuName is the test displayed in the hyperlink to the page. The ImageURL is the path to an associated image icon. The URL is the path to the actual page to be loaded.

```
Public Shared Function FetchSecurityMenuItems() As ArrayList

        Dim userItems As New ArrayList()
        userItems.Add(New AdminMenuItem("Users", "ManageUsers.aspx"))
        userItems.Add(New AdminMenuItem("New User", "AddEditUser.aspx"))
        userItems.Add(New AdminMenuItem("Roles", "ManageRoles.aspx"))
        userItems.Add(New AdminMenuItem("New Role", "AddEditRole.aspx"))

        Return userItems

End Function
```

The AdminMenuItem has several overloaded constructors; I am using the version that accepts the MenuName and URL. This creates a simple text-based navigation list. The FetchSecurityMenuItems method returns an ArrayList of AdminMenuItems that are ultimately bound to the ListView in the security panel of the Accordion control.

```
Private Sub BindNavItems()

        'Other Admin Menu ListView binding code

        lvSecurity.DataSource = AdminMenuItems.FetchSecurityMenuItems
        lvSecurity.DataBind()

End Sub
```

Each `AccordionPane` in the Accordion has a header that list what the pane contains, for example the Security pane holds links to manage users and roles. The Header template defines the content listed in the pane's header, which is always visible. When the user clicks on the header, it will expand if it is not the currently visible pane, and the open pane will contract.

The Content template defines the elements contained in the expanded pane. For the administration navigation, this means the `ListView` bound to the module's admin links. Each of the `ListView` holds an unordered list (`<UL>`), with each list item (`<LI>`) containing the navigational link.

```
<ajaxToolkit:AccordionPane ID="apSecurity" runat="server">
<Header>

<div>
                <span>Security</span>

</div>
</Header>
<Content>

<asp:ListView ID="lvSecurity" runat="server">

<LayoutTemplate>

   <ul>

       <li id="itemPlaceholder" runat="server" />

   </ul>

</LayoutTemplate>

<ItemTemplate>

   <li><a href="<%#Eval("URL")%>">

       <%#Eval("MenuName")%></a></li>

</ItemTemplate>

</asp:ListView>
</Content>
</ajaxToolkit:AccordionPane>
```

The Accordion completes its visual look by applying a series of styles that assigns background images and font colors.

```
/* Accordion */

.accordion
{
    font-size:8.5pt;
    font-family:Tahoma;
    background:url(images/item_bg.gif);
}
```

```css
.accordion .header
{
    cursor: pointer;
    background: url(images/hd_bg.gif) repeat-x;
    border-bottom: solid 1px #57566f;
    border-bottom-color: #800000;
}
.accordion .header DIV
{
    cursor:pointer;
    height:30px;
    padding-left:40px;
    background-color:Transparent;
    background-position:center left;
    background-repeat:no-repeat;
}
.accordion .header SPAN
{
    cursor:pointer;
    font-weight:bold;
    display:block;
    padding-top:8px;
    color:#fff;
}
.accordion .header:hover
{
    cursor:pointer;
    height:31px;
    background-color:Transparent;
    background:url(images/hd_hover_bg.gif) repeat-x;
    border-bottom:none;
}
.accordion UL
{
    padding:0;
    margin:5px 5px 5px 15px;
    list-style-type:none;
}
.accordion LI
{
    background-color:Transparent;
    background-repeat:no-repeat;
    background-position:left center;
    vertical-align:middle;
    padding:6px 5px 6px 25px;
    cursor:hand;
}
.accordion LI DIV
{
    padding-left: 10px;
    color: #993333;
    cursor: hand;
}
.accordion LI:hover
```

```
    {
        text-decoration:underline;
    }
```

The balance of the Admin master page is very similar to the public master page. The menu links refer to the primary management pages for the related modules instead of the public pages.

The ManageUsers Administrative Page

This page's user interface can be divided into three parts:

1. The first part tells the administrator the number of registered users and how many of them are currently online.

2. The second part provides controls for finding and listing the users. There is an "alphabet bar" with all the letters of the alphabet; when one is clicked, a grid is filled with all the users whose names start with that letter. Additionally, an All link is present to show all users with a single click. The search functionality allows administrators to search for users by providing a partial username or e-mail address.

3. The third part of the page contains a grid that lists users and some of their properties.

The following code provides the user interface for the first two parts:

```
<asp:UpdatePanel runat="server" ID="uppnlUsers">
                <ContentTemplate>
                    <table style="width: 95%">
                        <tr>
                            <td>
                                <p>
                                </p>
                                <b>- Total registered users:
                                    <asp:Literal runat="server" ID="lblTotUsers" />
<br />

                                    - Users online now:
                                    <asp:Literal runat="server" ID="lblOnlineUsers" />
</b>
                                <p>
                                </p>
                                Click one of the following link to display all
users whose name begins with that
                                letter:
                                <p>
                                </p>
                                <asp:ListView runat="server" ID="lvAlphabet">
                                    <LayoutTemplate>
                                        <span runat="server" id="itemPlaceHolder" />
                                    </LayoutTemplate>
                                    <ItemTemplate>
                                        <span>
                                            <asp:LinkButton ID="LinkButton1" runat=
"server" Text='<%# Container.DataItem %>'
                                                CommandArgument='<%# Container.DataItem
%>' />  </span>
```

```
                                    </ItemTemplate>
                                </asp:ListView>
                                <p>
                                </p>
                                Otherwise use the controls below to search users
        by partial username or e-mail:
                                <p>
                                </p>
                                <asp:DropDownList runat="server" ID=
        "ddlSearchTypes" CssClass="formStyleDropDown">
                                        <asp:ListItem Text="UserName" Selected="true" />
                                        <asp:ListItem Text="E-mail" />
                                </asp:DropDownList>
                                contain
                                <asp:TextBox runat="server" ID="txtSearchText"
        CssClass="formField" />
                                <asp:Button runat="server" ID="btnSearch" Text=
        "Search" />
                                <p>
                                </p>
                            </td>
                        </tr>
                        <tr>
                            <td align="right">
                                <asp:Literal runat="server" ID="ltlstatus" />
                                <asp:Button ID="Button1" runat="server" Text=
        "New User" />
                            </td>
                        </tr>
```

As you see, the alphabet bar is built by a `ListView` control, not a fixed list of links. The `ListView` will be bound to an array of characters, displayed as links. I used a `ListView` instead of static links for a couple of reasons. First, this will make it much easier to change the bar's layout, if you want to do so later, because you only need to change the template, not a series of links. Second, if you decide to add localization to this page later, the `ListView`'s template can remain exactly the same, and it is sufficient to bind it to a different array containing the selected language's alphabet.

The third part of the page, which lists users and some of their properties, contains a `ListView`. A `ListView` can automatically take care of sorting, paging, and editing, without requiring us to write a lot of code. Following is the complete code used to define the `ListView`:

```
<asp:ListView ID="lvUsers" runat="server">
    <LayoutTemplate>
        <table cellspacing="0" cellpadding="0" class="AdminList">
            <tr class="AdminListHeader">
                <td>
                    UserName
                </td>
                <td>
                    Edit
                </td>
                <td>
```

```
                        Delete
                </td>
            </tr>
            <tr id="itemPlaceholder" runat="server">
            </tr>
        </table>
    </LayoutTemplate>
    <EmptyDataTemplate>
        <tr>
            <td colspan="3">
                <p>
                    Sorry there are no Users available at this time.</p>
            </td>
        </tr>
    </EmptyDataTemplate>
    <ItemTemplate>
        <tr>
            <td class="ListTitle">
                <a href="AddEditUser.aspx?CurrentUserName=<%#Eval("UserName")%>">
                    <%#Eval("UserName")%></a>
            </td>
            <td>
                <a href="AddEditUser.aspx?CurrentUserName=<%#Eval("UserName")%>">
                    <img src="../images/edit.gif" alt="" width="16" height="16"
class="AdminImg" /></a>
            </td>
            <td>
<asp:ImageButton ID="btnDelete" AlternateText="Delete this User?" ImageUrl=
'~/images/delete.gif' CausesValidation="False" runat="server" CommandName=
"DeleteUser" OnClientClick="ConfirmMsg('User');" /></td>
        </tr>
    </ItemTemplate>
</asp:ListView>
<div class="pager">
    <asp:DataPager ID="pagerBottom" runat="server" PageSize="10" PagedControlID
="lvUsers"
QueryStringField="pageNo">
<Fields>
    <asp:NextPreviousPagerField ButtonCssClass="command" FirstPageText="«"
 PreviousPageText="<"
        RenderDisabledButtonsAsLabels="true" ShowFirstPageButton="true"
ShowPreviousPageButton="true"
        ShowLastPageButton="false" ShowNextPageButton="false" />
    <asp:NumericPagerField ButtonCount="7" NumericButtonCssClass="command"
 CurrentPageLabelCssClass="current"
        NextPreviousButtonCssClass="command" />
    <asp:NextPreviousPagerField ButtonCssClass="command" LastPageText="»"
 NextPageText=">"
        RenderDisabledButtonsAsLabels="true" ShowFirstPageButton="false"
ShowPreviousPageButton="false"
        ShowLastPageButton="true" ShowNextPageButton="true" />
</Fields>
    </asp:DataPager>
</div>
```

Deleting a user account is a serious action that can't be undone, so have the administrator confirm this action before proceeding! This can be done by adding a JavaScript "confirm" in the link's `onclick` client-side event, through the button's new `OnClientClick` property. This is done by adding the JavaScript to the button's markup, `OnClientClick="ConfirmMsg('User');"`, which calls the `ConfirmMsg` function defined in the `TBH.js` file. It will be used throughout the site to question users before they perform a delete operation.

```
function ConfirmMsg(entityName) {
    return confirm('Warning: This will delete the ' + entityName + ' from the
  database.');
}
```

Before looking at the code-behind file, I want to point out another small, but handy, new feature: the `ListView` has a `<EmptyDataTemplate>` section that contains the HTML markup to show when the list is bound to an empty data source. This is a very cool feature because you can use this template to show a message when a search produces no results.

In the page's code-behind file there is a class-level `MemershipUserCollecion` object that is initialized with all the user information returned by `Membership.GetAllUsers`. The `Count` property of this collection is used in the page's `Load` event to show the total number of registered users, together with the number of online users. In the same event, we also create the array of letters for the alphabet bar, and bind it to the `ListView` control. The code is:

```
    Protected Sub Page_Load(ByVal sender As Object, ByVal e As System.EventArgs)
Handles Me.Load

        If Not IsPostBack Then
            BindAlphabet()
        End If

    End Sub

    Private Sub BindAlphabet()
        Dim alphabet As Char() = {"A"c, "B"c, "C"c, "D"c, "E"c, "F"c, _
                    "G"c, "H"c, "I"c, "J"c, "K"c, "L"c, _
                    "M"c, "N"c, "O"c, "P"c, "Q"c, "R"c, _
                    "S"c, "T"c, "U"c, "V"c, "W"c, "X"c, _
                    "Y"c, "Z"c}

        lvAlphabet.DataSource = alphabet
        lvAlphabet.DataBind()

        lblTotUsers.Text = allUsers.Count.ToString()
        lblOnlineUsers.Text = Membership.GetNumberOfUsersOnline().ToString()
    End Sub

    Private Sub BindUsers()

        BindAlphabet()

        Dim users As MembershipUserCollection = Nothing

        Dim lSearchText As StringBuilder = New StringBuilder()
        If String.IsNullOrEmpty(lvUsers.Attributes("SearchText")) = False Then
```

```
        lSearchText.Append(lvUsers.Attributes("SearchText"))
    End If

    Dim searchByEmail As Boolean = False
    If String.IsNullOrEmpty(lvUsers.Attributes("SearchByEmail")) = False Then
        searchByEmail = Boolean.Parse(lvUsers.Attributes("SearchByEmail"))
    End If

    If lSearchText.Length > 0 Then
        If (searchByEmail) Then
            users = Membership.FindUsersByEmail(lSearchText.ToString())
        Else
            users = Membership.FindUsersByName(lSearchText.ToString())
        End If
    Else
        users = allUsers
    End If

    lvUsers.DataSource = users
    lvUsers.DataBind()

End Sub
```

The grid is not populated when the page first loads, but rather after the user clicks a link on the alphabet bar or runs a search. This is done in order to avoid unnecessary processing and, thus, have a fast-loading page. When a letter link is clicked, the `ListView`'s `ItemCommand` event is raised. You handle this event to retrieve the clicked letter and then run a search for all users whose name starts with that letter. If the All link is clicked, you'll simply show all users. Because this page also supports e-mail searches, a `"SearchByEmail"` attribute is added to the control and set to `false`, to indicate that the search is by username by default. This attribute is stored in the grid's `Attributes` collection so that it is persisted in the view state and doesn't get lost during a postback. Here's the code:

```
Private Sub lvAlphabet_ItemCommand(ByVal sender As Object, ByVal e As
System.Web.UI.WebControls.ListViewCommandEventArgs) Handles lvAlphabet.ItemCommand
    lvUsers.Attributes.Add("SearchByEmail", False.ToString())
    If (e.CommandArgument.ToString().Length = 1) Then

        lvUsers.Attributes.Add("SearchText", e.CommandArgument.ToString() + "%")
        BindUsers()
    Else
        lvUsers.Attributes.Add("SearchText", "")
        BindUsers()
    End If

End Sub
```

The code that actually runs the query and performs the binding is in the `BindUsers` method. It takes a Boolean value as an input parameter that indicates whether the `allUsers` collection must be repopulated (necessary just after a user is deleted). The text to search for and the search mode (e-mail or username) are not passed as parameters, but rather are stored in the grid's `Attributes`. Here is the code:

```
Private Sub BindUsers()

    Dim users As MembershipUserCollection = Nothing

    Dim lSearchText As StringBuilder = New StringBuilder()
```

```
        If String.IsNullOrEmpty(lvUsers.Attributes("SearchText")) = False Then
            lSearchText.Append(lvUsers.Attributes("SearchText"))
        End If

        Dim searchByEmail As Boolean = False
        If String.IsNullOrEmpty(lvUsers.Attributes("SearchByEmail")) = False Then
            searchByEmail = Boolean.Parse(lvUsers.Attributes("SearchByEmail"))
        End If

        If lSearchText.Length > 0 Then
            If (searchByEmail) Then
                users = Membership.FindUsersByEmail(lSearchText.ToString())
            Else
                users = Membership.FindUsersByName(lSearchText.ToString())
            End If
        Else
            users = allUsers
        End If

        lvUsers.DataSource = users
        lvUsers.DataBind()

    End Sub
```

The `BindUsers` method is also called when the Search button is clicked. In this case, the `SeachByEmail` attribute will be set according to the value selected in the `ddlSearchTypes` drop-down list, and the `SearchText` will be equal to the entered search string with the addition of a leading and a trailing "`%`", so that a full `LIKE` query is performed:

```
    Protected Sub btnSearch_Click(ByVal sender As Object, ByVal e As EventArgs)
Handles btnSearch.Click
        Dim searchByEmail As Boolean = (ddlSearchTypes.SelectedValue = "E-mail")
        lvUsers.Attributes.Add("SearchText", "%" + txtSearchText.Text + "%")
        lvUsers.Attributes.Add("SearchByEmail", searchByEmail.ToString())
        BindUsers()

    End Sub
```

When the trashcan icon is clicked, the `ListView` raises the `ItemDeleting` event. Notice the username is not accessible through the `DataKeys` property, but rather by accessing the `DataItem` property of the `ListView`. This is because the users were bound to the `ListView` as an array of strings and, therefore, do not have a primary key or even a field to access the values. This event handler then calls the `DeleteUser` method, passing the username. From inside this event handler, you can use the static methods of the `Membership` and `ProfileManager` classes to delete the user account and its accompanying profile. After that, `BindUsers` is called again with `true` as a parameter, so that the collection of all users is refreshed, and the label displaying the total number of users is also refreshed:

```
    Private Sub lvUsers_ItemDeleting(ByVal sender As Object, ByVal e As
    System.Web.UI.WebControls.ListViewDeleteEventArgs) Handles lvUsers.ItemDeleting
```

```
        DeleteUser(lvUsers.Items(e.ItemIndex).DataItem)
    End Sub

    Private Sub DeleteUser(ByVal UserName As String)

        If Membership.DeleteUser(UserName) Then

            BindUsers()

            ltlstatus.Text = "The user was deleted."

        Else

            ltlstatus.Text = "The user was not deleted."

        End If

    End Sub
```

Figure 4-19 shows the page listing all current users.

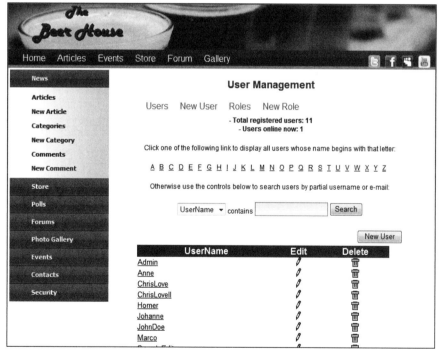

Figure 4-19

The AddEditUser Administrative Page

The AddEditUser.aspx page is linked from a row of the ManagedUsers.aspx list. It takes a username parameter on the querystring, and allows an administrator to see all the membership details about that user (i.e., the properties of the MembershipUser object representing that user), and supports editing the user's personal profile. The user interface of the page is simple and is divided in three sections:

1. The first section shows the data read from MembershipUser. All controls are read-only, except for those that are bound to the IsApproved and IsLockedOut properties. For IsLockedOut, you can set it to false to unlock a user account, but you can't set it to true to lock a user account, as only the membership provider can lock out a user.

2. The second section contains a CheckBoxList that displays all the roles defined for the application, and allows the administrator to add or remove users to and from roles. There is also a TextBox control and a button to create a new role.

3. The third and last section displays a user's profile and allows edits to the profile, through the UserProfile user control developed earlier.

Following is the code for AddEditUser.aspx:

```
<table id="Table1" cellspacing="1" cellpadding="1" width="525" align="center"
border="0">
                <tr>
                    <td>
                        <asp:Literal ID="ltlMessage" runat="server"></asp:Literal>
                    </td>
                </tr>
                <tr>
                    <td>
                        <table id="Table2" cellspacing="0" cellpadding="0" width=
"100%" align="center" border="0">
                            <tr>
                                <td class="fieldname">
                                    Username
                                </td>
                                <td width="10">
                                </td>
                                <td>
                                    <asp:Literal runat="server" ID="ltlUserName">
</asp:Literal>
                                    <div runat="server" id="dUserName">
                                        <asp:TextBox ID="txtUserName" runat="server"
CssClass="formField"></asp:TextBox><sup><font
                                            color="red" size="2">*</font></sup> 
                                        <asp:RequiredFieldValidator ID=
"RequiredFieldValidator3" runat="server" ControlToValidate="txtUserName"
                                            Display="None" ErrorMessage="You must supply
a Username."></asp:RequiredFieldValidator>
                                        <asp:ValidatorCalloutExtender ID=
"ValidatorCalloutExtender1" runat="server" TargetControlID=
"RequiredFieldValidator1">
                                        </asp:ValidatorCalloutExtender>
                                    </div>
```

```
                                    </td>
                                </tr>
                                <tr>
                                    <td class="fieldname">
                                        E-Mail
                                    </td>
                                    <td width="10">
                                    </td>
                                    <td>
                                        <asp:Literal runat="server" ID="ltlEMail">
</asp:Literal>
                                        <div runat="server" id="dEMail">
                                            <asp:TextBox ID="txtEmail" runat="server"
CssClass="formField"></asp:TextBox><span
                                                style="font-size: 10pt; vertical-align: super;
color: #ff0000">*</span>
                                            <asp:RequiredFieldValidator ID=
"RequiredFieldValidator2" runat="server" ControlToValidate="txtEmail"
                                                Display="None" ErrorMessage="You must supply
a valid E-Mail"></asp:RequiredFieldValidator>
                                            <asp:ValidatorCalloutExtender ID=
"ValidatorCalloutExtender2" runat="server" TargetControlID=
"RequiredFieldValidator2">
                                            </asp:ValidatorCalloutExtender>
                                        </div>
                                    </td>
                                </tr>
                                <tr runat="server" id="trQuestion">
                                    <td class="fieldname">
                                        <asp:Label runat="server" ID="lblQuestion"
AssociatedControlID="Question" Text="Security question:" />
                                    </td>
                                    <td width="10">
                                    </td>
                                    <td>
                                        <asp:TextBox runat="server" ID="Question" Width
="100%" />
                                        <asp:RequiredFieldValidator ID="valRequireQuestion"
runat="server" ControlToValidate="Question"
                                            SetFocusOnError="true" Display="Dynamic"
ErrorMessage="Security question is required."
                                            ToolTip="Security question is required."
ValidationGroup="CreateUserWizard1">*</asp:RequiredFieldValidator>
                                    </td>
                                </tr>
                                <tr runat="server" id="trAnswer">
                                    <td class="fieldname">
                                        <asp:Label runat="server" ID="lblAnswer"
AssociatedControlID="Answer" Text="Security answer:" />
                                    </td>
                                    <td width="10">
                                    </td>
                                    <td>
                                        <asp:TextBox runat="server" ID="Answer" Width=
```

```
                    "100%" />
                                    <asp:RequiredFieldValidator ID="valRequireAnswer"
runat="server" ControlToValidate="Answer"
                                    SetFocusOnError="true" Display="Dynamic"
ErrorMessage="Security answer is required."
                                    ToolTip="Security answer is required."
ValidationGroup="CreateUserWizard1">*</asp:RequiredFieldValidator>
                        </td>
                    </tr>
                    <tr runat="server" id="trRegistered">
                        <td class="fieldname">
                            Registered:
                        </td>
                        <td width="10">
                        </td>
                        <td>
                            <asp:Literal runat="server" ID="lblRegistered" />
                        </td>
                    </tr>
                    <tr runat="server" id="trLastLogin">
                        <td class="fieldname">
                            Last Login:
                        </td>
                        <td width="10">
                        </td>
                        <td>
                            <asp:Literal runat="server" ID="lblLastLogin" />
                        </td>
                    </tr>
                    <tr runat="server" id="trLastActivity">
                        <td class="fieldname">
                            Last Activity:
                        </td>
                        <td width="10">
                        </td>
                        <td>
                            <asp:Literal runat="server" ID="lblLastActivity" />
                        </td>
                    </tr>
                    <tr>
                        <td colspan="3">
                            <table runat="server" id="tUserStatus" cellspacing
="0" cellpadding="0" width="100%"
                                align="center" border="0">
                                <tr>
                                    <td class="fieldname">
                                        <asp:Label runat="server" ID
="lblOnlineNow" AssociatedControlID="chkOnlineNow" Text="Online Now:" />
                                    </td>
                                    <td width="10">
                                    </td>
                                    <td>
                                        <asp:CheckBox runat="server" ID
="chkOnlineNow" Enabled="false" />
```

```
                            </td>
                        </tr>
                        <tr>
                          <td class="fieldname">
                              <asp:Label runat="server" ID
="lblApproved" AssociatedControlID="chkApproved" Text="Approved:" />
                          </td>
                          <td width="10">
                          </td>
                          <td>
                              <asp:CheckBox runat="server" ID=
"chkApproved" AutoPostBack="true" />
                          </td>
                        </tr>
                        <tr>
                          <td class="fieldname">
                              <asp:Label runat="server" ID=
"lblLockedOut" AssociatedControlID="chkLockedOut" Text="Locked Out:" />
                          </td>
                          <td width="10">
                          </td>
                          <td>
                              <asp:CheckBox runat="server" ID=
"chkLockedOut" AutoPostBack="true" />
                          </td>
                        </tr>
                      </table>
                    </td>
                </tr>
                <tr>
                  <td colspan="3">
                  </td>
                </tr>
                <tr>
                  <td colspan="3">
                      <div runat="server" id="dPassword">
                          Password   
                          <asp:TextBox ID="txtPwd" runat="server"
TextMode="Password" CssClass="formField"></asp:TextBox><span
                              style="vertical-align: super; color: red">*
                          <asp:RequiredFieldValidator ID
="RequiredFieldValidator1" runat="server" ControlToValidate="txtPwd"
                              Display="None" ErrorMessage="You must
supply a Password."></asp:RequiredFieldValidator>
                          </span> <br />
                          <asp:ValidatorCalloutExtender ID
="ValidatorCalloutExtender3" runat="server" TargetControlID=
"RequiredFieldValidator3">
                          </asp:ValidatorCalloutExtender>
                          Confirm Password
                          <asp:TextBox ID="txtPwdConfirm" runat="server"
TextMode="Password" CssClass="formField"></asp:TextBox>
                          <asp:CompareValidator ID="CompareValidator1"
runat="server" ControlToCompare="txtPwdConfirm"
```

```
                                        ControlToValidate="txtPwd" Display="None"
ErrorMessage="The Passwords do not Match."></asp:CompareValidator>
                            <asp:ValidatorCalloutExtender ID=
"ValidatorCalloutExtender4" runat="server" TargetControlID="CompareValidator1">
                            </asp:ValidatorCalloutExtender>
                        </div>
                    </td>
                </tr>
                <tr>
                    <td colspan="3">
                    </td>
                </tr>
            </table>
        </td>
    </tr>
    <tr>
        <td>
            <div class="sectiontitle">
                Edit user's roles</div>
        </td>
    </tr>
    <tr>
        <td>
            <asp:CheckBoxList ID="cblRoles" runat="server"
RepeatColumns="3">
            </asp:CheckBoxList>
        </td>
    </tr>
    <tr>
        <td>
        <uc1:UserProfile ID="UserProfile1" runat="server" />
        </td>
    </tr>
    <tr>
        <td>
            <table id="Table11" cellspacing="1" cellpadding="1" width
="300" align="center" border="0">
                <tr>
                    <td class="AdminDetailsAction">
                        <asp:LinkButton ID="lbDelete" CssClass=
"AdminButton" runat="server" CausesValidation="false">Delete</asp:LinkButton>
                    </td>
                    <td class="AdminDetailsAction">
                        <asp:LinkButton ID="lbCancel" CssClass=
"AdminButton" runat="server" CausesValidation="false">Cancel</asp:LinkButton>
                    </td>
                    <td class="AdminDetailsAction">
                        <asp:LinkButton ID="lbUpdate" CssClass=
"AdminButton" runat="server">Update</asp:LinkButton>
                    </td>
                </tr>
            </table>
        </td>
```

```
        </tr>
    </table>
```

When the page loads, the `username` parameter is read from the querystring, a `MembershipUser` instance is retrieved for that user, and the values of its properties are shown by the first section's controls. Remember, as an administrator you are authenticated, so you must keep the username you want to edit separate from your account credentials. The membership provider assumes your account is to be used, if one is not specified, so there is some work required to keep these separated. The `CurrentUserName` property helps with this problem:

```
Private Property CurrentUserName() As String
    Get
        If Not IsNothing(ViewState("CurrentUserName")) Then
            Return ViewState("CurrentUserName").ToString
        Else
            If Not IsNothing(Request("CurrentUserName")) Then
                Return Request("CurrentUserName").ToString
            Else
                Return String.Empty
            End If
        End If
    End Get
    Set(ByVal value As String)
        ViewState("CurrentUserName") = value
    End Set
End Property
```

The `Page Load` event handler checks to see if a username was passed and either loads the user's information to be edited or clears the controls so a new user can be added to the site.

```
Protected Sub Page_Load1(ByVal sender As Object, ByVal e As System.EventArgs)
Handles Me.Load

    If Not IsPostBack Then

        If String.IsNullOrEmpty(CurrentUserName) = False Then 'Better make sure
            BindUser()
        Else
            ClearUser()
        End If

    End If

End Sub
```

The `GetMember` function wraps the `Membership.GetUser` method so that it can be consistently called as needed in the site.

```
Private Function GetMember() As MembershipUser
    Dim mu As MembershipUser = Membership.GetUser(CurrentUserName)
    Return mu
End Function
```

The `BindUser` method gets the `Membership` user object for the desired user and binds the controls to the corresponding values.

```
Private Sub BindUser()

    Dim mu As MembershipUser = GetMember()

    dUserName.Visible = False
    dEMail.Visible = False
    dPassword.Visible = False
    tUserStatus.Visible = True
    trRegistered.Visible = True
    trLastActivity.Visible = True
    trLastLogin.Visible = True
    trQuestion.Visible = False
    trAnswer.Visible = False

    lbUpdate.Text = "Update"

    ltlUserName.Text = mu.UserName
    ltlEMail.Text = mu.Email
    lblRegistered.Text = mu.CreationDate.ToString("f")
    lblLastLogin.Text = mu.LastLoginDate.ToString("f")
    lblLastActivity.Text = mu.LastActivityDate.ToString("f")

    chkOnlineNow.Checked = mu.IsOnline
    chkApproved.Checked = mu.IsApproved
    chkLockedOut.Checked = mu.IsLockedOut
    chkLockedOut.Enabled = mu.IsLockedOut

    BindRoles()

End Sub
```

In the `Page_Load` event handler you also call the `BindRoles` method, as follows, which fills a `CheckBoxList` with all the available roles and then retrieves the roles the user belongs to, and finally selects them in the `CheckBoxList`:

```
Protected Sub BindRoles()
        BindRoles(String.Empty)
End Sub

Protected Sub BindRoles(ByVal vUserName As String)

        cblRoles.DataSource = Roles.GetAllRoles
        cblRoles.DataBind()

        For Each role As String In Roles.GetRolesForUser(vUserName)
            cblRoles.Items.FindByText(role).Selected = True
        Next

End Sub
```

When the Update Roles button is pressed, the user is first removed from all her roles, and then is added to the selected ones. The removal that occurs first is necessary because a call to `Roles.AddUserToRole` will fail if the user is already a member of that role. This is a list collection that enables you to specify the datatype you wish to support for objects stored in the list. When you declare an instance of this collection, you have to indicate which datatype you want to store in it by enclosing it in angle brackets. Therefore, if you say `"List<string>"` you are asking for a list collection that is strongly typed to accept strings. You could have also asked for a collection of any other datatype, including any custom class you might create to hold related data.

Here's the code for the `UpdateRoles` method:

```
Private Sub UpdateRoles(ByVal mu As MembershipUser)

        Dim currRoles() As String = Roles.GetRolesForUser(mu.UserName)

        If currRoles.Length > 0 Then
            Roles.RemoveUserFromRoles(UserName, currRoles)
        End If

        ' and then add the user to the selected roles
        Dim newRoles As New List(Of String)
        For Each item As ListItem In cblRoles.Items
            If item.Selected Then
                newRoles.Add(item.Text)
            End If
        Next
        Dim userNames() As String = {mu.UserName}
        Roles.AddUsersToRoles(userNames, newRoles.ToArray)

        lblRolesFeedbackOK.Visible = True

    End Sub
```

As you see, you don't make individual calls to `Roles.AddUserToRole` for each selected role. Instead, you first fill a list of strings with the names of the selected roles and then make a single call to `Roles.AddUserToRoles`. When the Create Role button is pressed, you first check to see if a role with the same is already present, and if not, you create it. Then, the `BindRoles` method is called to refresh the list of available roles:

```
    Protected Sub btnNewRole_Click(ByVal sender As Object, ByVal e As EventArgs)
Handles btnNewRole.Click
        If Not Roles.RoleExists(txtNewRole.Text.Trim) Then
            Roles.CreateRole(txtNewRole.Text.Trim)
            BindRoles()
        End If
    End Sub
```

When the Approved checkbox is clicked, an auto-postback is made, and in its event handler you update the `MembershipUser` object's `IsApproved` property according to the checkbox's value, and then save the change:

```
    Protected Sub chkApproved_CheckedChanged(ByVal sender As Object, ByVal e As
System.EventArgs) Handles chkApproved.CheckedChanged
        Dim User As MembershipUser = Membership.GetUser(CurrentUserName)
        If Not IsNothing(User) Then
            User.IsApproved = chkApproved.Checked
            Membership.UpdateUser(User)
        End If
    End Sub
```

It works in a similar way for the Locked Out checkbox, except that the corresponding `MembershipUser` property is read-only, and the user is unlocked by calling the `UnlockUser` method. After this is done, the checkbox is made read-only because you can't lock out a user here (as mentioned previously). Take a look at the code:

```
Protected Sub chkLockedOut_CheckedChanged(ByVal sender As Object, ByVal e As
System.EventArgs) Handles chkLockedOut.CheckedChanged
        If chkLockedOut.Checked = False Then
            Dim user As MembershipUser = Membership.GetUser(CurrentUserName)
            If Not IsNothing(user) Then
                user.UnlockUser()
                chkLockedOut.Enabled = False
            End If
        End If
End Sub
```

Finally, when the Update button is clicked, a call to the `UserProfile`'s `SaveProfile` is made, as you've done in other pages:

```
Protected Sub lbUpdate_Click(ByVal sender As Object, ByVal e As System.EventArgs)
Handles lbUpdate.Click

        UpdateUser(Membership.GetUser(CurrentUserName))
        UserProfile1.SaveProfile()

End Sub
```

Figure 4-20 shows this page.

Figure 4-20

ManageRoles.aspx Page

The ManageRoles page provides a list of the site's roles with links to edit and delete them. The two role administration pages both derive from `RoleAdminPage`, which in turn derives from `AdminPage`. The `RoleAdminPage` contains the `RoleName` property, which is built upon the `PrimaryKeyIdAsString` property defined in the `BasePage` class.

```
Public Class RoleAdminPage
        Inherits AdminPage

#Region " Properties "

        Protected Property RoleName() As String
            Get
                Return PrimaryKeyIdAsString("Role")
            End Get
            Set(ByVal value As String)
                PrimaryKeyIdAsString("Role") = value
            End Set
        End Property

#End Region

End Class
```

The `PrimaryKeyIdAsString` property is a catch-all sort of pattern designed to catch string parameters entered in the querystring or stored in the page's view state. I call it the `PrimaryKeyIdAsString` property because it is primarily used to manage values associated with primary keys in tables. However it can be used for any value that might potentially be passed in the querystring. The main difference between `PrimaryKeyId` and `PrimaryKeyIdAsString` property is the string version returns an empty string when no matching parameter is found. The `PrimaryKeyId` returns 0 for an empty integer parameter.

```
Public Property PrimaryKeyIdAsString(ByVal vPrimaryKey As String) As String
Get
                If Not IsNothing(ViewState(vPrimaryKey)) Then
                    Return ViewState(vPrimaryKey)
                ElseIf Not IsNothing(Request.QueryString(vPrimaryKey)) Then
                    ViewState(vPrimaryKey) = Request.QueryString(vPrimaryKey)
                    Return Request.QueryString(vPrimaryKey)
                End If
                Return String.Empty
End Get
Set(ByVal Value As String)
                ViewState(vPrimaryKey) = Value
End Set
End Property
```

The ManageRoles page relies on a `ListView`, which follows a common pattern with a table used for the layout, and a column to display the role, and edit and delete it. The first row of the table defines a header row, with column titles and applies the `AdminList` style class. In the case of the DarkBeer theme, this uses a maroon background and bold white font.

The ItemTemplate defines the binding responsible for rendering the content for each record. This is more than just echoing the text, it also renders the links and buttons for the user to edit and delete an existing role. The role name itself is wrapped in an anchor tag that loads the AddEditRole.aspx page, passing the role to modify.

The delete ImageButton leverages the built-in Deleting event handler of the ListView to handle the deleting process. Notice the ListView's DataKeyNames property is left blank, this is because the collection of roles bound to the ListView is a collection of strings, and therefore does not contain any primary key values.

```
<asp:ListView ID="lvRoles" runat="server" DataKeyNames="Role">
        <LayoutTemplate>
            <table cellspacing="0" cellpadding="0" class="AdminList">
                <tr class="AdminListHeader">
                    <td>
                        Role
                    </td>
                    <td>
                        Edit
                    </td>
                    <td>
                        Delete
                    </td>
                </tr>
                <tr id="itemPlaceholder" runat="server">
                </tr>
            </table>
<!--Common Data Pager Control Here -- >
            </div>
        </LayoutTemplate>
        <EmptyDataTemplate>
            <tr>
                <td colspan="3">
                    <p>
                        Sorry there are no Roles available at this time.</p>
                </td>
            </tr>
        </EmptyDataTemplate>
        <ItemTemplate>
            <tr>
                <td class="ListTitle">
                    <a href="<%# String.Format("AddEditRole.aspx?Role
={0}", Container.DataItem.ToString()) %>">
                        <%# Container.DataItem.ToString() %></a>
                </td>
                <td>
                    <a href="<%# String.Format("AddEditRole.aspx?Role
={0}", Container.DataItem.ToString()) %>">
                        <img src="../images/edit.gif" alt="" width="16"
height="16" class="AdminImg" /></a>
                </td>
                <td>
                    <asp:ImageButton runat="server" ID=
"btnDeleteEvents" CommandArgument='<%# Eval("Role")%>'
                        CommandName="Delete" ImageUrl=
```

```
"~/images/delete.gif" AlternateText="Delete" CssClass="AdminImg"
                              OnClientClick="return confirm('Warning: This
will delete the Role from the database.');" />
                     </td>
                  </tr>
               </ItemTemplate>
            </asp:ListView>
```

Similarly to the ManageUsers page, when a user clicks the trash can icon to delete a row the `ItemDeleting` event fires, and the role name is passed to the `DeleteRoles` function. This function first purges any users from the role before it deletes it from the site.

```
Private Sub lvRoles_ItemDeleting(ByVal sender As Object, ByVal e As
   System.Web.UI.WebControls.ListViewDeleteEventArgs) Handles lvRoles.ItemDeleting
      DeleteRole(lvRoles.Items(e.ItemIndex).DataItem)
   End Sub

   Private Sub DeleteRoles(ByVal vRole As String)
      If Roles.GetUsersInRole(vRole).Length > 0 Then
         Roles.RemoveUsersFromRole(Roles.GetUsersInRole(vRole), vRole)
      End If
      Roles.DeleteRole(vRole)
      BindRoles()
End Sub
```

AddEditRole.aspx Page

In this edition of the Beer House, the user and user and role management is broken into two distinct groups of pages that enables you to add a little more functionality. The AddEditRole page allows us to add new roles, edit existing roles, and add users to a specific role.

When the page is loaded, it checks to see if there has been a role name passed to the page, if not it clears the controls by calling the `ClearRoleInfo` method. If there is a role to work on, it binds the role and any associated users to the controls.

```
    Protected Sub Page_Load(ByVal sender As Object, ByVal e As System.EventArgs)
Handles Me.Load

    If Not IsPostBack Then

       MultiView1.ActiveViewIndex = 0

       If String.IsNullOrEmpty(RoleName) = False Then
          BindRoleInfo()
       Else
          clearRoleinfo()
       End If

    End If

End Sub

  Private Sub ClearRoleInfo()

     txtRole.Text = String.Empty
```

```
            flUser.visible = False
            lvUsers.Items.Clear

    End Sub
```

The `BindRoleInfo` method sets the text of the `txtRole` to the role, if it exists. I did this because, if the role does not exist, it needs to be added. If the role exists, then it is bound to the `txtRole` and a list of `UsersInRole` is bound to the `lvUsers` ListView. The list just shows the users in this role. There is also a delete button to remove the user from the list.

```
        Private Sub BindRoleInfo()
            BindRoleInfo(RoleName)
        End Sub

        Private Sub BindRoleInfo(ByVal sRole As String)

            If Roles.RoleExists(sRole) = False Then
                txtRole.Text = String.Empty

                Exit Sub
            End If

            txtRole.Text = sRole

            lvUsers.DataSource = Roles.GetUsersInRole(sRole)
            lvUsers.DataBind()

        End Sub
```

The `MultiView` control, introduced with ASP.NET 2.0, allows the definition of different panes of information that can be displayed based on runtime logic. It is great for exchanging what is visible based on server-side logic. In the case of administering a role, it can display either the role information or a view where a new user can be added. When the Add User to Role button is clicked, the second view is displayed and the first view is hidden. In fact the content of the hidden view is not even sent to the browser, making the actual content sent to the client thinner. However, this does mean that any activity to hide or display a view must involve a round trip to the server to determine which view should be displayed. We will see in the next chapter how to hide and display DIVs using JavaScript in a similar fashion, but all the activity is managed on the client.

A `TextBox` is used to collect the username to be added to the role. A `TextBox` is a better solution in this situation because the list of usernames could be very large. The `TextBox` is extended with an `AutoCompleteExtender` that retrieves a list of potential usernames as the administrator types characters in the `TextBox`. The `AutoCompleteExtender` is part of the ASP.NET AJAX Control Toolkit, discussed earlier in this chapter. The `AutoCompleteExtender` provides a suggestion effect that allows the administrator to see potential accounts without being overwhelmed with a large list of usernames.

To make the `AutoCompleteExtender` work, there must be a web service with a web method it can call to retrieve the suggestions. The method signature has to be in the form of a `String` and an `Integer`. The `String` is the phrase to be used as the search filter, and the `Integer` is a count limit the `AutoCompleteExtender` wants. This is used to limit the size of the list displayed below the `TextBox`. If there were no limit, the list could be infinitely long. The `MaximumPrefixLength` property signals to the `AutoCompleteExtender` how many characters need to be entered before it queries the web service for a list. This again is useful to help limit any potential long list of results. The `ServicePath` is the URL to the web service, and the `ServiceMethod` is the name of the method in the web service used to perform the filtering.

```
<asp:View runat="server" ID="vAddUserToRole">
    <fieldset id="Fieldset1">
        <legend>Assign New User</legend>
        <br />
        Role:
        <asp:Literal runat="server" ID="ltlRole" />
        <br />
        User
        <asp:TextBox ID="txtUser" runat="server" CssClass=
"formField"></asp:TextBox>   
        <asp:Button runat="server" ID="btnAddUserToRole2" Text=
"Add User To Role" />   
        <asp:Button runat="server" ID="btnCancelAddUserToRole" Text="Cancel" /><br />
        <asp:AutoCompleteExtender runat="server" ID="autoComplete1" TargetControlID
="txtUser"
            ServicePath="~/MembersService.asmx" ServiceMethod="SearchUsersByName"
 MinimumPrefixLength="1"
            CompletionInterval="1000" EnableCaching="true" CompletionSetCount="12" />
    </fieldset>
</asp:View>
```

The `SearchUsersByName` method uses the same search routine used in the `ManageUsers.aspx` page, `Membership.FindUsersByName` method. The `AutoCompleteExtender` passes in each character as it is typed and builds a list of potential usernames that match the characters already entered. The `SearchUsersByName` method retrieves the list of potential `MembershipUsers` and adds the usernames to a `StringCollection`. This is then copied to an array of `Strings` and returned to the `AutoCompleteExtender` to display as a list below the targeted `TextBox` control.

```
<WebMethod()> _
<System.Web.Script.Services.ScriptMethod()> _
Public Shared Function SearchUsersByName(ByVal vName As String,
ByVal count As Integer) As String()

        Dim saUsers As String()
        Dim UserNames As New StringCollection

        Dim users As MembershipUserCollection = Membership.FindUsersByName(vName)

        For Each mu As MembershipUser In users
            UserNames.Add(mu.UserName)
        Next

        Dim saUsers As String() = New String(UserNames.Count - 1) {}
        UserNames.CopyTo(saUsers, 0)

        Return saUsers
End Function
```

Summary

This chapter covered a great deal of information regarding the membership and profiling features introduced in ASP.NET. The "Solution" section contains surprisingly little code yet produces a complete membership system! We even managed to reimplement and extend the Security area of the ASP.NET Web Administration Tool. In addition, much of the code is for HTML layout, which gives the pages a good appearance, but the code-behind code we've written is just over a hundred lines.

We have also extended the membership, role, and profile systems to the client using ASP.NET AJAX and the corresponding systems. While the code has a certain coolness factor to it, there is much more that could be exploited to make an even sexier experience for our users.

One thing that can be improved upon is the fact that the membership module only supports users and roles, not individual permissions. It might be useful in some cases to define a list of permissions, associate them with a role, add users to the role, and then check for the presence of a permission from code, instead of just checking whether the user belongs to a role. This would give much finer granularity to the security settings and is something that we did in the custom security module developed in the first edition of this book. However, while that level of security control is almost always required in large browser-based applications, it is overkill for many small-to-medium websites and unnecessarily complicates the code. By sticking with simple built-in role security, we are able to completely meet our requirements, and we can do so with simpler code that is easier to test and deploy. If you decide that your particular application requires a fine amount of control that can be enumerated in a list of permissions, you can extend the membership support by writing your own permissions module that links to the current users and roles.

5

News and Article Management

The example site is basically a container for content targeted to beer, food, and pub enthusiasts. Content can be in the form of news, articles, reports of special events, reviews, photo galleries, and so forth. This chapter describes the typical content-related problems that should be considered for a site of this type. You'll then design and develop an online article manager that allows the complete management of the site's content, in terms of acquiring articles; adding, activating, and removing articles; sharing articles with other parties, and so on.

Problem

Different sites use different methods of gathering news and information: some site administrators hunt for news events and write their own articles, while others get news and articles directly from their users (a great example of this is the Add Your News link at www.aspwire.com) or they rely upon a company whose business is to gather and organize news to be sold to third-party sites. In the old days, some sites did *screen-scraping*, retrieving data from an external site's page and showing it on their pages with a custom appearance (of course, you must have the authorization from the external company and you must know the format they use to show the news on their pages). During the last few years, we've seen an explosion in the use of RSS (Really Simple Syndication), a simple XML format for syndicating content, making it available to other clients. Atom is another XML-based syndication standard that was created to solve some problems of RSS — it is relatively new but already very popular. The basic idea with RSS and ATOM is for sites to provide an index of news items in the form of an XML document. A client program can fetch that XML document and provide users with a list of news items and hyperlinks that can direct them to the individual stories they are interested in. One site's XML index document is called a *newsfeed*. The client program is called a *news aggregator* (or *feed reader*) because it can extract newsfeeds from many sites and present them in one list, possibly arranged by categories. Users can subscribe to the XML feed and their aggregator program can periodically poll for new stories by fetching new XML documents automatically in the background. Because RSS and Atom are open standards, there are many web-based and fat-client desktop applications that can subscribe to any site that provides such feeds. Some popular open-source feed readers written in C# are RSS Bandit (www.rssbandit.org) and SharpReader (www.sharpreader.com). RSS and Atom are very convenient for users who want to keep up on the latest news and articles. You can advertise your new content via RSS and ATOM feeds, or you can even display a list of content from other sites by showing RSS links on one of your web pages. Your page can have an aggregator user control that makes it simple to display the content of specified RSS and ATOM feeds. This adds to any unique content you provide, and users will find value in returning to your site frequently to see your own updated content as well as a list of interesting links to updated news items on other sites.

It doesn't matter which methods you decide to use, but you must have fresh and updated content as often as possible for your site to be successful and entice users to return. Users will not return regularly to a site if they rarely find new content. You should use a variety of methods to acquire new content. You can't rely entirely on external content (retrieved as an RSS feed, by screen-scraping, or by inserting some JavaScript) because these methods often imply that you just publish a small extract of the external content on your site, and publish a link to the full article, thus driving traffic away from your site. It can be a solution for daily news about weather, stock exchanges, and the like, but not for providing original content, which is why users surf the web. You must create and publish some content on your own, and possibly syndicate that content as RSS feeds, so that other sites can consume it, and bring new visitors to your site.

Once you have a source of articles, a second problem arises: how do you add them to your site? You can immediately rule out manually updating pages or adding new static HTML pages — if you have to add news several times a day, or even just every week, creating and uploading pages and editing all the links becomes an administrative nightmare. Additionally, the people who administer the site on a daily basis may not have the skills required to edit or create new HTML pages. You need a much more flexible system, one that allows the site administrators to easily publish fresh content without requiring special HTML code generation tools or knowledge of HTML. You want it to have many features, such as the capability to organize articles in categories and show abstracts, and even to allow some site users to post their own news items. You'll see the complete list of features you're going to implement in the "Design" section of this chapter. For now, suffice it to say that you must be able to manage the content of your site remotely over the web, without requiring any other tools. Think about what this implies: you can add or edit news as soon as it is available, in a few minutes, even if you're not in your office and even if you don't have access to your own computer; all you need is a connection to the Internet and a browser. And this can work the same way for your news contributors and partners. They won't have to e-mail the news to you and then wait for you to publish it. They can submit and publish content without your intervention (although in our case we will give administrators and editors the option to approve or edit the content before publication).

The last problem is the implementation of security. We want to give full control to one or more administrators and editors, allow a specific group of users (contributors) to submit news, and allow normal users to just read the news. You could even prevent them from reading the content if they have not registered with the site.

Once new articles or news is made available, you need to promote the content. In today's Web 2.0 world, this involves pushing content to social media sites such as Twitter, Facebook, and many other locations. The other side of Web 2.0 design is allowing visitors to comment on the content. The Beer House already allows comments, but the user interface needs a slight facelift.

To summarize the problem, you need the following:

❑ An online tool for managing news content that allows specific users to add, update, and delete articles without knowing HTML or other publishing software.

❑ A common infrastructure to post announcements to Twitter. This will provide a way to get news to patrons through the web and SMS (Short Message Service). Twitter also allows the Beer House to reach a growing Web 2.0 crowd of very interactive customers.

❑ A common infrastructure to leverage Gravatar.com to create user avatars used to visually identify them on the site when they post a comment to an article.

❑ A method of allowing other sites to use your content so that they publish an extract and link to your site for the entire articles, thus bringing more traffic.

❑ A system that allows various users different levels of access to the site's content.

Design

This section introduces the design of the solution and an online tool for acquiring, managing, and sharing the content of our site. Specifically, we will do the following:

❑ Provide a full list of the features we want to implement.

❑ Design the database tables for this module.

❑ Create a list and a description of the stored procedures needed to provide access to the database.

❑ Design the object models of the data and business layers.

❑ Describe the user interface services needed for content management, such as the site pages and reusable user controls.

❑ Explain how we will ensure security for the administration section and for other access-restricted pages.

Features to Implement

Let's start our discussion by writing down a partial list of the features that the article manager module should provide to be flexible and powerful, but still easy to use:

❑ An article can be added to the database at any time, with an option to delay publication until a specified release date. Additionally, the person submitting the article must be able to specify an expiration date, after which the article will be automatically retired. If these dates are not specified, then the article should be immediately published and remain active indefinitely.

❑ Articles can have an approved status. If an administrator or editor submits the article, it should be approved immediately. If you allow other people, such as staff or users of the site (we will call them *contributors*), to post their own news and articles, then this content should be added to the database in a "pending" state. The site administrators or editors will then be able to control this content, apply any required modifications, and finally approve the articles for publishing once they are ready.

❑ The system must also track who originally submitted an article or news item. This is important because it provides information regarding whether a contributor is active, who is responsible for incorrect content, who to contact for further details if the article is particularly interesting, and so on.

❑ The administrator/editor must be able to decide whether an article can be read by all readers or only by registered users.

❑ There can be multiple categories, enabling articles to be organized in different virtual folders. Each category should have a description and an image that graphically represents it.

❑ There should be a page with the available categories as a menu. Each category should be linked to a page that shows a short abstract for each published article. Clicking on the article's title should allow the user to read the whole text.

❑ Articles can be targeted to users from a specified location, for example, country, state/province, or city. Consider the case where you might have stories about concerts, parties, and special events that will happen in a particular location. In Chapter 4, you implemented a registration and profiling system that includes the user's address. That will be used here to highlight events that are going to happen close to the user's location. This is a feature that can entice readers to provide that personal information, which you could use later for marketing purposes (ads can be geographically targeted also).

❑ Users can leave comments or ask questions about articles, and this feedback should be published at the end of the article itself, so that other readers can read it and create discussions around it (this greatly helps to increase traffic). You might recognize this approach as being common to blogs, which are web logs in which an individual publishes personal thoughts and opinions and other people add comments. As another form of feedback, users can rate articles to express how much they liked them.

❑ Each comment needs to be screened for spam. Letting comment spam infiltrate the site can quickly diminish the desirability of the site to users. It could also degrade the quality of the site in the eyes of search engines, meaning fewer potential customers. Automatic checking and manual approval must be implemented.

❑ The module must count how many times an article is read. This information will also be shown to the reader, together with the abstract, the author name, the publication date, and other information. But it will be most important for the editors/administrators because it greatly helps them understand which topics the readers find most interesting, enabling administrators to direct energy, money, and time to adding new content on those topics.

❑ The new content must be available as an RSS feed to which a reader can subscribe to read through his or her favorite RSS aggregator.

❑ Above all, the article manager and the viewer must be integrated with the existing site. In our case, this means that the pages must tie in with the current layout and that we must take advantage of the current authentication/authorization system to protect each section and to identify the author of the submitted content.

It's essential to have this list of features when designing the database tables, as we now know what information we need to store, and the information that we should retrieve from existing tables and modules (such as the user account data).

Designing the Database Tables

As described in Chapter 3 (where we looked at building the foundations for our site), we're going to use the `tbh_` prefix for all our tables, so that we avoid the risk of naming a table such that it clashes with another table used by another part of the site (this may well be the case when you have multiple applications on the site that store their data on the same shared DB). We need three tables for this module: one for the categories, another one for the articles, and the last one for the user feedback. The diagram shown in Figure 5-1 illustrates how they are linked to each other.

Figure 5-1

Let's start by looking at these tables and their relationship in more detail.

The tbh_Categories Table

Unsurprisingly, the `tbh_Categories` table stores some information about the article categories:

Column Name	Type	Size	Allow Null	Description
CategoryID	int - PK	4	No	Unique ID for the category.
AddedDate	datetime	8	No	Category creation date/time.
AddedBy	nvarchar	256	No	Name of the user who created the category.
Title	nvarchar	256	No	Category's title.

Continued

Column Name	Type	Size	Allow Null	Description
Importance	int	4	No	Category's importance. Used to sort the categories with a custom order, other than by name or by date.
Description	nvarchar	4000	Yes	Category's description.
ImageUrl	nvarchar	256	Yes	URL of an image that represents the category graphically.
Active	Bit	1	No	Indicates if the record has been deleted or is active.
UpdatedDate	datetime	8	No	Category last update date/time.
UpdatedBy	nvarchar	256	No	Name of the user who last updated the category.

This system supports a single-level category, meaning that we cannot have subcategories. This is plenty for small-to-midsized sites that don't have huge numbers of new articles on a wide variety of topics. Having too many categories in sites of this size can even hinder the user's experience, because it makes it more difficult to locate desired content. Enhancing the system to support subcategories is left as an exercise if you really need it, but as a suggestion, the DB would only require an additional ParentCategoryID column containing the ID of the parent category.

AddedDate, AddedBy, UpdatedDate, and UpdatedBy are four columns that you will find in all our tables — they record when a category/article/comment/product/message/newsletter was created and last updated, and by whom, to provide an audit trail. Of course, this will only provide information about when the record was created and last modified. For a more robust auditing system, you might look at adding a general table to log all changes to the database, but again this is a bit more than the Beer Houses needs at this point. You may have thought that, instead of having an nvarchar column for storing the username, we could use an integer column that would contain a foreign key pointing to records of the aspnet_Users table introduced in Chapter 4. However, that would be a bad choice for a couple of reasons:

1. The membership data may be stored in a separate database, and possibly on a different server.

2. The membership module might use a provider other than the default one that targets SQL Server. In some cases, the user account data will be stored in Active Directory or maybe an Oracle database, and thus there would be no SQL Server table to link to.

Another column that has been added to all the tables is Active. This is a bit value that is either true (1) or false (0) to indicate if the record has been deleted or not. One of the rules I was taught early in my development career is to retain all records and to set flags to indicate the state each record is in. Active allows records to be retained in the database, yet be considered deleted by the application. This is also pretty handy when a record was accidentally deleted by a user and needs to be restored. Simply flipping the bit back to true saves you from having to restore the record or, even worse, the entire database.

The tbh_Articles Table

The `tbh_Articles` table contains the content and all further information for all the articles in all categories. It is structured as follows.

Column Name	Type	Size	Allow Null	Description
ArticleID	int – PK	4	No	Unique ID for the article.
AddedDate	Datetime	8	No	Date/time the article was added.
AddedBy	Nvarchar	256	No	Name of the user who created the article.
CategoryID	int – FK	4	No	ID of the category to which the news item belongs.
Title	Nvarchar	256	No	Article's title.
Abstract	Nvarchar	4000	Yes	Article's abstract (short summary) to be shown in the page that lists the article, and in the RSS feed.
Body	Ntext		No	Article's content (full version).
Country	Nvarchar	256	Yes	Country to which the article (concert/event) refers.
State	nvarchar	256	Yes	State/province to which the article refers.
City	nvarchar	256	Yes	City to which the article refers.
ReleaseDate	datetime	8	Yes	Date/time the article will be publicly readable.
ExpireDate	datetime	8	Yes	Date/time the article will be retired and no longer readable by the public.
Approved	bit	1	No	Approved status of the article. If false, an administrator/editor has to approve the article before it is actually published and available to readers.
Listed	bit	1	No	Whether the article is listed in the articles page (indexed). If false, the article will not be listed, but will be still accessible if the user types the right URL, or if there is a direct link to it.
CommentsEnabled	bit	1	No	Whether the user can leave public comments on the article.
OnlyForMembers	bit	1	No	Whether the article is available to registered and authenticated users only or to everyone.

Continued

Column Name	Type	Size	Allow Null	Description
ViewCount	int	4	No	Number of times the article has been viewed.
Votes	int	4	No	Number of votes the article has received.
TotalRating	int	4	No	Total rating score the article has received. This is the sum of all the ratings posted by users.
Active	Bit	1	No	Indicates if the record has been deleted.
UpdateDate	Datetime	8	No	Datetime when the last update to the record was made.
UpdatedBy	nvarchar	256	No	Who made the last update to the record.

The `ReleaseDate` and `ExpireDate` columns are useful because the site's staff can prepare content in advance and postpone its publication, and then let the site update itself at the specified date/time. In addition to the obvious benefit of spreading out the workload, this is also great during vacation periods, when the staff would not be in the office to write new articles but you still want the site to publish fresh content regularly.

The `Listed` column is also very important, because it enables you to add articles that will be hidden from the main article list page, and from the RSS feeds. Why would you want to do this? Suppose that you have a category called Photo Galleries (we'll actually create it later in the chapter) in which you publish the photos of a past event or meeting. In such photo gallery articles, you would insert thumbnails of the photos with links to their full-sized version. It would be nice if the reader could comment and rate each and every photo, not just the article listing them all, right? You can do that if instead of linking the big photo directly you link a secondary article that includes the photo. However, if you have many photos, and thus many short articles that contain each of them, you certainly don't want to fill the category's article listing with a myriad of links to the single photos. Instead, you will want to list only the parent gallery. To do this, you set the `Listed` property of all the photo articles to `false`, and leave it set to `true` only on the article with the thumbnails.

The `Country`, `State`, and `City` fields enable you to specify an accurate location for those articles that refer to an event (such as parties, concerts, beer contests, etc.). You may recall that we created the same properties in Chapter 2 for the user's profile. If the location for the article matches a specific user's location, even partially, then you could highlight the article with a particular color when it's listed on the web page. You may be wondering why it was necessary to define the `Country` and `State` fields as varchar fields, instead of an `int` foreign key pointing to corresponding records of the `tbh_Countries` and `tbh_States` lookup tables. The answer is that I want to use the `City` field to support not only U.S. states, but states and provinces for any other country, so I defined this as free text field. It's also good for performance if we denormalize these fields. Using a lookup table is particularly useful when there is the possibility that some values may change; storing the information in one location minimizes the effort to update the data and makes it easier to ensure that we don't get out of sync. However, realistically, the list of countries will not change, so this isn't much of a problem. In the remote case that this might happen, you will simply execute a manual update for all those records that have `Country="USA"` instead of `"United States"`, for example. This design decision can greatly improve the performance of the application.

> Be aware that IP address databases are available that can be used to determine the user's location as close as his ZIP Code in the United States. The targeting detail varies among these databases, but even one that gets the general area correct can be very useful for most sites to target the user's content.

You may be wondering why I decided to put the `Votes` and `TotalRating` columns into this table, instead of using a separate table to store all the single votes for all articles. That alternative has its advantages, surely: you could track the name and IP address of the user who submits the vote, and produce interesting statistics such as the number of votes for every level of rating (from one to five stars). However, retrieving the total number of votes, the total rating, and the number of votes for each rating level would require several SUM operations, in addition to the SELECT to the `tbh_Articles` table. I don't think the additional features are worth the additional processing time and traffic over the network, and thus I opted for this much lighter solution instead.

The tbh_Comments Table

The `tbh_Comments` table contains the feedback (comments, questions, answers, etc.) for the published articles. The structure is very simple:

Column Name	Type	Size	Allow Null	Description
CommentID	int - PK	4	No	Unique ID for the comment.
AddedDate	datetime	8	No	Date/time the comment was added.
AddedBy	nvarchar	256	No	Name of the user who wrote the comment.
AddedByEmail	nvarchar	256	No	User's e-mail address.
AddedByIP	nchar	15	No	User's IP address.
ArticleID	int	4	No	Article to which the comment refers.
Body	ntext		No	Text of the comment.
Active	Bit	1	No	Indicates if the record has been deleted.
UpdatedDate	Datetime	8	No	When the record was last updated.
UpdatedBy	nvarchar	256	No	The username of the user who last updated the record.

We will track the name of the user posting the comment, but she could even be an anonymous user, so this value will not necessarily be one of the registered usernames. We also store the user's e-mail address, so that the reader can be contacted with a private answer to her questions. Storing the IP address might be legally necessary in some cases, especially when you allow anonymous users to post content on a public site. In case of offensive or illegal content, it may be possible to geographically locate the user if you know her IP address and the time when the content was posted. In simpler cases, you may just block posts from that IP (not a useful option if it were a dynamically assigned IP, though).

Creating the Entity Model

Chapter 3 walked through creating an Entity Data Model using the Entity Framework Wizard. The same process holds for the articles model, but uses the `tbh_Articles`, `tbh_Categories` and `tbh_Comments` tables.

But, just as you saw with the `SiteMap` model, the Articles model needs to be customized. The `thb_Articles` entity needs to have the Entity Set Name set to `Articles` and the Name set to `Article`. The navigational properties need to be changed to `Category` and `Comments`, respectively. For the `thb_Categories` entity, change the Entity Set Name to `Categories` and the Name to `Category`. Rename the `tbh_Articles` navigational property to `Article`. Similary rename the `tbh_Comments` entity appropriately, so the final result looks like Figure 5-2.

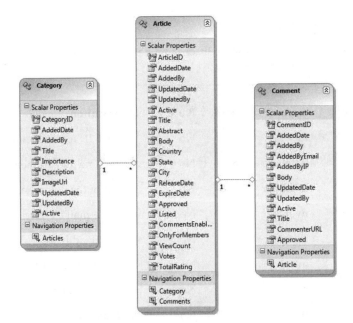

Figure 5-2

Once the model is generated, the classes in the model need to be placed in the `TheBeerHouse.BLL.Articles` namespace. This requires editing the generated code file by adding the namespace wrapper around classes. This is done below the Assembly definitions at the top of the file, which means an `Imports TheBeerHouse.BLL.Articles` directive at the top of the page. That's because the Assembly definitions reference the classes, now wrapped in the `Articles` namespace. Each of these entities is extended in corresponding partial classes defined in the class library.

One property exposed by the Comment entity is `EncodedBody`, which returns the same text returned by the `Body` property, but first performs HTML encoding on it. This protects us against the so-called script-injection and cross-site scripting attacks. As a very simple example, consider a page on which you allow users to anonymously post a comment. If you don't validate the input, they may write something like the following:

```
<script>document.location = 'http://www.usersite.com';</script>
```

This text is sent to the server, and you save it into the DB. Later, when you have to show the comments, you would retrieve the original comment text and send to the browser as is. However, when you output the preceding text, it won't be considered as text by the browser, but rather as a JavaScript routine that redirects the user to another website, hijacking the user away from your website! And this was just a basic attack — more complex scripts could be used to steal users' cookies, which could include authentication tickets and personal data, with potentially grave consequences. For our protection, ASP. NET automatically validates the user input sent to the server during a postback, and checks whether it matches a pattern of suspicious text. If so, it raises an exception and shows an error page. You should consider the case where a legitimate user tries to insert some simple HTML just to format the text, or maybe hasn't really typed HTML but only a < character. In that case, you don't want to show an error page; you only need to ensure that the HTML code isn't displayed in a browser (because you don't want users to put links or images on your site, or text with a font so big that it creates a mess with your layout). To make sure it isn't displayed, you can disable ASP.NET's input validation (only for those pages on which the user is actually expected to insert text, not for all pages!), and save the text into the DB, but only show it on the page after HTML encoding, as follows:

```
&lt;script&gt; document.location = 'http://www.usersite.com'; &lt;/script&gt;
```

This way, text inserted by the user is actually shown on the page, instead of being considered HTML. The link will show as a link, but it will not be a clickable link, and no JavaScript can be run this way. The `EncodedBody` property returns the HTML encoded text, but it can't completely replace the `Body` property, because the original comment text is still required in certain situations — for example, in the administration pages where you show the text in a textbox and allow the administrator to edit it.

> *Scripting-based attacks must not be taken lightly, and you should ensure that your site is not vulnerable. One good reference on the web is* www.technicalinfo.net/gunter/index.html, *but you can easily find many others. Try searching for "XSS," using your favorite search engine.*

There are two new features for the comment functionality of the Beer House, validating comments through Akismet and Gravatar support. Akismet is a comment spam-filtering service. Simply put a site can pass a comment through the Akismet API and it will return if Akismet thinks the comment is spam or not.

The last helper members help with accessing the user's Gravatar. Simply put, a Gravatar is a Globally Recognized Avatar and is managed at www.Gravatar.com. Anyone can go to Gravatar.com and create an account and assign images or photos to be used anywhere to represent them. If a commentor does not have a Gravatar account, the API returns a random image to represent the user, but more about that later, too.

Building Repository Classes

Instead of using stored procedures and a DAL (Data Access Layer) to access those stored procedures, with the Entity Framework and LINQ these tasks are contained within a repository class. As explained in Chapter 3, repository classes now manage the business aspect of the Beer House application. Repositories provide for some separation of concerns that will allow the architecture to be further extended in the future if desired. Figure 5-3 shows the class diagram for the Articles module.

Each of the entities related to the articles module has its own repository class. Each of these classes inherits a `BaseRepository` class that contains some common logic used by all the repository classes, such as the `Dispose` method and a common reference to the `ArticlesEntities DataContext` class to interact with the Entity Data Model for the articles module.

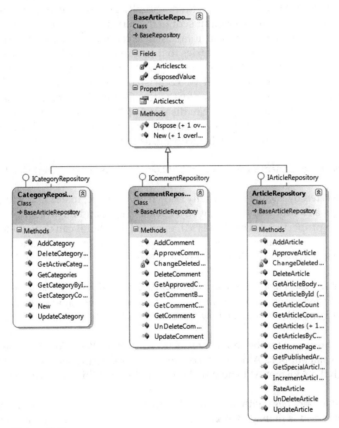

Figure 5-3

ArticleRepository

The `ArticleRepository` manages all the interactions with the Article entity, using LINQ to entities to build queries in the database. The repository is a class composed of methods to create, retrieve, update, and delete (CRUD) records in the tbh_Articles table, most manage retrieving and caching records in memory.

In the previous edition of the Beer House, the articles were retrieved in chunks or pages. This can still be done, but since the records are going to be cached in memory and pages using AJAX, this is not as important. If the site were to contain hundreds of thousands of records, then caching by page is slightly more feasible and can be done with LINQ by using the Skip and Take methods on the IQueryable(of Article) list returned by the LINQ query.

```
lArticles = (From lArticle In Articlesctx.Articles _
    Where lArticle.Published = True _
    Order By lArticle.ReleaseDate Descending).Skip(15).Take(15).ToList()
```

Skip accepts a numerical value that indicates how many rows to skip over before beginning the list of records to return. Similarly, the Take method accepts a numerical value to indicate how many records should be returned. So, the sample query returns the second displayed page of records.

Method	Description
GetArticles	Returns a list of Article instances and has three overloads to wrap all LINQ to Entities queries that retrieve the list of articles described above (to retrieve all articles, only published articles, etc.).
GetArticleCount	There are four overloads of this method that return the number of articles given no constraints (all articles), the parent category, the published status (but not the category), or the parent category plus the published status.
GetArticleByID	Returns an Article instance that fully describes the article identified by the input ID.
InsertArticle	Takes all the data for creating a new article, and returns its ID.
UpdateArticle	Updates data for an existing article and returns a Boolean value indicating whether or not the operation was successful.
DeleteArticle	Deletes the article identified by an ID and returns a Boolean value indicating whether or not the operation was successful.
ApproveArticle	Approves the article identified by an ID.
IncrementArticleViewCount	Increments the view count of the article identified by an ID.
RateArticle	Rates the article identified by the ID, with a value from 1 to 5.
GetPublishedArticles	A wrapper around the GetArticles overload passing a true value for the PublishedOnly parameter.
GetHomePageArticles	Returns a list of the three most recently added articles to have their titles and abstracts displayed on the home page.

The GetArticleById method returns a single article by its ID, but the method contains a couple of overloads. The primary returns just the article entity itself and does not retrieve the associated category or list of comments. This is the most efficient query but may not always meet the needs of the page asking for the article. In that case, the second overload accepts Boolean parameters to indicate if the associated category and comments should also be retrieved.

```
Public Function GetArticleById(ByVal ArticleId As Integer, ByVal
bIncludeCategories As Boolean, ByVal bIncludeComments As Boolean) As Article

        If ArticleId > 0 Then

            If bIncludeCategories And bIncludeComments Then

                Return (From lai In
Articlesctx.Articles.Include("Categories").Include("Comments") _
                    Where lai.ArticleID = ArticleId).FirstOrDefault

            ElseIf bIncludeCategories And Not bIncludeComments Then

                Return (From lai In Articlesctx.Articles.Include("Categories")
_ Where lai.ArticleID = ArticleId).FirstOrDefault

            ElseIf Not bIncludeCategories And Not bIncludeComments Then

                Return (From lai In Articlesctx.Articles _
                    Where lai.ArticleID = ArticleId).FirstOrDefault

            End If

        End If

        Throw New ArgumentException("The ArticleId is not valid.")

End Function
```

The RateArticle method is not necessarily the most efficient use of SQL because it retrieves an instance of the article's entity and changes the TotalRating and Votes members, then commits the changes to the database. What is more efficient is to change the values in an existing article entity you may be working with and save that to the database, but that may not always be possible. So, this method performs that duty for you using LINQ.

```
Public Function RateArticle(ByVal ArticleId As Integer,
ByVal rating As Integer) As Boolean

        Dim lArticle As Article = GetArticleById(ArticleId)

        lArticle.TotalRating += rating
        lArticle.Votes += 1

        Try
            Articlesctx.SaveChanges()
            MyBase.PurgeCacheItems(CacheKey)
```

```
                    Return True
              Catch ex As OptimisticConcurrencyException
                  ' catching this exception allows you to
                  ' refresh entities with either store/client wins
                  ' project the entities into this failed entities.
                  Dim failedEntities = From e1 In ex.StateEntries _
                                   Select e1.Entity

                  ' Note: in future you should be able to just pass the
opt.StateEntities in to refresh.
                  Articlesctx.Refresh(RefreshMode.ClientWins,
failedEntities.ToList())
                  Articlesctx.SaveChanges()

              Catch ex As Exception
                  Return False
              End Try

      End Function
```

The `RateArticle` method commits the changes to the database and also includes some special code to check for a `OptimisticConcurrencyException` and deals with it by specifying how the issue is to be resolved. While this should not be an issue with this method because the entity is being retrieved so fast, I thought it would be a good idea to include the code to demonstrate how this is done with the Entity Framework.

The `IncrementArticleViewCount` and `ApproveArticle` methods are structured in much the same way as the `RateArticle` method. They retrieve the article, change the relevant (ViewCount or Approved) value, and commit the change to the database.

The `AddArticle` method accepts an article entity and adds it to the database. There is a corresponding overload that accepts a series of parameters to create a new `Article` object. First, it checks to see if the `Article` already exists; if so, it uses the existing entity to make updates against. If it does not already exist, the method creates a new instance of an `Article`, and it is committed to the database by calling the other version of the `AddArticle` method.

```
    Public Function AddArticle(ByVal articleID As Integer, ByVal title As String,
    ByVal body As String, _
                ByVal approved As Boolean, ByVal listed As Boolean,
    ByVal commentsEnabled As Boolean, _
                ByVal onlyForMembers As Boolean, ByVal viewCount As Integer,
    ByVal votes As Integer, ByVal totalRating As Integer) As Article

            Dim article As Article

            If articleID > 0 Then

                article = GetArticleById(articleID)

                article.ArticleID = articleID
                article.UpdatedDate = Now
                article.UpdatedBy = Helpers.CurrentUserName
```

```
                article.Title = title
                article.Body = body
                article.Approved = approved
                article.Listed = listed
                article.CommentsEnabled = commentsEnabled
                article.OnlyForMembers = onlyForMembers
                article.ViewCount = viewCount
                article.Votes = votes
                article.TotalRating = totalRating

        Else
                article = article.CreateArticle(articleID, Now, _
    Helpers.CurrentUserName, Now, True, title, body, _
                        approved, listed, commentsEnabled, onlyForMembers, _
    viewCount, votes, totalRating)
            End If

            Return AddArticle(article)

    End Function
```

In the second `AddArticle` method leverages the built-in functionality of the Entity Framework to simply update the existing record. If the entity is not attached to the current context, it is added to the context before it is saved to the database. All the cache related to the `Article` entity is flushed from the system as well, to ensure that the freshest data is used by the application. Finally, a ternary `If` statement is used to return `True` or `False`, depending on if any records were affected, which typically will be true. If an exception occurs in the save operation, it is added to the `ActiveExceptions` list, which can then be used by the page working with the entity to inform the user about what happened.

```
    Public Function AddArticle(ByVal vArticle As Article) As Article

            Try
                If vArticle.EntityState = EntityState.Detached Then
                    Articlesctx.AddToArticles(vArticle)
                End If
                MyBase.PurgeCacheItems(CacheKey)
                Return If(Articlesctx.SaveChanges > 0, vArticle, Nothing)

            Catch ex As Exception
                ActiveExceptions.Add(CacheKey & "_" & vArticle.ArticleID, ex)
                Return Nothing
            End Try

    End Function
```

`ActiveExceptions` is a property defined in the `BaseRepository` class. It is a `Dictionary` of exceptions, so more than one exception can be caught and stored. I did this in case more than one exception was thrown, so that the page could loop through the exceptions and inform the user about each issue. Generally, there will be one exception, but there are some fringe cases where there might be more than one exception.

```
    Private _activeExceptions As Dictionary(Of String, Exception)
    Public Property ActiveExceptions() As Dictionary(Of String, Exception)
```

```
        Get
                    If IsNothing(_activeExceptions) Then
                        _activeExceptions = New Dictionary(Of String, Exception)
                    End If
                    Return _activeExceptions
                End Get
                Set(ByVal Value As Dictionary(Of String, Exception))
                    _activeExceptions = Value
            End Set
    End Property
```

The `AddEdit` pages in the site's admin all use the following routine to echo a list of the exceptions that occurred during a commit to the database:

```
Private Sub IndicateNotUpdated(ByVal vRepository As BaseRepository)

        ltlStatus.Text = String.Empty
        If vRepository.ActiveExceptions.Count > 0 Then
            For Each kv As KeyValuePair(Of String, Exception) In
vRepository.ActiveExceptions
                ltlStatus.Text += DirectCast(kv.Value, Exception).Message & "<BR/>"
            Next
        Else
            ltlStatus.Text = String.Format(My.Resources.EntityHasNotBeenUpdated,
"Article")
        End If

End Sub
```

`DeleteArticle` and `UnDeleteArticle` both call the `ChangeDeletedState` method but pass in either false to delete or true to undelete a record. The `ChangeDeleteState` method sets the `Active` field to the supplied `vState` parameter value, sets the `UpdatedDate` property to the current time and the `UpdatedBy` property to the current user's `UserName`.

```
Private Function ChangeDeletedState(ByVal vArticle As Article,
ByVal vState As Boolean) As Boolean
    vArticle.Active = vState
        vArticle.UpdatedDate = Now()
        vArticle.UpdatedBy = CurrentUserName

        Try
                Articlesctx.SaveChanges()
                MyBase.PurgeCacheItems(CacheKey)
                Return True
        Catch ex As Exception
                ActiveExceptions.Add(vArticle.ArticleID, ex)
                Return False
        End Try

End Function
```

CategoryRepository

The overall composition of the `CategoryRepository` class is very similar to the `ArticleRepository` as it applies to the basic CRUD operations.

Method	Description
GetCategories	Returns a list of `Category Entities`.
GetActiveCategories	Returns a list of all active `Category Entities`.
GetCategoryByID	Returns a `Category` entity by the `CategoryID`.
AddCategory	Takes all the data for creating a new category and returns true if the addition was successful.
UpdateCategory	Updates data for an existing category, and returns a Boolean value indicating whether the operation was successful.
DeleteCategory	Changes the `Active` flag for the category to indicate it is not active.
UnDeleteCategory	Changes the `Active` flag for the category to indicate it is active.
GetCategoryCount	Returns the number of categories stored in the database.

The `CategoryRepository`, located in the Articles folder of the class library, works much like the `ArticleRepository`. It does contain fewer members, since there are not many custom views of categories in the application. It differs from the previous edition of the Beer House; the `AllArticles` and `PublishedArticles` members have been removed and replaced with adequate corresponding members in the `ArticleRepository` class.

CommentRepository

The `CommentRepository` is a little simpler than the other two repository classes because it contains fewer methods and does not allow the deletion of comments. Instead, a comment is not going to be displayed unless it is approved.

Method	Description
GetComments	Returns a list of `Comment Entities`.
GetApprovedComments	Overloaded function that returns a list of all active `Comment Entities`, or all `Comments` by `Article` sorted in a desired order by date added.
GetCommentsByArticleId	Returns a list of `Comments` for an `Article` sorted in the specified order.
GetCommentCount	Returns the total number of `Comments`.
GetCommentByID	Returns a `Comment` entity by the `CommentID`.
AddComment	Takes all the data for creating a new comment and returns true if the addition was successful.

Method	Description
UpdateComment	Updates data for an existing comment and returns a Boolean value indicating whether the operation was successful.
ApproveComment	Changes the Approved flag for the Comment to indicate its approval state.
DeleteComment	Changes the Active flag for the Comment to indicate it has been deleted.
UnDeleteComment	Changes the Active flag for the Comment to indicate it has not been deleted.

The AddComment method does more than just add the comment to the database; it can also call the Akismet service to determine if the comment is spam or not. The method creates a new instance of the Akismet class, part of the Akismet.net library and passes an AkismetCommet object to the library, which subsequently calls Akisment to score the comment. If the comment is determined to be a spam comment, the method returns true; otherwise, it returns false to indicate the comment should be safe.

Working with Akismet requires having an account at WordPress.com, which is free to anyone who signs up (http://akismet.com). If you have higher traffic, there is a commercial license you might need to get, so check the Akismet website for more details.

The Akismet.net library has four methods that can be used to communicate with Akismet, VerifyKey, CommentCheck, SubmitSpam, and SubmitHam. If you want to verify your Word Press Key and blog, call the VerifyKey method, it returns True if you have a valid combination. To check a comment for spam, call the CommentCheck method, if Akismet returns false, then the comment should be safe. If you find items you want to submit to Akismet for their database, then use SubmitSpam, but only for something that is absolutely spam. Use the SubmitHam method if you are not quite sure if the comment is spam or not. Submitting suspect comments helps the Akismet system work better to protect the Internet from comment spam in the future!

We will not implement sorting features for the categories and the articles. This is because categories will always be sorted by importance (the Importance field) and then by name, whereas articles will always be sorted by release date, from the newest to the oldest, which is the right kind of sorting for these features. However, comments should be sorted in two different ways according to the situation:

❑ From the oldest to the newest when they are listed on the user page, under the article itself, so that users will read them in chronological order, allowing them to follow a discussion made up of questions and answers between the readers and the article's author, or among different readers.

❑ From the newest to the oldest in the administration page, so that the administrator finds the new comments at the top of the list, and in the first page (remember that comments support pagination), so they can be immediately read, edited, and, if necessary, deleted if found offensive.

Designing the Configuration Module

Chapter 3 introduced a custom configuration section named <theBeerHouse> that you must define in the root folder's web.config file, to specify some settings required in order for the site's modules to work. In that chapter, we also developed a configuration class that would handle the <contact> subelement of <theBeerHouse>, with settings for the Contact form in the Contact.aspx page. For the articles module of this chapter, you'll need some new settings that will be grouped into a new configuration subelement under <theBeerHouse>, called <articles>. This will be read by a class called ArticlesElement that will inherit from System.Configuration.ConfigurationElement and that will have the public properties shown in the following table.

Property	Description
ProviderType	Full name (namespace plus class name) of the concrete provider class that implements the data access code for a specific data store.
ConnectionStringName	Name of the entry in web.config's new <connectionStrings> section that contains the connection string to the module's database.
PageSize	Default number of articles listed per page. The user will be able to change the page size from the user interface.
RssItems	Number of items returned by the module's RSS feeds.
EnableCaching	Boolean value indicating whether the caching of data is enabled.
CacheDuration	Number of seconds for which the data is cached.
UrlIndicator	Used in the search engine friendly URLs to indicate the request is an article.
EnableTwitter	Boolean value indicating is posting to Twitter is enabled.
TwitterUserName	The site's Twitter account username.
TwitterPassword	The site's Twitter account password.
AkismetKey	Holds the Word Press Key needed to use Akismet.
EnableAkismet	Indicates if Akismet checking is turned on.
ReportAkismet	Indicates if automatic submission of comment spam to Akismet should be done.

The settings in the web.config file will have the same name, but will follow the camelCase naming convention; therefore, you will use providerType, connectionStringName, pageSize, and so on, as shown in the following example:

```
<theBeerHouse>
    <contactForm mailTo="thebeerhouse@wrox.com" />
    <articles pageSize="10" twitterUrserName="twitterBH"
twitterPassword="twitterPHPwd" enableTwitter="false" />
    :
</theBeerHouse>
```

A `Helpers` class is part of the BeerHouse class library that contains a series of shared (VB.NET) or static (C#) members. One of the members returns an instance of `theBeerHouse` configuration section.

```
Public Shared ReadOnly Settings As TheBeerHouseSection = _
    CType(WebConfigurationManager.GetSection("theBeerHouse"), TheBeerHouseSection)
```

An instance of `ArticlesElement` is returned by the `Articles` property of the `TheBeerHouseSection` class, described in Chapter 3, that represents the `<theBeerHouse>` parent section. This class will also have a couple of other new properties, `DefaultConnectionStringName` and `DefaultCacheDuration`, to provide default values for the module-specific `ConnectionStringName` and `CacheDuration` settings. These settings will be available for each module, but you want to be able to set them differently for each module. For example, you may want to use one database for storing articles data, and a second database to store forums data, so that you can easily back them up independently and with a different frequency according to how critical the data is and how often it changes. This is one of the reasons for having dedicated Entity Data Models for each module used in the site.

The same goes for the cache duration. However, in case you want to assign the same settings to all modules (which is probably what you will do for small to midsized sites), you can just assign the default values at the root section level, instead of copying and pasting them for every configuration subelement.

In addition to the properties listed earlier, the `ArticlesElement` will have another property, `ConnectionString`. This is a calculated property, though, not one that is read from `web.config`. It uses the `<articles>`'s connectionStringName or the `<theBeerHouse>`'s defaultConnectionStringName and then looks up the corresponding connection string in the `web.config` file's `<connectionStrings>` section, so the caller will get the final connection string and not just the name of its entry.

Designing the User Interface

The design of the ASP.NET pages in this module is not particularly special, so there's not much to discuss. We have a set of pages, some for the administrators and some for the end users, which allow us to manage articles, and navigate through categories and read articles, respectively. In the first edition of this book, the most important consideration for the UI section of the first chapters was the approach used to integrate the module-specific pages into the rest of the site. However, you've already seen from previous chapters that this is very straightforward in ASP.NET 2.0, thanks to master pages. Following are the pages we will code later:

❑ **~/Admin/ManageCategories.aspx** — Lists the current categories, and allows administrators to create new ones and delete and update existing ones.

❑ **~/Admin/AddEditCategory.aspx** — Allows administrators to create new categories and update existing categories.

❑ **~/Admin/ManageArticles.aspx** — Lists the current articles (with pagination support) and allows administrators to delete them. The creation of new articles and the editing of existing articles will be delegated to a secondary page.

❑ **~/Admin/AddEditArticle.aspx** — Allows administrators to create new articles and update existing articles.

- ❏ **~/Admin/ManageComments.aspx** — Lists the current comments for any article, has pagination support, and supports deletion and updates of existing comments.

- ❏ **~/ShowCategories.aspx** — An end-user page that lists all categories, with their title, description, and image.

- ❏ **~/BrowseArticles.aspx** — An end-user page that allows users to browse published articles for a specific category or for all categories. The page shows the title, abstract, author, release date, average rating, and location of the articles.

- ❏ **~/ShowArticle.aspx** — An end-user page that shows the complete article, along with the current comments at the bottom, and a box to let users post new comments and rate the article.

- ❏ **RSSFeed.vb** — A custom `HttpHandler` that is mapped to handle all requests for any .RSS resource in the Beer House site. It is intelligent enough to apply appropriate filtering to the list of RSS items it serves.

Writing Articles with a WYSIWYG Text Editor

The first and most important challenge you face is that the site must be easily updatable by the client herself, without requiring help from any technical support people. Some regular employees working in the pub must be able to write and publish new articles, and make them look good by applying various formatting, colors, pictures, tables, and so forth. All this must be possible without knowing any HTML, of course! This problem can be solved by using a WYSIWYG (the acronym for "what you see is what you get") text editor: these editors enable users to write and format text, and to insert graphical elements, much like a typical word processor (which most people are familiar with), and the content is saved in HTML format that can be later shown on the end-user page "as is." There are various editors available, some commercial and some free. Among the different options I picked FCKeditor (www .fckeditor.net), mainly because it is open source and because it is compatible with most Internet browsers, including IE 5.5+, Firefox 1.0+, Mozilla 1.3+, and Netscape 7+. Figure 5-4 shows a screenshot of an online demo from the editor's website.

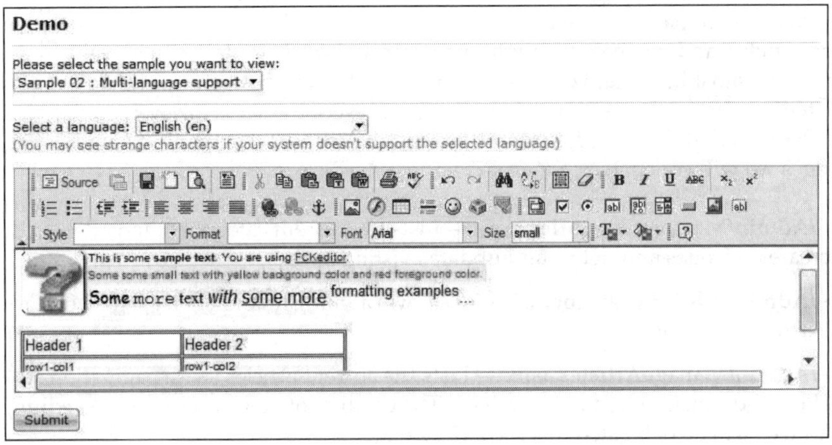

Figure 5-4

The editor is even localizable (language packs for many languages are already provided), and its user interface can be greatly customized, so you can easily decide what toolbars and what command buttons (and thus formatting and functions) you want to make available to users.

Uploading Files

The editor must be able to upload files, typically images for an article or to publish in a photo gallery, and maybe upload documents, screen savers, or other goodies that editors want to distribute to their end users. An administrator of a site would be able to use an FTP program to upload files, but an editor typically does not have the expertise, or the credentials, needed to access the remote server and its file system. An online file manager might be very helpful in this situation. In the first edition of this book, an entire chapter was devoted to showing you how to build a full-featured online file manager that would enable users to browse and remove folders and files; upload new files; download, rename, copy and delete existing files; and even edit the content of text files. However, this would be overkill in most situations, as the administrator is the only one who needs to have full control over the files and folders and structure of the site, and the administrator will presumably use an FTP client for this purpose. Editors and contributors only need the capability to upload new files. To implement this functionality, we will develop a small user control that allows users to upload one file at a time, and when done, displays the full URL of the file saved on the server, so the user can easily link to it using the WYSIWYG editor. The control will be used in various pages: in the page used to add and edit an article and in the page used to manage categories (as each category can have an image representing it); later in the book, we'll use this in the pages that send newsletters and submit forum posts.

This user control, named `FileUploader.ascx`, will utilize the new ASP.NET 2.0 `FileUpload` control to select the file, submit it, and save it on the server. This control simply translates to an `<input type="file" />` control, with server-side methods to save the image. Under ASP.NET 1.x there was no such control; you had to add the `runat="server"` attribute to a plain HTML control declaration.

One important design decision we need to consider is how to avoid the possibility that different editors might upload files with the same name, overwriting previous files uploaded by someone else. A simple, but effective, solution is to save the file under `~/Uploads/{UserName}`, where the `{UserName}` placeholder is replaced by the actual user's name. This works because only registered and authenticated users will have access to pages where they can upload files. We do want to let users overwrite a file that they uploaded themselves, as they might want to change the file.

> Remember that you will need to add NTFS write permission to the remote Uploads folder at deployment time, for the ASP.NET (Windows 2000 and XP) or Network Service user account (Windows Server 2003). It's easy to overlook this kind of thing, and you don't want to leave a bad impression with users when you set up a new site for them.

Article List User Control

You will need a way to quickly add the list of articles (with title, author, abstract, and a few more details) to any page. It's not enough to have entirely new articles; you also need to show them on existing pages so users will know about them! You'll need to show the list on the `BrowseArticles.aspx` page for end users and on the `ManageArticles.aspx` page for administrators. You may also want to show the article list on the home page. If you've got a good understanding of user controls, you may have already guessed that a user control is the best solution for this list because it enables us to encapsulate this functionality into a single code unit (the .ascx file plus the cs code-behind file), which enables us to write the code once and then place that user control on any page using one line of code.

This user control will be named `ArticleListing.ascx`. It produces different output according to whether the user is a regular user, an administrator, or an editor. If they belong to one of the special roles, each article item will have buttons to delete, edit, or approve them. This way, we can have a single control that will behave differently according to its context. Besides this, when the control is placed into an administration page, it must show all articles, including those that are not yet published (approved), or those that have already been retired (based on the date). When the control is on an end-user page, it must show only the active and published articles. The control will expose the following public properties (all Boolean), so that its content and its behavior can be changed in different pages:

Property	Description
EnableHighlighter	Indicates whether articles referring to events in the user's country, state/ province, or city are highlighted with different colors.
PublishedOnly	Indicates whether the control lists only articles that are approved, and whose `ReleaseDate`–`ExpireDate` interval includes the current date.
RatingLockInterval	The number of days that must pass before a user can again rate the same article.
ShowCategoryPicker	Indicates whether the control shows a drop-down list filled with all article categories, which lets the user filter articles by category. If the property is false the drop-down list will be hidden, and the control will filter the articles by category according to the CategoryID parameter passed on the querystring.
ShowPageSizePicker	Indicates whether the control shows a drop-down list representing the number of articles to be listed per page. If the property is true, the user will be able to change the page size to a value that best meets his desires and his connection speed (users with a slow connection may prefer to have fewer items per page so that it loads faster).
EnablePaging	Indicates whether the control will paginate the collection of articles resulting from the current filters (category and published status). When false, the control will have no paging bar and will only show the first n articles, where n is the page size. This allows us to use the control on the home page, for example, to list the n most recent additions. When true, it will show only the first n articles but will also show an indication of which page is displayed, and the user can switch between pages of articles.

Producing and Consuming RSS Feeds

You've already learned from the introduction that we're going to implement a mechanism to provide the headlines of the site's new content as an RSS feed, so that external (online or desktop-based) aggregator programs can easily consume them, adding new content to their own site, but also driving new traffic to our site. This process of providing a list of articles via RSS is called *syndication*. The XML format used to contain RSS content is simple in nature (it's not an accident that the RSS acronym stands for "Really Simple Syndication"), and here's an example of one RSS feed that contains an entry for two different articles:

```
<rss version="2.0">
 <channel>
  <title>My RSS feed</title>
  <link>http://www.contoso.com</link>
  <description>A sample site with a sample RSS</description>
  <copyright>Copyright 2005 by myself</copyright>

  <item>
   <title>First article</title>
   <author>Marco</author>
   <description>Some abstract text here...</description>
   <link>http://www.contoso.com/article1.aspx</link>
   <pubDate>Sat, 03 Sep 2005 12:00:34 GMT</pubDate>
  </item>
  <item>
   <title>Second article</title>
   <author>Mary</author>
   <description>Some other abstract text here...</description>
   <link>http://www.contoso.com/article2.aspx</link>
   <pubDate>Mon, 05 Sep 2005 10:30:22 GMT</pubDate>
  </item>
 </channel>
</rss>
```

As you can see, the root node indicates the version of RSS used in this file, and just below that is a `<channel>` section, which represents the feed. It contains several required subelements, `<title>`, `<link>`, and `<description>`, whose names are self-descriptive. There can also be a number of optional subelements, including `<copyright>`, `<webMaster>`, `<pubDate>`, `<image>`, and others. After all those feed-level elements is the list of actual posts/articles/stories, represented by `<item>` subsections. An item can have a number of optional elements, a few of which (`title`, `author`, `description`, `link`, `pubDate`) are shown in the preceding example. For details on the full list of elements supported by RSS, you can check the link `http://blogs.law.harvard.edu/tech/rss` or just search for "RSS 2.0 Specification."

One important thing to remember is that this must be a valid XML format, and therefore you cannot insert HTML into the `<description>` element to provide a visual "look and feel," unless you ensure that it meets XML standards (XHTML is the name for tighter HTML that meets XML requirement). You must ensure that the HTML is well formed, so that all tags have their closing part (`<p>` has its `</p>`) or are self-closing (as in `<img.../>`), among other rules. If you don't want the hassle of making sure that the HTML is XML compliant, you can just wrap the text into a CDATA section, which can include any kind of data. Another small detail to observe is that the value for the pubDate elements must be in the exact format "ddd, dd MMM yyyy HH:mm:ss GMT," as in "Thu, 03 Jan 2002 10:20:30 GMT." If you aren't careful to meet these RSS requirements, your users may get errors when they try to view your RSS feed. Some feed readers are more tolerant than others, so it's not sufficient to make sure that it works in your own feed reader — you need to meet the RSS specifications.

A custom HttpHandler returns the RSS feed much more efficiently than a Web Form can. An HttpHandler is the foundational unit that any request processed by the ASP.NET engine uses to return any content. The `Page` class implements `iHttpHandler`, which requires a class implement two members, `IsReusable` and `ProcessRequest`.

Once you have an RSS feed for your site, you can also consume the feed on this site itself, on the home page, to provide a list of articles! The `ArticleListing.ascx` user control we already discussed is good for a page whose only purpose is to list articles, but it's too heavy for the home page. On the home page you don't need details such as the location, the rating, and other information. The new article's title and the abstract is enough — when users click on the title, they will be redirected to the page with the whole article, according to the link entry for that article in the RSS feed. We'll build our own RSS reader user control to consume our own RSS feed. The control will be generic, so that it will be able to consume RSS feeds from other sources as well, such as the site forum's RSS, the products RSS, or some other external RSS feeds. Its public properties are listed in the following table:

Property	Description
RssUrl	Full URL of the RSS feed.
Title	Title to be displayed.
MoreUrl	URL of a page with the full listing of items (versus the last n items returned by the RSS items). In the case of the articles module, this will be the URL for the `BrowseArticles.aspx` page.
MoreText	Text used for the link pointing to `MoreUrl`.

The only question left is how you can take the XML of the RSS feed and transform it into HTML to be shown on the page. Here are two possible solutions:

❑ Use an XSL stylesheet to apply to the XML content, and use an XSLT transform to write the templates that define how to extract the content from the XML and represent it with HTML.

❑ Dynamically build a `DataTable` with columns for the title, author, description, and the other `<item>`'s elements. Then fill the `DataTable` with the data read from the RSS feed, and use it as the data source for a `Repeater`, `DataList`, or other template-based control.

Personally, I strongly prefer the latter option, mostly because I find it much faster to change the template of a `Repeater` rather than to change the template in an XSL file. Additionally, with a `DataTable` I can easily add calculated columns, apply filters and sorting, and merge feeds coming from different sources (consider the case where you have multiple blogs or sources of articles and want to show their RSS feeds in a single box, with all items merged together and sorted by date). The `DataTable` approach is more flexible and easier to work with.

The Need for Security

The articles manager module is basically divided into two parts:

❑ The administration section, which allows the webmaster, or another designated individual, to add, delete, or edit the categories, publish articles, and moderate comments.

❑ The end-user section, which has pages to navigate through the categories, read the articles, rate an article or post feedback, and display the headlines on the home page.

Obviously, different pages may have different security constraints: an administration page should not be accessible by end users, and an article with the `OnlyForMembers` flag set should not be accessible by the anonymous users (users who aren't logged in). In the previous chapter, we developed a very flexible module that allows us to administer the registered users, read or edit their profile, and dynamically assign them to certain roles. For the articles manager module, we will need the following roles:

❑ **Administrators and Editors:** These users have full control over the articles system. They can add, edit, or delete categories; approve and publish articles; and moderate comments. Only a very few people should belong to this role. (Note that Administrators also have full rights over the user management system and all the other modules of the site, so it might be wise if only a single individual has this role.)

❑ **Contributors:** These users can submit their own articles, but they won't be published until an administrator or editor approves them. You could give this permission to many users if you wanted to gather as much content as possible, or just to a selected group of people.

Enforcing these security rules is a simple task, as you've learned in the previous chapter. In many cases, it suffices to protect an entire page against unauthorized users by writing some settings in that page's folder's `web.config` file. Settings done in a configuration file are called *declarative coding,* and settings made with source code are called *imperative coding.* I favor declarative coding because it's easier to modify without recompiling source code, but in some more complex cases you have to perform some security checks directly from code. An example is the `AddEditArticle.aspx` page, which is used to post a new article or edit an existing one. The first action (post) is available to Contributors and upper roles, while the second (edit) is available only to Editors and Administrators. When the page loads you must understand in which mode the page is being loaded, according to some querystring settings, and check the user's roles accordingly.

Solution

In coding the solution, we'll follow the same path we used in the "Design" section: from database tables and stored procedure creation, to the implementation of security, passing through the DAL, BLL, and lastly the user interface.

The Database Solution

Creating the database tables is straightforward with Visual Studio's integrated Server Explorer and database manager, so we won't cover it here. You can refer to the tables in the "Design" section to see all the settings for each field. In the downloadable code file for this book, you will find the complete DB ready to go. Instead, here you'll create relationships between the tables and write some stored procedures.

You create a new diagram from the Server Explorer: drill down from Data Connections to your database (if you don't see your database, you can add it as a new Data Connection), and then Database Diagrams. Right-click on Database Diagrams and select Add New Diagram. By following the wizard, you can add the `tbh_Categories`, `tbh_Articles`, and `tbh_Comments` tables to your diagram. As soon as the three tables are added to the underlying window, Server Explorer should recognize a relationship between `tbh_Categories` and `tbh_Articles`, and between `tbh_Articles` and `tbh_Comments`, and automatically create a parent-child relationship between them over the correct fields, as shown in Figure 5-5. However, if it does not, click on the `tbh_Articles'` `CategoryID` field and drag and drop the icons that appear over the `tbh_Categories` table. Once you release the button, a dialog with the relationship's properties appears, and you can ensure that the foreign key is the `tbh_Articles'` `CategoryID` field, while the primary key is `tbh_Categories'` `CategoryID`.

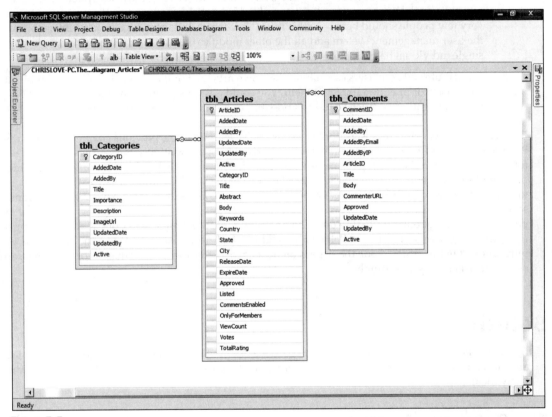

Figure 5-5

Now you have to create a relationship between `tbh_Comments` and `tbh_Articles`, based on the `ArticleID` field of both tables. As before, click the `tbh_Comments'` `ArticleID` field, drag and drop the icon over the `tbh_Articles` table, and complete the Properties dialog as before. When you're done with the diagram, go up to the tab, right-click on it, and save the diagram. Make sure that you let it change your tables as specified in the diagram.

Implementing the Configuration Module

The `ArticlesElement` class is implemented in the `~/App_Code/ConfigSection.cs` file. It descends from `System.Configuration.ConfigurationElement` and implements the properties that map the attributes of the `<articles>` element under the `<theBeerHouse>` custom section in the `web.config` file. The properties, listed and described in the "Design" section, are bound to the XML settings by means of the ConfigurationProperty attribute. Here's its code:

```vb
Public Class ArticlesElement
    Inherits ConfigurationElement

    <ConfigurationProperty("connectionStringName")> _
    Public Property ConnectionStringName() As String
        Get
            Return CStr(Me("connectionStringName"))
        End Get
        Set(ByVal value As String)
            Me("ConnectionStringName") = value
        End Set
    End Property

    Public ReadOnly Property ConnectionString() As String
        Get
            Dim connStringName As String
            If String.IsNullOrEmpty(Me.ConnectionStringName) Then
                connStringName = Globals.Settings.DefaultConnectionStringName
            Else
                connStringName = Me.ConnectionStringName
            End If
            Return WebConfigurationManager.ConnectionStrings(connStringName)
.ConnectionString
        End Get
    End Property

    <ConfigurationProperty("providerType", _
DefaultValue:="MB.TheBeerHouse.DAL.SqlClient.SqlArticlesProvider")> _
    Public Property ProviderType() As String
        Get
            Return CStr(Me("providerType"))
        End Get
        Set(ByVal value As String)
            Me("providerType") = value
        End Set
    End Property

    <ConfigurationProperty("ratingLockInterval", DefaultValue:="15")> _
    Public Property RatingLockInterval() As Integer
        Get
            Return CInt(Me("ratingLockInterval"))
        End Get
        Set(ByVal value As Integer)
            Me("ratingLockInterval") = value
        End Set
    End Property

    <ConfigurationProperty("pageSize", DefaultValue:="10")> _
    Public Property PageSize() As Integer
        Get
```

```vb
        Return CInt(Me("pageSize"))
    End Get
    Set(ByVal value As Integer)
        Me("pageSize") = value
    End Set
End Property

<ConfigurationProperty("rssItems", DefaultValue:="5")> _
Public Property RssItems() As Integer
    Get
        Return CInt(Me("rssItems"))
    End Get
    Set(ByVal value As Integer)
        Me("rssItems") = value
    End Set
End Property

<ConfigurationProperty("enableCaching", DefaultValue:="true")> _
Public Property EnableCaching() As Boolean
    Get
        Return CBool(Me("enableCaching"))
    End Get
    Set(ByVal value As Boolean)
        Me("enableCaching") = value
    End Set
End Property

<ConfigurationProperty("cacheDuration")> _
Public Property CacheDuration() As Integer
    Get
        Dim duration As Integer = CInt(Me("cacheDuration"))
        If duration > 0 Then
            Return duration
        Else
            Return Globals.Settings.DefaultCacheDuration
        End If
    End Get
    Set(ByVal value As Integer)
        Me("cacheDuration") = value
    End Set
End Property

<ConfigurationProperty("urlIndicator")> _
Public Property URLIndicator() As String
    Get
        Dim lurlIndicator As String = Me("urlIndicator").ToString
        If String.IsNullOrEmpty(lurlIndicator) Then
            lurlIndicator = "Article"
        End If
        Return lurlIndicator
    End Get
    Set(ByVal Value As String)
        Me("urlIndicator") = Value
    End Set
```

```
End Property

<ConfigurationProperty("akismetKey")> _
Public Property AkismetKey() As String
    Get
        Dim lakismetKey As String = Me("akismetKey").ToString
        If String.IsNullOrEmpty(lakismetKey) Then
            lakismetKey = ""
        End If
        Return lakismetKey
    End Get
    Set(ByVal Value As String)
        Me("akismetKey") = Value
    End Set
End Property

<ConfigurationProperty("enableAkismet", DefaultValue:="false")> _
Public Property EnableAkismet() As Boolean
    Get
        Return CBool(Me("enableAkismet"))
    End Get
    Set(ByVal value As Boolean)
        Me("enableAkismet") = value
    End Set
End Property

<ConfigurationProperty("reportAkismet", DefaultValue:="false")> _
Public Property ReportAkismet() As Boolean
    Get
        Return CBool(Me("reportAkismet"))
    End Get
    Set(ByVal value As Boolean)
        Me("reportAkismet") = value
    End Set
End Property

<ConfigurationProperty("enableTwitter", DefaultValue:="false")> _
Public Property EnableTwitter() As Boolean
    Get
        Return CBool(Me("enableTwitter"))
    End Get
    Set(ByVal value As Boolean)
        Me("enableTwitter") = value
    End Set
End Property

<ConfigurationProperty("twitterUrserName")> _
Public Property TwitterUrserName() As String
    Get
        Dim lurlIndicator As String = Me("twitterUrserName").ToString
        If String.IsNullOrEmpty(lurlIndicator) Then
            lurlIndicator = "TwitterUserName"
        End If
        Return lurlIndicator
```

```
            End Get
            Set(ByVal Value As String)
                Me("twitterUrserName") = Value
            End Set
        End Property

        <ConfigurationProperty("twitterPassword")> _
        Public Property TwitterPassword() As String
            Get
                Dim lurlIndicator As String = Me("twitterPassword").ToString
                If String.IsNullOrEmpty(lurlIndicator) Then
                    lurlIndicator = "TwitterPassword"
                End If
                Return lurlIndicator
            End Get
            Set(ByVal Value As String)
                Me("twitterPassword") = Value
            End Set
        End Property

    End Class
```

The ConnectionString property does not directly read/write a setting from/to the configuration file, but rather returns the value of the entry in the web.config's <connectionStrings> section identified by the name indicated in the <articles>'s connectionStringName attribute, or the <theBeerHouse>'s defaultConnectionStringName if the first setting is not present. The CacheDuration property returns the <articles>'s cacheDuration setting if it is greater than zero, or the <theBeerHouse>'s defaultCacheDuration setting otherwise.

DefaultConnectionStringName and DefaultCacheDuration are two new properties of the TheBeerHouseSection created in Chapter 3, now modified as shown here:

```
    Public Class TheBeerHouseSection
        Inherits ConfigurationSection

        Private Shared ReadOnly instance As TheBeerHouseSection =
    New TheBeerHouseSection

        <ConfigurationProperty("defaultConnectionStringName",
    DefaultValue:="LocalSqlServer")> _
        Public Property DefaultConnectionStringName() As String
            Get
                Return CStr(Me("defaultConnectionStringName"))
            End Get
            Set(ByVal value As String)
                Me("DefaultConnectionStringName") = value
            End Set
        End Property

        <ConfigurationProperty("siteDomainName", DefaultValue:="localhost")> _
        Public Property SiteDomainName() As String
            Get
```

```
                Return CStr(Me("siteDomainName"))
            End Get
            Set(ByVal value As String)
                Me("siteDomainName") = value
            End Set
        End Property


        <ConfigurationProperty("defaultCacheDuration", DefaultValue:="600")> _
        Public Property DefaultCacheDuration() As Integer
            Get
                Return CInt(Me("defaultCacheDuration"))
            End Get
            Set(ByVal value As Integer)
                Me("defaultCacheDuration") = value
            End Set
        End Property


        <ConfigurationProperty("contactForm", IsRequired:=True)> _
        Public ReadOnly Property ContactForm() As ContactFormElement
            Get
                Return CType(Me("contactForm"), ContactFormElement)
            End Get
        End Property


        <ConfigurationProperty("articles", IsRequired:=True)> _
        Public ReadOnly Property Articles() As ArticlesElement
            Get
                Return CType(Me("articles"), ArticlesElement)
            End Get
        End Property
    End Class
```

The updated <theBeerHouse> section in web.config looks like this:

```
<theBeerHouse defaultConnectionStringName="TheBeerHouseEntities"
siteDomainName="http://TheBeerHouseBook.com">
<contactForm mailTo="thebeerhouse@wrox.com" />
<articles pageSize="10" twitterUrserName="TheBeerHouse" twitterPassword="132456"
enableTwitter="true" akismetKey="11aaaaa11111" enableAkismet="true"/>
</theBeerHouse>
```

To read the settings from code you can do it this way: Helpers.Settings.Articles.RssItems.

Implementing the Business Logic Layer

As we did for the data access classes, the business classes are created in the TBHBLL class library, which needs to be compiled before any changes can be used. The basic architecture of the business layer used in this edition is explained in Chapter 3. For the Articles module this includes a series of repository classes and extensions of the ObjectContext and Entity classes generated by the Entity Framework Wizard.

The Repositories

The `Articles` module has three main repository classes, one for `Categories`, `Articles`, and `Comments`. But because each of these repositories share the same entity data model and thus a common `DataContext` class and base `CacheKey`, the `BaseArticleRepository` manages these members. It also manages the `Dispose` method.

The BaseArticleRepository

The `BaseArticleRepository` inherits the `BaseRepository` that was discussed in Chapter 3. Its constructors are very similar to the `SiteMapRepository`; they set the connection string and set the core `CacheKey` value.

```
Public Sub New(ByVal sConnectionString As String)
ConnectionString = sConnectionString
CacheKey = "Articles"
End Sub

Public Sub New()
ConnectionString = Globals.Settings.DefaultConnectionStringName
CacheKey = "Articles"
End Sub
```

The balance of the `BaseArticleRepository` follows the same patterns discussed in Chapter 3, as will all the remaining repositories in the application.

The ArticleRepository

The `ArticleRepository` class, in the Articles folder of the class library (`ArticlesRepository.vb`) contains all the worker methods that interact with the articles entity model to manage articles. These include the common CRUD methods as well as some specialized methods to return records according to specific needs in the application. Each of these methods uses LINQ to entities as much as possible.

In the previous edition, the values related to paging had to be calculated by calling an article count stored procedure, the list of articles, and so forth. In this edition, I use the `ListView` and the `DataPager` control to manage paging the list of records for all the list views of data. The `UpdatePanel` also makes it easier to do "seamless" paging from the client by using AJAX queries to the server to perform databinding. All this combined with caching the records in memory means managing the image around paging is no longer a concern.

```
Public Function GetArticles() As List(Of Article) Implements
IArticleRepository.GetArticles
Dim key As String = String.Format(CacheKey)

If EnableCaching AndAlso Not IsNothing(Cache(key)) Then
Return CType(Cache(key), List(Of Article))
End If

Dim lArticles As List(Of Article) = (From lArticle In Articlesctx.Articles _
Order By lArticle.ReleaseDate Descending).ToList()

If EnableCaching Then
```

```
    CacheData(key, lArticles)
    End If

    Return lArticles

    End Function
```

The `GetArticles` method returns an unfiltered generic list of articles and caches the results in memory. This is a basic LINQ to Entities query that does order the articles by release date in descending order. the Entity Framework translates this LINQ query into the following SQL statement that is executed in the database:

```
SELECT
[Project1].[C1] AS [C1],
[Project1].[ArticleID] AS [ArticleID],
[Project1].[AddedDate] AS [AddedDate],
[Project1].[AddedBy] AS [AddedBy],
[Project1].[UpdatedDate] AS [UpdatedDate],
[Project1].[UpdatedBy] AS [UpdatedBy],
[Project1].[Active] AS [Active],
[Project1].[Title] AS [Title],
[Project1].[Abstract] AS [Abstract],
[Project1].[Body] AS [Body],
[Project1].[Country] AS [Country],
[Project1].[State] AS [State],
[Project1].[City] AS [City],
[Project1].[ReleaseDate] AS [ReleaseDate],
[Project1].[ExpireDate] AS [ExpireDate],
[Project1].[Approved] AS [Approved],
[Project1].[Listed] AS [Listed],
[Project1].[CommentsEnabled] AS [CommentsEnabled],
[Project1].[OnlyForMembers] AS [OnlyForMembers],
[Project1].[ViewCount] AS [ViewCount],
[Project1].[Votes] AS [Votes],
[Project1].[TotalRating] AS [TotalRating],
[Project1].[Keywords] AS [Keywords],
[Project1].[CategoryID] AS [CategoryID]
FROM ( SELECT
[Extent1].[ArticleID] AS [ArticleID],
[Extent1].[AddedDate] AS [AddedDate],
[Extent1].[AddedBy] AS [AddedBy],
[Extent1].[UpdatedDate] AS [UpdatedDate],
[Extent1].[UpdatedBy] AS [UpdatedBy],
[Extent1].[Active] AS [Active],
[Extent1].[CategoryID] AS [CategoryID],
[Extent1].[Title] AS [Title],
[Extent1].[Abstract] AS [Abstract],
[Extent1].[Body] AS [Body],
[Extent1].[Keywords] AS [Keywords],
[Extent1].[Country] AS [Country],
[Extent1].[State] AS [State],
[Extent1].[City] AS [City],
[Extent1].[ReleaseDate] AS [ReleaseDate],
[Extent1].[ExpireDate] AS [ExpireDate],
```

```
[Extent1].[Approved] AS [Approved],
[Extent1].[Listed] AS [Listed],
[Extent1].[CommentsEnabled] AS [CommentsEnabled],
[Extent1].[OnlyForMembers] AS [OnlyForMembers],
[Extent1].[ViewCount] AS [ViewCount],
[Extent1].[Votes] AS [Votes],
[Extent1].[TotalRating] AS [TotalRating],
1 AS [C1]
FROM [dbo].[tbh_Articles] AS [Extent1]
) AS [Project1]
ORDER BY [Project1].[ReleaseDate] DESC
```

I am not an expert on optimized Transact SQL, but I do find it interesting to see almost the same SQL query nested inside itself to perform the sorting, since the Entity Framework has been designed to optimize SQL queries. Also notice that, instead of a `Select * from` statement, each field is explicitly stated. This is a requirement when you write Entity SQL; all fields in the query must be explicitly stated. You can monitor any activity in a SQL Server by running SQL Profiler, one of the tools you can install with SQL Server. Using this tool can help you understand how queries are being composed by Entity Framework to see where you might need to adjust a query.

I actually included three overloads of the `GetArticles` method so that you could see how to make various LINQ to Entities queries. The second overload accepts a parameter to filter for published articles, while the third adds `pageIndex` and `pageSize` parameters that allow you to retrieve just the desired pages of articles.

Another slight variation on the `GetArticles` methods is the `GetHomePage` articles method. It returns the three most recently published articles to be displayed on the home page. It filters for articles that are approved, listed, and have a release date that is before the current time. It then sorts by a descending date and takes the first three articles.

```
Public Function GetHomePageArticles() As List(Of Article)

        Dim lArticles As List(Of Article)

        Dim key As String = CacheKey & "_HomePage"

        If EnableCaching AndAlso Not IsNothing(Cache(key)) Then
            Return CType(Cache(key), List(Of Article))
        End If

        lArticles = (From lArticle In Articlesctx.Articles
.Include("Category") _
            Where lArticle.Active = True And lArticle.Approved = True And _
            lArticle.Listed = True And lArticle.ReleaseDate < Now() And
lArticle.ExpireDate > Now() _
            Order By lArticle.AddedDate Descending).Take(3).ToList()

        If EnableCaching Then
            CacheData(key, lArticles, CacheDuration)
        End If

        Return lArticles

End Function
```

The `GetArticleCount` method is a simple statement that uses the LINQ `Count` method to return the number of articles in the database. The problem with this approach is we might need to filter for the number of articles meeting specified criteria. In those cases, the `Count` member of the generic `List` class can be used to get a count of records matching the filter being applied to the database.

```
Public Function GetArticleCount() As Integer
Return Articlesctx.Articles.Count()
End Function
```

The CategoryRepository

The `CategoryRepository` class, in the Articles folder of the class library (`CategoriesRepository.vb`), contains all the worker methods that interact with the articles entity model to manage categories. These include the common CRUD methods as well as some specialized methods to return records according to specific needs in the application. Each of these methods uses LINQ to entities as much as possible. The members of this class use common LINQ query patterns that are explained in more detail under the `ArticleRepository` description.

The CommentRepository

The one special aspect of the `CommentRepository` class is the Add and Delete members. Each of these members interact with Akismet, assuming that this feature is enabled in the site's `web.config`.

The comment is still going to be added to the database, but instead of setting the initial Active flag to true, it is set to false. This means a site administrator can evaluate the comment to determine if it is really spam.

```
Public Function AddComment(ByVal vComment As Comment) As Comment

        Try

            If Helpers.Settings.Articles.EnableAkismet Then

                Dim lAkismet As New Akismet(Helpers.Settings.Articles
    .AkismetKey, _
                    "http://TheBeerHouseBook.com", "TheBeerHouse |
    Akismet/1.11")

                If lAkismet.CommentCheck(vComment.GetAkismetComment) Then
                    vComment.Active = False
                End If

            End If

            If vComment.EntityState = EntityState.Detached Then
                Articlesctx.AddToComments(vComment)
            End If
            Return If(Articlesctx.SaveChanges > 0, vComment, Nothing)

        Catch ex As Exception
            ActiveExceptions.Add(vComment.CommentID, ex)
            Return Nothing
```

```
                End Try

    End Function
```

The `ApproveComment` method accepts either a `CommentId` or a `Comment` entity and sets the `Approved` flag.

```
    Public Function ApproveComment(ByVal lComment As Comment) As Boolean

                lComment.Approved = True
                lComment.UpdatedDate = Now()
                lComment.UpdatedBy = CurrentUserName

                Try
                    Articlesctx.SaveChanges()
                    Return True
                Catch ocEx As OptimisticConcurrencyException
                    ActiveExceptions.Add(lComment.CommentID, ocEx)
                    Return False
                Catch Ex As Exception
                    ActiveExceptions.Add(lComment.CommentID, Ex)
                    Return False
                End Try

    End Function
```

When a comment is deleted, it can be assumed that it is spam in most cases. The Akismet API offers the ability for you to submit spam comments to add to its system for further analysis. How this analysis is applied to the scoring algorithm I am not sure. In case you do not want to automatically report deleted comments as spam, the `ArticlesElement` has a `ReportAkismet` Boolean property to turn that feature off.

```
    Public Function DeleteComment(ByVal vComment As Comment) As Boolean

                If Helpers.Settings.Articles.EnableAkismet And
        Helpers.Settings.Articles.ReportAkismet Then

                    'Submit uncaught Comment Spam to Akismet to add to their database.
                    Dim lAkismet As New
        Joel.Net.Akismet(Helpers.Settings.Articles.AkismetKey, _
                        "http://beerhouse.extremewebworks.com", "TheBeerHouse |
        Akismet/1.11")
                    lAkismet.SubmitSpam(vComment.GetAkismetComment)

                End If

                Return ChangeDeletedState(vComment, False)

    End Function
```

In the previous edition, a compromise was made to programmatically sort the generic list of comments with a custom sorting method. LINQ makes this operation even easier by allowing us to apply LINQ syntax to sort the list of comments. The `CommentRepository` list retrieval methods have overloads to allow specification of which order in which the comments are listed in the returned generic list.

```
Public Function GetApprovedComments(ByVal ArticleId As Integer,
ByVal bMostRecentFirst As Boolean) As List(Of Comment)

        Dim key As String = CacheKey & "_Comments_Approved_ArticleId_" &
ArticleId & "_MostRecent_" & bMostRecentFirst

        If EnableCaching AndAlso Not IsNothing(Cache(key)) Then
            Return CType(Cache(key), List(Of Comment))
        End If

        Dim lComments As List(Of Comment) = DirectCast(Cache(key),
List(Of Comment))

        If IsNothing(lComments) Then

            Articlesctx.Comments.MergeOption = MergeOption.NoTracking

            If bMostRecentFirst Then
                lComments = (From lComment In Articlesctx.Comments _
                        Where lComment.Approved = True And
lComment.Article.ArticleID = ArticleId _
                        Order By lComment.AddedDate Ascending).ToList()
            Else
                lComments = (From lC In Articlesctx.Comments _
                        Where lC.Approved = True And lC.Article.ArticleID =
ArticleId _
                        Order By lC.AddedDate Descending).ToList()
            End If

        End If

        CacheData(key, lComments)
        Return lComments

End Function
```

The Article Class

The `Article` class is extended in the class library's `Articles/Article.vb` file. It is placed in the `TheBeerHouse.BLL.Articles` namespace. The `Article` class adds custom members, including immutable properties composed from values supplied by the entity framework. Since each entity class in the Entity Data Model is a partial class, they can be extended by creating another class with the same name in another file. They cannot be inherited by another class, they but can implement any interface needed. In the case of The Beer House, all entities implement the `IBaseEntity` interface. This means that the entity will implement an `IsValid` property and four methods to validate activity permission (`CanRead`, `CanEdit`, `CanDelete`, and `CanAdd`).

```
Public ReadOnly Property IsValid() As Boolean Implements IBaseEntity.IsValid
Get
If String.IsNullOrEmpty(Me.Title) = False And _
```

```
                    String.IsNullOrEmpty(Me.Abstract) = False And _
                    String.IsNullOrEmpty(Me.Body) = False And _
                    Me.ReleaseDate < Me.ExpireDate Then
                Return True
            End If
            Return False
        End Get
    End Property
```

The IsValid property determines if the entity has required values and they are in an acceptable state. For the Article entity, this means that it must have Title, Abstract, and Body values. The ReleaseData must also be less than the ExpireDate, or the article will never be published.

For the article module site, Administrators and Editors are allowed to add or edit article related entities. Each one of the entities in the articles model is extended to have authorization properties that can be used to verify action authorization.

```
Public ReadOnly Property CanAdd() As Boolean Implements BLL.IBaseEntity.CanAdd
            Get
                If Helpers.CurrentUser.IsInRole("Administrator") Or
Helpers.CurrentUser.IsInRole("Editor") Then
                    Return True
                End If
                Return False
            End Get
End Property


Public ReadOnly Property CanDelete() As Boolean Implements IBaseEntity.CanDelete
            Get
                If Helpers.CurrentUser.IsInRole("Administrator") Or
Helpers.CurrentUser.IsInRole("Editor") Then
                    Return True
                End If
                Return False
            End Get
End Property

Public ReadOnly Property CanEdit() As Boolean Implements IBaseEntity.CanEdit
Get
                If Helpers.CurrentUser.IsInRole("Administrator") Or
Helpers.CurrentUser.IsInRole("Editor") Then
                    Return True
                End If
Return False
End Get
End Property


Public ReadOnly Property CanRead() As Boolean Implements IBaseEntity.CanRead
Get
Return True
End Get
End Property
```

The `Helpers.CurrentUser` property returns an `IPrincipal` that represents the current user. It can be used to determine if the user belongs to a role or not.

```
Public Shared ReadOnly Property CurrentUser() As IPrincipal
        Get
                Return HttpContext.Current.User
        End Get
End Property
```

Each property of an entity has two events associated with it for changing values: `[FieldName]Changing` and `[FieldName]Changed`. The `ArticleID` property cannot be less than 0, so in the `ArticleIDChanging` event, a check to ensure the value is greater than 0 is done. If the value is negative, an `ArgumentException` is thrown.

```
Private Sub OnArticleIDChanging(ByVal value As Integer)
If value < 0 Then
        Throw New ArgumentException("The ArticleId cannot be less than 0.")
    End If

If value <> ArticleID Then
        IsDirty = True
    End If

End Sub
```

This idea can be carried over to any field in any entity in an Entity Data Model to verify that the value being set passes the requirements to be properly set.

While this is how validation is to be done based on the pattern generated by the Entity Data Model Wizard, I find it less than ideal because it requires throwing an exception when values do not meet the validation requirements. I think the `IsValid` method should be used to ultimately perform validation because it can be used before the entity is committed to the data store. Throwing exceptions is never an optimal way to perform data validation as values are being set. The `IsValid` property gives you the opportunity to stop the commitment and report the issues.

One of the drawbacks of the Entity Framework is access to foreign key values. The Entity Data Model for a database does not expose foreign key values. For the `Article` entity, this would be `CategoryId` since each article belongs to a category that is defined in the `tbh_Categories` table. Accessing this value requires a bit of work by referencing the `EntityKey` value. The `Article` entity has a `CategoryReference` property which can be used to access the foreign key value. It is of type `System.Data.Objects.DataClasses .EntityReference(Of Category)`, which contains an `EntityKey` property. This property, in turn, contains a collection of `EntityKeyValues`, one for each member of the foreign key, which is typically one value. Since this value may not exist, you must check to see if the `CategoryReference` has been created before accessing it. In the case of the `CategoryId`, if there is no reference, then the property returns a 0.

```
Public Property CategoryId() As Integer
        Get
                If Not IsNothing(Me.CategoryReference.EntityKey) Then
                    Return Me.CategoryReference.EntityKey.EntityKeyValues(0).Value
                End If
```

287

```
                    Return 0
            End Get
            Set(ByVal Value As Integer)
                    If Not IsNothing(Me.CategoryReference.EntityKey) Then
                        Me.CategoryReference = Nothing
                    End If
                    Me.CategoryReference.EntityKey = New
    EntityKey("ArticlesEntities.Categories", "CategoryID", Value)

        End Set

        End Property
```

The `EntityKey` value can be set, but if there is an existing value, it must be destroyed and a new one created. In the case of the `CategoryId`, a new `EntityKey` is created by passing the entity object, the field name, and the value for the key.

If you are creating a new entity, the primary key value of the entity itself cannot be set; let the database create it for you. If you do set the value, an exception is thrown by the framework.

Carried over from the previous edition of the Beer House, immutable properties make up the `Article` entity. These are properties that are composed or calculated from values stored in the database for the article. Immutable properties for an article include the `ArticleReleaseDate`, `AverageRating`, `CategoryTitle`, `Location`, and `Published`.

The `ArticleReleaseDate` actually wraps around the `ReleaseDate` value because it can be null. The property is a string composed by calling the `ToShortDateString` property of the `DateTime` class. The `ReleaseDate` property is created as a nullable value, since the field can be null in the database. This can cause issues when dealing with the value in the user interface. This is solved by calling the `GetValueOrDefault` method and setting its value to a local variable.

```
        Public ReadOnly Property ArticleReleaseDate() As String
            Get

                If Not IsNothing(ReleaseDate.GetValueOrDefault) Then
                    Dim lRelaseDate As DateTime = ReleaseDate.GetValueOrDefault
                    Return lRelaseDate.ToShortDateString
                End If

                Return String.Empty

            End Get
        End Property

        Public ReadOnly Property AverageRating() As Double
            Get
                If Me.Votes >= 1 Then
                    Return CDbl(Me.TotalRating) / CDbl(Me.Votes)
                Else
                    Return 0.0
                End If
            End Get
```

```
        End Property

        Public ReadOnly Property CategoryTitle() As String
            Get
                If Not IsNothing(Me.Category) Then
                    Return Me.Category.Title
                End If
                Return String.Empty
            End Get
        End Property

        Public ReadOnly Property Location() As String
            Get
                Dim _location As String = String.Empty

                If Not IsNothing(Me.City) Then
                    _location = Me.City.Split(";")(0)
                End If

                If String.IsNullOrEmpty(Me.State) = False Then
                    If _location.Length > 0 Then
                        _location += ", "
                    End If
                    _location += Me.State.Split(";")(0)
                End If

                If String.IsNullOrEmpty(Me.Country) = False Then
                    If _location.Length > 0 Then
                        _location += ", "
                    End If
                    _location += Me.Country
                End If

                Return _location
            End Get
        End Property

        Public ReadOnly Property Published() As Boolean
            Get
                Return (Me.Approved And Me.ReleaseDate <= DateTime.Now And
    Me.ExpireDate > DateTime.Now)
            End Get
    End Property
```

The Category Class

The Category class has instance properties that fully describe a category of articles, instance methods to delete and update an existing category, and static methods to create, update, or delete one category. I won't describe all of them here as they are similar to the corresponding methods of the Article class. They're actually a little simpler because you don't need multiple overloads to support pagination and other filters. There are two properties, Articles and PublishedArticles, that use a couple of overloads of the Article.GetArticles static methods to return a list of Article objects. Like the Article .Comments property, these two properties also use the lazy load pattern, so articles are retrieved only once, when the property is read for the first time.

The IsValid property checks to make sure that the Category contains a Title and a positive Importance value.

```
Public ReadOnly Property IsValid() As Boolean Implements IBaseEntity.IsValid
        Get
                If String.IsNullOrEmpty(Title) And Importance > -1 Then
                    Return False
                End If
                Return True
        End Get
End Property
```

The authorization members are the same as the Article class:

```
#Region " Authorization "

        Public ReadOnly Property CanAdd() As Boolean Implements
BLL.IBaseEntity.CanAdd
            Get
                If Helpers.CurrentUser.IsInRole("Administrator") Or
Helpers.CurrentUser.IsInRole("Editor") Then
                    Return True
                End If
                Return False
            End Get
        End Property


        Public ReadOnly Property CanDelete() As Boolean Implements
IBaseEntity.CanDelete
            Get
                If Helpers.CurrentUser.IsInRole("Administrator") Or
Helpers.CurrentUser.IsInRole("Editor") Then
                    Return True
                End If
                Return False
            End Get
        End Property

        Public ReadOnly Property CanEdit() As Boolean Implements
IBaseEntity.CanEdit
            Get
                If Helpers.CurrentUser.IsInRole("Administrator") Or
Helpers.CurrentUser.IsInRole("Editor") Then
                    Return True
                End If
                Return False
            End Get
        End Property


        Public ReadOnly Property CanRead() As Boolean
```

```
Implements IBaseEntity.CanRead
        Get
                Return True
        End Get
    End Property

#End Region
```

The Comment Class

The Comment class is extended in several ways: to validate the data, give structured access to related data and to manage interactions with Akismet and Gravatar. The first is a property to allow managed access to the ArticleId foreign key value:

```
Public Property ArticleId() As Integer
Get
                If Not IsNothing(Me.ArticleReference.EntityKey) Then
                    Return Me.ArticleReference.EntityKey.EntityKeyValues(0).Value
                End If
                Return 0
End Get
Set(ByVal Value As Integer)
                If Not IsNothing(Me.ArticleReference.EntityKey) Then
                    Me.ArticleReference = Nothing
                End If
                Me.ArticleReference.EntityKey = New
EntityKey("ArticlesEntities.Articles", "ArticleID", Value)
End Set
End Property
```

Next is a ReadOnly property called DisplayTitle; it wraps access to the Article's Title. This property makes it easy to return the title if the related article has also been retrieved with the comment itself. But this is not always going to be the case, and to handle this a ternary If statement is used and "Not Supplied" is returned if the related Article does not exist.

```
Public ReadOnly Property DisplayTitle() As String
Get
Return If(String.IsNullOrEmpty(Me.Title), _
                    If(Not IsNothing(Me.Article), Me.Article.Title, _
"Not Supplied"), Me.Title)
End Get
End Property
```

The EncodedBody property returns an HTMLEncoded version of the comment body to guard against cross-site scripting attacks:

```
Public ReadOnly Property EncodedBody() As String
Get
Return HttpUtility.HtmlEncode(Me.Body)
End Get
End Property
```

The `IsValid` property checks to make sure that the comment has a `Body`; if there is nothing in the body of the comment, there is no comment after all. But as I discussed earlier, documenting who made the comment is important for a comment on a website, so their e-mail and IP addresses must be submitted.

```
Public ReadOnly Property IsValid() As Boolean Implements IBaseEntity.IsValid
Get
If String.IsNullOrEmpty(Me.Body) = False And _
                String.IsNullOrEmpty(Me.AddedByEmail) = False And _
                String.IsNullOrEmpty(Me.AddedByIP) = False Then
                Return True
        End If
        Return False
End Get
End Property
```

All comments must be scanned for spam because too many unscrupulous webmasters look to place unrelated comments on blogs trying to gain search engine placement and the occasional visitor. Akismet is a free scoring service available to anyone with a WordPress.com account. I will talk about that in more detail later in the chapter. But Akismet has a URL-based API that can be used to check a comment. For the Beer House, I decided to use a popular .NET library, Akismet.Net, available on CodePlex.com (`www.codeplex.com/AkismetApi`).

The Akismet.Net library requires that an `AkismetComment` class be created, which it then passes to Akismet for checking. The `Comment` entity has been extended to include the `GetAkismetComment` method, which builds an `AkismetComment` class:

```
Public Function GetAkismetComment() As AkismetComment

Dim lComment As New AkismetComment
lComment.Blog = "http://TheBeerHouseBook.com"
lComment.CommentAuthor = Me.AddedBy
lComment.CommentAuthorEmail = Me.AddedByEmail
lComment.CommentContent = Me.Body
lComment.CommentType = "comment"
lComment.UserIp = Me.AddedByIP
lComment.CommentAuthorUrl = Me.CommenterURL

Return lComment

End Function
```

The last custom property, `EMailHash`, returns a hash of the commentor's e-mail address. This is used to retrieve the user's Gravatar.

```
Public ReadOnly Property EMailHash() As String
Get
Return GravatarHelper.GetGravatarHash(Me.AddedByEmail)
End Get
End Property
```

Implementing Gravatars

Gravatar.com is a service that makes it easy for a person to store a standard Avatar in a central location. But it is also a very easy service to integrate into the Beer House site as an automatic service for visitors when they leave comments on the site or other content that may utilize an Avatar, such as the forums. The service works by calling a URL with a Hexidecimal MD5 hash of the commentor's e-mail address. The URL is in the form of `http://www.gravatar.com/avatar/[EMail Hash].jpg?s=XY`. The querystring is optional but is useful because it allows you to specify the image width. Additionally, you can pass a "d:" parameter to specify a default avatar to be used when one is not available for the user. More information can be found on the Gravatar implementation page, `http://en.gravatar.com/site/implement/url`.

Implementing the User Interface

The database design and the data access classes for the `Articles` module are now complete, so it's time to code the user interface. We will use the business classes to retrieve and manage `Article` data from the DB. We'll start by developing the administration console, so that we can use it later to add and manage sample records when we code and test the UI for end users.

The ManageCategories.aspx Page

The `ManageCategories.aspx` page, located under the `~/Admin` folder, allows the administrator and editors to add, delete, and edit article categories, as well as directly jump to the list of articles for a specific category. The screenshot of the page, shown in Figure 5-6, demonstrates what I'm talking about, and then you'll learn how to build it.

Figure 5-6

Each of the list administrative pages in the Beer House will typically consist of a `ListView` with a `DataPager` wrapped in an `UpdatePanel`. The `ListView` is a much leaner tabular data control that works in tandem with the `DataPage` control to allow easy navigation through a set of entities. Wrapping the `ListView` inside an `UpdatePanel` quickly adds AJAX capabilities without changing any of the code from normal ASP.NET Web Form authoring.

These same administrative pages will also follow a common layout with a title displayed at the top and some relevant navigational links to other activities in that module. Typically, these links will take you to other lists in the module, such as `Articles` or `Comments`, or give you the ability to add a new record to the site.

The `ListView` used to manage the article categories displays the category's Title, an Edit icon (a pencil), and a Delete icon (a trash can). Clicking the Edit link takes you to the `AddEditCategory.aspx` page, where the category can be changed.

The `ListView` is a templated data control that works in a slightly different way than the `ListView`, `DataList`, and `Repeater`. It is more of a hybrid of the `DataList` and `Repeater`, with the option of paging and sorting built into it. The overall layout of the `ListView` is defined in the `LayoutTemplate`. The layout of the individual records is defined the `ItemTemplate` and the `AlternatingItemTemplate`. There is also an `EmptyDataTemplate` to display a message to the user if there are no items available to display. There are other templates available to handle in-place editing, and so forth, but they will not be used in the Beer House.

```
<asp:UpdatePanel runat="server" ID="uppnlCategories">
    <ContentTemplate>
        <asp:ListView ID="lvCategories" runat="server" DataKeyNames=
"CategoryId">
            <LayoutTemplate>
                <table cellspacing="0" cellpadding="0"
class="AdminList">
    <thead>
                    <tr class="AdminListHeader">
                        <td>
                            Title
                        </td>
                        <td>
                            Edit
                        </td>
                        <td>
                            Delete
                        </td>
                    </tr>
    </thead>
    <tbody>
                    <tr id="itemPlaceholder" runat="server">
                    </tr>
    </tbody>
                <tfoot>
                    <tr>
                        <td colspan="3">
                            <div class="pager">
                                <asp:DataPager ID="pagerBottom"
runat="server" PageSize="15" PagedControlID="lvCategories">
                                    <Fields>
```

```
                                      <asp:NextPreviousPagerField
  ButtonCssClass="command" FirstPageText="«" PreviousPageText="<"
        RenderDisabledButtonsAsLabels="true" ShowFirstPageButton="true"
ShowPreviousPageButton="true"
                                        ShowLastPageButton="false"
ShowNextPageButton="false" />
                                      <asp:NumericPagerField
ButtonCount="7" NumericButtonCssClass="command"
CurrentPageLabelCssClass="current"
                                NextPreviousButtonCssClass="command" />
                                      <asp:NextPreviousPagerField
ButtonCssClass="command" LastPageText="»" NextPageText=">"
                                RenderDisabledButtonsAsLabels="true"
ShowFirstPageButton="false"
ShowPreviousPageButton="false"
                                        ShowLastPageButton="true"
ShowNextPageButton="true" />
                                  </Fields>
                              </asp:DataPager>
                          </div>
                      </td>
                  </tr>
              </tfoot>
            </table>
          </LayoutTemplate>
          <EmptyDataTemplate>
              <tr>
                  <td colspan="3">
                          Sorry there are no Categories
available at this time.
                  </td>
              </tr>
          </EmptyDataTemplate>
          <ItemTemplate>
              <tr>
                  <td class="ListTitle">
                      <a href='<%#
String.Format("AddEditCategory.aspx?categoryid={0}",
Eval("CategoryId")) %>'>
                          <%# Eval("Title") %></a>
                  </td>
                  <td align="center">
                      <a href="<%#
String.Format("AddEditCategory.aspx?categoryid={0}",
Eval("CategoryId")) %>">
                          <img src="../images/edit.gif" alt=""
width="16" height="16" class="AdminImg" /></a>
                  </td>
                  <td align="center">
                      <img src="../images/delete.gif" alt=""
width="16" height="16" class="AdminImg" />
                  </td>
              </tr>
          </ItemTemplate>
      </asp:ListView>
```

```
  </ContentTemplate>
  </asp:UpdatePanel>
```

Inside the `LayoutTemplate`, one of the elements needs to be declared to runat the server and either have the name `itemPlaceHolder` or match a custom id supplied in the `itemPlaceHolderID` property of the `ListView`. This element will automatically be replaced by the Item and `AlternatingItem` templates with the appropriate databinding. You should also set the `DataKeyNames` property to the name of the entity's primary key value. This will be used in the deleting operation.

The `DataPager` can be declared inside or outside the `LayoutTemplate`. I like to place it in the `LayoutTemplate` because it gives more control over positioning. You can place it outside the template as long as the `DataPager` sets the `PagedControlId` property to the `ListView`. This means the `DataPager` can be placed anywhere on the page. You can have more than one pager assigned to the `ListView`.

Clicking the Delete icon calls the `DeleteCategory` member and reloads the categories in the `ListView`. When an item is deleted using a `ListView` the `ListView`'s `ItemDeleting` event is called, then the `ItemDeleted`. You are still responsible for actually deleting the item and rebinding the list to the `ListView`.

```
    Protected Sub lvCategories_ItemDeleting(ByVal sender As Object, ByVal e As
    System.Web.UI.WebControls.ListViewDeleteEventArgs)
    Handles lvCategories.ItemDeleting
            Using lCategoryrpt As New CategoryRepository
                lCategoryrpt.DeleteCategory(lvCategories.DataKeys(e.ItemIndex).Value)
                BindCategories()
            End Using
    End Sub
```

In the `ItemDeleting` event handler a new `CategoryRepository` is created and the `DeleteCategory` method is called, passing the `CategoryId` of the record to be deleted. Then the `BindCategories` method is called to rebind the list. The `CategoryId` is retrieved from the `ListView` by accessing the `DataKeys` value for the selected row. This value was set by defining the `DataKeyNames` property in the `ListView`'s declaration, `DataKeyNames="CategoryId"`.

The ManageCategories.aspx.vb Code-Behind File

The code needed to manage the list of categories is very simple. The form's class inherits from the `AdminPage` class, which contains some helper members used by all the pages in the admin section. Specifically, for the administrative pages of the `Articles` module, the base admin page contains wrappers for the primary key parameters that are used to identify specific items. I will cover how that works in the `AddEditCategory` page.

The first thing the page does is check to ensure that the user is authorized to access this page. While the site's entire Admin folder is protected by the `web.config` security settings, it is always a good idea to check.

If the user is authorized, the `BindCategories` method is called. This method uses a `CategoryRepository` to bind a list of categories to the `ListView`.

```
    Imports TheBeerHouse.UI
    Imports TheBeerHouse.BLL.Articles
```

```
Imports System.Security

Partial Public Class ManageCategories
    Inherits AdminPage

    Protected Sub Page_Load(ByVal sender As Object, ByVal e As System.EventArgs)
Handles Me.Load

        If Not IsPostBack Then
            If Me.User.Identity.IsAuthenticated AndAlso _
                (Me.User.IsInRole("Administrators") Or _
                Me.User.IsInRole("Editors") Or _
                Me.User.IsInRole("Contributors") Or _
                Me.User.IsInRole("Posters")) Then

                BindCategories()
            Else
                Throw New SecurityException( _
                    "You are not allowed to edit existing articles!")
            End If

        End If

    End Sub
```

The BindCategories method creates a CategoryRepository, and the GetActiveCategories method returns a list of Categories that is bound to a list. This list is then bound to the ListView. As nice as the DataPager control is, it does not have a property to hide it when there is less than one page of records to display. So, I created a method, SetupListViewPager, and placed it in the BasePage class to handle this. It accepts the count of records and a reference to the DataPager. The SetUpListViewPager method then checks to see if the pager should be visible, which it should if there are more records being bound than records being displayed on a page. The method follows; remember this is not part of the ManageCategories.aspx page but part of the BasePage class.

```
Public Sub SetupListViewPager(ByVal vCount As Integer, ByVal vPager As DataPager)

    If Not IsNothing(vPager) Then
        vPager.Visible = IIf(vCount <= vPager.PageSize, False, True)
    End If

End Sub
```

You can see how this is applied in the BindCategories method:

```
Private Sub BindCategories()

    Using Categoryrpt As New CategoryRepository

        Dim lCategories As List(Of Category) =
Categoryrpt.GetActiveCategories()
        lvCategories.DataSource = lCategories
        lvCategories.DataBind()

        SetupListViewPager(lCategories.Count,
```

```
lvCategories.FindControl("pagerBottom"))

        End Using

    End Sub
```

The only task remaining is handling when the list is paged. The `ListView` control fires the `PagePropertiesChanged` event when the user pages the list. Since the `ListView` has a `DataPager` hooked into it, the `ListView` handles working with the records to display the desired set of records. Since the records are being cached in memory, this should be a pretty efficient way to manage paging through the records. If the site grows to have hundreds of thousands of categories, this strategy should be rethought. But for now it is sufficient.

```
    Protected Sub lvCategories_PagePropertiesChanged(ByVal sender As Object,
ByVal e As System.EventArgs) Handles lvCategories.PagePropertiesChanged
        BindCategories()
    End Sub

End Class
```

The AddEditCategory.aspx Page

The `AddEditCategory` page (see Figure 5-7) displays the data in an editable format for a `Category` specified in the `CategoryId` `QueryString` parameter. The data is displayed in a form with appropriate controls, such as `TextBoxes`, `DropDownList`, `FCKeditor`, and so forth. If a new `Category` is being created, the controls are set to their blank state and the administrator can create a new `Category`.

Figure 5-7

I won't go into the details of the page's markup because there is nothing too fancy in play here. I will go over the standard `AddEdit` page markup with the `AddEditArticle` page because there are more interesting user interface elements on that page.

The AddEditCategories.aspx.vb Code-Behind File

The one particular item I want to discuss on the Category administration page is managing the uploading of the category's image. This is done with a `FileUpload` control, an ASP.NET web control that manages a file upload from the client. I created a method to manage the uploading of a file for an admin page called `GetItemImage`. It accepts a reference to a `FileUpload` and a `TextBox` that echoes the URL to the image. The first thing that the method does is check the `FileUpload`'s `HasFile` property. If it is true, then there is a file being uploaded and the method saves the file to the "images" folder. The function then returns the URL reference to the stored image. If there is no file being uploaded, it checks to see if there is a value in the `txtImageURL` and returns that value. If none exists, it returns a reference to a stock image.

```
Protected Function GetItemImage(ByVal vFileUpload As FileUpload, _
ByVal txtImageURL As TextBox) As String
        If vFileUpload.HasFile Then

            vFileUpload.SaveAs(Path.Combine( _
                Path.Combine(Request.PhysicalApplicationPath, "images"), _
vFileUpload.FileName))

            Return Path.Combine("~/images", vFileUpload.FileName)
        ElseIf String.IsNullOrEmpty(txtImageURL.Text) = False Then
            Return txtImageURL.Text
        Else
            Return "~/Images/pencil45_32.png"
        End If
End Function
```

The ManageArticles.aspx Page

Similarly to the `ManageCategories.aspx` page the `ManageArticles.aspx` page gives site administrators the capability to view a list of articles and go edit them. It also lists the Article title with an Edit and a Delete button, displayed in Figure 5-8.

Figure 5-8

It uses the same basic coding patterns used in the `ManageCategory.aspx` page.

The AddEditArticle.aspx Page

The `AddEditArticle.aspx` page allows Administrators, Editors, and Contributors to add new articles or edit existing ones. It decides whether to use edit or insert mode according to whether an `ArticleID` parameter was passed on the querystring. If it was, then the page loads in edit mode for that article, but only if the user is an Administrator or Editor (the edit mode is only available to Administrators and Editors, while the insert mode is also available to Contributors). This security check must be done programmatically, instead of declaratively from the `web.config` file. Figure 5-9 shows the page in edit mode for an article.

Figure 5-9

As you might guess from studying this picture, the page is a table with a series of input fields, a few read-only fields (`ArticleID`, `AddedDate`, and `AddedBy` as usual, but also `ViewCount`, `Votes`, and `Rating`) and many other editable fields. The `Body` field uses the open-source FCKeditor described earlier. It is declared on the page as any other custom control, but it requires some configuration first. To set up FCK, you must download two packages from www.fckeditor.net:

1. FCKeditor (which at the time of writing is in version 2.6.3) includes the set of HTML pages and JavaScript files that implement the control. The control can be used not only with ASP.NET but also with ASP, JSP, PHP, and normal HTML pages. This first package includes the "host-independent" code, and some ASP/ASP.NET/JSP/PHP pages that implement an integrated file browser and file uploader.

2. `FCKedit.Net` is the .NET custom control that wraps the HTML and JavaScript code of the editor.

Unzip the first package into an FCKeditor folder, underneath the site's root folder. Then unzip the second package and put the compiled DLL underneath the site's bin folder. The .NET custom control class has a number of properties that let you customize the look and feel of the editor; some properties can only be set in the `fckconfig.js` file found under the FCKeditor folder. The global FCKConfig JavaScript editor enables you to configure many properties, such as whether the `File Browser` and `Image Upload` commands are enabled. Here's how to disable them in code (we already have our own file uploader, so we don't want to use it here, and we don't want to use the file browser for security reasons):

```
FCKConfig.LinkBrowser = false;
FCKConfig.ImageBrowser = false;
FCKConfig.LinkUpload = false;
FCKConfig.ImageUpload = false;
```

You can even create a customized editor toolbar by adding the commands that you want to implement. For example, this shows how you can define a toolbar named "TheBeerHouse" with commands to format the text, and insert smileys and images, but not insert input controls or Flash animations:

```
FCKConfig.ToolbarSets["TheBeerHouse"] = [
  ['Source','Preview','Templates'],
  ['Cut','Copy','Paste','PasteText','PasteWord','-','Print','SpellCheck'],
  ['Undo','Redo','-','Find','Replace','-','SelectAll','RemoveFormat'],
  ['Bold','Italic','Underline','StrikeThrough','-','Subscript','Superscript'],
  ['OrderedList','UnorderedList','-','Outdent','Indent'],
  ['JustifyLeft','JustifyCenter','JustifyRight','JustifyFull'].
  ['Link','Unlink','Anchor'],
  ['Image','Table','Rule','Smiley','SpecialChar','UniversalKey'],
  ['Style','FontFormat','FontName','FontSize'],
  ['TextColor','BGColor'],
  ['About']
];
```

Many other configurations can be set directly from the ASP.NET page that hosts the control, as you'll see shortly.

The `AddEditArticle.aspx` page uses typical ASP.NET Web controls such as `TextBoxes`, `DropDowns`, and the like, but also leverages a few controls and extenders from the ASP.NET AJAX Control Toolkit, `www.codeplex.com/AjaxControlToolkit`. Normally, a control reference is added to the top of the page for a set of controls not included with the core .NET Framework, but a sitewide reference can be made in the controls section of the `web.config` file. Scott Guthrie details this technique on this blog, `http://weblogs.asp.net/scottgu/archive/2006/11/26/tip-trick-how-to-register-user-controls-and-custom-controls-in-web-config.aspx`:

```
<add tagPrefix="asp" namespace="AjaxControlToolkit" assembly="AjaxControlToolkit,
  Version=3.0.20820.16598, Culture=neutral, PublicKeyToken=28f01b0e84b6d53e" />
```

Now the control toolkit has been registered for sitewide use the controls and extenders can be added to any form on the site as if they were common web controls. For articles, the `CalendarExtender`, `MaskEditExtender`, and `MaskEditValidator` are used. The `CalendarExtender` is used for the date related fields. The `MaskEditExtender` is used to limit the input a user can make to a valid date format.

The `MaskEditValidator` enforces the data format on the client. If the user happens to enter something that does not match the mask, a error message is displayed, as has been done with the traditional validator controls since ASP.NET was introduced.

The following excerpt shows the use of the `MaskEditExtendor`, `MaskEditValidator`, and `CalendarExtender` to manage a datetime input on the `AddEditArticle` page:

```
<tr>
    <td>
        Release Date :
    </td>
    <td>
        <asp:TextBox runat="server" ID="txtReleaseDate" Width="70"
CssClass="formField"></asp:TextBox>
        <asp:Image runat="Server" ID="iReleaseDate"
ImageUrl="~/images/Calendar.png" /><br />
        <asp:CalendarExtender ID="CalendarExtender1" runat="server"
TargetControlID="txtReleaseDate"
            PopupButtonID="iReleaseDate">
        </asp:CalendarExtender>
        <asp:MaskedEditExtender ID="MaskedEditExtender1"
runat="server" TargetControlID="txtReleaseDate"
            Mask="99/99/9999" MessageValidatorTip="true"
OnFocusCssClass="MaskedEditFocus"
            OnInvalidCssClass="MaskedEditError" MaskType="Date"
DisplayMoney="Left" AcceptNegative="Left" />
        <asp:MaskedEditValidator ID="MaskedEditValidator1"
runat="server" ControlExtender="MaskedEditExtender1"
            ControlToValidate="txtReleaseDate" IsValidEmpty="True"
EmptyValueMessage="Date is required"
            InvalidValueMessage="Date is invalid"
ValidationGroup="Demo1" Display="Dynamic"
            TooltipMessage="Input a Date" />
    </td>
</tr>
```

The declaration of the `FCKeditor` shows the use of the `ToolbarSet` property, which references the TheBeerHouse toolbar defined earlier in the JavaScript configuration file.

If the user decides to cancel the operation, the button does a response redirect to the `ManageArticles` `.aspx` page. This is done by using a `button` HTML element with the client-side `OnClick` event handler loading the `ManageArticles.aspx` page.

```
<button onclick ="window.location.assign('ManageArticles.aspx');"
value="">Cancel</button>
```

The AddEditArticle.aspx.vb Code-behind File

The `AddEditArticle` page allows Administrators, Editors, Contributors, and Posters to work with articles. However, if an article has been loaded, only site Administrators and Editors are allowed to perform this action. If an `ArticleId` is passed through the `QueryString` the `BindArticle` method is called and the article's data is bound to the controls on the page. If the user does not belong to these roles, the page will throw a SecurityException:

```
Protected Sub Page_Load(ByVal sender As Object, ByVal e As System.EventArgs)
Handles Me.Load

    If Not IsPostBack Then

        If Me.User.Identity.IsAuthenticated AndAlso _
           (Me.User.IsInRole("Administrators") Or _
           Me.User.IsInRole("Editors") Or _
           Me.User.IsInRole("Contributors") Or _
           Me.User.IsInRole("Posters")) Then

            txtBody.BasePath = Me.BaseUrl & "FCKeditor/"

            If ArticleId > 0 Then
                If Me.User.IsInRole("Administrators") Or _
                   Me.User.IsInRole("Editors") Then
                    BindArticle()
                Else
                    Throw New SecurityException( _
                        "You are not allowed to edit existent articles!")
                End If

            Else
                ClearItems()
            End If

        Else
            Throw New SecurityException( _
                "You are not allowed to edit existent or insert new articles!")
        End If

    End If

End Sub
```

If the page was loaded to create a new article the ClearItems method is called, which sets all the input controls to either empty (TextBox for example) or to a default selection (DropDownList for example). If the user is not a member of any of the preceding groups, a SecurityException is thrown, but most likely there are some other security issues with the site, since the Admin section of the site is closed off to anyone not in these groups in the web.config file!

The FCKeditor requires another property, BasePath, that points to the URL of the FCKeditor folder that contains all its HTML, JavaScript, and image files. This is also done in the page load event handler.

The ClearItems method is called when an article is being created. This clears all the TextBoxes and sets other controls to their initial state. You should preselect the checkboxes that make the article listed and to allow comments. You should also select and enable the Approved checkbox, but only if the current user belongs to the Administrators or Editors roles. This can be done by setting a local Boolean variable to the result of checking the user Role membership. The status Literal control should also have its text set to "Create a New Article" to describe what the user is doing:

```
Private Sub ClearItems()

        ltlArticleID.Text = String.Empty
        ltlAddedDate.Text = String.Empty
        ltlAddedBy.Text = String.Empty

        txtTitle.Text = String.Empty
        txtAbstract.Text = String.Empty
        txtBody.Value = String.Empty
        ddlState.ClearSelection()
        ddlCountry.ClearSelection()
        txtCity.Text = String.Empty
        txtReleaseDate.Text = String.Empty
        txtExpireDate.Text = String.Empty
        Dim bApprove As Boolean = (Me.User.IsInRole("Administrators") Or _
                        Me.User.IsInRole("Editors"))
        cbApproved.Checked = bApprove
        cbApproved.Enabled = bApprove
        cbListed.Checked = True
        cbCommentsEnabled.Checked = True
        cbOnlyForMembers.Checked = False
        ArticleHelper.BindCategoriesToListControl(ddlCategories, 0)

        ltlViewCount.Text = "0"
        ltlVotes.Text = "0"
        ltlRating.Text = "0"

        ltlUpdatedDate.Text = String.Empty
        ltlUpdateBy.Text = String.Empty

        ltlStatus.Text = "Create a New Article"

    End Sub
```

Notice the use of the ArticleHelper.BindCategoriesToListControl method. This is a little helper method that is useful to the Articles module for binding a list of categories to a DropDownList control. This method accepts a ListControl, which is the base class for several controls such as the DropDownList, and a selectedId or the CategoryId to be the selected Category. It then binds a list of active categories to the control and sets the selected value.

```
Public Shared Sub BindCategoriesToListControl(ByVal lCtrl As ListControl, _
ByVal selectedId As Integer)

        Using Categoryrpt As New CategoryRepository

            lCtrl.DataTextField = "Title"
            lCtrl.DataValueField = "CategoryID"

            lCtrl.DataSource = Categoryrpt.GetActiveCategories
```

```
            lCtrl.DataBind()

            lCtrl.SelectedValue = selectedId

        End Using

    End Sub
```

The `BindArticle` method binds the requested article, based on the `ArticleId` to the controls on the page:

```
    Private Sub BindArticle()

        Using Articlerpt As New ArticleRepository

            Dim lArticle As Article = Articlerpt.GetArticleById(ArticleId, False, _
    False)

            If Not IsNothing(lArticle) Then

                ltlArticleID.Text = lArticle.ArticleID
                ltlAddedDate.Text = lArticle.AddedDate
                ltlAddedBy.Text = lArticle.AddedBy

                txtTitle.Text = lArticle.Title
                txtAbstract.Text = lArticle.Abstract
                txtKeywords.Text = lArticle.Keywords
                txtBody.Value = lArticle.Body
                ddlState.SelectedValue = lArticle.State
                ddlCountry.SelectedValue = lArticle.Country
                txtCity.Text = lArticle.City
                txtReleaseDate.Text = lArticle.ReleaseDate
                txtExpireDate.Text = lArticle.ExpireDate
                cbApproved.Checked = lArticle.Approved
                cbListed.Checked = lArticle.Listed
                cbCommentsEnabled.Checked = lArticle.CommentsEnabled
                cbOnlyForMembers.Checked = lArticle.OnlyForMembers

                ArticleHelper.BindCategoriesToListControl(ddlCategories, _
    lArticle.CategoryId)

                ltlViewCount.Text = lArticle.ViewCount
                ltlVotes.Text = lArticle.Votes
                ltlRating.Text = lArticle.AverageRating
                ltlUpdatedDate.Text = lArticle.UpdatedDate
                ltlUpdateBy.Text = lArticle.UpdatedBy

                ltlStatus.Text = "Edit The Article."
            Else
                ArticleId = 0
                ltlStatus.Text = "Create a New Article."
            End If

        End Using

    End Sub
```

The FileUploader.ascx User Control

The `FileUploader.ascx` user control, located under the `~/Controls` folder, allows administrators and editors to upload a file (normally an image file) to the server and save it in their own private user-specific folder. Once the file is saved, the control displays the URL so that the editor can easily copy and paste it into the `ImageUrl` field for a property, or reference the image file in the article's WYSIWYG editor. The markup code is simple — it just declares an instance of the `FileUpload` control, a Submit button, and a couple of `Label`s for the positive or negative feedback:

```
Upload a file:
<asp:FileUpload ID="filUpload" runat="server" /> 
<asp:Button ID="btnUpload" runat="server" OnClick="btnUpload_Click"
    Text="Upload" CausesValidation="false" /><br />
<asp:Label ID="lblFeedbackOK" SkinID="FeedbackOK" runat="server"></asp:Label>
<asp:Label ID="lblFeedbackKO" SkinID="FeedbackKO" runat="server"></asp:Label>
```

The file is saved in the code-behind's `btnUpload_Click` event handler, into a user-specific folder under the `~/Uploads` folder. The actual saving is done by calling the `SaveAs` method of the `FileUpload`'s `PostedFile` object property. If the folder doesn't already exist, it is created by means of the `System.IO.Directory.CreateDirectory` static method:

```
Protected Sub btnUpload_Click(ByVal sender As Object, ByVal e As System.EventArgs)
  Handles btnUpload.Click
        If Not filUpload.HasFile Then
            Try
                ' if not already present, create a directory
                ' names /uploads/{CurrentUserName}
                Dim dirUrl As String = CType(Me.Page, BasePage).BaseUrl + _
                    "Uploads/" + Me.Page.User.Identity.Name
                Dim dirPath As String = Server.MapPath(dirUrl)
                If Not Directory.Exists(dirPath) Then
                    Directory.CreateDirectory(dirPath)
                End If
                ' save the file under the users's personal folder
                Dim fileUrl As String = dirUrl + "/" + _
                    Path.GetFileName(filUpload.PostedFile.FileName)
                filUpload.PostedFile.SaveAs(Server.MapPath(fileUrl))

                lblFeedbackOK.Visible = True
                lblFeedbackOK.Text = "File successfully uploaded: " + fileUrl
            Catch ex As Exception
                lblFeedbackKO.Visible = True
                lblFeedbackKO.Text = ex.Message
            End Try
        End If
End Sub
```

To register this control on a page, you write the following directive at the top of the page (for example, the `ManageCategories.aspx` page):

```
<%@ Register Src="~/Controls/FileUploader.ascx"
    TagName=" FileUploader" TagPrefix="mb" %>
```

And use this tag to create an instance of the control:

```
<mb:FileUploader ID="FileUploader1" runat="server" />
```

The ManageComments.aspx Page

The `ManageComments.aspx` page is located under the `~/Admin/` folder, and it displays all comments of all articles, from the newest to the oldest, and allows an administrator or an editor to moderate the feedback by editing or deleting comments that may not be considered suitable. The page uses a pagable `ListView` for displaying the comments. Figure 5-10 shows this page.

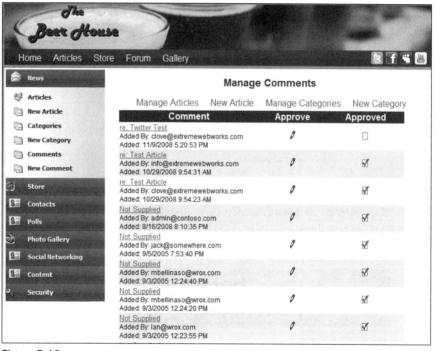

Figure 5-10

I won't cover the code for this page in detail because it's similar to other code that's already been discussed. The pagination for the `ListView` is implemented the same way as the pagination in the `ArticleListing` user control. You can refer to the downloadable code for the complete implementation.

There are a couple of visual differences from the majority of other admin list interfaces to note. The edit column is titled Approve because that is all you can do. I chose not to make this an inline process with AJAX because the comment itself is not displayed and I want to force the editor to read the comment before making the decision to ban it. The delete column is also absent for this same reason. I chose not to display comments in the grid because sometimes they can be rather long for this type of interface. Finally, the last column displays a graphic to indicate if the comment is approved or not. The following code shows the ListView, wrapped in an UpdatePanel. To view the full code, open the source file in Visual Studio.

```
<asp:UpdatePanel runat="server" ID="uppnlComments">
    <ContentTemplate>
        <asp:ListView ID="lvComments" runat="server">
            <LayoutTemplate>
...
            </LayoutTemplate>
            <EmptyDataTemplate>
...
            </EmptyDataTemplate>
            <ItemTemplate>
...
            </ItemTemplate>
            <AlternatingItemTemplate>
...
            </AlternatingItemTemplate>
        </asp:ListView>
        <div class="pager">
...
        </div>
    </ContentTemplate>
</asp:UpdatePanel>
```

The AddEditComment.aspx File

While the title of the AddEditComment.aspx page is slightly misleading, I wanted to keep a consistent naming convention for the details page. This page (see Figure 5-11) allows only administrators to approve or delete comments.

Figure 5-11

The only actionable control on the page is the Approved checkbox. This can either be true or false and is set from the value stored in the database. The Delete function flips the Active bit to false and also reports the comment to Akismet. This was covered in the section on the CommentRepository earlier, so check that out for more details.

The ShowCategories.aspx Page

ShowCategories.aspx is the first end-user page of this module, located in the site's root folder. Its only purpose is to display the article categories in a nice format, so that the reader can easily and clearly understand what the various categories are about and quickly jump to their content by clicking on the category's title. Figure 5-12 shows this page.

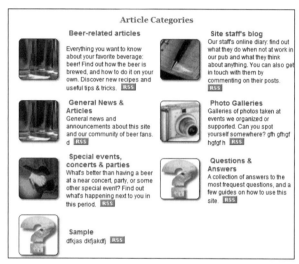

Figure 5-12

The list of categories is implemented as a ListView using grouping, with two columns (with GroupItemCount set to 2). We don't need pagination, sorting, or editing features here, so a simple ListView with support for repeated columns is adequate. Following is the code for the ListView:

```
<asp:UpdatePanel runat="server" ID="uppnlArticles">
    <ContentTemplate>
        <asp:ListView ID="lvCategories" runat="server" DataKeyField="CategoryID"
GroupItemCount="2">
            <LayoutTemplate>
                <table id="tblCategories" runat="server" cellspacing="0"
cellpadding="6" style="width: 100%;">
                    <tr runat="server" id="groupPlaceholder" />
                </table>
                <div class="pager">
                    <asp:DataPager ID="pagerBottom" runat="server" PageSize="4"
PagedControlID="lvCategories">
                        <Fields>
                            <asp:NextPreviousPagerField ButtonCssClass="command"
FirstPageText="«" PreviousPageText="<"
```

```
                                 RenderDisabledButtonsAsLabels="true"
ShowFirstPageButton="true" ShowPreviousPageButton="true"
                        ShowLastPageButton="false" ShowNextPageButton="false" />
                  <asp:NumericPagerField ButtonCount="7"
NumericButtonCssClass="command" CurrentPageLabelCssClass="current"
                        NextPreviousButtonCssClass="command" />
                  <asp:NextPreviousPagerField ButtonCssClass="command"
LastPageText="»" NextPageText=">"
                        RenderDisabledButtonsAsLabels="true"
ShowFirstPageButton="false" ShowPreviousPageButton="false"
                        ShowLastPageButton="true" ShowNextPageButton="true" />
                </Fields>
              </asp:DataPager>
            </div>
          </LayoutTemplate>
          <GroupTemplate>
            <tr runat="server" id="CategoriesRow" style="background-color:
#FFFFFF">
                <td runat="server" id="itemPlaceholder" />
            </tr>
          </GroupTemplate>
          <ItemTemplate>
            <td style="width: 1px">
                <asp:HyperLink ID="lnkCatImage" runat="server" NavigateUrl='<%#
"BrowseArticles.aspx?CategoryID=" & Eval("CategoryID") %>'>
                    <asp:Image ID="imgCategory" runat="server" BorderWidth="0px"
AlternateText='<%# Eval("Title") %>'
                        ImageUrl='<%# Eval("ImageUrl") %>' /></asp:HyperLink>
            </td>
            <td>
                <div class="sectionsubtitle">
                    <a class="articletitle" href='<%# SEOFriendlyURL( _
                        Path.Combine("Category", Eval("Title")), ".aspx") %>'>
                    <%# httputility.HTMLEncode(Eval("Title")) %></a>
                <br />
                <asp:Literal ID="lblDescription" runat="server" Text='<%#
Eval("Description") %>'></asp:Literal>
                    <a class="articletitle" href='<%# SEOFriendlyURL( _
                        Path.Combine("Category", Eval("Title")), ".rss") %>'>
                    <img src="Images/rss.gif" alt="Get the Rss for this
category" style="border-width: 0px;" /></a>
                </td>
            </ItemTemplate>
        </asp:ListView>
      </ContentTemplate>
  </asp:UpdatePanel>
```

The category's image and title both link to the BrowseArticles.aspx page, with a CategoryID parameter on the querystring equal to the CategoryID of the clicked row. If you look at the code, you will notice that a direct URL is not formulated, but rather there is a search engine friendly URL for both the BrowseArticles page and the corresponding RSS feed. The code-behind for this page contains nothing new to review.

The BrowseArticles.aspx Page

`BrowseArticles.aspx` is the end-user version of the `ManageArticles.aspx` page presented earlier. It shows only published content instead of all content, but otherwise it's the same as `ManageArticles.aspx`; it just declares an instance of the shared `ArticleListing` user control:

```
<mb:ArticleListing id="ArticleListing1" runat="server" PublishedOnly="True" />
```

Figure 5-13 represents a screenshot of the page. Note that the page is available to all users, but because the current user is anonymous and the two articles listed on the page have their `OnlyForMembers` property set to `false`, the key image is shown next to them. If the user clicks the article's title, she will be redirected to the login page.

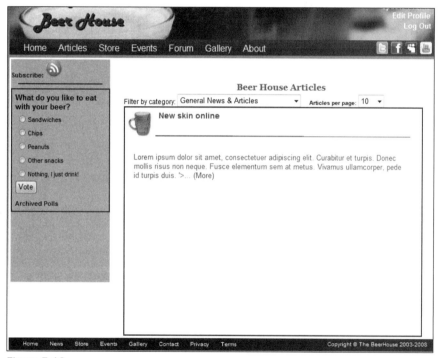

Figure 5-13

The ShowArticle.aspx Page

The `ShowArticle.aspx` end-user page outputs the article's entire text and all its other information (author, release date, average rating, number of views, etc.). It also lets the user rate the article (from one to five glasses of beer) and to submit comments. All comments are listed in chronological order, on a single page, so that it's easy to follow the discussion. When the page is loaded by an editor or an administrator, some additional buttons to delete, approve, and edit the article are also visible. Figure 5-14 shows a screenshot of the page as seen by an end user.

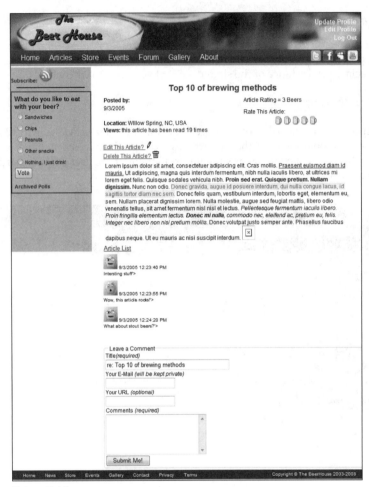

Figure 5-14

The Administrative links are displayed if the user is a site Administrator or an Editor. The Edit link is a `HyperLink` control that points to the `AddEditArticle.aspx` page in the site's Admin folder. The Approve and Delete links are `LinkButton` controls that post back to the server and perform the associated task. In the case of the Approve link, it is only displayed if the article has not been approved yet.

```
If Me.User.Identity.IsAuthenticated AndAlso _
(Me.User.IsInRole("Administrators") Or _
Me.User.IsInRole("Editors")) Then

hlnkEdit.NavigateUrl = String.Format("~/Admin/AddEditArticle.aspx?ArticcleId={0}",
  ArticleId)
hlnkEdit.Visible = True

lbtnApprove.Visible = IIf(lArticle.Approved, False, True)
lbtnDelete.Visible = True

End If
```

Approving and deleting an article are handled by using an `ArticleRepository` and calling the associated members. When an article is deleted, the user is redirected to the `ShowCategories.aspx` page.

```
Private Sub lbtnDelete_Click(ByVal sender As Object, ByVal e As System.EventArgs)
Handles lbtnDelete.Click
        Using lArticlerpt As New ArticleRepository

                lArticlerpt.DeleteArticle(ArticleId)
                Response.Redirect("~/ShowCategories.aspx")

        End Using
End Sub

Private Sub lbtnApprove_Click(ByVal sender As Object, ByVal e As System.EventArgs)
 Handles lbtnApprove.Click
        Using lArticlerpt As New ArticleRepository
            lArticlerpt.ApproveArticle(ArticleId)
            lbtnApprove.Visible = False
        End Using
End Sub
```

Another control available in the ASP.NET AJAX Control Toolkit is the `Rating` control. It provides a much improved way to collect and display ratings for articles. In the case of the Beer House, I decided to use beer mugs as a visual indicator of how readers liked the article. Again, since the Control Toolkit has been registered in the `web.config` file, the `Rating` control can be added just like any other control using the `asp` prefix. I did wrap it up in an update panel to make the rating a seamless process:

```
<asp:UpdatePanel ID="UpdatePanel1" runat="server">
<ContentTemplate>Rate This Article:<br />
<asp:Rating ID="ArticleRating" runat="server" BehaviorID="RatingBehavior1"
CssClass="ArticleRating" StarCssClass="ratingStar"
WaitingStarCssClass="savedRatingStar" FilledStarCssClass="filledRatingStar"
                        EmptyStarCssClass="emptyRatingStar">
</asp:Rating>
</ContentTemplate>
</asp:UpdatePanel>
```

The `Rating` control displays images based on the style assigned to corresponding properties of the control. An empty value is the `StarCssClass`, and a filled value is the `FilledStarCssClass`. These are defined in the stylesheet.

```
/* Rating */

.ArticleRating
{
    float: right;
    margin:3px 75px 10px 10px;
}

.ratingStar {
    font-size: 0pt;
    width: 19px;
    height: 19px;
```

```
    margin: 0px;
    padding: 0px;
    cursor: pointer;
    display: block;
    background-repeat: no-repeat;
}

.filledRatingStar {
    background-image: url(Images/filledbeer.gif);

}

.emptyRatingStar {
    background-image: url(Images/EmptyBeer.gif);
}

.savedRatingStar {
    background-image: url(Images/SavedBeer.gif);
}
```

The current rating of the article is set in the `BindArticle` method by setting the `Rating` Control's `CurrentRating` property to the `Rating` property of the `Article` entity. Remember, the `Rating` property is one of the immutable properties we added to the `Article` entity in the custom partial class. The `Rating` control has a `Tag` property, which I use to hold the `ArticleId` being rated.

```
Using Articlerpt As New ArticleRepository

Dim lArticle As Article = Articlerpt.GetArticleById(ArticleId)
ArticleRating.Tag = ArticleId
ArticleRating.CurrentRating = lArticle.AverageRating

End Using
```

When a user clicks the `Rating` control to select a rating for the article, it is quietly posted back to the server using the magical AJAX features of the `UpdatePanel`. The `Rating` control's `Change` event handler is handled by the page and passes the value of the vote to the database by calling the `RateArticle` member of the `ArticleRepository`.

```
Private Sub ArticleRating_Changed(ByVal sender As Object, ByVal e As
AjaxControlToolkit.RatingEventArgs) Handles ArticleRating.Changed
Using Articlerpt As New ArticleRepository
         Articlerpt.RateArticle(e.Tag, e.Value)
End Using
End Sub
```

Collecting Comments with AJAX

Allowing visitors to comment on articles is a great way to increase community activity around the Beer House. Doing this with AJAX is even cooler. The comments for an article are displayed in a `ListView`, wrapped in an `UpdatePanel`. This is nothing new based on what I have already reviewed. Below the comment list is a form, so the visitor can make a comment. This entire form is wrapped in a DIV, called "dComment". There are actually three nested DIVs contained within the fieldset element that wraps around the form. The first DIV contains the Input elements, including a button to submit the comment.

```
<div id="dComment">
    <fieldset id="commentform">
        <legend>Leave a Comment</legend>
        <div id="dMakeComment">
            <div>
                <label for="txtTitle">
                    Title</label><em>(required)</em></div>
            <div>
                <input id="txtTitle" type="text" value="re: <% =GetTitle()%>"
size="40" /></div>
            <div>
                <label for="txtEmail">
                    Your E-Mail</label>
                <em>(will be kept private)</em></div>
            <div>
                <input id="txtEmail" type="text" /></div>
            <div>
                <label for="txtURL">
                    Your URL</label>
                <em>(optional)</em></div>
            <div>
                <input id="txtURL" type="text" /></div>
            <div>
                <label for="txtComment">
                    Comments</label>
                <em>(required)</em><span id="sCommentReq" style="color: Red;
visibility: hidden;">*</span></div>
            <div>
                <textarea rows="5" cols="25" id="txtComment"></textarea></div>
            <button name="btnStoreComment" id="btnStoreComment"
onclick="StoreComment(); return false;">
                Submit Me!</button>
        </div>
        <div id="dThinking">
            Thinking....</div>
        <div id="dCommentPosted">
            Your Comment has been submitted, check back later to see it
 listed....</div>
    </fieldset>
</div>
```

The latter two DIVs are initially hidden from view because they will be displayed when the user submits their comment and when the response from the server indicating the comment has been posted is complete. These DIVs are hidden by a combination of CSS and JavaScript. When the page is loaded, it calls the SetPage JavaScript function, defined in the TBHComment.js file. This is added to the Body tag's Onload event in the Page Init event handler. Since the page uses a set of nested master pages a little magic needs to be done by casting the Master property to the correct type where the actual Body tag is located. The Body tag has to be declared as a server-side control by adding runat=server and assigning it an ID, <body runat="server" id="pageBody">.

```
Private Sub Page_PreInit(ByVal sender As Object, ByVal e As System.EventArgs)
Handles Me.PreInit

        Dim mp As TBHMain = CType(CType(Me.Master, CRMaster).Master, TBHMain)
        mp.pageBodyTag.Attributes.Add("onload", "SetPage();")

End Sub
```

In the ShowArticle page a ScriptManagerProxy has to be added along with a reference to each the JavaScript file with the client-side code to execute the storing of the comments and the web service:

```
<asp:ScriptManagerProxy ID="ScriptManagerProxy1" runat="server">
        <Services>
            <asp:ServiceReference Path="~/CommentService.asmx"
InlineScript="true" />
        </Services>
        <Scripts>
            <asp:ScriptReference Path="~/TBHComments.js" />
        </Scripts>
</asp:ScriptManagerProxy>
```

The submit button calls a JavaScript function, StoreComment, that makes an asynchronous call to a web service that stores the comment:

```
var dThinking = $get('dThinking');
var dCommentPosted = $get('dCommentPosted');

if (dCommentPosted != null) {
    HideElement('dCommentPosted');
    HideElement('dThinking');
}

function SetPage() {

    if ($get('dResults') != null) {
        HideElement('dResults');
    }

}

function StoreComment() {

    HideElement('dMakeComment');
    ShowElement('dThinking');

    var ArticleId = $get('ArticleId');
    var eMail = $get('txtEmail');
    var Title = $get('txtTitle');
```

```
        var Comment = $get('txtComment');
        var URL = $get('txtURL');

        if (eMail.value.length > 0 && Comment.value.length > 0 &&
Title.value.length > 0) {

            var objCat = new TheBeerHouse.BLL.Articles.Comment();
            objCat.ArticleId = ArticleId.value;
            objCat.addedByEmail = eMail.value;
            objCat.Title = Title.value
            objCat.Body = Comment.value;
            objCat.CommenterURL = URL.value;
            objCat.AddedByIP = UserIP.value;
            objCat.AddedBy = eMail.value;
            objCat.UpdatedBy = eMail.value;

            //   alert('calling the Service.');

            TBH_Web35.CommentService.PostComment(objCat, StoreCommentCompleteEvent,
StoreCommentErrorEvent);

            // alert('Called the Service.');

        } else {
            alert('Just not a valid form.');
        }

        return false;
}


function StoreCommentCompleteEvent(result, context) {

    HideElement('dThinking');
    ShowElement('dCommentPosted');

}

function StoreCommentErrorEvent(result, context) {
    alert('It blew up!');
    if (null != result) {
        alert(result.get_stackTrace());
    }

}


function ShowElement(ElementName) {
    $get(ElementName).style.display = '';
}

function ShowBlockElement(ElementName) {
    var a = $get(ElementName);
```

```
        a.style.display = 'block';
        a.style.overflow = 'auto';
        a.style.height = 'auto';
}

function HideElement(ElementName) {
        $get(ElementName).style.display = 'none';
}

function calcTaxes() {
        HideElement('dIntro');
        ShowBlockElement('dResults');
        return false;
}
```

The `StoreComment` function hides the `dMakeComment` DIV and displays the `dThinking` DIV while the comment is being stored. Next, it grabs references to each of the `Input` elements in the form and sets those values to JavaScript version of the `Comment` class after it does some basic validation of the data. Remember, the comment has to have a title, the person's e-mail address, and of course the comment. The user's IP address along with the `ArticleId` are held in `Hidden` input fields. These fields are accessed by the JavaScript and added to the `Comment` object before it is posted to the server. Next, the `PostComment` method of the `CommentService` is called, passing the `Comment` and the names of the functions to be called when the operation is complete or an error occurs.

When the web service completes and the comment has been posted, the `dCommentPosted` DIV is displayed and the `dThinking` DIV is hidden. This does not completely end the comment process; the comment still needs to be approved by an administrator before it will be displayed to the world.

The `CommentService` is a normal web service, except that it has a couple of AJAX-related attributes set, `ScriptService` at the class level and `ScriptMethod` at the method level. ASP.NET AJAX now knows how to communicate with the web service. The `PostComment` service itself calls the `AddComment` method of the `CommentRepository` and passes the comment provided by the client-side code.

```
Imports System.Web
Imports System.Web.Services
Imports System.Web.Services.Protocols
Imports System.Web.Script.Services
Imports TheBeerHouse.BLL.Articles


' To allow this Web Service to be called from script, using ASP.NET AJAX,
uncomment the following line.
' <System.Web.Script.Services.ScriptService()> _
<WebService(Namespace:="http://tempuri.org/")> _
<WebServiceBinding(ConformsTo:=WsiProfiles.BasicProfile1_1)> _
<ScriptService()> _
<Global.Microsoft.VisualBasic.CompilerServices.DesignerGenerated()> _
Public Class CommentService
        Inherits System.Web.Services.WebService

        <WebMethod()> _
        <ScriptMethod()> _
        Public Function PostComment(ByVal vComment As Comment) As Boolean

                Dim bRet As Boolean = False
```

```
            vComment.AddedByIP = HttpContext.Current.Request.UserHostAddress

            Using Commentrps As New CommentRepository
                bRet = Commentrps.AddComment(vComment)
            End Using

            Return bRet
        End Function

    End Class
```

The ShowArticle.aspx.vb Code-behind File

When the page loads, it reads the ArticleID parameter from the querystring. This is managed in the ShowArticle.vb code-behind file. The ArticleID parameter must be specified; otherwise, the page will throw an exception because it doesn't know which article to load. Since we are using the site map infrastructure described in Chapter 3, the URLRewriting module handles this for us by exchanging the friendly URL for the direct URL needed to display the article properly.

After an Article object has been loaded for the specified article, you must also confirm that the article is currently published (it is not a future or retired article) and that the current user can read it (if the OnlyForMembers property is true, they have to be logged in). You must check these conditions because a cheating user might try to enter an ArticleID in the URL manually, even if the article isn't listed in the BrowseArticles.aspx page. Of course, this type of hacking is one of the main reasons we are using search engine friendly URLs. If everything is OK, the article's view count is incremented, and Labels and other controls on the page are filled with the article's data:

```
    Private Sub ShowArticle_PreLoad(ByVal sender As Object,
    ByVal e As System.EventArgs) Handles Me.PreLoad
        If Not IsPostBack Then
            BindArticle()
        End If
    End Sub

    Private Sub BindArticle()

        Using Articlerpt As New ArticleRepository

            Dim lArticle As Article = Articlerpt.GetArticleById(ArticleId)
            ArticleRating.Tag = ArticleId
            Title = lArticle.Title
            lblLocation.Visible = (lArticle.Location.Length > 0)
            lblLocation.Text = String.Format(lblLocation.Text, lArticle.Location)
            lblViews.Text = String.Format(lblViews.Text, lArticle.ViewCount)
            ArticleRating.CurrentRating = lArticle.AverageRating

            ArticleDetails = lArticle

            lArticle.ViewCount += 1
            Articlerpt.UpdateArticle(lArticle)

        End Using

    End Sub
```

Some of the value are not bound directly to controls on the page. I did this to demonstrate how to call methods or properties defined in the page directly in the page's markup. The use of Literal and Label controls is not always necessary and can add to the page's overhead and weight. The thinner the better from a performance and search engine placement perspective. So, use this technique to keep your pages a little thinner.

The RSSFeed HttpHandler

As discussed in the "Design" section of this chapter, the RSSFeed handler composes and returns a valid RSS XML document composed of articles in the Beer House site. In the "Design" section of this chapter, you saw the schema of a valid RSS 2.0 document. HttpHandlers are composed of two members, IsReusable and ProcessRequest.

The IsReusable property is a Boolean that indicates to the ASP.NET framework if the request can be used by more than one request at a time. Typically, you want to return false since the content of most handlers is dynamic and each request needs to be sent down a different path. For an RSS feed, it could be set to True because the content being returned is the same and most likely does not change that often.

The ProcessRequest method is automatically called by the framework and accepts a reference to the HttpContext being used to process the request. The HttpContext object provides access to the current HttpRequest and HttpResponse objects, needed to evaluate what was being requested and to send content to the client.

```
Public ReadOnly Property Response() As System.Web.HttpResponse
        Get
            Return BaseContext.Response
        End Get
End Property

Public ReadOnly Property Request() As System.Web.HttpRequest
        Get
            Return BaseContext.Request
        End Get
End Property
```

Typically, I create properties to wrap the context, request, and response objects and refactor the worker code to a method that is called by the ProcessRequest method. In the RSSFeed handler The BaseContext property is set to the context parameter. This is then used by the Request and Response properties to return the associated objects to read and write. Finally the CreateRSSFeed method is called to actually produce the RSS feed.

```
Public Sub ProcessRequest(ByVal context As System.Web.HttpContext)
Implements System.Web.IHttpHandler.ProcessRequest

        BaseContext = context
        CreateRSSFeed()

End Sub
```

The `CreateRSSFeed` member reads the list of published articles from the database and produces the RSS feed, an XML document. This is where one of the major differences between VB.NET and C# comes into play, XML Literals (`http://msdn.microsoft.com/en-us/library/bb384629.aspx`). For the most part, there is little to no difference between the two dominant languages in the .NET world, and by that I mean capabilities that one has the other does not have. For the most part, the languages are differentiated by their syntax. VB has the `Dim` statement, and C# has a plethora of ;'s and case sensitivity. XML Literals are one clear advantage that VB.NET has over other languages and, as is typical of the Visual Basic experience, it is designed to make development faster.

Simply put, XML Literals allow you to integrate XML directly into your VB.NET code as a natural part of the syntax. For the RSS feed, an XML template can be added directly to the code and logic placed inside the XML to build an XML document.

```
Private Sub CreateRSSFeed()

  Response.ContentType = "application/xml"

  Using lArticlectx As New ArticleRepository

    Dim Settings As TheBeerHouseSection = Helpers.Settings

    Dim xRss As XDocument = <?xml version="1.0" encoding="utf-8"?>
                    <rss version="2.0" xmlns:geo=
"http://www.w3.org/2003/01/geo/wgs84_pos#">
                        <channel>
                            <title>The Beer House Articles</title>
                            <link>http://www.TheBeerHouseBook.com/</link>
                            <description>RSS Feed containing The Beer House
News Articles.</description>
                            <docs>http://www.rssboard.org/rss-specification</docs>
                            <image>

                                <link>http://www.TheBeerHouseBook.com/</link>
                                <title>The Beer House Articles</title>
                                <url>http://www.TheBeerHouseBook.com
/Images/tbh-logo.png</url>
                            </image>
                            <%= From lArticle In lArticlectx.GetRSSArticles
.AsEnumerable _
                                Select <item>
                                    <title><%= lArticle.Title %></title>
                                    <link><%= SEOFriendlyURL( _
                                        Path.Combine(Settings.Articles
.URLIndicator, lArticle.Title)) %></link>
                                    <description><%= lArticle.Abstract
%></description>
                                </item> %>
                        </channel>
```

```
                    </rss>

        Response.Write(xRss.ToString)

    End Using

    Response.Flush()
    Response.End()

  End Sub
```

The Response's ContentType property is not set to "text/xml". This is necessary for the browser to correctly recognize the output as an XML document. The XDocument's ToString method is called to get an XML string that is sent to the client by calling the Response.Write method. Finally, the Response.Flush and Response.End methods are called to ensure that any content remaining in the buffer is flushed to the client and to close off any more content from being sent.

An XDocument object, xRSS, is created by setting it to the XML template. Embedded within the XML template is a LINQ query that retrieves Article entities as an Enumerable by calling the AsEnumerable operator. The AsEnumerable operator changes the list of objects to an IEnumerable(Of T), which the XML Literal can traverse through. This is done with a special method in the ArticleRepository class, GetRSSArticles.

```
  Public Function GetRSSArticles() As IEnumerable(Of Article)

            Dim key As String = String.Format(CacheKey)

            If EnableCaching AndAlso Not IsNothing(Cache(key)) Then
                Return CType(Cache(key), List(Of Article))
            End If

            Dim lArticles As IEnumerable(Of Article) = (From lArticle In
  Articlesctx.Articles _
                Where lArticle.Active = True And lArticle.Approved = True And _
                lArticle.Listed = True And lArticle.ReleaseDate < Now() And _
                lArticle.ExpireDate > Now() _
                    Order By lArticle.ReleaseDate Descending).AsEnumerable

            If EnableCaching Then
                CacheData(key, lArticles)
            End If

            Return lArticles

  End Function
```

The RSSFeed handler uses the Title and Abstract fields to populate the RSS feed. The <link> element of the feed is built with a helper method, SEOFriendlyURL and the Path.Combine method. Path.Combine takes two strings related to a path, which can be a URL or a UNC file name, and combines them with the proper / or \ separation. I have found this method to be extremely helpful when composing file paths. The `SEOFriendlyURL` method accepts a `URLIndicator` and the article title. It then combines and massages these values to produce a search engine friendly URL that contains the article's title. The result can be seen in Figure 5-15, which shows FireFox consuming the feed.

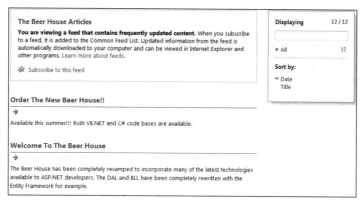

Figure 5-15

Also notice the URLs are fully composed and not relative. This is because the RSS feed will be consumed outside the Beer House's website and, thus, need the full URL to be included in the `<link>` elements.

The RssReader.ascx User Control

The final piece of code for this chapter's module is the `RssReader` user control. In the `ascx` file, you define a `ListView` that displays the title and description of the bound RSS items and makes the title a link pointing to the full article. It also has a header that will be set to the channel's title, a graphical link pointing to the source RSS file, and a link at the bottom that points to a page with more content:

```
<%@ Control Language="vb" AutoEventWireup="false" CodeBehind="RSSReader.ascx.vb"
    Inherits="TBH_Web35.RSSReader" %>
<asp:ListView runat="server" ID="lvRSSReader" ItemPlaceholderID="itemPlaceHolder">
    <LayoutTemplate>
        <dl runat="server" id="itemPlaceHolder">
        </dl>
    </LayoutTemplate>
    <ItemTemplate>
        <dt><a href="<%#Eval("Url")%>">
            <%#Eval("Title")%></a> </dt>
        <dd>
            <%#Eval("description")%>
            <a href="<%#Eval("Url")%>">...</a></dd>
    </ItemTemplate>
</asp:ListView>
```

The RssReader.ascx.cs Code-behind File

The first part of the `RssReader.ascx.cs` code-behind file defines all the custom properties defined in the "Design" section that are used to make this user control a generic RSS reader, and not specific to our site's content and settings:

```
Public Partial Class RSSReader
    Inherits System.Web.UI.UserControl

    Protected Sub Page_Load(ByVal sender As Object, ByVal e As System.EventArgs)
Handles Me.Load

        If Not IsPostBack Then
            BindData()
        End If
    End Sub

    Private Sub BindData()

        Trace.Write(Helpers.FormatUrl("TheBeerHouse.rss"))

        Dim rssFeed As XDocument =
XDocument.Load(Helpers.FormatUrl("TheBeerHouse.rss"))

        Dim rssItems = (From rss In rssFeed.<rss>.<channel>.<item> _
                        Select New With {.Title = rss.<title>.Value, _
                        .Url = rss.<link>.Value, _
                        .description = rss.<description>.Value}).Take(5).ToList

        lvRSSReader.DataSource = rssItems
        lvRSSReader.DataBind()

    End Sub
End Class
```

You don't need to persist the property values in the `ControlState` here as we did in previous controls because all properties wrap a property of some other server-side control, and it will be that other control's job to take care of persisting the values. All the real work of loading and binding the data is done in `BindData` method. With XML literals, a simple LINQ statement can be used over the RSS source to retrieve the items and bind them to the `ListView`.

```
<mb:RssReader id="RssReader1" runat="server" Title="Latest Articles"
    RssUrl="~/GetArticlesRss.aspx"
    MoreText="More articles..." MoreUrl="~/BrowseArticles.aspx" />
```

The output is shown in Figure 5-16.

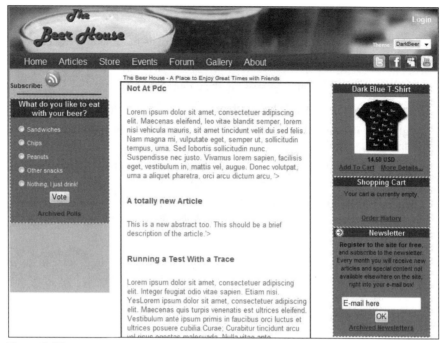

Figure 5-16

Configuring Security Settings

Many security checks have been implemented programmatically from the page's code-behind. Now you need to edit the Admin folder's web.config file to add the Contributors role to the list of allowed roles for the AddEditArticle.aspx page:

```
<configuration xmlns="http://schemas.microsoft.com/.NetConfiguration/v2.0">
   <system.web>
      <authorization>
         <allow roles="Administrators,Editors" />
         <deny users="*" />
      </authorization>
   </system.web>

   <location path="AddEditArticle.aspx">
      <system.web>
         <authorization>
            <allow roles="Administrators,Editors,Contributors" />
            <deny users="*" />
         </authorization>
      </system.web>
   </location>

   <!-- ManageUsers.aspx and EditUser.aspx pages... -->
</configuration>
```

Summary

This chapter showed you how to build a complex and articulate module to completely manage the site's articles and announcements. It covered all of the following:

❏   An administrative section for managing the data in the database.

❏   Pages for browsing the published content.

❏   Integration with the built-in membership system to secure the module and track the authors of the articles.

❏   A syndication service that publishes a RSS feed of recent content for a specific category, or for every category, by means of an ASP.NET page.

❏   A generic user control that consumes any RSS feed. It has been used in this chapter to list the new articles on the home page, but you could also use it in the forums module, and in other situations.

By following along in this chapter, you've seen some of the powerful things you can do with the `ListView` control, the Entity Framework, and a properly designed business logic layer (BLL).

This system is flexible enough to be utilized in many real-world applications, but you can also consider making some of the following improvements:

❏   Support multilevel categories (subcategories management).

❏   A search engine could be added to the public section of the modules. Currently, when users want to find a particular article, they have to go through all the content (which could fill several pages in the article list). You could add a Search box that searches for the specified words in the selected category, or in all the categories, and with further options.

❏   Extend the `ShowArticle.aspx` page, or create a separate page that outputs a printer-friendly version of the article, that is, the article without the site's layout (header, menus, footer, left- and right-hand columns). This could be done easily by adding a new stylesheet to the page (when the page is loaded with a `PrinterFriendly=1` parameter on the querystring) that hides some DIVs (use the `visibility:hidden` style).

❏   Create a web service that allows other applications to retrieve the list of articles as an alternative to the RSS feed. This could also be used by Contributors to submit new articles, or even by Administrators and Editors to perform their duties. You could use the Microsoft Web Service Extensions (WSE) to make authentication much easier and even to support encryption — otherwise, you'd have to pass credentials in the SOAP headers, and encryption would only be possible by using SSL.

In the next chapter, you'll work on a module for creating, managing, displaying, and archiving opinion polls, to implement a form of user-to-site communication.

6

Opinion Polls

Opinion polls consist of questions with a set of options from which users can select their response. Once a user votes in a poll, it's customary to show them current statistics about how the poll is going at that particular time. This chapter explains why polls are useful and important for different websites. Then you will learn how to design and implement a simple and maintainable voting module for the TheBeerHouse site.

Problem

There are basically two reasons why polls are used on a website: because the site's managers may be interested in what their users like (perhaps so they can modify their advertising or product offerings, or maybe in a more general sense to understand their users better) and to help users feel like they have some input to a site and are part of a community of users. Good polls always contain targeted questions that can help the site's managers learn who their users are and what they want to find on the site. This information can be used to identify which parts of the site to improve or modify. Polls are valuable for e-commerce sites, too, because they can indicate which products are of interest and in high demand. Armed with this information, e-commerce businesses can highlight those products, provide more detailed descriptions or case studies, or offer discounts to convince users to buy from their site. Another use for the information is to attract advertising revenue. Medium to large sites frequently display an "Advertise with Us" link or something similar. If you were to inquire about the possibility of advertising on a particular site, that site's advertising department would likely give you some demographics regarding the typical users of that site, such as age, the region or country they live in, common interests, and so on. This information is often gathered by direct or indirect polls. The more details you provide about your typical audience, the more chance you have of finding a sponsor to advertise on your site.

The other major benefit is user-to-user communication. Users generally like to know what their peers think about a product or a subject of interest to them. I must admit that I'm usually curious when I see a poll on a website. Even if I don't have a very clear opinion about the question being asked, I often vote just so I can see the statistics of how the other users voted! This explains why polls are usually well accepted, and why users generally vote quite willingly. Another reason why users may desire to cast a vote is that they think their opinion may influence other users or the site's managers. In addition, their votes really are important, as you've seen, and the results can definitely drive the future content of the site and perhaps even business decisions. For these reasons, you or your client may realize that you want the benefits of a poll feature, and thus you will implement some form of polling on the website.

There are some web poll design issues to consider — namely, the problems that you must address to successfully run a poll system. First of all, as with the news and other content, the same poll shouldn't remain active for too long. If you left the same poll on the page for, say, two months, you might gather some more votes, but you would lose the interest of users who voted early. If you keep a poll up for just a couple of days, you may not achieve significant results because some of your users may not have visited your site within that time frame. The right duration depends mostly on the average number of visitors you have and how often they return to your site. As a rule of thumb, if you know that several thousands of users regularly come to visit the site each week, then that is a good duration for the active poll. Otherwise, if you have fewer visitors, you can leave the poll open for two or more weeks, but probably not longer than a month.

> There are several services that enable you to easily retrieve statistics such as the frequency and number of visitors and much more for your site. Some of these services are commercial, but you can find some good free ones. If you have a hosted website, you probably have access to some statistics through your hosting company's control panel, which gathers information by analyzing the IIS (Internet Information Server) log files. Of course, you could implement your own hit counter — it would be pretty easy to track visitors and generate some basic statistics — but if you want to reproduce all the advanced features offered by specialized services, it would be quite a lot of work, and it may be cheaper in the long run to subscribe to a professional service.

When you change the active poll, a new question arises: What do you do with the old questions and their results? Throw them away? Certainly not! They might be very interesting for new users who didn't take part in the vote, and the information will probably remain valid for some time, so keep them available for viewing. Old polls can be part of the useful content of your site — you could build an archive of past polls.

If you allow a user to vote as many times as he wants to, you'll end up with incorrect results. The overall results will be biased toward that user's personal opinion. Having false results is just as useless as having no results at all, because you can't base any serious decisions on them. Therefore, you want to prevent users from voting more than once for any given question. There are occasions when you might want to allow the user to vote several times, though. For example, during your own development and testing stage, you may need to post many votes to determine whether the voting module is working correctly. The administrator could just manually add some votes by entering them directly into the SQL table, but that would not tell you if the polling frontend is working right. If you enter votes using the polling user interface that you'll build in this chapter, it's more convenient and it thoroughly tests the module. There are reasons for wanting to allow multiple votes after deployment, too. Imagine that you are running a competition to select the best resource on any selected topic. The resources might be updated frequently, and if the poll lasts a month, then users may change their mind in the meantime, after voting. You may then decide to allow multiple votes, but no more than once per week (but you probably won't want to go to the trouble of letting a user eliminate his earlier vote).

This discussion talks only about polls that allow a single option to be selected (poll boxes with a series of radio buttons). Another type of poll box enables users to vote for multiple options in a single step (the options are listed with checkboxes, and users can select more than one). That might be useful for a question like "What do you usually eat at pubs?" for which you want to allow multiple answers through multiple separate checkboxes. However, this type of poll is quite rare, and you could probably reword the question to ask what food they most like to eat at pubs to allow only one answer. The design of a multiple-answer poll would needlessly complicate this module, so the example here won't use that kind of functionality.

To summarize what we've discussed here: you want to implement a poll facility on the site to gauge the opinions of your users and to generate a sense of community. You don't want users to lose interest by seeing the same poll for a long time, but you do want a meaningful number of users to vote, so you'll add new questions and change the current poll often. You also want to allow users to see old polls because that helps to add useful content to your page, but they won't be allowed to vote in the old polls. Finally, you want to be able to easily add the poll to any page, and you want the results to be as unbiased and accurate as possible. Now let's look at the design in more detail, and consider how to meet these challenges.

Design

The poll functionality for the site will store the data (questions, answers, votes, and so on) in the database shared by all modules of this book (although the configuration settings do allow each module to use a separate database, if there's a need to do that). To easily access the DB you'll need tables, an Entity Data Model, and a business layer to keep the presentation layer separate from the DB and the details of its structure. Of course, some sort of user interface will allow administrators to see and manage the data using their favorite browser.

Here's the list of features needed in the polls module:

❑ An access-protected administration console to easily change the current poll and add or remove questions. It should allow multiple polls and their response options to be added, edited, or deleted. The capability to have multiple polls is important because you might want to have different polls in different sections of your site. The administration pages should also show the current statistical results for each poll, and the total number of votes for each poll, as a quick general summary.

❑ A user control that builds the poll box that can be inserted into any page. The poll box should display the question text and the available options (usually rendered as radio buttons to allow only one choice). Each poll will be identified by a unique ID, which should be specified as a custom property for the user control, so that the webmaster can easily change the currently displayed question by setting the value for that property.

❑ Prevent users from voting multiple times for the same poll. Or, even better, you should be able to dynamically decide if you want to allow users to vote more than once, or specify the period during which they will be prevented from voting again.

❑ You can only have one poll question declared as the current default. When you set a poll question as being current, the previous current one should change its state. The current poll will be displayed in a poll box unless you specify a nondefault poll ID. Of course, you can have different polls on the site at the same time depending on the section (perhaps one for the Beer-related article category, and one for party bookings), but it's useful to set a default poll question because you'll be able to add a poll box without specifying the ID of the question to display, and you can change the poll question through the administration console, without manually changing the page and redeploying it.

❑ A poll should be archived when you decide that you no longer want to use it as an active poll. Once archived, if a poll box is still explicitly bound to that particular poll, the poll will only be shown in Display state (read-only), and it will show the recorded results.

❑ A page that displays all the archived polls and their results. A page for the results of the current poll is not necessary because they will be shown directly by the poll box — instead of the list of response options — when it detects that the user has voted. This way, users are forced to express their opinion if they want to see the poll's results (before the poll expires), which will bring in more votes than we would get if we made the current results freely available to users who have not yet voted. There must also be an option that specifies whether the archive page is accessible by everyone, or just by registered users. You may prefer the second option to give the user one more reason to register for the site.

Now let's look at designing the database tables, stored procedures, data and business layers, user interface services, and security needed for this module.

Handling Multiple Votes

As discussed in the "Problem" section, we want to be able to control whether users can cast multiple votes, and allow them to vote again after a specified period. Therefore, you would probably like to give the administrator the capability to prevent multiple votes, or to allow multiple votes but with a specified lock duration (one week in the previous example). You still have to find a way to ensure that the user does not vote more times than is allowed. The simplest, and most common and reliable, solution is writing a cookie to the client's browser that stores the PollID of the poll for which the user has voted. Then, when the poll box loads, it first tries to find a cookie matching the poll. If a cookie is not found, the poll box displays the options and lets the user vote. Otherwise, the poll box shows the latest results and does not allow the user to vote again. To allow multiple votes, the cookie will have an expiration date. If you set it to the current date plus seven days, it means that the cookie expires in seven days, after which the user will be allowed to vote again on that same question.

Writing and checking cookies is straightforward, and in most cases it is sufficient. The drawback to this method is that users can easily turn off cookies through a browser option, or delete the cookies from their machine, and then be allowed to vote as many times as they want to. Only a very small percentage of users keep cookies turned off — except for company users where security is a major concern — because they are used on many sites and are sometimes actually required. Because of this, it shouldn't be much of an issue because most people won't bother to go to that much trouble to re-vote, and this is not a high-security type of voting mechanism that would be suitable for something very important, such as a political election.

There's an additional method to prevent multiple votes: IP locking. When users vote, their computer's IP address can be retrieved and stored in the cache together with the other voting details. Later in the same user session, when the poll box loads or when the user tries to vote again, you can check whether the cache contains a vote for a specific poll, by a specified IP. To implement this, the PollID and user's

IP address may be part of the item's key if you use the `Cache` class; otherwise, the `PollID` is enough, if you choose to store it in `Session` state storage, because that's already specific to one user. If a vote is found, the user has already voted and you can prevent further voting. This method only prevents re-voting within the same session — the same user can vote again the next day. We don't want to store the user's IP address in the database because it might be different tomorrow (because most users today have dynamically assigned IP addresses). Also, the user might share an IP with many other users if they are in a company using network address translation (NAT) addresses, and we don't want to prevent other users within the same company from voting. Therefore, the IP locking method is normally not my first choice.

There's yet another option. You could track the logged users through their usernames instead of their computer's IP address. However, this only works if the user is registered. In our case we don't want to limit the vote to registered users only, so we won't cover this method further.

In this module we'll provide the option to employ both methods (cookie and IP), only one of them, or neither. Employing neither of them means that you will allow multiple votes with no limitations, and this method should only be used during the testing stage. In a real scenario, you might need to disable one of the methods — maybe your client doesn't want to use cookies for security reasons, or maybe your client is concerned about the dynamic IP issue and doesn't want to use that method. I personally prefer the cookie option in most cases.

In conclusion, the polls module will have the following options:

❑ Multiple votes per poll can be allowed or denied.

❑ Multiple votes per poll can be prevented with client cookies or IP locking.

❑ Limited multiple votes can be allowed, in which case the administrator can specify the lock duration for either method (users can vote again in seven days, for example).

This way, the polls module will be simple and straightforward, but still flexible, and it can be used with the options that best suit the particular situation. Online administration of polls follows the general concept of allowing the site to be remotely controlled by managers and administrators using a web browser.

Designing the Database Tables

We will need two tables for this module: one to contain the poll questions and their attributes (such as whether a poll is current or archived) and another one to contain the polls' response options and the number of votes each received. Figure 6-1 shows how they are linked to each other.

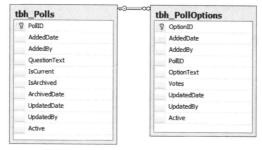

Figure 6-1

Here you see the primary and foreign keys, the usual AddedDate and AddedBy fields that are used in most tables for audit and recovery purposes, and a few extra fields that store the poll data. The tbh_Polls table has a QuestionText field that stores the poll's question, an IsArchived bit field to indicate whether that poll was archived and no longer available for voting, and an ArchivedDate field for the date/time when the poll was archived (this last column is the only one that is nullable). There is also an IsCurrent bit field, which can be set to 1 only for a single poll, which is the overall default poll. The other table, tbh_PollOptions, contains all the configurable options for each poll, and makes the link to the parent poll by means of the PollID foreign key. There is also a Votes integer field that contains the number of user votes received by the option.

Designing the Configuration Module

I've already mentioned that the polls module will need a number of configuration settings that enable or disable multiple votes, make the archive public to everyone, and more. Following is the list of properties for a new class, named PollsElement, which inherits from the framework's ConfigurationElement class and will read the settings of a <polls> element under the <theBeerHouse> custom configuration section (introduced in Chapter 3 and used again in Chapter 5).

Property	Description
ProviderType	Made obsolete with the Entity Framework. Retained from previous editions.
ConnectionStringName	The name of the entry in web.config's new <connectionStrings> section, which contains the connection string to the module's database.
VotingLockInterval	An integer indicating when the cookie with the user's vote will expire (number of days to prevent re-voting).
VotingLockByCookie	A Boolean value indicating whether a cookie will be used to remember the user's vote.
VotingLockByIP	A Boolean value indicating whether the vote's IP address is kept in memory to prevent duplicate votes from that IP in the current session.
ArchiveIsPublic	A Boolean value indicating whether the poll's archive is accessible by everyone, or if it's restricted to registered members.
EnableCaching	A Boolean value indicating whether the caching of data is enabled.
CacheDuration	The number of seconds for which the data is cached if there aren't inserts, deletes, or updates that invalidate the cache.

Creating the Entity Data Model

As in the previous chapters, a dedicated Entity Data Model (see Figure 6-2) is generated for the Poll module. It contains an entity for the Poll and PollOption. And as usual The EntitySet and relationships need to be renamed to something more friendly.

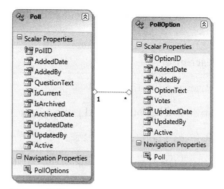

Figure 6-2

Designing the Business Layer

The BLL for this module is composed of a series of classes, Poll and PollOption, which wrap the data of the tbh_Poll and tbh_PollOption, respectively. Both the Poll and PollOption have dedicated repositories that handle calling the entity model to retrieve and manipulate the data. Just as you saw in Chapter 5, there is a BasePollRepository class that both repositories inherit common features from. The PollEntities class is the data model's DataContext class. Figure 6-3 illustrates the business classes and their relationships.

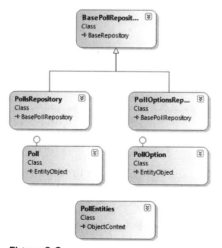

Figure 6-3

The PollRepository

The PollRepository contains the normal CRUD members, but also has a series of methods that allow it to manage the data for specific polling-related tasks. These include methods to archive and retrieve just archived polls, obtain a count of polls, get the current poll, and get its `PollId`. The following table describes those methods.

Method	Description
GetPolls	Retrieves a full list of polls.
GetArchivedPolls	Retrieves a list of archived polls.
GetPollById	Retrieves a poll by its `PollId`.
GetPollCount	Returns the number of polls in the database.
AddPoll	Adds a new poll to the database.
UpdatePoll	Updates an existing poll.
DeletePoll	Deletes a poll by setting the `Active` flag to false.
UnDeletePoll	Undeletes a poll by setting the `Active` flag to true.
ArchivePoll	Archives the designated poll by setting the `CurrentPoll` value to 0 and `IsArchived` to 1.
GetCurrentPollId	Returns the `PollId` of the poll designated as the currently active poll.
CurrentPoll	Retrieves an instance of the current `Poll`.

The PollOptionRepository

The `PollOptionRepository` is similar with common CRUD members and a few custom members. Custom members get the poll options for a poll and a method to register a vote. Here are the methods:

Method	Description
GetPollOptions	Retrieves a full list of poll options.
GetActivePollOptionsByPollId	Retrieves a list of active poll options by the specified `PollId`.
GetPollOptionsByPollId	Retrieves a list of poll options by the specified `PollId`.
GetPollOptionById	Retrieves the `PollOption` by the specified `PollOptionId`.
GetPollOptionCount	Returns a count of poll options.
AddPollOption	Adds a new poll option to the database.
UpdatePollOption	Updates an existing poll option.
DeletePollOption	Deletes a poll option by setting the `Active` flag to false.
UnDeletePollOption	Undeletes a poll option by setting the `Active` flag to true.
Vote	Returns the `PollId` of the poll designated as the currently active poll.

Designing the User Interface Services

Following are the pages and controls that constitute the user interface layer of this module:

❑ **~/Admin/ManagePolls.aspx:** This is the page through which an administrator or editor can view a list of polls. Icon buttons for each poll give the administrator the ability to archive, edit, or delete the poll. Before a poll is deleted, the administrator is prompted to confirm the action. Clicking the Edit button takes the administrator to the `AddEditPoll.aspx` page. This page only lists active polls, however. Once a poll is archived, it will be visible only in the archived polls page (you can't change history).

❑ **~/Admin/AddEditPoll.aspx:** This is the page through which an administrator or editor can manage a poll: add, edit, archive, and define poll options; see current results; and set the current poll.

❑ **~/ArchivedPolls.aspx:** This page lists the archived polls and shows their results. If the user accessing it is an administrator or an editor, she will also see buttons for deleting polls. The archived polls are not editable; they can only be deleted if you don't want them to appear on the archive page.

❑ The **PollBox user control** will enable us to insert the poll box into any page, with only a couple of lines of code. This control is central to the poll module and is described in further detail in the following section.

For now, let's look at the `PollBox` user control, which has two functions:

1. If it detects that the user has not voted for the question yet, the control will present a list of radio buttons with the various response options and a Vote button.

2. If it detects that the current user has already voted, instead of displaying the radio buttons, it displays the results. It will show the percentage of votes for each option, both as a number and graphically, as a colored bar. This will also happen if the poll being shown was archived.

In both cases, the control can optionally show header text and a link at the bottom. The link points to the archive page. This method of changing behavior based on whether the user has already voted is elegant, doesn't need an additional window, and intelligently hides the radio buttons if the user can't vote. The control's properties, which enable us to customize its appearance and behavior, are described in the following table.

Property	Description
PollID	The ID of the poll to display in the poll box. If no ID is specified, or if it is explicitly set to -1, the poll with the IsCurrent field set to 1 will be used.
HeaderText	The text for the control's header bar.
ShowHeader	Specifies whether the control's header bar is visible.
ShowQuestion	Specifies whether the poll's question is visible.
ShowArchiveLink	Specifies whether the control shows a link at the bottom of the control pointing to the poll's Archive page.

When you add this control to a page, you will normally configure it to show the header, the question, and the link to the archive page. If, however, you have multiple polls on the page, you may want to show the link to the archive in just one poll box, maybe the one with the poll marked as the current default. The control will also be used in the archive page itself, to show the results of the old polls (the second mode described previously). In this case, the question text will be shown by some other control that lists the polls, and thus the PollBox control will have the ShowHeader, ShowQuestion, and ShowArchiveLink properties set to false.

Solution

Now that the design is complete, you should have a very clear idea about what is required, so now we can consider how we're going to implement this functionality. You'll follow the same order as the "Design" section, starting with the creation of database tables and stored procedures, the configuration, DAL and BLL classes, and finally the ASPX pages and the PollBox user control.

Working on the Database

The tables required for this module are added to the same sitewide SQL Server database shared by all modules, although the configuration settings enable you to have the data and the db objects separated into multiple databases if you prefer to do it that way. It's easy to create the required objects with Visual Studio using the integrated Server Explorer or SQL Server Management Studio, right from within the Visual Studio IDE. Figure 6-4 is a screenshot of the IDE when adding columns to the tbh_Polls tables, and setting the properties for the PollID primary key column.

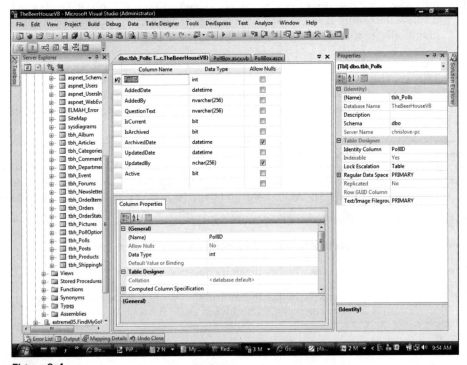

Figure 6-4

After creating the two tables with the columns shown in Figure 6-1, you need to create a relationship between them over the `PollID` column, and set up cascade updates and deletes (Select Data ⇨ Add New ⇨ Diagram to bring up the interactive diagram that enables you to create the relationship — as explained in Chapter 5). Figure 6-5 shows the relationship diagram with the Tables and Columns dialog displayed to select the primary and foreign key relationship.

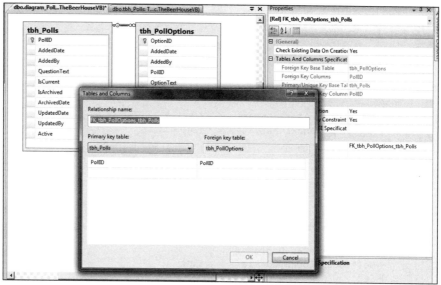

Figure 6-5

Implementing the Configuration Module

The custom configuration class must be developed before any other code because the custom settings are used in all other layers. This class is similar to the one seen in the previous chapter. It inherits from `ConfigurationElement` and has the properties previously defined:

```
Public Class PollsElement
    Inherits ConfigurationElement

    <ConfigurationProperty("connectionStringName")> _
    Public Property ConnectionStringName() As String
        Get
            Return CStr(Me("connectionStringName"))
        End Get
        Set(ByVal value As String)
            Me("connectionStringName") = value
        End Set
    End Property

    Public ReadOnly Property ConnectionString() As String
        Get
            Dim connStringName As String
```

```vbnet
                If String.IsNullOrEmpty(Me.ConnectionStringName) Then
                    connStringName = Globals.Settings.DefaultConnectionStringName
                Else
                    connStringName = Me.ConnectionStringName
                End If
                Return WebConfigurationManager.ConnectionStrings(connStringName)
.ConnectionString
            End Get
        End Property

        <ConfigurationProperty("votingLockInterval", DefaultValue:="15")> _
        Public Property VotingLockInterval() As Integer
            Get
                Return CInt(Me("votingLockInterval"))
            End Get
            Set(ByVal value As Integer)
                Me("votingLockInterval") = value
            End Set
        End Property

        <ConfigurationProperty("votingLockByCookie", DefaultValue:="true")> _
        Public Property VotingLockByCookie() As Boolean
            Get
                Return CBool(Me("votingLockByCookie"))
            End Get
            Set(ByVal value As Boolean)
                Me("votingLockByCookie") = value
            End Set
        End Property

        <ConfigurationProperty("votingLockByIP", DefaultValue:="true")> _
        Public Property VotingLockByIP() As Boolean
            Get
                Return CBool(Me("votingLockByIP"))
            End Get
            Set(ByVal value As Boolean)
                Me("votingLockByIP") = value
            End Set
        End Property

        <ConfigurationProperty("archiveIsPublic", DefaultValue:="false")> _
        Public Property ArchiveIsPublic() As Boolean
            Get
                Return CBool(Me("archiveIsPublic"))
            End Get
            Set(ByVal value As Boolean)
                Me("archiveIsPublic") = value
            End Set
        End Property

        <ConfigurationProperty("enableCaching", DefaultValue:="true")> _
        Public Property EnableCaching() As Boolean
            Get
                Return CBool(Me("enableCaching"))
            End Get
```

```vb
            Set(ByVal value As Boolean)
                Me("enableCaching") = value
            End Set
        End Property


        <ConfigurationProperty("cacheDuration")> _
        Public Property CacheDuration() As Integer
            Get
                Dim duration As Integer = CInt(Me("cacheDuration"))
                If duration <= 0 Then
                    duration = Globals.Settings.DefaultCacheDuration
                End If
                Return duration
            End Get
            Set(ByVal value As Integer)
                Me("cacheDuration") = value
            End Set
        End Property


        <ConfigurationProperty("urlIndicator")> _
        Public Property URLIndicator() As String
            Get
                Dim lurlIndicator As String = Me("urlIndicator").ToString
                If String.IsNullOrEmpty(lurlIndicator) Then
                    lurlIndicator = "Poll"
                End If
                Return lurlIndicator
            End Get
            Set(ByVal Value As String)
                Me("urlIndicator") = Value
            End Set
        End Property

    End Class
```

To make this class map a `<polls>` element under the top-level `<theBeerHouse>` section, we add a property of type `PollsElement` to the `TheBeerHouseSection` class developed in the previous chapter and then use the `ConfigurationProperty` attribute to do the mapping:

```vb
    <ConfigurationProperty("polls", IsRequired:=True)> _
    Public ReadOnly Property Polls() As PollsElement
            Get
                Return CType(Me("polls"), PollsElement)
    End Get
    End Property
```

To make the archive available to everyone and disable vote locking by the user's IP, use these settings in the `web.config` file:

```xml
    <theBeerHouse defaultConnectionStringName="LocalSqlServer">
       <contactForm mailTo="mbellinaso@wrox.com"/>
       <articles pageSize="10" />
       <polls archiveIsPublic="true" votingLockByIP="false"  />
    </theBeerHouse>
```

339

The default value will be used for all those settings not explicitly defined in the configuration file, such as `connectionStringName`, `providerType`, `votingLockByCookie`, `votingLockInterval`, and the others.

Implementing the Repositories

Similar to how things were structured in the Articles module in Chapter 5 the Polls module has a set of repository classes that are located in the Polls folder of the TBHBLL class library project. There is a `BasePollRepository`, which contains the common constructors, a reference to the entity model's `DataContext`, and the `Dispose` members. The `Poll` and `PollOption` entities each have a corresponding repository to manage the business logic associated for each. Since most of the patterns used in the repository members were discussed in Chapters 3 and 5, I will limit this chapter to new items.

Implementing the PollRepository

The `PollRepository` contains standard CRUD business members and some that perform targeted operations. These include archiving a poll and retrieving the current poll. All the queries are LINQ to Entities statements and cache the results when a list is retrieved according to the cache settings in the `web.config` file.

Implementing the PollOptionRepository

Like the `PollRepository`, the `PollOptionRepository` contains common CRUD members and a member to cast a vote for an option and another member to get options by a `PollId`.

Extending the Entity Model Entities

Each of the entity classes generated by the Entity Data Model Wizard is a partial class that can be extended. The Polling module has two entities, `Poll` and `PollOption`. The main extensions that I will discuss revolve around managing the votes for a poll and each of its options.

Extending the Poll Entity

The `Poll` entity has a property that holds the number of total votes cast in a poll by calculating the SUM of the votes for each option. This is done using a LINQ statement with a LAMBDA expression.

```
Private _Votes As Integer = 0
Public Property Votes() As Integer
Get

            If Me._Votes = 0 Then
                If PollOptions.IsLoaded = False Then
                    Me.PollOptions.Load()
                End If

                _Votes = (From po In Me.PollOptions _
                            Select New With {.Votes = po.Votes})
.Sum(Function(p) p.Votes)
                End If
                Return _Votes

    End Get
```

```
Set(ByVal value As Integer)
                _Votes = value
End Set
End Property
```

The Get section of the Votes property checks to see if the _Votes variable is set to 0 and if it is, it tries to calculate the votes. First, it checks to see if the associated PollOptions have been loaded in the Poll entity; if not, they are manually loaded. This is an example of when deferred loading is not desired but easily dealt with. Now that all poll options have been loaded, a simple LINQ statement is executed calling the Sum operator and passing in the Votes value of each poll option in a LAMBDA expression. Finally the total value is returned. This value is then used in the binding operation when the poll results are displayed.

Extending the PollOption Entity

The PollOption entity also has a few members added to the extended partial class, a custom ToString method, and PollId, TotalVotes, and Percentage properties. The ToString method returns a custom formatted string with the PollId, the OptionText, and the number of votes cast for that option. This can be used as a quick method to display information about the option. PollId is the property used to access the foreign key value of the associated Poll. The TotalVotes property is number of votes cast for the poll, this means a total of all the votes cast by all the poll's options. The Percentage property returns the percentage value of the option's votes in relation to the total number of votes cast in the poll.

```
Public Overrides Function ToString() As String
        Return String.Format("{0}, {1}, {2}", Me.PollId, Me.OptionText,
Me.Votes) ', {3:N1} , Me.Percentage)
End Function

Public Property PollId() As Integer
        Get
            If Not IsNothing(Me.PollReference.EntityKey) Then
                Return Me.PollReference.EntityKey.EntityKeyValues(0).Value
            End If
            Return 0
        End Get
        Set(ByVal Value As Integer)
            If Not IsNothing(Me.PollReference.EntityKey) Then
                Me.PollReference = Nothing
            End If
            Me.PollReference.EntityKey = New EntityKey("PollEntities.Polls",
 "PollID", Value)
        End Set
End Property

Private _TotalVotes As Double = 0
Public Property TotalVotes() As Integer
        Get
            If Not IsNothing(Me.Poll) Then
                _TotalVotes = Poll.Votes
            End If
            Return _TotalVotes
        End Get
```

```
                Set(ByVal value As Integer)
                    _TotalVotes = value
            End Set
    End Property

    Public ReadOnly Property Percentage() As Double
            Get
                If TotalVotes = 0 Then
                    Return -1D
                End If
                Return ((Votes * 100) / TotalVotes)
            End Get
    End Property
```

Implementing the User Interface

Now it's time to build the user interface: the administration page, the poll box user control, and the archive page.

The ManagePolls.aspx Page

The `ManagePolls.aspx` page (see Figure 6-6), located under the ~/Admin folder, allows the administrator to view a list of polls, add a new poll, and edit, delete, or archive existing polls. The page is composed of the common administration layout with a menu across the top and a combination of an `Accordion` and `ListView` of detailed navigation on the left. It uses the Admin master page to implement the common navigation features. The table listing the polls is a `ListView` with paging capabilities. The link to edit a poll is a pencil icon and the archive link is a file folder. The delete icon is the familiar trash can.

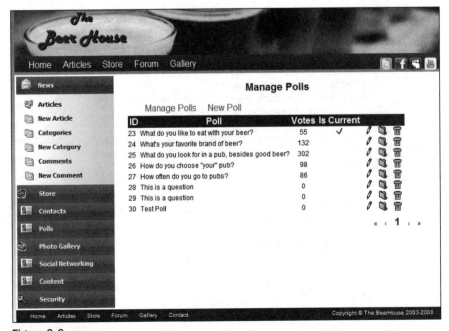

Figure 6-6

The ListView is wrapped in an UpdatePanel so that it can take advantage of ASP.NET AJAX without having to add any more code to the solution. The effects of the UpdatePanel can be seen when paging through the list, or archiving or deleting a poll. These operations will occur on the server and provide seamless updates in the browser. If the poll is the current poll a checkbox icon is displayed before the action items are listed. To the left of the current icon is a tally of the total votes. The following code shows the MainContent's markup:

```
<asp:Content ID="MainContent" ContentPlaceHolderID="AdminContent" runat="Server">
    <table cellpadding="0" cellspacing="0" class="AdminLayout">
        <tr>
            <td>
                <h1>
                    Manage Polls</h1>
            </td>
        </tr>
        <tr>
            <td>
                <div id="dAdminHeader">
                    <ul>
                        <li><a href="ManagePolls.aspx"><span>Manage Polls</span>
</a></li>
                        <li><a href="AddEditPoll.aspx"><span>New Poll</span>
</a></li>
                    </ul>
                </div>
            </td>
        </tr>
        <tr>
            <td>
                <asp:UpdatePanel runat="server" ID="uppnlCategories">
                    <ContentTemplate>
                        <asp:ListView runat="server" ID="lvPolls"
DataKeyNames="PollId">
                            <LayoutTemplate>
                                <table cellpadding="0" cellspacing="0" border="0">
                                    <tr class="AdminListHeader">
                                        <td>
                                            ID
                                        </td>
                                        <td>
                                            Poll
                                        </td>
                                        <td>
                                            Votes
                                        </td>
                                        <td>
                                            Is Current
                                        </td>
                                        <td colspan="3">
                                        </td>
                                    </tr>
                                    <tr id="itemPlaceholder" runat="server">
                                    </tr>
```

```
                        </table>
                    </LayoutTemplate>
                    <ItemTemplate>
                        <tr>
                            <td>
                                <%#Eval("PollId")%>
                            </td>
                            <td>
                                <%#Eval("QuestionText")%>
                            </td>
                            <td align="center">
                                <%#Eval("Votes")%>
                            </td>
                            <td align="center">
                                <asp:Image ID="imgIsCurrent" runat="server"
ImageUrl="~/Images/OK.gif" Visible='<%# Eval("IsCurrent") %>' />
                            </td>
                            <td align="center">
                                <a href="<%#
String.Format("AddEditPoll.aspx?PollID={0}", Eval("PollId")) %>">
                                    <img src="../images/edit.gif" alt=""
width="16" height="16" class="AdminImg" /></a>
                            </td>
                            <td align="center">
                                <asp:ImageButton runat="server"
ID="ibtnArchive" CommandArgument='<%# Eval("PollID").ToString() %>'
                                    CommandName="Archive"
ImageUrl="~/images/folder.gif" AlternateText="Archive"
                                    CssClass="AdminImg" />
                            </td>
                            <td>
                                <asp:ImageButton runat="server"
 ID="btnDeleteOption" CommandArgument='<%# Eval("PollID").ToString() %>'
                                    CommandName="Delete"
ImageUrl="~/images/delete.gif" AlternateText="Delete" CssClass="AdminImg"
                                    OnClientClick="return
confirm('Warning: This will delete the Event from the database.');" />
                            </td>
                        </tr>
                    </ItemTemplate>
                </asp:ListView>
                <div class="pager">
                    <asp:DataPager ID="pagerBottom" runat="server"
PageSize="15" PagedControlID="lvPolls">
                        <Fields>
                            <asp:NextPreviousPagerField
ButtonCssClass="command" FirstPageText="&laquo;" PreviousPageText="&lt;"
                                RenderDisabledButtonsAsLabels="true"
 ShowFirstPageButton="true" ShowPreviousPageButton="true"
                                ShowLastPageButton="false"
ShowNextPageButton="false" />
                            <asp:NumericPagerField ButtonCount="7"
NumericButtonCssClass="command" CurrentPageLabelCssClass="current"
                                NextPreviousButtonCssClass="command" />
```

```
                              <asp:NextPreviousPagerField
ButtonCssClass="command" LastPageText="»" NextPageText=">"
                              RenderDisabledButtonsAsLabels="true"
ShowFirstPageButton="false" ShowPreviousPageButton="false"
                              ShowLastPageButton="true"
ShowNextPageButton="true" />
                          </Fields>
                      </asp:DataPager>
                  </div>
              </ContentTemplate>
          </asp:UpdatePanel>
      </td>
    </tr>
  </table>
</asp:Content>
```

The `ListView` itself is composed of a table that is dynamically built as the `Poll` entities are bound to it. If the list of polls is less than needed to invoke paging the pager is suppressed from the bottom of the list.

Above the table are a couple of administrative links that are common in each of the Beer House module administrations. In the case of the Poll module, there are links to navigate to the `ManangePolls.aspx` page and to add a new poll via the AddEditPoll.aspx page. The Edit button on each poll's record is also a hyperlink to the `AddEditPoll.aspx` page, but it passes the `PollID`.

Notice the JavaScript added to the `Delete ImageButton`. It displays a confirmation `MessageBox` to the user before it executes the delete operation. Use this technique anyplace data is being deleted or affected in a major way.

The ManagePolls.aspx.vb Code-Behind File

In the code-behind for the `ManagePolls.aspx` page is the code to bind the polls to the `ListView`, `Delete`, and `Archive` selected polls. The `Page Load` event handler checks to see if this is a postback before binding the list of polls to the `ListView`. The `BindPolls` method uses a `PollsRepository` to get a list of polls and check whether the `ListView`'s `DataPager` should be visible:

```
Protected Sub Page_Load(ByVal sender As Object, ByVal e As System.EventArgs)
Handles Me.Load
        If Not IsPostBack Then
            BindPolls()
        End If
End Sub


Private Sub BindPolls()

Using Pollrpt As New PollsRepository

            Dim lPolls As List(Of Poll) = Pollrpt.GetPolls
            lvPolls.DataSource = lPolls
            lvPolls.DataBind()

            Dim pagerBottom As DataPager = lvPolls.FindControl("pagerBottom")

            If Not IsNothing(pagerBottom) Then
```

```
                If lPolls.Count <= pagerBottom.PageSize Then
                    pagerBottom.Visible = False
                Else
                    pagerBottom.Visible = True
                End If
            End If

        End Using

    End Sub
```

Each poll listed in the `ListView` has an archive and delete `ImageButton` on the row. When these buttons are clicked the `ListView`'s `ItemCommand` event is fired. Based on the command name associated with the `ImageButton`, the appropriate action is taken. Here's the event's code:

```
Private Sub lvPolls_ItemCommand(ByVal sender As Object, ByVal e As
System.Web.UI.WebControls.ListViewCommandEventArgs)
Handles lvPolls.ItemCommand

        Select Case e.CommandName
            Case "Delete"
                DeletePoll(e.CommandArgument)
            Case "Archive"
                ArchivePoll(e.CommandArgument)

        End Select

    End Sub
```

Both the `ArchivePoll` and `DeletePoll` methods use the associated methods of a `PollRepository` to execute the desired action:

```
Private Sub ArchivePoll(ByVal pollid As Integer)

        Using Pollrpt As New PollsRepository

            Pollrpt.ArchivePoll(pollid)

        End Using

    End Sub

Private Sub DeletePoll(ByVal pollId As Integer)

        Using Pollrpt As New PollsRepository

            Pollrpt.DeletePoll(pollId)

        End Using
```

```
        Me.BindPolls()
End Sub

Private Sub lvPolls_ItemDeleting(ByVal sender As Object,
ByVal e As System.Web.UI.WebControls.ListViewDeleteEventArgs)
Handles lvPolls.ItemDeleting
        DeletePoll(lvPolls.DataKeys(e.ItemIndex).Value)
End Sub
```

The AddEditPoll.aspx page

The AddEditPoll.aspx page (see Figure 6-7) provides the visual representation to manage the information about a poll, including the poll question and the associated poll options. When a new poll is being created, the poll options are suppressed until the poll question has been submitted. Once a poll exists, a list of editable poll options is displayed.

Figure 6-7

Figure 6-8 shows the page for editing an existing poll. Notice that the poll options are listed in a table on the right with the built-in capability to insert (add) a new option at the bottom of the list. Each option in the list can be edited by clicking the pencil, or deleted by clicking the trash can.

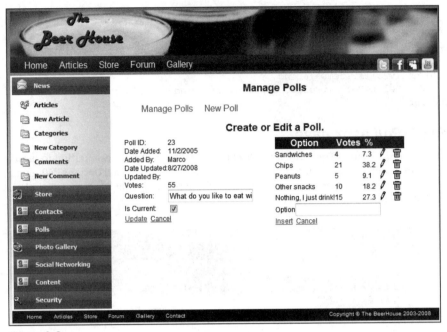

Figure 6-8

Editing the poll or a poll option can be canceled by clicking the associated Cancel hyperlink. When editing a poll is canceled, the administrator is taken to the `ManagePolls.aspx` page. When a poll option is canceled, the Option textbox is cleared.

The AddEditPoll.aspx.vb Code-Behind File

The code in the `AddEditPoll.aspx.vb` code-behind file that drives the managing of a specific poll is divided into two distinct sections, one related to the poll itself and one to manage the associated poll options. The `Page Load` event handler chooses either to bind the designated poll data to the corresponding controls or to clear the values for a new poll. If this is an edit operation, the `BindPollOptions` method is called to bind the associated options to a `ListView`. When the Update/Insert button is clicked by the administrator, the poll information is committed to the database.

```
Protected Sub Page_Load(ByVal sender As Object, ByVal e As System.EventArgs)
Handles Me.Load

    If Not IsPostBack Then

        If PollId > 0 Then
            BindPoll()
        Else
            ClearPoll()
        End If
    End If
End Sub
```

```
Private Sub BindPoll()

        Using Pollrpt As New PollsRepository

            Dim vPoll As Poll = Pollrpt.GetPollById(PollId)

            If Not IsNothing(vPoll) Then

                lblPollId.Text = vPoll.PollID
                lblDateAdded.Text = vPoll.AddedDate.ToShortDateString
                lblAddedBy.Text = vPoll.AddedBy
                lblDateUpdated.Text = vPoll.UpdatedDate.ToShortDateString
                lblUpdatedBy.Text = vPoll.UpdatedBy
                lblVotes.Text = vPoll.Votes
                txtQuestion.Text = vPoll.QuestionText
                cbIsCurrent.Checked = vPoll.IsCurrent

                BindPollOptions()

                lbtnInsertPoll.Text = "Update"

                tOptionDetail.Visible = True

            End If

        End Using

End Sub

Private Sub ClearPoll()

        lblPollId.Text = String.Empty
        lblDateAdded.Text = String.Empty
        lblAddedBy.Text = String.Empty
        lblDateUpdated.Text = String.Empty
        lblUpdatedBy.Text = String.Empty
        lblVotes.Text = String.Empty
        txtQuestion.Text = String.Empty
        cbIsCurrent.Checked = False
        lbtnInsertPoll.Text = "Insert"

        tOptionDetail.Visible = False

End Sub

Protected Sub lbtnInsertPoll_Click(ByVal sender As Object, ByVal e As EventArgs)
Handles lbtnInsertPoll.Click

        Using Pollrpt As New PollsRepository

            Dim vPoll As Poll = Pollrpt.GetPollById(PollId)

            If IsNothing(vPoll) Then
                vPoll = New Poll
```

```
            End If

            vPoll.QuestionText = txtQuestion.Text
            vPoll.IsCurrent = cbIsCurrent.Checked


            vPoll.UpdatedBy = UserName
            vPoll.UpdatedDate = Now

            If vPoll.PollID > 0 Then
                If Pollrpt.UpdatePoll(vPoll) Then
                    ltlStatus.Text = "The Poll Has Been Updated."
                Else
                    ltlStatus.Text = "The Poll Has Not Been Updated."
                End If
            Else
                vPoll.AddedBy = UserName
                vPoll.AddedDate = Now
                If Pollrpt.AddPoll(vPoll) Then
                    ltlStatus.Text = "The Poll Has Been Added."
                    tOptionDetail.Visible = True
                Else
                    ltlStatus.Text = "The Poll Has Not Been Added."
                End If
            End If

        End Using

End Sub
```

The poll options are bound to the ListView if an existing poll is being edited. If there are no options, a message lets the user know. As soon as a new option is added it is added to the option list. This list does not contain a pager because it is more feasible to have all the poll options listed on the page.

Updating or adding a poll option works just as with any other entity; if the option exists, the OptionText is updated and stored in the database. A new option is added to the database. The balance of the code manages deleting or selecting options from the ListView.

```
Private Sub BindPollOptions()

        Using PollOptionRpt As New PollOptionsRepository

            lvPollOptions.DataSource = PollOptionRpt.GetActivePollOptionsByPollId(
PollId)
            lvPollOptions.DataBind()

        End Using

End Sub

Protected Sub lbInsert_Click(ByVal sender As Object, ByVal e As EventArgs)
Handles lbInsert.Click
        UpdatePollOptions()
```

```
End Sub

Private Sub UpdatePollOptions()

        Using PollOptionsrpt As New PollOptionsRepository

            Dim lPollOption As PollOption

            If PollOptionId > 0 Then
                lPollOption = PollOptionsrpt.GetPollOptionById(PollOptionId)
            Else
                lPollOption = New PollOption()
            End If

            lPollOption.PollId = PollId
            lPollOption.OptionText = txtOption.Text

            lPollOption.UpdatedDate = Now
            lPollOption.UpdatedBy = UserName


            If lPollOption.OptionID > 0 Then
                If PollOptionsrpt.UpdatePollOption(lPollOption) Then
                    IndicateOptionUpdated()
                Else
                    IndicateOptionNotUpdated(PollOptionsrpt)
                End If
            Else
                lPollOption.Active = True
                lPollOption.AddedBy = UserName
                lPollOption.AddedDate = Now
                If PollOptionsrpt.AddPollOption(lPollOption) Then
                    IndicateOptionUpdated()
                Else
                    IndicateOptionNotUpdated(PollOptionsrpt)
                End If
            End If

            lbInsert.Text = "Insert"

        End Using

End Sub

Private Sub IndicateOptionNotUpdated(ByVal vRepository As BaseRepository)

        ltlStatus.Text = String.Empty
        If vRepository.ActiveExceptions.Count > 0 Then
            For Each kv As KeyValuePair(Of String, Exception) In
vRepository.ActiveExceptions
                ltlStatus.Text += DirectCast(kv.Value, Exception).Message & "<BR/>"
            Next
        Else
```

```
                    ltlStatus.Text = "The Option Has Not Been Updated."
            End If

    End Sub

    Private Sub IndicateOptionUpdated()
            ltlStatus.Text = "The Option Has Been Updated."
            '           cmdDelete.Visible = True
            txtOption.Text = String.Empty
            Me.BindPollOptions()
    End Sub

    Private Sub DeletePollOption(ByVal OptionId As Integer)
            Using PollOptionsrpt As New PollOptionsRepository
                PollOptionsrpt.DeletePollOption(PollOptionsrpt
    .GetPollOptionById(OptionId))
            End Using
            Me.BindPollOptions()
    End Sub

    Private Sub lvPollOptions_ItemDeleting(ByVal sender As Object, ByVal e As
    System.Web.UI.WebControls.ListViewDeleteEventArgs)
    Handles lvPollOptions.ItemDeleting
            DeletePollOption(lvPollOptions.DataKeys(e.ItemIndex).Value)
    End Sub

    Private Sub lvPollOptions_ItemEditing(ByVal sender As Object, ByVal e As
    System.Web.UI.WebControls.ListViewEditEventArgs)
    Handles lvPollOptions.ItemEditing
            PollOptionId = lvPollOptions.DataKeys(e.NewEditIndex).Value

            Using lPollOptionrpt As New PollOptionsRepository

            Dim lPollOption As PollOption =
    lPollOptionrpt.GetPollOptionById(PollOptionId)

                txtOption.Text = lPollOption.OptionText
                lbInsert.Text = "Update"

            End Using
    End Sub
```

The PollBox.ascx User Control

You'll plug the PollBox user control into the site's common layout (the master page). The PollBox.ascx user control is created under the ~/Controls folder, together with all other user controls.

This user control can be divided into four parts. The first defines a panel with an image and a label for the configurable header text. This content is placed into a Panel so that it can be hidden if the ShowHeader property is set to false. It also defines another label for the poll's question text. Here's the code:

```
<%@ Control Language="C#" AutoEventWireup="true" CodeFile="PollBox.ascx.cs"
 Inherits="PollBox" %>
<div class="pollbox">
```

```
<asp:Panel runat="server" ID="panHeader">
<div class="sectiontitle">
<asp:Image ID="imgArrow" runat="server" ImageUrl="~/images/arrowr.gif"
   style="float: left; margin-left: 3px; margin-right: 3px;"/>
<asp:Label runat="server" ID="lblHeader"></asp:Label>
</div>
</asp:Panel>
<div class="pollcontent">
<asp:Label runat="server" ID="lblQuestion" CssClass="pollquestion"></asp:Label>
```

The second part is a `Panel` to show when the poll box allows the user to vote (i.e., when it detects that the poll being shown is not archived, and the user has not already voted for it). The `Panel` contains a `RadioButtonList` to list the options, a `RequiredFieldValidator` that ensures that at least one option is selected when the form is submitted, and the button to do the postback:

```
<asp:Panel runat="server" ID="panVote">
   <div class="polloptions">
   <asp:RadioButtonList runat="server" ID="optlOptions"
      DataTextField="OptionText" DataValueField="ID" />
   <asp:RequiredFieldValidator ID="valRequireOption" runat="server"
      ControlToValidate="optlOptions" SetFocusOnError="true"
      Text="You must select an option." ToolTip="You must select an option"
      Display="Dynamic" ValidationGroup="PollVote"></asp:RequiredFieldValidator>
   </div>
   <asp:Button runat="server" ID="btnVote" ValidationGroup="PollVote"
      Text="Vote" OnClick="btnVote_Click" />
</asp:Panel>
```

The third part defines the `Panel` to be displayed when the control detects that the user has already voted for the current poll. In this situation, the control displays the results, which is done by means of a `Repeater` that outputs the option text and the number of votes it has received. It also creates a `<div>` element whose `width` style attribute is set to the option's `Percentage` value, so that the user will get a visual representation of the vote percentage, in addition to seeing the percentage as a number:

```
<asp:Panel runat="server" ID="panResults">
   <div class="polloptions">
<asp:ListView runat="server" ID="lvOptions">
<LayoutTemplate>
                        <div runat="server" id="itemPlaceHolder">
                        </div>
</LayoutTemplate>
<ItemSeparatorTemplate>
<img runat="server" src="~/Images/spacer.gif" height="5"
meta:resourcekey="imgSeparatorResource1"
                        alt="" /><br />
</ItemSeparatorTemplate>
<ItemTemplate>
<div>
                        <%# Eval("OptionText") %>
                        <small>(<%# Eval("Votes") %>
                            vote(s) -
                            <%# GetFixedPercentage(Eval("Votes"),
TotalVotes) %>
```

```
                                %)</small>
                             <br />
                      <div class="pollbar" style="width: <%#
GetFixedPercentage(Eval("Votes"), TotalVotes) %>%"> </div>
</div>
</ItemTemplate>
</asp:ListView>    <br />
    <b>Total votes: <asp:Label runat="server" ID="lblTotalVotes" /></b>
    </div>
</asp:Panel>
```

Finally, the last section of the control defines a link to the archive page, which can be hidden by means of the control's ShowArchiveLink custom property, plus a couple of closing tags for <div> elements opened earlier to associate some CSS styles to the various parts of the control:

```
<asp:HyperLink runat="server" ID="lnkArchive"
    NavigateUrl="~/ArchivedPolls.aspx" Text="Archived Polls" />
</div>
</div>
```

The PollBox.ascx.vb Code-Behind File

The PollBox.ascx control's code-behind file begins by defining all those custom properties described in the "Design" section. Most of these properties are just wrappers for the Text or Visible properties of inner labels and panels, so they don't need their values persisted:

```
Partial Public Class PollBox
    Inherits System.Web.UI.UserControl

#Region " Property "

    Private _pollID As Integer = -1

    <Personalizable(PersonalizationScope.Shared), _
        WebBrowsable(), _
        WebDisplayName("Show Archive Link"), _
        WebDescription("Specifies whether the link to the archive page is
displayed")> _
    Public Property ShowArchiveLink() As Boolean
        Get
            Return lnkArchive.Visible
        End Get
        Set(ByVal value As Boolean)
            lnkArchive.Visible = value
        End Set
    End Property

    Public Property ShowQuestion() As Boolean
        Get
            Return lblQuestion.Visible
        End Get
        Set(ByVal value As Boolean)
            lblQuestion.Visible = value
        End Set
```

```
          End Property

          Public Shared ReadOnly Settings As TheBeerHouseSection = Helpers.Settings

      #End Region
```

The PollID property does not wrap any other property, and therefore its value is manually stored in and retrieved from the control's state, as part of the control's ViewState collection. As already shown in previous chapters, this is done by overriding the control's LoadControlState and SaveControlState methods and registering the control to specify that it requires the control state, from inside the Init event handler:

```
          <Personalizable(PersonalizationScope.Shared), _
              WebBrowsable(), _
              WebDisplayName("Poll ID"), _
              WebDescription("The ID of the poll to show")> _
          Public Property PollID() As Integer
              Get
                  Return _pollID
              End Get
              Set(ByVal value As Integer)
                  _pollID = value
              End Set
          End Property

      Protected Sub Page_Init(ByVal sender As Object, ByVal e As System.EventArgs)
      Handles Me.Init
              Me.Page.RegisterRequiresControlState(Me)
      End Sub

      Protected Overrides Sub LoadControlState(ByVal savedState As Object)
              Dim ctlState() As Object = CType(savedState, Object())
              MyBase.LoadControlState(ctlState(0))
              Me.PollID = CInt(ctlState(1))
      End Sub

      Protected Overrides Function SaveControlState() As Object
              Dim ctlState() As Object
              ReDim ctlState(2)
              ctlState(0) = MyBase.SaveControlState()
              ctlState(1) = Me.PollID
              Return ctlState
      End Function
```

The control can be shown because it is explicitly defined on the page, or because it is dynamically created by some template-based control, such as ListView, Repeater, DataList, DataGrid, GridView, and DetailsView. In the first case, the code that loads and shows the response options (in either edit or display mode) will be run from the control's Load event handler. Otherwise, it will run from the control's DataBind method, which you can override. The code itself is placed in a separate method, DoBinding, and it's called from these two methods, as follows:

```
      Protected Sub Page_Load(ByVal sender As Object, ByVal e As System.EventArgs)
      Handles Me.Load
```

```
            If Not Me.IsPostBack Then DoBinding()
    End Sub

    Public Overrides Sub DataBind()
            ' the call to the base DataBind makes a call to OnDataBinding,
            ' which parses and evaluates the control's binding expressions, i.e.
    the PollID prop
            MyBase.DataBind()
            ' with the PollID set, do the actual binding
            DoBinding()
    End Sub
```

Note that in the `DataBind` method, the base version of `DataBind` is called before executing the custom binding code of `DoBinding`. The call to the base version, in turn, makes a call to the control's standard `OnDataBinding` method, which parses and evaluates the control's expressions. This is necessary because when the control is placed into a template, it will have the `PollID` property bound to some expression, and this binding expression must be evaluated before actually executing the `DoBinding` method, so that it will find the final `PollID` value.

The `DoBinding` method retrieves the data from the database (via the BLL), binds it to the proper `RadioButtonList` and the `Repeater` controls, and either shows or hides the options or results, depending on whether the user has already voted for the question being asked. However, before retrieving the poll and its options, it must check whether the `PollID` property is set to -1, in which case it must first retrieve the ID of the current poll:

```
    Public Property TotalVotes() As Integer
            Get
                If Not IsNothing(ViewState("TotalVotes")) AndAlso
    IsNumeric(ViewState("TotalVotes")) Then
                    Return CInt(ViewState("TotalVotes"))
                End If
                Return 0
            End Get
            Set(ByVal Value As Integer)
                ViewState("TotalVotes") = Value
            End Set
    End Property

    Protected Sub DoBinding()

            panResults.Visible = False
            panVote.Visible = False

            Using Pollrpty As New PollsRepository

                Dim lpollID As Integer = If(Me.PollID = -1, Pollrpty.CurrentPollID,
    Me.PollID)

                If lpollID > -1 Then

                    Dim lpoll As Poll = Pollrpty.GetPollById(lpollID, False)

                    If Not IsNothing(lpoll) Then

                        lblQuestion.Text = lpoll.QuestionText
```

```
                               TotalVotes = lpoll.Votes.ToString
                               lblTotalVotes.Text = TotalVotes
                               valRequireOption.ValidationGroup &= lpoll.PollID.ToString
                               btnVote.ValidationGroup = valRequireOption.ValidationGroup

                               If lpoll.IsArchived Or GetUserVote(lpollID) > 0 Then
                                   lvOptions.DataSource = lpoll.PollOptions
                                   lvOptions.DataBind()
                                   panResults.Visible = True
                               Else
                                   optlOptions.DataSource = lpoll.PollOptions
                                   optlOptions.DataBind()
                                   panVote.Visible = True
                               End If

                       End If

                  End If

          End Using

    End Sub
```

To check whether the current user has already voted for the poll, a call to the GetUserVote method is made. If the method returns a value greater than 0, it means that a vote for the specified poll was found. You'll see the code for this method in a moment, but first consider the code executed when the Vote button is clicked. The button's Click event handler calls the Poll.VoteOption business method to add a vote for the specified option (whose ID is read from the RadioButtonList's SelectedValue), and then shows the results panel and hides the edit panel. In order to remember that the user has voted for this poll, you create a cookie named Vote_Poll{x}, where {x} is the ID of the poll. The cookie's value is the ID of the option the user has voted for. The cookie is created only if the VotingLockByCookie configuration property is set to true (the default) and the cookie's expiration is set to the current date plus the number of days also stored in the <polls> custom configuration element (15 by default). Finally, it saves the votes in the cache (unless the VotingLockByIP setting is set to false), to ensure that it will be remembered at least for the current user's session even if the client has his cookies turned off. The cache's key is defined as {y}_Vote_Poll{x}, where {y} is replaced by the client's IP address. This is necessary because the Cache is not user-specific like session state, and thus you need to create different keys for different users. Here's the code of the Click event handler:

```
    Protected Sub btnVote_Click(ByVal sender As Object, ByVal e As System.EventArgs)
    Handles btnVote.Click

          Using Pollrpty As New PollsRepository

                  Dim lpollID As Integer = If(Me.PollID = -1, Pollrpty.CurrentPollID,
    Me.PollID)

                       ' check that the user has not already voted for this poll
                       Dim userVote As Integer = GetUserVote(lpollID)
                       If userVote = 0 Then
                           ' post the vote and then create a cookie to remember this user's vote
                           userVote = Convert.ToInt32(optlOptions.SelectedValue)

                           Using PollOptionRptry As New PollOptionsRepository
```

```
                    PollOptionRptry.Vote(userVote)
        End Using

        ' hide the panel with the radio buttons, and show the results
        DoBinding()
        panVote.Visible = False
        panResults.Visible = True

        Dim expireDate As DateTime = DateTime.Now.AddDays( _
            Settings.Polls.VotingLockInterval)
        Dim key As String = "Vote_Poll" & lpollID.ToString

        ' save the result to the cookie
        If Settings.Polls.VotingLockByCookie Then
            Dim cookie As New HttpCookie(key, userVote.ToString)
            cookie.Expires = expireDate
            Me.Response.Cookies.Add(cookie)
        End If

        ' save the vote also to the cache
        If Settings.Polls.VotingLockByIP Then
            Cache.Insert( _
                Me.Request.UserHostAddress.ToString & "_" & key, _
                userVote)
        End If
    End If

End Using

End Sub
```

The final piece of code is the GetUserVote method discussed earlier, which takes the ID of a poll, and checks whether it finds a vote in a client's cookie or in the cache, according to the VotingLockByCookie and VotingLockByIP settings, respectively. If no vote is found in either place, 0 is returned, indicating that the current user has not yet voted for the specified poll:

```
Protected Function GetUserVote(ByVal vpollID As Integer) As Integer
    Dim key As String = "Vote_Poll" & vpollID.ToString
    Dim key2 As String = Me.Request.UserHostAddress.ToString & "_" & key

    ' check if the vote is in the cache
    If Settings.Polls.VotingLockByIP And Not IsNothing(Cache(key2)) Then
        Return CInt(Cache(key2))
    End If

    ' if the vote is not in cache, check if there's a client-side cookie
    If Settings.Polls.VotingLockByCookie Then
        Dim cookie As HttpCookie = Me.Request.Cookies(key)
        If Not IsNothing(cookie) Then
            Return Integer.Parse(cookie.Value)
        End If
    End If

    Return 0
End Function
```

```
Protected Function GetFixedPercentage(ByVal vVotes As Integer,
ByVal vTotalVotes As Integer) As Integer
        Dim val As Double = (vVotes * 100) / If(vTotalVotes > 0, vTotalVotes, 1)
        Dim percentage As Integer = Convert.ToInt32(val)
        Select Case val
            Case 100
                percentage = 98
            Case -1
                percentage = 0
        End Select
        Return percentage
End Function
```

Plugging the PollBox Control into the Site's Layout

The PollBox user control is now ready, and you can finally plug it into any page. For this sample site we'll put it into the site's master page, so that the polls will be visible in all pages. As an example of adding more, you can add two PollBox instances to the master page: the first will have no PollID specified, so that it will dynamically use the current poll, and the second one has the PollID property set to a specific value so that it can reference a different poll and has the ShowArchiveLink property set to false to hide the link to the archive page, as it's already shown by the first poll box. Here's the code:

```
<%@ Register Src="Controls/PollBox.ascx" TagName="PollBox" TagPrefix="mb" %>
...
<mb:PollBox id="PollBox1" runat="server" HeaderText="Poll of the week" />
<mb:PollBox id="PollBox2" runat="server" HeaderText="More polls"
    PollID="18" ShowArchiveLink="False" />
```

Figure 6-9 shows the result: the home page with the two poll boxes displayed in the site's left-hand column. You can change the first poll simply by going to the administrative page and setting a different (existing or new) poll as the current one. If you want to change the second, you'll need to change the ID in the master page's source code file.

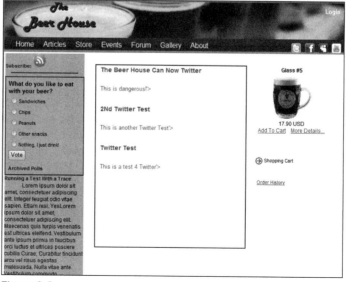

Figure 6-9

The ArchivedPolls.aspx Page

ArchivedPolls.aspx is the last page to develop for this module. It lists all archived polls, one per line, and when the user clicks one it has to expand and display its options and results. The page allows you to have multiple questions expanded at the same time if you prefer. It initially shows them in "collapsed" mode because you don't want to create a very long page, distracting users and making it hard for them to search for a particular question. Displaying the questions only when the page is first loaded produces a cleaner and more easily navigable page. If the current user is an administrator or an editor, she will also see command links on the right side of the listed polls to delete them. Figure 6-10 shows the page as seen by a normal anonymous user, with two of the three polls on the page expanded.

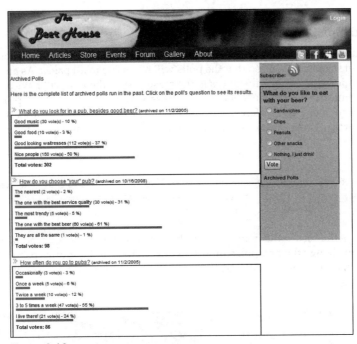

Figure 6-10

If you compare the poll results on the page's central section with the results of the poll in the left column, you'll notice that they look similar. Actually, they are nearly identical, except for the fact that in the former case the question text is shown as a link and not as bold text. As you can easily guess, the poll results rendered in the page's content section are created by PollBox controls, which have the ShowHeader, ShowQuestion, and ShowArchiveLink properties set to false. The link with the poll's text is created by a binding expression defined within the ItemTemplate of a parent ListView control. The PollBox control itself is defined inside the sample template section and has its PollID property set to a binding expression that retrieves the PollID value from the Poll object being bound to every row, and is wrapped by a <div> that is hidden by default (it has the display style attribute set to none). When the user clicks the link, he doesn't navigate to another page, but executes a local JavaScript function that takes the name of a <div> (named after poll{x}, where {x} is the ID of a poll) and toggles its display state (if set to none, it sets it to an empty string to make it visible, and vice versa). Following is the code for the JavaScript function, located in the TBH.js file, which hides and shows the <div> with the results:

```
function toggleDivState(divName)
{
   var ctl = window.document.getElementById(divName);
   if (ctl.style.display == "none")
      ctl.style.display = "";
   else
      ctl.style.display = "none";
}
```

Here is the HTML markup containing the ListView definition and other page information:

```
<div class="sectiontitle">Archived Polls</div>
<p>Here is the complete list of archived polls run in the past. Click on
the poll's question to see its results.</p>
<asp:ListView ID="lvPolls" runat="server" ItemPlaceholderID="itemPlaceHolder">
<LayoutTemplate>
        <div runat="server" id="itemPlaceHolder" />
    </LayoutTemplate>
    <ItemTemplate>
        <div>
            <img src="Images/ArrowR2.gif" />
            <a href="javascript:toggleDivState('poll<%# Eval("PollID") %>');">
                <%# Eval("QuestionText") %></a> <small>(archived on
                    <%# Eval("ArchivedDate", "{0:d}") %>)</small>
            <div style="display: none;" id="poll<%# Eval("PollID") %>">
                <uc1:PollBox ID="PollBox1" runat="server" PollID='
<%# Eval("PollID") %>' ShowHeader="False"
                    ShowQuestion="False" ShowArchiveLink="False" />
            </div>
            <asp:ImageButton runat="server" ID="ibtnDelete"
ImageUrl="~/Images/Delete.gif" CommandName ="Delete" />
        </div>
    </ItemTemplate>
    <EmptyDataTemplate>
        <div>
            <b>No polls to show</b></div>
    </EmptyDataTemplate>
</asp:ListView>
```

The ArchivedPolls.aspx.vb Code-Behind File

In the ListView just defined, an ImageButton is declared to create a Delete command for each of the listed polls. However, this command must be visible only to users who belong to the Editors and Administrators roles. When the page loads, if the user is not authorized to delete polls, then the delete ImageButton is hidden. Before doing this, however, you have to check whether the user is anonymous and, if so, whether the page is accessible to everyone or only to registered members. If the check fails, the `RequestLogin` method of the `BasePage` base class is called to redirect the user to the login page. Here's the code:

```
Protected Sub Page_Load(ByVal sender As Object, ByVal e As System.EventArgs)
Handles Me.Load
        If Not Me.User.Identity.IsAuthenticated AndAlso Not
Settings.Polls.ArchiveIsPublic Then
            Me.RequestLogin()
        End If

        If Not IsPostBack Then
            BindPolls()
        End If

End Sub
```

The list of archived polls is bound to the `ListView` by calling the `GetArchivedPolls` method of the `PollRepository` in a using statement.

```
Private Sub BindPolls()

        Using lPollrpty As New PollsRepository

            lvPolls.DataSource = lPollrpty.GetArchivedPolls
            lvPolls.DataBind()

        End Using

End Sub
```

The only other code in the code-behind file for this page is the event handler for the `ListView`'s `ItemCreated` event, from which you add the JavaScript confirmation pop-up to the `Delete` command buttons:

```
Private Sub lvPolls_ItemCreated(ByVal sender As Object, ByVal e As
System.Web.UI.WebControls.ListViewItemEventArgs) Handles
lvPolls.ItemCreated
        If e.Item.ItemType = ListViewItemType.DataItem Then
            Dim ibtnDelete As ImageButton = CType(e.Item
.FindControl("ibtnDelete"), ImageButton)

            ibtnDelete.Visible = Me.User.Identity.IsAuthenticated And _
                (Me.User.IsInRole("Administrators") Or Me.User.IsInRole("Editors"))

            ibtnDelete.OnClientClick = "if (confirm('Are you sure you want to
delete this poll?') == false) return false;"
        End If

End Sub
```

Summary

This chapter presents a working solution for handling multiple dynamic polls on your website. The complete polls module is made up of an administration console for managing the polls through a web browser, integration with the membership system to secure the administration and archive pages, and a user control that enables us to show different polls on any page using only a couple of lines of code. This module can easily be employed in many real-world sites as it is now, but of course you can expand and enhance it as desired. Here are a few suggestions:

- ❏ Add the capability to remind users which option they voted for. Currently, they can see the results, but the control does not indicate how they voted; the vote is stored in a cookie, which is easy to retrieve.

- ❏ Add a `ReleaseDate` and an `ExpireDate` to the polls, so that you can schedule the current poll to change automatically. We do this type of thing with the articles module.

- ❏ Provide the option to allow only registered users to vote.

- ❏ Expand the capabilities of the Poll module to create a survey by chaining questions together.

- ❏ Add the ability to let users register once they have completed a poll or survey for contest prizes.

- ❏ Allow voting to be multiple choice for selected questions.

In the next chapter, you continue the development of the TheBeerHouse site through the addition of another module that integrates with the rest of the site's architecture. The new module will be used for creating and sending out newsletters to users who subscribed to the newsletter at registration time.

7

Newsletters

In this chapter we'll design and implement a newsletter mailing list system that allows users to subscribe to online newsletters, and administrators to manage the newsletter content. First, we'll look at what newsletters can offer to web sites like the one developed in this book, and we'll examine the various management aspects that must be addressed in order to make the mailing list administrator's life as easy as possible. By the end of the chapter, we'll have a powerful newsletter module fully developed and integrated into our site.

Problem

Relationship marketing was developed back in the 1970s as a way to create a long term, more profitable customer relationship. It encourages customers to buy products and services from vendors with whom they have a long standing trust established. This relationship works best when there are competitive alternatives for the customer to choose from; for example, the Beer House competes with many other similar establishments for the same patrons.

The Beer House practices modern relationship marketing by letting customers create a profile and select different settings to reflect their preferences. One of those choices is to receive periodic newsletters. In today's competitive marketplace there needs to be more incentive for a user to visit the site than just announcing new web site content. Often this is in the form of a coupon and promotional and event announcements. Effective use of announcing things on social networking like Twitter and Facebook is great, but directly sending the information to existing customers compounds the chance of success. Many studies show that compound marketing efforts — using more than one medium to reach a customer — drastically increase positive response rates.

Part of good customer relations is managing how often you contact customers and of course which customers. We have already seen how profiles are used to allow customers to opt into the newsletter. We also need to keep track of what we have already sent and when. It is also a good idea not to over send promotional e-mails as this can become very annoying to customers and ultimately drive them away. For the purposes of the Beer House this can be accomplished with the basic administration structure we have already explained in previous chapters. Because the demands of the Beer House are relatively simple, displaying the dates newsletters were sent will suffice. In a more demanding scenario a scheduling mechanism might need to be employed that will que newsletters to be sent and automatically process them at the exact time desired.

In the previous version of the Beer House only one newsletter was allowed to be sent at once, which only makes sense from a marketing point of view. We are going to retain this feature, but change much of the user interface around sending newsletters. A newsletter module presents a great opportunity to explore how to send e-mail in .NET, how to run a long process on a background thread and how to use AJAX to monitor the progress of a long running background task. While there are many ways to execute the use of a newsletter, this chapter is going to stay focused on the technical requirements and leave the details of planning a complete marketing program around newsletters for an online marketing book, such as the *New Rules of Marketing and PR* by David Scott: (www.wiley.com/WileyCDA/WileyTitle/ productCd-0470379286.html).

Design

There are several issues that need to be addressed in a basic newsletter module, managing user subscriptions, sending e-mails and managing content. The previous edition of the Beer House took advantage of the Membership and Profile systems to track registered users who wanted to receive periodic newsletters from the Beer House. Since this is a very simple and adequate methodology this is not going to change. Sending e-mail can be a tricky thing to deal with programmatically; fortunately .NET offers a very rich set of classes to create and send messages. In particular it is pretty easy to create an e-mail message that contains both plain-text and HTML formatting by conforming to the e-mail RFCs and supporting multi-part MIME messages. Each user can also designate which format they would like to receive e-mail and have that stored as part of their profile.

Administering newsletters, sending them, and tracking those that have already been sent, this is going to be done by using the same Manage/AddEdit administration architecture we have used in previous chapters. One key difference is the use of a background thread and AJAX to send and monitor the progress of a newsletter. Because sending e-mail to a list can take a long time (for larger lists) there is no need for a page to be waiting on these e-mails to be sent when handing this task over to a background thread is a much better way to accomplish this task. Web servers are designed to receive requests for content and serve it up as quickly as possible. While this process can manage many long running tasks, often the request will hit a time threshold and timeout. This leaves the user hanging and ultimately unsure if the process completed or not.

Creating and Sending E-mails

The .NET framework has an entire namespace of classes devoted to managing e-mail communications, System.Net.Mail. While this namespace is composed of more than 60 classes, including all the Friend (VB.NET) or sealed (C#) classes (these are classes that cannot be accessed by us directly), we are only going to be concerned with the SMTPClient, MailMessage, and MailAddress classes. Before looking into how to use these classes to send e-mail there are some basic configuration settings that need to be made.

The system.net element in the web.config file can contain several child elements pertaining to configurations for objects within the namespace, but for our purposes we are going to focus on the mailSettings element, which contains one thing, the smtp section. Simple Mail Transport Protocol (SMTP, www.faqs.org/rfcs/rfc2554.html) is the protocol used to send e-mail. (Post Office Protocol (POP-3, www.faqs.org/rfcs/rfc1939.html) is the protocol used to check e-mail, which we won't cover because the Beer House site does not check e-mail.) Some configuration is needed so that things like the membership controls and the newsletter module can just send e-mail without having to explicitly set the values. While adding these values to web.config is not required to send e-mail, it is a great place to store it so you do not have to programmatically set it each place you need to send e-mail in the site. It does not mean you cannot also explicitly set the values at runtime.

The SMTPClient class has properties for both the Host and From addresses. The Host is either the DNS name of the server or its IP address used to send the e-mail. The From address is the e-mail address used to send the message, think of this as the return address on the envelope. An e-mail address is different from an e-mail account. Often addresses are aliases to accounts and the SMTP protocol does not care if the address is an account or an alias.

A lot of developers ask questions about sending e-mail and many times their problem lies with them not configuring the mailSettings in the config file. The primary issue is not configuring the Host, either because they are not aware they need to specify the host or they do not know what their SMTP host address is. Just because the classes exist to manage sending e-mail does not mean they automatically know which server to send the mail through; that has to be explicitly set somewhere. For small businesses like the Beer House the site is typically hosted in a shared hosting environment by a hosting provider. Generally the SMTP server address is supplied by the host as part of your setup or account information. In larger corporations you usually need to follow the IT department's SMTP policy, which includes using the designated SMTP server. Also, many IT departments have SMTP blocked except to and from the designated SMTP server. The main point is to know what SMTP server your site is supposed to use and add it to the web.config file as shown here, or set it at runtime:

```
<system.net>
<mailSettings>
<smtp from="thebeerhouse@wrox.com">
<network host="smtp.thebeerhouse.com"/>
</smtp>
</mailSettings>
</system.net>
```

Managing Long Operations on the Server

Sending groups of e-mails to a long list of recipients can be a time-consuming process that can tie up any user interface, even a desktop application. Web pages are designed to be a request and immediate response model. IIS or any web server is designed to timeout or kill the request if it takes too long to process. This helps keep the overhead on the server from getting out of control with an infinite loop, etc. It is also by design to help combat denile of service or other malicious attacks a site might see. A long list of e-mail recipients has a good chance at hitting the timeout threshold.

From a user's perspective seeing a blank web page is not very encouraging. Often a user will become frustrated and think they did something wrong, users need immediate feedback. Fortunately we can use background threads in ASP.NET to pass these long running tasks and AJAX to provide comforting feedback to the user confirming the process is working.

The `SMTPClient` class has built asynchronous methods to allow for e-mail to be sent on background threads, `SendAsync`, `SendAsyncCancel` and `SendCompleted`. These are good when sending a single message, but will throw an exception if a second message is attempted to be sent before the previous one has been sent. This is known as a blocking call. The Send method sends an e-mail synchronously, meaning the Send method keeps the application from executing the next line until the message has been sent. The SendAsynch moves the sending process to another thread and allows the next line to be called. While the SendAsynch may sound like the solution needed for the Newsletter module it actually is not because the sending process is already on a background thread.

Because the newsletter will be sent to a list of recipients, one after the other, taking the chance the SendAsynch has not completed gets a bit trickier. By sending the newsletter synchronously we can accurately increment the status of the newsletter progress, loop to the next recipient and send the next e-mail with confidence it will process correctly. The process that sends the newsletters is done on its own background thread.

Creating multithreaded applications can be very easy in .NET; the task of managing how a multithreaded application actually runs is the challenge on any platform. The `System.Threading` namespace is rich with classes to build such applications. The basic steps are as follows:

1. Create a `ThreadStart` delegate that points to the method that will run in the secondary thread. The method must return `void` and can't accept any input parameters.

2. Create a `Thread` object that takes the `ThreadStart` delegate in its constructor. You can also set a number of properties for this thread, such as its name (useful if you need to debug threads and identify them by name instead of by ID) and its priority. The `Priority` property, in particular, can be dangerous, because it can seriously affect the performance of the whole application. It's of type `ThreadPriority`, an enumeration, and by default it's set to `ThreadPriority.Normal`, which means that the primary thread and the secondary thread have the same priority, and the CPU time given to the process is equally divided between them. Other values of the `ThreadPriority` enumeration are `AboveNormal`, `BelowNormal`, `Highest`, and `Lowest`. In general, you should never assign the `Priority` property an `AboveNormal` or `Highest` value for a background thread. Instead, set the property to `BelowNormal`, so that the background thread doesn't slow down the primary thread any noticeable degree, and it won't interfere with ASP.NET.

3. Call the `Start` method of the `Thread` object. The thread starts, and you can control its lifetime from the thread that created it. For example, to affect the lifetime of the thread you can call the `Abort` method to start terminating the thread (in an asynchronous way), the `Join` method to make the primary thread wait until the secondary thread has completed, and the `IsAlive` property, which returns a Boolean value indicating whether the background thread is still running.

The following snippet shows how to start the `ExecuteTask` method, which can be used to perform a long task in a background thread:

```
' create and start a background thread
dim ts as new ThreadStart(Test)
Thread thread = new Thread(ts)
thread.Priority = ThreadPriority.BelowNormal
thread.Name = "TestThread"
thread.Start()
' main thread goes ahead immediately
```

```
...

' the method run asynchronously by the background thread
Public sub ExecuteTask()
    ' execute time consuming processing here
    ...
End sub
```

The Newsletter module only needs a fairly simple background thread to operate efficiently. The main problem lies in managing access to shared data between the user interface thread and the background process. The `ParameterizedThreadStart` delegate, which points to methods that take an object parameter, makes passing resources to a background thread fairly easy. Because an object can be anything, you can pass a custom object with properties that you define as parameters, or simply pass an array of objects if you prefer. The following snippet shows how you can call the `ExecuteTask` method and pass an array of objects to it, where the first object is a string, the second is an integer (that is boxed into an object), and the last is a `DateTime`. The `ExecuteTask` method takes the object parameter and casts it to a reference of type `object` array, and then it extracts the single values and casts them to the proper type, and finally performs the actual processing:

```
' create and start a background thread with some input parameters
Dim parameters As Object() = New Object() {"val1", 10, DateTime.Now}
Dim pts As New ParameterizedThreadStart(ExecuteTask)
Dim thread As New Thread(pts)
thread.Priority = ThreadPriority.BelowNormal
thread.Start(parameters)
' main thread goes ahead immediately
...


' the method run asynchronously by the background thread
Private Sub ExecuteTask(ByVal data As Object)
    ' extract the parameters from the input data object
    Dim parameters As Object() = DirectCast(data, Object())
    Dim val1 As String = DirectCast(parameters(0), String)
    Dim val2 As Integer = CInt(parameters(1))
    Dim val3 As DateTime = DirectCast(parameters(2), DateTime)

    ' execute time consuming processing here
    ...
End Sub
```

The most serious issue with multi-threaded programming is synchronizing access to shared resources. That is, if you have two threads reading and writing to the same variable, you must find some way to synchronize these operations so that one thread cannot read or write a variable while another thread is also writing it. If you don't take this into account, your program may produce unpredictable results and have strange behaviors, it may lock up at unpredictable times, and possibly even cause data integrity problems. A shared resource is any variable or field within the scope of the current method, including class-level public and private fields and static variables. The simplest way to synchronize access to these resources is through the `lock` statement. It takes a non-null object (i.e., a reference type — value types are *not* accepted), which must be accessible by all threads, and is typically a class-level field. The type of this object is not important, so many developers just use an instance of the root `System.Object` type for this purpose. You can simply declare an object field at the class level, assign it a reference to a new object, and use it from the methods running in different threads. Once the code enters a lock block, the execution must exit the block before another thread can enter a lock block for the same locking variable. Here's an example:

```
Private lockObj As New Object()
Private counter As Integer = 0

Private Sub MethodFromFirstThread()
    SyncLock lockObj
        counter = counter + 1
    End SyncLock
    ' some other work...
End Sub

Private Sub MethodFromSecondThread()
    SyncLock lockObj
        If counter >= 10 Then
            DoSomething()
        End If
    End SyncLock
End Sub
```

In many situations, however, you don't want to completely lock a shared resource against both read and write operations. That is, you normally allow multiple threads to read the same resource at the same time, but no write operation can be done from any thread while another thread is reading or writing the resource (multiple reads, but exclusive writes). To implement this type of lock, you use the ReaderWriterLock object, whose AcquireWriterLock method protects code following that method call against other reads or writes from other threads, until a call to ReleaseWriterLock is made. If you call AcquireReaderLock (not to be confused with AcquireWriterLock), another thread will be able to enter its own AcquireReaderLock block and read the same resources, but an AcquireWriterLock call would wait for all the other threads to call ReleaseReaderLock. Following is an example that shows how you can synchronize access to a shared field when you have two different threads that read it, and another one that writes it:

```
Public Shared Lock As New ReaderWriterLock()
Private counter As Integer = 0

Private Sub MethodFromFirstThread()
    Lock.AcquireWriterLock(Timeout.Infinite)
    counter = counter + 1
    Lock.ReleaseWriterLock()

    ' some other work...
End Sub

Private Sub MethodFromSecondThread()
    Lock.AcquireReaderLock(Timeout.Infinite)
    If counter >= 10 Then
        DoSomething()
    End If
    Lock.ReleaseReaderLock()
```

```
End Sub

Private Sub MethodFromThirdThread()
    Lock.AcquireReaderLock(Timeout.Infinite)
    If counter <> 50 Then
        DoSomethingElse()
    End If
    Lock.ReleaseReaderLock()
End Sub
```

In our specific case, you'll have a business class that runs a background thread to asynchronously send out the newsletters; after sending each mail, it updates a number of server-side variables that indicate the total number of mails to send, the number of mails already sent, the percentage of mails already sent, and whether the task has completed. Then, the web page from the presentation layer, and thus from a different thread, will read this information to update the status information on the client's screen. Because the information is shared between two threads, you'll need to synchronize the access, and the `ReaderWriterLock` will be used for this purpose.

> Multi-threaded programming is a very complex subject, and there are further considerations regarding the proper way to design code so that it performs well and doesn't cause deadlocks that may freeze the entire application. You should avoid creating too many threads if it's not strictly required, because the operating system and the thread scheduler (the portion of the OS that distributes the CPU time among the existing threads) consume CPU time and memory for managing them. There are also other classes that I haven't discussed here (such as `Monitor`, `Semaphore`, `Interlocked`, `ThreadPoll`, etc.) because they will not be necessary for implementing the solution of this specific module.

Designing the Database Tables

There is only one table in the Newsletter module, tbh_Newsletter (see Figure 7-1). There are fields to hold the subject, plainbody, HTML Body and a new field from the previous version `DateSent`. The remainder fields are the standard fields to track the reacord's activity. The `DateSent` field is nullable and holds the value for when the newsletter was actually sent.

Figure 7-1

Designing the Configuration Module

Like the other modules in this site, the newsletter module has its own configuration setting, which will be defined as attributes of the `<newsletter>` element under the `<theBeerHouse>` section in `web.config`. That element is mapped by a `NewsletterElement` class, which has the following properties:

Property	Description
ProviderType	The full name (namespace plus class name) of the concrete provider class that implements the data access code for a specific data store
ConnectionStringName	The name of the entry in `web.config`'s new `<connectionStrings>` section that contains the connection string to the module's database
EnableCaching	A Boolean value indicating whether the caching of data is enabled
CacheDuration	The number of seconds for which the data is cached if there aren't any inserts, deletes, or updates that invalidate the cache
FromEmail	The newsletter sender's e-mail address, used also as a reply address
FromDisplayName	The newsletter sender's display name, which will be shown by the e-mail client program
HideFromArchiveInterval	The number of days before a newsletter appears in the archive.
ArchiveIsPublic	A Boolean value indicating whether the polls archive is accessible by everyone, or restricted to registered members

The first four settings are common to all modules. You may argue that the sender's e-mail address can be read from the built-in `<mailSettings>` section of `web.config`, as shown earlier. However, that is usually set to the postmaster's or administrator's e-mail address, which is used to send service e-mails such as the confirmation for a new registration, the lost password e-mail, and the like. In other situations you may want to differentiate the sender's e-mail address, and use one for someone on your staff, so that if the user replies to an e-mail, his reply will actually be read. In the case of a newsletter, you may have a specific e-mail account, such as newseditor@contoso.com, used by your newsletter editor.

The `ArchiveIsPublic` property has the same meaning as the similarly named property found in the poll module's configuration class — it enables the administrator to decide whether the archived newsletters can be read only by registered members; she may want to set this to `True` to give users another reason to subscribe. `HideFromArchiveInterval` is also very important, because it allows you to decide how many days must pass before the newsletter just sent is available from the archive. If you set this property to zero, some users may decide not to subscribe to the newsletter, and just go to the archive occasionally to see it. If you set this to 15 instead (which is the default value), they will have to subscribe to the newsletter if they want to read it without waiting 15 days to see it in the archives.

Designing the User Interface Services

The last part of the design phase is to design the pages and user controls that make up the module's presentation layer. Here is list of the user interface files that we'll develop later in the "Solution" section:

❑ **~/Admin/AddEditNewsletter.aspx:** This page lets the administrator or editor send a newsletter to current subscribers. If another newsletter is already being sent when this page is first loaded, an error message appears instead of the normal form showing the other newsletter's subject and body, and a link to the page that displays that newsletter's progress. The page must also take into account situations in which no newsletter is being sent when the page loads, but later when the user clicks the Submit button to send this newsletter another newsletter is found to be under way at that time, because another user may have sent it from another location while the first editor was completing the form on her browser. In this case, the current newsletter is not sent and a message explaining the situation is shown, but the form showing the current newsletter's data is kept visible so that the data is not lost and can be sent later when the other newsletter has completed transmission. This page also allows viewing of previously sent newsletters, but not the editing of them.

❑ **~/Admin/ManageNewsletter.aspx:** This page simply lists all the newsletters that have been sent. It does not provide the ability to delete the newsletter, but does provide a link to view the content of the newsletter.

❑ **~/ArchivedNewsletters.aspx:** This page lists all past newsletters sent at least "x" days before the current date, where x is equal to the HideFromArchiveInterval custom configuration setting. Anonymous users will be able to access this page only if the ArchiveIsPublic setting is set to true in the web.config file's <newsletters> element, under the <theBeerHouse> section. The list of newsletters will show the date when each newsletter was sent and its subject. The subject is rendered as a link that points to another page showing the newsletter's entire content.

❑ **~/ShowNewsletter.aspx:** This page displays the full plain-text and HTML body of the newsletter whose ID is passed on the querystring.

❑ **~/Controls/NewsletterBox.ascx:** This user control determines whether the current site user is logged in; if not, it assumes she is not registered and not subscribed to the newsletter, and thus it displays a message inviting her to subscribe by typing her e-mail address into a textbox. When the user clicks the Submit button, the control redirects her to the Register.aspx page developed in Chapter 4, passing her e-mail on the querystring, so that Register.aspx will be able to read it and prefill its own e-mail textbox. If the user is already a member and is logged in, the control instead displays a message explaining that she can change her subscription type or cancel the subscription by going to the EditProfile.aspx page (also developed in Chapter 4) to which it links. In both cases, a link to the newsletter archive page is shown at the bottom of the control.

❑ **~/NewsLetterService.asmx:** While this is not a true user interface page, it is an interface used to both send a newsletter and check on the status of a newsletter being sent.

Solution

With all the features that are new and unique to the Newsletter module explained it is time to combine this knowledge with the patterns and features of the previous modules to create a fully functioning newsletter module.

Implementing the Configuration Module

The code for the `NewslettersElement` custom configuration element is found in the Config folder of the application's class library `ConfigSection.vb` file, together with the classes that map the other elements under the `<theBeerHouse>` section. Following is the whole class, which defines the properties listed in the design section, their default values, whether they are required or not, and their mapping to the respective attributes of the `<newsletters>` element:

```
Public Class NewslettersElement
    Inherits ConfigurationElement

    <ConfigurationProperty("connectionStringName")> _
    Public Property ConnectionStringName() As String
        Get
            Return CStr(Me("connectionStringName"))
        End Get
        Set(ByVal value As String)
            Me("connectionStringName") = value
        End Set
    End Property

    Public ReadOnly Property ConnectionString() As String
        Get
            Dim connStringName As String
            If String.IsNullOrEmpty(Me.ConnectionStringName) Then
                connStringName =
Globals.Settings.DefaultConnectionStringName
            Else
                connStringName = Me.ConnectionStringName
            End If
            Return WebConfigurationManager.ConnectionStrings( _
                connStringName).ConnectionString
        End Get
    End Property

    <Obsolete("No longer a factor with the Entity Framework.")> _
    Public Property ProviderType() As String
        Get
            Return CStr(Me("providerType"))
        End Get
        Set(ByVal value As String)
            Me("providerType") = value
        End Set
    End Property

    <ConfigurationProperty("fromEmail", IsRequired:=True)> _
```

```vbnet
    Public Property FromEmail() As String
        Get
            Return CStr(Me("fromEmail"))
        End Get
        Set(ByVal value As String)
            Me("fromEmail") = value
        End Set
    End Property

    <ConfigurationProperty("fromDisplayName", isrequired:=True)> _
    Public Property FromDisplayName() As String
        Get
            Return CStr(Me("fromDisplayName"))
        End Get
        Set(ByVal value As String)
            Me("fromDisplayName") = value
        End Set
    End Property

    <ConfigurationProperty("hideFromArchiveInterval", _
defaultvalue:="15")> _
    Public Property HideFromArchiveInterval() As Integer
        Get
            Return CInt(Me("hideFromArchiveInterval"))
        End Get
        Set(ByVal value As Integer)
            Me("hideFromArchiveInterval") = value
        End Set
    End Property

    <ConfigurationProperty("archiveIsPublic", defaultvalue:="false")> _
    Public Property ArchiveIsPublic() As Boolean
        Get
            Return CBool(Me("archiveIsPublic"))
        End Get
        Set(ByVal value As Boolean)
            Me("archiveIsPublic") = value
        End Set
    End Property

    <ConfigurationProperty("enableCaching", defaultvalue:="true")> _
    Public Property EnableCaching() As Boolean
        Get
            Return CBool(Me("enableCaching"))
        End Get
        Set(ByVal value As Boolean)
            Me("enableCaching") = value
        End Set
    End Property

    <ConfigurationProperty("cacheDuration")> _
    Public Property CacheDuration() As Integer
        Get
            Dim duration As Integer = CInt(Me("cacheDuration"))
```

375

```
                If duration > 0 Then
                    Return duration
                Else
                    Return Globals.Settings.DefaultCacheDuration
                End If
            End Get
            Set(ByVal value As Integer)
                Me("cacheDuration") = value
            End Set
        End Property

        <ConfigurationProperty("urlIndicator")> _
        Public Property URLIndicator() As String
            Get
                Dim lurlIndicator As String = Me("urlIndicator").ToString
                If String.IsNullOrEmpty(lurlIndicator) Then
                    lurlIndicator = "Newsletter"
                End If
                Return lurlIndicator
            End Get
            Set(ByVal Value As String)
                Me("urlIndicator") = Value
            End Set
        End Property

    End Class
```

A property named `Newsletters` of type `NewslettersElement` is added to the
`TheBeerHouseSection` (found in the same file), which maps the `<theBeerHouse>` section:

```
public class TheBeerHouseSection
Inherits ConfigurationSection
    ' other properties...

        <ConfigurationProperty("newsletters", IsRequired:=True)> _
        Public ReadOnly Property Newsletters() As NewslettersElement
            Get
                Return CType(Me("newsletters"), NewslettersElement)
            End Get
        End Property
End Class
```

Now you can go to the `web.config` file and configure the module with the attributes of the
`<newsletters>` element. The `SenderEmail` and `SenderDisplayName` are required, the others are
optional. The following extract shows how you can configure these two attributes, plus others that make
the archive public (it is not by default) and specify that 10 days must pass before a sent newsletter
appears in the archive:

```
<theBeerHouse defaultConnectionStringName="LocalSqlServer">
    <contactForm mailTo="mbellinaso@wrox.com"/>
    <articles pageSize="10" />
    <polls archiveIsPublic="true" votingLockByIP="false"  />
```

```
    <newsletters fromEmail="mbellinaso@wrox.com"
fromDisplayName="TheBeerHouse"
        archiveIsPublic="true" hideFromArchiveInterval="10" />
</theBeerHouse>
```

Implementing the Data Access Layer

Like the other chapters, the Newsletter module (see Figure 7-2) has a table that is mapped to a dedicated Entity Data Model, NewsletterModel.emdx. A corresponding repository (NewletterRepository) and entity extension class are also included to add the custom behavior needed for the Beer House application. Since there are no related tables to the tbh_Newsletters table, the only thing that needs to be done to the model created by the wizard is changing the name of the entity to Newsletter and the Entity Set Name to Newsletters.

Figure 7-2

Implementing the Business Logic Layer

The Newsletter's Business layer consists of the repository class, an extended entity class, NewsletterStatus class, SubscriberInfo class and SubscriptionType enum. The repository contains the normal CRUD methods that have been explained in the previous chapters, it does add some members to manage sending e-mails on a background thread. The Newsletter entity is extended by adding a few shared members to store information about an active newsletter during the e-mail process. The SubscriberInfo, NewsletterStatus and SubscriptionType enum are all helper classes to supplement the newsletter process.

Extending the Newsletter Entity

The Newsletter entity created by the Entity Data Model wizard is exending using a partial class to add shared (Static in C#) members used to monitor the status of a newsletter as it is being sent. The reason these members are shared is to make them available across threads; the values themselves will not be stored values for the newsletter.

The first member is a ReaderWriterLock, which is used to lock the values of the shared members across threads. A ReaderWriterLock is primarily used to synchronize access to a value across threads where the value is mostly read. This lock will be acquired anytime we are reading or writing to any of the Newletter shared members. I will discuss this more process in more detail in the repository section.

The next four members are all properties used to track the status of an active newsletter as it is being sent. The IsSending member is a Boolean that indicates if there is an active newsletter being sent. The TotalMails property indicates how many e-mails are ging sent with the active newsletter. Similarly SentMails is the number of e-mails sent during the active process; it is incremented as each e-mail is sent. Finally the PercentageComplete property is ReadOnly member that is calculated by dividing the number of SentMails by the TotalMails value. If there are no TotalMail, meaning there is no active newsletter at the moment, it returns zero. Otherwise it would cause a divide by zero exception.

```
Public Shared Lock As New ReaderWriterLock

Private Shared _isSending As Boolean = False
Public Shared Property IsSending() As Boolean
    Get
        Return _isSending
    End Get
    Set(ByVal value As Boolean)
        _isSending = value
    End Set
End Property

Public Shared ReadOnly Property PercentageCompleted() As Double
    Get
        If TotalMails = 0 Then
            Return 0D
        End If
        Return CDbl(SentMails) * 100 / CDbl(TotalMails)
    End Get
End Property

Private Shared _totalMails As Integer = -1
Public Shared Property TotalMails() As Integer
    Get
        Return _totalMails
    End Get
    Set(ByVal value As Integer)
        _totalMails = value
    End Set
End Property

Private Shared _sentMails As Integer = 0
Public Shared Property SentMails() As Integer
    Get
        Return _sentMails
    End Get
    Set(ByVal value As Integer)
        _sentMails = value
    End Set
End Property
```

Implementing the NewslettersRepository

The common CRUD operations are including in the `NewslettersRepository` and follow the patterns we have already reviewed. The repository does contain four extra members, two to manage sending e-mails and two methods to customize the message to the user.

The `HasPersonalizationPlaceholders` method reviews a string to determine if there are any customization placeholders in the text. It uses a set of regular expressions to see if there are any matches to a series of personalization placeholders in the text. There are four personalization placeholders that can be added to the newsletter: <username>, <email>, <firstname> and <lastname>. As they are entered in the body of the message they are added with the <> brackets on each side of the placeholder. The method also accepts the `isHtml` parameter to indicate if the string should be evaluated as HTML or plain text, an important distinction. The <> characters are HTML encoded, or changed to < and > respectively to avoid any parser confusion with the same characters being used as delimiters in HTML markup.

As the string is passed through the method, it is matched against the appropriate expressions for each placeholder. If a match is found the method immediately returns true and does not check the remaining placeholders. Since the main purpose of the method is to simply check to see if there are any placeholders to replace, as soon as one is found return true, saving processor cycles.

```
Private Shared Function HasPersonalizationPlaceholders(ByVal text _
As String, ByVal isHtml As Boolean) As Boolean
        If isHtml Then
            If Regex.IsMatch(text, "&lt;%\s*username\s*%&gt;", _
 RegexOptions.IgnoreCase Or _
                RegexOptions.Compiled) Then
                Return True
            End If
            If Regex.IsMatch(text, "&lt;%\s*email\s*%&gt;", _
RegexOptions.IgnoreCase Or _
                RegexOptions.Compiled) Then
                Return True
            End If
            If Regex.IsMatch(text, "&lt;%\s*firstname\s*%&gt;", _
RegexOptions.IgnoreCase Or _
                RegexOptions.Compiled) Then
                Return True
            End If
            If Regex.IsMatch(text, "&lt;%\s*lastname\s*%&gt;", _
 RegexOptions.IgnoreCase Or _
                RegexOptions.Compiled) Then
                Return True
            End If
        Else
            If Regex.IsMatch(text, "<%\s*username\s*%>", _
RegexOptions.IgnoreCase Or _
                RegexOptions.Compiled) Then
                Return True
            End If
```

```
                    If Regex.IsMatch(text, "<%\s*email\s*%>",
RegexOptions.IgnoreCase Or _
                       RegexOptions.Compiled) Then
                       Return True
                   End If
                   If Regex.IsMatch(text, "<%\s*firstname\s*%>",
RegexOptions.IgnoreCase Or _
                       RegexOptions.Compiled) Then
                       Return True
                   End If
                   If Regex.IsMatch(text, "<%\s*lastname\s*%>",
RegexOptions.IgnoreCase Or _
                       RegexOptions.Compiled) Then
                       Return True
                   End If
               End If
               Return False
           End Function
```

If there is a match found for any of the placeholders, then the ReplacePersonalizationPlaceholders method is called. You should note you do not have to call HasPersonalizationPlaceholders before calling ReplacePersonalizationPlaceholders, because the regular expressions used to perform the placeholder replacements will not replace any text that does not match the placeholders.

Again a set of regular expressions are used to process the text, but instead of looking for matches the RegEx is used to performa a replace operation. Regular Expressions, RegEx in .NET, are great to process a string and perform tasks like replace based on a pattern, instead of a set string. Using a Regex .Replace to perform a toke replacement, like being done in the ReplacePersonalizationPlaceholders method is more ideal because the String.Replace method does not match patterns, but instead the exact string being passed. Regular expressions also tend to perform much faster than methods like Replace, Contains, etc in the String class. *Beginning Regular Expressions*, www.wiley.com/WileyCDA/ WileyTitle/productCd-0764574892.html is a good place to start learning about regular expressions. www.Regexlib.com is one of the primary online resources for regular expressions in the .NET world and a definite site to bookmark.

```
    Private Shared Function ReplacePersonalizationPlaceholders(ByVal
    text As String, _
            ByVal subscriber As SubscriberInfo, ByVal isHtml As
    Boolean) As String

            If isHtml Then
                text = Regex.Replace(text, "&lt;%\s*username\s*%&gt;", _
                    subscriber.UserName, RegexOptions.IgnoreCase Or
    RegexOptions.Compiled)
                text = Regex.Replace(text, "&lt;%\s*email\s*%&gt;", _
                    subscriber.Email, RegexOptions.IgnoreCase Or
    RegexOptions.Compiled)
                Dim firstName As String = "reader"
                If subscriber.FirstName.Length > 0 Then
                    firstName = subscriber.FirstName
                End If
                text = Regex.Replace(text, "&lt;%\s*firstname\s*%&gt;",
    firstName, _
```

```
                    RegexOptions.IgnoreCase Or RegexOptions.Compiled)
            text = Regex.Replace(text, "&lt;%\s*lastname\s*%&gt;", _
                subscriber.LastName, RegexOptions.IgnoreCase Or
RegexOptions.Compiled)
        Else
            text = Regex.Replace(text, "<%\s*username\s*%>", _
                subscriber.UserName, RegexOptions.IgnoreCase Or
RegexOptions.Compiled)
            text = Regex.Replace(text, "<%\s*email\s*%>", _
                subscriber.Email, RegexOptions.IgnoreCase Or
RegexOptions.Compiled)
            Dim firstName As String = "reader"
            If subscriber.FirstName.Length > 0 Then
                firstName = subscriber.FirstName
            End If
            text = Regex.Replace(text, "<%\s*firstname\s*%>",
firstName, _
                RegexOptions.IgnoreCase Or RegexOptions.Compiled)
            text = Regex.Replace(text, "<%\s*lastname\s*%>", _
                subscriber.LastName, RegexOptions.IgnoreCase Or
RegexOptions.Compiled)
        End If
        Return text
    End Function
```

The worker methods in the `NewlettersRepository` are `SendNewsletter` and `SendEMails`. The `SendNewsletter` function accepts a `Newsletter` object and uses it to create a background thread to send a newsletter. First it creates a Writer Lock on the newsletter to initialize the the values used to track the progress of the newsletter as it is e-mailed to its recipients. Calling the `AquireWriterLock` method creates a lock where all attempts to read or write to the Newsletter's shared members will be blocked or this method will wait until other locks have been released. The writer lock is released by calling the `ReleaseWriterLock`.

After initializing the shared members an array of parameters is created to hold the values that comprise the newsletter, Subject, plainBody, HTMLBody and the current context of the request. These values are passed as a generic object to the constructor of a `ParameteriedThreadStart` object; this makes these values available to the `SendEmails` method once the thread is started.

```
Public Shared Function SendNewsletter(ByVal vNewsLetter As
Newsletter) As Integer

        If Not IsNothing(vNewsLetter) Then

            Newsletter.Lock.AcquireWriterLock(Timeout.Infinite)
            Newsletter.TotalMails = -1
            Newsletter.SentMails = 0
            Newsletter.IsSending = True
            Newsletter.Lock.ReleaseWriterLock()

            ' send the newsletters asyncronously
            Dim parameters() As Object = {vNewsLetter.Subject,
 vNewsLetter.PlainTextBody, vNewsLetter.HtmlBody, HttpContext.Current}
            Dim pts As New ParameterizedThreadStart(AddressOf
SendEmails)
```

```
                    Dim thread As New Thread(pts)
                    thread.Name = "SendEmails"
                    thread.Priority = ThreadPriority.BelowNormal
                    thread.Start(parameters)

            End If

    End Function
```

The `SendEmails` method performs the task of sending a copy of the newsletter to all the subscribers. It takes the data passed from the `SendNewsletter` method and parses it to use in building the messages. Before any e-mails are set the `TotalMails` value is set to an initial value of 0. The next step is to replace any personalization values. Next a loop is performed to check every member's profile to see if they have subscribed to receive newsletters; if so new SubscriberInfo object is created for the member and added to a list of recipients. As recipients are added to the list, the `TotalMails` value is incremented.

```
Public Shared Sub SendEmails(ByVal data As Object)

            Dim parameters() As Object = CType(data, Object())
            Dim subject As String = CStr(parameters(0))
            Dim plainTextBody As String = CStr(parameters(1))
            Dim htmlBody As String = CStr(parameters(2))
            Dim context As HttpContext = CType(parameters(3), HttpContext)

            Newsletter.Lock.AcquireWriterLock(Timeout.Infinite)
            Newsletter.TotalMails = 0
            Newsletter.Lock.ReleaseWriterLock()

            ' check if the plain-text and HTML bodies have
personalization placeholders
            ' the will need to be replaced on a per-mail basis. If not,
the parsing will
            ' be completely avoided later.
            Dim plainTextIsPersonalized As Boolean =
HasPersonalizationPlaceholders(plainTextBody, False)
            Dim htmlIsPersonalized As Boolean =
HasPersonalizationPlaceholders(htmlBody, True)
```

The final step is actually sending the e-mails. A new `SMTPClient` class is created. Then the list of subscribers is looped through and an individual e-mail is created and sent to them. Instead of using the from address defined in the `system.net` element of the web.config file, the from address defined in the Newsletter custom configuration section is used. The reason you might want the newsletters to originate from a different address than the overall site address is to give them a unique source, since it is a dedicated purpose.

Each subscriber is checked to see what type of e-mail they have requested plain text or HTML and assign the message's body appropriately. If the subscriber wants HTML e-mails then the `IsBodyHTML` property is set to true, otherwise it is false. Any personalization placeholders are also set. This information is stored in the `SubscriberInfo` class, a helper class used here to hold the nessecary information for each subscriber. The `SubscriberInfo` class has 5 public members; `Username`, `Email`, `FirestName`, `LastName` and `SubscriptionType` and a single constructor that accepts and sets all these values.

```
                ' retreive all subscribers to the plain-text and HTML
newsletter
                Dim subscribers As New List(Of SubscriberInfo)
                Dim profile As ProfileBase = CType(context.Profile,
ProfileBase)

                For Each user As MembershipUser In Membership.GetAllUsers
                    Dim userProfile As ProfileBase =
Helpers.GetUserProfile(user.UserName, False)
                    If Not Helpers.GetSubscriptionType(userProfile) <>
SubscriptionType.None Then
                        Dim subscriber As New SubscriberInfo(user.UserName,
user.Email, _
                        Helpers.GetProfileFirstName(userProfile), _
                        Helpers.GetProfileLastName(userProfile),
 Helpers.GetSubscriptionType(userProfile))
                        subscribers.Add(subscriber)
                        Newsletter.Lock.AcquireWriterLock(Timeout.Infinite)
                        Newsletter.TotalMails += 1
                        Newsletter.Lock.ReleaseWriterLock()
                    End If
                Next
```

Once all the MailMessage values have been set the message is sent using the synchronous Send member of the SMTPClient. As each message is sent the SentEmails value is incremented. Once all the messages have been sent the isSending property is set to false, allowing any other newsletters to be sent.

```
                ' send the newsletter
                Dim smtpClient As New Net.Mail.SmtpClient

                For Each subscriber As SubscriberInfo In subscribers
                    Dim mail As New MailMessage
                    mail.From = New MailAddress(
Helpers.Settings.Newsletters.FromEmail, _
                            Helpers.Settings.Newsletters.FromDisplayName)
                    mail.To.Add(subscriber.Email)
                    mail.Subject = subject
                    If subscriber.SubscriptionType =
SubscriptionType.PlainText Then
                        Dim body As String = plainTextBody
                        If plainTextIsPersonalized Then
                            body = ReplacePersonalizationPlaceholders(body,
subscriber, False)
                        End If
                        mail.Body = body
                        mail.IsBodyHtml = False
                    Else
                        Dim body As String = htmlBody
                        If htmlIsPersonalized Then
                            body = ReplacePersonalizationPlaceholders(body,
subscriber, True)
                        End If
                        mail.Body = body
                        mail.IsBodyHtml = True
```

```
                    End If
                    Try
                        smtpClient.Send(mail)
                    Catch

                    End Try

                    Newsletter.Lock.AcquireWriterLock(Timeout.Infinite)
                    Newsletter.SentMails += 1
                    Newsletter.Lock.ReleaseWriterLock()

                Next

                Newsletter.Lock.AcquireWriterLock(Timeout.Infinite)
                Newsletter.IsSending = False
                Newsletter.Lock.ReleaseWriterLock()

            End Sub
```

Implementing the User Interface

In this last part of the "Solution" section you'll implement the administration pages for sending out a newsletter and checking its progress, as well as the end-user pages that display the list of archived newsletters, and the content of a specific newsletter. Finally, there is the NewsletterBox user control that you will plug into the site's master page, which creates a subscription box and a link to the archive page.

The AddEditNewsletter.aspx Page

The AddEditNewsletter.asp page serves the same purpose as its sibling pages that allow administrators to edit individual records. It does differ drastically because it also sends newsletters to subscribers and provides real-time feedback on the progress of the process. One feature added to the newsletter is the capability to save a newsletter without sending it, so it can be retrieved later.

First let's review the layout of the page. It has two main panels, panSend and panWait. The first panel contains all the controls to edit a newsletter or view its contents after it has been sent. The panWait is displayed if there is an active newsletter being sent and provides continual progress updates. The Page Load event handler checks to see if a newsletter is being sent. If this is a request to edit an existing newsletter the page shows the appropriate edit fields with the stored information ready to edit. If this is a new newsletter request and one is currently being sent, the panWait panel is displayed and the progress of the current newsletter begins updating. Otherwise a clean page to create a new newsletter is rendered.

```
        Protected Sub Page_Load(ByVal sender As Object, ByVal e As
        System.EventArgs) Handles Me.Load

            If Not Me.IsPostBack Then

                Dim isSending As Boolean = False
                Newsletter.Lock.AcquireReaderLock(Timeout.Infinite)
                isSending = Newsletter.IsSending
                Newsletter.Lock.ReleaseReaderLock()
```

```
                    If NewsLetterId > 0 Then
                        BindNewsletter()
                    ElseIf isSending Then
                        ShowSending()
                    Else
                        ClearInfo()
                    End If

                End If
                txtHtmlBody.BasePath = Me.BaseUrl + "FCKeditor/"
        End Sub
```

The `panSend` contains a set of parallel controls to receive the newsletter subject, plain body and HTML body (see Figure 7-3). For each input control there is also a `Literal` control to display the values once the newsletter has been sent. The HTML body is created using the `FCKeditor`. This panel also contains two buttons, one to save and submit and the other to just save the newsletter.

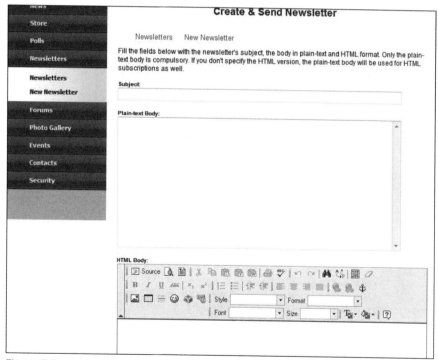

Figure 7-3

```
        <asp:Panel runat="server" ID="panSend">
                <asp:Literal runat="server" ID=
"ltlAddInstruction"></asp:Literal>
                Fill the fields below with the newsletter's subject,
the body in plain-text and
                HTML format. Only the plain-text body is compulsory.
```

If you don't specify the HTML
version, the plain-text body will be used for HTML
subscriptions as well.

```
            <asp:Literal runat="server" ID="ltlDateSent"></asp:Literal>
            <br />
            <br />
            <small><b>
                <asp:Literal runat="server" ID="lblTitle"
Text="Subject:" /></b></small><br />
            <asp:Literal ID="ltlSubject" runat="server"></asp:Literal>
            <asp:TextBox ID="txtSubject" runat="server"
MaxLength="256" Width="90%"></asp:TextBox>
            <asp:RequiredFieldValidator ID="valRequireSubject"
runat="server" ControlToValidate="txtSubject"
                Display="Dynamic" ErrorMessage="RequiredFieldValidator"
 SetFocusOnError="True"
                ValidationGroup="Newsletter">The Subject field
is required.</asp:RequiredFieldValidator>
            <br />
            <br />
            <small><b>
                <asp:Literal runat="server" ID="lblPlainTextBody"
Text="Plain-text Body:" /></b></small><br />
            <asp:Literal ID="ltlPlainTextBody"
runat="server"></asp:Literal>
            <asp:TextBox ID="txtPlainTextBody" runat="server"
Rows="14" TextMode="MultiLine"
                Width="90%"></asp:TextBox>
            <asp:RequiredFieldValidator ID="valRequirePlainTextBody"
runat="server" ControlToValidate="txtPlainTextBody"
                Display="Dynamic" ErrorMessage="RequiredFieldValidator"
 SetFocusOnError="True"
                ValidationGroup="Newsletter">The plain-text body
is required.</asp:RequiredFieldValidator>
            <br />
            <br />
            <small><b>
                <asp:Literal runat="server" ID="lblHtmlBody"
Text="HTML Body:" /></b></small><br />
            <asp:Literal ID="ltlHtmlBody" runat="server"></asp:Literal>
            <FCKeditorV2:FCKeditor ID="txtHtmlBody" runat="server"
Height="400px" ToolbarSet="TheBeerHouse">
            </FCKeditorV2:FCKeditor>
            <br />
            <br />
            <asp:Button ID="btnSave" runat="server" Text="Save"/>
            <asp:Button ID="btnSend" runat="server" Text="Send"
OnClientClick="if (confirm('Are you sure you want to send the
newsletter?') == false) return false;"
                ValidationGroup="Newsletter" />
        </asp:Panel>
```

Note that there are RequiredFieldValidators for the subject and plain body TextBoxes force input in each of these fields before a newsletter can be saved or sent. If there is no HTML body specified, the plain text version will be used for the HTML versions. The send button also has JavaScript to display a confirmation dialog to ask the user to confirm they want to send the newsletter. This saves the user from accidentally sending a newsletter instead of just saving it. This can be a real-life issue that can lead to some real problems if a draft is accidentally sent to subscribers. While the confirmation dialog is not fool-proof, it does provide a small layer of protection against this issue.

Figure 7-4 shows how the page is rendered for a newsletter that has been saved. The TextBox and FCKEditor are replaced with Literal controls and the plain and HTML versions of the newsletter are displayed with a yellow background.

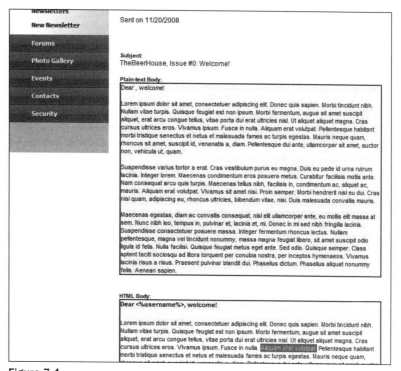

Figure 7-4

The `panWait` contains a series of DIV elements that will be used to display a progress bar as each of the e-mails is sent and the `SentMails` value is incremented. The `dProgress` DIV will have a text value that is set via JavaScript as it checks the progress of the newsletter. The progess bar is incremented by an AJAX driven script that periodically checks the progress of the newsletter and changes the style of the `progressbar` DIV element.

```
<asp:Panel ID="panWait" runat="server" Visible="false">
    <p>
        Another newsletter is currently being sent.
Please wait until it completes before
        compiling and sending a new one.</p>
    <div>
        <div id="dIsSending">
```

```
                    Checking to see if sending a NewsLetter....
                </div>
                <div id="dProgress">
                </div>
                <br />
                <div class="progressbarcontainer">
                    <div class="progressbar" id="progressbar">
                    </div>
                </div>
            </div>
        </asp:Panel>
```

Just like we examined with article comments, we can use AJAX to call a web service to monitor the progress of the newsletter and update the progressbar and dProgress DIV. The NewsletterService. asmx has one member, GetNewsletterStatus which returns a NewsletterStatus object with updated values using JSON. JSON stands for JavaScript Object Notation and is a lightweight data interchange format often used with AJAX to perform communication with the server. Traditionally web services transmit data using large XML data structures; JSON on the other hand uses a simple delineation schema to transmit data between a client and the server. It is defined in RFC 4627, www.ietf.org/mail-archive/web/ietf-announce/current/msg02778.html. You can also learn more about JSON at www.json.org. ASP.NET AJAX and .NET web services automatically serialize and deserialize objects using JSON when exchanging data between a client and the server.

```
<WebMethod()> _
<ScriptMethod()> _
Public Function GetNewsLetterStatus() As NewsletterStatus

        Dim lNewsletterStatus As New NewsletterStatus

        Newsletter.Lock.AcquireReaderLock(Timeout.Infinite)

        lNewsletterStatus.SentMails = Newsletter.SentMails
        lNewsletterStatus.TotalMails = Newsletter.TotalMails
        lNewsletterStatus.IsSending = Newsletter.IsSending

        Newsletter.Lock.ReleaseReaderLock()

        Return lNewsletterStatus

End Function
```

The Newsletter module also has its own JavaScript file, "~/scripts/Newsletter.js" that calls the GetNewsletterStatus method and updates the page. The function UpdateStatus calls the web services and assings the GetNewsletterStatus callback method to be used when the call to the web service completes.

```
function UpdateStatus() {
    NewsLetterService.GetNewsLetterStatus(GetNewsLetterStatusCompleted);
}
```

The GetNewsletterStatusCompleted function accepts the result, which is actually a NewsletterStatus object. The NewsletterStatus is another helper class used explicitly to send status information from the server through the web service to the page via AJAX. It is a class that contains 4 properties to report the number of e-mails, total sent, percentage sent and if a newsletter is being sent currently.

```vbnet
Public Class NewsletterStatus

    Private _isSending As Boolean = False
    Public Property IsSending() As Boolean
        Get
            Return _isSending
        End Get
        Set(ByVal value As Boolean)
            _isSending = value
        End Set
    End Property

    Public ReadOnly Property PercentageCompleted() As Double
        Get
            If TotalMails = 0 Then
                Return 0D
            End If
            Return CDbl(SentMails) * 100 / CDbl(TotalMails)
        End Get
    End Property

    Private _totalMails As Integer = -1
    Public Property TotalMails() As Integer
        Get
            Return _totalMails
        End Get
        Set(ByVal value As Integer)
            _totalMails = value
        End Set
    End Property

    Private _sentMails As Integer = 0
    Public Property SentMails() As Integer
        Get
            Return _sentMails
        End Get
        Set(ByVal value As Integer)
            _sentMails = value
        End Set
    End Property

End Class
```

The function takes these values and sets the width in perecent of the progressbar DIV and the text of the dIsSending DIV to verbally indicate the progress of the newsletter. Finally, as long as a newsletter is being sent the function sets a timer to call the UpdateStatus function in 5 seconds. This time can be adjusted to be faster or slower depending on the actual situation. For newsletters with fewer subscribers maybe a 1 second interval would be more desirable since it will not take long for the process to execute.

```
function GetNewsLetterStatusCompleted(result) {

    var lNewsletterStatus = result;

    var percentage = lNewsletterStatus.PercentageCompleted;
    var sentMails = lNewsletterStatus.SentMails;
    var totalMails = lNewsletterStatus.TotalMails;
    var isSending = lNewsletterStatus.IsSending;

    if (totalMails < 0)
        totalMails = '???';

    var dIsSending = $get('dIsSending');
    var progBar = $get('progressbar');

    progBar.style.width = percentage + '%';
    dIsSending.innerHTML = '<b>' + percentage + '% Complete: '
        '<b><br/>' + sentMails + ' out of ' + totalMails + '
emails have been sent.';

    if (isSending) {
        dIsSending.innerHTML = dIsSending.innerHTML + '<br/>Currently
sending a NewsLetter....';
        setTimeout(UpdateStatus, 5000);
    } else {
    dIsSending.innerHTML = dIsSending.innerHTML + '<br/>
Not sending a NewsLetter....';
    }

}
```

Using a tool like Fiddler, www.fiddlertools.com, you can examine the data travelling between the browser and the server. Below is the JSON returned from the server in response to a status update request. There is no data passed from the client in this case because the GetNewsletterStatus accepts no parameters.

{"d":{"__type":"TheBeerHouse.NewsletterStatus","IsSending":true,
"PercentageCompleted":20,"TotalMails":20,"SentMails":4}}

As the progress bar is expanded, beer mugs are displayed (see Figure 7-5). I thought this would be more fun than a solid bar! The corresponding style defines a background image of a beer mug that is 32x32 pixels. It is also set to repeat in the x or horizontal direction.

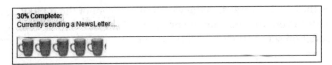

Figure 7-5

As the width of the DIV is expanded by the JavaScript, more and more beer mugs are displayed. For this layout the width of the progress bar container DIV is defined as 544 pixels, exactly the width of 17 beer mugs. This way there are no partial mugs displayed when the newsletter finishes, as this would lead to confusion for many end users. This technique can be employed in just about any progress bar scenario to provide a much richer effect than a plain colored bar or even a traditional gradient bar.

```
#progressbar
{
    width: 0px;
    height: 32px;
    background-repeat: repeat-x;
    background: url(images/glass1_small.jpg);
}
```

As I mentioned earlier the AddEditNewsletter page not only saves and sends a newsletter, but can also just store a draft of a newsletter to be edited and sent at a later time. The difference is setting the newsletter's DateSent value when the newsletter is actually sent. When the newsletter is loaded this value is checked, if it is null then the TextBoxes are displayed, if there is a value, then the literals are displayed. The click event handlers both call the SaveNewsletter method and pass either a true or false to indicate if the newsletter should be sent after it is saved to the database. If the newsletter is to be sent and another newsletter is already being sent, then the wait panel will be displayed, but any changes to the newsletter are committed to the database. If the newsletter can be sent, then it is stored and the send process begins.

```
Private Sub SaveNewsletter(ByVal bSendNow As Boolean)

    Dim isSending As Boolean = False

    If bSendNow Then

        Newsletter.Lock.AcquireReaderLock(Timeout.Infinite)
        isSending = Newsletter.IsSending
        Newsletter.Lock.ReleaseReaderLock()

        If isSending Then
            bSendNow = False

            panWait.Visible = True
            panSend.Visible = False

        End If
    End If

    Using lNewsletterrpt As New NewslettersRepository

        Dim lNewsletter As Newsletter = lNewsletterrpt.AddNewsletter(
NewsLetterId, txtSubject.Text, _
txtPlainTextBody.Text, txtHtmlBody.Value, bSendNow)

        If bSendNow And Not isSending Then
            panWait.Visible = True
            panSend.Visible = False

            NewslettersRepository.SendNewsletter(lNewsletter)
```

```
                    ShowSending()

              End If

         End Using

    End Sub
```

The ArchivedNewsletters.aspx Page

The `ArchivedNewsletters` page displays a list of previously sent newsletters. The list displays the newsletter's subject and the date it was sent. The subject is linked to the `ShowNewsletterpage`, passing the `NewsletterId`. The list is bound to a `List(of Newsletter)` retrieved from an overloaded version of the repository's `GetNewsletters` method that accepts a cutoff date. This feature allows old newsletters to gracefully degrade from the list as time passes. Of course any date could be used to ensure the list include a reference to every newsletter sent.

```
Public Function GetNewsletters(ByVal vToDate As DateTime)
As List(Of Newsletter)
            Return (From lNewsletter In Newsletterctx.Newsletters _
                    Where lNewsletter.DateSent < vToDate Order By
lNewsletter.DateSent Descending).ToList()
End Function
```

If viewing archived newsletters has been designated as a members-only activity, an unauthenticated user is redirected to the site's login page. This check is done in the Page Load event and not as a security setting in the site's `web.config`. Anonymous accesses to archived newsletters is an optional setting and by making it a module specific setting you make administration a little easier.

```
Protected Sub Page_Load(ByVal sender As Object,
ByVal e As System.EventArgs) Handles Me.Load

       ' check whether this page can be accessed by anonymous
users. If not, and if the
       ' current user is not authenticated, redirect to the login page
       If Not Me.User.Identity.IsAuthenticated AndAlso Not
Helpers.Settings.Newsletters.ArchiveIsPublic Then
           Me.RequestLogin()
       End If

       If Not IsPostBack Then
           BindArchivedNewsLetters()
       End If

    End Sub
```

The ShowNewsletter.aspx page incorporates the same security check before it binds the value of the newsletter content to the page.

The NewsletterBox User Control

The NewsletterBox user control (~/controls/newsletterbox.ascx) displays targeted content depending on the user's authentication status. If the user is logged into the site the LoggedInTemplate is displayed, showing instructions on how to change their subscription status. It also has a link to the ArchivedNewsletter page. If the user is not authenticated a simple registration field is displayed telling the user they can register for newsletters by supplying their e-mail address. Once the user submits their e-mail address they will be asked to create their account using the Register.aspx page. Because the LoginView automatically displays the correct template based on user authentication, there is no need to write any code.

```
<div class="SideBarbox">
    <div class="SideBarTitle">
        <asp:Image ID="imgArrow" runat="server" ImageUrl="~
/images/arrowr.gif" Style="float: left;
            margin-left: 3px; margin-right: 3px;"
GenerateEmptyAlternateText="True" meta:resourcekey=
"imgArrowResource1" />
        Newsletter
    </div>
    <div class="SideBarContent">
        <asp:LoginView ID="LoginView1" runat="server">
            <AnonymousTemplate>
                <asp:Localize runat="server" ID="locSubscribe1"
meta:resourcekey="locSubscribe1Resource1"
                    Text="
        &lt;b&gt;Register to the site for free&lt;/b&gt;, and
subscribe to the newsletter. Every month you will receive new
        articles and special content not available elsewhere on
the site, right into your e-mail box!
        "></asp:Localize>
                <br />
                <br />
                <input id="NewsletterEmail" style="width: 140px"
type="text" value="E-mail here"
                    onfocus="javascript:this.value = '';" />
                <input type="button" value="OK
onclick="javascript:SubscribeToNewsletter();" />
            </AnonymousTemplate>
            <LoggedInTemplate>
                <asp:Localize runat="server" ID="locSubscribe2"
meta:resourcekey="locSubscribe2Resource1"
                    Text="
        You can change your subscription type (plain-text, HTML or
no newsletter) from your"></asp:Localize>
                <asp:HyperLink runat="server" ID="lnkProfile"
NavigateUrl="~/EditProfile.aspx" Text="profile"
                    meta:resourcekey="lnkProfileResource1" />
                <asp:Localize runat="server" ID="locSubscribe3"
 meta:resourcekey="locSubscribe3Resource1"
```

```
                     Text="page. Click the link below to read
the newsletters run in the past."></asp:Localize>
            </LoggedInTemplate>
        </asp:LoginView>
        <br />
        <asp:HyperLink runat="server" ID="lnkArchive"
NavigateUrl="~/ArchivedNewsletters.aspx"
            Text="Archived Newsletters" meta:resourcekey=
"lnkArchiveResource1" />     </div>
</div>
```

Figure 7-6 shows content this code renders based on the user's subscription status.

Figure 7-6

Summary

In this chapter you've implemented a complete module for sending out newsletters to members who registered to receive them, either at initial registration time or later. The module sends out the e-mails from a background thread instead of the main thread used to process the page request, so that you don't risk page timeouts, and, above all, so that you don't leave the editor with a blank page that may last several minutes or more. To provide some feedback to the editor about the newsletter being sent, the AddEditNewsletter page uses AJAX to call a web service that updates a progress bar and shows the updated status information every couple of seconds. Finally, end users can look at past newsletters listed in an archive page.

To implement all this, you've used advanced features such as multi-threaded programming, script callbacks, and the `SmtpClient` and `MailMessage` classes to compose and send e-mail messages. However, although this module works fine, there's always room for enhancements. Here are some suggestions for improvements you may wish to make:

❑   Add the capability to send attachments with the newsletters. This can be very useful if you want to send HTML newsletters with images. Currently, you can only send e-mails with images, by referencing the full URL of the images on your server.

❑   Add support for setting the priority of the newsletter e-mails.

❑   Add the capability to have different mailing lists, for different topics, such as Parties, New Articles, or New Products in your store. This would require having more profile properties, and an expanded `SendNewsletter` page, so that you can choose the target mailing list.

❑ The personalization placeholder's list may be further expanded — to include placeholders for the subscriber's location, for example. You may also build a parser that manages custom tags defined into the newsletter's body, and includes or excludes their content according to the user's profile. For example, the content of a section `<profileProperty language="Italian">...` `</profileProperty>` could be included only in the newsletters for subscribers who choose Italian for the `Language` property in their profile. Or `<profileProperty state="NY">...` `</profileProperty>` could be used to include content only for subscribers living in New York state. This mechanism would not be difficult to implement, and it would allow editors to create very targeted newsletters, something that is especially important for commercial and marketing purposes.

❑ When the messages are sent out, you won't get an error or exception if the e-mail doesn't reach its destination because the e-mail address isn't valid. The SMTP server does its work without letting you know about the results. However, messages sent to non-existent addresses usually come back to the sender with an error message saying that the message couldn't be successfully delivered because the address does not exist. These error messages are sent to the server's post master and then forwarded to the site's administrator. At this point, when you get such a message, you can manually set that account's Newsletter profile property to `none`. However, a much better and automated approach would be to write a program (probably as a Windows service) that parses the incoming messages to find the error messages, automatically performing the unsubscribe operation.

❑ Create a newsletter queing system to allow administrators to create newsletters and designate a specific time to have the e-mails sent.

❑ Expand the user interface of the entire site to add a newsletter status visual on each page so the newsletter administrators can keep track of the progress without being tied to the newsletter's administrative page.

In the last few chapters we've developed modules to strengthen the site-to-user communications, such as the polls module and this newsletter manager. In the next chapter you're going to implement a module to manage forums, which is an important form of user-to-user communication.

8

Forums

Internet users like to feel part of a community of people with similar interests. A successful site should build a community of loyal visitors, providing a place where they can discuss their favorite subjects, ask questions, and reply to others. Community members return often to talk to other people with whom they've already shared messages, or to find comments and opinions about their interests. This chapter outlines some of the advantages of building such a virtual community, its goals, and the design and implementation of a new module for setting up and managing discussion boards.

Problem

User-to-user communication is important in many types of sites. For example, in a content site for pub enthusiasts, visitors to the site may want advice about the best way to brew their own beer, suggestions for good pubs in their area, to share comments on the last event they attended, and so on. Having contact with their peers is important so that they can ask questions and share their own knowledge. E-commerce sites have an added benefit of enabling users to review products online. Two ways to provide user-to-user communication are opinion polls and discussion boards. We've already looked at opinion polls in Chapter 6, and in this chapter we'll look at discussion boards, also known as forums. Visitors can browse the various messages in the forums, post their questions and topics, reply to other people's questions, and share ideas and tips. Forums act as a source of content, and provide an opportunity for users to participate and contribute. One reason why forums are especially attractive from a manager's perspective is that they require very little time and effort from employees because end users provide most of the content. However, a few minutes a day should be spent to ensure that nobody has posted any offensive messages, and that any problems that may be mentioned in a message receive some attention (maybe problems with the site or questions about products, locations, etc.).

As for TheBeerHouse site, we will offer discussion boards about brewing beers, pubs, concerts and parties, and more. These will be separate forums, used to group and categorize the threads by topic, so that it's easier for visitors to read what they are interested in. Early web forum systems often threw up long lists of messages on a single page, which took ages to load. This can be avoided by displaying lists in pages, with each page containing a particular number of messages. The website already has a way to identify users, and the forums will need to be integrated with that membership system. Besides being identified by username in the forum module, users may like something "catchy" in order to be recognized by the community: something such as an avatar image (a small picture that represents the user on their messages) and a signature line. This information will be added to every post and will help readers quickly identify the post's author. Of course, as with any other module you've developed so far, the site's administrators and editors must be able to add, remove, or edit forums, topics, and replies.

Design

Before looking at the design, let's consider a more accurate list of features to be implemented:

❑ Support for multiple categories, or subforums, that are more or less specific to a single topic/argument. Subforums are identified by name and description, and optionally by an image.

❑ Forums must support moderation. When a forum is moderated (this is a forum-level option), all messages posted by anyone except power users (administrators, editors, and moderators) are not immediately visible on the forum but must be approved by a member of one of the power user roles first. This is a useful option to ensure that posts are pertinent, not offensive, and comply with the forum's policy. However, this also places a bigger burden on the power users because posts have to be approved often (at least several times a day, even on weekends), or users will lose interest. Because of the timeliness needed for moderation, most forums are not moderated, but they are checked at least once a day to ensure that their policies have not been violated (with no particular need to check on weekends).

❑ The list of threads for a subforum, and the list of posts for a thread, must be paginable. In addition, the list of threads must be sortable by the last posting date, or the number of replies or views, in ascending or descending order. Sort options are very helpful if there are a lot of messages.

❑ Posting is only permitted by registered members, whereas browsing is allowed by everybody. An extension of the forum implemented in this chapter may include more options to specify that browsing also requires login or that posting is allowed by anonymous users.

❑ Users will be able to format their messages with a limited, and safe, set of HTML tags. This will be done by means of the FCKeditor control already used in Chapter 5, with a reduced toolbar.

❑ While creating a new thread, a user must be able to immediately close the thread so that other users cannot reply. If replies are allowed, they can later be disabled (and thus the thread closed) only by administrators, editors, and moderators.

❑ Users can modify their own posts anytime, but the operation must be logged in the message itself (a simple note in the message saying that it was edited will avoid confusion if another user remembers seeing something in a message but the next time they look it's gone).

❑ Users can have an avatar image associated with their account, which is displayed on every post they make. This helps them create a virtual, digital identity among other users of the forum. Users can also define a signature to be automatically added at the end of each post, so that it doesn't need to be copied and pasted every time. Signatures often include a special greeting, motto, old saying, or any other quote taken from a movie, taken from a famous person, or coined by the member herself. Sometimes it will contain a URL of that person's own site — this is normally OK, but you probably don't want any kind of advertising in this manner (e.g., www.BuyMyProduct.com).

❑ The messages posted by users are counted, and the count is displayed, together with the user's avatar, on each of the user's messages. This count is a form of recognition, and it lets other users know that this person might be more knowledgeable, or at least that they've hung around in the forums a lot (it tends to lend them more credibility). In addition, the forum system supports three special user levels; these are descriptions tied to the number of posts each user has made. The number of posts needed to advance to the next level can be configured, just like the descriptions.

❑ Full support for RSS 2.0 feeds should allow users to track new messages in an RSS aggregator program (such as the free SharpReader or RSS Bandit). There will be a flexible syndication system that provides distinct feeds to specific subforums, or all forums, and it will sort posts in different ways. This enables users to get a feed with the 10 newest threads posted into any forum, or with the 10 most popular threads (if sorted by number of replies). The feeds will be consumed by the generic RSS `Reader` control already developed in Chapter 5.

❑ Administrators, editors, and moderators can edit and delete any post. Additionally, they can move an entire thread to a different forum, which is helpful for ensuring that all threads are published in the appropriate place.

> Remember that you need some kind of policy statement somewhere in the forum pages that tells users what the rules are. This is usually needed for legal reasons in case a nasty, hateful, or untruthful message is posted and not caught quickly — just some kind of disclaimer to protect the site owners/administrators from lawsuits.

Designing the Database Tables

Since the last version of the book only one modification has been made to the Forum tables: a `Sticky` field was added to the `tbh_Post` table. This was added to allow administrators to make a post stick to the top of the list on the first page of the forum. The `Active`, `DateUpdated`, and `UpdatedBy` fields were also added. Figure 8-1 represents the tables as shown by the Database Diagram Editor window of VS 2008's Server Explorer tool (which is similar to what Enterprise Manager would show in SQL Server 2005).

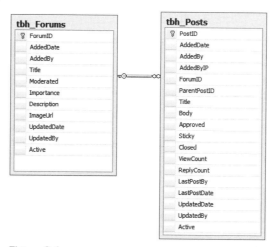

Figure 8-1

The `tbh_Forums` table is similar to the `tbh_Categories` table used in Chapter 5 for the articles module, with the addition of the `Moderated` column, which indicates whether the messages posted by normal users must be approved before they become visible in the forums' pages. The `tbh_Posts` table contains the following columns (the usual `AddedDate` and `AddedBy` fields aren't shown here):

- ❏ **PostID:** The primary key.

- ❏ **AddedByIP:** The IP of the user who authored the message — used for auditing purposes. Remember that you may become partially responsible for what users write (this also depends on the laws of your country). You should try to log information about the user who posted a message (such as the date/time and IP address), so you can provide this to legal authorities in the unlikely event that it might be needed.

- ❏ **ForumID:** The foreign key to a parent forum.

- ❏ **ParentPostID:** An integer referencing another record in the same table, which is the first message of a thread. When this field contains 0, it means that the post has no parent post; therefore, this is a thread post. Otherwise, this is a reply to an existing thread.

- ❏ **Title:** The title of the post. Reply posts also have a title; it will usually be `"Re: {thread title here}"`, but it's not absolutely necessary and the user will be free to change it while posting a new reply.

- ❏ **Body:** The body of the post, in HTML format (only limited HTML tags are allowed).

- ❏ **Approved:** A Boolean value indicating whether the post has been approved by a power user (administrators, editors, and moderators), and visible on the end-user pages. If the parent forum is not moderated, this field is automatically set to 1 when the post is created.

- ❏ **Sticky:** This field is only used for thread posts, and is a Boolean value indicating whether the thread is always be listed at the top of the thread list for the forum. Administrators will have the ability to turn this feature on an off.

- ❏ **Closed:** This field is only used for thread posts and is a Boolean value indicating whether the thread is closed and no more replies can be added. The user will be able to specify this option only while creating the thread. Once a thread has been created, only power users can close the thread.

- ❏ **ViewCount:** An integer indicating the number of times a thread has been read. If the record represents a reply, this field will contain 0.

- ❏ **ReplyCount:** The number of replies for the thread post. If the record represents a reply, this field will contain 0.

- ❏ **LastPostBy:** The name of the member who submitted the last post to this thread. As long as there are no replies, the field contains the name of the member who created the thread, which is also the name stored in the record's `AddedBy` field.

- ❏ **LastPostDate:** The date and time of the last post to this thread. As long as there are no replies, the field contains the date and time when the thread was created, which is also the value stored in the record's `AddedDate` field.

In the case of `ParentPostID`, the replies will always link to the first post of the thread, not to another reply. Therefore, the proposed structure does not support threaded discussions, such as those in Internet newsgroups. Instead, posts of nonthreaded discussions will be shown to the reader, sorted by creation date, from the oldest to the newest, so that they are read in chronological order. Both of these two types of forum systems, threaded or not, have their pros and cons. Threaded discussions make it easier to follow replies to previous posts, but nonthreaded discussions make it easier to follow the discussion with the correct temporal order (time-sequenced). To make it easier for the reader to follow the discussion, nonthreaded discussions usually allow users to quote a previous reply, even if the referenced reply is a number of posts prior to that one. In my research, nonthreaded discussions are more widely used, and easier to develop, so we'll use them for our sample site. If you want to modify the forum system to support threaded discussions, you'll be able to do that without modifying the DB; you just need to set the post's `ParentPostID` to the appropriate value.

Designing the Configuration Module

The configuration settings of the forums module are defined in a `<forums>` element within the `<theBeerHouse>` section of the `web.config` file. The class that maps the settings and exposes them is `ForumsElement`, which defines the properties in the following table.

Property	Description
ProviderType	The full name (namespace plus class name) of the concrete provider class that implements the data access code for a specific data store.
ConnectionStringName	The name of the entry in `web.config`'s new `<connectionStrings>` section containing the connection string for this module's database.
EnableCaching	A Boolean value indicating whether caching is enabled.
CacheDuration	The number of seconds for which the data is cached if there aren't any inserts, deletes, or updates that invalidate the cache.
ThreadsPageSize	The number of threads listed per page when browsing the threads of a subforum.
PostsPageSize	The number of posts listed per page when reading a thread.
RssItems	The number of threads included in the RSS feeds.
HotThreadPosts	The number of posts that make a thread *hot*. Hot threads will be rendered with a special icon to be distinguished from the others.
BronzePosterPosts	The number of posts that the user must reach to earn the status description defined by `BronzePosterDescription`.
BronzePosterDescription	The title that the user earns after reaching the number of posts defined by `BronzePosterPosts`.
SilverPosterPosts	The number of posts that the user must reach to earn the status description defined by `SilverPosterDescription`.
SilverPosterDescription	The title that the user earns after reaching the number of posts defined by `SilverPosterPosts`.
GoldPosterPosts	The number of posts that the user must reach to earn the status description defined by `GoldPosterDescription`.
GoldPosterDescription	The title that the user earns after reaching the number of posts defined by `GoldPosterPosts`.

Designing the Business Layer

The design of the core business layer follows the same rules as the previous modules, a set of entity model classes extended through the partial class functionality and a set of corresponding repository classes. Figure 8-2 is a class diagram of the Forum module Business classes.

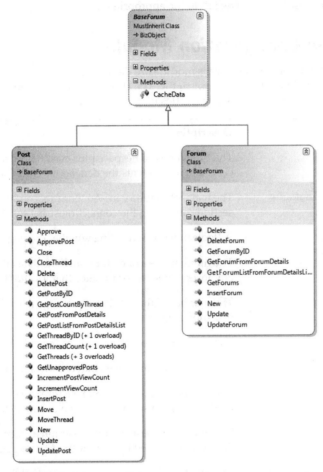

Figure 8-2

Designing the User Interface Services

The last thing we need to define are the UI pages and user controls that enable the user to browse forums and threads, post new messages, and administer the forum's content. Following is a list of the user interface pieces that you'll develop shortly in the "Solution" section:

❏ **~/Admin/ManageForums.aspx:** Lists forums and allows deletes.

❏ **~/Admin/AddEditForums.aspx:** Adds, updates, and deletes a designated forum.

- ❑ **~/Admin/ManageUnapprovedPosts.aspx:** Lists all unapproved posts (first thread posts and then replies, all sorted from the oldest to the newest), shows the entire content of a selected post, and approves or deletes it.

- ❑ **~/Admin/MoveThread.aspx:** Moves a thread (i.e., the thread post and all its replies) to another forum.

- ❑ **~/ShowForums.aspx:** Shows the list of all subforums, with their title, description, and image. Clicking on the forum's title will bring the user to another page showing the list of threads for that forum. For each forum, this also provides a link to its RSS feed, which returns the last "*n*" threads of that forum (where "*n*" is specified in `web.config`).

- ❑ **~/BrowseThreads.aspx:** Browses a forum's threads, page by page. The grid that lists the threads shows the thread's title, the number of times it was read, the number of replies, the author of the last post, and when the last post was created. Power users also see special links to delete, close, or move the thread. The results can be sorted by date, reply count, or view count.

- ❑ **~/ShowThread.aspx:** Shows all posts of a thread, in a paginated grid. For each post, it shows the title, body, author's signature, submission date and time, author's name, avatar image, and status description. Power users also see links to delete or edit any post, and a link to close the thread to stop replies. Normal members only see links to edit their own posts.

- ❑ **~/AddEditPost.aspx:** Creates a new thread, posts a new reply, or edits an existing message, according to the parameters on the querystring.

- ❑ **~/Forum.rss:** Returns an RSS feed of the forum's content. According to the querystring parameters, it can return the feed for a specific subforum or include threads from any subforum, and supports various sorting options. This can retrieve a feed for the sitewide threads (if sorting by date) or for the most active threads (if sorting by reply count).

- ❑ **~/Controls/UserProfile.ascx:** This control already exists, as it was developed in Chapter 4 while implementing the membership and profiling system. However, you must extend it here to support the Avatar image and Signature profile properties.

Solution

In this section, we'll cover the implementation of key parts of this module, as described in the "Design" section. But you won't find complete source code printed here, as many similar classes were discussed in other chapters. See the code download to get the complete source code.

Implementing the Database

The most interesting stored procedure is `tbh_Forums_InsertPost`. This inserts a new record into the `tbh_Posts` table, and if the new post being inserted is approved it must also update the `ReplyCount`, `LastPostBy`, and `LastPostDate` fields of this post's parent post. Because there are multiple statements in this stored procedure, a transaction is used to ensure that they are both either committed successfully or rolled back:

```
ALTER PROCEDURE dbo.tbh_Forums_InsertPost
(
    @AddedDate        datetime,
    @AddedBy          nvarchar(256),
```

```
        @AddedByIP          nchar(15),
        @ForumID            int,
        @ParentPostID       int,
        @Title              nvarchar(256),
        @Body               ntext,
        @Approved           bit,
        @Closed             bit,
        @PostID             int OUTPUT
)
AS
SET NOCOUNT ON

BEGIN TRANSACTION InsertPost

INSERT INTO tbh_Posts
    (AddedDate, AddedBy, AddedByIP, ForumID, ParentPostID, Title, Body, Approved,
        Closed, LastPostDate, LastPostBy)
    VALUES (@AddedDate, @AddedBy, @AddedByIP, @ForumID, @ParentPostID, @Title,
        @Body, @Approved, @Closed, @AddedDate, @AddedBy)

SET @PostID = scope_identity()

-- if the post is approved, update the parent post's
-- ReplyCount and LastReplyDate fields
IF @Approved = 1 AND @ParentPostID > 0
    BEGIN
    UPDATE tbh_Posts SET ReplyCount = ReplyCount + 1, LastPostDate = @AddedDate,
        LastPostBy = @AddedBy
        WHERE PostID = @ParentPostID
    END

IF @@ERROR > 0
    BEGIN
    RAISERROR('Insert of post failed', 16, 1)
    ROLLBACK TRANSACTION InsertPost
    RETURN 99
    END

COMMIT TRANSACTION InsertPost
```

If the post being inserted must be reviewed before being approved, its parent posts won't be modified because you don't want to count posts that aren't visible. When it gets approved later, the tbh_Forums_ ApprovePost stored procedure will set this post's Approved field to 1 and then update its parent post's fields mentioned previously. The ReplyCount field must also be incremented by one, but to update the parent post's LastPostBy and LastPostDate fields, the procedure needs the values of the AddedBy and AddedDate fields of the post being approved, so it executes a fast query to retrieve this information and stores it in local variables, and then it performs the parent post's update using those values, as shown here:

```
ALTER PROCEDURE dbo.tbh_Forums_ApprovePost
(
 @PostID   int
)
```

```
AS

BEGIN TRANSACTION ApprovePost

UPDATE tbh_Posts SET Approved = 1 WHERE PostID = @PostID

-- get the approved post's parent post and added date
DECLARE @ParentPostID    int
DECLARE @AddedDate       datetime
DECLARE @AddedBy         nvarchar(256)

SELECT @ParentPostID = ParentPostID, @AddedDate = AddedDate, @AddedBy = AddedBy
    FROM tbh_Posts
    WHERE PostID = @PostID

-- update the LastPostDate, LastPostBy and ReplyCount fields
-- of the approved post's parent post
IF @ParentPostID > 0
    BEGIN
    UPDATE tbh_Posts
        SET ReplyCount = ReplyCount + 1, LastPostDate = @AddedDate,
            LastPostBy = @AddedBy
        WHERE PostID = @ParentPostID
    END

IF @@ERROR > 0
    BEGIN
    RAISERROR('Approval of post failed', 16, 1)
    ROLLBACK TRANSACTION ApprovePost
    RETURN 99
    END

COMMIT TRANSACTION ApprovePost
```

Implementing the Data Access Layer

Most of the DAL methods are simply wrappers for stored procedures, so they won't be covered here. The GetThreads method is interesting: it returns the list of threads for a specified forum (a page of the results), and it is passed the page index and the page size. It also takes the sort expression used to order the threads. The method uses SQL Server 2005's ROW_NUMBER function to provide a unique auto-incrementing number to all rows in the table, sorted as specified, and then selects those rows with an index number between the lower and the upper bound of the specified page. The SQL code is very similar to the tbh_Articles_ GetArticlesByCategory stored procedure developed for the articles module in Chapter 5. The only difference (other than having the SQL code in a C# class instead of inside a stored procedure) is the fact that the sorting expression expected by the ORDER BY clause is dynamically added to the SQL string, as specified by an input parameter. Here's the method, which is implemented in the MB.TheBeerHouse .DAL.SqlClient.SqlForumsProvider class:

```csharp
public override List<PostDetails> GetThreads(
    int forumID, string sortExpression, int pageIndex, int pageSize)
{
    using (SqlConnection cn = new SqlConnection(this.ConnectionString))
    {
```

```
            sortExpression = EnsureValidSortExpression(sortExpression);
            int lowerBound = pageIndex * pageSize + 1;
            int upperBound = (pageIndex + 1) * pageSize;
            string sql = string.Format(@"
SELECT * FROM
(
    SELECT tbh_Posts.PostID, tbh_Posts.AddedDate, tbh_Posts.AddedBy,
    tbh_Posts.AddedByIP, tbh_Posts.ForumID, tbh_Posts.ParentPostID, tbh_Posts.Title,
    tbh_Posts.Approved, tbh_Posts.Closed, tbh_Posts.ViewCount, tbh_Posts.ReplyCount,
    tbh_Posts.LastPostDate, tbh_Posts.LastPostBy, tbh_Forums.Title AS ForumTitle,
    ROW_NUMBER() OVER (ORDER BY {0}) AS RowNum
    FROM tbh_Posts INNER JOIN tbh_Forums ON tbh_Posts.ForumID = tbh_Forums.ForumID
    WHERE tbh_Posts.ForumID = {1} AND ParentPostID = 0 AND Approved = 1
) ForumThreads
WHERE ForumThreads.RowNum BETWEEN {2} AND {3} ORDER BY RowNum ASC",
            sortExpression, forumID, lowerBound, upperBound);

            SqlCommand cmd = new SqlCommand(sql, cn);
            cn.Open();
            return GetPostCollectionFromReader(ExecuteReader(cmd), false);
        }
    }
```

At the beginning of the preceding method's body, the `sortExpression` string is passed to a method named `EnsureValidSortExpression` (shown below), and its result is assigned to the `sortExpression` variable. `EnsureValidSortExpression`, as its name clearly suggests, ensures that the input string is a valid sort expression that references a field in the `tbh_Posts` table, and not some illegitimate SQL substring used to perform a SQL injection attack. You should always do this kind of validation when building a dynamic SQL query by concatenating multiple strings coming from different sources (this is not necessary when using parameters, but unfortunately the ORDER BY clause doesn't support the use of parameters). Following is the method's implementation:

```
protected virtual string EnsureValidSortExpression(string sortExpression)
{
    if (string.IsNullOrEmpty(sortExpression))
        return "LastPostDate DESC";

    string sortExpr = sortExpression.ToLower();
    if (!sortExpr.Equals("lastpostdate") && !sortExpr.Equals("lastpostdate asc") &&
        !sortExpr.Equals("lastpostdate desc") && !sortExpr.Equals("viewcount") &&
        !sortExpr.Equals("viewcount asc") && !sortExpr.Equals("viewcount desc") &&
        !sortExpr.Equals("replycount") && !sortExpr.Equals("replycount asc") &&
        !sortExpr.Equals("replycount desc") && !sortExpr.Equals("addeddate") &&
        !sortExpr.Equals("addeddate asc") && !sortExpr.Equals("addeddate desc") &&
        !sortExpr.Equals("addedby") && !sortExpr.Equals("addedby asc") &&
        !sortExpr.Equals("addedby desc") && !sortExpr.Equals("title") &&
        !sortExpr.Equals("title asc") && !sortExpr.Equals("title desc") &&
        !sortExpr.Equals("lastpostby") && !sortExpr.Equals("lastpostby asc") &&
        !sortExpr.Equals("lastpostby desc"))
    {
        return "LastPostDate DESC";
    }
    else
    {
        if (sortExpr.StartsWith("title"))
```

```
        sortExpr = sortExpr.Replace("title", "tbh_posts.title");
      if (!sortExpr.StartsWith("lastpostdate"))
        sortExpr += ", LastPostDate DESC";
      return sortExpr;
    }
  }
```

As you see, if the `sortExpression` is null or an empty string, or if it doesn't reference a valid field, the method returns `"LastPostDate DESC"` as the default, which will sort the threads from the newest to the oldest.

Implementing the Business Logic Layer

The Entity Model and the BLL of this module are similar to those used in other chapters — Chapter 5 in particular. It employs the same patterns for retrieving and managing data by using LINQ to Entities, caching and purging data, and so on. The business layer is composed of two repositories, each inherit from `BaseForumRepository`. The `BaseForumRepository` then inherits from `BaseRepository`, the same architecture used in the Articles module where the `BaseForumRepository` holds values specific to the forums modules shared between the `PostsRepository` and the `ForumsRepository`. Both of the repositories should have methods that parallel the methods contained in the previous editions BLL classes.

The `GetUnapprovedPosts` method returns a list of post that need to be approved by an administrator. The main difference between this version and the last edition is the ability to sort by the `IsThreadPost` property. This is an immutable property and not actually part of the entity model and, therefore, cannot be used in the LINQ query used against the database.

```
Public Function GetUnapprovedPosts() As List(Of Post)

          Return (From lPost In MyBase.Forumctx.Posts.Include("Forum") _
            Where lPost.Approved = False _
            Order By lPost.AddedDate Descending).ToList

End Function
```

Implementing the User Interface

Before you start coding the user interface pages, you should modify the `web.config` file to add the necessary profile properties to the `<profile>` section. The required properties are `AvatarUrl` and `Signature`, both of type `string`, and a `Posts` property, of type `integer`, used to store the number of posts submitted by the user. They are used by authenticated users, and are defined within a `Forum` group, as shown here:

```
<profile defaultProvider="TBH_ProfileProvider">
    <providers>...</providers>
    <properties>
      <add name="FirstName" type="String" />
      <add name="LastName" type="String" />
      <!-- ...other properties here... -->
      <group name="Forum">
        <add name="Posts" type="Int32" />
        <add name="AvatarUrl" type="String" />
```

```
                <add name="Signature" type="String" />
        </group>
        <group name="Address">...</group>
        <group name="Contacts">...</group>
        <group name="Preferences">...</group>
    </properties>
</profile>
```

You must also change the UserProfile.ascx user control accordingly, so that it sets the new AvatarUrl and Signature properties (but not the Posts property, because that can only be set programmatically). This modification just needs a few lines of markup code in the .ascx file, and a couple of lines of C# code to read and set the properties, so I won't show them here. Once this "background work" is done, you can start creating the pages.

Administering and Viewing Forums

The definition of a *subforum* is almost identical to that of *article categories* employed in Chapter 5, with the unique addition of the Moderated field. The DAL and BLL code is similar to that developed earlier, but the UI for adding, updating, deleting, and listing forums is also quite similar. Therefore, I won't cover those pages here, but Figure 8-3 shows how they should look. As usual, consult the code download for the complete code.

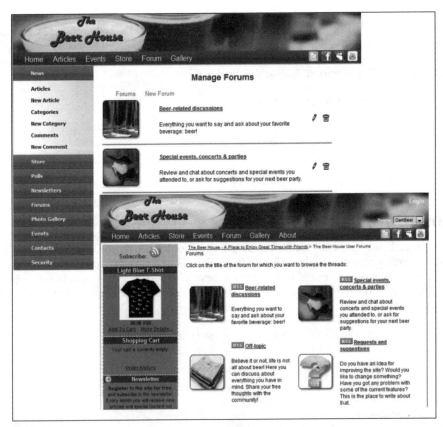

Figure 8-3

The AddEditPost.aspx Page

The AddEditPost.aspx page has a simple interface, with a textbox for the new post's title, a FCKeditor instance to create the post's body with a limited set of HTML formatting, and a checkbox to indicate that you won't allow replies to the post (the checkbox is only visible when a user creates a new thread and is not replying to an existing thread, or the user is editing an existing post). Figure 8-4 shows how it is presented to the user who wants to create a new thread.

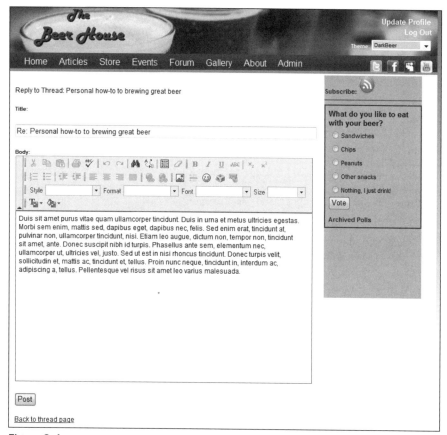

Figure 8-4

The page's markup is as simple, having only a few controls, so it's not shown here. The page inherits from the ForumPage class that defines a few properties that are driven by the querystring and use the PrimaryKey property pattern discussed in previous chapters.

```
Public Property ForumId() As Integer
    Get
        Return PrimaryKeyId("ForumId")
    End Get
```

```
            Set(ByVal Value As Integer)
                PrimaryKeyId("ForumId") = Value
            End Set
        End Property

        Public Property PostId() As Integer
            Get
                Return PrimaryKeyId("PostId")
            End Get
            Set(ByVal Value As Integer)
                PrimaryKeyId("PostId") = Value
            End Set
        End Property

        Public Property ThreadId() As Integer
            Get
                Return PrimaryKeyId("ThreadId")
            End Get
            Set(ByVal Value As Integer)
                PrimaryKeyId("ThreadId") = Value
            End Set
        End Property

        Public Property QuotePostID() As Integer
            Get
                Return PrimaryKeyId("QuotePostID")
            End Get
            Set(ByVal Value As Integer)
                PrimaryKeyId("QuotePostID") = Value
            End Set
        End Property
```

The page's code-behind class defines a few private variables used to store calculated values:

```
Private isNewThread As Boolean = False
Private isNewReply As Boolean = False
Private isEditingPost As Boolean = False
```

Not all variables are used in every function of the page. The following list defines whether these variables are used and how they are set for each function of the page:

❑ Creating a new thread:

  ❑ **forumID** — Set with the ForumID querystring parameter.

  ❑ **threadID** — Not used.

  ❑ **postID** — Not used.

  ❑ **quotePostID** — Not used.

  ❑ **isNewThread** — Set to true.

  ❑ **isNewReply** — Set to false.

  ❑ **isEditingPost** — Set to false.

❑ Posting a new reply to an existing thread:

    ❑ **forumID** — Set with the `ForumID` querystring parameter.

    ❑ **threadID** — Set with the `ThreadID` querystring parameter, which is the ID of the target thread for the new reply.

    ❑ **postID** — Not used.

    ❑ **quotePostID** — Not used.

    ❑ **isNewThread** — Set to false.

    ❑ **isNewReply** — Set to true.

    ❑ **isEditingPost** — Set to false.

❑ Quoting an existing post to be used as a base for a new reply to an existing thread:

    ❑ **forumID** — Set with the `ForumID` querystring parameter.

    ❑ **threadID** — Set with the `ThreadID` querystring parameter.

    ❑ **postID** — Not used.

    ❑ **quotePostID** — Set with the `QuotePostID` querystring parameter, which is the ID of the post to quote.

    ❑ **isNewThread** — Set to false.

    ❑ **isNewReply** — Set to true.

    ❑ **isEditingPost** — Set to false.

❑ Editing an existing post:

    ❑ **forumID** — Set with the `ForumID` querystring parameter.

    ❑ **threadID** — Set with the `ThreadID` querystring parameter (necessary for linking back to the thread's page after submitting the change, or if the editor wants to cancel the editing and go back to the previous page).

    ❑ **postID** — Set with the `PostID` querystring parameter, which is the ID of the post to edit.

    ❑ **quotePostID** — Not used.

    ❑ **isNewThread** — Set to false.

    ❑ **isNewReply** — Set to false.

    ❑ **isEditingPost** — Set to true.

The variables are set in the Page's Load event handler, which also calls the code to load the body of the post to edit or quote, sets the link to go back to the previous page, and checks whether the current user is allowed to perform the requested function. Here's the code:

```
Protected Sub Page_Load(ByVal sender As Object, ByVal e As System.EventArgs)
Handles Me.Load

        isNewThread = ((PostId = 0) And (ThreadId = 0))
```

```
        isEditingPost = Not (PostId = 0)
        isNewReply = (Not isNewThread And Not isEditingPost)

        ' show/hide controls and load data according to the parameters above
        If Not Me.IsPostBack Then

            lnkThreadList.NavigateUrl = String.Format(lnkThreadList.NavigateUrl,
    ForumId)
            lnkThreadPage.NavigateUrl = String.Format(lnkThreadPage.NavigateUrl,
    ThreadId)
            txtBody.BasePath = Me.BaseUrl & "FCKeditor/"
            chkClosed.Visible = isNewThread

            BindPost()

        End If
    End Sub
```

The `BindPost` method actually retrieves the post and binds the contents to the appropriate controls. The method takes care to bind the controls as needed for either editing or posting a new thread. It also has a security check to force a login is the user is not authorized to make edit the post. For example, if someone happened to figure out a hack to retrieve the post for editing and was not a site administrator or the original poster, it would ask them to authenticate.

```
    Private Sub BindPost()
        Using lPost As New PostsRepository

            If isEditingPost Then
                ' load the post to edit, and check that the current user has the
                ' permission to do so
                Dim post As Post = lPost.GetPostById(PostId)
                If Not isModerator AndAlso _
                   Not (Me.User.Identity.IsAuthenticated And _
                   Me.User.Identity.Name.Equals(post.AddedBy.ToLower)) Then
                   Me.RequestLogin()
                End If

                lblEditPost.Visible = True
                btnSubmit.Text = "Update"
                txtTitle.Text = post.Title
                txtBody.Value = post.Body
                panTitle.Visible = isModerator
            ElseIf isNewReply Then
                ' chech whether the thread the user is adding a reply to is still open
                Dim post As Post = lPost.GetPostById(ThreadId)
                If post.Closed Then
                    Throw New ApplicationException( _
                        "The thread you tried to reply to has been closed.")
                End If

                lblNewReply.Visible = True
                txtTitle.Text = "Re: " & post.Title
                lblNewReply.Text = String.Format(lblNewReply.Text, post.Title)
                ' if the ID of a post to be quoted is passed on the querystring, load
```

```
                        ' that post and prefill the new reply's body with that post's body
                    If quotePostID > 0 Then
                        Dim quotePost As Post = lPost.GetPostById(quotePostID)
                        txtBody.Value = String.Format( _
                            "<blockquote><hr noshade="""" size=""1"" />" & _
                            "<b>Originally posted by {0}</b><br /><br />{1}" & _
                            "<hr noshade="""" size=""1"" /></blockquote>", _
                            quotePost.AddedBy, quotePost.Body)
                    End If
                ElseIf isNewThread Then
                    lblNewThread.Visible = True
                    lnkThreadList.Visible = True
                    lnkThreadPage.Visible = False
                End If

            End Using
        End Sub
```

When the user clicks the Submit button, the previously discussed class fields are used again to determine whether an `AddPost` or an `UpdatePost` is required. When editing a post, a line is dynamically added at the end of the post's body to log the date and time of the update, and the editor's name. When the post is inserted, you must also check whether the target forum is moderated, and if it is, you can only pass `true` to the `InsertPost`'s `approved` parameter if the current user is a power user (administrator, editor, or moderator). After inserting the post, you also increment the author's `Posts` profile property. Here's the full code for the Submit button's `OnClick` event handler:

```
Protected Sub btnSubmit_Click(ByVal sender As Object, ByVal e As System.EventArgs) _
    Handles btnSubmit.Click

        Using lPostrpt As New PostsRepository

            If isEditingPost Then
                ' when editing a post, a line containing the current Date/Time and the
                ' name of the user making the edit is added to the post's body so that
                ' the operation gets logged
                Dim body As String = Helpers.FilterProfanity(txtBody.Value)
                body &= String.Format("<p>-- {0}: post edited by {1}.</p>", _
                    DateTime.Now.ToString, Me.User.Identity.Name)
                ' edit an existing post
                Dim lPostItem As Post = lPostrpt.GetPostById(PostId)
                lPostItem.Title = txtTitle.Text
                lPostItem.Body = body

                lPostItem.UpdatedDate = Now
                lPostItem.UpdatedBy = UserName

                lPostrpt.UpdatePost(lPostItem)
                panInput.Visible = False
                panFeedback.Visible = True
            Else

                Dim lPostItem As New Post

                Using lForumrpt As New ForumsRepository
```

```
                    Dim forum As Forum = lForumrpt.GetForumById(ForumId)

                    lPostItem.ForumId = ForumId
                    lPostItem.ParentPostID = ThreadId
                    lPostItem.Title = txtTitle.Text
                    lPostItem.Body = txtBody.Value
                    lPostItem.Closed = chkClosed.Checked
                    lPostItem.LastPostDate = Now
                    lPostItem.LastPostBy = UserName
                    lPostItem.UpdatedDate = Now
                    lPostItem.UpdatedBy = UserName

                    If (forum.Moderated) Then
                        If Not isModerator Then
                            lPostItem.Approved = False
                        End If
                    End If

                    lPostItem.Active = True
                    lPostItem.AddedDate = Now
                    lPostItem.AddedBy = UserName
                    lPostItem.AddedByIP = Request.UserHostAddress

                    ' insert the new post
                    If lPostrpt.AddPost(lPostItem) Then

                        panInput.Visible = False
                        ' increment the user's post counter
                        Dim lPosts As Integer =
          profile.GetProfileGroup("Forum").GetPropertyValue("Posts")
                        profile.GetProfileGroup("Forum").SetPropertyValue("Posts",
          lPosts + 1)

                        ' show the confirmation message saying that approval is
                        ' required, according to the target forum's moderated property

                        If forum.Moderated Then
                            If Not isModerator Then
                                panApprovalRequired.Visible = True
                            Else
                                panFeedback.Visible = True
                            End If
                        Else
                            panFeedback.Visible = True
                        End If

                        'Just in case they corrected an error.
                        ltlStatus.Visible = False
                    Else

                        ltlStatus.Visible = True

                        For Each kv As KeyValuePair(Of String, Exception) In
          lForumrpt.ActiveExceptions
```

```
                             ltlStatus.Text += "<BR/>" & DirectCast(kv.Value, Exception)
        .Message & "<BR/>"
                        Next

                End If

            End Using

        End If

    End Using

End Sub
```

The ManageUnapprovedPosts.aspx Page

The ManageUnapprovedPosts.aspx page enables power users to see the list of messages waiting for approval for moderated forums, and allows them to review their content and then either approve or delete them. The page is pretty simple, as there's just a ListView that shows the title and a few other fields of the posts, without support for pagination or sorting. Next to the poster's name is an icon to expand the body of the post for review. The entire ListView is wrapped in an UpdatePanel to make interacting with the items more seamless. A screenshot is shown in Figure 8-5.

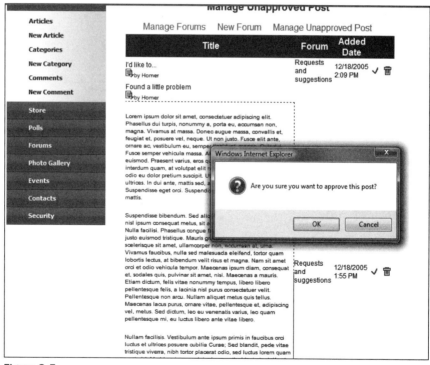

Figure 8-5

The code to manage this list has a small peculiarity: when the editor clicks on the post's title or the GoDown.gif icon the full body of the post is exposed. This way the administrator can review the body of the post before approving or deleting it. This is done through the ListView's ItemDataBound event handler by adding OnClick event handlers to a SPAN wrapping the title and the image. Both of these elements are designated as server-side controls.

The method first grabs an instance of each of the controls, the SPAN is cast as an HTMLGenericControl and the Image as an HTMLImage control. Then the same attribute is applied to use the toggleDivState function defined in the TBH.js file. The body of the post is contained in a DIV element that is dynamically named 'body' + PostId. I wanted to do this to have control over the ID on the client because ASP.NET would have made the ID hard to work with otherwise. I could have made the DIV a server-side element, too, and used the UniqueID property but chose not to, to make it simpler. Also notice the Approve and Delete ImageButtons also have a special confirmation message applied to their click events.

```vb
Private Sub lvPosts_ItemDataBound(ByVal sender As Object, ByVal e As
System.Web.UI.WebControls.ListViewItemEventArgs)
Handles lvPosts.ItemDataBound

        Dim lvdi As ListViewDataItem = DirectCast(e.Item, ListViewDataItem)

        If lvdi.ItemType = ListViewItemType.DataItem Then

            Dim iGoDown As System.Web.UI.HtmlControls.HtmlImage =
DirectCast(e.Item.FindControl("iGoDown"),
System.Web.UI.HtmlControls.HtmlImage)
            Dim btnApprove As ImageButton = DirectCast(
e.Item.FindControl("btnApprove"), ImageButton)
            btnApprove.OnClientClick = "if (
confirm('Are you sure you want to approve this post?') == false)
return false;"
            btnApprove.ToolTip = "Approve this post"
            Dim btnDelete As ImageButton =
DirectCast(e.Item.FindControl("btnDelete"), ImageButton)
            btnDelete.OnClientClick = "if (
confirm('Are you sure you want to delete this post?') == false)
 return false;"
            btnDelete.ToolTip = "Delete this post"
            Dim dTitle As HtmlGenericControl = DirectCast(e.Item.FindControl("dTitle")
, HtmlGenericControl)

            Dim lPost As Post = DirectCast(lvdi.DataItem, Post)

            If Not IsNothing(iGoDown) Then
                iGoDown.Attributes.Add("OnClick",
String.Format("toggleDivState('{0}');", "body" & lPost.PostID))
            End If

            If Not IsNothing(dTitle) Then
                dTitle.Attributes.Add("OnClick",
String.Format("toggleDivState('{0}');", "body" & lPost.PostID))
            End If

        End If

End Sub
```

When the administrator deletes a post, the `ListView`'s `ItemDeleting` event is fired and the typical delete routine is used. When the administrator approves a post the `ItemCommand` event handler is called and the `ApprovePost` method of the `PostRepository` is called.

```
Private Sub lvPosts_ItemCommand(ByVal sender As Object, ByVal e As
System.Web.UI.WebControls.ListViewCommandEventArgs)
Handles lvPosts.ItemCommand

    Select Case e.CommandName
        Case "Approve"

            Using lPostrpt As New PostsRepository

                lPostrpt.ApprovePost(Convert.ToInt32(e.CommandArgument))

            End Using

            BindUnapprovedPosts()

    End Select

End Sub
```

The BrowseThreads.aspx Page

The `BrowseThreads.aspx` page takes a `ForumID` parameter on the querystring with the ID of the forum the user wants to browse and fills a paginable `GridView` control with the thread list returned by the `Post.GetThreads` business method. Figure 8-6 shows a screenshot of this page.

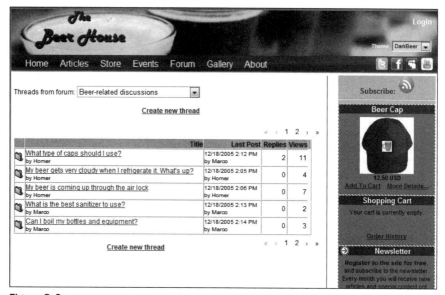

Figure 8-6

In addition to the `GridView` control with the threads, the page also features a `DropDownList` at the top of the page, which lists all available forums (retrieved by an `ObjectDataSource` that uses the `Forum.GetForums` business method) and allows users to quickly navigate to a forum by selecting one. The `DropDownList` onchange client-side (JavaScript) event redirects the user to the same `BrowseThreads.aspx` page but with the newly selected forum's ID on the querystring:

```
<asp:DropDownList ID="ddlForums" runat="server" DataSourceID="objForums"
    DataTextField="Title" DataValueField="ID"
    onchange="javascript:document.location.href='BrowseThreads.aspx?ForumID='
+ this.value;" />
<asp:ObjectDataSource ID="objForums" runat="server" SelectMethod="GetForums"
    TypeName="MB.TheBeerHouse.BLL.Forums.Forum" />
```

The `GridView` is bound to another `ObjectDataSource` control, which specifies the methods to select and delete data. Because you want to support pagination, you use the `GetThreadCount` method to return the total thread count. To support sorting you must set `SortParameterName` to the name of the parameter that the `SelectMethod` (i.e., `GetThreads`) will use to receive the sort expression; in this case, as shown earlier, it's `sortExpression`. Here's the complete declaration of the `ObjectDataSource`:

```
<asp:ObjectDataSource ID="objThreads" runat="server"
    TypeName="MB.TheBeerHouse.BLL.Forums.Post"
    DeleteMethod="DeletePost" SelectMethod="GetThreads"
    SelectCountMethod="GetThreadCount"
    EnablePaging="true" SortParameterName="sortExpression">
    <DeleteParameters>
        <asp:Parameter Name="id" Type="Int32" />
    </DeleteParameters>
    <SelectParameters>
        <asp:QueryStringParameter Name="forumID"
            QueryStringField="ForumID" Type="Int32" />
    </SelectParameters>
</asp:ObjectDataSource>
```

The following `GridView` control has both the `AllowPaging` and `AllowSorting` properties set to `true`, and it defines the following columns:

❑ A `TemplateColumn` that displays an image representing a folder, which is used to identify a discussion thread. A templated column is used in place of a simpler `ImageColumn`, because the image being shown varies according to the number of posts in the thread. If the post count reaches a certain value (specified in the configuration), it will be considered a *hot thread*, and a red icon will be used to highlight it.

❑ A `TemplateColumn` defining a link to the `ShowThread.aspx` page on the first line, with the thread's title as the link's text, and the thread's author's name in smaller text on the second line. The link on the first line also includes the thread's ID on the querystring so that the page will load that specific thread's posts.

❑ A `TemplateColumn` that shows the date of the thread's last post on the first line, and the name of the author who entered the thread's last post on the second line. The column's `SortExpression` is `LastPostDate`.

❑ A `BoundField` column that shows the thread's `ReplyCount` and has a header link that sorts threads on this column.

❑ A `BoundField` column that shows the thread's `ViewCount` and has a header link that sorts threads on this column.

❑ A `HyperLinkField` column pointing to the `MoveThread.aspx` page, which takes the ID of the thread to move on the querystring. This column will not be shown if the current user is not a power user.

❑ A `ButtonField` column to close the thread and stop replies to it. This column will not be shown if the current user is not a power user.

❑ A `ButtonField` column to delete the thread with all its posts. This column will not be shown if the current user is not a power user.

❑ Following is the complete markup code for the `GridView`:

```
<asp:GridView ID="gvwThreads" runat="server" AllowPaging="True"
    AutoGenerateColumns="False" DataSourceID="objThreads" PageSize="25"
    AllowSorting="True" DataKeyNames="ID" OnRowCommand="gvwThreads_RowCommand"
    OnRowCreated="gvwThreads_RowCreated">
<Columns>
    <asp:TemplateField ItemStyle-Width="16px">
        <ItemTemplate>
            <asp:Image runat="server" ID="imgThread" ImageUrl="~/Images/Thread.gif"
                Visible='<%# (int)Eval("ReplyCount") <
                    Globals.Settings.Forums.HotThreadPosts %>'
                GenerateEmptyAlternateText="" />
            <asp:Image runat="server" ID="imgHotThread"
                ImageUrl="~/Images/ThreadHot.gif"
                Visible='<%# (int)Eval("ReplyCount") >=
                    Globals.Settings.Forums.HotThreadPosts %>'
                GenerateEmptyAlternateText="" />
        </ItemTemplate>
        <HeaderStyle HorizontalAlign="Left" />
    </asp:TemplateField>
    <asp:TemplateField HeaderText="Title">
        <ItemTemplate>
            <asp:HyperLink ID="lnkTitle" runat="server" Text='<%# Eval("Title") %>'
                NavigateUrl='<%# "ShowThread.aspx?ID=" + Eval("ID") %>' /><br />
            <small>by <asp:Label ID="lblAddedBy" runat="server"
                Text='<%# Eval("AddedBy") %>'></asp:Label></small>
        </ItemTemplate>
        <HeaderStyle HorizontalAlign="Left" />
    </asp:TemplateField>
    <asp:TemplateField HeaderText="Last Post" SortExpression="LastPostDate">
        <ItemTemplate>
            <small><asp:Label ID="lblLastPostDate" runat="server"
                Text='<%# Eval("LastPostDate", "{0:g}") %>'></asp:Label><br />
            by <asp:Label ID="lblLastPostBy" runat="server"
                Text='<%# Eval("LastPostBy") %>'></asp:Label></small>
        </ItemTemplate>
        <ItemStyle HorizontalAlign="Center" Width="130px" />
        <HeaderStyle HorizontalAlign="Center" />
    </asp:TemplateField>
    <asp:BoundField HeaderText="Replies" DataField="ReplyCount"
        SortExpression="ReplyCount" >
        <ItemStyle HorizontalAlign="Center" Width="50px" />
```

```
            <HeaderStyle HorizontalAlign="Center" />
        </asp:BoundField>
        <asp:BoundField HeaderText="Views" DataField="ViewCount"
            SortExpression="ViewCount" >
            <ItemStyle HorizontalAlign="Center" Width="50px" />
            <HeaderStyle HorizontalAlign="Center" />
        </asp:BoundField>
        <asp:HyperLinkField
            Text="<img border='0' src='Images/MoveThread.gif' alt='Move thread' />"
            DataNavigateUrlFormatString="~/Admin/MoveThread.aspx?ThreadID={0}"
            DataNavigateUrlFields="ID">
            <ItemStyle HorizontalAlign="Center" Width="20px" />
        </asp:HyperLinkField>
        <asp:ButtonField ButtonType="Image" ImageUrl="~/Images/LockSmall.gif"
            CommandName="Close">
            <ItemStyle HorizontalAlign="Center" Width="20px" />
        </asp:ButtonField>
        <asp:CommandField ButtonType="Image" DeleteImageUrl="~/Images/Delete.gif"
            DeleteText="Delete thread" ShowDeleteButton="True">
            <ItemStyle HorizontalAlign="Center" Width="20px" />
        </asp:CommandField>
    </Columns>
    <EmptyDataTemplate><b>No threads to show</b></EmptyDataTemplate>
</asp:GridView>
```

There are just a few lines of code in the page's code-behind class. In the `Page_Init` event handler, you set the grid's `PageSize` to the value read from the configuration settings, overwriting the default hard-coded value used previously:

```
protected void Page_Init(object sender, EventArgs e)
{
    gvwThreads.PageSize = Globals.Settings.Forums.ThreadsPageSize;
}
```

In the `Page_Load` event handler, there's some simple code that uses the ID passed on the querystring to load a `Forum` object representing the forum: the forum's title read from the object is used to set the page's `Title`. Then the code preselects the current forum from the `DropDownList` at the top, sets the `ForumID` parameter on the hyperlinks that create a new thread, and hides the last three `GridView` columns if the current user is not a power user:

```
protected void Page_Load(object sender, EventArgs e)
{
    if (!this.IsPostBack)
    {
        string forumID = this.Request.QueryString["ForumID"];
        lnkNewThread1.NavigateUrl = string.Format(lnkNewThread1.NavigateUrl,
            forumID);
        lnkNewThread2.NavigateUrl = lnkNewThread1.NavigateUrl;

        Forum forum = Forum.GetForumByID(int.Parse(forumID));
        this.Title = string.Format(this.Title, forum.Title);
        ddlForums.SelectedValue = forumID;

        // if the user is not an admin, editor or moderator, hide the grid's column
```

```
        // with the commands to delete, close or move a thread
        bool canEdit = (this.User.Identity.IsAuthenticated &&
           (this.User.IsInRole("Administrators") || this.User.IsInRole("Editors") ||
            this.User.IsInRole("Moderators")));
        gvwThreads.Columns[5].Visible = canEdit;
        gvwThreads.Columns[6].Visible = canEdit;
        gvwThreads.Columns[7].Visible = canEdit;
    }
}
```

The click on the threads' Delete button is handled automatically by the GridView and its companion ObjectdataSource control. To make the Close button work, you have to manually handle the RowCommand event handler and call the Post.CloseThread method, as shown here:

```
protected void gvwThreads_RowCommand(object sender, GridViewCommandEventArgs e)
{
    if (e.CommandName == "Close")
    {
        int threadPostID = Convert.ToInt32(
            gvwThreads.DataKeys[Convert.ToInt32(e.CommandArgument)][0]);
        MB.TheBeerHouse.BLL.Forums.Post.CloseThread(threadPostID);
    }
}
```

The MoveThread.aspx Page

The MoveThread.aspx page contains a DropDownList with the list of available forums and allows power users to move the thread (whose ThreadID is passed on the querystring) to one of the forums, after selecting it and clicking the OK button. Figure 8-7 shows this simple user interface.

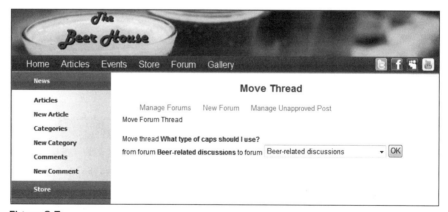

Figure 8-7

The DropDownList is filled with an instructional message by calling the BindForums method in the ForumPage class. The BindForums method uses a ForumsRepository to bind the ActiveForums to the supplied ListControl. Using a ListControl ultimately provides the flexibility to bind to a DropDownList, RadioButtonList, or any other web control derived from ListControl. Ultimately, they all work the same when it comes to binding. Finally, a customized instruction string is inserted at the top of the `ListContol`'s items collection. If the `ForumId` is greater than 0, then it is selected in the list.

```
Protected Sub BindForums(ByVal vListControl As ListControl, _
ByVal vInstruction As String)

        Using lforumRpt As New ForumsRepository

                vListControl.DataSource = lforumRpt.GetActiveForums
                vListControl.DataBind()

                vListControl.Items.Insert(0, New ListItem(vInstruction, "0"))

                If ForumId > 0 Then
                    vListControl.SelectedValue = ForumId
                End If

        End Using

End Sub
```

The MoveThread page calls the `BindPostInfo` method after it binds the forum's `DropDownList`. This method binds information about the post that is being moved to the associated controls.

```
Private Sub BindPostInfo()

        Using lPostrpt As New PostsRepository
            Dim post As Post = lPostrpt.GetPostById(ThreadId)
            lblThreadTitle.Text = post.Title
            lblForumTitle.Text = post.ForumTitle
            ddlForums.SelectedValue = post.ForumId.ToString()
        End Using

End Sub
```

When the user clicks the Submit button the `PostsRepository` is used to move the thread and then redirect to the BrowseThreads.aspx page at the root of the site.

```
Private Sub btnSubmit_Click(ByVal sender As Object, ByVal e As System.EventArgs) _
Handles btnSubmit.Click

        Using lPostrpt As New PostsRepository
            Dim lforumID As Integer = Integer.Parse(ddlForums.SelectedValue)
            lPostrpt.MoveThread(ThreadId, ForumId)
            Me.Response.Redirect("~/BrowseThreads.aspx?ForumID=" & forumID.ToString())
        End Using

End Sub
```

The ShowThread.aspx Page

The `ShowThread.aspx` page renders a paginable list showing all posts of the thread, whose `ThreadID` is passed on the querystring. Figure 8-8 shows this `ListView` in action.

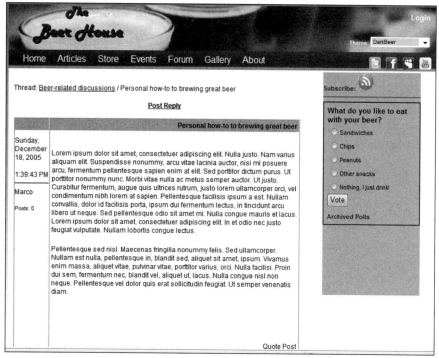

Figure 8-8

Some of the information (such as the post's title, body, author, and date/time) is retrieved from the bound data retrieved by calling the GetThread method of the PostRepository. Some other data, such as the author's avatar, number of posts, and signature are retrieved from the profile associated with the membership account named after the post author's name. The controls that show this profile data are bound to an expression that calls the GetUserProfile method, which takes the author's name and returns an instance of ProfileCommon for that user. Using the dynamically generated, strongly typed ProfileCommon object, you can easily reference the profile groups and subproperties. The following code declares the ListView's ItemTemplate, which defines the links to edit and delete the post (these will be hidden by code in the code-behind if the current user should not see them), and then defines controls bound to the user's Posts and AvatarUrl profile properties in the first table cell:

```
<ItemTemplate>
        <tr>
            <td valign="top">
                <div class="posttitle">
                    <asp:HyperLink runat="server" ID="lnkEditPost"
ImageUrl="~/Images/Edit.gif"
NavigateUrl="~/AddEditPost.aspx?ForumID={0}
&ThreadID={1}&PostID={2}" /> 
                    <asp:ImageButton runat="server" ID="btnDeletePost"
ImageUrl="~/Images/Delete.gif"
                        OnClientClick="if (
confirm('Are you sure you want to delete this {0}?') == false)
return false;" />  
```

```
                    </div>
                    <asp:Literal ID="lblAddedDate" runat="server"
        Text='<%# Eval("AddedDate", "{0:D}<br/><br/>{0:T}") %>' />
                    <hr />
                    <asp:Literal ID="lblAddedBy" runat="server"
        Text='<%# Eval("AddedBy") %>' /><br />
                    <br />
                    <small>
                        <asp:Literal ID="lblPosts" runat="server"
        Text='<%# "Posts: " &
        GetNoofPostForUser(Eval("AddedBy")).ToString() %>' />
                        <asp:Literal ID="lblPosterDescription" runat="server"
        Text='<%# "<br />" &
        GetPosterDescription(GetNoofPostForUser(Eval("AddedBy"))) %>'
                            Visible='<%# GetNoofPostForUser(Eval("AddedBy")) >=
        Settings.Forums.BronzePosterPosts %>' /></small><br />
                    <br />
                    <asp:Panel runat="server" ID="panAvatar" Visible='<%#
        GetPosterAvatar(Eval("AddedBy")).Length > 0 %>'>
                        <asp:Image runat="server" ID="imgAvatar"
        ImageUrl='<%# GetPosterAvatar(Eval("AddedBy")) %>' />
                        <br />
                        <br />
                    </asp:Panel>
                </td>
                <td valign="top">
                    <div class="posttitle">
                        <asp:Literal ID="lblTitle" runat="server"
        Text='<%# Eval("Title") %>' /></div>
                    <div class="postbody">
                        <asp:Literal ID="lblBody" runat="server"
        Text='<%# Eval("Body") %>' /><br />
                        <br />
                        <asp:Literal ID="lblSignature" runat="server"
        Text='<%# ConvertToHtml(GetPosterSignature(Eval("AddedBy")))
        %>' /><br />
                        <br />
                        <div style="text-align: right;">
                            <asp:HyperLink runat="server" ID="lnkQuotePost"
        NavigateUrl="~/AddEditPost.aspx?ForumID={0}&ThreadID={1}&QuotePostID={2}">
        Quote Post</asp:HyperLink>
                        </div>
                    </div>
                </td>
            </tr>
        </ItemTemplate>
```

The second cell renders the post's title, the body, and then the user's Signature profile property. Because the signature is in plain text, though, it first passes through a helper method named ConvertToHtml, which transforms the signature into simple HTML (it replaces carriage returns with <br/> tags, replaces multiple spaces and tabs with " ", etc.). At the bottom, it has a HyperLink to the AddEditPost.aspx page, which creates a new reply by quoting the current post's body.

There's some interesting code in the code-behind class: in the preceding code, you can see that the GetUserProfile method is called six times for every single post. This can cause performance problems when you consider how many times this might execute in one page cycle. The same thread will likely have multiple posts by the same user: in a typical thread of 20 posts, four of them might be from the same user. This means we make 24 calls to GetUserProfile for the same user. This method uses ASP.NET's Profile.GetProfile method to retrieve a ProfileCommon object for the specified user, which unfortunately doesn't cache the result. This means that every time you call Profile.GetProfile, it will run a query to SQL Server to retrieve the user's profile, and then build the ProfileCommon object to be returned. In our situation, this would be an incredible waste of resources, because after the first query for a specific user, the next 23 queries for that user would produce the same result. To prevent this kind of waste, we'll use the GetUserProfile method to wrap the call to Profile.GetProfile by adding simple caching support that will last as long as the page's lifetime. It uses a Hashtable, which uses the username as a key, and the ProfileCommon object as the value; if the requested profile is not found in the Hashtable when the method is called, it forwards the call to Profile.GetProfile and then saves the result in the Hashtable for future needs. Here's how it's implemented:

```
Dim profiles As New Hashtable()

Protected Function GetPostUserProfile(ByVal userName As Object) As ProfileBase
    Dim name As String = CStr(userName)
    If Not profiles.Contains(name) Then
        Dim profile As ProfileBase = Helpers.GetUserProfile(name)
        profiles.Add(name, profile)
        Return profile
    Else
        Return CType(profiles(userName), ProfileBase)
    End If
End Function
```

There's another helper method on the page, GetPosterDescription, which returns the user's status description according to the user's number of posts. It compares the number with the values of the GoldPosterPosts, SilverPosterPosts, and BronzePosterPosts configuration settings and returns the appropriate description:

```
Protected Function GetPosterDescription(ByVal posts As Integer) As String
    If posts >= Settings.Forums.GoldPosterPosts Then
        Return Settings.Forums.GoldPosterDescription
    ElseIf posts >= Settings.Forums.SilverPosterPosts Then
        Return Settings.Forums.SilverPosterDescription
    ElseIf posts >= Settings.Forums.BronzePosterPosts Then
        Return Settings.Forums.BronzePosterDescription
    Else
        Return String.Empty
    End If
End Function
```

The rest of the page's code-behind is pretty typical. For example, you handle the list's ItemDataBound event to show, or hide, the post's edit link according to whether the current user is the post's author or a power user, or just another user. It also sets the delete button's CommandName to either DeleteThread or

DeletePost or hides the link to quote the post according to whether the thread is closed. The following code shows this:

```vbnet
Private Sub lvPosts_ItemDataBound(ByVal sender As Object,
ByVal e As System.Web.UI.WebControls.ListViewItemEventArgs)
Handles lvPosts.ItemDataBound

    If e.Item.ItemType = ListViewItemType.DataItem Then

        Dim lvdi As ListViewDataItem = DirectCast(e.Item, ListViewDataItem)
        Dim lPost As Post = CType(lvdi.DataItem, Post)
        Dim threadID As Integer = lPost.ParentPostID
        If lPost.IsFirstPost Then threadID = lPost.PostID

        If Not IsNothing(lPost) Then

            ' the link for editing the post is visible to the post's author, and to
            ' administrators, editors and moderators
            Dim lnkEditPost As HyperLink =
CType(e.Item.FindControl("lnkEditPost"), HyperLink)


            lnkEditPost.NavigateUrl = String.Format(lnkEditPost.NavigateUrl,
lPost.ForumId, threadID, lPost.PostID)
            lnkEditPost.Visible = IsModeratorOrPoster(lPost.AddedBy.ToLower())

            ' the link for deleting the thread/post is visible only to
administrators, editors and moderators
            Dim btnDeletePost As ImageButton =
CType(e.Item.FindControl("btnDeletePost"), ImageButton)
            If lPost.IsFirstPost Then
                btnDeletePost.OnClientClick =
String.Format(btnDeletePost.OnClientClick, "entire thread")
                btnDeletePost.CommandName = "DeleteThread"
            Else
                btnDeletePost.OnClientClick =
String.Format(btnDeletePost.OnClientClick, "post")
                btnDeletePost.CommandName = "DeletePost"
            End If
            btnDeletePost.CommandArgument = lPost.PostID.ToString()
            btnDeletePost.Visible = isModerator

            ' if the thread is not closed, show the link to quote the post
            Dim lnkQuotePost As HyperLink =
CType(e.Item.FindControl("lnkQuotePost"), HyperLink)
            lnkQuotePost.NavigateUrl = String.Format(lnkQuotePost.NavigateUrl, _
                lPost.ForumId, threadID, lPost.PostID)
            If lPost.IsFirstPost Then
                lnkQuotePost.Visible = Not lPost.Closed
            Else
                lnkQuotePost.Visible = Not lPost.ParentPost.Closed
```

```
        End If

      End If

    End If

  End Sub
```

You also handle the grid's `ItemCommand` event to process the click action of the post's Delete button. You always call `Post.DeletePost` to delete a single post, or an entire thread (the situation is indicated by the `CommandName` property of the method's e parameter), but in the first case you just rebind the `ListView` to its data source, whereas in the second case you redirect to the page that browses the thread's parent forum's threads after deleting it:

```
Private Sub lvPosts_ItemCommand(ByVal sender As Object,
ByVal e As System.Web.UI.WebControls.ListViewCommandEventArgs)
Handles lvPosts.ItemCommand

    Select e.CommandName
      Case "DeleteThread"
        Using lPostrpt As New PostsRepository
          Dim threadPostID As Integer = Convert.ToInt32(e.CommandArgument)
          Dim forumID As Integer = lPostrpt.GetPostById(threadPostID).PostID
          lPostrpt.DeletePost(threadPostID)
          Me.Response.Redirect("BrowseThreads.aspx?ForumID=" &
forumID.ToString())
        End Using

      Case "DeletePost"
        Using lPostrpt As New PostsRepository
          Dim postID As Integer = Convert.ToInt32(e.CommandArgument)
          lPostrpt.DeletePost(postID)

          Dim pagerBottom As DataPager =
DirectCast(lvPosts.FindControl("pagerBottom"), DataPager)
          pagerBottom.SetPageProperties(0,
Settings.Forums.PostsPageSize, False)
          lvPosts.DataBind()
        End Using

    End Select

  End Sub
```

Producing and Consuming RSS Feeds

The forums module includes the `RSSForum` handler, which returns an RSS feed of the forums' threads, either for a single subforum or for all subforums, depending on whether a `ForumID` parameter is passed on the querystring or not. It also supports a `SortExpr` parameter that specifies one of the supported sort expressions, such as `"LastPostDate DESC"` (the default), `"ReplyCount DESC"`, and so forth.

The main difference between the handler and the previous edition is the use of a custom `httpHandler` instead of a Web Form to produce the RSS. As discussed in the Article's module chapter, this is a much more efficient method to produce an RSS feed. The handler uses the same XML Literal mechanisms for VB.NET used in Chapter 5 and LINQ to XML, XDocument, methodology used for C#. The only real difference is the specific query used to retrieve the posts.

```
Public Function GetRSSForum(ByVal vForumId As Integer) As IEnumerable(Of Post)

        Dim key As String = CacheKey & "_IEnumerable"

        Forumctx.Posts.MergeOption = Objects.MergeOption.NoTracking
        Dim lPosts As IEnumerable(Of Post)

        If vForumId > 0 Then

            lPosts = (From lPost In Forumctx.Posts _
                    Order By lPost.LastPostDate Descending).Take(10).AsEnumerable

        Else

            lPosts = (From lPost In Forumctx.Posts _
                Where lPost.Forum.ForumID = vForumId _
                    Order By lPost.LastPostDate Descending).Take(10).AsEnumerable

        End If

        Return lPosts

End Function
```

Remember to make the custom handler actually execute, it must be registered in the `web.config` file. Since we set the `*.rss` to invoke the articles handler, this declaration must be before that declaration.

```
<add verb="*" path="forum.rss" validate="false" type="TheBeerHouse.RSSForum,
TBHBLL, Version=3.5.0.1, Culture=neutral, PublicKeyToken=null" />
<add verb="*" path="*.rss" validate="false" type="TheBeerHouse.RSSFeed,
TBHBLL, Version=3.5.0.1, Culture=neutral, PublicKeyToken=null" />
```

Securing the Forum Module

While developing the pages, we've already inserted many checks to ensure that only certain users can perform actions such as closing, moving, deleting, and editing posts. Programmatic security is required in some circumstances, but in other cases it suffices to use declarative security to allow or deny access to a resource by a given user or role. For example, the `AddEditPost.aspx` page must never be accessed by anonymous users in this implementation, and you can easily enforce this restriction by adding a declaration to the `web.config` file found in the site's root folder: you just need to add a new `<location>` section with a few `<allow>` and `<deny>` elements. There's one other aspect of the `AddEditPost.aspx` page that should be considered: if a member doesn't respect the site's policies and repeatedly submits messages with spam or offensive language, then you'd like to be able to ban the member from adding any new posts. One way to do this is to block messages coming from that IP address, but it's even better to block that user account from accessing the page. However, you don't want to block that account completely; otherwise, that member would lose access to any other section of the site, which would be too restrictive for that particular crime! The easiest way to handle this is to add a new role called "Posters" to all new users at registration time and then add a declarative restriction to web.config that ensures that only users who belong to the Administrators, Editors, Moderators, or Posters role can access the AddEditPost.aspx page, as shown here:

```
<location path="AddEditPost.aspx">
   <system.web>
      <authorization>
         <allow roles="Administrators,Editors,Moderators,Posters" />
         <deny users="*"/>
      </authorization>
   </system.web>
</location>
```

To automatically add a user to the Posters role immediately after the user has registered, you must modify the Register.aspx page developed in Chapter 4 to handle the CreateUserWizard's CreatedUser event (which is raised just after the user has been created), and then call the AddUserToRole method of ASP.NET's Roles class, like this:

```
Protected Sub CreateUserWizard1_CreatedUser(ByVal sender As Object,
ByVal e As System.EventArgs) Handles CreateUserWizard1.CreatedUser
        Roles.AddUserToRole(CreateUserWizard1.UserName, "Posters")
End Sub
```

In the future, if you want to remove a given user's right to post new messages, you only need to remove the user from the Posters role, using the EditUser.aspx administration page developed in Chapter 4. This module's administration page also has some <location> section restrictions in the web.config file located under the Admin folder to ensure that only Administrators, Editors, and Moderators can access them.

Summary

In this chapter, you've built a forums system from scratch, and you did it by leveraging much of the work done in earlier chapters, and many of the new features in ASP.NET 2.0. This was a further example showing how to integrate the built-in membership and profile systems into a custom module, as well as reusing other pages and controls (such as the RssReader control) developed previously. Our forums module supports multiple subforums, with optional moderation; it lists threads and replies through custom pagination (with different sorting options), offers support for publishing and consuming standard RSS feeds, and extends the user profiles with forum-specific properties. We also created administration features for deleting, editing, approving, moving, and closing threads and posts. This is a fairly complete forums module that should work well with many small to midsized sites. However, the subject of user forums in general is a big area, and there are many possible options and features that you might want to consider adding to your forums module. Here are a few suggestions to get you started:

❑ Add support for some open forums, as a subforum-level option, which would be accessible by anonymous posters.

❑ Allow some subforums to have different moderators for more granular security control (especially useful for larger sites that may have multiple moderators who specialize in certain subforums).

❏ Add e-mail notification of new forum activity, or you can even send out e-mail message digests. E-mails could also be used by moderators to be notified about new messages waiting to be approved, and you might even allow the moderator to approve a message simply by clicking a link contained in the e-mail, after reviewing the post's body, also included in the e-mail.

❏ Support a list of banned words and use regular expressions to replace them with acceptable alternatives, or maybe just a generic "###" pattern. Or, you can just tag offending messages for moderation, even if the forum is not a moderated forum (would require a little more work on the plumbing).

❏ Add private forums, whereby members can send each other messages, but each member can only read messages that were specifically addressed to them. This is a handy way to encourage people to communicate with each other, while allowing them to keep their own personal e-mail address hidden from other users (which is often desirable as a means of limiting spam). To make this easier to use, whenever you see the username of someone who posted a message in a forum, that username could have a link to another page that gives you the option to send that user a private message. To ensure that she will read your message, you could add an automatic check for private messages that would occur each time a registered user logs in.

❏ Implement a search feature to enable users to locate messages containing certain words or phrases.

❏ Let members upload their own attachments, which would be accessed from a link in a forum message (be sure to make this an option, because some site owners may not like this idea for security and bandwidth reasons). You could allow configurable filename extensions (disallowing .exe, .bat, .vbs, and so forth, but allowing .doc, .txt, and the like) and a configurable limit on allowable file size. You might also want to force any messages containing an attachment to be moderated so that a power user can review the attachment before allowing it (this is especially important if you want to allow images to be uploaded).

There are numerous very complex and complete forums systems for ASP.NET, and many of them are free. You might want to use one of them if the simple forums module presented here doesn't meet your needs, or you might just want to study the others to get ideas for features you might want to add to your own forum module. One of the best, and most feature-rich, forums modules for ASP.NET is the Community Server, available at www.communityserver.org. This is 100% free for nonprofit sites, and fairly inexpensive for use on commercial sites. This is the same forums module used by the famous www.asp.net site, Microsoft's official ASP.NET developer site. But don't be too quick to discard the forums module developed in this chapter, because even though it's missing some of the more advanced features, it still has several big benefits, including the fact that it's already integrated with the site's common layout and membership system (while others do not, unless you modify them, as they need to be installed on a separate virtual folder that makes it more difficult to share pieces of the parent site); it uses many of the features in ASP.NET 2.0, and it is fairly easy to maintain and understand.

In the next chapter, we'll implement another common requirement in a modern, full-featured website: an e-commerce store with support for real-time electronic payments.

9

E-Commerce Store

In this chapter, we'll implement a simple working e-commerce store for The Beer House, to enable users to shop for mugs, T-shirts, and other gadgets for beer-fanatics. In addition to the existing patterns and knowledge we have covered in this book the store gives us a chance to extend the application of AJAX and custom profile objects. We'll also drill down into e-commerce-specific design and coding issues as we implement a persistent shopping cart, and we'll integrate a third-party payment processor service to support real-time credit card transactions. At the end of the chapter you'll have a complete e-commerce module that you can easily adapt to suit your own needs.

Problem

The Beer House wants to extend its brand and turn the website into a direct revenue stream instead of just a promotional vehicle. Many bars and restaurants sell branded products to customers, which is both profitable and actually provides valuable free advertising. Nothing like customers who are willing to pay you to promote your business!

This chapter covers the design and implementation of an e-commerce store — this option was chosen for our demo website because it's a good example of nontrivial design and coding, and it gives you a chance to examine some additional ASP.NET technology in a real-world scenario. Building an e-commerce store from scratch is one of the most difficult jobs for a web developer, and it requires a good design up front, including accounting for security, leading the shopper to place a profitable order, and the most important thing — collecting money. It's not just a matter of building the site to handle the catalog, the orders, and the payments; a complete business analysis is required. You must identify your audience (potential customers), your competitors, a marketing strategy to promote your site, marketing offers to convince people to shop on your site rather than somewhere else, and plan for offers and other incentives to turn an occasional buyer into a repeat buyer. You also need to arrange a supplier for products that you can sell (if you are not producing them yourself), which involves the order management and shipping functions, and some consideration of local laws (licenses, tax collection, etc.). All of this could require a considerable amount of time, energy, and money, unless you are already running some kind of physical store that you merely want to extend. In this case, we assume that the sample site will use a pub that already has the business knowledge needed to answer the marketing-related questions, and we'll focus on the technical side of this project (a reasonable assumption because we are software developers and not marketing specialists).

> *I recommend any web developer building public-facing sites take some time to learn some basic online marketing skills because doing so can go a long way toward understanding how to effectively build a business's public interface.*

For the sample project, let's say that the owner of TheBeerHouse wants to add an electronic store to the site — to sell beer glasses, T-shirts, key chains, and other gift items for beer enthusiasts. She needs the capability to create an online catalog that lists products divided into categories, one that provides a detailed and appealing description for each product, has pictures of products, and allows users to add them to an electronic shopping cart and pay for them online using a credit card (with a possible option of letting users phone in their orders in case they don't want to divulge their credit card information online). The owner needs the capability to run special promotions by setting up discounts for certain products, and to offer multiple shipping options at different prices. All this must be easily maintainable by the store keeper herself, without routine technical assistance, so you must also provide a very complete and intuitive administrative user interface. Finally, she also needs some kind of order-reporting page that retrieves and lists the latest orders, the orders with a specific status (completed orders, orders that were confirmed but not yet processed, etc.) or orders for a specific customer. It should also enable her to change the order status, the shipment date, and the shipment tracking information, and, of course, see all order details, such as the customer's full address and contact information. In the next section, you'll find a detailed list of requirements and features to be implemented.

Customer service is a very important aspect of any retail business, but there are differences between online and brick-and-mortar service. In person, a customer with a question or product problem can interface directly with a clerk or manager. This is not always the case with online stores, but there are steps that can be taken to improve the user experience when something goes wrong. The most basic features include a contact form or phone number prominently displayed on the site. This gives customers a sense of comfort; they can always contact you if they need help. Because the Beer House site is a demonstration site, no phone number is displayed, but you should do this for any small online store.

One of the most overlooked customer service features any online store can have is a policies or terms and conditions page. Simply put this is your policies and procedures concerning common issues that happen, such as broken merchandise, lost items in shipping, returns, and the like. My experience over the years is this is the one statement that can give you leverage against a bad customer. Most of the time you will not have to deal with this situation, but it will occur. The other important aspect is a privacy policy; this should also be have a link from every page in the site.

Design

As you can gather from the "Problem" section, implementing a custom e-commerce module can easily be a big challenge, and entire books have been devoted to this subject. With this in mind, and because of space constraints, this is the only chapter to cover that subject, including selected features that any such store must have. Although this module won't compete with sites like Amazon.com in terms of features, it will be complete enough to actually run a real, albeit small, e-store. As you've done in other chapters, you'll leverage much of the other functionality already developed, such as membership and profile management (see Chapter 4), and our general DAL/BLL design, ASP.NET AJAX, and URL Rewriting (see Chapter 3). Therefore, the following list specifies the new functionality you'll implement in this chapter:

❑ Support for multiple store departments, used to categorize products so that they're easy to find if the catalog has a lot of items

❑ Products need a description with support for rich formatting, and images to graphically represent them. Because customers can't hold the product in their own hands, any written details and visual aids will help them understand the product and may lead to a sale. It is also very important in earning high search engine position for search phrases. A small thumbnail image will be shown in the products listing and on the product page, while a bigger image can be shown when the user clicks on the small image to zoom in.

❑ Products will support a discount percentage that the storekeeper will set when she wants to run a promotion for that item. The customer will still see the full price on the product page, along with the discount percentage (so that she can "appreciate" the sale, and feel compelled to order the product), and the final price that she will pay to buy the product.

❑ As you've already done for the articles and forums modules, this module will also expose an RSS feed for the products catalog, which can be consumed on the home page of the site itself, or by external RSS readers set up by customers who want to be notified about new products.

❑ Also the use of Search Engine Friendly URLS will be implemented like the Articles module. Both the store department and individual product pages will use friendly URLs.

❑ Some simple stock availability management will be needed, such as the possibility to specify how many units of a particular item are in stock. This value will be decreased every time someone confirms an order for that product, and the storekeeper will be able to see which products need to be reordered (i.e., when there are only a few units left in stock).

❑ The storekeeper will be able to easily add, remove, and edit shipping methods, such as Standard Ground, Next Business Day, and Overnight, each with a different price. Customers will be able to specify a preferred shipping option when completing the order.

❑ The module needs a persistent shopping cart for items that the customer wants to purchase. Making it persistent means that the user can place some items in the shopping cart, close the browser, and end her session, and come back to the site later and still find her shopping cart as she left it, so that she doesn't need to browse the entire catalog again to find the products she previously put in the cart. The customer may want time to consider the purchase before submitting it, she may want to compare your price with competitors first, or she may not have her credit card with her in that moment, so it's helpful for users to be able to put items in the cart and come back later to finalize the deal.

❑ The current content of the shopping cart (the names of the items that were put inside it, as well as their quantity and unit price) and the subtotal should be always visible on each page of the catalog, and possibly on the entire site, so that the user can easily keep it in mind (you want it to be easy for customers to check out when they are ready, and you don't want them to forget to check out).

❑ A user account is required to complete the order, because you'll need some way to identify users when they come back to the site after submitting the order, to see the status of their order. However, a well-designed e-commerce module should not ask users to log in or create a user account until actually required, to ease the shopping process. If a new user is asked to create an account (and thus fill up a long form, providing personal information, etc.) before even beginning to shop, this may be a bother and prevent visitors from even looking at your products. If, instead, you allow visitors to browse for products, add them to a shopping cart, and only ask them to log in or create a new account just before confirming the order, they'll consider this request as a normal step of the checkout process, and won't complain about it (and you've already hooked them into putting items in their cart).

❑ To make the checkout process as smooth as possible, the shipping address information should be prefilled with the address stored in the user's profile, if found (remember that those details were optional at registration time). However, the shipping address may be different from the customer's address (possibly because the purchase is a gift for someone else), and thus the address may be edited for any order. The profile address should only be used as the default value. The billing address may be different also, but that will be collected by the payment processor service (more details later).

❑ The storekeeper must have a page that lists the orders of any specific interval of dates, using the last *n* days as a default interval (*n* is configurable in the default `web.config` file). She may also need to retrieve all orders for a specific customer, or jump directly to a particular order if she already knows its ID. The list will show a few order details, while a separate page will show the complete information, including the list of items ordered, the customer's contact information, and the shipping address. Besides this read-only history data, the storekeeper must be able to edit the order's status (the number and title of order statuses must also be customizable by the store's administrator), the shipping date, and optionally the transaction ID and tracking ID (if tracking is available by the shipping method chosen by the customer during checkout).

❑ Add a Privacy and Terms and Conditions page to the site.

As anticipated, you may want, or need, to add many additional features. However, the features in the preceding list will give you a basic starting point for a working solution. In the following sections, you'll read more about some e-commerce-specific issues, such as choosing a service for real-time credit card processing, and then you'll create the typical design of the Entity Model, BLL, and UI parts of the module.

Choosing an Online Payment Solution

The user has visited your site, browsed the catalog, read the description of some products, and put them into the shopping cart. She finally decides that the prices and conditions are good, and wants to finalize the order. This means providing her personal information (name, contact details, and shipping address) and, of course, paying by credit card. You should plan for, and offer, as many payment solutions as you can, to satisfy all types of customers. Some prefer to send a check via snail mail; others prefer to provide the credit card information by fax or phone, and others are fine with paying via their credit card online.

The best option for the storekeeper is, of course, the online transaction, as it is the most secure (information is encrypted and no physical person sees it), it gives immediate feedback to the user, and it doesn't require the storekeeper to do anything. Several third-party services, called *payment gateways*, provide this service. They receive some order details, perform a secure transaction for the customer, and keep a small fee for each order — typically a percentage of the transaction amount, but it may also be a fixed fee, or possibly a combination of the two. You can integrate your site with these services in one of two ways:

❑   HTML forms
❑   Fully integrated payments

Implementing HTML Forms

The customer clicks the button on your site to confirm the order and pays for it. At this point, the user is redirected to the external site of the payment gateway. That site will ask your customer for her billing information (name, address, and credit card number) and will execute the transaction. The gateway's site resides on a secure server, that is, a server where the SSL protocol is used to encrypt the data sent between the customer's browser and the server. After the payment, the customer is redirected back to your site. Figure 9-1 illustrates the process.

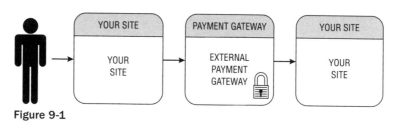

Figure 9-1

The Secure Sockets Layer (SSL) is a secure web protocol that encrypts all data between a web server and a user's computer to prevent anyone else from knowing what information was sent over that connection. SSL certificates are used on web servers and are issued by third-party certificate authorities (CA), which guarantee to the customer that the site they're shopping at really has the identity it declares. A customer can identify the use of SSL by the presence of "https:" instead of "http:" in the URL, and by the padlock icon typically shown in the browser's status bar. To learn more about SSL, you can search on Google or visit the websites of CAs such as GeoTrust, VeriSign, or Comodo. These providers ultimately offer the same security product, but their prices and requirements vary.

Our store's checkout page sends the payment gateway's page the amount to charge, the recipient account where it should place the money, the currency, and the URL where the customer will be redirected in case of a successful or canceled order, using an HTML form that posts the data contained in a few hidden fields. Here's an example:

```
<form method="post" action="https://payment_gateway_url_here">
    <input type="hidden" name="LoginName" value="THEBEERHOUSE">
    <input type="hidden" name="OrderAmount" value="46.50 ">
    <input type="hidden" name="OrderCurrency" value="USD">
    <input type="hidden" name="OrderID" value="#12345">
    <input type="hidden" name="OrderDescription" value="Beer Glass #2 (4 pieces)"
    <input type="hidden" name="ConfirmUrl"
      value="http://www.yoursite.com/order_ok.aspx">
    <input type="hidden" name="CancelUrl"
      value="http://www.yoursite.com/order_ko.aspx">
    <input type="submit" value="CLICK HERE TO PAY NOW!">
</form>
```

Every payment gateway has its own parameters, with different names, and accepts data following their own conventions, but the overall principle is the same for all of them. Many gateways also accept the expected parameters through a GET request instead of a POST, which means that parameters are passed on the querystring: in this case, you can build the complete URL on your site, possibly from within the Click event handler of your ASP.NET form's Submit button, and then redirect the customer to it (but this method is less desirable because the querystring is visible).

Most of the information you pass to the gateway is also forwarded to the store site once the customer comes back to it, either in the Order Confirmed or the Order Canceled page, so that the original order is recognized (by means of its ID) and the record representing it in your database is updated with the appropriate status code. Some payment gateway services encrypt the data they send to you and give you a private key used to decrypt the data, so that you can ensure that the customer did not manually jump directly to your order finalization page. Others use different mechanisms, but you always have some way to be notified whether payment was made (despite this automatic notification, it would be wise to validate that the payment was actually processed to ensure that a hacker has not tried to give us a false indication that a payment was made).

The advantage of using an external payment service is its ease of integration and management. You only forward the user to the external gateway (to a URL built according the gateway's specifications guide), and handle the customer's return after she has paid for the order, or canceled it. You don't have to deal with the actual money transaction, nor do you have to worry about the security of the transaction, which would at least imply setting up SSL on your site, and you don't have to worry about keeping the customer's credit card information stored in a safe manner and complying with privacy laws (if you only keep the customer's name and address you don't have to worry about the kinds of laws that protect account numbers).

The disadvantage is that the customer actually leaves your site for the payment process, which may be disorienting and inconvenient. While it's true that most payment gateway services allow the site's owner/developer to change their payment page's colors and insert the store's logo inside it, the customization often does not go much further, so the difference between the store's pages and the external payment page will be evident. This would not be a problem if you've just created and launched an e-commerce site that nobody knows and trusts. A customer may be more inclined to leave her credit card information on the site of a well-known payment gateway, instead of on your lesser known site. In that case, the visibility of the external payment service may actually help sales. For larger e-commerce sites that already have a strong reputation and are trusted by a large audience, this approach won't be as appealing because it looks less professional than complete integration.

Implementing Fully Integrated Payments

The second approach to handling online payments also relies on an external payment gateway, but instead of physically moving the user to the external site and then bringing her back to your site, she never leaves your site in the first place: she enters all her billing and credit card information on our page, which you then pass to the external service behind the scenes (and you don't store it within your own system). The gateway will ultimately return a response code that indicates the transaction's success or failure (plus some additional information such as the transaction ID), and you can display some feedback to the user on your page. This approach is depicted in Figure 9-2.

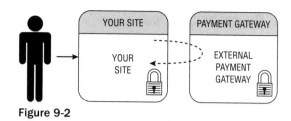

Figure 9-2

The manner in which your page communicates and exchanges data with the gateway service may be a web service or some other simpler server-to-server technology, such as programmatically submitting a POST request with the System.Net.HttpWebRequest class of the .NET Framework, and handling the textual response (usually a simple string with some code indicating success or failure). The obvious advantage of this approach is that the customer stays at your site for the entire process, so that all the pages have the same look and feel, which you can customize as you prefer, and you don't need to worry about fake or customer-generated confirmation requests from the payment gateway, because everything happens from server to server during a single postback.

A disadvantages of this approach is that you're in charge of securing the transmission of sensitive information from the customer's browser to your site (even though you don't store the info, it will still be transferred to and from your web server), by installing a SSL certificate on your server, and using HTTPS to access your own checkout pages. If credit card information is hijacked somehow during the transmission, or if you don't comply with all the necessary security standards, you may get into big legal trouble, and you may lose all your other customers if they hear about the problem. Another disadvantage is that if your site is small and unknown, then some customers may be reluctant to give you their credit card number, something they would feel comfortable doing with a large and well-known credit card–processing service.

It should be clear by now which of the two approaches you may prefer, and this will be influenced by the size of the store, its transaction volume, its popularity among the customers, and how much money the store owner wants to invest. Implementing the second approach requires buying and installing a SSL certificate, it leaves more responsibilities to both you and the store's owner, so you might choose the first approach, which is simpler, more cost-effective, and still very good for small sites. Conversely, if you're implementing a new e-commerce storefront for a large site that is already selling online and is very popular, then the complete integration of the payment process into the store is definitely the best and most professional option.

For the e-commerce store of TheBeerHouse, we'll follow the simpler approach and implement a payment solution that forwards the customer to the external payment service's page. As the store grows, you may wish to upgrade the site to use a fully integrated payment mechanism in the future.

There are many payment services to choose from, but some of them can only be used in one country, or may only accept a small variety of credit cards. Because I wanted to implement a solution that could work for as many readers as possible and be simple to integrate with, I selected PayPal. PayPal is widely known as the main service used by eBay, and it accepts many popular credit cards and works in many countries.

Using PayPal as the Payment Service

PayPal started as a service that enabled people to exchange money from one user's account to another, or to have payment sent to the user's home in the form of a check, but it has grown into a full-featured payment service that is used by a huge number of merchants worldwide as their favorite payment method, for a number of reasons:

- ❑ Competitive transaction fees, which are lower than most payment gateways.

- ❑ Great recognition among customers worldwide. At the time of writing, it reports more than 86 million registered users. Much of their popularity stems from their relationship with eBay, but PayPal is definitely not restricted to use within eBay.

- ❑ It is available to 56 countries, and it supports multiple languages and multiple currencies.

- ❑ It supports taking orders via phone, fax, or mail, and processes credit cards from a management console called Virtual Terminal (available in the United States only).

- ❑ Support for automated recurring payments, which is useful for sites that offer subscription-based access to their content, and need to bill their members regularly — on a monthly basis, for example.

- ❑ Easy integration. Just create an HTML form with the proper parameters to redirect the customer to the payment page, and specify the return URL for confirmed and canceled payments.

- ❑ Multiple products that target business of all sizes for online payment processing. PayPal offers integrated gateway products as well as PayPal hosted payment forms.

- ❑ Almost immediate setup. However, your store needs to use a validated PayPal account, which requires a simple process whereby they can send a small deposit to your linked bank account, and you verify the amount and date of the transfer. This validation step is simple but necessary to prove that the electronic transfer works with your bank account, and it proves your identity.

- ❑ It has some good customization options, such as changing the payment pages' colors and logo, so that it integrates, at least partially, with your site's style.

- ❑ Multiple payment integration opportunities, including both types of gateway interfaces previously described.

- ❑ It offers complete control over which customers can make a purchase (for example, only U.S. customers with a verified address) and enables merchants to set up different tax and shipping amounts for different countries and states.

- ❑ It provides a robust sandbox to allow developers to test their applications without fear of running up transaction fees against the live payment gateway.

Choosing PayPal as the payment processor for TheBeerHouse allows you to start with its Website Payments Standard option, `https://www.paypal.com/cgi-bin/webscr?cmd=_wp-standard-overview-outside`, (the HTML form that redirects the customer to the PayPal's pages) and later upgrade to Website Payments Pro, `https://www.paypal.com/cgi-bin/webscr?cmd=_wp-pro-overview-outside`, or PayFlow Pro gateway, `https://www.paypal.com/cgi-bin/webscr?cmd=_payflow-gateway-overview-outside`. if you want to completely integrate the payment process into your site, hiding PayPal from the customer's eyes. All in all, PayPal offers a lot of options for flexibility, as well as support and detailed guides for merchants and developers who want to use it. I'll outline a few steps for setting up the PayPal integration here. See the official documentation at `https://cms.paypal.com/us/cgi-bin/?cmd=_render-content&content_ID=developer/howto_html_landing` and `http://developer.paypal.com` for further details and examples. Even without prior knowledge of PayPal, it's still trivial to set up, and it works well.

Of special interest for developers is the Sandbox, a complete replication of PayPal used for development and testing of systems that interact with PayPal (including all the administrative and management pages, where you configure all types of settings). This test environment doesn't make real transactions but works with test credit card numbers and accounts. Developers can create an account for free (on developer.paypal.com) and then create PayPal test business accounts for use within the Sandbox. These test accounts can then be used as the recipient for sample transactions. You only need to know a few basic parameters, described in the following table:

Property	Description
cmd	Specifies in which mode you're using PayPal's pages. A value equal to _xclick specifies that you're using the Pay Now mode, whereby the customer lands on the PayPal's checkout page, types in her billing details, and completes the order. If the value is _cart, then you'll be using PayPal's integrated shopping cart, which allows users to keep going back and forth from your store site to PayPal to add multiple items to a cart managed by PayPal, until the customer wants to check out. In this case, you'll be implementing your own shopping cart and only use PayPal only for the final processing, so you'll use the _xclick value.
upload	A value of 1 indicates that you're using your own shopping cart.
currency_code	Specifies the currency in which the other amount parameters (see below) are denoted. If not specified, the default value is USD (United States Dollar). Other possible values are AUD (Australian Dollar), CAD (Canadian Dollar), EUR (Euro), GBP (Pound Sterling), and JPY (Japanese Yen). We'll allow our site administrator to configure this setting.
business	The e-mail address that identifies the PayPal business account that will be the recipient for the transaction. For example, I've created the account thebeerhouse@wrox.com through the Sandbox, to use for my tests. You should create a Sandbox account of your own for testing.
item_number	A number/string identifying the order.
first_name	First name
last_name	Last name
address1	Street (1 of 2 fields)
city	City
state	State
zip	Postal code
custom	A custom variable that can contain anything you want. This is called a pass-through parameter, because its value will be passed back to your store site when PayPal notifies you of the outcome of the transaction by calling our server-side page indicated by the notify_url page (see below).
item_name	A descriptive string for the order the customer is going to pay for, for example, Order #25, or maybe "TheBeerHouse order 12345."

Continued

Property	Description
amount	The amount the user will pay, in the currency specified by `currency_code`. You must use the point (.) as the separator for the decimal part of the number, regardless of the currency and language being used, for example, 33.80.
shipping	The cost of the shipping, specified in the same currency of the amount, and in the same format. This will be added to the amount parameter to calculate the total price the customer must pay. Example: 6.00
return	The URL the customer will be redirected to after completing the payment on PayPal's page, for example, `www.yoursite.com/paypal/orderconfirmed.aspx`. In this page, you'll typically provide some form of static feedback to your customer that provides further instructions to track the order status, and will mark the order as confirmed. The URL must be encoded, so the previous URL would become `http%3a%2f%2fwww.yoursite.com%2fPayPal%2fOrderCompleted.aspx`.
cancel_return	The URL to which the customer will be redirected after canceling the payment on PayPal's page, for example, `www.yoursite.com/paypal/ordercancelled.aspx`. In this page, you'll typically provide your customer some information to make the payment later. This URL must be encoded as explained for the return parameter.
notify_url	The URL used by PayPal's Instant Payment Notification (IPN) to asynchronously notify you of the outcome of a transaction. This is done in addition to the redirection to the return URL, which happens just after the payment, and which you can't trust because a smart customer might manually type in the URL for your site's order confirmation page, once she has discovered its format (possibly from a previous regular order). IPN is a mechanism based on server-to-server communication: PayPal calls your page by passing some information that identifies the transaction (such as the order ID, the amount paid, etc.), and you interrogate PayPal to determine whether this notification is real or was created by a malicious user. To verify the notification, you forward all the parameters received in the notification back to PayPal, making a programmatic asynchronous POST request (through the `HttpWebRequest` class), and see if PayPal responds with a "VERIFIED" string. If that's the case, you can finally mark the order as confirmed and verified.

Instead of creating a form making an HTTP POST (and thus passing the required parameters in the request's body), you can make a GET request and pass all parameters in the querystring, as in the example that follows:

```
https://www.sandbox.paypal.com/us/cgi-bin/webscr?cmd=_xclick&upload=1&rm=2
&no_shipping=1&no_note=1&currency_code=USD&business=thebeerhouse%40wrox.com
&item_number=25&custom=25&item_name=Order+%2325&amount=33.80
&shipping=6.00&notify_url=http%3a%2f%2fwww.yoursite.com%2fPayPal%2fNotify.aspx
&return=http%3a%2f%2fwww.yoursite.com%2fPayPal%2fOrderCompleted.aspx%3fID%3d25
&cancel_return=http%3a%2f%2fwww.yoursite.com%2fPayPal%2fOrderCancelled.aspx
```

The preceding URL would redirect the customer to the Sandbox test environment. To handle real payments later, all you need to do is replace the "`https://www.sandbox.paypal.com/us/cgi-bin/`"

webscr" part with "https://www.paypal.com/us/cgi-bin/webscr". Later in the chapter you'll see how to dynamically build URLs for order-specific checkout pages, and how to implement the return and verification pages. For now, however, you should have enough background information to get started! So let's proceed with the design of the database, and then the DAL, BLL, and UI.

Designing the Database Tables

The e-commerce store module uses six tables for the catalog of products and order management, as shown in Figure 9-3.

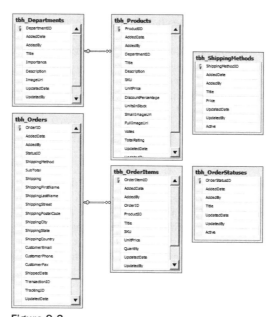

Figure 9-3

All catalog data is stored in tbh_Departments (the categories of products, which is similar to tbh_Categories used by the articles module in Chapter 5) and tbh_Products, which contains the title, price, description, images, and other information about specific products. Note that it contains a UnitPrice field and a DiscountPercentage field, but the final price is not saved in the database; rather, it is dynamically calculated on the BLL. Similarly, there are the Votes and TotalRating fields (which have a similar usage to the tbh_Articles table), and the AverageRating information will be dynamically calculated later. The relationship between the two tables makes tbh_Products.DepartmentID a foreign key and establishes cascade updates and deletes, so that if a department is deleted, then all of its products are automatically deleted as well.

A similar relationship exists between tbh_Orders and tbh_OrderItems. The former stores information about the order, such as its subtotal and shipping amount, the complete customer's contact information and shipping address, shipping method, current order status, and transaction and tracking ID. The latter is the Details table of the master-detail relationship, and stores the order lines of the product, whereby a line describes each ordered product, with its title, ID, unit price, quantity, and stock-keeping unit (SKU) — a SKU is a marketing term designating a product; it's basically a model number (you will use the SKU to reorder more items of a given type). There are also two more support tables, which store shipping options and order status.

You may be wondering why the tbh_Orders and tbh_OrderItems tables maintain a copy of many values that could be retrieved by joining two tables. Take, for example, the tbh_Orders.ShippingMethod and tbh_Orders.Shipping fields, which you may assume could be replaced with a single ShippingMethodID foreign key that references a record in tbh_ShippingMethods. As another example, consider that tbh_OrderItems contains the title, price, and SKU of the ordered product, even if it already has a reference to the product in the tbh_Products table through the ProductID foreign key. However, think about the situation when a shipping method is deleted or edited, which changes its title and price. If you only linked an order record to a record of ShippedMethods, this would result in a different total amount and a different shipping method after the change, which obviously can't be permitted after an order was submitted and confirmed (you can't modify data of a confirmed order because it would be too late). The same is true for products: you can delete or change the price of a product, but orders made before the change cannot be modified, and they must keep the price and all other information as they were at the time of the order. If a product is deleted, the storekeeper must still be able to determine the product's name, SKU, and price, to identify and ship it correctly. All this wouldn't be possible if you only stored the ID of the product because that would become useless once the product were deleted. The product ID is still kept in the tbh_OrderItems table, but only as optional information that would enable you to create a hyperlink to the product page if the product is still available. The tbh_Orders and tbh_OrderItems tables are self-contained history tables.

The exception to this rule is the tbh_Orders.StatusID field, which actually references a record of tbh_OrderStatuses: there will be three built-in statuses in this table (of which you can customize at least the title), which identify an order waiting for payment, a confirmed order (PayPal redirected to the OrderConfirmed.aspx page), and a verified order (an order for which you've verified the payment's authenticity by means of PayPal's IPN notification). The tbh_Orders and tbh_OrderItems tables are also read-only for the most part, except for some information in the tbh_Orders table, such as the StatusID, ShippedDate, TrackingID, and TransactionID fields, which must be updatable to reflect the changes that happen to the order during its processing.

Designing the Configuration Module

The configuration settings of the store module are defined in a <store> element within the <theBeerHouse> section of the web.config file. The class that maps the settings is StoreElement, which defines the following properties:

Property	Description
RatingLockInterval	Number of days that must pass before a customer can rate a product that she has already rated previously.
PageSize	Default number of products listed per page. The user will be able to change the page size from the user interface.
RssItems	Number of products included in the RSS feeds.
DefaultOrderListInterval	Number of days from the current date used to calculate the start date of the default date interval in which to retrieve the orders in a specific state (in the storekeeper's management console). The interval's start and end date can be changed in the administration page.

Property	Description
SandboxMode	Boolean value indicating whether the transactions will be run in PayPal's Sandbox test environment or in the real PayPal.
BusinessEmail	E-mail address of the PayPal business account that will be the recipient for the money transfer executed on PayPal to pay for the order.
CurrencyCode	String identifying the currency for the amounts that the customer will pay on PayPal. The default is USD. This currency code will also be used in the amounts shown in the end-user pages on the right side of the amounts (e.g., 12.50 USD).
LowAvailability	Lower threshold of units in stock that determines when a product should be reordered to replenish the stock. This condition will be displayed graphically on the page with special icons.
ProductURLIndicator	The string designating the path token used in the Search Engine Friendly URL to retrieve a Catalog Department page.
DepartmentURLIndicator	The string designating the path token used in the Search Engine Friendly URL to retrieve a Product Detail page.

Designing the Entity Model

As usual, the Entity Model is created by running the wizard, which creates the entities for each table in the database and their relationships. After the wizard completes, the entity names and relationships should be adjusted to make them more human readable by removing the `tbh_` prefix and adjusting the singular and plural state for the Set and entity name. Figures 9-4 through 9-6 show the Entity Model with the final names.

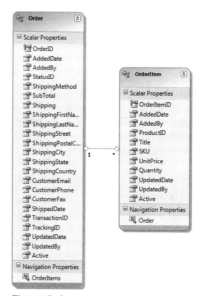

Figure 9-4

443

Figure 9-5

Figure 9-6

Designing the Business Layer

The business layer for the E-Commerce module follows the same rules that have been reviewed in previous chapters. Each entity has a corresponding repository class that inherits from a `BaseShoppingCartRepository` class. Each of these repositories contains members that manage querying, inserting, and updating records. Each entity also has a class that extends the partial class nature of the entity class. Here additional properties and validation logic is managed. Figure 9-7 shows the classes that manage the store's catalog.

Figure 9-8 illustrates the classes needed for managing orders: the shopping cart, the shipping methods, the order statuses, and the actual order storage.

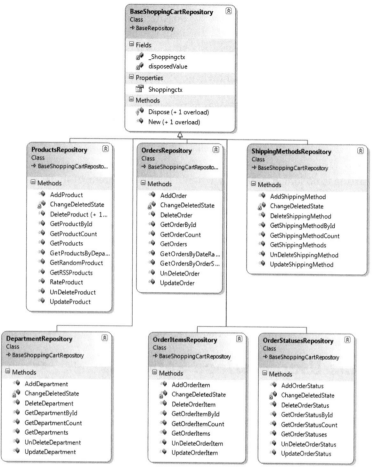

Figure 9-7

Figure 9-8

Most of the classes displayed in the figure don't require further explanation. However, the classes related to the shopping cart are not typical, and we'll examine these now. As mentioned earlier, we want to make the shopping cart persistent between different sessions of the same user. Prior to ASP.NET 2.0, projects like this would have required creating your own tables, stored procedures or SQL statements, and classes for saving the shopping cart data in a durable medium, instead of using `Session` variables that would only last a short time. Now, however, we can create a domain class that represents the cart, and, assuming the class is serializable, you can use it as a data type for a profile variable, and let ASP. NET's profile module persist and load it for the current user automatically, including anonymous users!

The `ShoppingCart` class displayed earlier is such a class: its methods add, modify, and remove items (represented by `ShoppingCartItem` objects) to and from an internal `Dictionary` object (the generic version of `Dictionary` actually, which has been specialized for storing `ShoppingCartItem` objects, so that explicit casting is no longer necessary when retrieving an item from it), and its `Total` property dynamically calculates the shopping cart's total amount by multiplying the quantity by the unit price of each product, adding the result for each item. The other class, `CurrentUserShoppingCart`, provides static methods that just call the similarly named method of the `ShoppingCart` object for the current user. The `CurrentUserShoppingCart` class is used as the object referenced because it cannot directly reference a `profile` property in its `TypeName` property.

Finally, note the `Order.InsertOrder` method does not take a list of items, with all their details, to be copied into records of `thb_OrderItems`, but rather, takes an instance of the `ShoppingCart` class, which already contains all this data. Additionally, it also takes the customer's details and the shipping address, which is not contained in the `ShoppingCart`.

Designing the User Interface Services

This module is made up of many pages. As usual, there is a complete administration console that allows you to edit practically all the data it uses. In addition to the existing roles (Administrators, Editors, Contributors, and Posters) a new role named StoreKeepers should be created to designate which users will be allowed to administer the store. A new role, separate from the current Editors role, was necessary because people managing articles, polls, and newsletters are not necessarily the same people who will manage products and orders (and vice versa). However, there are a few sensitive functions that only an Administrator can perform, such as deleting orders. Here is a complete list of pages and user controls used by the module:

❑ **~/Admin/ManageDepartments.aspx:** Let's an administrator or storekeeper add, edit, and delete store departments.

❑ **~/Admin/AddEditDepartment.aspx:** Lets an administrator or storekeeper add a new department or edit an existing one.

❑ **~/Admin/ManageShippingMethods.aspx:** Lets an administrator or storekeeper add, edit, and delete shipping methods.

❑ **~/Admin/AddEditShippingMethod.aspx:** Lets an administrator or storekeeper add a new shipping method or edit an existing one.

❑ **~/Admin/ManageOrderStatuses.aspx:** Lets an administrator or storekeeper add, edit, and delete store order statuses.

❑ **~/Admin/AddEditOrderStatus.aspx:** Lets an administrator or storekeeper add a new order status or edit an existing one.

❑ **~/Admin/ManageDepartments.aspx:** Lets an administrator or storekeeper view the list of departments, with their title, description, and associated image. Also contains links and commands to edit, delete departments, and display the administration of the department's products.

❑ **~/Admin/AddEditDepartment.aspx:** Lets an administrator or storekeeper add a new department or edit an existing one.

❑ **~/Admin/ManageProducts.aspx:** Lets an administrator or storekeeper view the list of products, with their title, unit price, average rating, availability, and other information. Also contains links and commands to edit and delete products.

❑ **~/Admin/AddEditProduct.aspx:** Lets an administrator or storekeeper add a new product or edit an existing one.

❑ **~/Admin/ManageOrders.aspx:** Lets an administrator or storekeeper find and review orders by customer name, status, or ID. However, only administrators can delete orders.

❑ **~/Admin/EditOrder.aspx:** Lets an administrator or storekeeper manage a specific order, that is, review all of its details and edit a few of its properties, such as the status, the shipping date, and the transaction and tracking ID.

❑ **~/ShowDepartments.aspx:** This end-user page displays the list of store departments, with an image and a description for each of them, along with a link to browse their products.

❑ **~/BrowseProducts.aspx:** Renders a list of products with paging support, for a specific department or for all departments. Information such as the product's title, unit price, discount, average rating, availability, and a small image are displayed.

❑ **~/ShowProduct.aspx:** Shows all details about a specific product, allows a customer to rate the product, and allows them to add the product to their shopping cart, for later review or purchase.

❑ **~/ShoppingCart.aspx:** Shows the current contents of the customer's shopping cart, allowing them to change the quantity of any item, remove an item, choose a shipping method, and then recalculate the subtotal, shipping, and total amounts. This page also provides a three-step wizard for checkout: the first step is the actual shopping cart just described; in the second step, the customers provide the shipping address (by default this is retrieved from the user's address, stored in their profile, if present), and in the final step customers can review all the order information, that it, the list of items they're about to order (with unit price and quantity), the subtotal, the shipping method and its cost, the total amount, and the address to which the products will be shipped. After the last step is confirmed, the order is saved in the database, and the customer is sent to the PayPal site to pay for the order.

❑ **~/PayPal/OrderCompleted.aspx:** This is the page to which PayPal redirects customers after they pay for the order. The page provides some feedback to the user and marks the order as confirmed.

❑ **~/PayPal/OrderCancelled.aspx:** This is the page to which PayPal redirects customers after they have canceled the order. The page provides some feedback to the customer, explaining that the order was saved, and that it can be paid for later.

❑ **~/PayPalIPN.ashx:** This is the page to which PayPal sends the transaction's result, as part of the Instant Payment Notification. It confirms that the notification is verified, and if so, marks it as such.

❑ **~/OrderHistory.aspx:** This lets customers review their past orders, to check their status, or if/when they were shipped, and so forth. For orders that were canceled during payment, a link to return to PayPal and complete the payment is provided.

❑ **~/Products.rss:** This is a custom `HttpHandler` that produces the RSS feed for the store catalog, returning a number of products (the number is specified by the `RssItems` configuration setting described earlier) sorted according to a querystring parameter. For example, it may return the 10 most recent products, the 10 least expensive products, or the 10 most discounted products (great for immediate syndication of special offers).

❑ **~/Controls/ShoppingCartBox.ascx:** This user control statically displays the current contents of the customer's shopping cart, with the name and quantity of the products. It doesn't support editing but provides a link to the `ShoppingCart.aspx` page where this can be done. It also has a link to the `OrderHistory.aspx` page. The control will be plugged into the site's shared layout, so that these links and information are easily reachable from anywhere on the site.

❑ **~/Privacy.aspx:** A static page contains the site's privacy policy.

❑ **~/Terms.aspx:** A static page contains the site's terms and conditions.

Solution

We'll go very quickly through much of the implementation of the solution, as the structure of many classes and pages is similar to those developed for previous modules. In particular, creation of the database tables, the Entity Data Model, and the configuration code is completely skipped in this chapter, because of space constraints. Of course, you'll find the complete details in the code download. Instead, I'll focus this space on the implementation of code containing features not already discussed, and code containing interesting logic, such as the shopping cart profile class and the companion classes, as well as the checkout process and the integration with PayPal.

Implementing the Business Logic Layer

First, we'll examine the BLL classes related to the shopping cart, starting with the `ShoppingCartItem` class, which is a class that wraps data for an item in the cart, with its title, SKU, ID, unit price, and quantity. This class is decorated with the `[Serializable]` attribute, which is necessary to allow the ASP.NET profile system to persist the `ShoppingCartItem` objects. Here's the code:

```
<Serializable()> _
Public Class ShoppingCartItem

        Private _id As Integer = 0
        Private _title As String = String.Empty
        Private _sku As String = String.Empty
        Private _unitPrice As Decimal
        Private _quantity As Integer = 1

        Public Property ID() As Integer
            Get
                 Return _id
            End Get
            Private Set(ByVal value As Integer)
```

```vbnet
                    _id = value
            End Set
        End Property

        Public Property Title() As String
            Get
                Return _title
            End Get
            Private Set(ByVal value As String)
                _title = value
            End Set
        End Property

        Public Property SKU() As String
            Get
                Return _sku
            End Get
            Private Set(ByVal value As String)
                _sku = value
            End Set
        End Property

        Public Property UnitPrice() As Decimal
            Get
                Return _unitPrice
            End Get
            Private Set(ByVal value As Decimal)
                _unitPrice = value
            End Set
        End Property

        Public Property Quantity() As Integer
            Get
                Return _quantity
            End Get
            Set(ByVal value As Integer)
                _quantity = value
            End Set
        End Property

        Public Sub New(ByVal id As Integer, ByVal title As String, _
    ByVal sku As String, ByVal unitPrice As Decimal)
            Me.ID = id
            Me.Title = title
            Me.SKU = sku
            Me.UnitPrice = unitPrice
        End Sub
End Class
```

The ShoppingCart class exposes a number of methods for inserting, removing, and retrieving multiple ShoppingCartItem objects to and from an internal Dictionary object instantiated for that type. When an item is inserted, the class checks whether the Dictionary already contains an item with the same ID: if not, it adds it; otherwise, it increments the Quantity property of the existing item. The RemoveItem method works similarly, but it decrements the Quantity if the item is found; if the Quantity reaches 0, it completely removes the item from the shopping cart. RemoveProduct suggests the same action, but it's actually different, because it removes a product from the cart, regardless of its quantity. UpdateItemQuantity updates an item's quantity, and is used when the customer edits the quantities in the shopping cart page. Finally, the Clear method empties the shopping cart by clearing the internal Dictionary. Here's the complete code:

```vb
<Serializable()> _
Public Class ShoppingCart
        Private _items As New Dictionary(Of Integer, ShoppingCartItem)()

        Public ReadOnly Property Items() As ICollection
            Get
                 Return _items.Values
            End Get
        End Property

        ' Gets the sum total of the items' prices
        Public ReadOnly Property Total() As Decimal
            Get
                Dim sum As Decimal = 0.0
                For Each item As ShoppingCartItem In _items.Values
                    sum += item.UnitPrice * item.Quantity
                Next
                Return sum
            End Get
        End Property

        ' Adds a new item to the shopping cart
        Public Sub InsertItem(ByVal id As Integer, ByVal title As String, _
ByVal sku As String, ByVal unitPrice As Decimal)
            If _items.ContainsKey(id) Then
                _items(id).Quantity += 1
            Else
                _items.Add(id, New ShoppingCartItem(id, title, sku, unitPrice))
            End If
        End Sub

        ' Removes an item from the shopping cart
        Public Sub DeleteItem(ByVal id As Integer)
            If _items.ContainsKey(id) Then
                Dim item As ShoppingCartItem = _items(id)
                item.Quantity -= 1
                If item.Quantity = 0 Then _
                    _items.Remove(id)
            End If
        End Sub

        ' Removes all items of a specified product from the shopping cart
        Public Sub DeleteProduct(ByVal id As Integer)
            If _items.ContainsKey(id) Then
                _items.Remove(id)
            End If
        End Sub

        ' Updates the quantity for an item
```

```
        Public Sub UpdateItemQuantity(ByVal id As Integer, _
ByVal quantity As Integer)
            If _items.ContainsKey(id) Then
                Dim item As ShoppingCartItem = _items(id)
                item.Quantity = quantity
                If item.Quantity <= 0 Then _
                _items.Remove(id)
            End If
        End Sub


        ' Clears the cart
        Public Sub Clear()
            _items.Clear()
        End Sub
End Class
```

If you now go to the root's `web.config` file and change the `<profile>` section according to what is shown here, you'll have a fully working persistent shopping cart, also available to anonymous users:

```
<profile defaultProvider="TBH_ProfileProvider">
    <providers>...</providers>
    <properties>
        <add name="FirstName" type="String" />
        <add name="LastName" type="String" />
        ...
        <add name="ShoppingCart" type="TheBeerHouse.BLL.Store.ShoppingCart"
serializeAs="Binary" allowAnonymous="true" />
    </properties>
</profile>
```

> The `ShoppingCartItem` class is not serializable to XML, because a default constructor for the `ShoppingCartItem` is not present, and the ShoppingCart's `Item` property does not have a setter accessory. These requirements do not exist for binary serialization, though, and because of this I chose to use this serialization method and create more encapsulated classes.

With a few dozen lines of code we've accomplished something that in previous versions of .NET and most other frameworks would have required hours of work to accomplish by creating database tables, stored procedures, and DAL classes. Remember to update the `Profile_MigrateAnonymous` event handler in the `global.asax` file to migrate the `ShoppingCart` property from the anonymous user's profile to the profile of the member who just logged in. However, you must do it only if the anonymous customer's shopping cart is not empty, because otherwise you would always erase the registered customer's shopping cart:

```
Sub Profile_MigrateAnonymous(ByVal sender As Object,
ByVal e As ProfileMigrateEventArgs)
        ' get a reference to the previously anonymous user's profile
        Dim anonProfile As ProfileBase = ProfileBase.Create(e.AnonymousID)
    ' if set, copy its Theme and ShoppingCart to the current user's profile
        If anonProfile.GetPropertyValue("ShoppingCart").Items.Count > 0 Then
            Me.Profile.ShoppingCart = anonProfile.GetPropertyValue("ShoppingCart")
```

```
        End If
    ...
End sub
```

Next we'll look at the `Order` class, for which `GetOrderByID` looks like all the `Get{xxx}ByID` methods of the other business classes in other modules:

```
Public Function GetOrderById(ByVal OrderId As Integer) As Order

Dim key As String = CacheKey & "_" & OrderId

If EnableCaching AndAlso Not IsNothing(Cache(key)) Then
                Return CType(Cache(key), Order)
End If

Shoppingctx.Orders.MergeOption = MergeOption.NoTracking
Dim lOrder As Order = (From lai In Shoppingctx.Orders _
                Where lai.OrderID = OrderId).FirstOrDefault

If EnableCaching Then
        CacheData(key, lOrder)
End If

Return lOrder

End Function
```

Another interesting method is `InsertOrder`, which accepts an instance of `ShoppingCart` with all the order items, and other parameters for the customer's contact information and the shipping address. It must insert multiple records (a record into `tbh_Orders`, and one or more records into `tbh_OrderDetails`). Thanks to the transactional nature of the Entity Framework, you do not have to use a `TransActionScope` object to manage the insertion process. Each item in the customer's shopping cart is added to the Order's `OrderItems` list before the object graph is committed to the database in one single transaction. `TransactionScope` can still be used to wrap code using the Entity Framework to update the database but is best served in situations where the transaction involves coordination with external services such as MSMQ. The following code shows how it's used in a real situation:

```
Public Function InsertOrder(ByVal vshoppingCart As ShoppingCart,
ByVal shippingMethod As String, _
            ByVal shipping As Decimal, ByVal shippingFirstName As String,
ByVal shippingLastName As String, _
            ByVal shippingStreet As String, ByVal shippingPostalCode As String,
ByVal shippingCity As String, _
            ByVal shippingState As String, ByVal shippingCountry As String,
ByVal customerEmail As String, _
            ByVal customerPhone As String, ByVal customerFax As String,
ByVal transactionID As String) As Order

        Dim lOrder As Order

        Dim userName As String = Helpers.CurrentUserName

        ' insert the master order
```

```
lOrder = Order.CreateOrder(0, DateTime.Now, _
    userName, 1, shippingMethod, vshoppingCart.Total, shipping, _
    shippingFirstName, shippingLastName, shippingStreet,
shippingPostalCode, _
    shippingCity, shippingState, shippingCountry, customerEmail,
customerPhone, _
    customerFax, Now, True)

lOrder.TransactionID = transactionID

'insert the child order items
For Each item As ShoppingCartItem In vshoppingCart.Items
    lOrder.OrderItems.Add(OrderItem.CreateOrderItem(0,
DateTime.Now, userName, _
        item.ID, item.Title, item.SKU, item.UnitPrice,
item.Quantity, DateTime.Now, True))
Next

lOrder = Me.AddOrder(lOrder)

Return lOrder

End Function
```

The `StatusCode` enumeration used in the preceding code includes the three built-in statuses required by the module: waiting for payment, confirmed, and verified, and is defined as follows:

```
Public Enum StatusCode As Integer
    WaitingForPayment = 1
    Confirmed = 2
    Verified = 3
    Shipped = 4
    Canceled = 5
End Enum
```

Note, however, that because the `StatusID` property is an integer, an explicit cast to `int` is required. The `StatusID` type is `int` and not `StatusCode` because users can define their own additional status codes, and thus working with numeric IDs is more appropriate in most situations.

The Store module has a dedicated helper class, `StoreHelper`, which contains several methods to help with common routines that could be used in various places in the store. The `GetPayPalPaymentUrl` returns the URL to redirect the customer to PayPal to pay for the order. A valid `Order` entity must be passed to the method to compile a valid URL to post to PayPal. It dynamically builds the URL shown in the "Design" section with the amount, shipping, and `OrderID` values taken from the current order, plus the recipient business e-mail and currency code taken from the configuration settings, and the return URLs that point to the `OrderCompleted.aspx`, `OrderCancelled.aspx`, and `PayPalIPN.ashx` pages described earlier:

```
Public Shared Function GetPayPalPaymentUrl(ByVal vOrder As Order) As String

    If Not vOrder.IsValid Then
        Return "Not a valid order"
```

```
        End If

        Dim serverUrl As String
        If Globals.Settings.Store.SandboxMode Then
            serverUrl = "https://www.sandbox.paypal.com/us/cgi-bin/webscr"
        Else
            serverUrl = "https://www.paypal.com/us/cgi-bin/webscr"
        End If
        Dim amount As String = vOrder.SubTotal.ToString("N2").Replace(",", ".")
        Dim shipping As String = vOrder.Shipping.ToString("N2").Replace(",", ".")

        Dim firstname As String = HttpUtility.UrlEncode(vOrder.ShippingFirstName)
        Dim lastname As String = HttpUtility.UrlEncode(vOrder.ShippingLastName)
        Dim address As String = HttpUtility.UrlEncode(vOrder.ShippingStreet)
        Dim city As String = HttpUtility.UrlEncode(vOrder.ShippingCity)
        Dim state As String = HttpUtility.UrlEncode(vOrder.ShippingState)
        Dim zip As String = HttpUtility.UrlEncode(vOrder.ShippingPostalCode)

        Dim baseUrl As String =
HttpContext.Current.Request.Url.AbsoluteUri.Replace
(HttpContext.Current.Request.Url.PathAndQuery, "") & _
            HttpContext.Current.Request.ApplicationPath
        If Not baseUrl.EndsWith("/") Then baseUrl &= "/"

        Dim notifyUrl As String = HttpUtility.UrlEncode(baseUrl
& "PayPal/PayPalIPN.ashx")
        Dim returnUrl As String = HttpUtility.UrlEncode(baseUrl
& "PayPal/OrderCompleted.aspx?OrderID=" & _
            vOrder.OrderID.ToString())
        Dim cancelUrl As String = HttpUtility.UrlEncode(baseUrl
& "PayPal/OrderCancelled.aspx")
        Dim business As String = HttpUtility.UrlEncode(
Globals.Settings.Store.BusinessEmail)
        Dim itemName As String = HttpUtility.UrlEncode(
"Order #" & vOrder.OrderID.ToString())

        Dim url As New StringBuilder()
        url.AppendFormat( _
            "{0}?cmd=_xclick&upload=1&rm=2&no_shipping=1&no_note=1&currency_code={1}
&business={2}&item_number={3}&custom={3}&item_name={4}&amount={5}
&shipping={6}&notify_url={7}&return={8}&cancel_return={9}
&first_name={10}&last_name={11}&address1={12}&city={13}
&state={14}&zip={15}", _
            serverUrl, Globals.Settings.Store.CurrencyCode, business,
vOrder.OrderID, itemName, _
            amount, shipping, notifyUrl, returnUrl, cancelUrl, firstname,
lastname, address, city, state, zip)

        Return url.ToString()
End Function
```

Note that the method uses a different base URL according to whether the store runs in real or test mode, as indicated by the Sandbox configuration setting. Also note that PayPal expects all amounts to use the period (.) as a separator for the amount's decimal parts, and only wants two decimal digits. You use `variable.ToString("N2")` to format the double or decimal variable as a string with two decimal digits. However, if the current locale settings are set to Italian or some other country's settings for which a comma is used, you'll get something like "33,50" instead of "33.50." For this reason you also do a `Replace` for "," with "." just in case.

Implementing the User Interface

As stated earlier, the Shopping Cart module is composed of many pages to manage the store and allow customers to shop. There are really two distinct user interface sections: administrative and consumer.

Implementing the Store Administration Pages

Many administrative and end-user pages of this module are similar in structure of those in previous chapters, especially to those of the articles module described and implemented in Chapter 5. For example, in Figure 9-8 you can see how similar the page to manage departments is to the page to manage article categories.

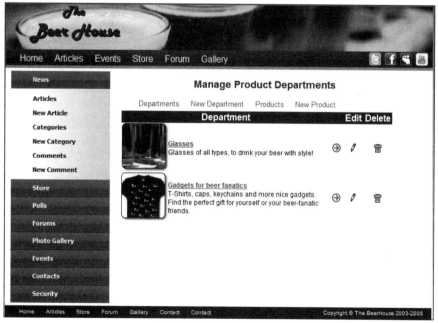

Figure 9-9

The page to manage a shipping option (see Figure 9-10) is also similar: the controls used to list and insert/modify records just define different fields, but the structure of the page is nearly identical.

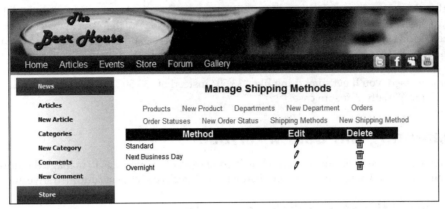

Figure 9-10

In the page for managing order status, status records with IDs from 1 to 5 cannot be deleted, because they identify special, hard-coded values. For example, you've just seen in the implementation of the Order class that the UpdateOrder method checks whether the current order status is 2, in which case it decrements the UnitsInStock field of the ordered products. Because of this, you should handle the ItemDataBound event of the ListView displaying the records, and ensure that the Delete ImageButton is hidden for the first three records. Following is the code to place into this event handler, and Figure 9-11 shows the final result on the page:

```
Protected Sub lvOrderStatuses_ItemDataBound(ByVal sender As Object,
ByVal e As System.Web.UI.WebControls.ListViewItemEventArgs)
Handles lvOrderStatuses.ItemDataBound

        Dim lvdi As ListViewDataItem = DirectCast(e.Item, ListViewDataItem)

        If lvdi.ItemType = ListViewItemType.DataItem Then

            Dim btnDelete As ImageButton = CType(lvdi.FindControl("btnDelete"),
ImageButton)
            Dim lOrderStatus As OrderStatus = CType(lvdi.DataItem, OrderStatus)

            If Not IsNothing(lOrderStatus) And Not IsNothing(btnDelete) Then

                If lOrderStatus.OrderStatusID <= 5 Then
                    btnDelete.Visible = False
                End If

            End If

        End If

End Sub
```

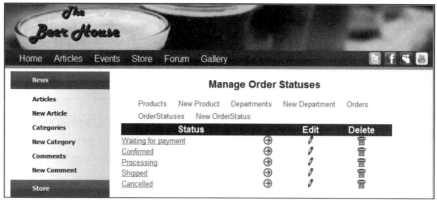

Figure 9-11

The `AddEditProduct.aspx` page uses a familiar set of controls with some AJAX control extenders to provide client-side validation, and enables to you to edit an existing product or insert a new one according to the presence of an `ProductID` parameter on the querystring. The same thing was done (and shown in detail) in Chapter 5, so please refer to that chapter to see the implementation. Figure 9-12 shows the resulting page.

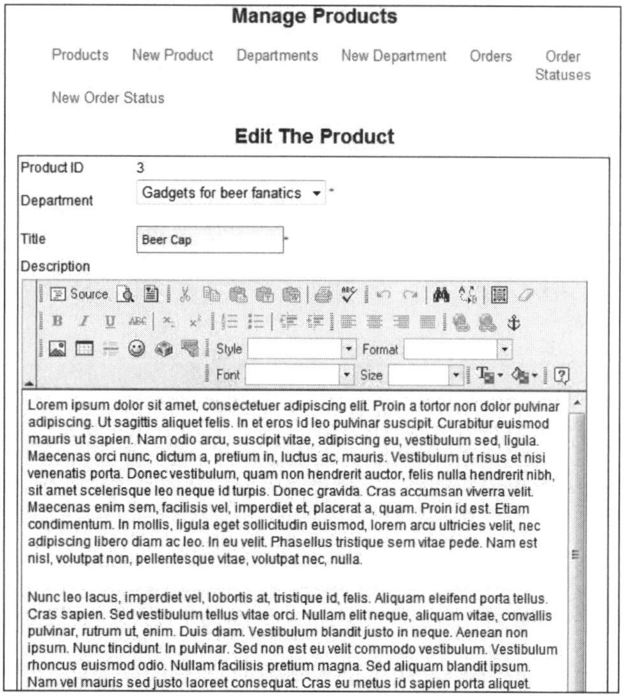

Figure 9-12

The `ManageProducts.aspx` page shows the list of the products of a specific department if a `DepartmentID` parameter is found on the querystring; otherwise, it shows products from all departments. The page contains a `ListView` control that defines the following columns:

❏ An `IMG` tag that shows the product's small image, whose URL is stored in the `SmallImageUrl` field. The IMG is wrapped by an anchor tag that links to the product's detail admin page (`AddEditProduct.aspx`).

❏ A column containing the product's Title, anchored to its detailed admin page. Below the title the product's SKU is displayed.

❏ A column that displays all the pricing information, including the `UnitPrice`, the Discount Percent and the units currently available.

❏ The final two columns contain the edit and delete Image Buttons used in all the admin list pages.

Finally the `ListView` contains an `AlternatingItemTemplate` that uses a slightly different background color to help differentiate the rows. Here's the code that defines the `ListView` just described:

```
<asp:ListView ID="lvProducts" runat="server">
    <LayoutTemplate>
        <table cellspacing="0" cellpadding="0" class="AdminList">
            <tr class="AdminListHeader">
                <td colspan="2">
                    Product
                </td>
                <td>
                    Price Info
                </td>
                <td>
                    Edit
                </td>
                <td>
                    Delete
                </td>
            </tr>
            <tr id="itemPlaceholder" runat="server">
            </tr>
            <tr>
                <td colspan="5">
                    <div class="pager">
<asp:DataPager ID="pagerBottom" runat="server" PageSize="10"
PagedControlID="lvProducts">
    <Fields>
        <asp:NextPreviousPagerField ButtonCssClass="command"
FirstPageText="«" PreviousPageText="<"
            RenderDisabledButtonsAsLabels="true" ShowFirstPageButton="true"
ShowPreviousPageButton="true"
            ShowLastPageButton="false" ShowNextPageButton="false" />
        <asp:NumericPagerField ButtonCount="7" NumericButtonCssClass-"command"
CurrentPageLabelCssClass="current"
            NextPreviousButtonCssClass="command" />
        <asp:NextPreviousPagerField ButtonCssClass="command" LastPageText="»"
```

```
NextPageText=">"
                RenderDisabledButtonsAsLabels="true" ShowFirstPageButton="false"
ShowPreviousPageButton="false"
                ShowLastPageButton="true" ShowNextPageButton="true" />
    </Fields>
</asp:DataPager>
                        </div>
                    </td>
                </tr>
            </table>
        </LayoutTemplate>
        <EmptyDataTemplate>
            <tr>
                <td colspan="5">
                    <p>
                        Sorry there are no Productss available at this time.</p>
                </td>
            </tr>
        </EmptyDataTemplate>
        <ItemTemplate>
            <tr>
                <td>
                    <a href="<%# String.Format("AddEditProduct.aspx?ProductId={0}",
 Eval("ProductId")) %>">
                        <img id="Img1" runat="server"
src='<%# Eval("SmallImageUrl") %>' alt='<%# Eval("Title") %>'
border="0" /></a>
                </td>
                <td>
                    <a href="<%# String.Format("AddEditProduct.aspx?ProductId={0}",
Eval("ProductId")) %>">
                        <%# Eval("Title") %></a>
                    <br />
                    <%# Eval("SKU") %>
                </td>
                <td>
                    <%#FormatPrice(Eval("UnitPrice"))%>
                    <br />
                    Discount:
                    <%# Eval("DiscountPercentage") %>%
                    <br />
                    Units in Stock:
                    <%# Eval("UnitsInStock") %>
                </td>
                <td align="center">
                    <a href="<%# String.Format("AddEditProduct.aspx?ProductId={0}",
 Eval("ProductId")) %>">
                        <img src="../images/edit.gif" alt="" width="16"
height="16" class="AdminImg" /></a>
                </td>
                <td align="center">
                    <asp:ImageButton runat="server" ID="btnDelete"
CommandArgument='<%# Eval("DepartmentID").ToString() %>'
                        CommandName="Delete" ImageUrl="~/images/delete.gif"
```

459

```
            AlternateText="Delete" CssClass="AdminImg"
                        OnClientClick="return confirm('Warning: This will delete the
Product from the database.');" />
                </td>
            </tr>
        </ItemTemplate>
        <AlternatingItemTemplate>
            <tr class="AltAdminRow">
                <td>
                    <a href="<%# String.Format("AddEditProduct.aspx?ProductId={0}",
Eval("ProductId")) %>">
                        <img id="Img1" runat="server"
src='<%# Eval("SmallImageUrl") %>' alt='<%# Eval("Title") %>'
border="0" /></a>
                </td>
                <td>
                    <a href="<%# String.Format("AddEditProduct.aspx?ProductId={0}",
Eval("ProductId")) %>">
                        <%# Eval("Title") %></a>
                    <br />
                    <%# Eval("SKU") %>
                </td>
                <td>
                    <%#FormatPrice(Eval("UnitPrice"))%>
                    <br />
                    Discount:
                    <%# Eval("DiscountPercentage") %>%
                    <br />
                    Units in Stock:
                    <%# Eval("UnitsInStock") %>
                </td>
                <td align="center">
                    <a href="<%# String.Format("AddEditProduct.aspx?ProductId={0}",
Eval("ProductId")) %>">
                        <img src="../images/edit.gif" alt="" width="16" height="16"
class="AdminImg" /></a>
                </td>
                <td align="center">
                    <asp:ImageButton runat="server" ID="btnDelete"
CommandArgument='<%# Eval("DepartmentID").ToString() %>'
                        CommandName="Delete" ImageUrl="~/images/delete.gif"
AlternateText="Delete" CssClass="AdminImg"
                        OnClientClick="return confirm('Warning: This will delete
the Product from the database.');" />
                </td>
            </tr>
        </AlternatingItemTemplate>
        <ItemSeparatorTemplate>
            <tr>
                <td colspan="5">
                    <hr />
                </td>
```

```
        </tr>
    </ItemSeparatorTemplate>
</asp:ListView>
```

There are other controls on the page, such as `DropDownList` controls to choose the parent department and the number of products to list on the page. The Department's `DropDownList` is bound in the `Page Load` event by calling the `BindDepartmentsToListControl` method defined in the `AdminPage` class. This method is used to bind a list of departments to a `ListControl`, which the `DropDownList` control inherits. I chose to bind the list to the base `ListControl` class because the `RadioButtonList`, `BulletedList`, `RadioButtonList` and `ListBox` all inherit from `ListControl` and the members needed to accomplish the data binding are all defined in the `ListControl` class. The method takes two parameters, the `ListControl` and a `Boolean` to indicate if an extra instructional item should be added at the top of the list. It also automatically sets the `SelectedValue` based on the current value of the `DepartmentId` property also defined in the `AdminPage` class:

```
Public Sub BindDepartmentsToListControl(ByVal vDepartmentListControl
As ListControl, ByVal bAddInstruction As Boolean)

        Using lDepartmentrpt As New DepartmentRepository

            vDepartmentListControl.DataValueField = "DepartmentId"
            vDepartmentListControl.DataTextField = "Title"

            vDepartmentListControl.DataSource = lDepartmentrpt.GetDepartments
            vDepartmentListControl.DataBind()

            If bAddInstruction Then
                vDepartmentListControl.Items.Insert(0,
New ListItem("All Departments", 0))
            End If

            vDepartmentListControl.SelectedValue = DepartmentId

        End Using

End Sub
```

If you look closely at the column that displays the product's price, you'll see that it calls a method named `FormatPrice` to show the amount. This method is added to the `Helpers` class and wrapped in `BasePage` class to help with legacy code based on previous versions of TheBeerHouse. It formats the input value as a number with two decimal digits, followed by the currency code defined in the configuration settings:

```
Public Shared Function FormatPrice(ByVal vPrice As Object) As String
Return Convert.ToDecimal(vPrice).ToString("N2") & " " &
 Globals.Settings.Store.CurrencyCode
End Function
```

Amounts are not displayed on the page with the default currency format (which would use the "C" format string) because you may be running the store in another country, such as Italy, which would display the euro symbol in the string, but you want to display USD regardless of the current locale settings. Figure 9-13 shows the page at runtime.

Figure 9-13

Implementing the Consumer Interface

Presenting a good clean, easy to use store front is one of the most important things to make an e-commerce site work. This does not mean there has to be over the top graphics and eye candy, but customers must feel they can trust you, find the products they want, and be able to check out easily and intuitively. Making a customer think or work hard to place an order quickly leads to an investment that loses the company money.

The ShowProduct.aspx Page

The `BrowseProducts.aspx` page is a very simple page that displays a list of store departments with links to a product listing for each department. So we can jump straight to the product-specific `ShowProduct.aspx` page. This shows all the possible details about the product whose `ProductID` is passed on the querystring: the title, the average rating, the availability icon, the HTML long description, the small image (or a default "no image available" image if the `SmallImageUrl` field is empty), a link to the full-size image (displayed only if the `FullImageUrl` field is not empty), and the product's price. As for the product listing, the `UnitPrice` amount is shown if the `DiscountPercentage` is 0; otherwise, that amount is rendered as crossed out, and `DiscountPercentage` along with the `FinalUnitPrice` are displayed. Finally, there's a button on the page that will add the product to the customer's shopping cart and will redirect the customer to the `ShoppingCart.aspx` page. Following is the content of the .aspx markup page:

```
<div>
    <div id="ContentTitle">
        <h1>
            <asp:Label runat="server" ID="lblTitle" /></h1>
        <asp:Panel runat="server" ID="panEditProduct">
```

```
                <asp:HyperLink runat="server" ID="lnkEditProduct"
ImageUrl="~/images/edit.gif" ToolTip="Edit product"
                    NavigateUrl="~/Admin/AddEditProduct.aspx?ID={0}" />
                 
                <asp:ImageButton runat="server" ID="btnDelete"
CausesValidation="false" AlternateText="Delete product"
                    ImageUrl="~/Images/Delete.gif" OnClientClick="if
(confirm('Are you sure you want to delete this product?') == false)
return false;" />
            </asp:Panel>
        </div>
        <div id="ContentBody">
            <div id="ProductImage">
                <asp:HyperLink runat="server" ID="HyperLink1"
Target="_blank"></asp:HyperLink>
            </div>
            <div id="productinfo">
                <b>Price: </b>
                <asp:Literal runat="server" ID="lblDiscountedPrice"><s>{0}</s>
 {1}% Off = </asp:Literal>
                <asp:Literal runat="server" ID="lblPrice" />
                <br />
                <b>Availability: </b>
                <asp:AvailabilityImage runat="server" ID="availDisplay" />
                <br />
                <b>Rating: </b>
                <asp:Literal runat="server" ID="lblRating" Text="{0} user(s)
have rated this product " />
                <br />
                <div class="ProductThumb">
                    <img runat="Server" id="imgProduct" class="ProductThumb"
src="~/Images/noimage.gif" /><br />
                </div>
                <asp:HyperLink runat="server" ID="lnkFullImage"
Target="_blank"></asp:HyperLink>
                <asp:Literal runat="server" ID="lblDescription" />
                <br />
                <asp:Button ID="btnAddToCart" runat="server" Text="Add to
Shopping Cart" />
                <br />
                <hr class="ProductHR" />
                <div class="sectiontitle">
                    How would you rate this product?
                    <asp:UpdatePanel ID="UpdatePanel1" runat="server">
                        <ContentTemplate>
                            Rate This Product:<br />
                            <asp:Rating ID="ProductRating" runat="server"
BehaviorID="ratDisplay" CssClass="ArticleRating"
                                StarCssClass="ratingStar"
WaitingStarCssClass="savedRatingStar"
FilledStarCssClass="filledRatingStar"
                                EmptyStarCssClass="emptyRatingStar">
                            </asp:Rating>
                        </ContentTemplate>
                    </asp:UpdatePanel>
```

```
                    </div>
                    <asp:Literal runat="server" ID="ltlAvgRating" Text="The average
rating for {1} is {0} beer(s)." />
                    <asp:Literal runat="server" ID="lblUserRating" Visible="False"
Text="Your rated this product {0} beer(s). Thank you for your feedback." />
                </div>
            </div>
```

You can see that there's no binding expression in the preceding code, because everything is done in the BindProduct method, which is called from the Page_Load event handler, after loading a Product object according to the ProductID value read from the querystring; actually, it is a PrimaryKey property defined in the base page classes. Remember the shopping cart is using search engine friendly URLs, just like we used in the Articles module. So, there should be a valid ProductId passed in the URL via the URL Rewrite function. If not, the page throws an ApplicationException with the message a parameter is missing in the querystring. Assuming that there is a ProductId, the product BindProduct method is called, and then the user rating for the product is set:

```
        Protected Sub Page_Load(ByVal sender As Object, ByVal e As System.EventArgs)
Handles Me.Load
            If Me.ProductId < 1 Then
                Throw New ApplicationException("Missing parameter on the querystring.")
            End If

            If Not Me.IsPostBack Then
                ' try to load the product with the specified ID, and raise an
exception if it doesn't exist
                BindProduct()

                ' hide the rating box controls if the current user has already voted
for this product
                Dim userRating As Integer = GetUserRating()
                If userRating > 0 Then _
                    ShowUserRating(userRating)
            End If
        End Sub
```

The BindProduct method follows the standard pattern we have used to bind value to the controls on the page. Notice the method is the use of String.Format to apply values to specific textual controls on the page. For example, the lblRating Literal control has its Text property defined in the markup as "{0} user(s) have rated this product". In the BindProduct method the number of users that have submitted product ratings is inserted to the control's Text.

```
    Private Sub BindProduct()

        Using lProductrpt As New ProductsRepository

            Dim lproduct As Product = lProductrpt.GetProductById(ProductId)
            If IsNothing(lproduct) Then _
                Throw New ApplicationException("No product was found for the
specified ID.")

            ' display all article's data on the page
            lblTitle.Text = lproduct.Title
```

```
                Title = lproduct.Title
                lblRating.Text = String.Format(lblRating.Text, lproduct.Votes)
                availDisplay.Value = lproduct.UnitsInStock
                lblDescription.Text = lproduct.Description
                panEditProduct.Visible = Me.UserCanEdit
                lnkEditProduct.NavigateUrl = String.Format(lnkEditProduct.NavigateUrl,
    ProductId)
                lblPrice.Text = Me.FormatPrice(lproduct.FinalUnitPrice)
                lblDiscountedPrice.Text = String.Format(lblDiscountedPrice.Text, _
                    Me.FormatPrice(lproduct.UnitPrice), lproduct.DiscountPercentage)
                lblDiscountedPrice.Visible = (lproduct.DiscountPercentage > 0)

                ltlAvgRating.Text = String.Format(ltlAvgRating.Text,
    lproduct.AverageRating, lproduct.Title)

                If lproduct.SmallImageUrl.Length > 0 Then _
                    imgProduct.Src = lproduct.SmallImageUrl
                imgProduct.Alt = lproduct.Title
                If lproduct.FullImageUrl.Length > 0 Then
                    lnkFullImage.NavigateUrl = lproduct.FullImageUrl
                    lnkFullImage.Visible = True
                Else
                    lnkFullImage.Visible = False
                End If

        End Using

    End Sub
```

The page's markup lays out where the product image and details are displayed. The image is wrapped in its own DIV tag to make it easier to apply different styles to the image via themes. The balance of the product descriptive information is a series of Hyperlink and Literal controls to hold the product's information. It also has the very important Add to Shopping Cart button, this does just what it says, adds the product to the customer's shopping cart. Below that is a Rating control, wrapped in a dedicated UpdatePanel. The functionality of the rating control was discussed in the Article module chapter. Another important feature is the availability control. I will detail this web control very shortly.

```
            <div id="ProductImage">
                <asp:HyperLink runat="server" ID="HyperLink1"
    Target="_blank"></asp:HyperLink>
            </div>
            <div id="productinfo">
                <b>Price: </b>
                <asp:Literal runat="server" ID="lblDiscountedPrice"><s>{0}</s>
    {1}% Off = </asp:Literal>
                <asp:Literal runat="server" ID="lblPrice" />
                <br />
                <b>Availability: </b>
                <asp:AvailabilityImage runat="server" ID="availDisplay" />
                <br />
                <b>Rating: </b>
                <asp:Literal runat="server" ID="lblRating" Text="{0} user(s) have
    rated this product " />
                <br />
```

```
                    <div class="ProductThumb">
                        <img runat="Server" id="imgProduct" class="ProductThumb"
src="~/Images/noimage.gif" /><br />
                    </div>
                    <asp:HyperLink runat="server" ID="lnkFullImage"
Target="_blank"></asp:HyperLink>
                    <asp:Literal runat="server" ID="lblDescription" />
                    <br />
                    <asp:Button ID="btnAddToCart" runat="server" Text="Add to
Shopping Cart" />
                    <br />
                    <hr class="ProductHR" />
                    <div class="sectiontitle">
                        How would you rate this product?
                        <asp:UpdatePanel ID="UpdatePanel1" runat="server">
                            <ContentTemplate>
                                Rate This Product:<br />
                                <asp:Rating ID="ProductRating" runat="server"
 BehaviorID="ratDisplay" CssClass="ArticleRating"
                                    StarCssClass="ratingStar"
WaitingStarCssClass="savedRatingStar"
FilledStarCssClass="filledRatingStar"
                                    EmptyStarCssClass="emptyRatingStar">
                                </asp:Rating>
                            </ContentTemplate>
                        </asp:UpdatePanel>
                    </div>
                    <asp:Literal runat="server" ID="ltlAvgRating" Text="The average
rating for {1} is {0} beer(s)." />
                    <asp:Literal runat="server" ID="lblUserRating" Visible="False"
Text="Your rated this product {0} beer(s). Thank you for your feedback." />
                </div>
```

Figure 9-14 shows the result.

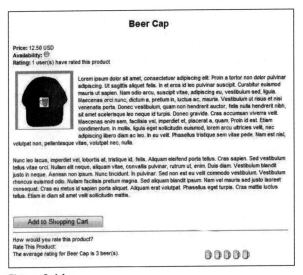

Figure 9-14

When the customer clicks the Add to Shopping Cart button, we call the `InsertItem` method of the `ShoppingCart` object returned by the `profile` property, and pass in the product's data read from the `Product` object. Finally, we redirect the customer to the `ShoppingCart.aspx` page, where he can change the quantity of the products to order and proceed to the checkout process:

```
Protected Sub btnAddToCart_Click(ByVal sender As Object,
ByVal e As System.EventArgs) Handles btnAddToCart.Click
        Using lProductrpt As New ProductsRepository
            Dim lProduct As Product = lProductrpt.GetProductById(ProductId)
            Dim lprofile As ProfileBase = Helpers.GetUserProfile
            Dim lShoppingCart As ShoppingCart = Profile.ShoppingCart
            lShoppingCart.InsertItem(lProduct.ProductID, lProduct.Title,
lProduct.SKU, lProduct.FinalUnitPrice)
            Profile.ShoppingCart = lShoppingCart

            Me.Response.Redirect("ShoppingCart.aspx", False)
        End Using

    End Sub
```

The AvailabilityImage Web Control

In the previous edition of TheBeerHouse a user control was defined called `AvailabilityImage.ascx`, which was used to visually indicate how many items were in stock for a particular product. Red meant it was out of stock, yellow meant running low, and green meant there were plenty available. There was one public property, `Value`, that was set when a product was bound to indicate how many units were in stock. For this edition, I took that user control and made a `WebControl` out of it, `AvailablityImage`. By making this into a more flexible `WebControl`, it can potentially be used for more than just an indicator of units in stock and on many other sites when a three-way visual indicator is needed.

Like the Country and State `DropDownList` controls inherited from an existing `WebControl`, I have already discussed, the `AvailabilityImage` control inherits from an `Image WebControl`. There are eight public properties available to customize the way the image is rendered. Three properties — `RedImage`, `YellowImage`, and `GreenImage` — set the corresponding images that can be used. The `RedAlt`, `YellowAlt`, and `GreenAlt` properties set the `Alt` attribute values rendered for the image. The `LowAvailability` property is the value used to indicate an item is in short supply. Finally, `Value` indicates the number of units in stock for the product.

```
<ToolboxData("<{0}:AvailabilityImage runat=server></{0}:AvailabilityImage>")> _
Public Class AvailabilityImage
    Inherits System.Web.UI.WebControls.Image

    Private _RedAlt As String = "Currently not available"
    <Category("The Beer House"), DefaultValue("Currently not available")> _
Public Property RedAlt() As String
        Get
            Return _RedAlt
        End Get
        Set(ByVal value As String)
            _RedAlt = value
        End Set
    End Property

    Private _YellowAlt As String = "Few units available"
```

467

```vb
        <Category("The Beer House"), DefaultValue("Few units available")> _
    Public Property YellowAlt() As String
            Get
                Return _YellowAlt
            End Get
            Set(ByVal value As String)
                _YellowAlt = value
            End Set
        End Property

        Private _GreenAlt As String = "Available"
        <Category("The Beer House"), DefaultValue("Available")> _
    Public Property GreenAlt() As String
            Get
                Return _GreenAlt
            End Get
            Set(ByVal value As String)
                _GreenAlt = value
            End Set
        End Property

        Private _RedImage As String = "~/images/lightred.gif"
        <Category("The Beer House"), DefaultValue("~/images/lightred.gif")> _
    Public Property RedImage() As String
            Get
                Return _RedImage
            End Get
            Set(ByVal value As String)
                _RedImage = value
            End Set
        End Property

        Private _YellowImage As String = "~/images/lightyellow.gif"
        <Category("The Beer House"), DefaultValue("~/images/lightyellow.gif")> _
    Public Property YellowImage() As String
            Get
                Return _YellowImage
            End Get
            Set(ByVal value As String)
                _YellowImage = value
            End Set
        End Property

        Private _GreenImage As String = "~/images/lightgreen.gif"
        <Category("The Beer House"), DefaultValue("~/images/lightgreen.gif")> _
    Public Property GreenImage() As String
            Get
                Return _GreenImage
            End Get
            Set(ByVal value As String)
                _GreenImage = value
            End Set
```

```
        End Property

        Private _lowAvailability As Integer = 5
        <Category("The Beer House"), DefaultValue("5")> _
        Public Property LowAvailability() As Integer
            Get
                Return _lowAvailability
            End Get
            Set(ByVal Value As Integer)
                _lowAvailability = Value
            End Set
        End Property

        Private _value As Integer = 0
        <Category("The Beer House"), DefaultValue("0")> _
    Public Property Value() As Integer
            Get
                Return _value
            End Get
            Set(ByVal value As Integer)
                _value = value
                SetProperties()
            End Set
        End Property

        Private Sub SetProperties()
            If _value <= 0 Then
                MyBase.ImageUrl = RedImage
                MyBase.AlternateText = RedAlt
            ElseIf _value <= LowAvailability Then
                MyBase.ImageUrl = YellowImage
                MyBase.AlternateText = YellowAlt
            Else
                MyBase.ImageUrl = GreenImage
                MyBase.AlternateText = GreenAlt
            End If
        End Sub

        Protected Overloads Overrides Sub OnInit(ByVal e As EventArgs)
            SetProperties()
            MyBase.OnInit(e)
        End Sub

    End Class
```

The ShoppingCart.aspx Page

As described earlier in the "Design" section for the user interface, this page is actually more complex than a page that just manages the shopping cart, as it includes a complete wizard for the checkout process, which includes steps to provide the contact information and the shipping address, and to review the order a last time before being redirected to PayPal for the payment. The page uses the `Wizard` control, which allows you to define different views within it, and it automatically creates and manages the buttons/links at the bottom of the wizard to move backward and forward through the wizard's steps. The control's structure is outlined in the following code:

```
<asp:Wizard ID="wizSubmitOrder" runat="server" ActiveStepIndex="0"
 CancelButtonText="Continue Shopping"
    CancelButtonType="Link" CancelDestinationPageUrl="~/BrowseProducts.aspx"
DisplayCancelButton="True"
    DisplaySideBar="False" FinishPreviousButtonType="Link"
StartNextButtonText="Proceed with order"
    StartNextButtonType="Link" Width="100%" StepNextButtonText="Proceed with order"
    StepNextButtonType="Link" StepPreviousButtonText="Modify data in previous step"
    StepPreviousButtonType="Link" FinishCompleteButtonText="Submit Order"
FinishCompleteButtonType="Link"
    FinishPreviousButtonText="Modify data in previous step">
    <WizardSteps>
        <asp:WizardStep ID="WizardStep1" runat="server" Title="Shopping Cart">
        </asp:WizardStep>
        <asp:WizardStep ID="WizardStep2" runat="server" Title="Shipping Address">
        </asp:WizardStep>
        <asp:WizardStep runat="server" Title="Order Confirmation">
        </asp:WizardStep>
    </WizardSteps>
    <StepNextButtonStyle CssClass="BHButton" />
    <StartNextButtonStyle CssClass="BHButton" />
    <FinishCompleteButtonStyle CssClass="BHButton" />
    <FinishPreviousButtonStyle CssClass="BHButton" />
    <StepPreviousButtonStyle CssClass="BHButton" />
</asp:Wizard>
```

There's a <WizardSteps> section used to define one <asp:WizardStep> control for each step you want the wizard to have. The WizardStep is a template-based control used to declare the content of that step. The parent Wizard control has a number of properties that enable you to completely customize the visual appearance of the commands at the bottom, in addition to their text. The properties used in the preceding code are self-explanatory. The Wizard control also exposes a number of methods that a developer can handle to run code when the current step changes, or when the user clicks the button to complete the wizard. There will also be a Cancel command in each step that we'll use as the command to continue shopping, so it just redirects the user to the BrowseProducts.aspx page.

The entire Wizard is wrapped by an UpdatePanel, which makes stepping through the check out process seamless to the end user. It does however introduce some changes to the code that runs behind the scenes to manage the shopping cart information. Stepping through the wizard is an automatic operation; it is managing changes to the quantity of items and shipping selection that has to be effectively handled differently than in the previous version of TheBeerHouse, but more on that later.

Let's start with the first step. It defines a ListView control that binds to the list of ShoppingCartItem objects returned by CurrentUserShoppingCart.GetItems in the BindShoppingCart method in the code-behind. The BindShoppingCart method is called when the page first loads or a change is made to the contents of the shopping cart by the user. The list has a column for the item's title, a column that shows the item's price, a column with an editable textbox with the quantity for that product, and finally a column with a command link to completely remove that item from the shopping cart (which would be the same as manually setting the product's quantity to 0 and clicking the button to update the totals).

```
<asp:ListView ID="lvOrderItems" runat="server" DataKeyNames="ID">
    <LayoutTemplate>
        <table>
            <tr class="AdminListHeader">
                <td class="CartProductName">
                    Product
                </td>
                <td>
                    Price
                </td>
                <td>
                    Quantity
                </td>
                <td>
                </td>
            </tr>
            <tr runat="server" id="itemPlaceHolder">
            </tr>
        </table>
    </LayoutTemplate>
    <ItemTemplate>
        <tr>
            <td>
                <asp:HyperLink runat="server" ID="hlnkProduct"
ForeColor="#800000" NavigateUrl='<%# SEOFriendlyURL( _
                            Path.Combine(Settings.Store.ProductURLIndicator,
Eval("Title").ToString()), ".aspx") %>'>
<%# Eval("Title") %></asp:HyperLink>
            </td>
            <td class="AdminRightCell">
                <%# FormatPrice(Eval("UnitPrice")) %>
            </td>
            <td class="AdminRightCell">
                <asp:TextBox runat="server" ID="txtQuantity"
Text='<%# Bind("Quantity") %>' MaxLength="6"
                    Width="30px" AutoPostBack="true"
OnTextChanged="QtyChanged"></asp:TextBox>
                <asp:RequiredFieldValidator ID="valRequireQuantity"
runat="server" ControlToValidate="txtQuantity"
                    SetFocusOnError="true" ValidationGroup="ShippingAddress"
Text="The Quantity field is required."
                    ToolTip="The Quantity field is required."
 Display="Dynamic"></asp:RequiredFieldValidator>
                <asp:CompareValidator ID="valQuantityType"
runat="server" Operator="DataTypeCheck"
                    Type="Integer" ControlToValidate="txtQuantity"
Text="The Quantity must be an integer."
                    ToolTip="The Quantity must be an integer."
Display="dynamic" />
            </td>
```

```
            <td>
                    <asp:ImageButton runat="server" ID="btnDelete"
CommandArgument='<%# Eval("ID").ToString() %>'
                        CommandName="Delete" ImageUrl="~/images/delete.gif"
AlternateText="Delete" CssClass="AdminImg"
                        OnClientClick="return confirm('Warning: This will delete
the Product from the shopping cart.');" />
                </td>
            </tr>
    </ItemTemplate>
    <EmptyDataTemplate>
            <b>The shopping cart is empty</b></EmptyDataTemplate>
    </asp:ListView>
```

Below the list you define a Panel containing several controls that display the total cost of the order, a drop-down to select shipping method and a grand total including the shipping. The Update Totals button is retained from the previous version of TheBeerHouse, just in case a user has disable JavaScript, or there just happens to be an unforeseen JavaScript error on the client. The totals are recalculated as soon as an item's quantity or shipping selection is changed by the user. The UpdatePanel makes this possible because the quantity TextBoxes and shipping method DropDownList are set to AutoPostback and a server-side event handler is defined to handle the OnTextChanged and SelectedIndexChanged events. The event handlers call the UpdateTotal method that review the quantity values in the cart list and the selected shipping method to update the active shopping cart and the values echoed in the browser.

```
        <asp:Panel runat="server" ID="panTotals">
            <div style="text-align: right; font-weight: bold; padding-top: 4px;">
                Subtotal:
                <asp:Literal runat="server" ID="lblSubtotal" />
                <p>
                    Shipping Method:
                    <asp:DropDownList ID="ddlShippingMethods" runat="server"
DataTextField="TitleAndPrice"
                        DataValueField="Price" AutoPostBack="true">
                    </asp:DropDownList>
                    <asp:RequiredFieldValidator ID="valRequireQuantity"
runat="server" ControlToValidate="ddlShippingMethods"
                        SetFocusOnError="true" ValidationGroup="ShippingMethod"
Text="A Shipping method is required."
                        ToolTip="A Shipping method is required."
Display="Dynamic" InitialValue="0"></asp:RequiredFieldValidator>
                </p>
                <p>
                    <u>Total:</u>
                    <asp:Literal runat="server" ID="lblTotal" />
                </p>
                <asp:Button ID="btnUpdateTotals" runat="server" Text="Update totals" />
                <br />
                <br />
            </div>
        </asp:Panel>
```

The UpdateTotals method is also called when a row is deleted from the ListView (a product was completely removed from the shopping cart). Before calling UpdateTotals after a product has been removed, the BindShoppingCart method must be called. If UpdateTotals was called without rebinding the ListView to the items in the shopping cart, UpdateTotals would operate over the previous version of the cart. If you call BindShoppingCart first, the ListView will reflect the most current shopping cart list. UpdateTotals loops through the rows of the ListView control, and for each row it finds the textbox control with the product's quantity, reads its value, and uses it to update the quantity of the product stored in the shopping cart, by means of the ShoppingCart.UpdateItemQuantity method.

Notice that I also used an index i to track the cart item being processed; this is because access to the row's ShoppingCartItem DataItem is not guaranteed upon postback not initiated by a ListView event, such as the OnTextChanged event. After looping through the cart items the order's subtotal and total amounts are displayed according to the updated quantities and the currently selected shipping method. Finally, it checks whether the shopping cart actually contains something, because if that's not the case, it doesn't make sense for the customer to proceed to the next step of the checkout wizard. Curiously, the Wizard control has no properties to explicitly disable the Next and Previous commands, but you can do that by setting the command's text to an empty string, so that they won't be visible. The property to set in this case is StartNextButtonText, because you are in the Start step (i.e., the first one), and you want to disable the Next command. Here's the implementation for this first part of the wizard:

```
Protected Sub UpdateTotals()

    Dim i As Integer = 0

    For Each lvdi As ListViewDataItem In lvOrderItems.Items

        Dim lCartItem As ShoppingCartItem =
DirectCast(lShoppingCart.Items(i), ShoppingCartItem)

        If Not IsNothing(lCartItem) Then

            Dim id As Integer = lCartItem.ID
            Dim quantity As Integer = Convert.ToInt32(CType(lvdi.FindControl(
"txtQuantity"), TextBox).Text)
            lShoppingCart.UpdateItemQuantity(id, quantity)

        End If

        i += 1

    Next

    ' display the subtotal and the total amounts
    lblSubtotal.Text = FormatPrice(lShoppingCart.Total)
    lblTotal.Text = FormatPrice(lShoppingCart.Total + _
        Convert.ToDecimal(ddlShippingMethods.SelectedValue))

    ' if the shopping cart is empty, hide the link to proceed
    If lShoppingCart.Items.Count = 0 Then
        wizSubmitOrder.StartNextButtonText = String.Empty
        panTotals.Visible = False
```

```
       Else
            wizSubmitOrder.StartNextButtonText = "Proceed with order"
       End If

       Profile.ShoppingCart = lShoppingCart

       BindShoppingCart()

   End Sub
```

Figure 9-15 shows this first step at runtime.

Shopping Cart

Review and update the quantity of the products added to the cart before proceeding to checkout, or continue shopping.

Product	Price	Quantity	
Beer Cap	12.50 USD	2	🗑
Orange T-Shirt	13.60 USD	1	🗑
Light Blue T-Shirt	17.00 USD	5	🗑
Glass #5	17.90 USD	1	🗑

Subtotal: 141.50 USD

Shipping Method: Select Shipping Method ▼

Total: 141.50 USD

Update totals

Proceed with order   Continue Shopping

Figure 9-15

The second step is simpler than the first one; it's just a form that asks for contact information and the shipping address. This information is prefilled with the information stored in the customer's profile, if provided, but customers can change everything in this form if they're buying a gift for someone and want the product(s) to be shipped directly to that person. Also, at this point a user account is required to proceed, so if the current user is anonymous, then she will be asked to log in or create a new user account, instead of displaying the input form. To do this, a `MultiView` control with two views is used, and the index of the desired view will be dynamically set when the page loads if the index of the wizard's current step is 1 (second step), according to whether the user is authenticated. This version uses a `MaskedEditExtender` to format data such as a phone number as the user enters it and the `StateDropDown` control. In practice, it's just a wizard control under the hood without the automatically created buttons to move forward and backward. Here's the markup code:

```
<asp:MultiView ID="mvwShipping" runat="server">
    <asp:View ID="vwLoginRequired" runat="server">
        <p>
            An account is required to proceed with the order submission. If you
already have
            an account please log in now, otherwise <a href="Register.aspx">
```

```
create a new account</a>
               for free.</p>
       </asp:View>
       <asp:View ID="vwShipping" runat="server">
           <p>
               Fill the form below with the shipping address for your order.
All information is
               required, except for phone and fax numbers.
           </p>
           <table cellpadding="2" width="410">
               <tr>
                   <td width="110" class="fieldname">
                       <asp:Label runat="server" ID="lblFirstName"
 AssociatedControlID="txtFirstName" Text="First name:" />
                   </td>
                   <td width="300">
                       <asp:TextBox ID="txtFirstName" runat="server"
Width="100%" />
                       <asp:RequiredFieldValidator ID="valRequireFirstName"
runat="server" ControlToValidate="txtFirstName"
                           SetFocusOnError="True"
ValidationGroup="ShippingAddress" Text="The First Name field is required."
                           ToolTip="The First Name field is required."
 Display="Dynamic"></asp:RequiredFieldValidator>
                   </td>
               </tr>
               <tr>
                   <td class="fieldname">
                       <asp:Label runat="server" ID="lblLastName"
AssociatedControlID="txtLastName" Text="Last name:" />
                   </td>
                   <td>
                       <asp:TextBox ID="txtLastName" runat="server"
Width="100%" />
                       <asp:RequiredFieldValidator ID="valRequireLastName"
runat="server" ControlToValidate="txtLastName"
                           SetFocusOnError="True"
ValidationGroup="ShippingAddress" Text="The Last Name field is required."
                           ToolTip="The Last Name field is required."
Display="Dynamic"></asp:RequiredFieldValidator>
                   </td>
               </tr>
               <tr>
                   <td class="fieldname">
                       <asp:Label runat="server" ID="lblEmail"
AssociatedControlID="txtEmail" Text="E-mail:" />
                   </td>
                   <td>
                       <asp:TextBox runat="server" ID="txtEmail" Width="100%" />
                       <asp:RequiredFieldValidator ID="valRequireEmail"
runat="server" ControlToValidate="txtEmail"
                           SetFocusOnError="True"
ValidationGroup="ShippingAddress" Text="The E-mail field is required."
                           ToolTip="The E-mail field is required."
```

```
Display="Dynamic"></asp:RequiredFieldValidator>
                        <asp:RegularExpressionValidator runat="server"
ID="valEmailPattern" Display="Dynamic"
                        SetFocusOnError="True"
ValidationGroup="ShippingAddress" ControlToValidate="txtEmail"
                        ValidationExpression=
"\w+([-+.']\w+)*@\w+([-.]\w+)*\.\w+([-.]\w+)*"
Text="The E-mail address you specified is not well-formed."
                        ToolTip="The E-mail address you specified is not
well-formed."></asp:RegularExpressionValidator>
                    </td>
                </tr>
                <tr>
                    <td class="fieldname">
                        <asp:Label runat="server" ID="lblStreet"
AssociatedControlID="txtStreet" Text="Street:" />
                    </td>
                    <td>
                        <asp:TextBox runat="server" ID="txtStreet" Width="100%" />
                        <asp:RequiredFieldValidator ID="valRequireStreet"
runat="server" ControlToValidate="txtStreet"
                        SetFocusOnError="True"
ValidationGroup="ShippingAddress" Text="The Street field is required."
                        ToolTip="The Street field is required."
 Display="Dynamic"></asp:RequiredFieldValidator>
                    </td>
                </tr>
                <tr>
                    <td class="fieldname">
                        <asp:Label runat="server" ID="lblPostalCode"
 AssociatedControlID="txtPostalCode"
                        Text="Zip / Postal code:" />
                    </td>
                    <td>
                        <asp:TextBox runat="server" ID="txtPostalCode"
Width="100%" />
                        <asp:RequiredFieldValidator ID="valRequirePostalCode"
 runat="server" ControlToValidate="txtPostalCode"
                        SetFocusOnError="True"
ValidationGroup="ShippingAddress" Text="The Postal Code field is required."
                        ToolTip="The Postal Code field is required."
Display="Dynamic"></asp:RequiredFieldValidator>
                    </td>
                </tr>
                <tr>
                    <td class="fieldname">
                        <asp:Label runat="server" ID="lblCity"
AssociatedControlID="txtCity" Text="City:" />
                    </td>
                    <td>
                        <asp:TextBox runat="server" ID="txtCity" Width="100%" />
                        <asp:RequiredFieldValidator ID="valRequireCity"
runat="server" ControlToValidate="txtCity"
                        SetFocusOnError="True"
```

```
ValidationGroup="ShippingAddress" Text="The City field is required."
                            ToolTip="The City field is required."
Display="Dynamic"></asp:RequiredFieldValidator>
                        </td>
                    </tr>
                    <tr>
                        <td class="fieldname">
                            <asp:Label runat="server" ID="lblState"
 AssociatedControlID="ddlState" Text="State / Region:" />
                        </td>
                        <td>
                            <asp:StateDropDownList runat="server" ID="ddlState"
Width="100%" CssClass="formField">
                            </asp:StateDropDownList>
                            <asp:RequiredFieldValidator ID="valRequireState"
runat="server" ControlToValidate="ddlState"
                            SetFocusOnError="True"
ValidationGroup="ShippingAddress" Text="The State field is required."
                            ToolTip="The State field is required."
InitialValue="0" Display="Dynamic"></asp:RequiredFieldValidator>
                        </td>
                    </tr>
                    <tr>
                        <td class="fieldname">
                            <asp:Label runat="server" ID="lblCountry"
AssociatedControlID="ddlCountries" Text="Country:" />
                        </td>
                        <td>
                            <asp:CountryDropDownList ID="ddlCountries" runat="server"
 CssClass="formField">
                            </asp:CountryDropDownList>
                        </td>
                    </tr>
                    <tr>
                        <td class="fieldname">
                            <asp:Label runat="server" ID="lblPhone"
AssociatedControlID="txtPhone" Text="Phone:" />
                        </td>
                        <td>
                            <asp:TextBox runat="server" ID="txtPhone" Width="100%" />
                            <asp:MaskedEditExtender ID="MaskedEditExtender1"
runat="server" TargetControlID="txtPhone"
                            Mask="(999)999-9999" MaskType="Number"
ClearMaskOnLostFocus="false">
                            </asp:MaskedEditExtender>
                        </td>
                    </tr>
                    <tr>
                        <td class="fieldname">
                            <asp:Label runat="server" ID="lblFax"
AssociatedControlID="txtFax" Text="Fax:" />
                        </td>
                        <td>
                            <asp:TextBox runat="server" ID="txtFax" Width="100%"
```

```
/><asp:MaskedEditExtender ID="MaskedEditExtender2"
                          runat="server" TargetControlID="txtFax"
Mask="(999)999-9999" MaskType="Number"
                          ClearMaskOnLostFocus="false">
                </asp:MaskedEditExtender>
            </td>
        </tr>
    </table>
  </asp:View>
</asp:MultiView>
```

Following is the code-behind that prefills the various textboxes if the current user is logged in. Also note that UpdateTotals is called in this event so that the totals are updated correctly even when the customer has changed some quantities and proceeded to the next step without clicking the Update Total button and the AJAX updates did not fire:

```
Private Sub wizSubmitOrder_ActiveStepChanged(ByVal sender As Object,
ByVal e As System.EventArgs) Handles wizSubmitOrder.ActiveStepChanged

    If wizSubmitOrder.ActiveStepIndex = 1 Then

        UpdateTotals()

        If Me.User.Identity.IsAuthenticated Then

            If txtFirstName.Text.Trim().Length = 0 Then _
               txtFirstName.Text = Profile.FirstName
            If txtLastName.Text.Trim().Length = 0 Then _
               txtLastName.Text = Profile.LastName
            If txtEmail.Text.Trim().Length = 0 Then _
               txtEmail.Text = Membership.GetUser().Email
            If txtStreet.Text.Trim().Length = 0 Then _
               txtStreet.Text = Profile.Address.Street
            If txtPostalCode.Text.Trim().Length = 0 Then _
               txtPostalCode.Text = Profile.Address.PostalCode
            If txtCity.Text.Trim().Length = 0 Then _
               txtCity.Text = Profile.Address.City

            If ddlState.SelectedIndex = 0 AndAlso Not
String.IsNullOrEmpty(Profile.Address.State) Then _
                ddlState.SelectedValue = Profile.Address.State

            If ddlCountries.SelectedIndex = 0 AndAlso Not
String.IsNullOrEmpty(Profile.Address.Country) Then _
                ddlCountries.SelectedValue = Profile.Address.Country

            If txtPhone.Text.Trim().Length = 0 Then _
               txtPhone.Text = Profile.Contacts.Phone
            If txtFax.Text.Trim().Length = 0 Then _
               txtFax.Text = Profile.Contacts.Fax
        End If
' Code to handle the last step ...
End Sub
```

Figure 9-16 shows what this step looks like on the page at runtime.

Shipping Address

Fill the form below with the shipping address for your order. All information is required, except for phone and fax numbers.

First name:	Chris
Last name:	Love
E-mail:	info@extremewebworks.com
Street:	123 Main St
Zip / Postal code:	27607
City:	Raleigh
State / Region:	North Carolina
Country:	United States
Phone:	(919)182-3823
Fax:	(919)383-7373

Modify data in previous step   Proceed with order   Continue Shopping

Figure 9-16

The last step allows the customer to review all data inserted so far: the name, price, and quantity of the products she's about to order; the subtotal amount; the shipping method and its cost; and the total amount, as well as her personal contact information and the shipping address. The `WizardStep` template defines a number of `Labels` for most of this information, and a `Repeater` control bound to the items in the shopping cart:

```
<div id="ContentBody">
    <p>
        Please carefully review the order information below.
If you want to change something
        click the link below to go back to the previous pages and
make the corrections.
        If everything is ok go ahead and submit your order.
    </p>
    <img src="Images/paypal.gif" style="float: right" alt="" />
    <b>Order Details</b>
    <br />
    <asp:Repeater runat="server" ID="repOrderItems">
        <ItemTemplate>
            <img src="Images/ArrowR3.gif" border="0" alt="" />
            <%# Eval("Title") %>
            -
            <%# FormatPrice(Eval("UnitPrice")) %>
              <small>(Quantity =
                <%# Eval("Quantity") %>)</small>
            <br />
        </ItemTemplate>
    </asp:Repeater>
    <br />
    Subtotal =
    <asp:Literal runat="server" ID="lblReviewSubtotal" />
    <br />
```

```
                Shipping Method =
                <asp:Literal runat="server" ID="lblReviewShippingMethod" />
                <br />
                <u>Total</u> =
                <asp:Literal runat="server" ID="lblReviewTotal" />
                <br />
                <b>Shipping Details</b>
                <br />
                <asp:Literal runat="server" ID="lblReviewFirstName" />
                <asp:Literal runat="server" ID="lblReviewLastName" /><br />
                <asp:Literal runat="server" ID="lblReviewStreet" /><br />
                <asp:Literal runat="server" ID="lblReviewCity" />,
                <asp:Literal runat="server" ID="lblReviewState" />
                <asp:Literal runat="server" ID="lblReviewPostalCode" /><br />
                <asp:Literal runat="server" ID="lblReviewCountry" />
        </div>
```

When this step loads, you confirm that the wizard's `ActiveStepIndex` is 2 and then show all the information in the controls:

```
ElseIf wizSubmitOrder.ActiveStepIndex = 2 Then
    lblReviewFirstName.Text = txtFirstName.Text
    lblReviewLastName.Text = txtLastName.Text
    lblReviewStreet.Text = txtStreet.Text
    lblReviewCity.Text = txtCity.Text
    lblReviewState.Text = ddlState.SelectedValue
    lblReviewPostalCode.Text = txtPostalCode.Text
    lblReviewCountry.Text = ddlCountries.SelectedValue

    lblReviewSubtotal.Text = Me.FormatPrice(lShoppingCart.Total)
    lblReviewShippingMethod.Text = ddlShippingMethods.SelectedItem.Text
    lblReviewTotal.Text = Me.FormatPrice(lShoppingCart.Total + _
        Convert.ToDecimal(ddlShippingMethods.SelectedValue))

    repOrderItems.DataSource = lShoppingCart.Items
    repOrderItems.DataBind()
```

The results of this step are displayed as shown in Figure 9-17.

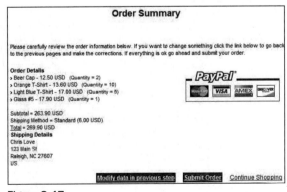

Figure 9-17

If the Finish button is clicked, the wizard's `FinishButtonClick` event handler will save the shopping cart's content as a new order in the database, clear the shopping cart, and use the `StoreHelper`'s `GetPayPalPaymentUrl` method to get the PayPal URL with the customer's shipping information, then you'll redirect the customer to pay for the ordered products. However, before doing all this, you must determine whether the customer is still authenticated. In fact, consider the situation in which the customer gets to this last step and then goes away from the computer, maybe to find her credit card. When she comes back, her authentication cookie may have expired, in which case you'd get an empty shopping cart for an anonymous user when accessing `Profile.ShoppingCart`. Therefore, if the current user is not authenticated at this point, you'll redirect her to the page that requests the login; otherwise, you'll go ahead and send her to the PayPal site:

```
Private Sub wizSubmitOrder_FinishButtonClick(ByVal sender As Object, _
ByVal e As System.Web.UI.WebControls.WizardNavigationEventArgs) _
Handles wizSubmitOrder.FinishButtonClick

        If Me.User.Identity.IsAuthenticated Then

            Dim shippingMethod As String = ddlShippingMethods.SelectedItem.Text
            shippingMethod = shippingMethod.Substring(0, _
shippingMethod.LastIndexOf("(")).Trim

            Dim lorder As Order
            Using lorderrpt As New OrdersRepository

                Dim lShoppingCart As ShoppingCart = Profile.ShoppingCart

                lorder = lorderrpt.InsertOrder(lShoppingCart, shippingMethod, _
                    Convert.ToDecimal(ddlShippingMethods.SelectedValue), _
                    txtFirstName.Text, txtLastName.Text, txtStreet.Text, _
txtPostalCode.Text, txtCity.Text, _
                    ddlState.SelectedValue, ddlCountries.SelectedValue, _
txtEmail.Text, txtPhone.Text, txtFax.Text, "")

                lShoppingCart.Clear()

                Profile.ShoppingCart = lShoppingCart

            End Using

            Me.Response.Redirect(StoreHelper.GetPayPalPaymentUrl(lorder), False)

        Else
            Me.RequestLogin()
        End If
    End Sub
```

Figure 9-18 shows the PayPal payment page run from inside the Sandbox test environment. The subtotal, shipping, and total amounts are exactly the same as those in the previous figures.

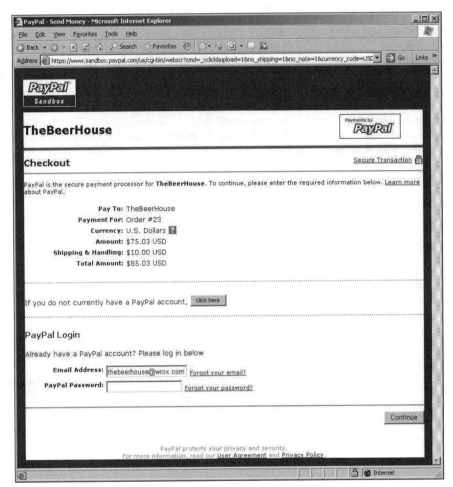

Figure 9-18

Handing the Customer's Return from PayPal

When the customer cancels the order while she's on PayPal's page, she is redirected to the OrderCancelled
.aspx page, which has just a couple of lines of static feedback instructions explaining how she can pay
at a later time. If she completes the payment, she'll be directed to the OrderCompleted.aspx page
instead. It expects the ID of the order paid by the customer on the querystring, so that it can load an
Order object for it. It then it updates its StatusID property from "waiting for payment" to "confirmed"
but not yet "verified":

```
Protected Sub Page_Load(ByVal sender As Object, ByVal e As System.EventArgs)
Handles Me.Load

        Using lorderrpt As New OrdersRepository

            Dim order As Order = lorderrpt.GetOrderById(Convert.ToInt32(
```

```
Me.Request.QueryString("OrderID")))
                If order.StatusID = CInt(StatusCode.WaitingForPayment) Then
                    order.StatusID = CInt(StatusCode.Confirmed)
                    lorderrpt.AddOrder(order)
                End If

            End Using

    End Sub
```

Figure 9-19 shows both pages.

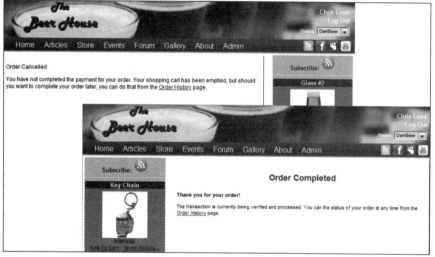

Figure 9-19

The `PayPalIPN.ashx` generic handler is the one that receives the IPN notification. (In a previous version of TheBeerHouse, this was a full-blown Web Form, which is completely unnecessary because a browser never opens the response and a form is not needed.) As explained earlier, the first thing you do in this page is verify that the notification is real and was not faked by a dishonest user. To do this, you send the notification data back to PayPal using `HttpWebRequest`, and see if PayPal responds with a `VERIFIED` string:

```
Protected Function IsVerifiedNotification() As Boolean
    Dim response As String = String.Empty
    Dim post As String = Request.Form.ToString() & "&cmd=_notify-validate"
    Dim serverUrl As String
    If Helpers.Settings.Store.SandboxMode Then
        serverUrl = "https://www.sandbox.paypal.com/us/cgi-bin/webscr"
    Else
        serverUrl = "https://www.paypal.com/us/cgi-bin/webscr"
    End If

    Dim req As HttpWebRequest = CType(WebRequest.Create(serverUrl), _
HttpWebRequest)
```

```
        req.Method = "POST"
        req.ContentType = "application/x-www-form-urlencoded"
        req.ContentLength = post.Length

        Dim writer As New StreamWriter(req.GetRequestStream(), _
System.Text.Encoding.ASCII)
        writer.Write(post)
        writer.Close()

        Dim reader As New StreamReader(req.GetResponse().GetResponseStream())
        response = reader.ReadToEnd()
        reader.Close()

        Return (response = "VERIFIED")
    End Function
```

This method is called from inside the ProcessRequest method, and if the check succeeds, you extract some data from the request's parameters, such as custom (the order ID), payment_status (a string describing the current status for the order transaction), and mc_gross (the order's total amount). Then you get a reference to the Order object according to the order ID obtained from the notification, and you check whether the total amount stored in the database matches the amount indicated by the PayPal notification. If so, you update the order status to "verified." Here's the code:

```
Public Sub ProcessRequest(ByVal context As HttpContext)
Implements IHttpHandler.ProcessRequest

        Request = context.Request
        response = context.Response

        If IsVerifiedNotification() Then

            Dim orderID As Integer = Convert.ToInt32(Me.Request.Params("custom"))
            Dim status As String = Me.Request.Params("payment_status")
            Dim amount As Decimal = Convert.ToDecimal(
Me.Request.Params("mc_gross"), _
                CultureInfo.CreateSpecificCulture("en-US"))

            Using lorderrpt As New OrdersRepository

                Dim order As Order = lorderrpt.GetOrderById(Convert.ToInt32(
Me.Request.QueryString("OrderID")))
                Dim origAmount As Decimal = (order.SubTotal + order.Shipping)
                If amount >= origAmount Then
                    order.StatusID = CInt(StatusCode.Confirmed)
                    lorderrpt.AddOrder(order)
                End If

            End Using

        End If

    End Sub
```

In the preceding code, when parsing the `mc_gross` string to a decimal value, a `CultureInfo` object for `en-US` (English for U.S.) is passed to the `Convert.ToDecimal` call. This is because PayPal always uses a period (.) as separator for the decimal part of the number, but if the current thread's locale is set to some other culture that uses a comma for the separator, the string would have been parsed incorrectly without this code.

You should also make a mental note that supplying PayPal with an Instant Pay Notification URL on your local machine (using the built-in development server with localhost in its URL) will not allow you to test that page. PayPal is an external party and it cannot see your localhost, so to test the handler you must have this on a public server.

> There can be many more parameters that PayPal passes to your page in the IPN notifications than those used here. I strongly suggest you to refer to PayPal's documentation for the full coverage of these parameters, and for the guide on how to activate and set up the IPN notifications from your PayPal's account settings, which is not covered here.

The ShoppingCart.ascx User Control

So far I haven't shown any links to the `ShoppingCart.aspx` page, but we want the cart to be visible on any page. The shopping cart's current content should always be visible as well, so that the customer does not need to go to `ShoppingCart.aspx` just to see whether she's already put a product into the cart. We also want customers to see the subtotal so they won't get any surprises when they proceed to checkout. All this information can easily be shown on a user control that will be plugged into the site's master page, so it will always be present. The `ShoppingCart.ascx` control defines a `ListView` control that's similar to the one used earlier in the last step of the `ShoppingCart.aspx` page, which shows the current list of shopping cart items with their name, unit price, and quantity. Below that is a label for displaying the shopping cart's total amount, and a hyperlink to the full `ShoppingCart.aspx` page, where the customer can change quantities and proceed with the checkout. It also defines a link to the `OrderHistory.aspx` page, which you'll create next:

```
<asp:ListView runat="server" ID="lvOrderItems" ItemPlaceholderID="itemPlaceHolder">
        <LayoutTemplate>
            <div runat="server" id="itemPlaceHolder">
            </div>
        </LayoutTemplate>
        <ItemTemplate>
            <div id="ShoppingCartItem">
                <asp:Image runat="Server" ID="imgProduct"
ImageUrl="~/Images/ArrowR3.gif" GenerateEmptyAlternateText="true" />
                <%# Eval("Title") %>
                -
                <%#CType(Me.Page, BasePage).FormatPrice(Eval("UnitPrice"))%>
                  <small>(<%# Eval("Quantity") %>)
                    <br />
                </small>
            </div>
        </ItemTemplate>
        <EmptyDataTemplate>
            <div>
```

```
                            <asp:Literal runat="server" ID="lblCartIsEmpty"
Text="Your cart is currently empty."
                                meta:resourcekey="lblCartIsEmptyResource1" /></div>
                </EmptyDataTemplate>
</asp:ListView>
<br />
<b><asp:Literal runat="server" ID="lblSubtotalHeader"
Text="Subtotal = " meta:resourcekey="lblSubtotalHeaderResource1" /><asp:Literal
                runat="server" ID="lblSubtotal" /></b>
<br />
<asp:Panel runat="server" ID="panLinkShoppingCart"
meta:resourcekey="panLinkShoppingCartResource1">
<asp:HyperLink runat="server" ID="lnkShoppingCart"
NavigateUrl="~/ShoppingCart.aspx"
                meta:resourcekey="lnkShoppingCartResource1">
Detailed Shopping Cart</asp:HyperLink><br />
</asp:Panel>
<asp:HyperLink runat="server" ID="lnkOrderHistory"
NavigateUrl="~/OrderHistory.aspx"
                meta:resourcekey="lnkOrderHistoryResource1">Order History
</asp:HyperLink>
```

In the control's code-behind class, you just handle the Load event to bind the ListView with the data returned by the Items property of the Profile.ShoppingCart object, show the total amount in the label, and hide the panel with the link to ShoppingCart.aspx if the cart is empty:

```
Protected Sub Page_Load(ByVal sender As Object, ByVal e As System.EventArgs)
Handles Me.Load
        If Not Me.IsPostBack Then

                Dim lBasePage As BasePage = CType(Me.Page, BasePage)
                Dim lShoppingCart As ShoppingCart = Profile.ShoppingCart
                lvOrderItems.DataSource = lShoppingCart.Items
                lvOrderItems.DataBind()

                If Not IsNothing(lShoppingCart) AndAlso
lShoppingCart.Items.Count > 0 Then

                        lblSubtotal.Text = lBasePage.FormatPrice(lShoppingCart.Total)
                        lblSubtotal.Visible = True
                        lblSubtotalHeader.Visible = True
                        panLinkShoppingCart.Visible = True
                Else
                        lblSubtotal.Visible = False
                        lblSubtotalHeader.Visible = False
                        panLinkShoppingCart.Visible = False
                End If
        End If
End Sub
```

Figure 9-20 shows how the control looks — both empty and with items.

Figure 9-20

The FeaturedProduct.ascx Control

Constantly promoting catalog products on every page in the site is a great way to tempt visitors to place an order. The FeaturedProducts.ascx control does just that by randomly selecting an active product from the database and displaying its details in promotional square on the side of selected pages in the site. Like the Shopping cart control, it tries to take up just a small piece of the page to promote the product, so it shows only the title, thumbnail image, price, and links to add the product to the shopping cart or view the product details.

```
<asp:HyperLink ID="hlnkProductImage" runat="server"></asp:HyperLink>
<br />
<b>
    <asp:Literal ID="ltlUnitPrice" runat="server"></asp:Literal></b>
<br />
<asp:LinkButton ID="lbtnAddToCart" runat="server">
Add To Cart</asp:LinkButton>   
<asp:HyperLink ID="hlnkMoreDetails" runat="server">More Details...</asp:HyperLink>
```

The product is retrieved in a way similar to that used by the ShowProduct.aspx page; if there happens to be a ProductId passed in the querystring, it will display that product; if not, a random product is selected.

```
Private Sub BindData()

    Using Productrpt As New ProductsRepository

        Dim lProduct As Product

        If ProductId > 0 Then
            lProduct = Productrpt.GetProductById(ProductId)
        Else
            lProduct = Productrpt.GetRandomProduct()
            ProductId = lProduct.ProductID
        End If

        If Not IsNothing(lProduct) Then

            ltlTitle.Text = String.Format("<b>{0}</b>", lProduct.Title)

            Dim sURL As String = Helpers.SEOFriendlyURL("~/" & _
                            Path.Combine(
Helpers.Settings.Store.ProductURLIndicator,
lProduct.Title), ".aspx")

            hlnkProductImage.Text = lProduct.Title
```

487

```
            hlnkProductImage.ImageUrl = ResolveUrl(lProduct.SmallImageUrl)
            hlnkProductImage.NavigateUrl = sURL

            ltlUnitPrice.Text = Helpers.FormatPrice(lProduct.UnitPrice)

            hlnkMoreDetails.NavigateUrl = sURL

        End If

    End Using

End Sub
```

The `GetRandomProduct` function returns a randomly selected product by retrieving a list of products then getting a random number and returning the product matching that index in the list.

```
Public Function GetRandomProduct() As Product

    Dim lProductList As List(Of Product) = Me.GetProducts
    Dim lRandProdIndex As Integer = MyBase.GetRandItem(0, lProductList.Count - 1)
    Return lProductList.Item(lRandProdIndex)

End Function
```

The OrderHistory.aspx Page

This page contains a `ListView` wrapped in an `UpdatePanel` that lists all past orders for the current authenticated user. The `ListView`'s template section shows the order's title, the total amount, and the title of the current status, plus the detailed list of all items in the order, rendered by a `Repeater`, similar to those used earlier. If the order's `StatusID` is 1 (waiting for payment), it also renders a link to the PayPal payment page, retrieved by means of the order's `GetPayPalPaymentUrl` method, already used in the last step of the `ShoppingCart.aspx` page's Checkout Wizard. At the end of the template, it also displays the subtotal amount, and the shipping method's title and cost:

```
<asp:ListView runat="server" ID="lvOrders" DataKeyNames="OrderId">
    <LayoutTemplate>
        <div runat="server" id="itemPlaceHolder">
        </div>
        <div class="pager">
            <asp:DataPager ID="pagerBottom" runat="server"
PageSize="5" PagedControlID="lvOrders">
                <Fields>
                    <asp:NextPreviousPagerField ButtonCssClass="command"
FirstPageText="&#171;" PreviousPageText="&#60;"
                        RenderDisabledButtonsAsLabels="true"
ShowFirstPageButton="true" ShowPreviousPageButton="true"
                        ShowLastPageButton="false"
ShowNextPageButton="false" />
                    <asp:NumericPagerField ButtonCount="7"
NumericButtonCssClass="command" CurrentPageLabelCssClass="current"
                        NextPreviousButtonCssClass="command" />
                    <asp:NextPreviousPagerField
```

```
                ButtonCssClass="command" LastPageText="»" NextPageText=">"
                                    RenderDisabledButtonsAsLabels="true"
        ShowFirstPageButton="false" ShowPreviousPageButton="false"
                                    ShowLastPageButton="true" ShowNextPageButton="true" />
                        </Fields>
                    </asp:DataPager>
                </div>
            </LayoutTemplate>
            <ItemTemplate>
                <div class="sectionsubtitle">
                    Order #<%#Eval("OrderID")%>
                    -
                    <%# Eval("AddedDate", "{0:g}") %></div>
                <br />
                <img src="Images/ArrowR4.gif" border="0" alt="" />
                <u>Total</u> =
                <%# FormatPrice(CDec(Eval("SubTotal")) + CDec(Eval("Shipping"))) %>
<br />                  .
                <img src="Images/ArrowR4.gif" border="0" alt="" />
                <u>Status</u> =
                <%# Eval("StatusTitle") %>
                   
                <asp:HyperLink runat="server" ID="lnkPay" Font-Bold="true"
Text="Pay Now" NavigateUrl='<%# StoreHelper.GetPayPalPaymentUrl
(CType(Container.DataItem, Order)) %>'
                    Visible='<%# (CInt(Eval("StatusID"))) = 1 %>' />
                <br />
                <br />
                <small><b>Details</b><br />
                    <small>
                        <asp:Repeater runat="server" ID="repOrderItems">
                            <ItemTemplate>
                                <img src="../Images/ArrowR3.gif" border="0" alt="" />
                                [<%# Eval("SKU") %>]
                                <asp:HyperLink runat="server" ID="lnkProduct"
Text='<%# Eval("Title") %>' NavigateUrl=
'<%# "~/ShowProduct.aspx?productID=" & Eval("ProductID") %>' />
                                - (<%# Eval("Quantity") %>)
                                <br />
                            </ItemTemplate>
                        </asp:Repeater>
                    </small>
                    <br />
                    Subtotal =
                    <%# FormatPrice(Eval("SubTotal")) %><br />
                    Shipping Method =
                    <%# Eval("ShippingMethod") %>
                    (<%# FormatPrice(Eval("Shipping")) %>) </small>
            </ItemTemplate>
            <ItemSeparatorTemplate>
                <hr style="width: 99%;" />
            </ItemSeparatorTemplate>
</asp:ListView>
```

The page's code-behind contains only a couple of lines that bind the `ListView` with the list of orders returned by the `Order.GetOrdersByUser` method, which accepts the name of the current user:

```
Dim lOrders As List(Of Order) = lOrderrpt.GetOrdersByUser(Helpers.CurrentUserName)
lvOrders.DataSource = lOrders
lvOrders.DataBind()
```

Figure 9-21 shows the page.

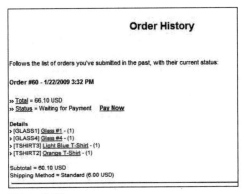

Figure 9-21

The ManageOrders.aspx and AddEditOrder.aspx Pages

This administrative page is used by storekeepers to retrieve the list of orders in a certain status created in a specified date interval, or to retrieve the list of all orders made by a given customer. If the store-keeper already knows the `OrderID` of a specific order and wants to update it, there's a form that lets her enter the `OrderID` and click the button to jump to the edit page.

The form utilizes some of the AJAX extenders and the Membership web service introduced back in Chapter 4 to provide some client-side help. First the Order Status drop-down sets the `AutoPostBack` property to true, meaning anytime a new selection is made the list of orders is changed to reflect that choice. The `OrderStatusId` property is set the selected value and the `BindOrders` method is called. `BindOrders` has logic that checks for each of the possible filters and applies them as needed.

Next, the date range can be selected by the user to limit the number of orders. It uses two `TextBoxes` extended with the AJAX `Calendar` and `MaskedEdit` extenders. There is an accompanying Submit button to apply the desired date range. The filter is designed to let the user specify either a from or to date or both. If only one of the date values is entered, it is used as a cutoff point in the desired direction. Additionally, a `CompareValidator` is employed to make sure that the two values entered are not the same; if they were, then no records would be displayed.

Next, orders can be filtered for specific users. A `TextBox` allows the user to type in the username. Once the username is entered, there is a Submit button that can be pressed to submit the user filter. While the user is typing the username, an `AutoCompleteExtender` displays a list of possible matches in a hint drop-down. This helps when the user is not quite sure what the username actually is.

```
<fieldset>
        <legend>Orders by status</legend>Status:
```

```
        <asp:DropDownList ID="ddlOrderStatuses" runat="server"
DataTextField="Title" DataValueField="OrderStatusID"
            AutoPostBack="True" />
        <br />
        Order Date from:
        <asp:TextBox ID="txtFromDate" runat="server" Width="80px" />
<asp:Image runat="Server"
            ID="iFromDate" ImageUrl="~/images/Calendar.png" />
        <asp:CalendarExtender ID="ceEventDate" runat="server"
TargetControlID="txtFromDate"
            PopupButtonID="iFromDate">
        </asp:CalendarExtender>
        <asp:MaskedEditExtender ID="meeEventDate" runat="server"
TargetControlID="txtFromDate"
            Mask="99/99/9999" MessageValidatorTip="true"
OnFocusCssClass="MaskedEditFocus"
            OnInvalidCssClass="MaskedEditError" MaskType="Date"
DisplayMoney="Left" AcceptNegative="Left" />
        to:
        <asp:TextBox ID="txtToDate" runat="server" Width="80px" />
        <asp:Image runat="Server" ID="Image1" ImageUrl="~/images/Calendar.png" />
        <asp:CalendarExtender ID="CalendarExtender1" runat="server"
TargetControlID="txtToDate"
            PopupButtonID="iToDate">
        </asp:CalendarExtender>
        <asp:MaskedEditExtender ID="MaskedEditExtender1" runat="server"
 TargetControlID="txtToDate"
            Mask="99/99/9999" MessageValidatorTip="true"
OnFocusCssClass="MaskedEditFocus"
            OnInvalidCssClass="MaskedEditError" MaskType="Date"
DisplayMoney="Left" AcceptNegative="Left" />
        <asp:Button ID="btnListByStatus" runat="server" Text="Load"
 ValidationGroup="ListByStatus" />
        <asp:RequiredFieldValidator ID="valRequireFromDate" runat="server"
 ControlToValidate="txtFromDate"
            SetFocusOnError="true" ValidationGroup="ListByStatus" Text="<br />
The From Date field is required."
            ToolTip="The From Date field is required."
Display="Dynamic"></asp:RequiredFieldValidator>
        <asp:CompareValidator runat="server" ID="valFromDateType"
ControlToValidate="txtFromDate"
            SetFocusOnError="true" ValidationGroup="ListByStatus" Text="<br />
The format of the From Date is not valid."
            ToolTip="The format of the From Date is not valid."
Display="Dynamic" Operator="DataTypeCheck"
            Type="Date" />
        <asp:RequiredFieldValidator ID="valRequireToDate"
runat="server" ControlToValidate="txtToDate"
            SetFocusOnError="true" ValidationGroup="ListByStatus"
Text="<br />The To Date field is required."
            ToolTip="The To Date field is required."
Display="Dynamic"></asp:RequiredFieldValidator>
        <asp:CompareValidator runat="server" ID="valToDateType"
ControlToValidate="txtToDate"
            SetFocusOnError="true" ValidationGroup="ListByStatus"
```

```
Text="<br />The format of the To Date is not valid."
            ToolTip="The format of the To Date is not valid."
Display="Dynamic" Operator="DataTypeCheck"
            Type="Date" />
        <br />
        <div class="sectionsubtitle">
            Orders by customer</div>
        Name:
        <asp:TextBox ID="txtCustomerName" runat="server" />
        <asp:Button ID="btnListByCustomer" runat="server"
Text="Load" ValidationGroup="ListByCustomer" />
        <asp:RequiredFieldValidator ID="valRequireCustomerName"
runat="server" ControlToValidate="txtCustomerName"
            SetFocusOnError="true" ValidationGroup="ListByCustomer"
Text="<br />The Customer Name field is required."
            ToolTip="The Customer Name field is required."
Display="Dynamic"></asp:RequiredFieldValidator>
        <asp:AutoCompleteExtender runat="server"
ID="autoComplete1" BehaviorID="AutoCompleteEx"
            TargetControlID="txtCustomerName"
ServicePath="~/MembersService.asmx" ServiceMethod="SearchUsersByName"
            MinimumPrefixLength="2" CompletionInterval="500"
EnableCaching="true" CompletionSetCount="12" />
        <br />
        <div class="sectionsubtitle">
            Order Lookup</div>
        ID:
        <asp:TextBox ID="txtOrderID" runat="server" />
        <asp:Button ID="btnOrderLookup" runat="server"
Text="Find" ValidationGroup="OrderLookup" />
        <asp:Label runat="server" ID="lblOrderNotFound" SkinID="FeedbackKO"
Text="Order not found!"
            Visible="false" />
        <asp:RequiredFieldValidator ID="valRequireOrderID" runat="server"
ControlToValidate="txtOrderID"
            SetFocusOnError="true" ValidationGroup="OrderLookup"
Text="<br />The Order ID field is required."
            ToolTip="The Order ID field is required."
Display="Dynamic"></asp:RequiredFieldValidator>
    </fieldset>
```

The filter criteria are shown in Figure 9-22

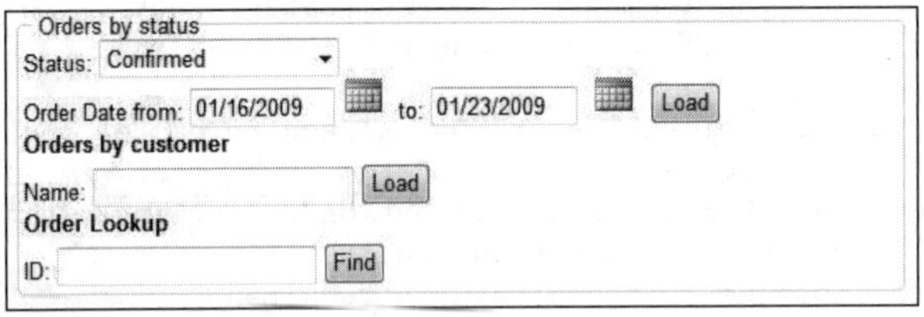

Figure 9-22

Finally the `OrderId` lookup lets the user type in an `OrderId` to bring up the order information. If the `OrderId` does not exist, an informational message is displayed to the right of the Submit button. All the filtering and potential empty result messages is done pretty seamlessly because the entire form is wrapped in an `UpdatePanel`, which means without writing any code all the filter submissions are done instantaneously without a full page postback.

```vb
Protected Sub btnOrderLookup_Click(ByVal sender As Object, _
    ByVal e As System.EventArgs) _
    Handles btnOrderLookup.Click

        Using lOrderrpt As New OrdersRepository

            Dim lOrder As Order = lOrderrpt.GetOrderById(txtOrderID.Text)
            If IsNothing(lOrder) Then
                lblOrderNotFound.Visible = True
                Exit Sub
            End If

            Response.Redirect("AddEditOrder.aspx?orderid=" & txtOrderID.Text)

        End Using

    End Sub
```

The `ListView` that actually displays the found orders, with their title, list of order items (through the usual `Repeater` as utilized in other areas of the store, which shows the SKU field in addition to the others, as this is useful information for storekeepers), the subtotal amount, and the shipping amount. On the right side of each order row, there's also a button to delete the order, but that will only be shown to Administrators, not to `StoreKeepers`, as it's a sensitive operation that should only be performed rarely, and never by accident:

```html
<asp:ListView ID="lvOrders" runat="server">
    <LayoutTemplate>
        <table cellspacing="0" cellpadding="0" class="AdminList">
            <tr class="AdminListHeader">
                <td>

                </td>
                <td>
                    Items
                </td>
                <td>
                    Cost
                </td>
                <td>
                    Edit
                </td>
                <td>
                    Delete
                </td>
            </tr>
            <tr id="itemPlaceholder" runat="server">
            </tr>
```

```
            <tr>
                <td colspan="5">
                    <div class="pager">
<asp:DataPager ID="pagerBottom" runat="server" PageSize="15"
PagedControlID="lvOrders">
    <Fields>
        <asp:NextPreviousPagerField ButtonCssClass="command"
FirstPageText="&#171;" PreviousPageText="&lt;"
            RenderDisabledButtonsAsLabels="true"
ShowFirstPageButton="true" ShowPreviousPageButton="true"
            ShowLastPageButton="false" ShowNextPageButton="false" />
        <asp:NumericPagerField ButtonCount="7"
NumericButtonCssClass="command" CurrentPageLabelCssClass="current"
            NextPreviousButtonCssClass="command" />
        <asp:NextPreviousPagerField ButtonCssClass="command"
LastPageText="&#187;" NextPageText="&gt;"
            RenderDisabledButtonsAsLabels="true"
ShowFirstPageButton="false" ShowPreviousPageButton="false"
            ShowLastPageButton="true" ShowNextPageButton="true" />
    </Fields>
</asp:DataPager>
                    </div>
                </td>
            </tr>
        </table>
    </LayoutTemplate>
    <EmptyDataTemplate>
        <tr>
            <td colspan="5">
                <p>
                    Sorry there are no Orders available at this time.</p>
            </td>
        </tr>
    </EmptyDataTemplate>
    <ItemTemplate>
        <tr>
            <td>
                <%#Eval("AddedBy")%>
                on
                <%#String.Format("{0:d}", Eval("AddedDate"))%><br />
                Shipping: <%#Eval("ShippingMethod")%>
            </td>
            <td>
                <small>
                    <asp:Repeater runat="server" ID="repOrderItems"
DataSource='<%# Eval("OrderItems") %>'>
<ItemTemplate>
    <img src="../Images/ArrowR3.gif" border="0" alt="" />
    [<%# Eval("SKU") %>]
    <asp:HyperLink runat="server" ID="lnkProduct" Text='<%# Eval("Title") %>'
 NavigateUrl='<%# "~/ShowProduct.aspx?productID=" & Eval("ProductID") %>' />
    - (<%# Eval("Quantity") %>)
    <br />
</ItemTemplate>
```

```
                </asp:Repeater>
            </small>
        </td>
        <td>
            Sub Total:
            <%#String.Format("{0:C2}", Eval("SubTotal"))%><br />
            Shipping:
            <%#String.Format("{0:C2}", Eval("Shipping"))%><br />
            Grand Total:
            <%#String.Format("{0:C2}", Eval("GrandTotal"))%>
        </td>
        <td align="center">
            <a href="<%# String.Format("AddEditOrder.aspx?OrderId={0}",
 Eval("OrderId")) %>">
                <img src="../images/edit.gif" alt="" width="16"
height="16" class="AdminImg" /></a>
        </td>
        <td align="center">
            <asp:ImageButton runat="server" ID="btnDelete"
CommandArgument='<%# Eval("OrderId").ToString() %>'
                CommandName="Delete" ImageUrl="~/images/delete.gif"
 AlternateText="Delete" CssClass="AdminImg"
                OnClientClick="return confirm('Warning: This will
delete the Product from the database.');" />
        </td>
    </tr>
    </ItemTemplate>
</asp:ListView>
```

When the page loads, the textbox for the end date of the date interval is prefilled with the current date, while the textbox for the start date is prefilled with the current date minus the number of days specified in the `DefaultOrderListInterval` configuration setting:

```
Protected Sub Page_Load(ByVal sender As Object, ByVal e As System.EventArgs)
Handles Me.Load

If Not IsPostBack Then
        BindOrderStatuses(ddlOrderStatuses)

        txtToDate.Text = DateTime.Now.ToShortDateString()
        txtFromDate.Text = DateTime.Now.Subtract( _
            New TimeSpan(Helpers.Settings.Store.DefaultOrderListInterval, _
            0, 0, 0)).ToShortDateString()

        BindOrders()
    End If

End Sub
```

The `BindOrders` method takes on the responsibility of tracking what filters are in play. It is designed to allow one or more filter criteria to be applied to the list of orders by first retrieving the entire list of orders and applying the criteria one at a time, until the desired list is finally bound to the `ListView` control. Now here is where an architectural decision was made out of convenience. If the site gets large numbers of orders a complicated ESQL query will be more desirable because it will apply these filters before it queries the database, which is more efficient. This is not the easiest thing to achieve. And because the list of orders in TheBeerHouse is still relatively small this is a much faster way to get things running.

```
Private Sub BindOrders()
    Using lOrdersrpt As New OrdersRepository

        Dim lOrders As List(Of Order)

        lOrders = lOrdersrpt.GetOrders

        If OrderId > 0 Then
            lOrders = (From lOrder In lOrders Where
lOrder.OrderID = OrderId).ToList
        End If

        If OrderStatusId > 0 Then
            lOrders = (From lOrder In lOrders Where
lOrder.StatusID = OrderStatusId).ToList
        End If

        If OrderStatusId > 0 Then
            lOrders = (From lOrder In lOrders Where
lOrder.AddedBy.StartsWith(CustomerName)).ToList
        End If

        If FromDate > DateTime.MinValue Then
            lOrders = (From lOrder In lOrders Where
lOrder.AddedDate > FromDate).ToList
        End If

        If ToDate > DateTime.MinValue Then
            lOrders = (From lOrder In lOrders Where
lOrder.AddedDate < ToDate).ToList
        End If

        lvOrders.DataSource = lOrders
        lvOrders.DataBind()

        Dim pagerBottom As DataPager = lvOrders.FindControl("pagerBottom")

        If Not IsNothing(pagerBottom) Then
            If lOrders.Count <= pagerBottom.PageSize Then
                pagerBottom.Visible = False
            Else
                pagerBottom.Visible = True
            End If
        End If
    End Using
End Sub
```

Figure 9-23 shows this page in action.

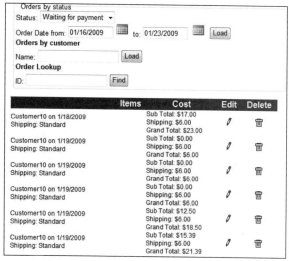

Figure 9-23

The `EditOrder.aspx` page defines a form with controls that allows an administrator to edit a few fields of the order whose `OrderID` is passed on the querystring. The code is not presented here because it's similar to the other `AddEdit{xxx}.aspx` pages developed for this module (but actually simpler because most of the data is read-only), and other modules. Figure 9-24 shows the page, however, so that you can get an idea of what it looks like and what it can do.

Edit The Order

Order ID	60
Order Date	1/22/2009 3:32:27 PM
Ordered By	Customer10

Ordered Items

SKU	Title	Unit Price	QTY
[GLASS1]	Glass #1	$13.00	(1)
[GLASS4]	Glass #4	$18.50	(1)
[TSHIRT3]	Light Blue T-Shirt	$17.00	(1)
[TSHIRT2]	Orange T-Shirt	$13.60	(1)

Status	Waiting for payment
Shipping Method	Standard
Sub Total	$60.10
Shipping	$6.00
Shipped Date	
Customer Email	info@extremewebworks.com
Customer Phone	(919) 182-3823
Customer Fax	(919) 383-7373
Address	Chris Love 123 Main St Raleigh NC 27607 US
Transaction ID	
Tracking ID	
Updated Date	1/22/2009 3:32:27 PM
Updated By	
Active	True

Cancel   Update

Figure 9-24

Creating a Policies and Procedures Page

As mentioned in the "Problem" section, a Policies page can go a long way toward making customers feel comfortable doing business with you, as well as give you a firm standing when problems escalate. Because you are not a lawyer and The Beer House's owner is not either, you need to get a lawyer to draft a policy page for the site, copy and modify one from a similar site, or use the online Policy Wizard at `www.the-dma.org/privacy/privacypolicygenerator.shtml` (see Figure 9-25).

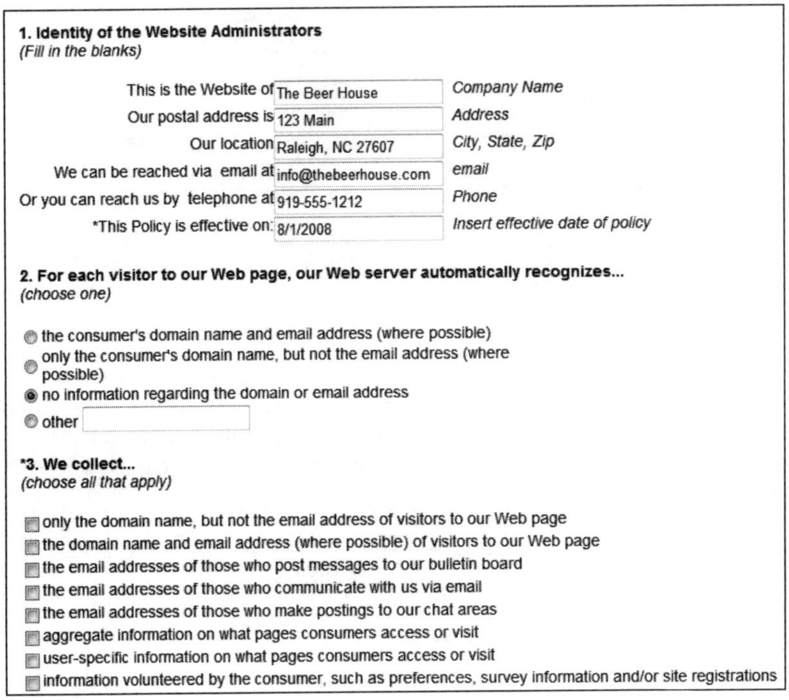

Figure 9-25

The wizard asks a series of questions about how you collect and use visitor data. Based on the answers you select, it will produce a privacy policy you can use on your site. Figure 9-26 shows a basic privacy page for The Beer House site.

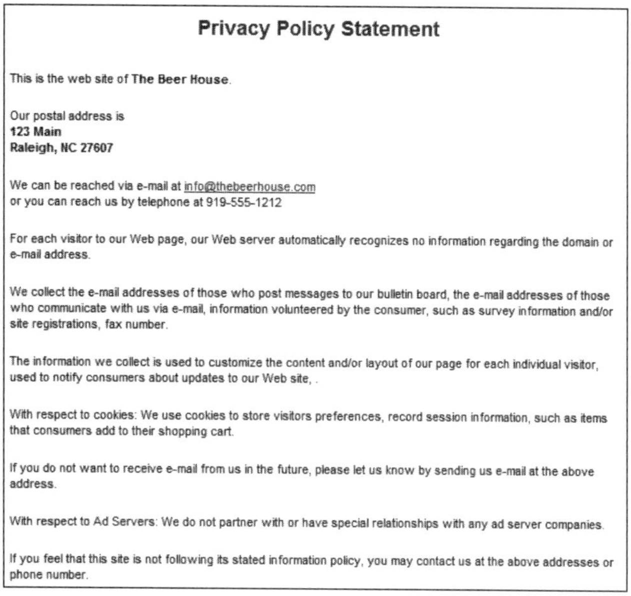

Privacy Policy Statement

This is the web site of **The Beer House**.

Our postal address is
123 Main
Raleigh, NC 27607

We can be reached via e-mail at info@thebeerhouse.com
or you can reach us by telephone at 919-555-1212

For each visitor to our Web page, our Web server automatically recognizes no information regarding the domain or e-mail address.

We collect the e-mail addresses of those who post messages to our bulletin board, the e-mail addresses of those who communicate with us via e-mail, information volunteered by the consumer, such as survey information and/or site registrations, fax number.

The information we collect is used to customize the content and/or layout of our page for each individual visitor, used to notify consumers about updates to our Web site, .

With respect to cookies: We use cookies to store visitors preferences, record session information, such as items that consumers add to their shopping cart.

If you do not want to receive e-mail from us in the future, please let us know by sending us e-mail at the above address.

With respect to Ad Servers: We do not partner with or have special relationships with any ad server companies.

If you feel that this site is not following its stated information policy, you may contact us at the above addresses or phone number.

Figure 9-26

Summary

An e-commerce module is a big challenge for any site developer, and there are a lot of features we couldn't implement in this chapter that you may find useful, especially for larger sites. In fact, you can find many commercial modules for managing electronic stores among third-party vendors, and sometimes it can be cheaper to buy one than to develop one yourself. You need to consider the features that you want and weigh the cost of commercial solutions against the cost of doing it yourself. One thing that seems to be very common is that customers always want a highly customized solution but do not always want to pay what it takes, so find the best compromise to get a viable solution online in a timely manner. The module in this chapter may be entirely adequate for small sites, or for a small store of a larger site, but you might also want to add some advanced features such as the capability to list a product under multiple categories, handle tax calculations on the store itself instead of leaving it to PayPal, support products with variations (color, size, etc.) that could also affect their price, support customer-level discounts (so that loyal customers get a better discount percentage, for example), support bundle offers and discounts based on the quantity of ordered products and the total price reached, integrate the shipment tracking offered by some shipping companies such as FedEx and UPS, and much more.

Nevertheless, in this chapter we've implemented a fully working e-commerce store with most of the basic features, including complete catalog and order management, a persistent shopping cart, integrated online payment via credit card, product rating, and more. All this required a fairly short amount of time to design and implement.

10

Calendar of Events

Offering a list of upcoming and even past events is a very important feature a successful business' online presence can offer its patrons. Everyday life for people keeps getting faster and faster paced and keeping track of everything one needs to do is hard enough, knowing when they can have fun can easily get lost. Providing patrons easy access to a schedule of events at the Beer House is a great way method to boost response in the pub. Giving customers the means to quickly add events to their calendar as reminders is another great way to remind them of the fun things they can do after they have worked all day or all week long.

Problem

The Beer House tries to maintain a regular schedule of popular events and activities to increase traffic in the pub on a nightly basis. Fortunately with sporting events and holidays the schedule has many nights covered. But the Beer House also likes to fill in the night where there is not something already scheduled that will attract folks in such as Karaoke, Ladies night and live entertainment. Promoting these events in the bar is one thing, but it is common for customers to forget these activities once they leave the bar, especially if they have enjoyed a bit too much of the Beer!

Because most of the potential Beer House customers are active online keeping an up to date schedule available on the web site is very important to keeping them informed. It gives them a way to quickly check to see what is happening and refer their friends as well. Offering a natural way to add a reminder to their digital calendars is another great way to let them be more active in scheduling their time to include a trip to the Beer House.

Design

Here's the list of features needed in the Events module:

- ❑ Display a list of upcoming events.
- ❑ Display events in a calendar format.
- ❑ Allow visitors to see full event details.
- ❑ Allow visitors to easily add an event reminder to their calendar.
- ❑ Promote upcoming events in the common layout of the site.
- ❑ For some events allow customers to RSVP.

Designing the Database Tables

The Events Module consists of two tables, one for Events and one for Event RSVPs. Instead of calling the event table Event, I called it EventInfo because using the name Event tends to cause issues because Event is a keyword in the .NET languages.

The tbh_EventInfo table contains a title, description, event time and duration, location, an AllowRegistration fields. The tbh_EventRSVP table contains some basic fields to collect information about the user attending, or not attending the event. The tables are related by a one-to-many relationship on the EventId field (see Figure 10-1).

Figure 10-1

Creating the Entity Data Model

As in the previous chapters a dedicated Entity Data Model is generated for the Event module, called CalendarofEvents. It contains an entity for EventInfo and EventRSVP, shown in Figure 10-2. And as usual the EntitySet and relationships need to be renamed to something more friendly. The module namespace is `Bll.EventCalendar`, so after the model is generated this namespace needs to be added to the accompanying designer file.

Figure 10-2

Designing the Business Layer

Like the other module business layers, each of the tables has corresponding entities and repositories. Each one inherits from the `BaseEventRepository` (see Figure 10-3) that manages the disposing members and wraps the `DataContext` in a common property.

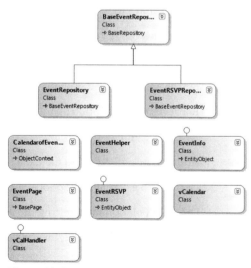

Figure 10-3

The EventRepository

Like all the entity repositories in the site, the `EventRepository` contains members to do basic retrieval, inserting, and updating of `EventInfo` entities. There are a few custom retrieval methods to retrieve a list of events based on a specified date. They're described in the following table.

Method	Description
GetEvents	Retrieves a full list of events
GetActiveEvents	Retrieves a list of active events
GetEventInfoById	Retrieves an event by its EventId
GetEventInfoCount	Returns the number of events in the database
AddEventInfo	Adds a new event to the database
UpdateEventInfo	Updates an existing event
DeleteEventInfo	Deletes an event by setting the Active flag to false
UnDeleteEventInfo	UnDeletes an event by setting the Active flag to true
DaysEvents	Returns a list events for the day passed to the method
GetTodaysEvents	Returns a list events for the current day
GetUpcomingEvents	Retrieves a list of events after the day passed to the method

The EventRSVPRepository

The `EventRSVPRepository` contains the basic repository members to perform CRUD operations against the entity data model. Here's a look at them:

Method	Description
GetEventRSVPs	Retrieves a full list of poll optionss
GetActiveActiveEventRSVPs	Retrieves a list of active poll options by the specified PollId
GetEventRSVPById	Retrieves a list of poll options by the specified PollId
GetEventRSVPByEventId	Retrieves the PollOption by the specificied PollOptionId
GetEventRSVPCount	Returns a count of poll options
AddEventRSVP	Adds a new poll option to the database
UpdateEventRSVP	Updates an existing poll option
DeleteEventRSVP	Deletes a poll option by setting the Active flag to false
UnDeleteEventRSVP	Undeletes a poll by setting the Active flag to true

Designing the User Interface Services

Following are the pages and controls that constitute the user interface layer of this module:

❑   **~/Admin/ManageEvents.aspx:** An administrative list of events with icons to edit or delete the event.

❑   **~/Admin/AddEditEvent.aspx:** Allows adding or editing of an event.

❑   **~/Admin/ManageEventRSVPs.aspx:** An administrative list of event RSVPs with icons to edit or delete the RSVP. The list can be edited by event.

❑   **~/Admin/AddEditEventRSVP.aspx:** Allows a site admin to either add or edit an event RSVP.

❑   **~/BrowseEvents.aspx:** List upcoming events and displays a calendar that highlights days with events scheduled.

❑   **~/ShowEvent.aspx:** Displays the details of the event, with a link to RSVP is the event allows registrations.

❑   **~/MakeEventRSVP.aspx:** Allows visitors to RSVP for an event.

❑   The **EventiCal Httphandler**: Returns an iCal card to the user that can be imported into Outlook or personal information manager.

Let's look at the user control now, and we'll cover the ASP.NET pages as we go through the rest of the chapter.

The vCalendar Httphandler

The `vCalendar Httphandler` control sends an iCal card to the user. iCalendar is based on the vCalendar standard defined to exchange personal calendar information. Often used in group situations to coordinate meetings, free/busy services allow users to publish their schedules to others. The Beer House can use this to enable patrons to easily track what is happening in their favorite watering hole, which also meets the overall goals of distributing information about the Beer House. Fortunately distributing this type of information is very easy with a custom `HttpHandler` because it is just a formatted text document. For more information, see Request for Comment (RFC) 2445 (www.ietf.org/rfc/rfc2445.txt), which defines the format, and RFCs 2446 and 2447 (www.ietf.org/rfc/rfc2446.txt and www.ietf .org/rfc/rfc2447.txt), which define interoperability of the content between systems and free/busy services.

Several years ago I found a couple of useful projects on CodeProject.com (www.codeproject.com/KB/vb/vcalendar.aspx) to easily manage vCalendar and vCard documents. They work by adding values to the object graph that represents the data format, vCalendar in this case. Once the data has been added to the object calling the `ToString` method returns the properly formatted data as a string. This string can be returned however desired, for a web site this means setting the MIME type and adding the resulting string to the output stream. The MIME type for an `iCalendar` file is "text/calendar", which tells the browser which application should consume the resource being loaded. For most people this will be Outlook, but with the proliferation of mobile devices this could be almost anything, and because this is an open standard format it is nothing we need to be concerned with.

The handler's `ProcessRequest` method checks to make sure there is an `EventId` value passed in the `QueryString`. If not it calls the `SendNoEventMessage` to the browser, a nice message to the user letting them know what is wrong without throwing a hard exception that may not help the end user.

```
If Not IsNothing(Request.QueryString("EventId")) Then

BuildVCal()

Else

SendNoEventMessage()

End If

Private Sub SendNoEventMessage()
        'Instead of throwing an error, let the user know what they did wrong
in a graceful manner.
        CurrentContext.Response.ContentType = "text/HTML"
        CurrentContext.Response.Write("<P>Sorry, Please supply a valid EventId.</P>")
        CurrentContext.Response.Flush()
        CurrentContext.Response.End()
        Exit Sub
End Sub
```

If an `EventId` value is present the `BuildVCal` method is called. It again does a quick test to make sure the `EventId` value is positive, if not the `SendNoEventMessage` is called. Next the event is retrieved from the database and the values are passed to a `vCalendar` object. The way the `vCalendar` works is it can contain multiple `vEvent` and `vAlarm` objects, both defined within the `vCalendar` class. The handler is concerned with just a single event, so only one `vEvent` object is created. The `Description`, `Location`, and `URL` properties are set first. Then the event date and times are set.

Setting the event date and time takes a little extra effort because the event start and end times are defined in separate database fields from the start and end dates. A new composite `DateTime` value must be created for each. The logic has to be aware of empty end dates and times. The time fields are stored as a string, so I used a regular expression to parse the Hour, Minute and AM/PM values. I chose to keep this pretty simple, assuming the data should be formatted in the format according to the `MaskEditExtender` I will talk about in the Solution section.

Be aware the `EventEndDate` value is a `Nullable` type and therefore you need to convert this to a real `DateTime` class using the `GetValueOrDefault` method. If the `EventEndDate` is null, then the `EventDate` is assumed to be the `EventEndDate`. This will be the case for most events because they should be more like appointments that last a few minutes or a few hours.

Dealing with Null Values

Null values are a common problem for programmers in any language and platform. Null dates in particular seem to be a common issue developers experience when they start dealing with null values. The .NET framework provides three things that can help the situation: nullable types in C# and VB.NET, a coalesce operator in C# (int x = y ?? 5), and the inline `If` statement in VB.NET (Dim x as integer = If(y, 5)).

In .NET value types can be declared as a nullable type, which ultimately gets compiled to the `Nullable(of T)` structure. This structure has four members: Value, `HasValue`, `GetValueOrDefault` and `GetValueOrDefault(defaultValue as T)`.

When the Entity Data Model Wizard encounters a field that allows null values, it creates the corresponding property as a nullable value:

```
Public Property EventEndDate() As Global.System.Nullable(Of Date)
        Get
            Return Me._EventEndDate
        End Get
        Set(ByVal value As Global.System.Nullable(Of Date))
            Me.OnEventEndDateChanging(value)
            Me.ReportPropertyChanging("EventEndDate")
            Me._EventEndDate = Global.System.Data.Objects.DataClasses
.StructuralObject.SetValidValue(value)
            Me.ReportPropertyChanged("EventEndDate")
            Me.OnEventEndDateChanged()
        End Set
End Property
```

In addition to using the `GetValueOrDefault` member I have also found the use of the Coalesce functionality to be very valuable. In C# this is represented by `??`; here's an example:

```
int? x = null;
int y = x ?? 5;
```

VB.NET uses a hybrid of the `if` statement to manage coalescing:

```
Dim x as Integer? = Nothing
Dim y as Integer = if(x, 5)
```

This is why the following line is used to set the actual event end date:

```
Dim dtEnd As DateTime = If(lEventInfo.EventEndDate, lEventInfo.EventDate)
Private Sub BuildVCal()

    Using lEventrpt As New EventRepository

        Dim lEventId As Integer = CInt(Request.QueryString("EventId"))

        If lEventId <= 0 Then
            SendNoEventMessage()
        End If

        Dim lEventInfo As EventInfo = lEventrpt.GetEventInfoById(lEventId)

        If Not IsNothing(lEventInfo) Then

            Dim lvCal As New vCalendar
            Dim lEvent As New vCalendar.vEvent

            lEvent.Description = lEventInfo.EventTitle
```

```vb
lEvent.Location = lEventInfo.EventLocation
lEvent.URL = String.Format("{0}?eventid={1}", _
            Path.Combine(Helpers.WebRoot, "ShowEvent.aspx"), _
            lEventId)
lEvent.Summary = lEventInfo.EventDesc

Dim rgTime As New Regex("^(\d{2}):(\d{2}):(\d{2})\ (PM|AM)$")

Dim mHour As Integer = 0
Dim mMinute As Integer = 0

For Each m As Match In rgTime.Matches(lEventInfo.EventTime)

    If m.Groups.Count > 3 Then

        If m.Groups(4).Value = "PM" Then
            mHour = 12 + m.Groups(1).Value
        Else
            mHour = m.Groups(1).Value
        End If

        mMinute = m.Groups(2).Value

    End If

Next

    lEvent.DTStart = New Date(lEventInfo.EventDate.Year,
lEventInfo.EventDate.Month, lEventInfo.EventDate.Day, _
                        mHour, mMinute, 0)

mHour = 0
mMinute = 0

For Each m As Match In rgTime.Matches(lEventInfo.EndTime)

    If m.Groups.Count > 3 Then

        If m.Groups(4).Value = "PM" Then
            mHour = 12 + m.Groups(1).Value
        Else
            mHour = m.Groups(1).Value
        End If

        mMinute = m.Groups(2).Value

    End If

Next

    'EventEndDate is a Nullable type, so we need to convert it
to a hard date and time.
    Dim dtEnd As DateTime = If(lEventInfo.EventEndDate,
lEventInfo.EventDate)

    If mHour > 0 Then
```

```
                lEvent.DTEnd = New Date(dtEnd.Year, dtEnd.Month,
    dtEnd.Day, mHour, mMinute, 0)
            End If

        lvCal.Events.Add(lEvent)

        CurrentContext.Response.ContentType = "text/calendar"
        CurrentContext.Response.ContentEncoding = Text.Encoding.UTF8
        CurrentContext.Response.Write(lvCal.ToString)
        CurrentContext.Response.Flush()
        CurrentContext.Response.End()

    Else

        SendNoEventMessage()

    End If

    End Using

End Sub
```

Just like the other `HttpHandlers` I have introduced in this version of the book, the custom handler needs to be registered in the web.config file and associated with a URL. For the iCalendar file type the standard extension is `.ics`, so we will stick with that standard and associate any request for an `.ics` file with the custom handler:

```
<add verb="*" path="*.ics" validate="false" type="TheBeerHouse.vCalHandler,
TBHBLL, Version=3.5.0.1, Culture=neutral, PublicKeyToken=null"/>
```

With these pieces in place, iCalendar files can be streamed dynamically from the Beer House's web site with the click of a hyperlink and added to the patron's personal schedule Figure 10-4.

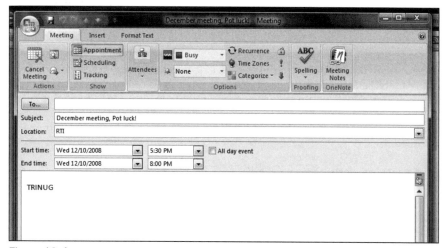

Figure 10-4

Solution

Again, we will discuss the details of implementing the Calendar of Events modules, but not repeat common patterns and features that have already been explored in previous chapters.

Implementing the Repositories

For the most part the business layer repositories follow the same patterns for the CRUD operations and will not be reviewed. Custom methods for each one will be added, but for the most part the module is implemented with very basic functionality.

Implementing the EventRepository

In addition to the basic CRUD methods that follow the same patterns used in previous repositories there are three custom functions in the EventRepository to return a list of events based on specified dates.

The GetDaysEvents function runs a LINQ to Object query over the results of the GetActiveEvents function to return just a list of events for the specified day. The GetTodaysEvents function returns a list of events for the current date by passing the current date to the GetDaysEvents function. The results of the GetActiveEvents are cached (assuming that is enabled), so these methods should be very fast because they are querying against an in-memory list.

```
Public Function GetTodaysEvents() As List(Of EventInfo)

Return GetDaysEvents(Today)

End Function

Public Function GetDaysEvents(ByVal vDate As DateTime) As List(Of EventInfo)

Return (From lEventInfo In GetActiveEvents() Where lEventInfo.EventDate =
vDate).ToList

End Function
```

The GetUpcomingEvents function retrieves a list of events occurring on the current day and after. Because it is a LINQ statement, the EventDate property can be compared against the Today value using the >= operator. Notice I am still using the Active=True filter. I tend to do this because you will very rarely work with inactive records in the database; remember the default GetEvents or get a list method in each repository does not apply this filter, so retrieving and working with inactive data can always be done.

```
Public Function GetUpcomingEvents() As List(Of EventInfo)

        Dim key As String = CacheKey & "_Upcoming_" & Today

    If EnableCaching AndAlso Not IsNothing(Cache(key)) Then
        Return CType(Cache(key), List(Of EventInfo))
    End If
```

```
            Dim lEvents As List(Of EventInfo)
            Eventctx.EventInfos.MergeOption = Objects.MergeOption.NoTracking

            lEvents = (From lEventInfo In Eventctx.EventInfos _
                Where lEventInfo.EventDate >= Today _
                And lEventInfo.Active = True).ToList()

            If EnableCaching Then
               CacheData(key, lEvents)
            End If

            Return lEvents

      End Function
```

Implementing the EventRSVPRepository

Outside the standard repository methods, the EventRSVPRepository has a the GetEventRSVPByEventId method, which returns a list of EventRSVP entities for the specified event.

```
Public Function GetEventRSVPByEventId(ByVal EventId As Integer) As List(Of
EventRSVP)

Dim key As String = CacheKey & "_List_By_EventId_" & EventId

If EnableCaching AndAlso Not IsNothing(Cache(key)) Then
            Return CType(Cache(key), List(Of EventRSVP))
End If

Dim lEventRSVPs As List(Of EventRSVP)
Eventctx.EventRSVPs.MergeOption = Objects.MergeOption.NoTracking

lEventRSVPs = (From lEventRSVP In Eventctx.EventRSVPs.Include("EventInfo") _
                        Where lEventRSVP.Active = True And
lEventRSVP.EventInfo.EventId = EventId).ToList()

If EnableCaching Then
            CacheData(key, lEventRSVPs)
End If

Return lEventRSVPs

End Function
```

Extending the Entity Model Entities

There is not much beyond what has already been covered as far as entity patterns to extend the base entity generated by the Entity Data Model Wizard. So I will omit filling these pages with the source code and advise you to review the previous chapters where I go into detail about the patterns employed by the partial class extensions of the generated entities.

The `IsValid` property of the `EventRSVP` entity checks to make sure the person's First and Last name have been supplied, if not it returns false.

```
Public ReadOnly Property IsValid() As Boolean Implements IBaseEntity.IsValid
        Get
            If String.IsNullOrEmpty(Me.FirstName) = False And _
              String.IsNullOrEmpty(Me.LastName) = False Then
                Return True
            End If
            Return False
        End Get
End Property
```

The `FullName` property concatenates the First and Last Name properties into a string for the full name for convenience. The `EventTitle` property returns the event's title the person RSVPed, if the associated `EventInfo` object was not retrieved, it returns "NA".

```
Public ReadOnly Property FullName() As String
        Get
            Return String.Format("{0} {1}", Me.FirstName, Me.LastName)
        End Get
End Property

Public ReadOnly Property EventTitle() As String
        Get
            If Not IsNothing(Me.EventInfo) Then
                Return EventInfo.EventTitle
            End If
            Return "NA"
        End Get
End Property
```

Implementing the User Interface

Now it's time to build the user interface: the administration pages, the Upcoming Events user control, and the public pages. The module's administration pages consist of the usual list and Add/Edit pages for events and the corresponding RSVPs.

The ManageEvents.aspx page

This page, located under the ~/Admin folder, allows the administrator to view a list of events, add a new event, edit and event, and delete an event. The page is composed of a `ListView` surrounded by an `UpdatePanel` to list the events. Each event list the event title and the date in the first column. The `ListView` also contains the familiar Pencil icon that is a hyper link to edit the event and the delete icon is the familiar trash can icon. The RSVP column contains a hot linked image that opens the `ManageEventRSVPs.aspx` page, filtered for the specified event. Figure 10-5 is a screenshot of the page.

Figure 10-5

The AddEditEvent.aspx page

The `AddEditEvent.aspx` page provides the visual representation to manage the information about an event. The page uses some of the ASP.NET AJAX control toolkit controls and extenders to add to the user experiences of the page. Primarily it uses the `CalendarExtender` and the `MaskedEditExtender`. The use of these controls to help users enter valid dates was covered in Chapter 4. But for a quick review, the `CalendarExtender` is used to display a Calendar control when the user clicks on the calendar icon to the right of the corresponding `TextBox`. The `MaskEditExtender` uses a mask, which looks somewhat like a regular expression, to format a date. For a date the `Mask` property is set to "99/99/9999" and the `MaskType` is set to Date.

The Allow Registration checkbox (near the bottom of Figure 10-6) is important to note simply because checking this control will enable users to RSVP for the event. If this is left unchecked, then registration is suppressed for visitors. Because some events need to have a projected attendance ahead of time for planning purposes, while others to do not, keep this in mind when defining an event.

Figure 10-6

The BrowseEvents.aspx Page

The BrowseEvents.aspx page uses a Calendar control and a ListView to display information about the event calendar. The Calendar is used to display highlighted days when events are scheduled. The ListView displays a list of upcoming events, but when a date is selected on the Calendar control a list of events for that date is displayed. The list displays the event title, date, start time, and location along with the title and a More Information link to the ShowEvent.aspx page for the event. The actual business area of the page is wrapped in an UpdatePanel to make filtering for specific days pretty seamless for the user's experience.

The Calendar control is styled so the current day and days with events stand out from other days, which helps users know when events are scheduled:

```
<asp:Calendar ID="objCalendar" runat="server" BorderColor="Black"
BorderStyle="Solid" BorderWidth="1px">
<TodayDayStyle CssClass="TodayDayStyle"></TodayDayStyle>
<DayStyle CssClass="DayStyle"></DayStyle>
<DayHeaderStyle CssClass="DayHeaderStyle"></DayHeaderStyle>
```

```
<TitleStyle CssClass="TitleStyle"></TitleStyle>
<OtherMonthDayStyle CssClass="OtherMonthDayStyle"></OtherMonthDayStyle>
</asp:Calendar>
```

Figure 10-7 shows the page in action.

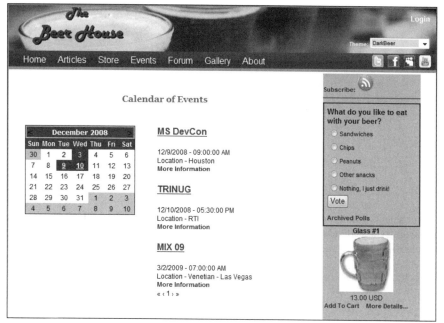

Figure 10-7

The BrowseEvents.aspx.vb Code-Behind File

The real work in the BrowseEvents.aspx page is in the event handlers for the Calendar control. As the Calendar is being rendered the DayRender event is executed, letting you format and add content to the cell for the day on the calendar. For the Beer House calendar, it checks to see if there are any events on the day and, if so, sets the background color to a dark red and the number to white. It also sets the IsSelectable property to true. This is important because for a user to filter just for that specific day the cell has to have some sort of post back mechanism in place. The IsSelectable property determines if this is the case. If there are no events on the day being rendered, then this is set to false, and the user cannot use this day to filter for events. Here's the code:

```
Protected Sub objCalendar_DayRender(ByVal sender As Object, ByVal e _
As System.Web.UI.WebControls.DayRenderEventArgs) Handles objCalendar.DayRender

    Using lEventrpt As New EventRepository

        Dim lEventList As List(Of EventInfo) =
lEventrpt.GetDaysEvents(e.Day.Date.ToShortDateString())
        If lEventList.Count > 0 Then
```

```
            Dim EventStyle As New Style()
            With EventStyle

                .BackColor = System.Drawing.Color.DarkRed
                .Font.Bold = True
                .ForeColor = Drawing.Color.White

            End With

            e.Day.IsSelectable = True
            e.Cell.ApplyStyle(EventStyle)

        Else

            e.Day.IsSelectable = False

        End If

    End Using

End Sub
```

When a user selects a day the `SelectionChanged` event is fired, which calls the `BindDaysEvents` method, passing the Calendar's `SelectedDate` value. This in turn binds the list of events for the selected date to the `ListView`.

```
Protected Sub objCalendar_SelectionChanged(ByVal sender As Object, ByVal e
As System.EventArgs) Handles objCalendar.SelectionChanged
        BindDaysEvents(objCalendar.SelectedDate)
End Sub
```

If the user pages the `Calendar` control to a new month, the `BindData` method is called, which resets the `ListView` to the list of upcoming events:

```
Protected Sub objCalendar_VisibleMonthChanged(ByVal sender As Object, ByVal e
As System.Web.UI.WebControls.MonthChangedEventArgs) Handles
objCalendar.VisibleMonthChanged
        BindData()
End Sub
```

This is an often overlooked event to create a handler for because as the user pages through the months, it is a good idea to keep the ListView up to date. You could also create a method to bind just the events for the displayed month.

The `BindDaysEvents` method binds the events for the specified date to the `ListView`, and also shows or hides the `DataPager` control depending on how many events are bound to the `ListView`:

```
Private Sub BindDaysEvents(ByVal vDate As DateTime)

        Using lEventrpt As New EventRepository
```

```
                     Dim lEventList As List(Of EventInfo) =
        lEventrpt.GetDaysEvents(objCalendar.SelectedDate)

           If lEventList.Count > 0 Then

               lvEvents.DataSource = lEventList
               lvEvents.DataBind()

               Dim pagerBottom As DataPager = lvEvents.FindControl("pagerBottom")

               If Not IsNothing(pagerBottom) Then
                  If lEventList.Count <= pagerBottom.PageSize Then
                     pagerBottom.Visible = False
                  Else
                     pagerBottom.Visible = True
                  End If
               End If

           Else

               lvEvents.Items.Clear()

           End If

        End Using

     End Sub
```

MakeEventRSVP.aspx Page

If an event has the `AllowRegisration` flag set to true the user can RSVP for the event. A link to do so is available on the event's ShowEvent.aspx page and loads the `MakeEventRSVP.aspx` page. This page operates almost exactly like an entity Add/Edit page in the site's Admin section. The main difference is the use of the `MultiView`. Initially the registration form is displayed, but once the RSVP has been successfully submitted a confirmation view is displayed to the user.

```
<asp:MultiView runat="server" ID="mvRegistration">
<asp:View runat="server" ID="vRegister">
'Registration Form
</asp:View>
<asp:View runat="server" ID="vConfirmation">
'Confirmation Form
</asp:View>
</asp:MultiView>
```

Figure 10-8 shows the registration and confirmation views.

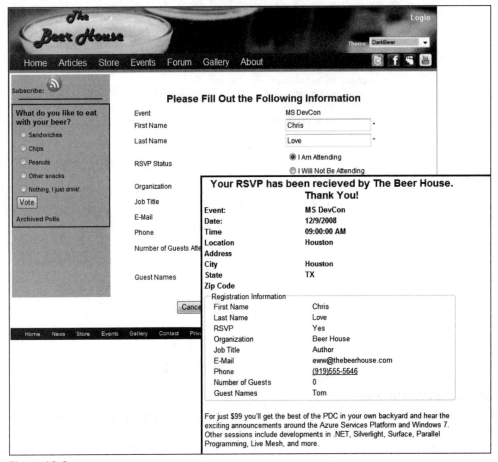

Figure 10-8

Summary

This chapter has presented a working solution for a calendar of events. The complete calendar of events module is made up of an administration console for managing the events and their corresponding RSVPs through a web browser. The module takes advantage of the `Calendar` control to provide a rich display of upcoming events for the Beer House to share with its patrons. This module can easily be employed in many real-world sites as it is now, but of course you can expand and enhance it as desired. Here are a few suggestions:

❑ Add the capability for users to forward event, iCalendar, reminders to friends.

❑ Add an Event Type filter and identifier to an event definition. For example the Beer House might have live entertainment, sporting events, etc and filtering them by type might be helpful to patrons.

❑ Correlate events with photo gallery albums.

11

Photo Gallery

With the proliferation of digital cameras these days, photo galleries have become a very popular component of websites over the past few years. Since the nature of the Beer House is a social setting, sharing photos of events at the Beer House is a natural use of the website.

Problem

Photo galleries are a great way to let visitors see the atmosphere in the pub. Showing happy patrons' having a good time in the Beer House is a great way to show what happened at previous events in the bar and maybe the food and beverages and the variety of entertainment offered by the Beer House.

A modern photo gallery should be easy to administer and allow users to organize the photos in albums. When photos are uploaded to the site, the creation of thumbnails and "display" versions should be done automatically. Visitors should be able to see a list of albums, with a featured or sample photo from each. An album should show all the photos as thumbnails and allow visitors to see a display version of the image and possibly the original image.

Design

Here's the list of features needed in the Photo Gallery module:

- ❏ Display a list of albums.
- ❏ Display the photos in an album.
- ❏ Display each photo using an AJAX invoked dialog/lightbox.

- ❑ Allow site administrators to create albums.
- ❑ Allow site administrators to upload photos to an album.
- ❑ Automatically create thumbnail and a display version of each photo as it is uploaded.
- ❑ Set the name of each photo to a URL-friendly name by replacing non-URL characters with "-".
- ❑ Automatically create the album directory structure when the album is created.

Designing the Database Tables

The Photo Gallery module consists of two tables: Albums and Pictures. The two tables are related in a one-to-many relationship on the AlbumId field in the tbh_Album table to the PictureAlbumId field in the tbh_Pictures table. Figure 11-1 shows the database diagram.

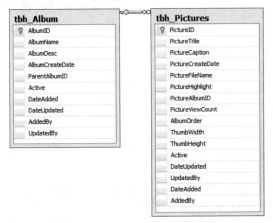

Figure 11-1

Albums can be nested beneath albums by setting the ParentAlbumId to the AlbumId of the parent album. The tbh_Picture's AlbumOrder field stores a numerical value that allows you to sort the images in a designated order. This means images can be displayed by more than just the PictureTitle or the PictureId.

Creating the Entity Data Model

As in the previous chapters a dedicated Entity Data Model is generated for the Photo Gallery module, called GalleryModel. It contains entities for the Album and Picture tables. And, as usual, the EntitySet and relationships need to be renamed to something more friendly. The module namespace is Bll.Gallery, so after the model is generated, this namespace needs to be added to the accompanying Designer file. Figure 11-2 shows the Entity Model from the Designer.

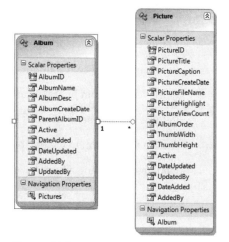

Figure 11-2

Designing the Business Layer

Like the other module business layers, each of the tables have corresponding entities and repositories. Each one inherits from the `BaseGalleryRepository` (see Figure 11-3) that manages the disposing members and wraps the `DataContext` in a common property.

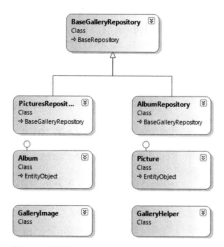

Figure 11-3

The AlbumRepository

Like all the entity repositories in the site, the `AlbumRepository` contains members to do basic retrieval, inserting, and updating of Album entities. There are a few custom retrieval methods to retrieve a list of events based on a specified date, shown in the following table.

Method	Description
GetAlbums	Retrieves a full list of albums.
GetActiveAlbums	Retrieves a list of active albums.
GetAlbumById	Retrieves an album by its AlbumId.
GetAlbumCount	Returns the number of albums in the database.
AddAlbum	Adds a new album to the database.
UpdateAlbum	Updates an existing album.
DeleteAlbum	Deletes an album by setting the Active flag to false.
UnDeleteAlbum	Undeletes an album by setting the Active flag to true.
GetChildAlbums	Returns a list albums with the specified ParentAlbumId.
GetActiveChildAlbums	Returns a list of active albums with the specified ParentAlbumId.
GetAlbumByIdWithPictures	Returns an album with a list of its pictures.

The PictureRepository

The PictureRepository contains the basic repository members to perform CRUD operations against the entity data model.

Method	Description
GetPictures	Retrieves a full list of pictures.
GetActivePictures	Retrieves a list of active pictures.
GetPictureById	Retrieves a list of pictures by the specified PictureId.
GetPicturesByAlbumId	Retrieves the pictures by the specified AlbumId.
GetPictureCount	Returns a count of pictures.
AddPicture	Adds a new picture to the database.
UpdatePicture	Updates an existing picture.
DeletePicture	Deletes a picture by setting the Active flag to false.
UnDeletePicture	Undeletes a picture setting the Active flag to true.

Designing the Configuration Module

Like any other module of this book, the photo gallery module has its own configuration setting, which will be defined as attributes of the `<galleryElement>` element under the `<theBeerHouse>` section in `web.config`. That element is mapped by a `GalleryElement` class, which has the following properties.

Property	Description
PhotosDirectory	The name of the root or parent photo gallery directory of all photo galleries.
OriginalsDirectory	The name of the album originals directory.
AlbumThumbnailsDirectory	The name of the album thumbnail directory.
AlbumDisplayDirectory	The name of the album display directory.
ThumbWidth	An integer used to define the maximum width for a thumbnail image.
ThumbHeight	An integer used to define the maximum height for a thumbnail image.
DisplayHeight	An integer used to define the maximum height for a display image.
DisplayWidth	An integer used to define the maximum width for a display image.

The first four settings allow flexibility in the naming conventions used to define the photo gallery folder structure. One thing to be aware is that if the names are changed the existing folder names will not be changed to match the settings and will have to be adjusted manually.

The next four properties manage the maximum height and width properties of the display and thumbnail images. These values can be changed to match the layout of your site, but again be aware that making any changes after the site is live means the display and thumbnail images should be reset manually.

If you look in the `web.config` file that comes with the Beer House application, there is no entry for the `galleryElement`. This is because all the default settings are used and, therefore, no customizations are needed.

```
<ConfigurationProperty("photosDirectory", DefaultValue:="Photos")> _
Public Property PhotosDirectory() As String
        Get
                Return CStr(Me("photosDirectory"))
        End Get
        Set(ByVal value As String)
                Me("photosDirectory") = value
        End Set
End Property
```

The Photo Gallery Storage

Storing the gallery images is one of the most important choices of the gallery module. There are several options used by photo galleries: store the original image in the database, store just the original image on disk, or store the original image and resized versions on disk at creation. I chose the latter because I have found it to be the easiest to work with in the long run. But I want to examine each strategy before proceeding.

Storing the images as a binary field in the database is one of the most popular choices. The problem with this strategy is that the image has to be transferred from a byte array to a file stream using a custom `HttpHandler` each time a version of the image is requested. On top of converting the bytes to a stream each time, the image dimensions need to be calculated and the image resized as it is being served. I find this to be a lot of overhead for each request, thus slowing the performance of the site under high demand. While SQL Server is perfectly capable of holding binary data, it and the .NET Framework are not optimized to serve files this way.

The next option is to store the original file to the disk and serve a resized version upon each request. Again, this will use a custom `HttpHandler` to perform the image resizing for each request, and while it resizes fairly quickly, it still adds some overhead. I do like this approach because it keeps the disk requirements to a minimum. This and the previous strategy both employ custom `HttpHandlers` to serve the requested image. This means that either all image file extensions must be configured to be processed by the ASP.NET engine, adding much more overhead to each request, or a generic handler or custom file extension must be mapped through ASP.NET.

When a file extension is mapped to be processed by ASP.NET that means each request for a resource of that file type will invoke the entire processing pipeline, all 20-plus events. For images, this is a lot of overhead because every image request would invoke this pipeline, even if it were a normal image used in the site layout. Yuk! The next option is to use a custom file extension to serve the gallery images. Again, this is not ideal because then the images might not get mapped properly by the search engines, and we have to be responsible for serving the correct MIME type for each image. Finally, we could map to a generic handler, an `.ashx` file, but this would just get us back to the previous problem. The use of a generic handler is one of the most common ways to solve this problem, but I think not the most optimal.

The choice I have settled on over the years is to let the administrator upload the image file in its original format and create resized versions for the photo gallery at that time. This means that the resizing operation only occurs once. The resized images are then processed just by IIS as a static resource when they are requested and the client-side caching rules will be applied to them by IIS. The only downside to this strategy is the amount of disk space it requires, but since hard drives are very cheap these days, I do not see this as a real issue.

Another advantage this strategy could have is letting the site administrator change the dimensions of the displayed images. Since the original picture is stored on the server, any time the administrator decides to change the dimensions used for thumbnails and display images, the stored files can be quickly replaced with new versions. To preserve space used in the book, I am going to refrain from demonstrating this process, but it would be a rather trivial set of code to add to the site.

Now how to decide on an actual storage strategy? First, all albums will be stored in the Photos folder. I am going to assume that each photo album will have its own unique name and that name will be used to create a dedicated folder for that album. Since the use of spaces is a bad idea, these will be replaced with "-" to make them more URL-friendly. Under the album folder there are three folders created, one to hold each version of the picture: Original, Display, and Thumbnails.

I have referred to a display image several times and not explained it. This is the version of the picture that is displayed when the thumbnail is clicked. I call it a display image because it is the one that is displayed within the framework of the web page. With today's digital cameras, high-resolution photos are very common and often are 3–5 times the size of most users' monitors, so the original version of the photo is not ideal to display to the user. Sometimes, when creating an online catalog or photo gallery, I provide links from the display version to open the original in a new window and let the users decide how they want to view the photo's details.

The main advantages I have found to using this strategy is the original photo is preserved, the photos are stored in the desired format needed to run the site and the photos can be quickly resized to meet the needs of a changing site if needed. Figure 11-4 shows this directory hierarchy.

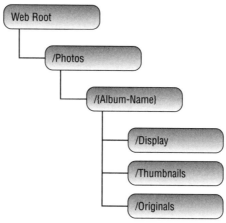

Figure 11-4

Designing the User Interface Services

This section describes the pages and controls that constitute the user interface layer of this module. In particular, there are two ASP.NET pages, and one user control:

- ❑ **~/Admin/ManageAlbums.aspx** — An administrative list of events with icons to edit or delete the album.

- ❑ **~/Admin/AddEditAlbum.aspx** — Allows adding or editing of an album.

- ❑ **~/Admin/AddEditPicture.aspx** — Allows a site admin to either add or edit a picture.

- ❑ **~/BrowseAlbums.aspx** — List albums with a featured or sample picture from the album.

- ❑ **~/ShowAlbum.aspx** — Displays the pictures in the album and displays each picture in an AJAX dialog when clicked.

Solution

As in the previous chapters, we will discuss the details of implementing the Photo Gallery module but not repeat common patterns and features that have already been explored in previous chapters. This one will vary slightly in how the data is managed and the use of another AJAX framework to add some pizzazz to the site.

Implementing the Repositories

For the most part, the business layer repositories follow the patterns for the CRUD operations and will not be reviewed. Custom methods for each one will be added, but for the most part the module is implemented with very basic functionality.

Implementing the AlbumRepository

The `AlbumRepository` uses the basic CRUD methods that follow the patterns used in previous repositories, so I will not review them. `GetAlbumByIdWithPictures` uses the `Include` operator to tell LINQ to Entities to include the related `Picture` entities for the album.

```
Public Function GetAlbumByIdWithPictures(ByVal AlbumId As Integer) As Album

        Return (From lai In Galleryctx.Albums.Include("Pictures") _
            Where lai.AlbumID = AlbumId).FirstOrDefault

End Function
```

Implementing the PictureRepository

Again, there is nothing really new in the `PictureRepository` class that has not been discussed. The `UpdatePicOrder` method changes just the `AlbumOrder` value of the picture and commits it to the database. This will create an `Update` SQL statement that just updates the one field instead of the entire record.

```
Public Function UpdatePicOrder(ByVal PictureId As Integer,
ByVal AlbumOrder As Integer) As Boolean

        Dim vPicture As Picture = Me.GetPictureById(PictureId)
        vPicture.AlbumOrder = AlbumOrder
        Return AddPicture(vPicture)

End Function
```

Extending the Entity Model Entities

There is not much beyond what has already been covered as far as entity patterns to extend the base entity generated by the Entity Data Model Wizard. So I will omit filling these pages with the source code and advise you to review the previous chapters, where I go into detail about the patterns employed by the partial class extensions of the generated entities.

Extending the Picture Entity

The `IsValid` property of the `Picture` entity checks to make sure the `PictureTitle`, `PictureCaption` and `PictureFileName` have been supplied, if not it returns false. It also checks to make sure the `ThumbHeight` and `ThumbWidth` are greater than 0 and that there is an `AlbumId` greater than 0.

```
Public ReadOnly Property IsValid() As Boolean Implements IBaseEntity.IsValid
        Get
            If String.IsNullOrEmpty(Me.PictureTitle) = False And _
               String.IsNullOrEmpty(Me.PictureCaption) = False And _
               String.IsNullOrEmpty(Me.PictureFileName) = False And _
               Me.ThumbHeight > 0 And Me.ThumbWidth > 0 And _
               Me.AlbumId > 0 Then
                Return True
            End If
            Return False
        End Get
End Property
```

The GalleryHelper

The `GalleryHelper` class contains a series of methods to help with managing the directory structures and URLs to the actual images. The methods are arranged into three regions: Directory Helpers, URL Helpers, and Directory Maintenance. The first series of functions manage retrieving the actual folder names. The first function, `GetPhotosDirectory`, returns the physical path to the root Photos folder that all albums sit below. The next function, `GetAlbumDirectory`, combines the result of the `GetPhotosDirectory` with a formatted `AlbumName` to return the path to the album's folder. The next three functions combine the result of the `GetAlbumDirectory` with the corresponding child folder to return the path to each image type's physical path.

Also, notice how the directory names are not hard-coded, but call the settings value from the `web.config` file. Whenever an album-specific folder name is needed the `Helpers.Settings.Gallery.<FolderName>` is used.

```
Public Class GalleryHelper

#Region " Directory Helpers "

    Public Shared Function GetPhotosDirectory() As String
        Return Helpers.GetPhyscialPath(Helpers.Settings.Gallery.PhotosDirectory)
    End Function

    Public Shared Function GetAlbumDirectory(ByVal AlbumName As String) As String
        Return Path.Combine(GetPhotosDirectory(),
Helpers.FormatSpacesForURL(AlbumName))
    End Function

    Public Shared Function GetAlbumOriginalsDirectory(ByVal AlbumName As String)
As String
        Return Path.Combine(GetAlbumDirectory(AlbumName),
Helpers.Settings.Gallery.OriginalsDirectory)
```

```
    End Function

    Public Shared Function GetAlbumThumbNailsDirectory(ByVal AlbumName As String)
As String
        Return Path.Combine(GetAlbumDirectory(AlbumName),
Helpers.Settings.Gallery.AlbumThumbNailsDirectory)
    End Function

    Public Shared Function GetAlbumDisplayDirectory(ByVal AlbumName As String)
As String
        Return Path.Combine(GetAlbumDirectory(AlbumName),
Helpers.Settings.Gallery.AlbumDisplayDirectory)
    End Function

#End Region
```

The next set of functions perform the same type of work, but instead of returning a physical folder path, it returns the full URL to the folder. It does this by combining the WebRoot value with the corresponding folder name. Again, the functions build on top of each other to build the appropriate URL. GetPictureURL is called by each of the three image type folder functions. Since there should be no one directly accessing the folders in a browser, the GetPictureURL function is marked as private and only used by the three folder-specific functions. Each of these functions takes two parameters, the AlbumName and the FileName, which are used to combine with the folder settings to produce a full URL to the desired image file.

```
#Region " URL Helpers "

    Private Shared Function GetPictureURL(ByVal vAlbumName As String,
ByVal vPictureType As String, ByVal vFileName As String) As String
        Return Path.Combine(Helpers.WebRoot, _
                        Path.Combine(Helpers.Settings.Gallery.PhotosDirectory,
Path.Combine(Helpers.FormatSpacesForURL(
vAlbumName), Path.Combine(vPictureType, vFileName))))
    End Function

    Public Shared Function GetThumbnailURL(ByVal vAlbumName As String,
ByVal vFileName As String)
        Return GetPictureURL(vAlbumName,
Helpers.Settings.Gallery.AlbumThumbNailsDirectory, vFileName)
    End Function

    Public Shared Function GetDispalyURL(ByVal vAlbumName As String,
ByVal vFileName As String)
        Return GetPictureURL(vAlbumName,
Helpers.Settings.Gallery.AlbumDisplayDirectory, vFileName)
    End Function

    Public Shared Function GetOriginalURL(ByVal vAlbumName As String,
ByVal vFileName As String)
        Return GetPictureURL(vAlbumName,
Helpers.Settings.Gallery.OriginalsDirectory, vFileName)
    End Function

#End Region
```

The final set of helper methods work to create the desired folder structure. There are four creation methods that call the `Helpers` class `MakeDirectory` method. This method checks to see if the folder exists; if so, it returns the folder's `DirectoryInfo`. If the folder does not exist, it creates the folder and returns the new folder's `DirectoryInfo`.

```
Public Shared Function MakeDirectory(ByVal vDirectoryPath As String)
  As DirectoryInfo

        Dim di As DirectoryInfo

        If Directory.Exists(vDirectoryPath) = True Then
            di = New DirectoryInfo(vDirectoryPath)
        Else
            di = Directory.CreateDirectory(vDirectoryPath)
        End If

        Return di

End Function
```

There is a creation method for each of the four folders that an album needs: the album name and the three image types. The next three methods are concerned with making sure that the album folder structure exists correctly. The `CreateAlbumTree` function creates the folder structure for an album. The `EnsureAlbumExists` function returns true or false, depending on whether the album tree already exists. The `UpdateAlbumTree` function is used when an album is renamed. It simply checks to see if the original album exists, and if so, it moves the folder to the new album name's corresponding folder. If the old album does not exist, `UpdateAlbumTree` simply creates the album tree.

```
#Region " Directory Maintenance "

    Public Shared Sub CreateAlbumDirectory(ByVal AlbumName As String)
        Helpers.MakeDirectory(GetAlbumDirectory(AlbumName))
    End Sub

    Public Shared Sub CreateAlbumOriginalsDirectory(ByVal AlbumName As String)
        Helpers.MakeDirectory(GetAlbumOriginalsDirectory(AlbumName))
    End Sub

    Public Shared Sub CreateAlbumThumbNailsDirectory(ByVal AlbumName As String)
        Helpers.MakeDirectory(GetAlbumThumbNailsDirectory(AlbumName))
    End Sub

    Public Shared Sub CreateAlbumDisplayDirectory(ByVal AlbumName As String)
        Helpers.MakeDirectory(GetAlbumDisplayDirectory(AlbumName))
    End Sub

    Public Shared Sub CreateAlbumTree(ByVal AlbumName As String)
        CreateAlbumDirectory(AlbumName)
        CreateAlbumOriginalsDirectory(AlbumName)
        CreateAlbumThumbNailsDirectory(AlbumName)
        CreateAlbumDisplayDirectory(AlbumName)
    End Sub

    Public Shared Function EnsureAlbumTreeExist(ByVal AlbumName As String)
```

```
    As Boolean

        If Directory.Exists(GetAlbumDirectory(AlbumName)) = False Then
            Return False
        End If

        If Directory.Exists(GetAlbumOriginalsDirectory(AlbumName)) = False Or _
            Directory.Exists(GetAlbumDisplayDirectory(AlbumName)) = False Or _
            Directory.Exists(GetAlbumThumbNailsDirectory(AlbumName)) = False Then
            Return False
        End If

        Return True

    End Function

    Public Shared Sub UpdateAlbumTree(ByVal OldAlbumName As String, _
ByVal AlbumName As String)
        If Directory.Exists(GetAlbumDirectory(OldAlbumName)) = True Then
            Directory.Move(GetAlbumDirectory(OldAlbumName), _
GetAlbumDirectory(AlbumName))
        Else
            CreateAlbumTree(AlbumName)
        End If
    End Sub

#End Region

End Class
```

The GalleryImage Class

When .NET was first released, I was very excited to see that the Image class contained a GetThumbnailImage function, but found that it often created pixilated or less than desirable results for my clients. So I invested the time to research and create a custom routine to create better quality photo thumbnails. The GalleryImage uses the core logic to produce resized images. I want to point out that making an image larger than the original image will most likely not result in a desirable outcome. The image resizing algorithm has to assume or interpolate pixels to fill the gaps, often resulting in a poor quality image. This is one of the reasons why I keep the original version of any image file uploaded to the server and use that file to create any resized versions.

The Photo Gallery logic prevents this from happening by choosing either desired dimensions or the original image itself. So, if you uploaded an image smaller than the display image, the original image will be used as the display version, resulting in a smaller than desired image, but nonetheless one not distorted from its original state. The resizing logic actually checks the dimensions of the original image and chooses to first limit the resulting width over the height. The reasoning behind this is that visitors do not like to scroll horizontally, but find vertical scrolling to be natural. So any image that is resized is actually resized to make a best fit to the desired box dimensions without distorting the image scale. So, a 300x400 pixel image would be resized to 75x100 to fit a maximum height and width of 100 pixels. But a 400x300 image would be resized to 100x75 pixels.

The `GalleryImage` class ultimately uses two functions, `StoreImage` and `MakeThumbnail`, and each have several overloads. The `StoreImage` function checks to make sure a file by the same name does not already exist; if so it deletes the existing file before a thumbnail is created.

```
Public Function StoreImage(ByVal DestinationPath As String,
 ByVal DestinationFileName As String, _
        ByVal ImageFileName As String, ByVal ImageWidth As Integer, _
        ByVal ImageHeight As Integer, ByVal CurrentImageFileName As String,
 ByVal ImageQuality As Integer) As String

        If String.IsNullOrEmpty(DestinationFileName) = False Then

            DestinationFileName = Path.GetFileName(DestinationFileName).Replace(
"#", String.Empty)
            DestinationFileName = Path.Combine(DestinationPath,
StoreImageExtracted(DestinationFileName))
            CheckFileExists(DestinationFileName)

            MakeThumbnail(ImageFileName, DestinationFileName, ImageWidth,
 ImageHeight, _
                Drawing.Drawing2D.InterpolationMode.HighQualityBicubic,
 ImageQuality)

            Return Path.GetFileName(DestinationFileName)

        End If

        Return String.Empty

 End Function
```

The `MakeThumbnail` method opens the original image in a `Bitmap` object and calculates the original dimensions and calculates the dimensions for the resized image based on the `MaxWidth` and `MaxHeight` passed to the method. Ultimately, the best height-to-width ratio is chosen to fit the desired containing box. Once the new height and width are determined, a new `Bitmap` object is created using those dimensions. Next, a new graphics object, `objGraphics`, is created by using the shared `Graphics.FromImage` method, which takes the new `Bitmap` object as its only parameter. The content of the original image is copied to the new `Graphics` object by passing the `DrawImage` method the original image and the four points that designate the new image size. For this, the first two parameters are both 0, specifying the top-left corner of the image and the new width and height, to complete the full image size. There are many overloads of the `DrawImage` method that take every possible combination of points and rectangles to produce the image.

Next, a new `EncoderParameters` object is created, actually as a one-dimensional array to match the expectations of the `Image.Save` method. The one parameter is set to a quality setting, which should be 100 for the best, but could be anything ranging from 0 to 100. The top quality setting produces the largest file size, but the highest-quality results. The lower the quality value, the smaller the file size, but reducing the file size sacrifices image quality.

Finally, the image is saved by calling the Save method on the new Bitmap object. The process is actually using the Save method of the base Image class. The overload used in the MakeThumbnail method uses the file destination, the type of image (GIF, JPG, or PNG) and the quality parameter just discussed to produce the new, resized image. Performing the image resizing like this gives you more control over the image quality and size that calling the Image.GetThumbnailImage method.

```
Public Sub MakeThumbnail(ByRef sSource As String, _
                ByVal sDestination As String, _
                ByRef MaxWidth As Integer, ByRef MaxHeight As Integer, _
                ByVal nMode As Drawing2D.InterpolationMode, _
                Optional ByVal iJPGQuality As Integer = 100)

        Dim objImage As System.Drawing.Image
        Dim objBitmap As Bitmap
        Dim objGraphics As Graphics
        Dim iWidth As Integer
        Dim iHeight As Integer
        Dim objEncoder As Imaging.EncoderParameters

        '       Try
        ' Open the source image
        objImage = New Bitmap(sSource)

        'get image original width and height
        Dim intOldWidth As Integer = objImage.Width
        Dim intOldHeight As Integer = objImage.Height
        Dim dblCoef As Double

        If intOldWidth > MaxWidth Then
            iWidth = MaxWidth

            dblCoef = MaxWidth / CDbl(intOldWidth)

            If MaxHeight <= Convert.ToInt32((dblCoef * intOldHeight)) Then
                iHeight = MaxHeight
                dblCoef = MaxHeight / CDbl(intOldHeight)
                iWidth = Convert.ToInt32((dblCoef * intOldWidth))
            Else
                iHeight = Convert.ToInt32((dblCoef * intOldHeight))
            End If

        ElseIf intOldHeight > MaxHeight Then
            iHeight = MaxHeight
            dblCoef = MaxHeight / CDbl(intOldHeight)
            iWidth = Convert.ToInt32((dblCoef * intOldWidth))
        Else
            iWidth = intOldWidth
            iHeight = intOldHeight
        End If

        ' Create a new bitmap object with the thumbnail's dimensions
```

```
    objBitmap = New Bitmap(iWidth, iHeight)

    ' Create a graphics object, used for resizing
    objGraphics = Graphics.FromImage(objBitmap)

    ' Set the graphics object's InterpolationMode
    objGraphics.InterpolationMode = nMode

    ' Draw the actual thumbnail
    objGraphics.DrawImage(objImage, 0, 0, iWidth, iHeight)

    ' Now, create a new Imaging Encoder...
    objEncoder = New Imaging.EncoderParameters(1)

    ' Tell it to be "Encoder.Quality" with the desired iJPGQuality
    objEncoder.Param(0) = New Imaging.EncoderParameter(
Imaging.Encoder.Quality, iJPGQuality)

    ' Using function GetEncoderInfo, write the thumbnail to disc
    sDestination = sDestination.ToLower

    If Path.GetExtension(sDestination) = ".gif" Then
        objBitmap.Save(sDestination, GetEncoder(ImageFormat.Gif), objEncoder)
    ElseIf Path.GetExtension(sDestination) = ".jpg" Then
        objBitmap.Save(sDestination, GetEncoder(ImageFormat.Jpeg), objEncoder)
    ElseIf Path.GetExtension(sDestination) = ".png" Then
        objBitmap.Save(sDestination, GetEncoder(ImageFormat.Png), objEncoder)
    End If

    objBitmap.Dispose()
    objImage.Dispose()

End Sub
```

Implementing the User Interface

Now it's time to build the user interface: the administration pages and the public pages. The module's administration pages consist of the usual list and Add/Edit pages for albums and the corresponding pictures.

The ManageAlbums.aspx Page

The ManageAlbums.aspx page, located under the ~/Admin folder, allows the administrator to view a list of albums, add a new album, and edit and delete an existing album. The page is composed of a ListView surrounded by an UpdatePanel to list the albums. Each album lists the Album Name preceded by a sample thumbnail image. The ListView also contains the familiar Pencil icon that is a hyperlink to edit the album and the delete icon is the familiar trash can icon. Figure 11-5 is a screenshot of the page.

Figure 11-5

The thumbnail image is bound in the ItemDataBound event handler. This involves casting a reference to the item's ListViewDataItem.DataItem value to the bound Album entity. The image is an HTMLImage and an instance of the control is created using the ListViewDataItem's FindControl method. Once both of these have been created the iThumb's Src property is set to the image of the first picture in the album. If there are no photos in the album, a default image is used.

```
Private Sub lvAlbums_ItemDataBound(ByVal sender As Object, _
 ByVal e As System.Web.UI.WebControls.ListViewItemEventArgs) _
 Handles lvAlbums.ItemDataBound

        Dim lvdi As ListViewDataItem = DirectCast(e.Item, ListViewDataItem)

        If lvdi.ItemType = ListViewItemType.DataItem Then

            Dim iThumb As HtmlImage = CType(lvdi.FindControl("iThumb"), HtmlImage)
            Dim lAlbum As Album = DirectCast(lvdi.DataItem, Album)

            If Not IsNothing(lAlbum) And Not IsNothing(iThumb) Then

                If Not IsNothing(lAlbum.Pictures) AndAlso
lAlbum.Pictures.Count > 0 Then
                    iThumb.Src = String.Format("~/Photos/{0}/thumbnails/{1}", _
                        Helpers.FormatSpacesForURL(lAlbum.AlbumName), _
lAlbum.Pictures(0).PictureFileName)
```

```
            Else
                iThumb.Src = "~/Images/generic.jpg"
            End If

            iThumb.Alt = lAlbum.AlbumName
        End If

    End If

End Sub
```

The AddEditAlbum.aspx Page

The `AddEditEvent.aspx` page provides the visual representation to manage the information about an album. This page really uses two forms, one to edit the values of the album; name, description, and any parent album. There are a series of `Hyperlinks` to perform specific actions such as adding a new photo to the album, returning to the `ManageAlbums.aspx` page, deleting the album, and of course updating or adding the album.

The "second form" is a `ListView` of the album's photos and their display order. The photo list displays the thumbnail for each photo in the album, a `TextBox` with the photo's `AlbumOrder` value, and a delete icon. Clicking the thumbnail takes you to the `AddEditPhoto.aspx` page for the photo. Clicking the trash can (delete icon) deletes the photo. Changing the Album order value does not do anything directly, but once the numerical values are set for the photos clicking either of the Update Order button will update the `AlbumOrder` values of each photo and reload the photos to represent the order. Figure 11-6 shows the page for a sample album.

Figure 11-6

The AddEditPhoto.aspx Page

The `AddEditPhoto.aspx` page functions pretty much like all the other entity-editing pages in the Beer House. The photo's `Title` and `Album` are required fields and have `RequiredFieldValidators` assigned to them. The form does allow you to set the thumbnails' width and height, but the default values from the configuration will always be set. This gives you some flexibility in defining the thumbnail constraint box. The thumbnail dimensions and the `AlbumOrder` field use the ASP.NET AJAX Control Toolkit's Numeric Up/Down extender to display helpful buttons to set the numeric values. They also have `MaskedEditEtenders` associated with them to force a numeric value be entered.

The `FileUpload` control has a `RegularExpressionValidator` assigned to it to enforce only upload-ing image files. This is something I have found invaluable over the years when I have built forms for clients to upload images. Inevitably, they will try to upload PDFs, Word Documents, Excel files, and so forth. This is one of those instances where you cannot assume that users will do what is expected of them, and I learned this the hard way many years ago. The web really only uses three image types: GIF, JPG and PNG. Internet Explorer can also render BMP files, but it is a good idea to avoid them. You could implement a conversion routine in the image storage routine, but I am not going to cover that in this book because there are all sorts of issues this could introduce that would go outside the scope of this book.

```
<asp:FileUpload ID="fPicture" runat="server" CssClass="formField" />
<asp:RegularExpressionValidator runat="server" ID="rvfPicture"
 ControlToValidate="fPicture"
 ValidationExpression="^(((([a-zA-Z]:)|
(\\{2}\w+)\$?)(\\(\w[\w].*))+(.jpg|.JPG|.png|.PNG|.gif|.GIF)$"
  ErrorMessage="You can only upload .jpg, .gif or .png image types." />
```

The one thing that stands out is the creation of the display and thumbnail images when a new photo is uploaded. First, the `HasFile` property is checked on the `FileUpload` control. If the control contains a new file the `PictureFileName` is set to the name of the file and the `StorePics` method is called. Otherwise, the `ResizeThumbnail` method is called.

```
If fPicture.HasFile Then
lPicture.PictureFileName = Helpers.FormatSpacesForURL(
Path.GetFileName(fPicture.FileName))
StorePics()
Else
    If lPicture.ThumbWidth <> txtWidth.Text Or _
        lPicture.ThumbHeight <> txtHeight.Text Then
        ResizeThumbnail()
    End If
End If
```

The `StorePics` method takes the file contained in the `FileUpload` control and saves it as the original photo first. This file is then used to create the display and thumbnail images. These versions are created by calling the `GalleryImage.StoreImage` method discussed earlier.

```
Private Sub StorePics()

        Dim sfName As String = ViewState("PictureFileName").ToString
        Dim lgi As New GalleryImage

        Dim lOriginalFileName As String = String.Empty
```

```
            Dim lDisplayFileName As String = String.Empty
            Dim lThumbnailFileName As String = String.Empty


        If fPicture.HasFile Then

            If PhotoExtension.ToLower.Contains("jpg") = False And _
                PhotoExtension.ToLower.Contains("gif") = False Then
                Response.Write("<B>You can Only Upload JPGs or GIFs</B>")
                Exit Sub
            End If

            If Not GalleryHelper.EnsureAlbumTreeExist(Helpers.FormatSpacesForURL(
ddlAlbums.SelectedItem.Text)) Then
                GalleryHelper.CreateAlbumTree(ddlAlbums.SelectedItem.Text)
            End If

            'Save Original
            lOriginalFileName = Path.Combine(
GalleryHelper.GetAlbumOriginalsDirectory( _
                ddlAlbums.SelectedItem.Text), UploadedFileName)

            If File.Exists(lOriginalFileName) = True Then
                File.Delete(lOriginalFileName)
            End If

            fPicture.PostedFile.SaveAs(lOriginalFileName)

            lThumbnailFileName = Path.Combine(
GalleryHelper.GetAlbumThumbNailsDirectory( _
                ddlAlbums.SelectedItem.Text), UploadedFileName)

            'Save Thumbnails
            If File.Exists(lThumbnailFileName) = True Then
                File.Delete(lThumbnailFileName)
            End If

            lgi.StoreImage(GalleryHelper.GetAlbumThumbNailsDirectory( _
                ddlAlbums.SelectedItem.Text), _
                Path.GetFileName(lThumbnailFileName), _
                lOriginalFileName, _
                Convert.ToInt32(txtWidth.Text), _
                Convert.ToInt32(txtHeight.Text))

            'Save Display or Large Version
            lDisplayFileName = Path.Combine(
GalleryHelper.GetAlbumDisplayDirectory( _
                ddlAlbums.SelectedItem.Text), UploadedFileName)

            If File.Exists(lDisplayFileName) = True Then
                File.Delete(lDisplayFileName)
            End If

            lgi.StoreImage(GalleryHelper.GetAlbumDisplayDirectory(
```

```
ddlAlbums.SelectedItem.Text), _
            Path.GetFileName(lDisplayFileName), _
            lOriginalFileName, _
            lGallerySettings.DisplayWidth, _
            lGallerySettings.DisplayHeight)

    End If

End Sub
```

The `ResizeThumbnail` method is called if there is not a new image present to make sure the thumbnail fits the constraining box defined in the form. It is only called if either the height or width has been changed. Again, it uses the `StoreImage` method to create the new thumbnail.

```
Private Sub ResizeThumbnail()

    Dim ei As New GalleryImage

    If File.Exists(GalleryHelper.GetAlbumOriginalsDirectory( _
            ddlAlbums.SelectedItem.Text) & UploadedFileName) = True Then

        ei.StoreImage(GalleryHelper.GetAlbumOriginalsDirectory( _
            ddlAlbums.SelectedItem.Text), UploadedFileName, _
            GalleryHelper.GetAlbumThumbNailsDirectory( _
            ddlAlbums.SelectedItem.Text) & UploadedFileName, _
            Convert.ToInt32(txtWidth.Text), _
            Convert.ToInt32(txtHeight.Text))

    End If

End Sub
```

Figure 11-7 shows this page in action.

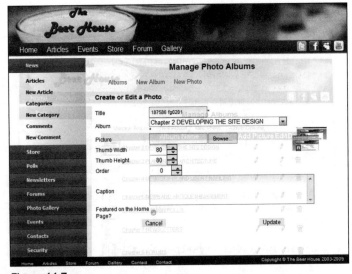

Figure 11-7

The BrowseAlbums.aspx Page

The `BrowseAlbums.aspx` page uses a `ListView` to display a representative thumbnail from each active photo album and the album's title. The `ListView` uses its grouping capabilities to display a row of `ItemTemplates`, in this case up to five. Each `ItemTemplate` is a table cell that contains two `DIV` elements, one with the thumbnail and the second with the album name. Each one is surrounded by a hyperlink that points to the `ShowAlbum.aspx` page for the album.

```
<ItemTemplate>
<td>
<div class="dAlbumImage">
<a href="ShowAlbum.aspx?albumid=<%#Eval("AlbumId") %>">
                                    <img runat="server" id="iThumb" border="0"
 width="50" align="middle" /></a>
</div>
<div class="dAlbumTitle">
                                <a href='<%# String.Format(
"AddEditAlbum.aspx?Albumid={0}", Eval("AlbumId")) %>'>
                                <%# Eval("AlbumName") %></a>
</div>
</td>
</ItemTemplate>
```

Just as you saw in the `AddEditAlbum.aspx` code-behind, the representative thumbnail is bound in the `ItemDataBound` event handler. If there are no active photos in the album, then a generic image is displayed.

```
Private Sub lvPictures_ItemDataBound(ByVal sender As Object,
ByVal e As System.Web.UI.WebControls.ListViewItemEventArgs)
 Handles lvPictures.ItemDataBound

        Dim lvdi As ListViewDataItem = DirectCast(e.Item, ListViewDataItem)

        If lvdi.ItemType = ListViewItemType.DataItem Then

            Dim iThumb As HtmlImage = CType(lvdi.FindControl("iThumb"), HtmlImage)
            Dim lAlbum As Album = DirectCast(lvdi.DataItem, Album)

            If Not IsNothing(lAlbum) And Not IsNothing(iThumb) Then
                If Not IsNothing(lAlbum.Pictures) AndAlso
lAlbum.Pictures.Count > 0 Then
                    Dim lPicture As Picture = lAlbum.Pictures(0)
                    iThumb.Src = String.Format("~/Photos/{0}/thumbnails/{1}", _
                        Helpers.FormatSpacesForURL(lAlbum.AlbumName),
 lPicture.PictureFileName)
                    iThumb.Alt = lPicture.PictureCaption
                Else
                    iThumb.Src = "~/Images/generic.jpg"
                    iThumb.Alt = "No Pictues Yet."
                End If

            End If

        End If

End Sub
```

Figure 11-8 shows the `BrowseAlbums.aspx` page.

Figure 11-8

ShowAlbum.aspx Page

The `ShowAlbum.aspx` page displays thumbnails of each photo in the album with a title below it. It does this in a grid that shows images side by side with a vertical line separating each image. This layout leverages the `GroupTemplate` and `EmptyItemTemplate`.

The `ListView` combines functionalities of the `Repeater`, the `DataList`, and the `GridView` to accomplish much of its functionality. To display the album, as you saw on the previous page, we have to leverage the `GroupTemplate` to display the images side by side. The `ListView`'s `GroupItemCount` property is declaratively set to 5, meaning that five pictures can be displayed on each row. The `GroupItemTemplate` has to have an `itemPlaceHolder` control to emit the actual content.

```
<asp:ListView ID="lvPictures" runat="server" GroupItemCount="5"
 GroupPlaceholderID="groupPlaceHolder" ItemPlaceholderID="itemPlaceHolder">
<LayoutTemplate>
<table id="tblPictures" runat="server" cellspacing="0" cellpadding="2">
                    <tr runat="server" id="groupPlaceholder" />
</table>
</LayoutTemplate>
<GroupTemplate>
```

```
<tr runat="server" id="ContactsRow" style="background-color: #FFFFFF">
                    <td runat="server" id="itemPlaceholder" />
</tr>
</GroupTemplate>
<ItemTemplate>
…
</ItemSeparatorTemplate>
</asp:ListView>
```

The `ItemTemplate` holds the layout for the actual image and its caption. I will go over the `ItemTemplate`'s layout detail in the lightbox section. Figure 11-9 shows an album with each picture's image and title displayed.

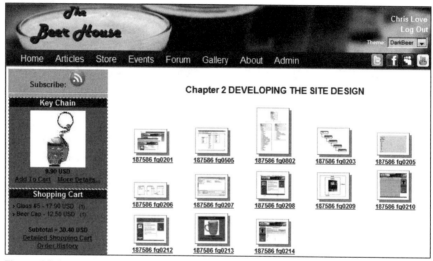

Figure 11-9

Implementing an AJAX Lightbox

The `ShowAlbum.aspx` page displays a grid of photo thumbnails using the `ListView`'s grouping capabilities, but it does not link to a `ShowPicture.aspx` page. Instead, I chose to go outside the box and implement a lightbox script, written by Lokesh Dhakar that runs on top of Scriptaculous (`http://script.aculo.us`), another AJAX framework, `www.huddletogether.com/projects/lightbox2`. I did this because there was a great script with animation already done and available to display the image to the user. It also has built-in paging capabilities, making it even more user-friendly.

Lightbox, as far as the web is concerned, is a term to describe isolating a photo from its surroundings for viewing. This combination of CSS and JavaScript create a very stunning lightbox to display the individual photos in the album. As the image is being loaded, the page is covered in a dark opaque layer, just as we did for the Login dialog in Chapter 4. A white dialog layer is created on top and resizes to fit the dimensions of the display image with an animation effect. Once that is done, a caption area is built below the image, displaying the image's `Title` property, the image number in the album, and a Close image to take the user back to the page. An example of the result is shown in Figure 11-10.

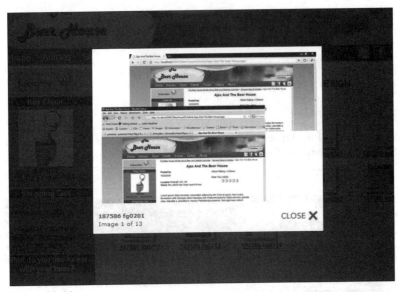

Figure 11-10

Implementing the lightbox script is very easy. First, the support images for the lightbox should be added to the Images folder, then the included script files are added to the site. I chose to keep them in a "js" folder to keep them isolated from the rest of the site. Finally, the CSS file should be added to the site.

The tricky part was deciding how to include the CSS and script files in the page's header section, since the Beer House leverages nested master pages. If you examine the TBHMain.master markup, there is a ContentPlaceHolder control in the layout's header tag that can be used to insert the file references. The remaining issue is how to do this through the nested master page CRMaster.master. The answer is to add a ContentPlaceHolder control inside its Content control that manages the content emitted in the desired ContentPlaceHolder in the primary master page.

```
<asp:Content ID="headContent" ContentPlaceHolderID="head" runat="Server">
    <asp:ContentPlaceHolder ID="cphMainHeader" runat="server">
    </asp:ContentPlaceHolder>
</asp:Content>
```

Ultimately, the normal script and link references can be added to the ShowAlbum.aspx page. This enables the page to leverage the lightbox script and keeps the scripts from being downloaded to the client unless they are viewing an album in the photo gallery.

```
<asp:Content ID="headContent" ContentPlaceHolderID="cphMainHeader" runat="Server">
    <link rel="stylesheet" href="lightbox.css" type="text/css" media="screen" />
    <script type="text/javascript" src="js/prototype.js"></script>
    <script type="text/javascript"
src="js/scriptaculous.js?load=effects,builder"></script>
    <script type="text/javascript" src="js/lightbox.js"></script>
</asp:Content>
```

The only thing left is to have the HTML created as `Picture` entities are bound to the `ListView` control. The lightbox script only requires the `rel` tag specify the "lightbox," but to get the Previous and Next paging feature, a group name must be added to the attribute value in brackets (`[]`). The script interrogates the page to find the other images that are part of the group automatically. It gets the links to the images by evaluating the `href` targets of the `<a..>` tags associated with the album's images. One thing to note is I included an extra `'img'` on the `rel` attribute value. I did this because the image and the associated caption have separate links in the album's layout, If they both had the same group name value, it would cause the lightbox to include duplicate images. To include a caption below the image in the lightbox, it must be added to the title attribute of the anchor tag.

```
<a href='<%#GetDisplayPicturePath(Eval("AlbumName"), Eval("PictureFileName"))%>'
rel="lightbox[<%#Eval("AlbumName") %>img]" title='<%#Eval("PictureTitle")%>'>
<img runat="server" id="iThumb" border="0" width="50" src='' />
</a>
```

The reference to the display image is built by calling a function I added to the page's code-behind, `GetDisplayPicturePath`. It takes the album and picture's name to combine into a string that fits the path I discussed earlier. Finally, notice that the album name is scrubbed to format the spaces that might be in the name and replace them with the more friendly "-".

```
Public Function GetDisplayPicturePath(ByVal vAlbumName As String,
ByVal vPicture As String) As String
Return String.Format("{2}Photos/{0}/Display/{1}", _
Helpers.FormatSpacesForURL(vAlbumName), vPicture, Helpers.WebRoot)
End Function
```

Summary

This chapter presents a working solution for a photo gallery. The complete Photo Gallery module is made up of an administration console for managing the albums and their photos. The module takes advantage of the .NET graphics classes and the `FileUpload` control to let administrators upload only a single photo that can be manipulated as needed by the site to produce thumbnails and display images. On top of that we also integrated a powerful lightbox script built on Scriptaculous. This module can easily be employed in many real-world sites as it is now, but of course you can expand and enhance it as desired. Here are a few suggestions:

❑ Let users comment on and rate the photos. This could be done by leveraging the `Rating` control and the comment infrastructure we examined in Chapter 5.

❑ Allow users to tag photos with the names of people they know, similarly to what Facebook allows.

❑ Correlate the Photo Gallery albums with events, articles, and other content in the site.

❑ Enable administrators to upload more than one photo at a time and possibly select an entire folder on their computer to upload. This would involve using an ActiveX control to interact with the user's file system, but there are many large image-hosting sites that do just this.

12

Localizing the Site

We live in a global community consisting of people from many countries. The term *localizing* refers to the capability to present a site in the language of the local user, and to use the correct symbols for currency, decimals, dates, and so on. ASP.NET 2.0 added some new features to its arsenal for localizing a site that make it easier than ever before. Since then the proliferation of AJAX means there is a new set of issues that need to be tackled. The developer is freed from writing clumsy code for managing multiple languages and locale settings, and translated strings and other resources can be compiled into independent files that can be easily plugged into the site, even after deployment, to add support for a new language that wasn't even considered when the site was designed. In this chapter, you'll look at the importance of localization and learn how ASP.NET features can help you localize your site with little effort.

Problem

These days, it seems that the word globalization is used everywhere. The beauty of the Internet and the World Wide Web is that you can reach anyone who has a computer and a phone line or some other sort of Internet connection, be it for fun, passion, business, or another purpose. Nevertheless, if you want to be able to communicate with people, you must speak (or write) a language the people can understand. Due to the proliferation of English as a primary or second-ary language, many sites use English as their base language, even if they are not run by people for which this language is the main tongue. However, offering a site in the user's first language is often a great advantage over competitors that don't, because all users find it easier and more comfortable reading their primary language even when they can understand others. This is true not only for text but also for the format used to display and parse numbers, dates, and currency names. In fact, an Italian would interpret 07/02/2006 as the February 2, whereas an American would interpret it to be July 2. And while this may cause misunderstandings when reading the date, it may cause errors when users insert data in one format when the system expects a different one. For this reason, any modern site that wants to target a worldwide audience must be multi-language, displaying numbers and dates according to the user's local settings, and translating the full site's text (or at least the most important parts) into the user's primary language.

Fully localizing a site based on dynamic content (articles, products, forums, polls, etc.) is an extremely difficult task, and there are a number of ways to approach it. The difficulty varies considerably, depending on whether you intend to localize everything or just static content (text on the page layouts, menus, links, and page, section and field titles and descriptions, and so forth). ASP.NET has features that significantly simplify localizing static parts of a site, and this is what I'll cover in this chapter. The ASP.NET AJAX framework has also been designed to be conscience of language needs. Conversely, localizing the dynamic content would be much harder and would require quite a lot of rework on the database, the UI structure, and the object model. If that's what you really need to achieve, it's usually better to create separate language-specific sites with their own content.

Design

The first thing you need to decide when localizing a site is whether you want to localize only static content (menus, links, copyright notices, usage agreement, titles and descriptions for pages, tables, fields, buttons, and other controls) or whether you want to provide a translation for everything, including articles, poll questions, product listings, and so on. Let me state up front that adding support for complete localization would be very difficult at this stage of development, as it would require a complete reworking of the database design, the DAL, the BLL, and the UI. It's something that should be planned very early, during the initial site design and the foundations development. Complete localization in a single website is not a common requirement: you normally wouldn't translate every article on the site, forums, polls, and newsletters, but rather, only those that have a special appeal to one country or language-specific audience. You may also want to present information differently for different languages — changing something in the site's layout, for example. Because of this, most sites that want to be fully localized "simply" provide multiple copies of their pages under different subdomains or folders, one copy for each language. For example, there could be www.contoso.com/en and www.contoso.com/it or http://en.contoso.com/ and http://it.contoso.com/. Each copy of the site would target an independent database that only contains data for that specific language. If you take this approach, you'll only need to make static content localizable, and then install the site multiple times for multiple languages. Another advantage of this strategy is that, with completely separate websites, you can have different people managing them independently, who would be able to create content that best suits the audience for that particular language. In this chapter, we'll localize the site's static content, and we'll support the different locale settings for dates and numbers in different languages.

Our sample site will only be installed once, and the language for which the site is localized will be specified by each user at registration time or later from the Edit Profile page. This setting is mapped to the Preferences.Culture profile property, which was described and implemented in Chapter 4. An alternative would be to detect the user's favorite language from her browser's settings, which is sent to the web server with the request's header. However, many nontechnical users don't understand how to set this, and it would be difficult to explain it on your site and answer support questions from people who don't understand this. Therefore, it's better to directly ask users which language they'd like to use, so they understand what the language choice is for and how to change it. The next section provides an overview of the ASP.NET features regarding localization of static content.

Localization Features of ASP.NET

Although the previous framework had technology for localizing sites, the solution outlined in the preceding section had a number of problems that made the process unwieldy and prone to error. The most significant issues were as follows:

❑ You had to create the resource files manually, in a folder of your choice. However, the final name of the resource class would change because of the inclusion of the folder name, and many developers didn't realize this. This often resulted in errors whereby resources could not be found.

❑ You had to specify the resource key as a string, and if you misspelled this string, it resulted in errors whereby resources could not be found. If this were an enumeration, you could avoid the possibility of misspelling it.

❑ You had to invent your own naming convention to choose key names that would identify the same resource but for different pages, such as `Page1_Title` and `Page2_Title`. This was the case because there were only sitewide global resources, and not page-specific resources. You could also create different `.resx` files, one for each page and thus simulate page specific resources. This was merely a way to physically separate resources as they were still accessible by any other page.

❑ Above all, you had to manually write the code to set the `Text` property (or any other localizable property) to the proper string loaded by means of a `ResourceManager`, as there wasn't a declarative way to do it from the .aspx markup file.

With ASP.NET 2.0, all this changed considerably, and even though under the cover things work pretty much the same, from the developer's viewpoint, things are much easier and more intuitive now. Here's a list of improvements, which are described in detail in the following subsections:

❑ **Strongly typed global resources:** Once you create a global resource file (like the ones you may have used under ASP.NET 1.*x*), it is dynamically compiled into a class, and you can immediately see and access the class listed under the `Resources` namespace. Each resource of the file is accessible as a property, and IntelliSense is provided by Visual Studio to make it easier to select the right one. No more mistyped resource names!

❑ **Page-level resources:** In addition to global resource files, you also have page-specific resource files, so that you can place the resource strings only in the page that uses them. This enables you to have a resource called `Title` for every page, with different values, as they are stored in separate files. You no longer have to come up with a naming convention such as using the page name as the prefix for the resource keys.

❑ **New localization expressions:** Similar to data binding expressions, these enable a developer to associate an expression to the properties to localize directly in the .aspx markup file, so you don't need any C# code. A special declarative syntax is also available to bind all localizable properties to resources in a single step. Programmatic localization is still possible, of course, and has been improved as mentioned before for the global resources.

❑ **Improved Visual Studio designer support:** This enables you to graphically associate a localization expression to a resource string from a dialog box, without requiring the developer to write any code. There's also a command to automatically generate the neutral language page-level resource file for the current page, which you can copy, rename, or translate to another language.

❑ **Auto detection of the Accept-Language HTTP header:** This is used to automatically set the page's UICulture and Culture properties, which correspond to the current thread's CurrentUICulture and CurrentCulture properties.

❑ **Custom providers:** Should you want to store localized resources in a data store other than .resx files, such as a database, you can do that by writing your own custom provider. This enables you to build some sort of online UI for managing existing resources, and create new ones for additional languages, without the need to create and upload new resource files to the server.

Using Global Resources

Global resources are shared among all pages, controls, and classes, and are best suited to store localized data used in different places. When I say "data," I don't just mean strings but also images, icons, sounds, and any other binary content. Although this was already possible in ASP.NET 1.*x*, VS.NET 2003 had worse graphical support for resource files. Now you access a resource file item (from the Add Item dialog box) under a folder named App_GlobalResources, which is a special folder, handled by the ASP. NET runtime and VS2008; and you can insert data into the grid-style editor represented in Figure 12-1.

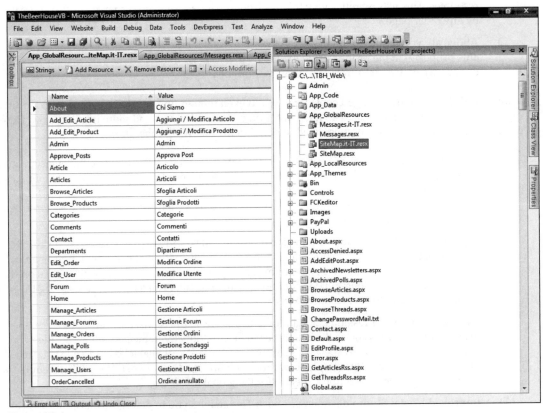

Figure 12-1

If you click the arrow on the right side of the editor's Add Resource toolbar button, you will be able to create an image or icon, or insert any other file. Figure 12-2 shows the window after choosing Images from the drop-down menu of the first toolbar icon (where Strings was selected in Figure 12-1) and after adding a few image files.

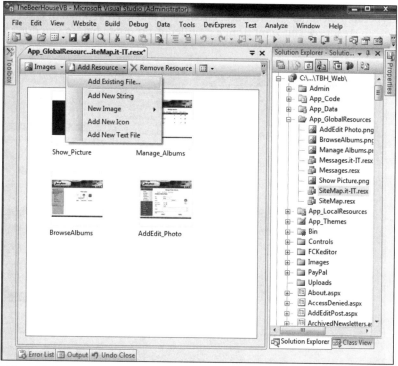

Figure 12-2

After adding a few strings and a few images, you can go to a .vb file in the editor and type **Resources**. IntelliSense will pop up a drop-down list with the names of the resource files added to the project, that is, Messages in the example shown in Figure 12-1. Then, when you type **Resources.Messages**, it will list the string and image resources added earlier; and if you look closely at Figure 12-3, you'll also note that image resources are returned with the proper type of System.Drawing.Bitmap.

Figure 12-3

This results in less manual typing, less probability of mistyping a resource or key name, and less casting.

Programmatic access of resources is necessary in some cases, particularly when you need to retrieve them from business or helper classes, and in this case you'll be happy to know that IntelliSense for dynamically compiled resources works also! However, when the resource will be used as the value for a property of a control on a page, there's an even easier approach: just select the control in the page's graphical designer and click the ellipses button on the right side of the "(Expressions)" item in the Properties window. From the dialog box that pops up, you can select the property you want to localize, select Resources as the expression type, and select then the resource class name and key, as shown in Figure 12-4. Note that you just select the resource you want from a prefilled drop-down list, so you don't need to type that yourself.

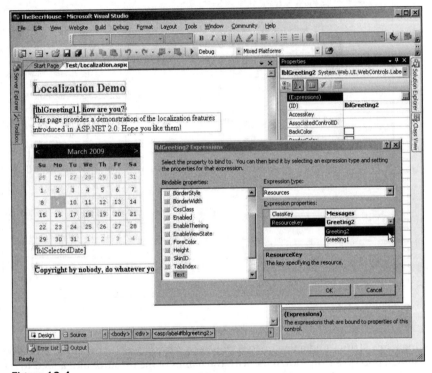

Figure 12-4

After using this dialog box on an ASP control, if you go to the Source View, the declaration of the localized `Label` control will look like this:

```
<asp:Label ID="lblGreeting2" runat="server"
    Text='<%$ Resources:Messages, Greeting2 %>' / >
```

The `Text` property is set to a new localization expression (also called *dollar-expression*, because of the leading $ character), which at runtime will return the resource string from the `Greeting2` item of the `Messages` class. You can also write these expressions yourself if you prefer coding your pages directly in the Source View (as I do). In either case, these expressions in the `.aspx` code are much better than manually writing C# code in the code-behind file, as you had to do with ASP.NET 1.*x*.

Using Page-Level Resources

You can create page-level resources by generating resource files, just as you do for global resources, but placing them under a folder named `App_LocalResources` (as opposed to `App_GlobalResources` used for global resources) located at the same level as the page to localize. For example, if the page is in the root folder, then you'll create the `App_LocalResources` under the root folder, but if the page is under `/Test`, then you'll create a `/Test/App_LocalResources` folder. This means you can have multiple `App_LocalResources` folders, whereas you can only have one `App_GlobalResources` folder for the whole site. The name of the resource filename is also fundamental, as it must be named after the page or control file for which it contains the localized resources, and include the culture name: for example, a culture-neutral resource file for `Localization.aspx` would be named `Localization.aspx.resx`, whereas it would be named `Localization.aspx.it-IT.resx` for the Italian resources. In Figure 12-5, you can see the organization of files in the Solution Explorer and the resource file being edited in the grid editor.

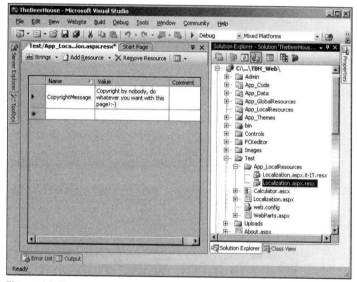

Figure 12-5

You can still use the Expressions dialog shown in Figure 12-4 to bind a control's property to an expression pointing to a localized resource: when you point to a page-specific resource you just leave the `ClassKey` textbox empty. Following is the generated expression:

```
<asp:Label ID="lblCopyright" runat="server"
    Text="<%$ Resources:CopyrightMessage %>" / >
```

It differs from the expression shown in the previous section, as it doesn't include the class name; it just specifies the resource key. If you want to access local resources programmatically, you use the page's `GetLocalResourceObject` method, which takes the resource key name and returns an `Object` that you must cast to `string` or to the proper destination type (such as `Bitmap` if you stored an image):

```
string copyrightMsg = (string)this.GetLocalResourceObject("CopyrightMessage");
```

Even with localization expressions and local resources, localizing full pages will be a slow task if you need to create the expressions for dozens of controls, and things get worse if you need to localize multiple properties for the same control, such as Text, ToolTip, ImageUrl, NavigateUrl, and so on, which is often the case. To speed things up, Visual Studio offers the Tools ➪ Generate Local Resource command, which generates a local resource file for the current page, and creates entries for all localizable properties of all controls on the page, following the ControlName.PropertyName naming convention for the names of the resources. Resource items are also automatically set with the value extracted from the page's markup; if a property is not used in the control's declaration, a resource item for it is generated anyway and left empty.

Localizable properties are those that are decorated with a [Localizable(true)] *attribute, which you can add to the properties of your custom controls. However, even when you add it to properties of user controls, resources for those properties will not be automatically generated by the Generate Local Resource command. You can create the local resources for those properties yourself, and write the localization expressions to make the association: everything will work perfectly at runtime, so this is only a design-time limitation. In addition, you'll have to write the localization expressions manually, because the (Expressions) item is not available from the Properties window when a user control is selected.*

Figure 12-6 shows the resource editor for the Localization.aspx.resx local resource file after executing the Generate Local Resource command on the test page.

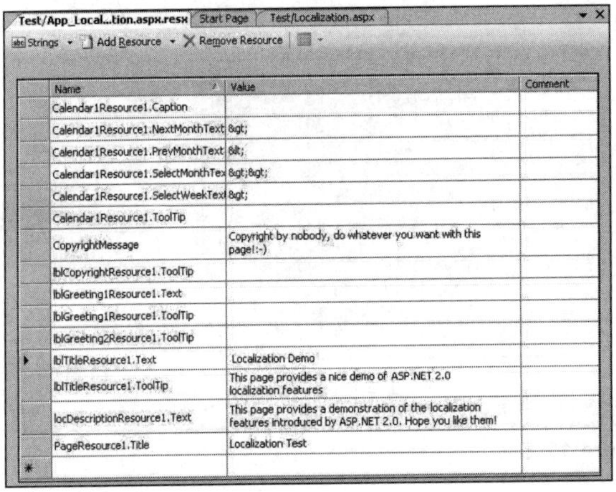

Figure 12-6

Besides the automatic generation of the resource file (or the addition of the resource items, if a resource file for that page was already present in the proper folder), what's even more interesting is that each control's declaration is modified as follows (note the code in bold):

```
<asp:Label ID="lblTitle" runat="server" Font-Size="X-Large" ForeColor="#C00000"
    meta:resourcekey="lblTitleResource1" Text="Localization Demo"
    Text="This page provides a nice demo of new ASP.NET 2.0 localization features"
/>
```

A meta:resourcekey attribute is added to the declaration and is set to the prefix used in the local resource file to identify all localized properties of that control, such as lblTitleResource1.Text and lblTitleResource1.ToolTip. These are called *implicit localization expressions* (expressions used earlier are considered *explicit*). At runtime, the framework parses all resources and applies them to the properties of the corresponding controls, making the mapping of the first part of the key with the value of meta:resourcename. This means that the control's declaration is decorated with just a single new attribute, but may make multiple properties localizable. Later, if you want to localize a property that you didn't take into account originally, you just need to go to the resource editor and add an item following the naming schema described above, or edit its value if it already exists.

> Note that the controls retain their original property declarations after running the Generate Local Resource command. These declarations are no longer necessary, though, as the property's value will be replaced at runtime with the values saved in the resource file; therefore, you can completely remove the definition of the Text, ToolTip, and the other localized properties, from the .aspx files to avoid confusion.

This behavior works with the page's title as well, originally defined in the @Page directive, which is modified as follows:

```
<%@ Page Language="C#" meta:resourcekey="PageResource1" …other attributes… %>
```

Localizing More Static Content

All content that you want to localize must be displayed by some sort of server-side control, such as the Label or Literal controls. You'll typically want to use a Literal over a Label if you don't need the appearance properties of a Label, either because you don't need to format the text or because the formatting is done through raw HTML tags present directly within the text, which is frequently the case for static text such as section and field titles, descriptions, copyright notices, and so on. An alternative to Literal is the new Localize control, listed in the last position under the Toolbox's Standard tab. If you declare it manually from the Source View, it's identical to a Literal. If, however, you work in the graphical designer, you'll notice that it doesn't have any properties listed in the Properties window beside the ID, not even a Text property. The way you fill it with text in the Designer is to place the caret inside it and type the text directly. Figure 12-7 shows the test page with the description text under the title placed inside a Localize control.

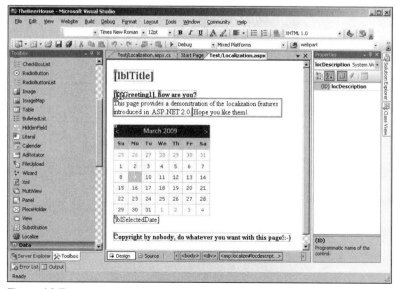

Figure 12-7

Specifying Alternate Language Pages

A LINK element can be added to the header of a page that specifies the `hreflang` attribute to associate an alternate version of the page in a specific language.

The declaration produced, after executing the Generate Local Resource command, is the following:

```
<asp:Localize ID="locDescription" runat="server"
    meta:resourcekey="locDescriptionResource1" Text="The page provides a demo... "
/>
```

As mentioned earlier, you can completely remove the `Text` property from the declaration, as it will be set from the localized resources at runtime.

> When wrapping static content in a `Localize` or `Literal` control, it's advisable that you don't include HTML formatting tags in the control's `Text`, because that would go into the resource when the page is localized. If you were to pass that resource file to a nontechnical translator, she may not understand what those HTML tags are and may modify them in some undesirable way. Because of this, if you have static content with HTML tags in the middle, then it may be wise to split it into multiple `Localize` controls, leaving the HTML formatting outside.

Setting the Current Culture

Once you've modified your page with localization expressions for the various controls displaying static content, and you've created local or global resource files for the different languages you want to support, it's time to implement some way to enable users to change the page's language. One method is to read the Accept-Language HTTP header sent by the client to the server, which contains the array of cultures set in the browser's preferences, as shown in the dialog box in Figure 12-8.

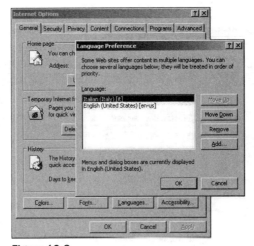

Figure 12-8

In ASP.NET 1.*x*, you would set the current thread's `CurrentCulture` and `CurrentUICulture` properties to the first item of the `UserLanguage` array of the `Request` object, which would contain the first language in the list. You would execute this code in the `Init` or `Load` event of a page (typically a `BasePage` class, so that all others would inherit the same behavior), or from the Application's `BeginRequest` event, as shown here:

```
Private Sub Application_BeginRequest(ByVal sender As Object, ByVal e As EventArgs)
    If Request.UserLanguages.Length > 0 Then
        Dim culture As CultureInfo =
CultureInfo.CreateSpecificCulture(Request.UserLanguages(0))
        Thread.CurrentThread.CurrentCulture = culture
        Thread.CurrentThread.CurrentUICulture = culture
    End If
End Sub
```

In ASP.NET 2.0 and above, however, you only need to set the `culture` and `uiCulture` attributes of the `web.config` file's `<globalization>` element to `"auto"`, so that the user's favorite language will be retrieved and used automatically:

```
<configuration>
    <system.web>
        <globalization culture="auto" uiCulture="auto" />
        ...
    </system.web>
</configuration>
```

You can also specify these setting at the page-level, with the `Culture` and `UICulture` attributes of the `@Page` directive:

```
<%@ Page Culture="auto" UICulture="auto" ... %>
```

Figure 12-9 shows what the same page looks like when loaded for the American English or Italian language selected in the browser.

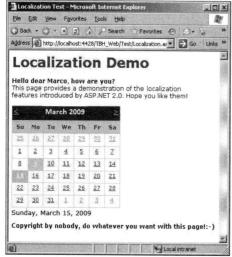 

Figure 12-9

The `"auto"` setting only saves a few lines of code, but it's nice to have. In many situations, however, you'll prefer to set the culture by yourself anyway, because you'll need to extract the current culture from the user's profile, from a session variable, or according to some other logic (I mentioned earlier that it's a good idea to let users specify their language of choice). If that's the case, the preceding code showing how to handle the application's `BeginRequest` is still valid, but you may actually prefer handling the application's `PostAcquireRequestState` event, so that the profile and session variables have been initialized already with the proper values. An even better solution is to override the page's new `InitializeCulture` method, to programmatically set the page's `Culture` and `UICulture` properties to the culture string (and not to a `CultureInfo` object as you do with the `Thread` properties). Here's an example:

```
Protected Overloads Overrides Sub InitializeCulture()
    Dim culture As String = Helpers.GetCurrentCulture()
    Me.Culture = culture
    Me.UICulture = culture
End Sub
```

`Helpers.GetCurrentCulture` is a custom function that would return something like "en-US" or "it-IT" after reading the desired current culture from somewhere. In the "Solution" section, you'll read the culture from the user's profile, and override this method in the custom `BasePage` class, so that all pages inherit this behavior without the need to replicate the code more than once.

> **The Generate Local Resource command automatically sets the** `Culture` **and** `UICulture` **attributes of the** `@Page` **directive to** `auto`**. If you use one of the application's events in the** `Global.asax` **file to programmatically set the current culture, you must remember to remove those attributes from the** `@Page` **directive after running the command on .aspx pages; otherwise, the automatic settings will override what you do by hand, because the page is parsed after the** `global.asax` **events you would typically use. (There is no such problem when generating localization resources for user controls, though, because the** `@Control` **directive doesn't have those page-level attributes, of course.) If you follow the approach of overriding the page's** `InitializeCulture` **event, this isn't important, because this method is raised after the page is parsed, so your code will override the culture set by the framework, as desired.**

Solution

As a sample implementation for this chapter, I fully localized the command layout stored in the `template.master` file, and most of the user controls, especially those that are part of the site's common structure, such as `NewsletterBox`, `PollBox`, `ShoppingCartBox`, `ThemeSelector`, `WelcomeBox`, and `PersonalizationManager`. To do this, you start by editing the `template.master` file and wrapping the static text you want to localize (such as the copyright notices, or the acknowledgments to Template Monster for providing the sample layout) in `Localize` controls. Then, from the Design View, you execute the Generate Local Resource command for the master page, thus creating a `Template.master.resx` file under the root `App_LocalResources` special folder. You copy this file into the same folder, rename it to `Template.master.it-IT.resx` (for Italian), open it in Visual Studio's resource editor, and translate all string values to the destination language. Figure 12-10 shows the resource file for Italian opened in the editor.

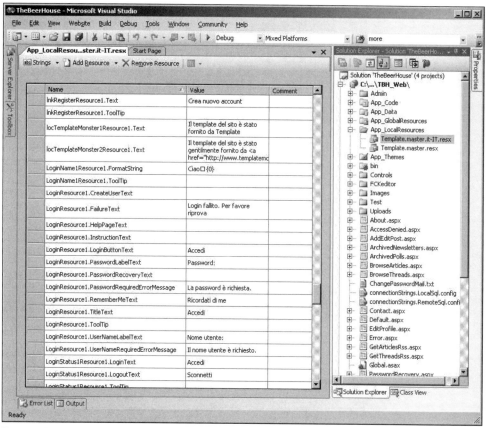

Figure 12-10

Then you follow the exact same process for the previously mentioned controls, which will produce a number of resource files under `/Controls/App_LocalResources`, as shown in Figure 12-11.

Yet another thing you want to localize is the `Web.sitemap` file. There isn't a command that localizes this automatically for you, however, so you must manually create global resource files for it, named `SiteMap.resx` and `SiteMap.it-IT.resx`, and located under the root `App_GlobalResources` folder. You create a key-value pair for each link defined in the site map, and translate them to the other language. At this point, the Solution Explorer and the resource file for the localized site map look like the example shown in Figure 12-12.

Figure 12-11

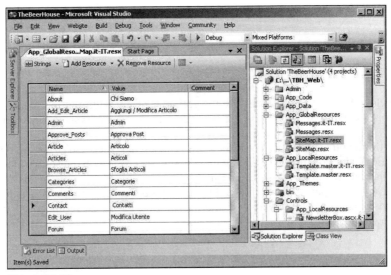

Figure 12-12

You then modify the original `Web.sitemap` file, by replacing the value of the `title` attribute with a localization expression referencing the proper key in the shared `SiteMap` resource file. Here is partial content of the modified file:

```
<siteMap xmlns="http://schemas.microsoft.com/AspNet/SiteMap-File-1.0"
    enableLocalization="true" >

    <siteMapNode title="$Resources: SiteMap, Home" url="~/Default.aspx">
        <siteMapNode title="$Resources: SiteMap, Articles"
            url="~/ShowCategories.aspx">
            <siteMapNode title="$Resources: SiteMap, Browse_Articles"
                url="~/BrowseArticles.aspx">
                <siteMapNode title="$Resources: SiteMap, Article"
                    url="~/ShowArticle.aspx" />
            </siteMapNode>
        </siteMapNode>
        <!-- more nodes here... -->
    </siteMapNode>
</siteMap>
```

Finally, you override the `InitializeCulture` method in the custom `BasePage` class, from which all your pages inherit, and set the page's `Culture` and `UICulture` properties to the `Preferences.Culture` `profile` property:

```
Public Class BasePage
    Inherits System.Web.UI.Page
    Protected Overloads Overrides Sub InitializeCulture()
        Dim culture As String = TryCast(HttpContext.Current.Profile,
ProfileCommon).Preferences.Culture
        Me.Culture = culture
        Me.UICulture = culture
    End Sub
' the rest of the class here...
End Class
```

Recall that in Chapter 4 this `profile` property was made accessible for anonymous users also, with a default value of `"en-US"`, so you don't need to verify that the current user is authenticated to safely read this property. You're now ready to test the localized home page: run the site and log in with your test user, go to your profile page, switch the language to Italian (or to whatever language you've added support for), and return to the home page to see how it is translated. Figure 12-13 shows the home page fully translated to Italian, except for the dynamic data (such as poll questions and options, and forum thread and article titles) stored in the database, of course.

If you intend to fully localize all the pages of the site, you'll find some hard-coded strings in a few .cs code-behind files. To localize them you can add resource strings into the `Messages.resx` and `Messages.it-IT.resx` global resource files created earlier as a test in the "Design" section, and replace the hard-coded strings with something like `Resources.Messages.ResourceKeyName`, as described earlier.

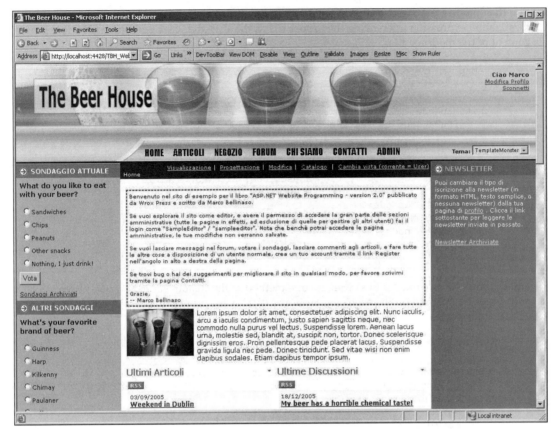

Figure 12-13

Localizing ASP.NET AJAX

While much of an AJAX application should be concerned with application logic, there are still times when resources might need to be localized in the scripts. ASP.NET AJAX is sensitive to this need and provides a way to embed localized scripts in assemblies. The framework actually uses this to create debug and release versions of the scripts, too. Scripts are added to an assembly with the culture appended to the file name before the `.js` extension, `Script.en-CA.js` for Canadian English or `Script.it-IT.js` for Italian, and the like.

To embed localized scripts you must be using Visual Studio 2008, as the Visual Web Developer Express does not allow class libraries to be created. Once you have an AJAX-enabled website created, add a class library project to the solution and make the website reference the class library project. The class library must also reference the `System.Web` and `System.Web.Extensions` libraries.

Add the script file to the class library, `Validation.js`. Then add `ValidationResources.resx` for language-neutral resources and `ValidationResources.it.resx` for Italian resources. In the script file add the following code:

```
function IsValidFirstName(firstName) {
    if (firstName == '') {
        alert(Validation.InValidFirstName);
    } else {
    alert(Validation.InValidFirstName);
    }
}
```

The script uses `Validation` as a placeholder to reference the desired resource strings. In the `ValidationResources.resx` file add two resource strings, `ValidFirstName` and `InValidFirstName`. Add the following values respectively: `'This is a valid First Name.'` and `'This not is a valid First Name.'` Next open the Italian resource file and add the same two resource strings, but this time set the values to the following phrases: `'Ciò è un nome valido.'` and `'Ciò è un ne nome valido.'` Before compiling the class library, the following code should be added to the assembly's `AssemblyInfo.vb` file:

```
<Assembly: System.Web.UI.WebResource("LocalizingResources.Validation.js",
"text/javascript")>
<Assembly: System.Web.UI.ScriptResource("LocalizingResources.Validation.js",
"LocalizingResources.ValidationResources", "Validation")>
```

Compile the class library. Not only do you get the normal `.dll` assembly, but there is also a subfolder "it" created that contains the Italian resources in its own assembly, `TBHBLL.resources.dll`. You can really see this if you examine the binary files created in the ASP.NET AJAX Control Toolkit, shown in Figure 12-14.

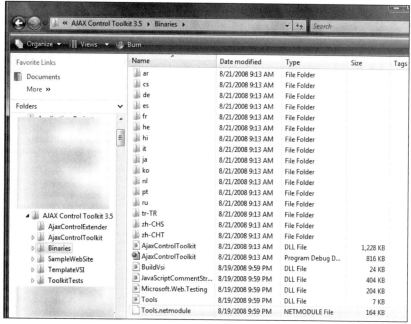

Figure 12-14

To enable the `ScriptManager` control to leverage the language resources, the `EnableScriptLocalization` property must be set to true. In addition, the `UICulture` and `Culture` page directives must be set to `"auto"`. In the Beer House application this can be accomplished in the `TBHMain.master` file.

```
<%@ Master Language="VB" AutoEventWireup="false" CodeBehind="TBHMain.master.vb"
Inherits="TBH_Web35.TBHMain"
    UICulture="auto" Culture="auto" %>


....
    <form id="form1" runat="server">
    <asp:ScriptManager ID="ScriptManager1" runat="server"
AllowCustomErrorsRedirect="true"
        EnablePartialRendering="true" LoadScriptsBeforeUI="false"
ScriptMode="Auto" EnableScriptLocalization="true">
        <Scripts>
            <asp:ScriptReference Path="~/TBH.js" />
            <asp:ScriptReference Assembly="TBHBLL"
Name="LocalizingResources.Validation.js" />
        </Scripts>
    </asp:ScriptManager>
```

If you run a page that calls the `IsValidFirstName` function, the response string will be returned in the appropriate language.

Summary

This chapter described the localization features of ASP.NET. Automatic resource generation, implicit and explicit localization expressions, strongly typed, dynamically compiled global resources, and good Visual Studio Designer support can all greatly speed up the implementation of localization support in your website. The "Solution" section of this chapter was fairly short because you only need to follow a few simple steps, repeating them for all the pages you want to localize. It only took me a couple of hours to fully localize the site's common layout and the home page. I know from personal experience that this would have taken much longer with the previous version of ASP.NET and, of course, infinitely longer with even older technologies. If this power and flexibility still isn't enough for your needs, I invite you to go deeper and study the provider model for localization, which enables you to store and retrieve resources to and from any data store you prefer.

Now that the site is 100% feature complete, you can start thinking about its packing, distribution, and publication to the Internet for global usage. The next chapter shows you how to deploy the site to both a shared hosted server and a dedicated server under your control, and how to create redistributable installers for packaged applications.

13

Deploying the Site

You've come to the end of the development: your site is ready, you've tested it locally and it all works fine, and now you have to publish it online. If you've ever had any experience with older legacy ASP/COM applications, and later with ASP.NET 1.*x* applications, you already know that .NET made deployment much easier: you no longer had any COM components to register, or shared components that might overwrite an existing version and thus break other applications. For pure ASP.NET applications, it may suffice to do an XCOPY of all your deployment-related files (such as .aspx, .dll, .config, and image files) to the remote server, and then deploy the database. However, in the real world, things usually tend to get a little more complex than that because you have constraints and company policies to respect regarding the deployment of your application. Database deployment and configuration are also nontrivial, and you should consider this carefully before you start rolling out the site. In this final chapter, I will guide you through all of the different options to successfully deploy your website's files and the database, explaining why and when some techniques are more suitable than another.

Problem

The problem described and solved here was a real problem that I faced while completing the sample site. I wanted to put the site online somewhere so that potential readers could browse it and consider whether it was worth the purchase, and so that I could show it to clients and colleagues during presentations about ASP.NET 2.0.

Not having a private dedicated server connected to the Internet available for this project, I chose to deploy the site to a typical shared web hosting service that uses servers running Windows Server and supports ASP.NET 2.0 and SQL Server. Most of these Microsoft-centric web hosting companies now support this platform, and several of them offer plans that cost as little as $10 per month. When evaluating hosting service companies, you need to ensure that they offer you enough disk space and bandwidth, and that you factor in the cost of SQL Server (some companies charge extra for this). Of course, your specific hosting requirements may vary according to the type of project you're working on. For large or high-usage sites, or just sites that require high availability, you'll want dedicated servers configured as a web farm (whereby a number of servers are running the same applications and load-balancing is used to determine which server will process a specific web request).

> *IIS and ASP.NET is a very scalable web platform where most websites have a very over abundant hardware allocation. Marcus Frind has a great discussion about his experiences with ASP.NET 2.0 with the demand Plentyoffish.com receives,* http://plentyoffish.wordpress.com/2006/06/10/ microsoft-aspnet-20-performance. *This article is a little outdated. With the release of IIS 7.0 the numbers are even better.*

Also consider that our sample website is 100% pure ASP.NET, with no legacy COM components, COM+ services, or Windows services: these things would require special installation and are usually not allowed by basic low-cost hosting plans. In our case, we don't need the benefits of a dedicated server or web farm, so a shared hosting plan is fine. For the situation just described, the problem statements are pretty simple to formulate:

❑ What files do I need to deploy?

❑ How do I deploy those files?

❑ How can I protect my source code against prying eyes once the website has been published on a shared remote server?

❑ How do I move my local SQL Server Express database into a full SQL Server 2005 database (when SQL Server Express has been used to develop the site)?

❑ How do I create an installer that automates the whole site's setup, which would be useful if I sold the website as a product, or if I wish to deploy to a dedicated web server?

In the following pages you'll find answers for all of these questions.

Design

The complete deployment is basically split into two parts: deploying the database and deploying the site's files. If your web server supports SQL Server Express (only recommended for small workgroups), deploying the database is as simple as copying the contents of the App_Data folder to the remote server's App_Data folder, and the .mdf and .ldf files will automatically be attached to the remote SQL Server Express that is installed on the web server! However, production deployment normally requires a full-featured SQL Server (not the Express edition), for security, performance, and scalability reasons. Because of this, you need to find some way to turn the current SQL Server Express database into a SQL Server database. As for the site's files, you have different options here, as you'll see shortly.

Make the effort to know the version the destination SQL Server. Most corporate environments are still using SQL Server 2005 or even 2000. There is nothing in the Beer House's database that should cause any problems with these earlier versions, but you may have to adjust the database properties to the proper version.

One important point to consider is the fact that we did all our development using VS2008's integrated web server and not IIS. The integrated web server is fine for local testing but your site must be tested on IIS before deploying to a production server. Therefore, before deploying the site to the remote server, you'll first test it on a local installation under IIS, replicating the configuration you have on the production server as much as possible. This will be a test of your deployment procedures and configuration, in addition to the obvious test of your code and pages. The following sections provide a detailed tutorial of the steps to take for a complete local deployment of the database and the application, and later you can follow the same steps for production deployment.

There are several common website deployment options: shared hosting, dedicated hosting/co-location, or an internal infrastructure. Shared hosting is great for the vast majority of websites because they have relatively low traffic and have minimal disk space needs, but there is limited administrative control over the server. A shared hosting environment has one instance of IIS running, with numerous websites. Think of it as leasing an office in a large office building. You have a key to your office but share the vast majority of infrastructure with other tenants. Some hosting companies stuff as many sites on the server as it physically can hold; often they will oversell the capacity on the server to make it profitable. It pays to do background research on any company you are thinking of choosing before committing your site to them.

Dedicated hosting provides much more control over the server and provides a more private experience, since there is no one else sharing the machine. You should note that it is very common for large hosting companies to offer virtual dedicated servers. This is not a dedicated physical server but a dedicated virtual server with several other dedicated virtual servers running on the same hardware. Typically, this will use a technology like Windows Hyper-V as the core operating system and run several virtual machines at once. You should also determine which type of dedicated hosting you are using. Virtualization is a great way to manage servers because the operating system image is not bound to the physical hardware and can be easily backed up and restored in the case of a hardware failure. Co-location is similar to renting a dedicated server environment from a hosting provider, except that you own the box and only rent the cabinet space, power, and bandwidth from the data center. Often it is slightly cheaper, but it places some extra responsibilities on you that you would not have in shared and dedicated environments.

Finally, most large enterprise operations have a dedicated IT staff and possibly a data center. They may actually utilize a third party and use the dedicated or co-location solutions described earlier. Either way, there will typically be a set of policies, procedures, and rules that must be followed for deployment. Often they will not allow you any sort of access to the servers hosting your database and site. You will instead have to provide them with the database or database script, the website files, and detailed instructions on installation. Understanding how to use the tools provided by SQL Server and Visual Studio 2008 should make this process much easier for any of the possible hosting scenarios.

Deploying the Database to SQL Server 2008

When using a shared hosting service, you will typically have an empty database on a shared SQL Server database, which you can access remotely through the SQL Server Management Studio (SSMS) desktop application (the new replacement for both Enterprise Manager and Query Analyzer), or with an online web front end provided by the hoster. However, they usually don't give you the access rights to upload an .MDF file and attach it by running the `sp_attach_db` stored procedure (which was introduced in Chapter 3), because that would require administrative rights, and nor do you have permission to restore a database from backup files generated on your local server. Your hosting company's support staff may do this for you if you make a special request, but they may not. However, most hosting companies have some kind of web application that lets you run queries and SQL scripts on your remote database; and as mentioned earlier, they do allow you to connect remotely with SSMS (SSMS is usually better than the hosting company's web application).

When deploying to a particular server under your control (as opposed to a shared hosting company server), you can just create a new database on the server, and then create a new login and give that login permissions in your new database. This is *not* an end-user account; it's the account that your website will use to access the database. The following SQL commands will do this (please select a good password in place of 'password'):

```
USE Master
GO
CREATE DATABASE TheBeerHouse
GO
USE TheBeerHouse
GO
EXEC sp_addlogin 'BeerHouseUser', 'password', 'TheBeerHouse'
EXEC sp_grantdbaccess 'BeerHouseUser', 'BeerHouseUser'
EXEC sp_addrolemember 'db_owner', 'BeerHouseUser'
EXEC sp_addrolemember 'db_datareader', 'BeerHouseUser'
EXEC sp_addrolemember 'db_datawriter', 'BeerHouseUser'
GO
```

To set up a remote database just like your local database, you need to create all its objects: tables, stored procedures, views, triggers, indexes, constraints, roles, and so forth. In addition to your own objects, you also have to re-create all the objects required by the SQL Server providers used by ASP.NET for features such as membership, profiling, personalization, and web events.

There are many ways to create all the database objects in a new remote database, but the following are among the best options (only the first option is covered in detail due to space constraints):

1. Make SQL scripts from your development server and execute those scripts on the new server (the code download for this book has SQL scripts, or you can make them yourself).

2. Use SQL Server Management Studio (SSMS) to copy the whole database from your local development database directly to the new server.

3. Copy your .mdf (database file) and .ldf (log file) from your local computer to the remote computer, and attach them to the remote instance of SQL Server.

4. Use SSMS or SQL commands to create a backup of your local database to a file, and restore from the file on the new server.

5. Use the new SQL Server Integration Services, which is a powerful and flexible replacement for the older DTS services.

6. Write your own data migration program using the SQL Server Management Objects (SMO), which is a new set of classes that enable you to manipulate SQL objects from a .NET program (SMO replaces the older SQL-DMO COM objects).

Option 2 is the easiest, but it requires you to have administrator access on both computers (not possible for a shared hosting deployment). In fact, options 2, 3, and 4 are normally not available for shared hosted sites, and options 5 and 6 may not be available in some shared hosting environments. This leaves option 1 as the most portable option that will always work for every situation. The only problem with option 1 is that you can't script data for image columns (used in the aspnet_profile table), so you need an alternate way to populate the data once the objects have been created.

Most of the aforementioned options are easiest to implement using SQL Server Management Studio (SSMS) on your local development computer, where both the local and remote databases are registered in the configuration. Either edition of SSMS (full or express) can be used for this purpose. Because of space constraints here, I can't cover SSMS in detail, but I'll walk you through some of its most useful features that are helpful for deployment.

Create the Standard ASP.NET Objects

There's a convenient shortcut for creating the ASP.NET required objects (for profiles, membership, etc.): if you remember from Chapter 4, all those objects can be created by executing the `aspnet_regsql` command-line tool and specifying the target server and database. Of course, this requires that you can access the remote SQL Server over the Internet (i.e., you can connect to it from your desktop and not only from the web server running your site). This is the syntax you can use to install the ASP.NET tables on a remote server at a specified IP address:

```
aspnet_regsql.exe -U username -P password -S 111.222.333.444 -d DBname -A all
```

An alternative, in case you can't access your remote database this way, is to use the hoster's database manager (or SSMS) to manually run a set of SQL scripts to create those objects. Microsoft has provided these scripts under the `C:\WINDOWS\Microsoft.NET\Framework\v2.0.50727` folder. The files have not changed since ASP.NET 2.0 was released. These script files must be run in the following order:

- ❑ `InstallCommon.sql`
- ❑ `InstallMembership.sql`
- ❑ `InstallPersonalization.sql`
- ❑ `InstallProfile.sql`
- ❑ `InstallRoles.sql`
- ❑ `InstallWebEventSqlProvider.sql`

> **Important!** All of these scripts reference a database named `aspnedb`. Your database is probably named differently, so you'll need to edit the scripts to specify the name of your database (you should make copies and only edit the copies, of course).

As you can see, it's very easy to create the standard objects, but you normally don't have to do this as a separate step. Instead, you can just script these objects along with your own objects, as you'll see in the following section.

Script All Your Database Objects

You can generate SQL CREATE scripts from your local development database, and then execute them on the remote database server. Although Visual Studio 2008 is not quite as good as SSMS when it comes to generating scripts, it can be used for this. Using Visual Studio 2008, open the Server Explorer Window (select View ➪ Server Explorer or press Ctrl+Alt+S). If your database is not already listed, you will need to add it by clicking the Connect to Database button at the top of the window. This displays the Add Connection dialog (see Figure 13-1).

Figure 13-1

Script objects can be created one by one by browsing the local database on Visual Studio's Server Explorer window and clicking the Generate Create Script to Project command from the object's context menu, see Figure 13-2.

Although this method of creating SQL scripts works fine, it's not the most convenient approach because you have to generate scripts one object at a time, in separate files, and then merge everything.

It's easier to generate one script that contains all the objects using SSMS. If you loaded the .MDF data file on your computer but haven't attached it to the local database yet, you can do this by means of the Attach command from the Databases item's context menu (see Figure 13-3).

From the dialog box that pops up you select the .MDF file to attach and the name you want to give it in the SQL Server 2008 instance. For example, in Figure 13-4 the AdventureWorksLT.MDF file is being named after AdventureWorksLTDemo.

> *If you receive an error when attaching the file from SQL Server's dialog box, ensure that it is not being used by some other process, and is not already attached to Visual Studio's Server Explorer tool. In the former case, just stop the guilty process; in the latter case, simply detach the file by means of the Detach comment, reachable from the database file's context menu.*

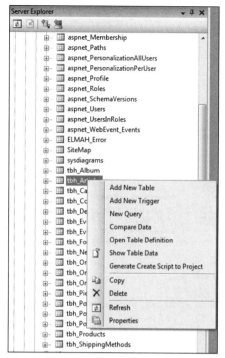

Figure 13-2

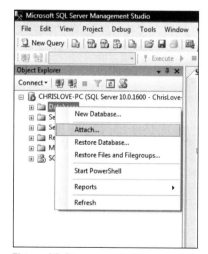

Figure 13-3

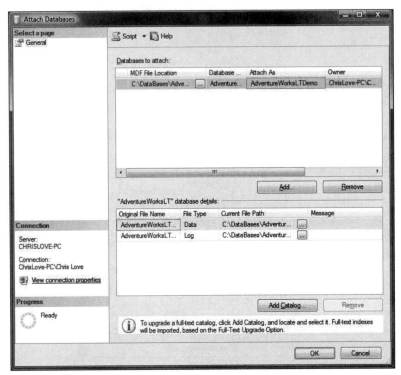

Figure 13-4

Once the database is attached to your local database, you can launch the Script Wizard by selecting the database from the Explorer window and then selecting Tasks ➪ Generate Scripts from the context menu (see Figure 13-5).

This launches the Script Wizard, which allows you to select the objects you want to include in the script. You can select all the objects by checking the "Script all objects in the selected database" option at the bottom of the dialog. In the next step, you can choose to script all tables, stored procedures, user-defined functions, roles, and views, and you have many more options to optionally script primary and foreign keys, check constraints, triggers, indexes, and so on (see Figure 13-6). This includes all the objects required by the ASP.NET features and providers, so if you follow this approach there will be no need to execute the individual scripts previously listed.

Once you have generated the script to create all the objects, you can execute the script on your new database to recreate the whole schema. This can be done with SSMS or any other tool that lets you execute SQL commands on your new database. First, you have to register your remote database in SSMS (select View ➪ Registered Servers, and then right-click in that window to add a new registered server). Then do a File ➪ Open on your creation script, and have it connect to the remote server (make sure that your database is selected in the drop-down list in the toolbar area), and run your creation script by pressing Execute or using the F5 shortcut key (see Figure 13-7).

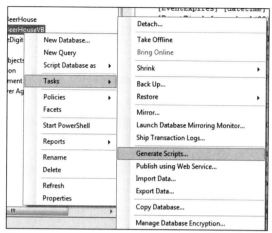

Figure 13-5

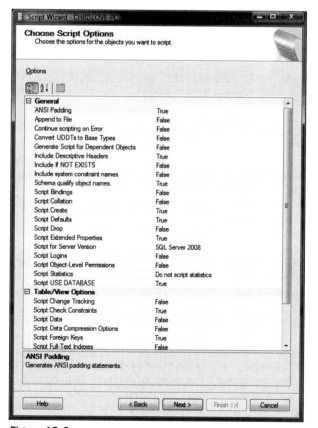

Figure 13-6

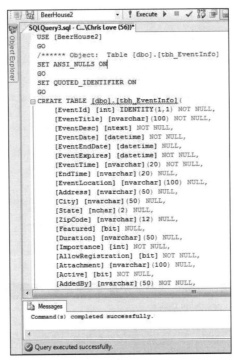

Figure 13-7

Importing Existing Data

The script we created and executed created the objects but didn't populate the tables with data. While developing the site on your local computer, you created quite a lot of data to define article categories, forums, polls, products, users, and so on, and you'll want to import all that information into the new database instead of recreating it from scratch. You might think that you could generate a script with `INSERT` statements for all the records from all your tables and then execute it on the new database. However, neither Visual Studio's Server Explorer nor your local installation of SSMS have the ability to create SQL `INSERT` scripts for your data, and you may end up coding the statements manually. If you only need to script a few dozen records, writing statements by hand may be feasible, but if you have to generate hundreds or thousands of `INSERT` statements for any table, then you will want to look at one of the many third-party tools that can automatically generate the script for you.

If you can connect to both the local and remote database by means of SQL Server Management Studio (SSMS), things are much easier. When you use the tool's Import Data feature, it allows you to choose all tables, but you can't select the order in which they will be imported, and you'll get many import errors if the tool tries to insert data into a detail table that has a foreign key to a master table for which the data hasn't been imported yet. To solve the problem, you need to temporarily disable the referential integrity checks during the import, so that the tool can insert data into a table even if the records reference other records that are not present in the master table yet. To do this, you use the `ALTER TABLE <tablename> NOCHECK CONSTRAINT ALL` statement for every table, as follows:

```
ALTER TABLE tbh_Articles NOCHECK CONSTRAINT ALL
ALTER TABLE tbh_Categories NOCHECK CONSTRAINT ALL
```

```
ALTER TABLE tbh_Comments NOCHECK CONSTRAINT ALL
...do the same for all other tables required by ASP.NET and your application
```

After disabling constraints, select the target database in which you want to import the data (this may be a local database or a database on the remote server) in the Object Explorer, and select Tasks ➪ Import Data from its context menu (see Figure 13-8) to open the Import and Export Wizard.

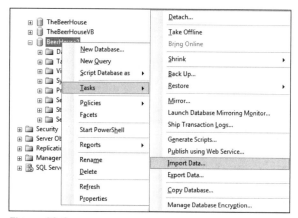

Figure 13-8

In the first wizard step, you select the source database, which will be the TheBeerHouse database attached to the .MDF SQL Server Express file (see Figure 13-9).

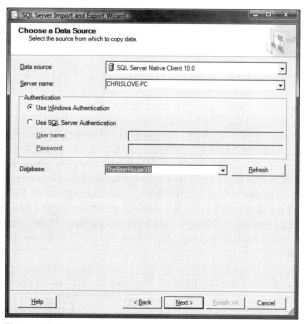

Figure 13-9

In the second step you choose the destination database, which will already be selected. If you're targeting a remote database (not on your own computer), you probably also need to modify the options to choose SQL Server Authentication, and enter your credentials to connect to it. In the next step, you select all the tables you want to import, which will be all tables starting with aspnet_ and tbh_ (see Figure 13-10).

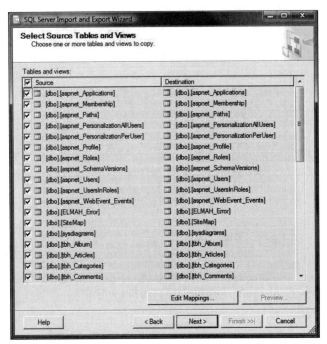

Figure 13-10

You could omit the following tables if you prefer: sysdiagrams and aspnet_WebEventEvents. Also, make sure you do not select the objects beginning with vw_aspnet, as these are views that don't contain their own data in reality. Before proceeding to the next step, you must go into the import options of each selected table, by clicking the Edit button on the right side of the grid listing the objects. Select the Enable Identity Insert option (see Figure 13-11) to ensure that records are imported with their original identity values (for columns such as ApplicationID, CategoryID, ArticleID, PollID, etc.). This is necessary so that inserted rows will respect the referential integrity (other tables have foreign keys that reference the specific values in these identity columns, so we have to insert the original values instead of letting it assign new values). You might think it's a good idea to select Delete Rows in Destination Table so that you won't get duplicate key errors if you're re-importing the data. This won't work, however, because it will try to use truncate statements that don't work on any table that has foreign keys (even if the constraints are off). So you need to use a script to delete all rows first if you want to re-import data, rather than use this checkbox.

Complete the wizard and check the box that lets you save the SSIS package, and check File System. When you see the Package Protection dialog, select "Encrypt all data with password" and specify a password. Select a filename for this package and run the actual process; it will import all rows as specified. Save the SSIS package in a file so that you can easily rerun this import in the future without having to do all the setup steps again (just double-click on that file). However, be careful because you have to empty your tables before doing this and you don't want to do this once you have real users in a production environment! Figure 13-12 shows the screen providing feedback about the process.

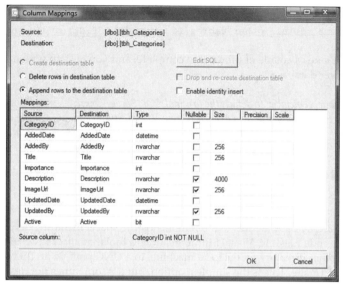

Figure 13-11

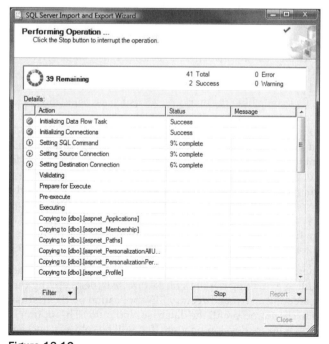

Figure 13-12

The last thing to do is reenable the constraints you previously disabled, by running the following statements on the remote database, from a query window:

```
ALTER TABLE tbh_Articles CHECK CONSTRAINT ALL
ALTER TABLE tbh_Categories CHECK CONSTRAINT ALL
ALTER TABLE tbh_Comments CHECK CONSTRAINT ALL
...do the same for all other tables required by ASP.NET and custom features
```

The entire import takes a couple of minutes to complete, and you end up with a perfect replication of the local SQL Server database.

When you're done, remember to detach the original SQL Server Express .MDF file used as a source; otherwise, you will no longer be able to open it from Visual Studio and run the site against it. This is not a concern if you used a full edition of SQL Server on your development computer.

Deploying the Site

There are three main methods to deploy the site's files:

❏ You can simply copy all files to the remote hosting space, including .aspx and .ascx files, .vb/.cs source code files, etc. Visual Studio includes a tool that allows you to copy the web project's file to another directory on the local machine, to a UNC path, to an IIS virtual application, or to a remote FTP site. This is the simplest option, but it's sometimes not desirable because your source code files will be copied as is, in "clear-text" format on the server, and many developers don't like this. As long as you deploy the site on your own in-house server that's fine, of course, but as soon as you need to deploy on a shared hosting space you'll probably want to precompile the source code so that you protect it (at least a bit, as it can always be decompiled if someone really wants to see your code) from prying eyes.

Even if your source code files are deployed to the server, they still cannot be downloaded by users because of the IIS settings, but it's probably best not to have them on the server at all.

❏ In addition to precompiling the site's source code files (the .vb or .cs files), you can also precompile the files containing the markup code (such as .aspx and .ascx files). Then, you'll only deploy the compiler-generated .dll assemblies, plus the .aspx/.ascx files as usual. However, because you precompiled the markup files, their content was stripped out by the compilation process, and they now only contain a placeholder string. For the actual deployment you can use an FTP client to copy the precompiled files to the server. In addition to offering better protection of your code, you're also making it harder for anyone to change your site's UI: this is particularly important if you sell the site as a packaged product and you put copyright notices and logos on the pages, and you don't want your client to remove or change them. Another advantage is that your code won't have to be compiled the first time a user accesses the site (but there will still be a JIT compile to go from IL to native code), which leads to slightly better performance the first time your site is accessed after deployment, or after IIS recycles the application.

You can generate an installer program that takes care of the complete setup of the web application, including extracting the site's files from CAB files, copying them to a folder selected by the user, creating a virtual directory/IIS application on the destination server, executing SQL scripts to create and prefill the database, and more. This option is particularly attractive to those of you who are developing a site that will be sold as a packaged application. In that case, it's standard to give users an installer program that takes care of the application's setup as much as possible. Note, however, that this approach isn't always useful because the user must have administrative rights on the destination server to install the site, and he needs to launch your installer program directly on the server itself. Therefore, this is not viable if you're targeting a shared hosting space. You can, however, create the installer anyway, so that clients will have the option to use it if they decide to deploy the site to their own server, or they can use FTP to deploy the site to a shared hosting service. The following sections explore these options in more detail.

Copying the Site Locally or Remotely

One of the problems that developers need to be aware of when developing websites with Visual Studio is that the built-in web server is not equivalent to IIS. It's normally very good, but you need to be aware that your website may function differently in some ways when deployed to a real IIS server. For this reason, you should always deploy your site to IIS and test it before deploying it to a production server. To demonstrate the Visual Studio Copy Website built-in tool, I'll show you how to copy the site to an IIS application, so that you can test the site on a real web server. *Only professional and server versions of Windows have IIS*, and even then it's not installed by default. If you have a home version of Windows, you'll have to deploy to a different system that has IIS installed. First, create a virtual folder/IIS application from the IIS Administration console, as shown in Figure 13-13.

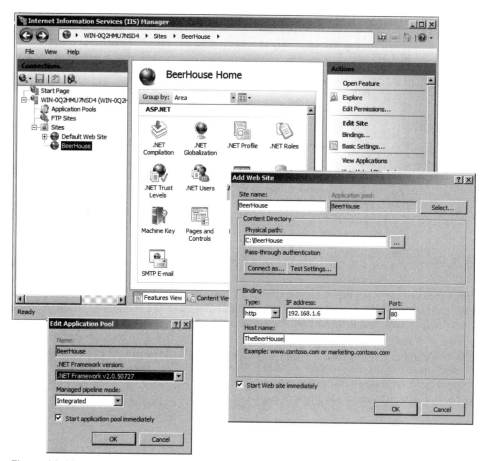

Figure 13-13

Ensure that ASP.NET version 2.0 is selected in the Edit Application Pool dialog: IIS 7.0 only offers the 2.0 framework by default. ASP.NET 3.5 uses the .NET 2.0 CLR, so there is no ASP.NET 3.5 version available in IIS. Also note the Managed Pipeline Mode is set to Integrated as opposed to Classic. IIS 7.0 adds a new processing model known as integrated. In integrated mode `HttpModules` are executed as part of IIS and not the website directly. This does not mean that all custom `HttpModules`, such as the URL Rewrite module you created in Chapter 3, have to be executed at the server level. For more detailed information about IIS 7, I recommend *Professional IIS*, ISBN: 978-0-470-09782-3, `www.wiley.com/WileyCDA/WileyTitle/productCd-0470097825.html`.

Once the website has been created in IIS, it can be copied directly from Visual Studio, click the Copy Website item from the IDE's Web Site menu. First you must connect to the destination, which can be a normal folder, an IIS/HTTP site, or an FTP site. In Figure 13-14, I'm connecting to the TheBeerHouse application folder (created previously) on my local IIS server.

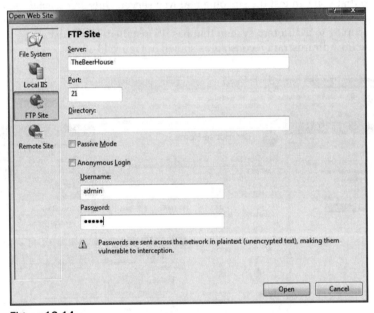

Figure 13-14

The tool's user interface is simple: once you select the destination, you can choose to copy everything from the source (the local copy of the site's files) to the destination, to copy everything from the destination back to the source (useful when someone else has updated the site and you want to download the latest version to your computer), or to synchronize the files on the source and destination according to their date. To deploy all your files, including source code, first make sure that your `web.config` file has the connection string for your remote database. Then, connect to your remote site on the right side and select everything on the left, except for the `App_Data` folder, and copy it to the right side. Figure 13-15 shows the tool after a successful complete copy.

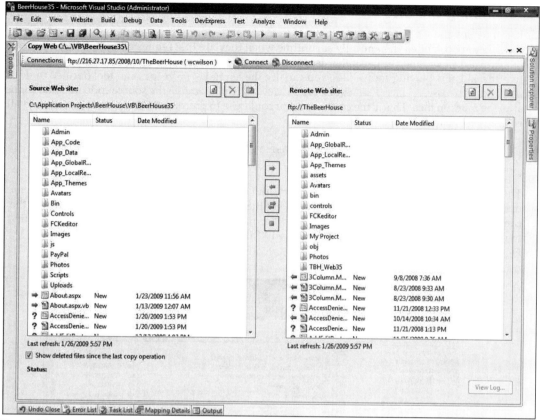

Figure 13-15

Although you can choose an FTP site as the destination for the copy, Visual Studio's Copy Web Site feature is slower than most third-party FTP clients, and it hung a few times while I was testing this feature. Therefore I prefer using an external FTP client instead of the Copy Web Site feature when I am deploying to a remote site using FTP. Personally, I like the freeware FileZilla FTP client (`http://filezilla.sourceforge.net/`). However, the Copy Web Site feature works well when copying to a local folder or an IIS application.

It is a good idea to hide the updating process from site visitors because as the files are being updated the application will most likely not respond and will throw numerous exceptions until the update process is complete. This has been a problem since applications have been on the web. When ASP.NET 2.0 was released, there was a feature added called app_offline.htm. Whenever this file is present in the site's root directory it is displayed in response to any request. This gives you the opportunity to put up a sign about the site being temporarily closed, without any ugly errors occurring. As soon as this file is removed or renamed, the normal application execution resumes.

Precompiling the Site

If you deploy the site by copying all the files (including the source code), the pages and the source code files are compiled dynamically at runtime when they are first requested by a user. This is called *in-place compilation,* and the generated assemblies are compiled into a temporary folder. As an alternative, instead of deploying source files, you can use the `aspnet_compiler.exe` tool (located under `C:\WINDOWS\Microsoft.NET\Framework\v2.0.50727`) to precompile the source code files and (optionally) the markup files. This is the command you could use to precompile everything (this should all be entered on one line):

```
aspnet_compiler.exe -p c:\Projects\ASP.NET\TheBeerHouse\TBH_Web
-v /TheBeerHouse c:\Deployment\TheBeerHouse
```

The `-p` parameter specifies the source directory, and the `-v` parameter specifies the virtual directory used at runtime by the site. The path at the end of the command is the destination directory for the compiler output files. If you look under the `c:\Deployment\TheBeerHouse\bin` folder, you'll find multiple `.dll` assembly files, plus one `.compiled` XML file for each `.aspx` and `.ascx` file (see Figure 13-16).

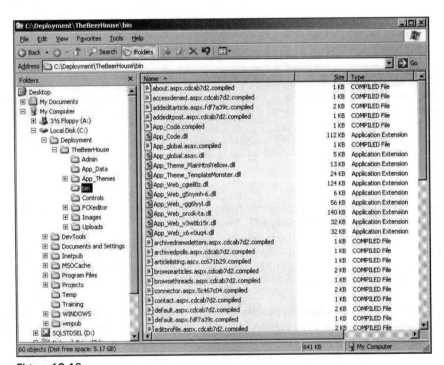

Figure 13-16

The files named with a `.compiled` extension contain XML text that shows the relationship between the virtual path of a page or user control and the corresponding type compiled into one of the assemblies.

If you look into any of the .aspx files, you won't find any HTML/ASPX markup code, but rather the following markup string:

```
This is a marker file generated by the precompilation tool,
and should not be deleted!
```

After executing the `aspnet_compiler`, you take all the output generated by this tool and upload it to the remote server, typically via FTP. If you're deploying to a server within your network you might simply copy the files to a shared folder on that server. However, even local servers are often isolated behind a firewall, so FTP may be needed anyway.

Compiling the markup code may definitely be appealing in some circumstances, such as for packaged commercial products for which you don't want the client to change anything; however, if you're deploying to your own site, this may not be particularly useful or necessary. Furthermore, it would complicate updates, because every time you needed to change a line of markup you'd have to recompile everything and redeploy the generated files. In the case of deploying to your own sites, it's simpler to precompile only the source code files but not the markup files. To do this, just add the –u switch (which stands for *updateable*) to the command line, as follows:

```
aspnet_compiler.exe -p c:\Projects\ASP.NET\TheBeerHouse\TBH_Web
-v /TheBeerHouse -u c:\Deployment\TheBeerHouse
```

With this command no `.compiled` files will be generated under the `/bin` folder, and the content of the .aspx and .ascx files won't be removed. However, the `CodeFile` attribute of the `@Page` and `@Control` directives will be removed, and the `Inherits` will be updated with a reference to the type compiled into one of the generated assemblies.

> **All static files (images, `.htm` files, `.css` stylesheet files, etc.) are always copied "as is" to the target folder. These are never included as part of a precompile.**

However, there's a small deployment issue when using one of the two precompile commands described previously: the assemblies they generate always have a different name, which makes it difficult to update the site locally and then replicate the changes remotely, because the assembly names will be different after each precompile. If you don't want to leave old and unused assemblies in the remote `/bin` folder, you need to delete them first and then upload all new `.dll` files. This is very annoying and time-consuming, so you can add the `–fixednames` compiler switch to cause the `aspnet_compiler` to create an assembly for each file it compiles, using a fixed name scheme. This is good because it allows you to update the site locally, recompile it, and then upload only the changed assembly file. This is the modified command line:

```
aspnet_compiler.exe -p c:\Projects\ASP.NET\TheBeerHouse\TBH_Web
-v /TheBeerHouse -u -fixednames c:\Deployment\TheBeerHouse
```

I covered the syntax of the command-line tool for completeness (and because many of you will want to script this procedure), but you don't have to remember all the various switches because Visual Studio provides a simple integrated UI for `aspnet_compiler`, which you can access by clicking Build ⇨ Publish Web Site. Figure 13-17 shows the graphical front end that it provides, making it easy to select your options, and to select a local or remote IIS site, or an FTP site, as the destination for the operation, in addition to a local folder.

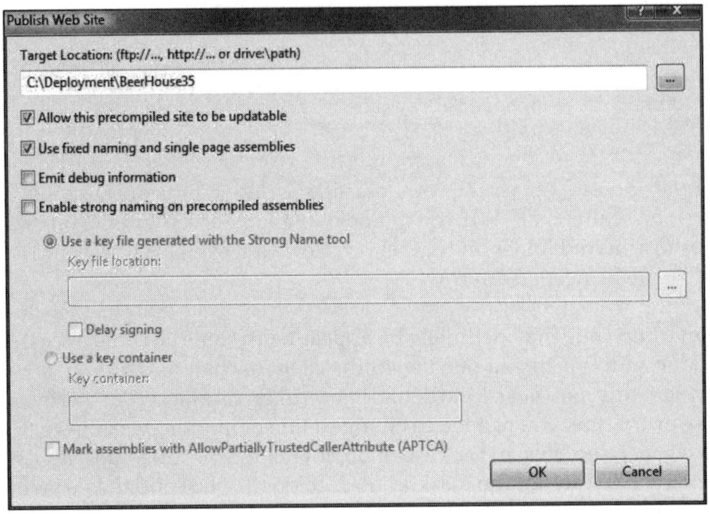

Figure 13-17

Some of you may be concerned about the large quantity of assemblies produced by the precompilation step. In large projects with hundreds of pages, the /bin folder will contain a lot of files, and it may be more convenient for deployment if you could combine all those .dll files into a single assembly file. This is done with a tool called asp_merge.exe. You can read more detail about the tool at http://msdn.microsoft.com/en-us/library/bb397866.aspx. It is located under the C:\Program Files\Microsoft SDKs\Windows\v6.0A\Bin folder. As its name suggests, it enables you to merge the multiple assemblies generated by the aspnet_compiler tool into a single dll. When you run this program you only need to specify the path of the precompiled website where it can find the assemblies you want to merge:

```
aspnet_merge.exe c:\Deployment\TheBeerHouse
```

The preceding command generates a dll for each of the website's folders containing files that were precompiled by aspnet_compiler. This is useful when you have folders that include a subapplication supported by different developers (such as the administration console), and you want to have separate assemblies for separate sections so that you can update them independently on the production server. In other cases, however, you may prefer to merge everything into a single assembly; you can do so with the -o switch, which specifies the name of the assembly being generated:

```
aspnet_merge.exe c:\Deployment\TheBeerHouse -o TheBeerHouse.dll
```

> **The tool can be used whether** aspnet_compiler.exe **precompiled the markup code or not. But the tool never merges in any external libraries referenced by the website's source files and pages, such as the** FredCK.FCKEditorV2.dll **assemblies. It only merges assemblies generated by** aspnet_compiler.exe**.**

Using the Visual Studio Web Deployment Projects

As for `aspnet_compiler`, there's also a front end UI for `aspnet_merge`. The Visual Studio Web Deployment Projects package, www.microsoft.com/downloads/details.aspx?FamilyId=0AA30AE8-C73B-4BDD-BB1B-FE697256C459&displaylang=en, is installed as an add-in for VS, and it adds a new project type called a "Deployment Project." You add a new deployment project to your solution by clicking the Add Web Deployment Project option on the IDE's Build menu or via the same option on the context menu of the website in the Solution Explorer window. You create the project by choosing its name and location from the dialog box shown in Figure 13-18.

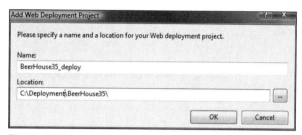

Figure 13-18

The project added to the Solution Explorer contains no files; you have to double-click the project name to open its configuration dialog box, from which you can specify a number of options. Among other things, you can specify how you want the precompiler to work, and how you want the files merged. In the first field of the dialog box (see Figure 13-19), you specify the output folder and choose whether the user interface pages and controls should be precompiled (which is the updatable option, corresponding to the -u switch of the `aspnet_compiler.exe` tool).

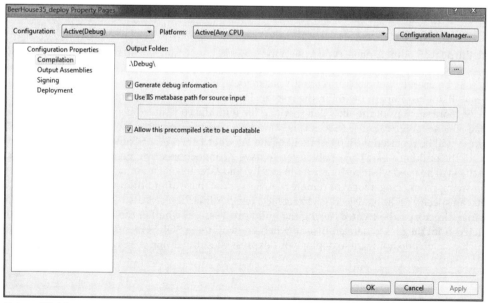

Figure 13-19

In the second tab, Output Assemblies (see Figure 13-20), you specify whether you want to compile every-thing into a single assembly, have an assembly for each folder, have an assembly for the user interface pages and controls, or have an assembly for each class and page being compiled (this last option means you don't want to use aspnet_merge.exe). From here, you can also specify the version information of the generated assemblies. If this information is not provided, the settings specified in the web.config file located under the /App_code folder will be used instead (if the file is present, which is not a requirement).

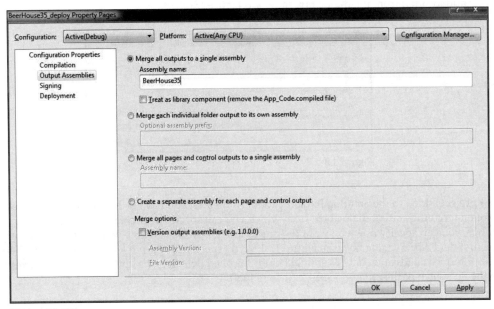

Figure 13-20

The third tab, Signing, enables you to sign the generated assemblies with a key file generated by the sn.exe command-line tool, to give them a strong name. This isn't normally desired for your own sites, but may be useful when you're creating a packaged application and you want to ensure that your assem-blies will not be tampered with. In the last tab, Deployment (see Figure 13-21), you can choose to replace one or more sections of the site's web.config file with the content from another file. For example, if you write connectionStrings=productionConnectionStrings.config, the whole <connectionStrings> section will be replaced with the content of the ProductionConnectionStrings.config file at the end of the build process. This enables you to have a connection string pointing the SQL Server Express database to be used while testing the site locally, and later have it automatically replaced with a connec-tion string referencing a local or remote SQL Server database after building the project for deployment. You can specify additional sections to replace, one per line. You can also use this window to specify a virtual directory to be created during the build process, and whether the App_Data folder will be deleted from the files generated (useful when you will use a SQL Server database after the build, in which case you do not want to deploy your express files under App_Data).

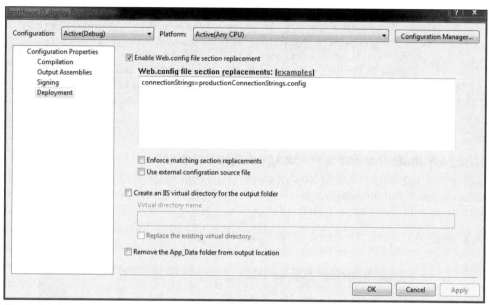

Figure 13-21

Once you've completed the configuration, you can build the project. At the end of the build process, you'll find a copy of the site with the precompiled and merged assemblies, plus all other files such as pages, controls, images, stylesheets, and so on in the output folder. You can then take this entire output and upload everything to the production server, typically via FTP.

Deployment projects simply consist of an XML file used to pass options to MSBuild.exe, the new Microsoft build tool capable of compiling and building complex projects and solutions. MSBuild is an extensible tool that uses configuration files that can contain many different options. And if an option or a task that you'd like doesn't exist yet, you can create it as a class and have MSBuild call it. Many of the configuration settings described here were implemented as custom settings and tasks by the developers of the Web Deployment Projects add-in. There are many more available options in addition to those you can configure from the Properties window explored earlier, such as the option to exclude files from the build, create new folders, grant the ASP.NET account write access to a folder (only on your local machine, though — you'll still need to replicate these security settings on the remote production server), execute external programs, and much more. You can add more settings and tasks (i.e., operations to run before or after the build and the merge processes) directly from the XML configuration file, which can be opened by clicking the Open Project File option from the Web Deployment project's context menu. Covering MSBuild is beyond the scope of this book, but you can find a lot of good documentation about this on the web and in the documents that come with the Web Deployment Projects package.

By default, all projects added to the solution are built in Visual Studio when you launch the primary project, that is, the website. Building the deployment project takes quite a lot of time, however, depending on the size of the site (on my machine it takes around 30 seconds to generate the precompiled site), and it is not something you want to do while testing the site locally. In order to avoid this waste of time, you can just exclude the project from the Debug Build from the Build ➪ Configuration Manager dialog box.

Creating an Installer for a Packaged Application

Creating an installer package that you can give to your clients, and that completely installs and sets up your site automatically, may be simpler than you think. In the old days, the setup programs were typically created with tools such as InstallShield or Wise Installation System, but starting with VS.NET 2003 they can be created with VS itself, thanks to the Web Setup Project types you find by selecting Other Project Types ➪ Setup and Deployment, from the Add New Project dialog box (see Figure 13-22).

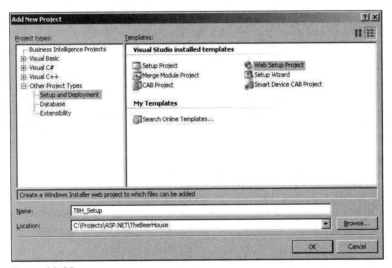

Figure 13-22

The Web Setup Project is tailor-made for creating installers for web-based applications. You add one such project to your current solution, and then you must tell it which files you want to include in the package. You could choose files one by one, but there may be thousands of files (including images and all static content files), so instead you can add the output of another project to the package (see Figure 13-23), and, in particular, the output of the Web Deployment project created earlier (see Figure 13-24). This includes everything you need (pages, controls, precompiled assemblies, and static content), so you shouldn't need to add anything else. If you do, however, then you could still add individual files from other sources — for example, if you wanted to include a manual that isn't among the website's deployment-related files.

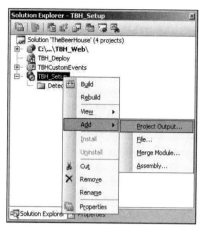

Figure 13-23

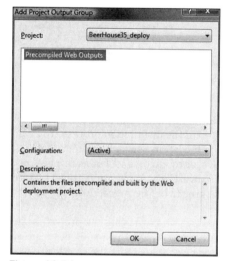

Figure 13-24

After you create the project, it preconfigures the creation of a Web Folder in the File System editor, as the destination for the installation process (see Figure 13-25). You can change its default name, the default page, application mappings, and related options that you would have manually configured from the virtual directory's Properties window in the IIS Administration console.

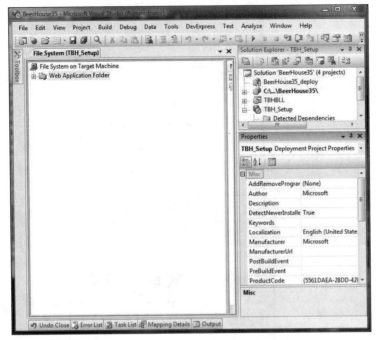

Figure 13-25

The default user interface includes steps for choosing the destination server and the folder name, and default options for the execution of the installation process. You can, however, open the User Interface editor (click the sixth icon from the left in Server Explorer's toolbar, after ensuring that the Setup project is selected) and add, remove, or modify steps. For example, you can put an image banner on them to customize their default appearance. Or, as shown in Figure 13-26, you can add a step that shows a license file, which users must agree to before proceeding.

After you've configured everything, you can build the project, and you'll end up with a setup.exe file that launches an .MSI file. Figure 13-27 shows the installer at runtime, demonstrating the step where you choose the destination server and folder, and the classic progress bar.

Creating a setup program in a matter of minutes is very cool! This basic setup does quite a lot of things (it creates a destination folder, turns it into an IIS virtual application with the proper settings, and copies all the necessary files into it), but it could be further extended with custom steps and actions. For example, you could create an additional step that enables users to choose whether they want to use a SQL Server Express database or a SQL Server database, and in the latter case it could execute .SQL scripts to automatically create the database and the required objects. Covering these advanced topics is beyond the scope of this book, as it pertains to the Installer projects and desktop programming in general, but I wanted you to know that you can create some useful setup programs using only Visual Studio. However, in some situations where you have advanced needs, there is still some benefit to be obtained from third-party installation builders such as InstallShield and Wise.

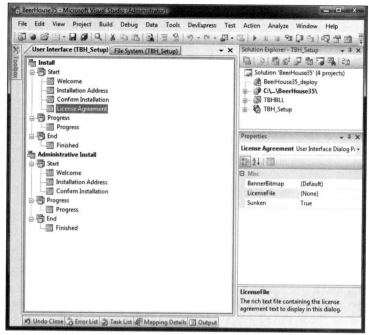

Figure 13-26

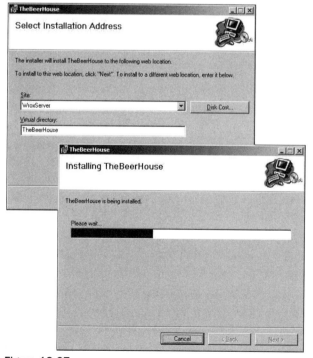

Figure 13-27

Solution

The "Solution" section of this chapter was actually merged with the "Design" section when I demonstrated how to solve the deployment problems while discussing some of the ASP.NET features, and I provided the background knowledge necessary to deploy the site. The solution I actually implemented for deploying the sample site consisted of using a Web Deployment Project to create a local precompiled copy of the site in an IIS virtual application, which I later deployed to the production server by means of an FTP client. I also switched from using SQL Server Express on my development computer to using the full SQL Server as my deployed target. To see my result, you can browse the sample site online by going to `www.beerhouse.extremewebworks.com`. I also created a web installer so that I could easily redistribute the site to colleagues, friends, and other people.

Summary

In this chapter, you've looked at all the options for deploying an ASP.NET 3.5 site, either on a local IIS server or to a remote production site. The new ASP.NET compilation model enables you to use a simple `XCOPY` deployment that includes everything but lacks protection of source code and takes a little time to compile upon the first page request. If that's a problem for you, you can use the command-line tools and the Visual Studio wizards to precompile the site and generate one or more assemblies to deploy. Different options for different needs; this new model is very flexible, and everyone will find something they like! This brings us to the end of our journey. I hope you like what you have read, and I wish you happy coding!

Index

V

Get more from Wrox.

978-0-470-18757-9   978-0-470-19137-8   978-0-470-19136-1

wrox™
An Imprint of **WILEY**

Available wherever books are sold or visit wrox.com